Norway

Svalbard
p348

The Far North
p312

Nordland
p270

Trøndelag
p253

**The Western
Fjords**
p207

**Central
Norway**
p119

**Bergen &
the Southwestern
Fjords** p152

**Southern
Norway**
p86

Oslo
p46

THIS EDITION WRITTEN AND RESEARCHED BY

Anthony Ham,
Stuart Butler, Donna Wheeler

Oslo pass
airport to hotel
hotel to Central Station

PLAN YOUR TRIP

OSLO P46

AURORA BOREALIS NEAR
TROMSØ P313

ON THE ROAD

Contents

Welcome to Norway

Norway is a once-in-a-lifetime destination and the essence of its appeal is remarkably simple: this is one of the most beautiful countries on earth.

Stirring Landscapes

The drama of Norway's natural world is difficult to overstate. Impossibly steep-sided fjords of extraordinary beauty cut gashes from a jagged coastline deep into the interior. The fjords' fame is wholly merited, but this is also a land of glaciers, grand and glorious, snaking down from icefields that rank among Europe's largest. Elsewhere, the mountainous terrain of Norway's interior resembles the ramparts of so many natural fortresses, and yields to rocky coastal islands that rise improbably from the waters like apparitions. And then, of course, there's the primeval appeal of the Arctic. Such landforms provide a backdrop for some of Europe's most charismatic wildlife – polar bears (in Svalbard), reindeer and musk oxen to name just three – and the setting for many a picturesque wooden village.

Scandinavian Sophistication

The counterpoint to so much natural beauty is found in Norway's vibrant cultural life. Norwegian cities are cosmopolitan and brimful of architecture that showcases the famous Scandinavian flair for design through the ages. At the same time, a busy calendar of festivals, many of international renown, are worth planning your trip around.

The Call of the Wild

In Norway, nature is very much an active pursuit, and Norwegians' passion for exploring their natural world has created one of Europe's most exciting and varied adventure-tourism destinations. Some activities may only be for the young, energetic and fearless, but most – such as world-class hiking, cycling and white-water rafting in summer; dog-sledding, skiing and snowmobiling in winter – can be enjoyed by anyone of reasonable fitness. On our travels we've encountered 93-year-old snowmobilers and whole families racing down rapids. Whether you're here in summer when the possibilities seem endless, or in winter for the soul-stirring spectacle of the northern lights, these activities are an exhilarating means of getting close to nature.

Worth the Expense

If one topic above all others dominates conversations among travellers to Norway, it's the formidable cost of travel here. Make no mistake: Norway is one of the most expensive countries on earth, which is yet another reason why saving up to come here is akin to planning the trip of a lifetime. But is it worth it? Absolutely: Norway will pay you back with never-to-be-forgotten experiences many times over.

Why I Love Norway

By Anthony Ham, Coordinating Author

The first time I stood on the waterfront at Aurland and contemplated the fjords, not long after having passed among the peaks of Jotunheimen National Park, I was utterly convinced that there was no more beautiful country anywhere on earth. On my many Norwegian journeys since then, in winter and in summer, I've never lost that feeling. Even more than the fjords and the high country, I now find myself drawn to the gravitas of Svalbard, to the perfect juxtaposition of water, rock and human habitation in the Lofoten Islands, and to the far horizons and Sami encampments of Norway's Arctic North.

For more about our authors, see page 448.

Above: Farms beside Sognefjorden (p210)

Norway

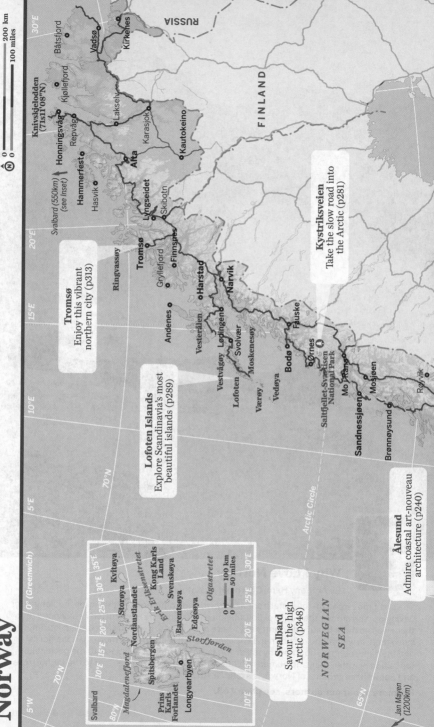

200 km
100 miles

RUSSIA

Båtsfjord
Vadsø
Kirkenes
Kjøllefjord
Knivskjelodden ('71s11'08"N)
Repvåg
Honningsvåg
Lakselv
Hammerfest
Hasvik
Karasjok
Alta
Skibotn
Lyngseidet
Kautokeino

FINLAND

Tromsø
Enjoy this vibrant northern city (p313)

Ringvassøy
Grylletfjord
Finnsnes
Tromsø
Harstad
Narvik
Andenes
Vesterålen
Langøya
Svolvær
Fauske
Moskenesøy
Bodø
Værøy
Vedøya
Sørnes
Mo i Rana
Saltfjellet-Svartisen National Park
Mosjøen
Sandnessjøen
Brønnøysund
Rørvik

Kystriksveien
Take the slow road into the Arctic (p281)

Lofoten Islands
Explore Scandinavia's most beautiful islands (p289)

Lofoten

Arctic Circle

Ålesund
Admire coastal art-nouveau architecture (p240)

Svalbard

Svalbard (550km) (see Inset)

100 km
50 miles

Kvitøya
Storøya
Nordaustlandet
Kong Karls Land
Svenskøya
Edgeøya
Barentsøya
Olgastretet
Storfjorden
Magdalenefjord
Spitsbergen
Prins Karls Forlandet
Longyearbyen

Svalbard
Savour the high Arctic (p348)

NORWEGIAN SEA

Jan Mayen (1200km)

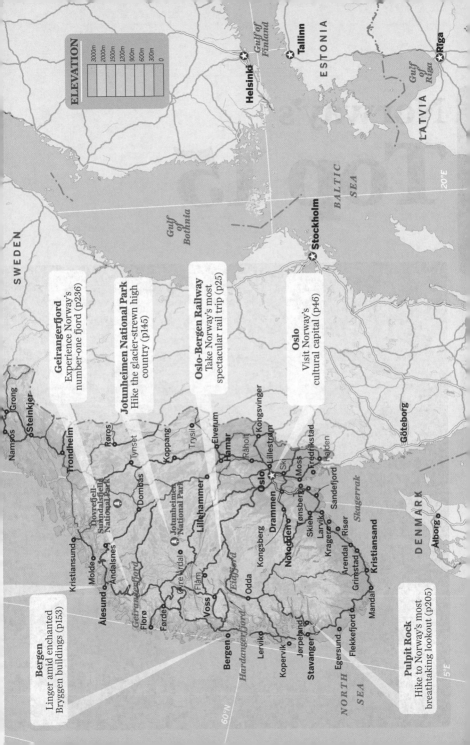

ELEVATION

3000m
2000m
1500m
1200m
900m
600m
300m
0

Geirangerfjord
Experience Norway's number-one fjord (p236)

Jotunheimen National Park
Hike the glacier-strewn high country (p146)

Oslo-Bergen Railway
Take Norway's most spectacular rail trip (p25)

Oslo
Visit Norway's cultural capital (p46)

Bergen
Linger amid enchanted Bryggen buildings (p153)

Pulpit Rock
Hike to Norway's most breathtaking lookout (p205)

Gulf of Finland

Tallinn

ESTONIA

Gulf of Riga

★Riga

LATVIA

20°E

★ Helsinki

BALTIC
SEA

Gulf of Bothnia

★ Stockholm

SWEDEN

Göteborg

DENMARK

Ålborg

Skagerrak

Grong
Steinkjer
Namsos
Trondheim
Røros
Tynset
Koppang
Trysil
Elverum
Hamar
Råholt
Kongsvinger
Lillestrøm
Ski
Moss
Fredrikstad
Halden
Dovrefjell-
Sundalsfjell
National Park
Dombås
Lillehammer
Jotunheimen
National Park
Kristiansund
Molde
Ålesund
Åndalsnes
Øvre Årdal
Flåm
Oslo
Drammen
Tønsberg
Sandefjord
Kongsberg
Notodden
Skien
Larvik
Kragerø
Arendal
Risør
Grimstad
Kristiansand
Mandal
Florø
Førde
Geirangerfjord
Voss
Odda
Eidfjord
Hardangerfjord
Leirvik
Bergen
Kopervik
Jørpeland
Stavanger
Egersund
Flekkefjord

NORTH
SEA

60°N

5°E

Norway's
Top 15

Geirangerfjord

1 The 20km chug along Geirangerfjord (p236), a Unesco World Heritage Site, must rank as the world's loveliest ferry journey. Long-abandoned farmsteads still cling to the fjord's near-sheer cliffs while ice-cold cascades tumble, twist and gush down to emerald-green waters. Take it from Geiranger and enjoy the calm as you leave this small, heaving port or hop aboard at altogether quieter Hellesylt. Prime your camera, grab a top-deck open-air seat and enjoy what's literally the only way to travel Geirangerfjord's secluded reaches.

Lofoten Islands

2 Few visitors forget their first sighting of the Lofoten Islands (p289). The jagged ramparts of this astonishing island chain rise abruptly from the sea in summer greens and yellows or the stark blue and white of winter, their razor-sharp peaks stabbing at a clear, cobalt sky or shrouded mysteriously in swirling mists. Postcard-perfect villages with wooden *rorbuer* (fishing huts) cling to the shoreline while the A-frame racks for drying fish tell of a land and a culture intimately entwined with the sea.

ADINA TOVY/GETTY IMAGES ©

SVEN BROECKX/GETTY IMAGES ©

3

Aurora Borealis

3 There is no more uplifting natural phenomena than the aurora borealis (p379), or northern lights. Visible throughout the long night of the Arctic winter from October to March, they dance across the sky in green or white curtains of light, shifting in intensity and taking on forms that seem to spring from a child's vivid imagination. While there's no guarantee that the northern lights will appear at any given time, if you are lucky enough to see them, it's an experience that will live with you forever.

Hiking the Jotunheimen

4 The high country of central Norway ranks among Europe's premier summer destinations. Although there are numerous national parks crisscrossed by well-maintained hiking trails, it's Jotunheimen National Park ('Home of the Giants'; p145) that rises above all others. With 60 glaciers and 275 summits over 2000m, Jotunheimen is exceptionally beautiful and home to iconic trails such as Besseggen, Hurrungane and those in the shadow of Galdhøpiggen, Norway's highest peak. Jotunheimen's proximity to the fjords further enhances its appeal.

Hurtigruten Coastal Ferry

5 So much more than merely a means of getting around, the iconic Hurtigruten coastal ferry (p420) takes you on one of the most spectacular coastal journeys anywhere on earth. On its daily path between Bergen and Kirkenes, it dips into coastal fjords, docks at isolated villages barely accessible by road, draws near to dramatic headlands and crosses the Arctic Circle only to return a few days later. In the process, it showcases the entire length of Norway's most glorious coast.

Bryggen, Bergen

6 Set amid a picturesque and very Norwegian coastal landscape of fjords and mountains, Bergen is one of Europe's most beautiful cities. A celebrated history of seafaring trade has bequeathed to the city the stunning (and Unesco World Heritage–listed) waterfront district of Bryggen (p153), an archaic tangle of wooden buildings. A signpost to a history at once prosperous and tumultuous, the titled and colourful wooden buildings of Bryggen now shelter the artisan boutiques and traditional restaurants for which the city is increasingly famous.

Oslo–Bergen Railway

7 Often cited as one of the world's most beautiful rail journeys, the Oslo–Bergen rail line (p25) is an opportunity to sample some of Norway's best scenery. After passing through the forests of southern Norway, it climbs up onto the horizonless beauty of the Hardangervidda Plateau and then continues down through the pretty country around Voss and on into Bergen. En route it passes within touching distance of the fjords and connects (at Myrdal) with the steep branch line down to the fjord country that fans out from Flåm.

VISIONS OF OUR LAND/GETTY IMAGES ©

IMAGEBROKER/ALAMY ©

Pulpit Rock

8 As lookouts go, Preikestolen (Pulpit Rock; p205) has few peers. Perched atop an almost perfectly sheer cliff that hangs more than 600m above the waters of gorgeous Lysefjord, Pulpit Rock is one of Norway's signature images and most eye-catching sites. It's the sort of place where you'll barely be able to look as travellers dangle far more than seems advisable over the precipice, even as you find yourself drawn inexorably towards the edge. The hike to reach it takes two hours and involves a full-day trip from Stavanger.

Svalbard

9 The subpolar archipelago of Svalbard (p348) is a true place of the heart. Deliciously remote and yet surprisingly accessible, Svalbard is Europe's most evocative slice of the polar north and one of the continent's last great wilderness areas. Shapely peaks, massive icefields (60% of Svalbard is covered by glaciers) and heartbreakingly beautiful fjords provide the backdrop for a rich array of Arctic wildlife (including around one-sixth of the world's polar bears), and for summer and winter activities that get you out amid the ringing silence of the snows.

Kystriksveien Coastal Route

10 The lightly trafficked coastal route through Nordland (p281) is an experience of rare and staggering beauty. You may not have time for the full 650km but a sample (preferably from Sandnessjøen to Storvik) is all but mandatory if you're progressing northwards. It's not one to be rushed. The frequent ferry hops offer compulsory, built-in breaks and stunning seascapes, while both inland glaciers and accessible offshore islands – such as Vega, famous for its eider ducks, or Lovund, home to 200,000 puffins – are seductive diversions.

GRANT DIXON/GETTY IMAGES ©

FRANZ ABEHVAM/GETTY IMAGES ©

VLADA Z/SHUTTERSTOCK ©

Tromsø

11 Tromsø (p313), a cool 400km north of the Arctic Circle, is northern Norway's most significant city with, among other superlatives, the world's northernmost cathedral, brewery and botanical garden. Its busy clubs and pubs – more per capita than in any other Norwegian town – owe much to the university (another northernmost) and its students. In summer, Tromsø's a base for round-the-clock, 24-hour daylight activity. Once the first snows fall, the locals slip on their skis or snowshoes, head out of town and gaze skywards for a glimpse of the northern lights. Arctic Cathedral

Wildlife-Watching

12 Norway is the last refuge for some of Europe's most intriguing wildlife (p384). While you may stumble upon polar bears (in Svalbard), Arctic foxes, Eurasian lynx, wolverine, reindeer and other species during your explorations of the Norwegian wilds, dedicated safaris in the Norwegian interior will take you within sight of the otherworldly musk ox, as well as the rather loveable elk (moose). Along the coast, Norway's bird life is abundant and filled with interest, while whale-watching outings are a staple of the Nordland coast, especially around Lofoten and Vesterålen. Eurasian lynx

Art Nouveau in Ålesund

13 Snug, tidy Ålesund (p240) owes much of its charm to a devastating fire that ripped through its wooden structures a century ago, destroying everything except the jail and a church. From its ashes rose a brand-new town, mostly of stone and mostly designed by young Norwegian architects who had trained in Germany. Strongly influenced by the Jugendstil (art-nouveau) movement of the time, they designed buildings rich in ornamentation, with turrets, spires, gargoyles and other fanciful elements based on local motifs.

Stave Churches

14 All over southern and central Norway you'll come across wooden stave churches. They come in all forms, from the monumental to the pocket-sized and cute. There's something about them that will stir up hazy memories of childhood. That's because the stave churches of Norway, many of which come enveloped in stories of trolls and adorned with fantastically carved creatures, are without doubt the very definition of fairy-tale churches, none more so than the spectacular Heddal Stave Church (p111). Heddal Stave Chruch

Oslo

15 Oslo (p46) is reinventing itself. This is a city that is aiming to become nothing less than a world-renowned centre of art and culture. It's already bursting at the seams with top-notch museums, art galleries and a glacier-white opera house that could make even Sydney jealous, but in the past couple of years it's achieved a striking rebirth of its waterfront district complete with daring architecture, a grade-A modern-art gallery, new restaurants and even a beach. Oslo Opera House (p47), architect Tarald Lundevall for Snøhetta

DOUGLAS PEARSON/GETTY IMAGES ©

ARCHITECT: TARALD LUNDEVALL FOR SNØHETTA. IMAGE: IVAN BRODEY/GETTY IMAGES ©

Need to Know

For more information, see Survival Guide (p405).

Currency
Norwegian kroner (Nkr)

Language
Norwegian

Money
ATMs widely available. Credit cards accepted in most hotels, restaurants, ferries and shops.

Visas
Generally not required for stays of up to 90 days (not required for members of EU or Schengen countries). Some nationalities need a Schengen visa.

Mobile Phones
Local SIM cards are widely available and can be used in most international mobile phones. Mobile coverage in all but wilderness areas.

Time
GMT/UTC +1 hour

When to Go

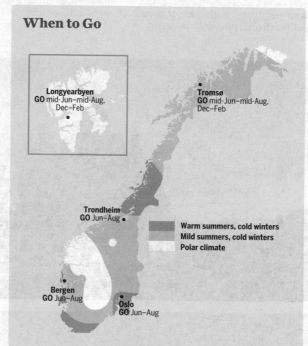

Longyearbyen
GO mid-Jun–mid-Aug, Dec–Feb

Tromsø
GO mid-Jun–mid-Aug, Dec–Feb

Trondheim
GO Jun–Aug

Bergen
GO Jun–Aug

Oslo
GO Jun–Aug

Warm summers, cold winters
Mild summers, cold winters
Polar climate

High Season
(mid-Jun–mid-Aug)

➡ Accommodation and transport often booked out in advance.

➡ Accommodation prices at their lowest (except in Lofoten).

➡ No guarantees with the weather – can be warm and sunny or cool and rainy.

Shoulder
(May–mid-Jun & mid-Aug–Sep)

➡ A good time to travel, with generally mild, clear weather and fewer crowds.

➡ Accommodation prices can be high, except on weekends.

➡ Book accommodation well ahead for festivals.

Low Season
(Oct–Apr)

➡ Can be bitterly cold.

➡ Many attractions are closed.

➡ March is considered high season in Svalbard.

➡ Accommodation prices high, except on weekends.

Useful Websites

Fjord Norway (www.fjordnorway.com) Focused on Norway's star attractions.

LonelyPlanet.com (www.lonelyplanet.com/norway) Destination information, hotel bookings, forums etc.

Northern Norway (www.nordnorge.com) Everything you need to know about northern Norway.

Svalbard (www.svalbard.net) Online guide with accommodation and activities bookings.

Visit Norway (www.visitnorway.com) Norwegian Tourist Board site ranging from practical to inspirational.

Important Numbers

From outside Norway, dial your international access code, Norway's country code, then the number. There are no area codes in Norway.

Directory assistance	☎180
International access code	☎00
Norway country code	☎47
Ambulance	☎113
Police	☎112

Exchange Rates

Australia	A$1	Nkr5.90
Canada	C$1	Nkr6.23
Europe	€1	Nkr8.81
Japan	¥100	Nkr5.95
New Zealand	NZ$1	Nkr5.47
UK	UK£1	Nkr11.17
USA	US$1	Nkr7.12

For current exchange rates, see www.xe.com.

Daily Costs

**Budget:
Less than €140**

➡ Dorm beds: from €31

➡ Huts or cabins: from €49

➡ Doubles in B&Bs/guesthouses: from €60/80

➡ Excellent supermarkets and cheaper lunch specials

Midrange: €140–200

➡ Double room in midrange hotel (weekends and high season): €90–175

➡ Lunch or dinner in decent local restaurant

➡ Car rental: from €75 per day

**Top end:
More than €200**

➡ Double room in top-end hotel: €175 and up

➡ Lunch and dinner in decent local restaurants

Opening Hours

These standard opening hours are for high season and tend to decrease outside that time for tourist-related sites.

Banks 8.15am to 3pm Monday to Wednesday and Friday, to 5pm Thursday

Central Post Offices 8am to 8pm Monday to Friday, 9am to 6pm Saturday; otherwise 9am to 5pm Monday to Friday, 10am to 2pm Saturday

Restaurants noon to 3pm, 6pm to 11pm. Some don't close between lunch and dinner.

Shops 10am to 5pm Monday to Wednesday and Friday, to 7pm Thursday, to 2pm Saturday

Supermarkets 10am to 9pm Monday to Friday, to 6pm Saturday

Arriving in Norway

Gardermoen International Airport (Oslo) Trains and buses connect the airport to the city centre (22 to 40 minutes) one to six times hourly from 4.05am to midnight. Taxis cost €80 to €120 (30 minutes to one hour).

Flesland Airport (Bergen) Airport bus connects the airport with downtown Bergen (45 minutes) up to four times hourly from 3.49am to just after midnight.

Getting Around

Train The rail network reaches as far north as Bodø, with an additional branch line connecting Narvik with Sweden further north. Book in advance for considerably cheaper *minipris* tickets.

Car Picking up your rental car in neighbouring Sweden *can* reduce costs. Roads are in good condition, but travel times can be slow thanks to winding roads, heavy summer traffic with few overtaking lanes, and ferries.

Bus Buses go everywhere that trains don't, and services along major routes are fast and efficient. Services to smaller towns can be infrequent, sometimes with no services at all on weekends.

Air SAS and Norwegian have an extensive, well-priced domestic network, while Widerøe hops from one small town to the next.

Boat Ferries, many of which will take cars, connect offshore islands to the mainland, while the Hurtigruten sails from Bergen to Kirkenes and back every day of the year.

For much more on
getting around,
see p416.

If You Like...

Fjords

Norway's epic landscapes rank among Europe's most varied and beautiful, but the sheer drama of the fjords alone is worth the effort of coming to this remarkable country.

Geirangerfjord Iconic Norwegian fjord that always inspires. (p236)

Nærøyfjord Unesco World Heritage–listed fjord region of extraordinary beauty. (p213)

Lysefjord A near-perfect fjord watched over by the world-famous Pulpit Rock. (p204)

Magdalenefjord, Svalbard One of the most beautiful places on earth. (p361)

Hardangerfjord Stunning network of fjords with lovely fjord-side villages. (p184)

Hiking

From central Norway's high country to sweeping panoramas in the Arctic North, Norway is a dream destination for those eager to explore the wilderness step by step.

Jotunheimen National Park Stunning trails amid glaciers and Norway's highest peaks. (p148)

Rondane National Park Shapely peaks and plenty of trails to escape the crowds. (p139)

Hardangervidda National Park A vast upland plateau with reindeer and glacier hikes. (p148)

Saltfjellet-Svartisen National Park One of the best places for glacier hikes just inside the Arctic Circle. (p276)

Aurlandsdalen Classic four-day trek from source to sea. (p212)

Lysefjord Hike to some of Norway's most spectacular lookouts. (p204)

Femundsmarka National Park Often-overlooked hikes through lake, forest and tundra. (p134)

Wildlife

Polar bears, whales, reindeer, musk ox, Arctic fox, elk (moose), epic bird colonies...Norway is home to some of Europe's most charismatic wildlife and most are accessible even to casual wildlife-watchers.

Svalbard Home to polar bears, Arctic foxes, reindeer and bird life. (p348)

Dovrefjell-Sunndalsfjella National Park Track down bird life and musk ox on safari from Oppdal or Dombås. (p138)

Hardangervidda National Park Home to Norway's largest herd of reindeer. (p148)

Gjesvær Remote and rewarding with millions of seabirds. (p332)

Andenes Whale-watching expeditions with birds, moose and seals thrown in. (p306)

Evje Track an elk in the southern Norwegian interior. (p117)

Winter Activities

The alter ego to Norway's world-famous summer attractions is its extraordinary range of winter activities. Many take place in the Arctic North, with dog-sledding, snowmobiling and skiing the marquee attractions.

Dog-sledding & snowmobiling, Svalbard Head off into Norway's most beautiful frozen wilderness. (p354)

Dog-sledding, Karasjok Get a lesson from a husky master. (p344)

Reindeer- and dog-sledding, Tromsø Arctic trails close to the Swedish border. (p317)

Snowmobiling, Kirkenes Explore the Pasvik Valley by day or moonlight alongside the Russian border. (p340)

Skiing, Lillehammer Ski the downhill runs used during the 1994 Winter Olympics. (p122)

King crab safaris, Kirkenes Arguably Norway's strangest (and most delicious) winter 'sport'. (p340)

Extreme skiing, Åndalsnes Fabulous ski up/ski down experience in Romsdalen. (p233)

Viking History

The coastal inlets along Norway's southern and southwestern coast is where the Vikings launched their longships in their quest for world domination and then returned with the spoils of victory.

Kaupang Archaeological ruins with the traces of a 9th-century Viking town. (p90)

Karmøy Island A Viking festival and fine Viking-themed museums. (p196)

Stiklestad Scene of an epic battle that changed Viking history. (p266)

Balestrand Intriguing Viking archaeology site in fjord country. (p216)

Eidfjord Easily accessible Viking grave mounds on a small plateau above the fjord. (p186)

Lindesnes Viking canal, historical centre and rock paintings. (p104)

Stave Churches

These fantastical structures evoke Norway's medieval past with dark-wood walls rising to turrets and ornamental flourishes, at times suggesting seemingly mythical creatures, at others the prow of a Viking ship.

Top: Mothing reindeer bull, Svalbard (p348)
Bottom: Aker Brygge (p48), Oslo

Heddal Stave Church, Notodden An astonishing flight of architectural fancy. (p111)

Urnes Unesco World Heritage–listed church on the shores of a fjord. (p220)

Lom Perfectly sited structure where valleys meet. (p142)

Borgund One of the best-preserved examples, with a medieval wooden bell tower. (p217)

Fantoft Stave Church, Bergen Poignantly reconstructed church that burned to the ground in 1992. (p158)

Ringebu A lovely little church set on a wooded hillside. (p142)

Scenic Drives

Norway has some extraordinarily beautiful roads, 18 designated as National Tourist Routes. But these only scratch the surface.

Sognefjellet Road, Jotunheimen National Park Breathtaking route across the roof of Norway. (p145)

Kystriksveien Coastal Route Norway's premier coastal road. (p281)

Trollstigen A dizzying succession of steep hairpin bends between fjords. (p233)

SnøVegen Short but nerve-wrackingly steep trail with unrivalled views over fjords. (p214)

E10, Lofoten Islands Takes you through the famous dramatic landscapes. (p289)

Gamle Strynefjellsvegen Among the loveliest drives in western Norway. (p229)

Ulvik to Odda, Hardangerfjord Hugs the fjord shoreline with some fine vistas. (p159)

City Life

Mostly set against picturesque backdrops, Norway's cities overflow with museums, architectural landmarks and large student populations who bring life and personality to often-pedestrianised streets.

Bergen Norway's prettiest and most cosmopolitan city. (p153)

Trondheim A fine cathedral and buzzing student population. (p254)

Ålesund Art-nouveau architecture and a lovely coastal setting. (p240)

Tromsø Vibrant student town deep in the Arctic. (p313)

Stavanger Museum-rich port city with an engaging old quarter. (p197)

Oslo Norway's cultural and political capital. (p46)

Villages

Norway's small, isolated settlements have been the lifeblood of Norwegian existence, from fishing villages and fjord-side hamlets to former mining settlements deep in the interior.

Røros Unesco World Heritage–listed former mining settlement with splendid wooden buildings. (p129)

Å A gloriously preserved Lofoten fishing village. (p300)

Sogndalstrand One of the prettiest wooden villages along the southern coast. (p106)

Nyksund Once-abandoned village now an artists' colony. (p308)

Utne Charming fjord-side village with Norway's oldest hotel. (p190)

Solvorn One of fjord country's loveliest villages. (p219)

Nusfjord An artsy Lofoten village. (p299)

Contemporary Architecture

Norway's contemporary architecture scene is one of Europe's most exciting, combining the clean lines of Scandinavian design with forms inspired by Norway's natural environment.

Arctic Cathedral, Tromsø The Ishavskatedralen has echoes of Arctic mountains and curtains of light from the aurora borealis. (p313)

Northern Lights Cathedral, Alta The latest addition to Arctic-inspired forms with an extraordinary swirl of silver titanium. (p324)

Opera House, Oslo Rises from Oslo's waterfront like a glacier floating above the fjord. (p47)

Astrup Fearnley Museet, Oslo An eye-catching, relatively recent addition to Oslo's waterfront. (p48)

Sámi Parliament, Karasjok Evokes a traditional Sami meeting place rendered in the signature woods of northern Norwegian forests. (p344)

Viking Ship Sports Arena, Hamar Olympic ice-skating rink that resembles an upturned Viking ship. (p126)

Hamsunsenteret, Hamarøy Daring homage to Norway's literary giant, Knut Hamsun. (p279)

Norwegian Wild Reindeer Centre Pavilion, Dovrefjell-Sunndalsfjella National Park Wavy timber, mirrored glass and a perfect setting. (p138)

Month by Month

January

Despite bitterly cold temperatures, January is a popular time for snowmobiling, dog-sledding and seeing the northern lights. By the end of January, the sun has returned to much of mainland Norway.

◉ Northern Lights

The aurora borealis, one of the natural world's most astonishing phenomena, is reason enough to visit northern Norway in winter. To combine the experience with more earthbound festivities, visit Tromsø in late January for the Northern Lights Festival.

☆ Midwinter Jazz

Held deep in the months-long Arctic night, Svalbard's Polar Jazz festival, the world's northernmost jazz festival, serves as a rhythmic reminder that life continues even in the depths of the polar winter. Late January or early February.

February

Generally Norway's coldest month, February is ideal for viewing the northern lights, participating in winter activities and joining two celebrations that capture the spirit of the Norwegian winter. Booking ahead is recommended, especially in northern Norway.

🎉 The Sami Winter

No one endures the Arctic winter quite like the Sami, the indigenous inhabitants of Norway's north. During Sami Week in early February, Tromsø's main street is the scene of the national reindeer sledge championship.

🎉 Rørosmartnan

Norway's largest winter festival in Røros dates back centuries and runs from Tuesday to Saturday in the second-last week of February. It's the perfect tonic for the long Norwegian winter with cultural programs, markets and live entertainment.

March

Days are lengthening as Norway awakes from its reluctant slumber with a full program of festivals (celebrating either winter's end or traditional Norwegian activities). It's one of the most popular months for visiting Svalbard.

🎉 Sami Easter Week

Easter among the indigenous Sami people in Kautokeino sees celebrations to mark the end of the polar night, with weddings, reindeer racing, the Sami Grand Prix (actually a *yoik* – a rhythmic-poem contest) and other traditional events.

🎉 Here Comes the Sun

The inhabitants of Longyearbyen in the high-Arctic archipelago of Svalbard must withstand the winter darkness longer than any other Norwegians. Their week-long Sunfest, in early March, is celebrated with special fervour.

✨ Winter's-End Dog-Sledding

Alta's Borealis Alta winter festival in March has concerts and other cultural events aimed at saying good riddance to winter. The festival also marks the beginning of Europe's longest dog-sled endurance race, the epic Finnmarksløpet.

April

April has surprisingly few festivals of note and represents something of a breathing space before the end-of-winter celebrations and action-packed Norwegian summers. The weather is improving and few tourists are around.

🍷 Food & Wine in Stavanger

Stavanger is a port city *par excellence* and its culinary culture is one of Norway's most varied. In mid-April, the local love of food and wine takes on special significance with the Stavanger Vinfest.

May

By May, Norway has a real spring in its step: the weather's warming up, Norway's renowned music festivals get under way and tourists have yet to arrive in great numbers.

✨ Constitution Day

On 17 May the country becomes engulfed in a wave of patriotism during Norway's most popular nationwide festival. It's celebrated with special fervour in Oslo,

where locals descend on the Royal Palace dressed in the finery of their native districts.

☆ Night Jazz Festival (Nattjazz)

Norway's calendar is replete with world-renowned jazz festivals and this fine Bergen festival in late May is one of the happiest, with serious jazz to be heard as the city's large student population gets into the swing.

✨ Bergen International Festival

One of the biggest events on Norway's cultural calendar, this two-week Bergen festival, beginning in late May, showcases dance, music and folklore presentations. In a typically Bergen twist, it's at once international and a return to the city's roots.

☆ Northern Blues & Soul

Close to the end of May or in early June, Alta's blues and soul festival is a worthy prelude to the summer-long program of music festivals. Held in the far north, it draws a respected international cast of bands.

June

The main tourist season begins in earnest and it's always worth booking ahead for accommodation. Some of Norway's best festivals take place and the weather can be mild and clear, although poor weather is possible.

✨ Viking Festival

The southwest is Norway's Viking heartland and in early or mid-June, Karmøy island provides a focal point for this fascinating history with Viking feasts, processions and saga evenings.

✨ Middle Ages Festival

Locals in period costume and Gregorian chants in the glass cathedral of Hamar are the highlights of this popular local festival. Held in June, it provides an alternative slant on the long-distant Norwegian past in a fantastic setting.

🏃 Midnight Sun Marathon

A midnight marathon could only happen in Norway, and Tromsø is the place to try the world's northernmost 42km road race. It's held in June and is possibly the only marathon in the world where the participants are still straggling in at 5am.

🏃 Extreme Sports Festival

Adventure junkies from across the world converge on Voss in late June for a week of skydiving, paragliding, parasailing and base jumping; local and international music acts keep the energy flowing.

July

July is the peak tourist season throughout most of Norway with the year's best weather and cheapest prices for hotels. Tourist sights can be crowded and we strongly recommend advance reservations for accommodation.

☆ Kongsberg Jazz Festival

Kongsberg's Jazz Festival, Norway's second largest, begins in early July, lasts four days and pulls in some of the biggest international names. As it precedes the Moldejazz festival, this is a great season for jazz-lovers.

🎿 Mountain Festival

In early July, Åndalsnes hosts what could be northern Europe's largest gathering of mountaineers and rock-climbers, swapping stories and inching their way up the sheer cliffs. The Norsk Fjellfestival has a full program of folk events to liven up the evenings.

☆ Moldejazz

Norway has a fine portfolio of jazz festivals, but Molde's version in mid-July is the most prestigious. With 100,000 spectators, world-class performers and a reputation for consistently high-quality music, it's easily one of Norway's most popular festivals.

🎿 St Olav Festival

This nationwide commemoration of Norway's favourite saint in late July is celebrated with special gusto in Trondheim, with processions, medieval markets, Viking dress-ups, concerts and a local food festival. In Stiklestad the saint is celebrated with a prestigious five-day pageant.

August

August is the scene of musical festivals across all genres. The weather should be fine and cheaper high-season prices continue, although in some cases only until the middle of the month. Book ahead.

☆ Rauma Rock

If Norway's regular diet of jazz and blues festivals doesn't suit your musical tastes, Central Norway's largest musical gathering is held in Åndalsnes over two days in early August, with everything from indie to hard rock.

☆ Notodden Blues Festival

This outstanding blues festival held in early August offers proof that even smaller Norwegian towns play their part in the country's festival obsession. You'll find it in nondescript Notodden; it draws a massive international crowd.

☆ International Chamber Music Festival

Most Norwegian music festivals cater more to a young and energetic audience, but Stavanger provides an antidote in early August with this stately festival; some concerts take place in the architecturally distinguished Stavanger Cathedral.

☆ Nordland Music Festival

The combining of diverse musical genres appears to be the only unifying theme when Bodø celebrates 10 days of music from symphony orchestras to jazz trios, folk groups and rock bands. It's held from early to mid-August.

☆ Oslo International Jazz Festival

A worthy member of Norway's coterie of terrific jazz festivals, this one takes over Oslo for six days of live music in August. It's so popular that many locals plan their summer holidays to be back in town for this event.

☆ Voss Blues & Roots Festival

If you're around the western fjords in late August, head to Voss for one of Norway's better music festivals. It serves as something of a last farewell to summer, with an especially festive feeling to proceedings.

☆ Norwegian Film

The highlight of the year for Norway's small but respected film industry, the Norwegian International Film Festival in Haugesund showcases innovative new works and coincides with the national film awards. It's held in mid- to late August.

☆ Green Rock

Norway's largest rock and indie music festival takes place in Oslo and is one of Europe's finest such festivals. It's also one of the greenest with impeccable environmental credentials. Hedonism without the guilt – it's a terrific combination.

☆ West Coast Jazz

Norway has a fabulous array of jazz festivals, but Silda Jazz in Haugesund is one of the country's most underrated jam sessions. Respected enough to draw big names but far enough off traveller routes to draw a predominantly local crowd, Silda Jazz is worth the trip out west.

September

The crowds have largely disappeared, but so have most of the cheaper summer deals; in some areas, many hotels and restaurants actually close down. In short, it's a quieter but often more expensive time to visit.

✲ Dyrsku'n Festival

Seljord's premier annual festival centres on Norway's largest traditional market and cattle show, and is one of the best ways to get a feel for traditional Norwegian culture. Held in the second week of September, it attracts 60,000 visitors annually.

◉ Kristiansund Photos

Arguably Norway's premier celebration of contemporary photography, the Nordic Light Photo Festival in Kristiansund draws massive crowds and world-renowned photographers, while also bringing a touch of sophistication to this busy oil port town.

October

Summer is a distant memory and by the end of October the months-long polar night begins in Svalbard. Temperatures have begun to drop and business travellers far outnumber those travelling for pleasure.

☆ Lillehammer Jazz Festival

This former Olympic city farewells the now-distant summer with the last major jazz festival of the Norwegian year; like any ski town, Lillehammer rocks (so to speak) during festival time, which is sometimes late September but more often October.

✲ UKA

Norway's largest cultural festival involves three weeks of concerts, plays and general celebration led by Trondheim's 25,000-strong university-student population. It takes place in odd-numbered years, beginning in October and not stopping until well into November.

☆ Svalbard Blues

In late October, with the long polar night just around the corner, Longyearbyen hosts a well-regarded blues festival, with scheduled concerts and improvised jam sessions.

Itineraries

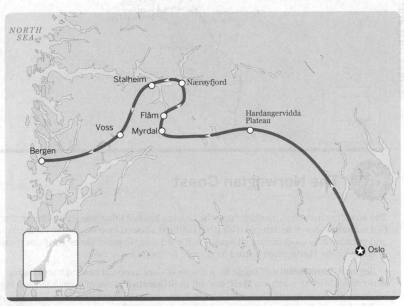

1 WEEK Norway in Microcosm

Even with only a week to spare, you can still see the best that Norway has to offer. This itinerary begins with Oslo's considerable charms, traverses the drama of Norway's high country and precipitous fjords, and ends up in beautiful Bergen. This journey can just as easily be taken in reverse order.

After a couple of days exploring the fine galleries and museums of **Oslo**, take the scenic Oslo–Bergen railway, one of the most spectacular rail journeys on earth. From Oslo, the line climbs gently through forests, plateaus and ski centres to the beautifully desolate **Hardangervidda Plateau**, home to Norway's largest herd of wild reindeer and numerous hiking trails. At **Myrdal**, take the Flåmsbana railway down to **Flåm**, from where fjord cruises head up the incomparable **Nærøyfjord**. Travel via Gudvangen, sleep overnight in **Stalheim**, and then continue on to **Voss**, where thrill-seekers love the easily accessible activities on offer. Trains then carry you on to **Bergen**, arguably Norway's prettiest city – wander its historic wooden waterfront, climb the surrounding mountains for sweeping views or soak up the atmosphere of the bars and restaurants that so distinguish this cosmopolitan city.

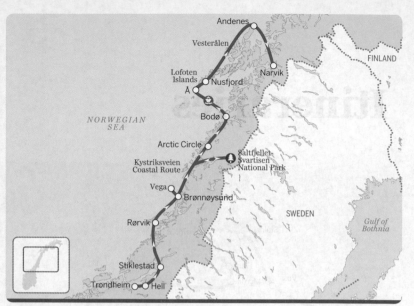

(2 WEEKS) The Norwegian Coast

The coastline between Trondheim and the Lofoten Islands takes you across the Arctic Circle along a shoreline fissured with deep inlets, shadowed by countless offshore islands and populated by quiet fishing villages. You'll need a car to make the most of this route, or consider the Hurtigruten coastal ferry, even for just a leg or two.

Begin in **Trondheim** and linger for a couple of days in one of Norway's most agreeable cities. Heading north, via **Hell**, stop off in **Stiklestad**, a site of great historical significance for Norwegians. Overnight here or continue on to **Rørvik**, where a fascinating multimedia display is the perfect introduction to coastal life.

The Rv17 travels north to picturesque **Brønnøysund**, and don't miss the offshore detour to the fascinating, Unesco World Heritage–listed island of **Vega**; count on a couple of nights in Brønnøysund and Vega. Back on the mainland, the extraordinary **Kystriksveien coastal route** hugs the coastline. A candidate for Norway's most spectacular drive, this road passes an estimated 14,000 islands. It can be slow going with all the ferries and inlet-hugging stretches of road, but it is unquestionably worth it. The entire route could be done in a couple of days, but four or five is far more enjoyable. Factor in time as well for a detour to the **Saltfjellet-Svartisen National Park**, home to Norway's second-largest icefield and accessible glacier tongues. The most beautiful section of the Kystriksveien route is between Sandnessjøen and Storvik, and it's along this section that you'll cross the **Arctic Circle**.

The primary appeal of **Bodø** is as the gateway (by ferry) to the **Lofoten Islands**. Unlike any other landscape in Norway, the Lofoten could easily occupy a week of your time, although it can be experienced much more rapidly for those in a hurry – make three days a minimum. All of the islands and villages are worth visiting, but on no account miss **Nusfjord** and **Å**, the latter a charmingly preserved village at the southern tip of Moskenesøy. Like Lofoten but with far fewer visitors, **Vesterålen** is wild and beautiful and worth two days, including summer whale-watching off **Andenes**, before you head on to your journey's end at **Narvik**.

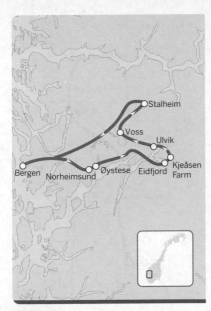

5 DAYS · A Bergen Long Weekend

Bergen is one of northern Europe's most popular short-break trips, with good reason. While there's more than enough to keep you occupied for five days in Bergen itself, the city's hinterland might entice you to consider a two-night excursion to see what all the fuss is about out in the fjords.

Bergen is the reason you came here and you've a busy time ahead of you if you hope to pack it all into two very full days of museums, wining and dining, shopping and simply wandering the postcard-perfect streets.

Although ranging beyond Bergen can be done using public transport, we recommend renting a car and driving on your third day through **Norheimsund**, the peaceful gateway to the stirring panoramas of the Hardangerfjord network. Pause in **Øystese** long enough to enjoy an unlikely contemporary art fix, then overnight in dramatic **Eidfjord**. The next morning, after a detour to **Kjeåsen Farm**, drive to gorgeous **Ulvik** for extraordinary views, stop for lunch in **Voss**, then drive to **Stalheim** for more spectacular views. Go for a hike in the morning, then drive back to **Bergen** in time for your flight home.

2 WEEKS · Best of the Fjords

Few natural attractions have come to define a country quite like Norway's fjords. This meandering route through Norway's fjord country, with a detour up and over the roof of Norway, is one of Europe's most beautiful. You'll need your own vehicle. Take as long as you can.

Begin in the far south, in **Stavanger**. After a day or two, take a day trip to **Lysefjord**, including the hike up to the signature lookout of Preikestolen (Pulpit Rock). A long day's drive north brings you to Hardangerfjord, and a string of villages you'll never want to leave, among them **Utne** and **Eidfjord**. Overnight in the latter, then continue on to **Flåm**; if you've still enough left in the tank, make for far lovelier **Aurland** for a couple of nights surrounded by extraordinary views. Wind your way north to pretty **Solvorn** on Lustrafjord, climb up and over the Sognefjellet Road through **Jotunheimen National Park**, then overnight in **Lom** with its perfectly sited stave church. Then it's on to peerless **Geirangerfjord**, up another breathtaking mountain road, the **Trollstigen**, down to **Åndalsnes** and then follow the coast to quiet and lovely **Ålesund**.

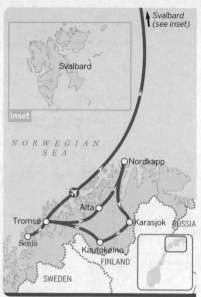

The Arctic North

2 WEEKS

The mystique of the extreme north has drawn explorers for centuries. Here is a horizonless world seemingly without end, a frozen wilderness that inspires the awe reserved for the great empty places of our earth. If you're really lucky, you might see a polar bear.

Tromsø is a university town par excellence. Its Polar Museum captures the spirit of Arctic exploration, its Arctic Cathedral wonderfully evokes the landscapes of the north, while the surrounding peaks host a wealth of summer and winter activities. You could also visit lovely **Senja** for a day. After three days on the road, head east for the rock carvings of **Alta**, then **Nordkapp**: as far north as you can go in Norway without setting out to sea. Next, head inland to **Karasjok** and **Kautokeino**, to the heartland of the Sami people. No exploration of the Arctic North would be complete without **Svalbard**. Return to Tromsø and catch a flight deep into the polar regions where the Svalbard archipelago is one of Europe's last great wildernesses. Allow at least four days to tap into the many activities that get you out into the wilderness.

 The Heart of Norway

1 WEEK

The high country of central Norway is simply spectacular and, provided you're willing to rent a car for part of the time, it offers some unparalleled opportunities to explore the region's quiet back roads; serious cyclists could also follow many of the same routes.

After a couple of days in **Oslo**, it's a short trip to **Lillehammer**, which hosted the 1994 Winter Olympics and remains one of central Norway's most pleasing spots; it has a wealth of Olympic sites and a lovely setting. Continuing north after a night in Lillehammer, **Ringebu** has one of Norway's prettiest stave churches. Having a car enables you to take the quiet Rv27, which draws near to the precipitous massifs of the **Rondane National Park**, before continuing northeast to Unesco World Heritage–listed **Røros**, one of Norway's most enchanting villages, with painted timber houses and old-world charm. After one or two nights in Røros, it's an easy detour north to **Trondheim**, a delightful coastal city with a stunning cathedral, large student population and engaging cultural scene; it's worth a two- or three-night stay.

Plan Your Trip
Outdoor Norway

Norway's portfolio of activities is simply extraordinary, from Europe's best summer hiking to fabulous winter sports, and it all caters as much for first-timers looking to leave the car behind as it does for hard-core adventurers who think nothing of leaping off a cliff. And whatever activity you choose, you'll do it against an utterly magnificent backdrop.

Planning Your Trip
When to Go

Norway has two major – and radically different – seasons for activities. Outside these periods, you'll probably find that the operators have simply shut up shop and, in many cases, followed their passion elsewhere in the world wherever the weather suits.

The summer season – when signature activities include hiking, kayaking, whitewater rafting and high-thrill pursuits that usually have 'para' attached as a prefix (namely parasailing etc) – most reliably runs from mid-June until mid-August. That's when there are enough travellers around to ensure regular departures and hence a wider range of options that suit your schedule. Depending on the weather, many operators, however, open in May and/or remain open until the middle or end of September.

Winter – when skiing, snowmobiling and dog-sledding take over – usually runs from December (or late November) until late February or early March.

What to Take

There are few requirements for most summer activities and operators who organise white-water rafting, kayaking, parasailing

Best Cycle Route
Cycle along the Rallarvegen from Finse to Flåm from mid-June to mid-August.

Best Extreme Sport
Para-bungee jumping in Voss from May to September.

Best Salmon Fishing
Tana Bru in eastern Finnmark from mid-June to mid-August.

Best Glacier Hike
Hardangerjøkulen on the Hardangervidda Plateau from mid-June to mid-August.

Best Hike
Besseggen in Jotunheimen National Park from mid-June to mid-August.

Best Dog-Sledding
Engholm's Husky in Karasjok from December to March.

Best Winter Skiing
Olympic ski slopes at Lillehammer from December to March.

and other similar 'sports' will provide the necessary equipment.

The major exception is hiking. Most hikers head out onto the trail under their own steam, but even those who plan on joining an organised hike will usually need to bring their own equipment.

In winter, you won't need much in the way of equipment for most of the activities – skis etc can be rented at ski stations and there are no special requirements for snowmobiling or dog-sledding.

Summer Activities

Norway is one of the world's premier wilderness destinations and it has a world-class adventure industry to match. Just about anything is possible and summer is the perfect time to wed an appreciation of Norway's wild beauty to a true sense of adventure.

Cycling

Whether you're keen to take a two-wheeled amble around the flat shoreline of your favourite fjord or are a serious cyclist with your sights set on the ultimate Norwegian challenge, Norway won't disappoint.

For the ambler, many tourist offices, some hotels and most bicycle shops rent out bicycles and provide information on cycling trails in their local area.

TOP FIVE CYCLING EXPERIENCES

➡ Sognefjellet Road (p145), through the Jotunheimen National Park.

➡ The exhilarating descent from Finse down to the shores of Aurlandsfjorden Flåm along the Rallarvegen (p151).

➡ Lofoten (p289), with its leisurely cycling through some wonderful, rugged scenery.

➡ Across the Hardangervidda Plateau (p116) near Rjukan.

➡ The steep and spectacular SnøVegen (p214) route above the fjords.

Cycling Resources

Bike Norway (www.bike-norway.com) This excellent website has route descriptions, maps and other advice for some of the better long-distance cycling routes around the country. They can also link you up with guided and self-guided package cycling and mountain-bike tours.

Norsk Bygdeopplevelser (☑61 28 99 70; www.norske-bygdeopplevelser.no/english) Private company that organises self-guided cycling tours, as well as hiking and ski tours.

Syklistenes Landsforening (☑22 47 30 30; www.slf.no; Storgata 23c, Oslo; ◷10am-5pm Mon-Fri) The main contact point for Norway's cycling clubs is useful for information on long-distance cycling routes and tunnels. It also sells *Sykkelruter i Norge* (Nkr120); it's only available in Norwegian, but the English-text Sykkelguide series of booklets with maps is available for Nkr125 each, and includes Lofoten, Rallarvegen, the North Sea Cycleway from the Swedish border at Svinesund to Bergen, and other routes.

Extreme Sports

Norway is gaining traction as a favoured destination for thrill-seekers thanks to its combination of highly professional operators and spectacular settings. Those who either have no fear or would simply love a bird's-eye view of some of Europe's most spectacular country have numerous possibilities, although they're almost exclusively centred on the fjord region in the western part of the country.

Voss in particular is arguably Norway's adventure capital and one of the world epicentres for extreme sports. Devotees of high-speed airborne pursuits converge on this lovely town in late June for the Extreme Sports Festival (p181).

Extreme Sports Destinations

Some of the best places to get the adrenaline flowing:

➡ **Kjeragbolten, Lysefjord** Base jumping from the sheer cliffs of Lysefjord close to the famous chock-stone of Kjeragbolten.

➡ **Rjukan** Norway's highest land-based bungee jump (84m), located in the southern Norwegian interior.

➡ **Voss** Paragliding, parasailing, a 180m-high bungee jump from a parasail (which claims to be Europe's highest bungee jump) and skydiving.

ALLEMANNSRETTEN

Anyone considering camping or hiking in Norway should be aware of *allemanns-retten* (every man's right, often referred to as 'right of access'). This 1000-year-old law, in conjunction with the modern Friluftsleven (Outdoor Recreation Act), entitles anyone to:

➡ camp anywhere for up to two days, as long as it's more than 150m from a dwelling (preferably further and out of sight);

➡ hike or ski across uncultivated wilderness areas, including outlying fields and pastures (except in fields with standing crops and close to people's houses);

➡ cycle or ride on horseback on all paths and roads; and

➡ canoe, kayak, row and sail on all rivers and lakes.

However, these freedoms come with responsibilities, among the most important of which are the prohibition against fires between 15 April and 15 September and the requirement that you leave the countryside, any wildlife and cultural sights as pristine as you found them.

Fishing

Norway's rivers and lakes have drawn avid anglers since the 19th century and salmon fishing is the undisputed star attraction. Norway's salmon runs are still legendary and, in June and July, you can't beat the rivers of Finnmark. In addition to salmon, 41 other fish species inhabit the country's 200,000 rivers and lakes. In the south, you'll find the best fishing from June to September, and in the north, in July and August.

The 175-page book *Angling in Norway,* available from tourist offices for Nkr200, details the best salmon- and trout-fishing areas, as well as fees and regulations, of which there are many.

Regulations vary between rivers but, generally, from mid-September to November, fish under 20cm must be thrown back. At other times between August and May, the limit is 30cm. Fishing is prohibited within 100m of fish farms, or cables and nets that are anchored or fastened to the shore, and fishing with live bait is illegal.

Anyone over 16 who wishes to fish in Norway needs to purchase an annual licence (Nkr240 for salmon, trout and char), which is sold at post offices. Check out fiskeravgift.miljodirektoratet.no for more information on the fee. To fish on private land, you must also purchase a local licence (Nkr75 to Nkr500 per day), which is available from sports shops, hotels, campgrounds and tourist offices. Some areas require a compulsory equipment disinfection certificate (Nkr125).

Fishing Destinations

➡ **Gjesvær** Expeditions near Nordkapp.

➡ **Moskenesøy** Deep-sea fishing off the Lofoten islands.

➡ **Reisa National Park** Another good salmon venue.

➡ **Saltstraumen Maelstrom** Popular fishing where two fjords collide.

➡ **Tana Bru** Legendary salmon fishing.

➡ **Tromsø** Ice fishing in winter.

Glacier Hiking

Glacier walking is one of Norway's most memorable summer pastimes, but you should only set out with an experienced local guide. Among our favourite places for a glacier hike are the following:

➡ **Folgefonna National Park** One of Norway's largest icefields, with glacier hikes at various points around the perimeter.

➡ **Hardangerjøkulen glacier on Hardangervidda** Said by some to be Norway's most breathtaking glacier hike.

➡ **Nigardsbreen** The pick of the accessible glaciers in the Jostedalsbreen area.

➡ **Saltfjellet-Svartisen National Park** Some of Europe's lowest-lying (and hence most easily accessible) glacier tongues just inside the Arctic Circle.

➡ **Svalbard** With 60% of Svalbard covered by glaciers, there are plenty of opportunities here, including some close to Longyearbyen.

Hiking

Norway has some of Europe's best hiking, including a network of around 20,000km of marked trails that range from easy strolls through the green zones around cities, to long treks through national parks and wilderness areas. Many of these trails are maintained by Den Norske Turistforening and are marked either with cairns or

Hiking season runs roughly from late May to early October; it's much shorter in higher mountain areas and the far north. In the highlands, snow often stays until June and returns in September, meaning many routes are only possible in July and August.

Hiking Resources

Den Norske Turistforening (DNT; Norwegian Mountain Touring Club; ☑40 00 18 70; www.

PERSONAL HIKING EQUIPMENT CHECKLIST

Summer

➡ Sturdy hiking boots; if you're heading to Svalbard, knee-high rubber hiking boots are recommended.

➡ A high-quality sleeping bag – even in summer, the weather can turn nasty at short notice.

➡ Warm clothing, including a jacket, jersey (sweater) or anorak (windbreaker) that can be added or removed, even in summer.

➡ A bed sheet – most huts charge extra for bedlinen.

➡ A sturdy but lightweight tent.

➡ Mosquito repellent.

➡ A lightweight stove.

➡ Airline-style sleeping mask for light-filled Norwegian summer nights.

➡ Membership of Den Norske Turistforening (DNT).

➡ Good topographical maps.

Winter

➡ Warm boots (ideally with a thick insulation of wool) big enough to wear double socks and to move your toes inside.

➡ At least one long underwear top and bottom (not cotton, but preferably underwear made of polypropylene).

➡ Multiple pairs of light synthetic (polypropylene) socks and heavy wool socks (again, not cotton).

➡ Flannel or polypropylene shirts.

➡ Trousers for walking, preferably made from breathing waterproof (and windproof) material such as Gore-Tex.

➡ Fleece sweater.

➡ Windproof and waterproof jacket with hood that's big enough to let you wear a lot of clothes underneath.

➡ One knitted, fur or fleece hat (such as a balaclava) to protect your face and another windproof one to cover your head and ears.

➡ Long woollen scarf.

➡ Woollen mittens plus windproof and waterproof mittens.

➡ Air-filled sleeping pad.

➡ Arctic-strength sleeping bag filled with synthetics or down; only necessary if 'u're likely to be sleeping out overnight.

iss Army knife.

(flashlight) with extra batteries or headlamp.

turistforeningen.no) Den Norske Turistforening is the Norwegian hiker's best friend and it's an important resource for anyone heading out on the trail. Its various chapters maintain a network of around 460 staffed and unstaffed mountain huts and lodges throughout the country.

Excellent hiking books include the following:
➡ Erling Welle-Strand, *Mountain Hiking in Norway* (1993)
➡ Constance Roos, *Walking in Norway* (2003)
➡ Anthony Dyer et al, *Walks and Scrambles in Norway* (2006)
➡ DNT, *Norwegian Mountains on Foot* – the English edition of the Norwegian classic *Til Fots i Fjellet*.

Hiking Routes

The list of possibilities for hiking in Norway is almost endless, but if we had to list our top 10, it would be the following:

➡ **Jotunheimen National Park** The doyen of Norwegian hiking destinations, with countless routes and incomparable high country.

➡ **Rondane National Park** Less-crowded trails than those of Jotunheimen, but arguably as beautiful.

➡ **Hardangervidda Plateau** Trails criss-cross this magnificent plateau, the home of reindeer.

➡ **Aurlandsdalen** Historic four-day hike following ancient trading routes from Geiteryggen to Aurland.

➡ **Trollstigen** Some wonderful treks through the dramatic Trollstigen range.

➡ **Dovrefjell-Sunndalsfjella National Park** Wildlife- and bird-rich park with the Knutshøene massif as a centrepiece.

➡ **Stabbursdalen National Park** Roadless park with tracks through glacial canyons and the world's northernmost pine forest.

➡ **Femundsmarka National Park** Lakes and forests with musk ox, close to the Swedish border and Røros.

➡ **Saltfjellet-Svartisen National Park** Icecaps and treeless uplands lend these trails an epic Arctic quality.

➡ **Trollheimen** Rolling mountains and high-altitude lakes make for memorable walking.

Kayaking

With all the hype surrounding hiking, white-water rafting and extreme summer sports, Norway's kayaking possibilities rarely receive the attention they deserve. And yet the chance to take to the water is a wonderful way to experience Norway's waterways without the crowds.

Kayaking Resources

Norges Padleforbund (☏21 02 98 35; www.padling.no) Norges Padleforbund has lists of kayaking operators and routes in Norway, although those sections of the website are only in Norwegian.

Kayaking Destinations

Norway's premier kayaking sites are clustered around (although by no means restricted to) the western fjords and there are numerous operators offering guided kayaking excursions. It's possible in many places to rent kayaks and the accompanying equipment from fjord-side campgrounds and tourist offices.

Top kayaking destinations include the following:

➡ **Flåm** Takes you away from the crowds on one of Norway's prettiest but busiest fjords.

➡ **Geiranger** Coastal kayaking trips from a spectacular Geiranger base.

➡ **Jostedalsbreen National Park** Guided kayaking and hiking trips that get up close to a glacier.

➡ **Langøya, Vesterålen** Introductory and more advanced courses around the time of the 170km Arctic Sea Kayak Race in July.

➡ **Lustrafjord** Four-hour kayaking tours on this lovely arm of Sognefjorden.

➡ **Svalbard** Difficult to imagine a more dramatic backdrop for your paddle.

➡ **Voss** One- to three-day kayaking trips on gorgeous Nærøyfjord.

Rock Climbing & Mountaineering

Norway's astounding vertical topography is a paradise for climbers interested in rock, ice and alpine pursuits. In fact, outside the Alps, Norway is probably Europe's finest climbing venue, although Norway's climatic extremes mean that technical climbers face harsh conditions, short seasons and strict restrictions. The western fjords region in particular is all the rage among serious climbers.

Climbing Resources

In addition to the rock-climbers' classic *Climbing in the Magic Islands* by Ed Webster, which describes most of the feasible routes in Lofoten, look for *Ice Fall in Norway* by Sir Ranulph Fiennes, which describes a 1970 sojourn around Jostedalsbreen. The more practical *Scandinavian Mountains* by Peter Lennon introduces the country's finest climbing venues.

Norsk Tindeklub (☑93 06 15 13; www.ntk.no) For general information on climbing in Norway.

Climbing Destinations

The most popular alpine venues in Norway include the following. Ice climbers should head to Rjukan.

➡ **Henningsvær, Lofoten** Site of a good climbing school that organises expeditions on the islands' vertiginous rock walls.

➡ **Lyngen Alps** Remote climbing and mountaineering but only for the experienced and self-sufficient.

➡ **Trollveggen or Romsdalshorn, Åndalsnes** Norway's prime climbing routes. Åndalsnes also hosts a very popular mountaineering festival, Norsk Fjellfestival (p233), in early July.

➡ **Uskedalen** A well-guarded but much-celebrated secret in the world climbing community, close to Rosendal.

Skiing

Numerous cross-country trails remain snow-bound throughout the year and a number of summer ski centres allow both cross-country (Nordic) and downhill skiing. These include the following:

➡ **Folgefonn Sommar Skisenter** (p192) A well-regarded centre high on the icefields of the southwestern fjord region.

➡ **Galdhøpiggen Summer Ski Centre** (p145) At 1850m above sea level but still in the shadow of Norway's highest peak, this is one of the prettiest places to ski at any time, although it's inaccessible in the depths of winter.

➡ **Stryn Summer Ski Centre** (p226) Norway's largest 'sommar skisenter' with good cross-country and downhill trails.

White-Water Rafting

The cascading, icy-black waters and white-hot rapids of central Norway are a rafter's paradise during the short season from mid-June to mid-August. A number of reputable operators offer trips, primarily in central Norway. These range from short, Class II doddles to Class III and IV adventures and rollicking Class V punishment. Rates include all requisite equipment and waterproofing.

Norges Padleforbund (p33) provides a list of rafting operators.

The best places to go rafting include the following:

➡ Drivadalen, Oppdal

➡ Heidalen, Sjoa

➡ Jostedalsbreen National Park

➡ Setesdalen, Evje

➡ Voss

Winter Activities

Skiing is the most popular winter activity (both as a leisure pursuit and a means of getting around), while snowmobiling serves a similar purpose in the far north and on the sub-polar archipelago of Svalbard. Dog-sledding is another major drawcard.

Dog-Sledding

This is easily our favourite winter activity because it enables you to experience Arctic and sub-Arctic wilderness areas by slowing you down to a pace that suits the quiet beauty of the terrain, free from engine noise. It's also one of Norway's most environmentally sound means of getting around.

Expeditions can range from half-day tasters to multiday trips with overnight stays in remote forest huts. With most operators, you'll have the option (depending on the number of travellers in your group) of *mushing* your own sled (after a brief primer course before setting out) or sitting atop the sled and watching the world pass by as someone else urges the dogs onwards.

There are long-distance endurance dog-sled races where you can see how the professionals do it.

Femundlopet (www.femundlopet.no) The Femundlopet starts and ends in Røros in early February.

Above: Hiking in Jotunheimen (p148)

Right: Rafting on the Otra River, near Evje (p117)

ANDERS BLOMQVIST/GETTY IMAGES ©

Finnmarkslopet (www.finnmarkslopet.no) The 1000km-long Finnmarkslopet starts and ends in Alta in March and traverses the length of the far north en route.

Dog-Sledding Destinations

Although most of the dog-sledding possibilities are to be found in Norway's high Arctic, Røros, in central Norway, is another option.

➡ **Alta** Three-hour excursions to five-day expeditions not far from Alta.

➡ **Karasjok** Wonderful short and long expeditions run by Sven Engholm (who has won the Finnmarkslopet a record 11 times) and his team.

➡ **Kirkenes** Mostly short-haul excursions but longer options are possible.

➡ **Røros** From a few hours to a few days in one of Norway's coldest corners.

➡ **Svalbard** The most spectacular landscapes bar none that can be reached by husky.

➡ **Tromsø** Up to four-day treks from Kvaløya island, south of town, with reindeer-sledding also possible.

Skiing

'Ski' is a Norwegian word and thanks to aeons-old rock carvings depicting hunters travelling on skis, Norwegians make a credible claim to having invented the sport. Interest hasn't waned over the years and these days it's the national pastime.

Cross-Country Skiing

Most skiing is of the cross-country (Nordic) variety, and Norway has thousands of

---

THE TELEMARK MANOEUVRE

The Telemark region of Norway has lent its name to the graceful turn that has made Nordic (cross-country) skiing popular around the world. Nordic ski bindings attach the boot at the toes, allowing free movement of the heel; to turn, one knee is dropped to the surface of the ski while the other leg is kept straight. The skis are positioned one behind the other, allowing the skier to smoothly glide around the turn in the direction of the dropped knee.

---

kilometres of maintained cross-country ski trails. Visitors should only set off after closely studying the trails/routes (wilderness trails are identified by colour codes on maps and signposts) and ensuring that they have appropriate clothing, sufficient food and water, and emergency supplies, such as matches and a source of warmth. You can either bring your own equipment or hire it on site.

Most towns and villages provide some illuminated ski trails, but elsewhere it's still worth carrying a good torch, as winter days are very short and in the north there's no daylight at all in December and January. The ski season generally lasts from early December to April. Snow conditions vary greatly from year to year and region to region, but February and March, as well as the Easter holiday period, tend to be the best (and busiest) times.

Downhill Skiing

Norway has dozens of downhill winter ski centres, although it can be an expensive pastime due to the costs of ski lifts, accommodation and the après-ski drinking sessions. The spring season lasts longer than in the Alps and the snow is of better quality, too.

Skiing Resources

The Norwegian Tourist Board (p414) publishes the useful annual *Skiing in Norway* brochure.

Skiing Destinations

Norway's better and more popular skiing locations include the following:

➡ **Geilo** The Oslo–Bergen railway line leaves you within sight of the ski lifts.

➡ **Holmenkollen, Oslo** Has 2400km of cross-country trails, many of them floodlit.

➡ **Hovden** A popular winter resort in the southern Norwegian interior.

➡ **Karasjok** Cross-country skiing in the far north.

➡ **Lillehammer** The chance to ski the downhill slopes used in the 1994 Winter Olympics.

➡ **Myrdalen** One of Norway's newer ski resorts, close to Voss.

➡ **Trysil** The largest network of trails in the country, with something to suit every standard and style.

WEATHER WARNING

Always check weather and other local conditions before setting out cross-country. This applies whenever traversing any exposed area, but is particularly an issue for hikers and cross-country skiers (two Scottish cross-country skiers died after being caught in snow and freezing fog in March 2007 on the Hardangervidda Plateau despite, according to some reports, being warned by local experts not to set out). At any time of the year, you should always be prepared for sudden inclement weather and stay aware of potential avalanche dangers, which are particularly rife in Jotunheimen but are a possibility anywhere in Norway's high country. Also, never venture onto glacial ice without the proper equipment and experience. And trust the advice of locals, who understand the conditions better than even the most experienced out-of-town hikers or skiers – if they say not to go, don't go.

➡ **Voss** Good trails in the Stølsheimen mountains high above Voss.

Snowmobiling

While snowmobiling may have its critics as a less-than-environmentally-sound means of getting around, life for many in the high Arctic would simply not be possible in winter without the snowmobile. For the traveller, snowmobiling also enables you to go much further than is possible with dog-sleds.

Most operators allow you to ride as a passenger behind an experienced driver or (usually for an additional charge) as the driver yourself; for the latter, a valid driving licence may be required.

Snowmobiling Destinations

Snowmobiling is generally restricted to the far north and Svalbard. Possibilities include the following:

➡ **Svalbard** Norway's premier snowmobiling location, with trails taking you deep into the main Spitsbergen island of this extraordinary place; there are some restrictions on where you can go.

➡ **Kirkenes** Day and night trips into the beautiful Pasvik Valley wedged between Finland and Russia.

➡ **Alta** One of the snowmobile hubs of mainland Norway.

➡ **Tromsø** Good trails close to Norway's northern capital.

Snowshoeing

Like most winter activities, strapping on a pair of snowshoes is a time-honoured way of getting around in snowbound regions and one that has morphed into a popular winter activity. That said, in our experience snowshoeing is something of a novelty to try for short distances rather than longer excursions – it can be exhausting and it takes a long time to get anywhere.

Throughout the Arctic North, hotels and operators who organise other winter activities rent out snowshoes and some also organise expeditions in Narvik, Lofoten and Tromsø.

Tour Operators

Norwegian Tour Operators

Many Norwegian tour operators offer activities and adventure expeditions. Although it is sometimes possible to simply turn up and join a tour, we always recommend that you make contact in advance, especially during the peak summer and winter seasons, to make sure that you don't turn up and find that all available places have been taken or that the departures don't fit within your travelling schedule.

Local operators can be reached via local tourist offices.

International Tour Operators

Many companies outside the country offer adventure- or activities-based tours to Norway. In most cases, tours are all-inclusive: the cost of your tour includes all accommodation, airfares, the cost of the activities and, in *some* cases, equipment.

In short, what you lose in flexibility you gain in convenience.

Arcturus Expeditions (www.arcturusexpeditions.co.uk) UK operator specialising in Arctic boat cruises but with at least two dog-sledding options.

Borton Overseas (www.bortonoverseas. com) US company specialising in adventure travel with dozens of Norwegian tours, including hiking, cycling, cross-country skiing and a full range of winter options.

Exodus (www.exodus.co.uk) Cross-country skiing and trips to Svalbard.

Go Fishing Worldwide (www.gofishing worldwide.co.uk) Salmon fishing on numerous Norwegian rivers.

High & Wild (www.highandwild.co.uk) Allows you to join the April reindeer-herding migration of the Sami by snowmobile.

Norway Direct (www.norwaydirect.com) Dog-sledding, snowmobiling, rock-climbing, white-water rafting and more.

Responsible Travel (www.responsibletravel. com) Not an operator as such, but a handy collection of sustainable tours in Norway, including many with an activities focus.

Plan Your Trip
Travel with Children

Norway is a terrific destination in which to travel as a family. This is a country that has become world famous for creating family-friendly living conditions and most hotels, restaurants and many sights are accordingly child-friendly. It's worth remembering, however, that the old parental adage of not trying to be too ambitious in how far you travel is especially relevant in Norway – distances are vast and, such is the terrain, journey times can be significantly longer than for equivalent distances elsewhere.

Norway for Kids

Domestic tourism is often organised around the assumption that many Norwegians will be travelling as a family, with everything from hotels to museums more than willing to not only accommodate children but make sure they have a good time.

Museums

Some of Norway's museums will immediately appeal to children (such as natural history museums), but even where the subject matter is more adult in focus, some museums have interactive exhibits and/or children's play areas with toys and activities. In summer (especially July), numerous museums with a historical focus organise programs for children, with games, activities and staff dressed up in period costumes.

On a practical level, most attractions allow free admission for children up to six years of age and half-price (or substantially discounted) admission for those aged up to 16. Family tickets are available at many of Norway's sights. Unfortunately some museums in Oslo insist that you use their baby strollers and not your own.

Best Regions for Kids

Oslo
Plenty of green parklands and a large array of museums, some interactive, mean there's plenty to keep children happy. Note not all sights and restaurants are that welcoming to younger travellers.

Central Norway
Lillehammer's (sometimes-interactive) Winter Olympic sites may appeal, as will activities around Røros and safaris in search of elk and musk ox.

Bergen & the Southwestern Fjords
Bergen and Stavanger have numerous child-oriented attractions; elsewhere there are boat trips on the fjords, interactive museums, water-based activities and the occasional Viking landmark.

Nordland
Whale-watching is the main draw here with ample opportunities on Lofoten, Vesterålen and nearby.

The Far North
Primarily winter activities such as dog-sledding thrill travellers of any age, while the northern lights are something the kids will never forget.

Theme Parks

Dotted around the country are some terrific theme parks that allow you to pass a day on rides and in themed pavilions; the focus is usually local in character, with trolls and other mythical Norwegian creatures the recurring themes. Larger towns and some coastal regions also have excellent aquariums.

Activities & Wildlife-Watching

Adventure tourism is one of Norway's major attractions, and there are a whole range of activities that kids can enjoy, although obviously the older your children, the wider the range of possibilities. For young travellers, wildlife safaris in search of whales, elk and musk ox are a terrific option. Dog-sledding is also possible in Svalbard, the far north and around Røros.

For older children, you may be surprised at what can be accomplished, from short hikes to kayaking and family white-water-rafting trips, and even some of the higher-octane thrills around Voss may be possible for travellers as young as 10 or 12.

Children's Highlights

Museums

➡ **Arkeologisk Museum, Stavanger** (p199) Viking-themed activities in summer.

➡ **Kon-Tiki Museum, Oslo** (p63) Guaranteed to inspire the inner explorer.

➡ **Nordvegen Historiesenter, Karmøy** (p196) Part museum, part Viking farm.

➡ **Norsk Luftfartsmuseum, Bodø** (www.luftfart.museum.no; Olav V gata; adult/child Nkr110/55; ☉10am-6pm mid-Jun–mid-Aug, 10am-4pm Mon-Fri, 11am-5pm Sat rest of year) Ideal for the aeroplane enthusiast.

➡ **Norsk Oljemuseum, Stavanger** (p197) The Petroleum Museum is one of Norway's most interactive.

➡ **Norwegian Glacier Museum, Fjærland** (p221) Hands-on exhibits of Norway's icefields.

➡ **Norwegian Museum of Childhood, Stavanger** (p199) Wonderful indoor playground for younger kids.

➡ **Vikingskipshuset, Oslo** (p55) Reconstructed Viking ships at the Viking Ship Museum.

➡ **Zoological Museum, Oslo** (p64) Stuffed Arctic wildlife.

Theme Parks

➡ **Atlanterhavsparken, Ålesund** (p241) Atlantic Ocean Park is one of northern Europe's best aquariums.

➡ **Bergen Akvariet** (p187) Fantastic aquarium that you can reNorskach by boat.

➡ **Hunderfossen Familiepark** (p126) Water rides, wandering trolls and fairy-tale palaces.

➡ **Kristiansand Dyrepark** (p98) Outstanding zoo and funfair in Norway's far south.

➡ **Lofoten Aquarium, Kabelvåg** (p295) Seals, sea otters and other marine creatures.

➡ **Olympic sights, Lillehammer** (p122) Everything from simulators to bobsled runs.

➡ **Polar Park, Setermoen** (p323) An excellent animal park with Arctic species.

➡ **Senjatrollet, Senja** (p322) The world's biggest troll, with accompanying attractions.

Activities

➡ **Dog-sledding** Possible from Røros in central Norway to Svalbard in winter, with sleds on wheels in summer.

➡ **Kayaking** Shorter family-friendly trips in Voss, Svalbard and the fjords.

➡ **Skiing** Year-round skiing at centres used to catering for kids, including Lillehammer, Trysil and, in summer, Stryn.

➡ **White-water rafting** Family-friendly trips in Sjoa and elsewhere.

Wildlife-Watching

➡ **Elk safaris** Free-range moose in southern and central Norway.

➡ **Musk-ox safaris** Search for this otherworldly beast in central and southern Norway.

➡ **Reindeer and Arctic foxes** Often seen within Longyearbyen (Svalbard) itself.

➡ **Whale-watching** See the giants of the sea off the Nordland coast.

Other Highlights

➡ **Hurtigruten coastal ferry** Kids' activities on board, and an alternative to long car journeys.

→ **Midnight sun** Endless days have huge novelty appeal.

→ **Myths of Seljord** Troll-rich country home to Selma the Serpent.

→ **Northern lights** One of the natural world's most mysterious phenomena.

Planning

As you'd expect, children's products such as baby food, infant formula, soy and cow's milk, and disposable nappies (diapers) are widely available in Norway (in supermarkets, pharmacies and more expensive convenience stores), but they're much more expensive than back home. You may want to bring a reasonable supply in order to keep costs down.

When to Go

Easily the best time to travel in Norway with children is the main tourist season that runs from mid-June to mid-August – this is when hotels offer the best deals for families, all sights and attractions are open and the weather is more conducive to a happy family holiday.

If you've come to Norway for the northern lights or activities such as dog-sledding, don't be put off by the bitterly cold weather. It's all about coming prepared with the appropriate clothes (Norwegian families don't hide in their homes for 10 months of the year!) and winter can be a magical time to be here.

Accommodation

Hotels, hostels, campsites and other accommodation options often have 'family rooms' or cabins that accommodate up to two adults and two children. Although many hotels do have larger, dedicated family rooms, other places simply squeeze in cots and/or extra beds when space allows, always for an additional fee.

One hotel chain that makes a special effort to cater for families from mid-June to mid-August is **Thon Hotels** (www.thonhotels. no), where family rooms can cost as little as Nkr1090 – stunning value by Norwegian standards. Most Thon Hotels also have a small children's play area and nice touches such as children's check-in steps.

Restaurants

Even in some upmarket restaurants, children will be made to feel welcome and, as a result, Norwegians are often seen eating out as a family group. Many restaurants offer children's menus with smaller portions and prices to match. And most of those that don't are willing to serve a smaller portion if you ask.

The high cost of meals can mean it's a challenge in Norway to ensure that your children eat well, but the general availability of hot dogs, hamburgers and pizzas do provide a fall-back option in case of emergency. Supermarkets are also good if you're stocking up for a family picnic and many have pre-made meals. Most restaurants have baby-change areas and a limited number of high chairs.

Transport

Norway's impressive public transport system is at once a comfortable means of getting from A to B and – given the variety, which spans trains, buses, tourist boats and ferries – may also carry considerable appeal for children.

On trains and buses, children under four generally travel for free (although they won't have a seat), while those aged between four and 15 (16 on the Hurtigruten coastal ferry) pay 50% of the adult fare. Some long-distance trains have a special family carriage complete with a children's play area!

Car-rental firms hire out children's safety seats at a nominal cost, but it's essential that you book them in advance, especially in summer and on weekends when demand is high.

Regions at a Glance

Oslo

Museums & Galleries
Architecture
Activities

Norway's Cultural Home

If it happened in Norwegian history, there's probably a museum in Oslo dedicated to the event, from the Vikings to Thor Heyerdahl and beyond. Some of the towering icons of national culture have wall space here as well.

Beautiful Buildings

Oslo's growing architectural reputation was cemented with the opening of the award-winning Opera House in 2008, but there's plenty more to turn the head, from a 14th-century fortress to the distinctive parliament and town hall and a new contemporary-art gallery.

The Great Outdoors

Escape the pressures of city life and take to the stands of green that surround Oslo. Much of the activity coalesces around the Holmenkollen Ski Jump and the Nordmarka woodland.

p46

Southern Norway

Festivals
Villages
Landscapes

Festivals

The summer tourist season draws Norwegians to the southern coast in droves. Yes, they come partly for the beaches, but some of Norway's most popular festivals and celebrations of coastal life also loom large.

Seaside Hamlets

Southern Norway's seaside villages showcase the white-washed timber architecture for which the region is famous.

Beyond Fjords

Coastal inlets of the kind that once sheltered Vikings are the topographical mainstay of the south, but there's drama aplenty in Jøssingfjord, the rolling hills of Setesdalen and the peak of Gausta.

p86

Central Norway

Hiking
Wildlife
Architecture

Hikes

Jotunheimen National Park has the most celebrated trails, although the parks of Hardangervidda and Rondane are every bit as good.

Wildlife

There aren't many places where it's easier to see three signature species of the north: wild reindeer roam the Hardangervidda Plateau, the musk ox inhabits two central Norwegian national parks and the humble elk (moose) is easy to see.

History in Wood

The stave churches at Lom and Ringebu, the mining town of Røros and Lillehammer's Maihaugen Folk Museum take you on a journey through Norwegian architectural history.

p119

Bergen & the Southwestern Fjords

Fjords
Villages
Cities

Fantastic Fjords

Spectacular Hardangerfjor is far less trammelled by tourists than the fjords further north. To the south, Lysefjord is picture-perfect with two iconic vantage points.

Timeless Hamlets

Some of Norway's prettiest villages – Ulvik, Eidfjord and Utne to name just three – are at once worthy destinations in their own right and front-row seats for stunning fjord country.

Beautiful Bergen

There is no more picturesque city in northern Europe than Bergen, with its harbourside district, mountainous backdrop and vibrant cultural life. Stavanger, too, is filled with energy and charm.

p152

The Western Fjords

Fjords
Activities
Architecture

Best Fjords

Norway's western fjords region – home to Geirangerfjord, as well as Nærøyfjord, Aurlandsfjorden and the other vertiginous tributaries of the vast Sognefjorden – is one of the most beautiful places on earth.

Ice-Bound

Take to the water in a kayak or hike up a mountainside, but the main drawcard here is the chance to venture onto the glacier tongues of the epic Jostedalsbreen icefield.

Stave Churches & Art Nouveau

Norway's prettiest stave churches – including Stordal, Kaupanger, Borgund and Urnes – are set against a postcard-perfect backdrop of fjords and mountains. To the northeast, art-nouveau Ålesund is magnificent.

p207

Trøndelag

Hiking
Cities
History

Sacred Path

Few Norwegian hiking trails resonate so strongly with the sacred. The Pilgrims' Way is an ancient pilgrimage trail with Trondheim as its goal. The Bymarka wilderness also contains fine trails.

Terrific Trondheim

A worthy rival to Bergen for the title of Norway's most agreeable city, Trondheim boasts excellent museums, a thriving culinary and cultural scene, and a slew of architecturally distinguished buildings.

Medieval Echoes

Trondheim's 12th-century Nidaros Cathedral is Scandinavia's largest medieval building. Stiklestad marks the site of St Olav's martyrdom and one of the most significant battles in Viking history.

p253

Nordland

Scenery
Islands
Nature

Enter the Arctic

Whether you choose the snaking Kystriksveien or the Arctic Highway (and we prefer the former), there are no finer passages into the Arctic anywhere in the world.

Jagged Coast

More than 14,000 islands sit just off the Nordland coast. The Vega archipelago consists of low-lying skerries; Vesterålen is wild and untrammelled, while Lofoten is arguably Europe's most spectacular island chain.

Whales & Glaciers

Nordland's coastal landscapes are the scene of Norway's best whale-watching possibilities, notably from Andenes. Inland, Saltfjellet-Svartisen National Park is Norway's second-largest icefield.

p270

The Far North

Activities
Sami People
Landscapes

Arctic Winter

While the rest of Norway hibernates for winter, the far north takes to the snow aboard snowmobiles, skis and sleds pulled by teams of huskies.

Sami Homeland

The indigenous Sami are Arctic Norway's most enduring human inhabitants and their emergence from centuries of persecution and an extreme climate is celebrated most powerfully in Karasjok and Kautokeino, now proud bastions of Sami culture.

Coast & Cathedrals

From the remote national parks of the interior to the coastal splendours of Senja, the Lyngen Alps and Nordkapp, Norway's high-Arctic landscapes inspire travellers and architects alike.

p312

Svalbard

Activities
Landscapes
Wildlife

Year-Round Adventure

Dog-sledding and snowmobiling in winter, hiking, cruises and kayaking in summer – there's not much you can't do here.

Frozen Wilderness

Svalbard's natural beauty – ice-bound for much of the year – defies superlatives. Much of the archipelago ranks among Europe's most beautiful wilderness areas, with mountainous ramparts, epic icefields and lonely fjords.

Arctic Wildlife

Here be polar bears. And walrus. And whales, reindeer, Arctic fox and more than 160 bird species. Svalbard offers a rare opportunity to see the inhabitants of this accessible slice of the polar north.

p348

On the Road

Oslo

POPULATION 0.59 MILLION

Best Places to Eat

➡ Hos Thea (p70)
➡ Fauna (p70)
➡ Punjab Tandoori (p71)
➡ Mathallen Oslo (p72)
➡ The Kasbah (p72)

Best Places to Stay

➡ Ellingsens Pensjonat (p68)
➡ The Thief (p68)
➡ Hotel Folketeateret (p68)
➡ Grand Central (p68)
➡ Oslo Vandrerhjem Central (p67)

Why Go?

To the rest of the world, Norway is where Mother Nature has created one of her finest works of art. Against such a wonderful natural canvas, it's easy to forget that man can also be artistic, and many a visitor has been left surprised to discover that Oslo is home to world-class museums and galleries rivalling anywhere else on the European art trail.

But even here Mother Nature has managed to make her mark, and Oslo is fringed with forests, hills and lakes awash with opportunities for hiking, cycling, skiing and boating.

Add to this mix a thriving cafe and bar culture, top-notch restaurants, nightlife options ranging from opera to indie rock, and a large and visible immigrant community who add their own colourful touch to the city and the result is a thoroughly intoxicating place in which to forget about the fjords for a while.

When to Go
Oslo

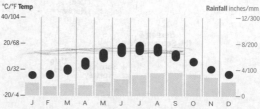

Apr–May Spring flowers fill the parks and National Day (17 May) brings crowds.

Jul The days are long, the sights are open and there's a packed cultural calendar.

Dec The first snow falls and Christmas markets and concerts bring seasonal magic.

History

The name Oslo is derived from the words *Ás,* the Old Norse name for the Norse Godhead, and *lo,* meaning 'pasture', yielding roughly 'the fields of the gods'.

The city was originally founded in 1049 by King Harald Hardråde (Harald Hard-Ruler), whose son Olav Kyrre (Olav the Peaceful) set up a cathedral and a corresponding bishopric here. In the late 13th century, King Håkon V created a military presence by building the Akershus Festning (Akershus Fortress) in the hope of deterring the Swedish threat from the east. After the mid-14th-century bubonic plague wiped out half of the country's population, Norway united with Denmark, and from 1397 to 1624 Norwegian politics and defence were handled from Copenhagen. Oslo slipped into obscurity, and in 1624 it burned to the ground. It was resurrected by King Christian IV, who rebuilt it on a more easily defended site and renamed it Christiania, after his humble self.

For three centuries, the city held on as a seat of defence. In 1814 the framers of Norway's first constitution designated it the official capital of the new realm, but their efforts were effectively nullified by Sweden, which had other ideas about Norway's future and unified the two countries under Swedish rule. In 1905, when that union was dissolved and Norway became a separate kingdom, the stage was set for Christiania to flourish as the capital of modern Norway. It reverted to its original name, Oslo, in 1925 and the city has never looked back.

☉ Sights

Oslo's main street, Karl Johans gate, forms a ceremonial axis westward through the heart of the city to the Royal Palace. Most sights, including the harbour front and Akershus Festning, are within a 15-minute walk of Karl Johans gate.

Whether you're artistic or literary, a peacenik or a history enthusiast, an explorer or an athlete, chances are there is a museum in Oslo tailor-made for you. Most are clustered around the city centre, on Bygdøy Peninsula or near Vigeland Park.

☉ Central Oslo

★ **Oslo Opera House** ARCHITECTURE
(Den Norske Opera & Ballett; Map p56; ☑21 42 21 21; www.operaen.no; Kirsten Flagstads plass 1;

admission to foyer free; ☉ foyer 10am-9pm Mon-Fri, 11am-9pm Sat, noon-9pm Sun) Hoping to transform the city into a world-class cultural centre, the city leaders have embarked on a massive waterfront redevelopment project (which is scheduled to last until 2020), the centrepiece of which is the magnificent Opera House, a creation which is fast becoming one of the iconic modern buildings of Scandinavia.

Designed by Oslo-based architectural firm Snøhetta and costing around €500 million to build, the Opera House, which opened in 2008, has been designed to resemble a glacier floating in the waters off Oslo. It's a subtle building that at first doesn't look all that impressive, but give it time and it will leave you spellbound. Impressive at any time, it's probably at its most magical in the winter when snow provides it with a gleaming coat and the surrounding harbour fills with sparkling sheets of ice.

Before venturing inside be sure to walk up onto the roof, which was designed to act as a 'carpet' of sloping angles and flat surfaces. It's a symbolism that obviously works because Norwegians love to sprawl out across it on sunny days and sunbathe. Also, don't miss 'playing' the musical rods that sit both up on the roof and near the entrance. Floating just offshore of the Opera House is Monica Bonvicini's *She Lies,* a three-dimensional interpretation of Caspar David Friedrich's 1823–24 painting *Das Eismeer* (The Sea of Ice). As the tides rush in and out of the harbour, the steel and glass sculpture spins and twists, creating a constantly changing perspective for the viewer.

The main entrance to the Opera House is purposely small and unimpressive, which serves only to add to the sense of vastness that greets you on entering the main foyer (the windows alone are 15m high and flood the foyer with light). Aside from the windows, the other dominating feature of the foyer is the Wave Wall. Made of strips of golden oak, the wall curves up through the centre of the foyer and provides access to the upper levels of the building. Opposite the wave wall, green lights create playful patterns on the wall (and make the toilets and coat room they hide the most artistic you will ever visit!).

Also in the foyer is a **restaurant** (Map p56; Kirsten Flagstads plass 1, Oslo Opera House; mains from Nkr148, set menus from Nkr375), serving suitably modern and arty takes on old Norwegian classics.

To see more of the building's interior, you will have to join one of the **guided tours** (☑21 42 21 21; Kirsten Flagstads plass 1; adult/child Nkr100/60; ⊘11am, noon & 1pm daily Jul-early Aug, 11am, noon & 1pm Mon-Fri, noon & 1pm Sat, 1pm Sun early Aug-31 Aug, 1pm Mon-Fri & Sun, noon Sat rest of year). These run in English and Norwegian and take you into some of the building's 1100 rooms. The guide will explain much of the artistic symbolism of the building, and reveal something of life behind the scenes at the Opera House. In high season it's a good idea to book a space on a tour in advance.

While wandering around the building, it can be easy to forget that it's not just there to serve as eye candy for tourists, and that its prime role is to act as a showcase for top-notch opera and ballet performances. Upcoming performances are listed on the website and ticket prices vary from Nkr100 to Nkr745.

★ **Astrup Fearnley Museet**   GALLERY
(Astrup Fearnley Museum; Map p52; ☑22 93 60 60; www.afmuseet.no; Strandpromenaden 2; adult/student/child Nkr100/60/free, guided tours Nkr50; ⊘noon-5pm Tue-Wed & Fri, noon-7pm Thu, 11am-5pm Sat & Sun) Recently reopened in a stunning architectural creation at the centre of Oslo's waterfront, this museum, which contains all manner of zany contemporary art, is Oslo's latest flagship project and the artistic highlight of the city.

Designed by Renzo Piano and completed in 2012, the museum resides within a wonderful wooden building floating on jetties and rafts, with sail-like roofs that, appropriately, gives the building the look of an old wooden boat. Incorporated into the overall design are canals, parks, a not-quite-yet-complete shopping and restaurant complex and, a favourite with Oslo families in summer, a small pebble beach.

Rather than a collection from a specific historical period, or from a certain artistic movement, the museum concentrates on individual pieces of work or artists who have pushed artistic boundaries. Saying that, the bulk of the original collection is focused on American artists from the 1980s, but today it has become far more wide-ranging in its outlook and the collection hosts pieces by Tom Sachs, Cindy Sherman and Cai Guo-Qiang. Its most famous piece is the gilded ceramic sculpture *Michael Jackson and Bubbles*, by Jeff Koons.

Guided **tours** in English taking in the best of the collection run at 5.30pm on Thursdays in July and August. Tours in Norwegian run at 1pm and 2pm every Saturday and Sunday year round.

Nobels Fredssenter   MUSEUM
(Nobel Peace Center; Map p56; ☑48 30 10 00; www.nobelpeacecenter.org; Rådhusplassen 1; adult/student/child Nkr90/60/free; ⊘10am-6pm daily

---

OSLO IN...

Two Days

Start your day at the **Nasjonalgalleriet** (p50) for a representative dose of artwork by Edvard Munch. Afterwards, try an alfresco, pier-side seafood lunch at one of the new restaurant developments at **Aker Brygge** (p71). Take a ferry from here to Bygdøy Peninsula, and spend your afternoon learning about the exploits of Norway's greatest explorers at the **Polarship Fram Museum** (p62) or **Vikingskipshuset** (p55). On day two head to the breathtaking **Oslo Opera House** (p47), timing your visit to coincide with one of the guided tours. Afterwards, explore the medieval **Akershus Festning & Slott** (p51) and then take a look at all that's cool and modern at the amazing new **Astrup Fearnley Museet** (p48). Finally, if time allows, learn how to make the world a better place at the **Nobel Fredssenter** (p48).

Four Days

If you have a couple of extra days, wander among the bold, earthy statues at **Vigeland Park** (p54) and consider launching yourself off the enormous **Holmenkollen Ski Jump** (p64), although it's probably better to content yourself with a virtual attempt in the nearby simulator. The energetic might also spend a day walking, skiing or biking in the **Nordmarka** (p64); otherwise simply make a lazy day trip to pretty **Fredrikstad** (p79).

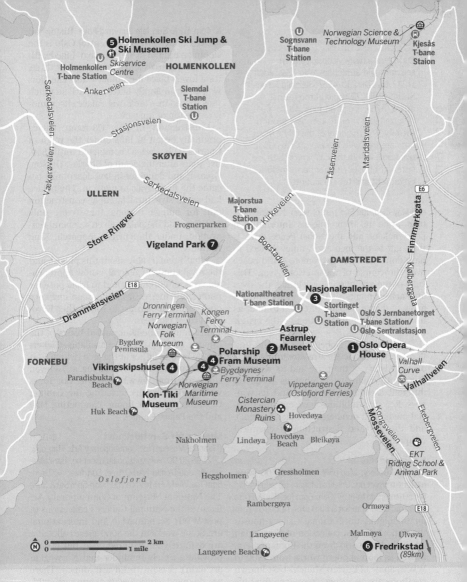

Oslo Highlights

1 Sing like a soprano while admiring the **Oslo Opera House** (p47).

2 Check out the arresting artwork at the **Astrup Fearnley Museet** (p48).

3 Scream with delight at *The Scream* in the **Nasjonalgalleriet** (p50).

4 Examine the ships of the **Vikingskipshuset** (p55), **Kon-Tiki Museum** (p63) and **Polarship Fram Museum** (p62).

5 Conquer your fear of heights at the **Holmenkollen Ski Jump** (p64).

6 Stroll the fortress walls and explore the boutiques of Fredrikstad's **Gamlebyen** (p80).

7 Reconsider parenthood while looking at Gustav Vigeland's works at **Vigeland Park** (p54).

ⓘ OSLO PASS

Oslo Pass (www.visitoslo.com/en/activities-and-attractions/oslo-pass; adult 1/2/3 days Nkr290/425/535, child & senior Nkr145/215/270), sold at the tourist office (p76), is one popular way of cutting transport and ticket costs around the city. The majority of the city's museums are free with the pass, as is public transport within the city limits (barring late-night buses). Other perks include restaurant and tour discounts.

---

mid-May–Sep, Tue-Sun rest of year) Norwegians take pride in their role as international peacemakers, and the Nobel Peace Prize is their gift to the men and women judged to have done the most to promote world peace over the course of the previous year. This state-of-the-art museum celebrates the lives and achievements of the winners with an array of digital displays intended to offer as much or as little information as the visitor desires.

Don't miss the Nobel Book on the 2nd floor or the movie theatre streaming films on the history of the prize and its winners. Frequently changing exhibitions focus on different aspects of the prize and its winners. Recent exhibitions have examined social media and democracy (or lack thereof), and the use and destruction of chemical weapons.

Nasjonalgalleriet   GALLERY
(National Gallery; Map p56; ☑ 21 98 20 00; www.nasjonalmuseet.no; Universitetsgata 13; adult/child Nkr50/free, Sun free; ☉ 10am-6pm Tue, Wed & Fri, to 7pm Thu, 11am-5pm Sat & Sun) One of Oslo's major highlights, the National Gallery houses the nation's largest collection of Norwegian art, including works from the Romantic era, as well as more-modern works from 1800 to WWII. Some of Edvard Munch's best-known creations are on display here, including his most renowned work, *The Scream*. There's also an impressive collection of European art, with works by Gauguin, Picasso and El Greco, and impressionists such as Manet, Degas, Renoir, Matisse, Cézanne and Monet.

Royal Palace & Slottsparken   PALACE, PARK
(Det Kongelige Slott; Map p56; ☑ 81 53 31 33; www.royalcourt.no; Slottsparken; park free, palace tours adult/child Nkr95/85; ☉ guided tours in English noon, 2pm & 2.20pm Mon-Thu & Sat, 2pm, 2.20pm & 4pm Fri & Sun late Jun–mid-Aug) Rising up above the western end of central Oslo is the sloping parkland of Slottsparken. Filled with stately royal trees and a duck pond or three, it's a lovely place for a quiet walk. The Norwegian royal family liked the park so much they moved in – the Royal Palace sits grandly at the top of the park.

Construction of the 173-room palace originally began in 1825 under the reign of Charles III but wasn't completed until 1849, five years after the death of Charles. His son, Oscar I, and daughter-in-law, Josephine, became the first royals to move in. The palace had some structural faults at construction but, for budget reasons, these were only rectified, and the palace given a general renovation, under the current monarch, King Harald V.

What's remarkable about this palace, and the royal family in general, is how approachable it is: children play and tourists pose for photos just metres from the main entrance door – quite a contrast to some other European royal palaces.

In summer one-hour guided **tours** of the interior of the palace are available. Tickets can be bought either at the gate (which is at the rear of the palace), by phone, at 7-Eleven stores or from www.billetservice.no. Tours visit a dozen rooms including the Cabinet Cloakroom, Mirror Room, Banqueting Hall and the Palace Chapel.

Museet for Samtidskunst   GALLERY
(National Museum for Contemporary Art; Map p56; ☑ 21 98 20 00; www.nasjonalmuseet.no; Bankplassen 4; adult/child Nkr50/free, Sun free; ☉ 11am-5pm Tue, Wed & Fri, to 7pm Thu, noon-5pm Sat & Sun) The National Museum of Contemporary Art features the National Gallery's collections of post-WWII Scandinavian and international art. Some works in the 3000-piece collection are definitely an acquired taste, but it does provide a timely reminder that Norwegian art didn't cease with Edvard Munch. There are frequent cutting-edge temporary exhibitions. The in-house cafe is also worthy of praise.

Stenersen Museum   GALLERY
(Stenersenmuseet; Map p56; ☑ 23 49 36 00; www.stenersen.museum.no; Munkedamsveien 15; adult/child Nkr60/free, Tue & with Oslo Pass free; ☉ noon-5pm Tue-Wed & Fri, 11am-7pm Thu, 11am-5pm Sat & Sun) This museum of Modernism, Realism and avant-garde art contains three formerly private collections of works, dating

from 1850 to 1970, by Norwegian artists. The museum and much of the art, which includes works by Ludvig Karsten and Amaldus Nielsen, were a gift to the city by Rolf E Stenersen.

Ibsen Museet
MUSEUM

(Ibsen Museum; Map p56; ☑40 02 36 3040 02 36 30; www.ibsenmuseet.no; Henrik Isbens Gate 26; adult/child Nkr95/30; ☺guided tours hourly 11am-6pm mid-May–mid-Sep, 11am-4pm Mon-Wed & Fri-Sun, 11am-6pm Thu rest of year) Housed in the last residence of Norwegian playwright Henrik Ibsen, the Ibsen Museum is a must-see for Ibsen fans. The study remains exactly as he left it, and other rooms have been restored to the style and colours popular in Ibsen's day. Visitors can even glance into the bedroom where he uttered his famously enigmatic last words 'Tvert imot!' ('To the contrary!'), before dying on 23 May 1906.

Historisk Museum
MUSEUM

(Map p56; ☑22 85 19 00; www.khm.uio.no; Frederiks gate 2, University of Oslo; adult/child Nkr50/free, with Oslo Pass free; ☺10am-5pm Tue-Sun mid-May–mid-Sep, 10am-4pm rest of year) The Historical Museum is actually three museums under one roof. Most interesting is the ground-floor **National Antiquities Collection** (Oldsaksamlingen), which has displays of Viking-era coins, jewellery and ornaments. Look out for the 9th-century **Hon treasure** (2.5kg), the largest such find in Scandinavia. A section on medieval religious art includes the doors and richly painted ceiling of the Ål stave church (built around 1300).

The second level has an **Arctic exhibit** and the Myntkabinettet, a collection of the earliest Norwegian coins from as far back as AD 995. Also on the second level, and continuing on the top floor, is the **Ethnographic Museum**, with changing exhibits on Asia, Africa and the Americas.

Oslo Cathedral
CATHEDRAL

(Domkirke; Map p56; Stortorvet 1; ☺24hr) FREE Dating from 1697, the highlights of a visit to Oslo Cathedral are the elaborate stained-glass windows by Emanuel Vigeland (brother of Gustav) and the painted ceiling, completed between 1936 and 1950. The exceptional altarpiece, a 1748 model of the *Last Supper and the Crucifixion* by Michael Rasch, was an original feature of the church (from 1700), but it was moved all over the country before being returned from Prestnes church in Majorstue in 1950.

The bazaar halls, around the back of the church, date from 1858 and are currently used by summer handicraft sales outlets and cafes.

Rådhus
ARCHITECTURE

(Map p56; Fridtjof Nansens plass; ☺9am-6pm, guided tours 10am, noon & 2pm Mon-Sat, also 4pm Sun Jun-Aug, Wed only rest of year) FREE This twin-towered town hall, completed in 1950 to commemorate Oslo's 900th anniversary, houses the city's political administration. Something of an Oslo landmark, its red-brick functionalist exterior is unusual, if not particularly attractive. It's here that the Nobel Peace Prize is awarded on 10 December each year.

Parliament Building
BUILDING

(Stortinget; Map p56; ☑23 31 33 33; www.stortinget.no; Karl Johans gate 22; ☺guided tours in English 10am & 1pm, in Norwegian 11.30am Jul & Aug, Sat only rest of year) FREE Built in 1866, Norway's yellow-brick parliament building is one of Europe's more charming parliaments. If you find yourself really hooked on Norwegian political debate, you can tune into the live action through the Stortinget website.

Akershus Festning & Slott

Strategically located on the eastern side of the harbour, dominating the Oslo harbourfront, are the medieval castle and fortress, arguably Oslo's architectural highlights. The complex as a whole is known as **Akershus Festning** (Akershus Fortress; Map p56; ☺6am-9pm) FREE. Inside the expansive complex are a couple of museums and interesting buildings. Entry to the fortress is through a gate at the end of Akersgata or over a drawbridge spanning Kongens gate at the southern end of Kirkegata. After 6pm in winter, use the Kirkegata entrance.

When Oslo was named capital of Norway in 1299, King Håkon V ordered the construction of Akershus to protect the city from external threats. It has since been extended, modified and had its defences beefed up a number of times.

When Oslo was rebuilt after a devastating fire in 1624, the city, renamed Christiania, was shifted to the less vulnerable and more defensible site behind the protective fortress walls. By 1818 the need for defence had been superseded by the need for space and most of the outer rampart was destroyed to accommodate population growth. From 1899 to 1963 it underwent major renovations, and nowadays the parklike grounds serve as

Oslo

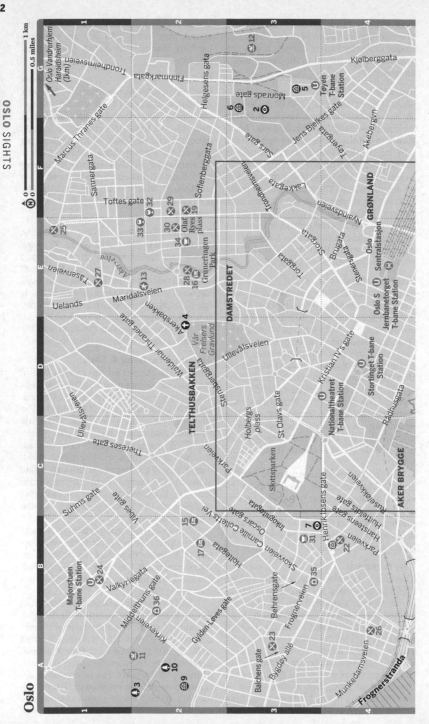

0.5 miles / 1 km

Oslo Vandrerhjem Haraldsheim (1km)

Trondheimsveien

Marcus Thranes gate

Sannergata

Toftes gate

Finnmarkgata

Helgesens gata

Monrads gate

Kjølberggata

Tøyen T-bane Station

Jens Bjelkes gate

Tøyengata

Akebergvn

Sars gate

Sofienberggata

32

29

19

33

30

34

Olaf Ryes plass

Grünerhagen Park

Trondheimsveien

Lakkegata

GRØNLAND

Nylandsveien

25

27

Tåsenveien

Akerselva

13

Maridalsveien

Uelands

Akersbakken

28

16

Grünerløkka

4

Vår Frelsers Gravlund

DAMSTREDET

Storgata

Brugata

Torggata

Steenstrupsgt

Nyvandsgata

Oslo Sentralstasjon

Oslo S

Jernbanetorget T-bane Station

Waldemar Thranes gate

Steenstrupsgata

Ueland Slellteveien

Ullevålsveien

Ullevålsveien

TELTHUSBAKKEN

Parkveien

St Olavs gate

Holbergs plass

Kristian IV's gate

Nationaltheatret T-bane Station

Stortinget T-bane Station

Rådhusgata

Thereses gate

Suhms gate

Vibes gate

Slottsparken

Inkognitogata

Camilla Colletts Vei

Oscars gate

Skovveien

Holtegata

17

15

Henrik Ibsens gate

Huitfeldts gate

Ruseløkkveien

AKER BRYGGE

Majorstuen T-bane Station

24

Valkyriegata

Middelthuns gate

36

Kirkeveien

Gylden Løves gate

Behrensgate

Frognerveien

35

7

31

Parkveien

Hansteens gate

22

3

11

10

9

Balchens gate

Bygdøy allé

23

26

Munkedamsveien

Frognerstranda

a venue for concerts, dances and theatrical productions – a far cry from its warlike origins and a welcome departure from its grim history. Note, however, that this complex remains a military installation and may be closed to the public whenever there's a state function.

The **Akershus Fortress Information Centre** (Map p56; ☎ 23 09 39 17; Akershus Slott; guided tours adult/child Nkr50/30; ⏰ 10am-5pm Mon-Fri, 11am-5pm Sat & Sun May-Aug, 10am-4pm Mon-Fri, 11am-5pm Sat & Sun rest of year), inside the main gate, has permanant exhibits recounting the history of the Akershus complex, as well as temporary exhibits highlighting aspects of Oslo's history. Staff can organise guided tours. At 1.30pm you can watch the changing of the guard at the fortress.

Akershus Slott
CASTLE

(Akershus Castle; Map p56; ☎ 22 41 25 21; www.nasjonalefestningsverk.no; adult/child Nkr70/30, with Oslo pass free; ⏰ 10am-4pm Mon-Sat, noon-4pm Sun May-Aug, noon-5pm Sat & Sun Sep-Apr, guided tours 11am, 1pm, 3pm mid-Jun–mid-Aug, shorter hours May–mid-Jun & mid-Aug–Sep) In the 17th century, Christian IV renovated Akershus Castle into a Renaissance palace, although the front remains decidedly medieval. In its dungeons you'll find dark cubbyholes where outcast nobles were kept under lock and key, while the upper floors contained sharply contrasting lavish banquet halls and staterooms.

The castle chapel is still used for army events, and the crypts of King Håkon VII and Olav V lie beneath it. The guided **tours** are led by university students in period dress and, while not compulsory, they do offer an entertaining anecdotal history of the place that you won't get by wandering around on your own.

Norwegian Resistance Museum
MUSEUM

(Norges Hjemmefront Museet; Map p56; ☎ 23 09 31 38; www.forsvaretsmuseer.no; adult/child Nkr50/25, with Oslo Pass free; ⏰ 10am-5pm Mon-Sat, 11am-5pm Sun Jun-Aug, 10am-4pm Mon-Fri, 11am-4pm Sat & Sun rest of year) Within the Akershus fortress complex, the Norwegian Resistance Museum stands adjacent to a memorial for resistance fighters executed on the spot during WWII. The small but worthwhile museum covers the dark years of German occupation, as well as the jubilant day of 9 May 1945 when peace was declared. Artefacts include underground newspapers, numerous maps and photographs, and, most

OSLO SIGHTS

Oslo

intriguingly, a set of dentures that belonged to a Norwegian prisoner of war in Poland that were wired to receive radio broadcasts.

⊙ Frognerparken & Vigeland Park

Frognerparken PARK
(Map p52) This park attracts locals with its broad lawns, ponds, stream and rows of shady trees. On a sunny afternoon it's ideal for picnics, strolling or lounging on the grass.

To get here, take tram 12 to Vigelandsparken from the city centre.

Vigeland Park PARK
(Map p52) The centrepiece of Frognerparken is an extraordinary open-air showcase of work by Norway's best-loved sculptor, Gustav Vigeland. Statistically one of the top tourist attractions in Norway, Vigeland Park is brimming with 212 granite and bronze Vigeland works. His highly charged work ranges from entwined lovers and tranquil elderly couples to contempt-ridden beggars. His most renowned work, *Sinnataggen* (Little Hot-Head), portrays a London child in a mood of particular ill humour.

Oslo City Museum MUSEUM
(Oslo Bymuseet; Map p52; ☑23 28 41 70; www.oslomuseum.no; Frognerveien 67; ⊙11am-4pm Tue-Sun, closed last week Dec–mid-Jan) **FREE** Near the southern entrance to Vigeland Park lies this museum. Housed in the 18th-century Frogner Manor (built on the site of a Viking-era manor), it contains exhibits of minor interest on the city's history.

Vigeland Museum GALLERY
(www.vigeland.museum.no; Nobelsgata 32; adult/child Nkr60/30, with Oslo Pass free; ⊙10am-5pm Tue-Sun May-Aug, noon-4pm Tue-Sun rest of year) For an in-depth look at Gustav Vigeland's work, visit the Vigeland Museum, opposite the southern entrance to Frognerparken. It was built by the city in the 1920s as a home and workshop for the sculptor in exchange for the donation of a significant propor-tion of his life's work. It contains his early collection of statuary and monuments to public figures, as well as plaster moulds, woodblock prints and sketches.

When he died in 1943, his ashes were de-posited in the tower, and the museum was opened to the public four years later. Guided **tours** are available (in English), with prior notice, from Nkr800 per group. In addition to the works of Vigeland, the museum also has a changing schedule of modern art.

Bygdøy Peninsula

The Bygdøy Peninsula holds some of Oslo's top attractions. You can rush around all the sights in half a day, but allotting a few extra hours will be more rewarding.

Although only minutes from central Oslo, Bygdøy maintains its rural character. The royal family has a summer home here, as do many foreign ambassadors and Oslo's most well-to-do residents.

Ferry No 91 (☑23 35 68 90; onboard adult/child Nkr50/25, from kiosks on departure jetty adult/child Nkr30/15, with the Oslo Pass free) makes the 15-minute run to Bygdøy every 20 minutes from 11.05am to 4.25pm from early April to early October, and every 30 minutes from 8.45am to 10.45am and 4.45pm to 8.45pm between mid-May and late August, with earlier final departures during the rest of the year. Keep an eye out for the king's ship KS *Norge* on the ride over, as well as the king's and queen's royal yacht clubs *(Kongen* and *Dronningen),* which face one another on either side of the Frognerkilen.

The ferries leave from **Rådhusbrygge 3** (Map p56; opposite the Rådhus) and stop first at Dronningen ferry terminal, from where it's a 10 minute walk to the Norsk Folkemuseum and a 15-minute walk to the Vikingskipshuset. Beyond the ships it's a further 20 minutes' walk to Bygdøynes, where the Kon-Tiki, Polarship Fram and Norwegian Maritime Museums are clustered; the route is signposted and makes a pleasant walk. Alternatively, the ferry continues to Bygdøynes. You can also take bus 30 from Jernbanetorget T-bane station.

Vikingskipshuset MUSEUM
(Viking Ship Museum; ☑22 13 52 80; www.khm. uio.no; Huk Aveny 35; adult/child Nkr60/30, with Oslo Pass free; ⊙9am-6pm May-Sep, 10am-4pm rest of year) Even in repose, there is something intimidating about the sleek, dark hulls of the Viking ships *Oseberg* and *Gokstad* – the best-preserved such ships in the world. There is also a third boat at the Vikingskipshuset, the *Tune,* but only a few boards and fragments remain. This museum is a must for anyone who enjoyed childhood stories of Vikings (so that's everyone).

OSLO SIGHTS

GUSTAV VIGELAND

The sculptor Gustav Vigeland (1869–1943) was born to a farming family near Mandal, in the far south of Norway. As a child and teenager he became deeply interested in Protestantism, spirituality, woodcarving and drawing – a unique combination that would dominate his life's work. In 1888 Vigeland secured an apprenticeship to sculptor Brynjulf Bergslien. The following year he exhibited his first work at the State Exhibition of Art. It was the break he needed, bringing his talents to national and international attention.

In 1891 he travelled to Copenhagen and then to Paris and Italy, where he worked with various masters; he was especially inspired by the work of French sculptor Auguste Rodin. When his public grants ran out he returned to Norway to make a living working on the restoration of the Nidaros Cathedral in Trondheim and producing commissioned portraits of prominent Norwegians.

In 1921 the City of Oslo recognised his talents and built him a spacious studio in which to work; it's now a museum (p54).

The highlight of Vigeland Park (p54), an open-air showcase of Vigeland's work in Frognerparken, is the 14m-high granite *Monolith,* which crowns the park's highest hill. This incredible production required three stone carvers working daily from 1929 to 1943 and was carved from a single stone pillar quarried from Iddefjorden in southeastern Norway. It depicts a writhing mass of 121 detailed human figures, both entwined with and undermining each other in their individual struggle to reach the top. The circle of steps around it supports rows of stone figures. The figures, together with the pillar, have been interpreted in many ways: as a phallic representation, the struggle for existence, yearnings for the spiritual spheres and transcendence of cyclic repetition.

Leading down from the plinth bearing this column is a series of steps that support sculptures depicting people experiencing the full range of human emotions and activities. The numerous sculptures dominating the surrounding park carry the artist's themes, from the realistic to the ludicrous.

Central Oslo

Parkveien
Pilestredet
Hegdehaugsveien
26
67
Inkognitogata
68
Wergelandsveien
Parkveien
Holbergs gate
Tullins Gate
Nordahl Bruns gate
Slottsparken
St Olavs gate
St Olavs plass
St Olavs gate
12
Pilestredet
52
St Olavs gate
Frederiks gate
Kristian Augusts gate
15
Kristian Augusts gate
5
8
CJ Hambros plass
Kristian IV's gate
53
69
Henrik Ibsens gate
Nationaltheatret
T-bane Station
6 44
31
33
Arbins gate
Kronprinsens gate
70
61
21
Karl Johans gate
28
54
Grensen
64
49
Eidsvolls-plass
Ruseløkkveien
16
Oslo Tourist Office
Stortingsgata
22
Haakon VII's gate
13
Fridtjof Nansens plass
Universitetsgata
Stortinget
T-bane Station
Dronning Mauds gate
Munkedamsveien
9
14
Olav V's gate
Rådhusplassen
Thorvald Meyers gate
Rosenkrantz gate
Øvre Vollgate
Nedre Vollgate
Prinsens gate
20
Rådhusbrygge
42
Akersgata
Nedre Slottsgate
Kongens gate
Kirkegata
AKER BRYGGE
38
Rådhusbrygge
Rådhusgata
32
17
Rådhusbrygge Quay (Boat Terminal)
36
29
Aker Brygge Pier
45
7
18
Akershus Fortress Information Centre
Myntgata
Pipervika
10
2
3
Hovedøya

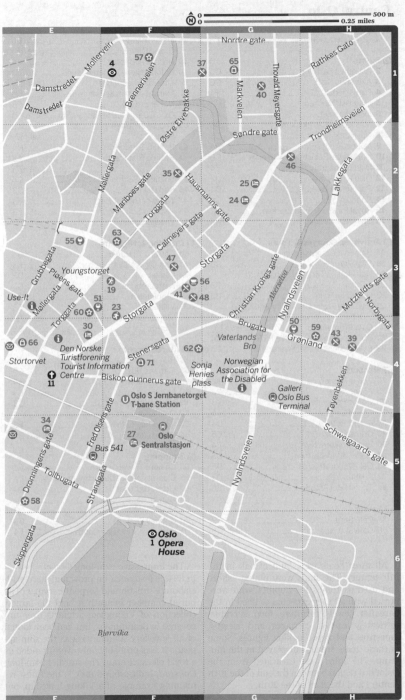

Central Oslo

All three boats were built of oak in the 9th century. The ships were pulled ashore and used as tombs for nobility, who were buried with all they expected to need in the hereafter: jewels, furniture, food, servants, intricately carved carriages and sleighs, tapestries and fierce-looking figures. Some of these items are also displayed in the museum. The ships were excavated from the Oslofjord region between the end of the 19th century and the start of the 20th.

The impressive 22m-long *Oseberg,* buried in 834, is festooned on prow and stern with elaborate dragon and serpent carvings. The burial chamber beneath it held the largest collection of Viking-age artefacts ever uncovered in Scandinavia, but had been looted of all jewellery. As daunting as the ship appears, it was probably only ever intended as a royal pleasure craft. The sturdier 24m-long *Gokstad,* built around 890, is the finest remaining example of a Viking longship, but when it was unearthed its corresponding burial chamber had also been looted and few artefacts were uncovered. In addition to the three ships, there are displays of skeletons found alongside the boats.

Norsk Folkemuseum MUSEUM
(Norwegian Folk Museum; ☏ 22 12 37 00; www.norskfolkemuseum.no; Museumsveien 10; adult/child Nkr110/30, with Oslo Pass free; ◷10am-6pm mid-May–mid-Sep, 11am-3pm Mon-Fri, 11am-4pm Sat & Sun mid-Sep–mid-May) Norway's largest open-air museum and one of Oslo's premier attractions is this folk museum. The museum includes more than 140 buildings, mostly from the 17th and 18th centuries, gathered from around the country, rebuilt and organised according to region of origin. Paths wind past old barns, elevated *stabbur* (raised storehouses) and rough-timbered farmhouses with sod roofs sprouting wildflowers. Children will be entertained by the numerous farm animals, horse-and-cart rides and other activities (some of which cost extra).

The Gamlebyen (Old Town) section is a reproduction of an early-20th-century Norwegian town and includes a village shop and an old petrol station; everyday throughout the summer you can see demonstrations of weaving, pottery-making and other artisan and cultural activities. Another highlight is the restored stave church, built around 1200 in Gol and shifted to Bygdøy in 1885.

LOCAL KNOWLEDGE

THE WORLD'S MOST PRESTIGIOUS PRIZE

Most Nobel prizes – physics, chemistry, medicine, literature and economics – are awarded every October in Stockholm, but the most prestigious prize of all, the Peace Prize, is reserved for Oslo. In his will in 1895, Alfred Nobel, the Swedish founder of the prize and the inventor of dynamite, instructed that the interest on his vast fortune be awarded each year 'to those who, during the preceding year, shall have conferred the greatest benefit on mankind'.

It is unclear why Nobel chose Norway to administer the Peace Prize, but whatever the reason, it is a committee of five Norwegians, appointed for six-year terms by the Norwegian *storting* (parliament), that chooses the winner each year. Their meetings, held in a room of the Nobel Institute (Map p52) that is decorated with the pictures of winners past, from Mother Teresa (1979) to Mikhail Gorbachev (1990) and Al Gore (2007), are closed-door affairs presided over by the chairman of the Norwegian Nobel Committee, Thorbjørn Jagland. Meetings are also attended by the institute's director, Geir Lundestad. Appointed director in 1990, Lundestad filled us in on some prize history.

What's the difference between being nominated and short-listed for the Peace Prize? Anyone can be nominated, from President George Bush to Madonna, and this often causes a huge outcry, but there is a big difference between being nominated and being selected as the winner! We start from almost 200 candidates in February. The list is cut down to 30, then five, and the rest of the time is spent focusing on the qualifications of the candidates on the short list.

Is the committee ever criticised for being too secretive? The committee is transparent, but it is true that the list of nominees is closed for 50 years and no minutes are kept, though some of the members keep notes, which they have made public.

How has the nature of the prize changed while you've been director? The definition of peace has slowly broadened to include elements that reflect the changing world. Human rights, for example, was initially a very controversial interpretation when it [the prize] was given in 1960 to South African activist Albert Lutuli. The environment was added as a road to peace in 2004 and there is always pressure to widen the definition further.

Describe the ideal candidate? Many see the prize as a declaration of sainthood, but winners are often just more or less ordinary people who have tried to do something useful for peace. Their efforts have been heroic, but they are all very different. At the same time, they share a vision and they have the courage to carry it out.

As told to Kari Lundgren

Oslo

Avert your gaze for an instant and Oslo changes. The waterfront is undergoing a facelift that's conjured up the Oslo Opera House, the Astrup Fearnley Museet and even a man-made beach, but the powers that be don't want to stop there: they want Oslo to become the cultural capital of Scandinavia.

RUDI SEBASTIAN/GETTY IMAGES ©

1. Oslo Opera House (p47)
Cafes and bars outside the opera house

2. Architecture
Vibrant night cityscape highlights modern Norwegian design

3. Aker Brygge (p48)
Boats in the harbour in this newly developed area

4. Astrup Fearnley Museet (p48)
Visitors admire the artwork moonrise.east.november by Ugo Rondinone

JACKIETRAVELLER OSLO/ALAMY ©

SABINE LUBENOW/ROBERT HARDING ©

OSLO FOR CHILDREN

After the long, dark winter nights, the arrival of spring and summer brings masses of baby carriages out onto the streets (we wonder if there is a connection between said long, dark nights and the amount of children in Oslo...). Despite this, Oslo is not one of Europe's more child-friendly cities, as many of the sights and restaurants are aimed squarely at adults, and it can sometimes feel as if children are tolerated more than welcomed. Note also that most of the museums and galleries insist on making you use one of their own baby carriages – something guaranteed to please every parent who has just managed to get their little darling off to sleep!

Despite this, you can still visit Oslo with children and enjoy the experience. Most Oslo parents will tell you that the best activities are often the simplest and are free. There are no rules against climbing the statues at Frognerparken (p54), for example, or chasing your little sister around the garden's 3000m mosaic labyrinth. The park also has one of the city's best playgrounds. Nearer the centre, the cannons and fortifications at Akershus Festning (p51) are great for sparking the imagination. The Norsk Folkemuseum (p59) also has regular events geared towards children.

Oslo City Train (Map p56; ☑ 48 17 44 44; www.oslocitytrain.no; adult/child/child under 5yrs/family Nkr100/50/free/280; ☻ 9.30am-5pm late Jun-Aug) Chuff and toot around central Oslo on one of two different steam 'trains'. Tours depart every half-hour from Aker Brygge and University Square (Map p56) on Karl Johans gate.

EKT Riding School & Animal Park (EKT Rideskole og Husdyrpark; ☑ 22 19 97 86; www.rideskole.no; Bekkelagshøgda 12; animal park Nkr50, pony ride Nkr40; ☻ 9.30am-5.30pm Mar-Oct, 10am-5pm Nov-Feb) For a more rural version of Oslo, the EKT Riding School and Animal Park in the Ekeberg forest southeast of the city centre has sheep, goats, pigs and rabbits, as well as Norwegian fjord ponies which children can trot about on between 11am and 3pm on weekdays and until 5pm on weekends between March and October (shorter hours during

The exhibition hall located near the main entrance includes exhaustive displays on Norwegian folk art, historic toys, national costumes (including traditional clothing used for weddings, christenings and burials), domestic and farming tools and appliances, as well as visiting exhibits. However, the most interesting exhibition focuses on the life and culture of the Sami. It examines their former persecution and looks at how they have adapted to life in a modern Norway. Temporary exhibitions can be as varied as church art or 1950s pop culture. Sunday is a good day to visit, as this day tends to have the most activities.

As most of the exhibits are outdoors, it makes sense to go on a nice day!

Polarship Fram Museum   MUSEUM
(☑ 23 28 29 50; www.frammuseum.no; adult/child Nkr80/30, with Oslo Pass free; ☻ 9am-6pm Jun-Aug, 10am-5pm May & Sep, 10am-4pm rest of year) Nature is often the best architect. Which is why, when well-known shipbuilder Colin Archer was asked to design a ship whose hull could withstand the crush of polar ice, he looked no further than an egg for inspiration – the oval design ensures that when ice is contracting against it, the boat is pushed up and onto the ice rather than being merely crushed by it. This museum is the final resting place of his creation, the *Polarship Fram*.

Launched in 1892, the *Polarship Fram*, at the time the strongest ship ever built, spent much of its life trapped in the polar ice. From 1893 to 1896 Fridtjof Nansen's North Pole expedition took the 39m schooner to Russia's New Siberian Islands, passing within a few degrees of the North Pole on their return trip to Norway.

In 1910 Roald Amundsen set sail in the *Fram* (meaning 'forward'), intending to be the first explorer to reach the North Pole, only to discover en route that Robert Peary had beaten him to it. Not to be outdone, Amundsen turned the *Fram* around and, racing Robert Falcon Scott all the way, became the first man to reach the South Pole. Otto Sverdrup also sailed the schooner around southern Greenland to Canada's Ellesmere Island between 1898 and 1902, travelling over 18,000km.

In addition to the *Fram*, the museum also houses the *Gjøa*, the first ship to successfully navigate the Northwest Passage.

the winter). Take tram 19 towards I jabru to Sportsplassen and walk 15 minutes uphill until you reach the farm.

Oslo Reptilpark (Map p56; www.reptilpark.no; St Olavs gate 2; adult/child Nkr100/70, with Oslo Pass free; ⊙10am-6pm daily Apr-Aug, Tue-Sun Sep-Mar) For something slippery, most kids will love meeting the snakes and lizards (as well as the odd monkey) at the Oslo Reptilpark.

Akerforeningen (www.akeforeningen.no; Holmenkollen; adult/child from Nkr100/80; ⊙9am-9pm Mon-Sat, 10am-6pm Sun winter) In the winter try sledding down the 'legendary' Korketrekkeren (corkscrew) toboggan run. The 2km-long track drops 255m and began its life as a bobsledding run for the 1952 Olympics. Sleds can be rented at the Akerforeningen, next to the Frognerseteren restaurant. To get here, take the T-bane to Frognerseteren and follow the signs downhill.

Norwegian Science & Technology Museum (Norsk Teknisk Museum & Telemuseum; ☏22 79 60 00; www.tekniskmuseum.no; Kjelsåsveien 143; adult/child Nkr100/50, with Oslo Pass free; ⊙10am-6pm daily late Jun–late Aug, 9am-4pm Mon-Fri, 11am-6pm Sat & Sun rest of year) A popular rainy-day distraction near Lake Maridal, Norwegian Science & Technology Museum has Norway's first car and tram, water wheels, clocks and enough gadgetry to keep the whole family busy for a few hours at least.

TusenFryd (☏64 97 64 97; www.tusenfryd.no; Vinterbro; height over/under 120cm Nkr369/299, under 95cm free; ⊙10.30am-7pm mid-Jun–Aug, shorter hours rest of year) TusenFryd, an amusement park 10km south of the city, is enormously popular with kids from all over the Oslo region. The park offers carousels, a fantasy farm and an excellent wooden roller coaster, which creates zero gravity 12 times each circuit. You'll find it just off the E6. The TusenFryd bus (bus 546) departs from the corner of Fred Olsens gate and Prinsens gate roughly hourly between 10am and 4pm.

You're allowed to thoroughly explore the ship, peek inside the cramped bunk rooms and imagine life at sea. In addition, there are detailed exhibits, complete with maps, pictures and artefacts, that bring the various expeditions to life, from Nansen's attempt to ski across the North Pole to Amundsen's discovery of the Northwest Passage and the fateful rescue attempt that ended in his disappearance. Other exhibitions look at life in the polar regions and the wildlife of the area; there's even a polar simulator.

Kon-Tiki Museum   MUSEUM
(☏23 08 67 67; www.kon-tiki.no; Bygdøynesveien 36; adult/child Nkr90/40, with Oslo Pass free; ⊙9.30am-6pm Jun-Aug, 10am-5pm Mar-May & Sep-Oct, 10am-4pm Nov-Feb) A favourite among children, this worthwhile museum is dedicated to the balsa raft *Kon-Tiki,* which Norwegian explorer Thor Heyerdahl sailed from Peru to Polynesia in 1947. The museum also displays the totora-reed boat *Ra II,* built by Aymara people on the Bolivian island of Suriqui in Lake Titicaca. Heyerdahl used it to cross the Atlantic in 1970.

Norwegian Maritime Museum   MUSEUM
(Norsk Maritimt Museum; Map p52; www.marmuseum.no; Bygdøy-nesveien 37; adult/child Nkr80/30, with Oslo Pass free; ⊙10am-5pm mid-May–Aug, 10am-3pm Tue-Fri, 10am & 4pm Sat & Sun rest of year) Author Roald Dahl once said that in Norway everyone seems to have a boat, and there is no better place to explore that theory than here. The museum depicts Norway's relationship with the sea, including the fishing and whaling industries, the seismic fleet (which searches for oil and gas), shipbuilding and wreck salvaging. The highlight for many is a 20-minute film with footage of the Norwegian coastline.

⊙ Grünerløkka Area

Munchmuseet   GALLERY
(Munch Museum; Map p52; ☏23 49 35 00; www.munchmuseet.no; Tøyengata 53; adult/child Nkr95/40, with Oslo Pass free; ⊙10am-5pm mid-Jun–Sep, 11am-5pm Wed-Mon rest of year) Fans of Edvard Munch (1863–1944) won't want to miss the Munch Museum, which is dedicated to his life's work and has most of the pieces not contained in the National Gallery. The

museum provides a comprehensive look at the artist's work, from dark (*The Sick Child*) to light (*Spring Ploughing*). With over 1100 paintings, 4500 watercolours and 18,000 prints and sketching books bequeathed to the city by Munch himself, this is a landmark collection.

To get here, take bus 20 or the T-bane to Tøyen, followed by a five-minute signposted walk.

Botanical Garden
GARDENS

(Botanisk Hage; Map p52; Sars gate 1; ⊙7am-9pm Mon-Fri, 10am-9pm Sat & Sun mid-Mar–Sep, to 5pm rest of year) **FREE** Oslo's 15-acre Botanical Garden features over 7500 plants from around the world. There are also plants from the Oslo fjords, including four that are almost extinct in nature. However, most visitors don't actually care what the plants are and just content themselves with lolling about under a tree!

Natural History Museum
MUSEUM

(Naturhistorisk Museum; Map p52; www.nhm.uio.no; Sars gate 1; adult/child Nkr50/25; ⊙11am-4pm Tue-Sun) Under the trees of Oslo's Botanical Garden, the university's Natural History Museum comprises two different museums: the **Zoological Museum** (Map p52), which as you might guess is stuffed full of stuffed (excuse the pun) native wildlife. Adjacent to this is the **Geological-Palaeontological Museum** (Map p52), which contains displays on the history of the solar system and Norwegian geology, as well as examples of myriad minerals, meteorites and moon rocks.

The palaeontological section includes Ida, the world's oldest complete primate fossil. In addition you can ogle a 10m-long iguanodon skeleton and a nest of dinosaur eggs. The admission fee also allows you to get green-fingered with the tropical plants inside the greenhouses.

Damstredet
OLD TOWN

(Map p56) The quirky 18th-century wooden homes of the Damstredet district and the nearby Telthusbakken are a nice change of pace from the modern architecture of the city centre. Once an impoverished shanty town, Damstredet has become a popular residential neighbourhood for artists. To get there, walk north on Akersgata and turn right on Damstredet gate. Telthusbakken is a little further up Akersgata, also on the right.

On the way, you'll pass **Vår Frelsers Gravlund**, the graveyard where Ibsen,

Munch and Bjørnstjerne Bjørnson are buried.

Gamle Aker Kirke
CHURCH

(Map p52; Akersbakken 26; ⊙noon-2pm Mon-Sat) **FREE** This medieval stone church, located north of the centre on Akersbakken, dates from 1080 and is Oslo's oldest building. Take bus 37 from Jernbanetorget to Akersbakken, then walk up past the churchyard.

⊙ Greater Oslo

Holmenkollen Ski Jump & Museum
MUSEUM

(⊘91 67 19 47; www.holmenkollen.com; adult/child Nkr120/60, with Oslo Pass free; ⊙9am-8pm Jun-Aug, 10am-5pm May & Sep, 10am-4pm rest of year) The Holmenkollen Ski Jump, perched on a hilltop overlooking Oslo, offers a panoramic view of the city and doubles as a concert venue. During Oslo's annual **ski festival**, held in March, it draws the world's best ski jumpers. Even if you're not a daredevil ski jumper, the complex is well worth a visit thanks to its ski museum and a couple of other attractions.

The **Ski Museum** (Kongeveien 5; entry incl in ticket for Holmenkollen; ⊙9am-8pm Jun-Aug, 10am-5pm May & Sep, 10am-4pm rest of year) leads you through the 4000-year history of Nordic and downhill skiing in Norway. There are exhibits featuring the Antarctic expeditions of Amundsen and Scott, as well as Fridtjof Nansen's slog across the Greenland icecap (you'll see the boat he constructed from his sled and canvas tent to row the final 100km to Nuuk).

Admission also includes a visit to the **ski-jump tower**. Part of the route to the top of the tower is served by a lift, but you're on your own for the final 114 steep steps. Outside, the **ski-jump simulator** (⊘90 01 20 46; www.skisimulator.no; adult/child Nkr65/40; ⊙9am-8pm Jun-Aug, 10am-5pm May & Sep, 10am-4pm rest of year) is good for a laugh, but don't try it if you have a weak stomach. To get to the museum, take T-bane line 1 to Holmenkollen and follow the signs uphill.

Nordmarka
FOREST

The woodland north of the Holmenkollen Ski Jump, known as Nordmarka, is a prime destination for hiking, mountain biking, sledding and skiing. It's also the geographical centre of the city, which must make Oslo, quite appropriately, about the only capital in the world to have a wild forest at its heart!

For skiers, there is **Tryvan Vinterpark**. In the summer the **Tryvannstårnet observation tower** is a good place to start a hike or a bike trip.

Make sure you take a container for picking blueberries in summer. From the Holmenkollen T-bane station, take the scenic ride to the end of the line at Frognerseteren and look for the signposted walking route.

Henie-Onstad Art Centre MODERN ART
(Henie-Onstad Kunstsenter; ☑ 67 84 48 80; www.hok.no; Høvikodden; adult/child Nkr80/free; ⊙ 11am-7pm Tue-Thu, to 5pm Fri-Sun) This private art museum contains works by Joan Miró and Pablo Picasso, as well as assorted impressionist, abstract, expressionist and modern Norwegian works. There's a free bus from the Thon Hotel near the Opera House to the museum every half-hour in summer; otherwise take bus 151 to Høvikodden.

Activities

Avid skiers, hikers and sailors, Oslo residents will do just about anything to get outside. That's not too hard given that there are over 240 sq km of woodland, 40 islands and 343 lakes within the city limits.

Climbing

The best local climbing is on the prebolted faces of Kolsåstoppen, which is accessible on T-bane line 3 to Kolsås.

Vulkan Climbing Centre CLIMBING
(Map p52; ☑ 22 11 28 90; www.kolsaas.no; Maridalsveien 17; adult/child from Nkr70/60; ⊙ 10am-10pm Mon-Thu, 10am-9pm Fri, 10am-8pm Sat & Sun mid-Aug–May) Indoor climbing centre with challenges for all skill levels. The centre has climbing walls and bouldering walls.

Cycling

Mountain bikers will find plenty of trails on which to keep themselves occupied in the Oslo hinterland. The tourist office (p76) has free cycling maps, with *Sykkelkart Oslo* tracing the bicycle lanes and paths throughout the city, and *Idrett og friluftsliv i Oslo* covering the Oslo hinterland. It also has a pamphlet called *Opplevelsesturer i Marka,* which contains six possible cycling and/or hiking itineraries within reach of Oslo.

Two especially nice rides within the city (which are also suitable to do on an Oslo city bike) are along the Akerselva up to Lake Maridal (Maridalsvannet; 11km), and in the woods around Bygdøy. The trip to Maridal will pass several waterfalls and a number of

converted factories at the edge of Grünerløkka and cross several of Oslo's more unique bridges, including the Anker, or *eventyr* (fairy-tale), bridge. Cyclists should be sure to stop for coffee and a waffle at **Hønse-Louisas Hus** (Map p52; www.honselovisashus.no; Sandakerveien 2; ⊙ 11am-6pm May-Aug, 11am-4pm Mar-Apr & Sep). This can also be done on foot by taking the T-bane to Kjesås and following the path back into the city. Cycling, or walking, around Bygdøy is far more pastoral and provides ample opportunity for swimming breaks. There is a bike rack in front of the Norwegian Folk Museum. For more serious cycling, take T-bane line 1 to Frognerseteren and head into the Nordmarka.

Hiking

A network of 1200km of trails leads into Nordmarka from Frognerseteren (at the end of T-bane line 1), including a good trail down to Sognsvann lake, 6km northwest of the centre at the end of T-bane line 5. If you're walking in August, be sure to take a container for blueberries, and a swimsuit to cool off in the lake (bathing is allowed in all the woodland lakes around Oslo except Maridalsvannet and Skjersjøen lakes, which are drinking reservoirs). The pleasant walk around Sognsvann itself takes around an hour, or for a more extended trip, try hiking to the cabin at **Ullevålseter** (www.ullevalseter.

no; ☺ Tue-Sun), a pleasant old farmhouse that serves waffles and coffee. The round trip (about 11km) takes around three hours.

The Ekeberg woods to the southeast of the city centre – take bus 34 or 46 from Jernbanetorget to **Ekeberg Camping** (Map p52; ☑ 22 19 85 68; www.ekebergcamping.no; Ekebergveien 65; 4-person tent with/without car Nkr270/180; ☺ Jun-Aug; P) – is another nice place for a stroll. During the summer weekends, it's a popular spot for riding competitions and, more recently, cricket matches. There is an Iron Age heritage path through the woods. For a piece of architectural history, don't miss the **Ekeberg Restaurant** (Map p52; ☑ 23 24 23 00; www.ekebergrestauranten.com; Kongsveien 15; mains Nkr220, set menus from Nkr375; ☺ 11am-midnight Mon-Sat, noon-10pm Sun), one of the earliest examples of functionalism. On the way down, stop at the Valhall Curve to see the view that inspired Edvard Munch to paint *The Scream*.

The Den Norske Turistforening office (p76), which maintains several mountain huts in the Nordmarka region, can provide information and maps covering longer-distance hiking routes throughout Norway.

Ice Skating

There are several ice-skating rinks in and around the city.

Spikersuppa Outdoor Ice Rink   ICE-SKATING
(Map p56; Karl Johans gate) FREE The most central, and romantic, ice skating in Oslo can be found at the Spikersuppa outdoor ice rink, where you can skate for free whenever it's cold enough to freeze over (around November to March). The rink often closes around 3pm to allow for ice preparation. Skates can be hired from the ice rink for Nkr100.

Skiing

Oslo's ski season runs roughly from December to March. There are over 2400km of prepared Nordic tracks (1000km in Nordmarka alone), many of them floodlit, as well as a ski resort within the city limits. Easy-access tracks begin at the end of T-bane lines 1 and 5. The **Skiservice Centre** (☑ 22 13 95 00; www.skiservice.no; Tryvannsveien 2; ☺ 10am-8pm), at Voksenkollen station, one T-bane stop before Frognerseteren, hires out snowboards and Nordic skis. The downhill slopes at **Tryvann Vinterpark** (☑ 40 46 27 00; www.oslovinterpark.no; ☺ 10am-10pm Mon-Fri, to 5pm Sat & Sun Dec–mid-Apr) are open in the ski season. Check out www.holmenkollen.com for more ski-related info.

Swimming at Islands & Beaches

When (or perhaps, if) the weather heats up, there are a few reasonable beaches within striking distance of central Oslo. Ferries to half-a-dozen islands in the Oslofjord region leave from Vippetangen Quay (p76), southeast of Akershus Festning. Boats to Hovedøya and Langøyene are relatively frequent in summer (running at least hourly), while other islands are served less often. The last ferry leaves Vippetangen at 6.45pm in winter and 9.05pm in summer.

The southwestern shore of otherwise rocky Hovedøya, the nearest island to the mainland, is popular with sunbathers. The island is ringed with walking paths to old cannon emplacements and the 12th-century **Cistercian monastery ruins**.

South of Hovedøya lies the undeveloped island of Langøyene, which has superb swimming from rocky or sandy beaches (one on the southeastern shore is designated for nude bathing). Boat 94 will get you there, but it only runs during the summer.

The Bygdøy Peninsula has two popular beaches, **Huk** and **Paradisbukta**, which can be reached on bus 30 from Jernbanetorget to its last stop. While there are some sandy patches, most of Huk comprises grassy lawns and large smooth rocks ideal for sunbathing. Separated into two beaches by a small cove, the beach on the northwestern side is open to nude bathing. If Huk seems too crowded, a 10-minute walk through the woods north of the bus stop leads to the more secluded Paradisbukta.

Finally, just in front of the Astrup Fearnley Museet and bang in the heart of Oslo, there's a tiny, **artificial pebble beach** with very safe swimming that's popular with local families.

The waters around Oslo *can* get surprisingly warm – up to 22°C isn't unusual. So now you've got no excuse!

Swimming Pools

Oslo has two outdoor municipal swimming pools.

Frognerbadet Swimming Pool   SWIMMING
(Map p52; ☑ 23 27 54 50; Middelthuns gate 28; adult/child Nkr86/40; ☺ Jun–mid-Aug) A large outdoor pool complex inside the Frognerparken (entry via Middelthuns gate).

Tøyenbadet Swimming Pool   SWIMMING
(Map p52; ☑ 23 30 44 70; Helgesens gata 90; adult/child Nkr86/40; ☺ 7am-7pm) Near the Munchmuseet, this complex has a mixture

of large indoor pools and summer-only outdoor pools. The exact opening times for public swimming depends on the day and what lessons are running.

Tours

The best Oslo tours offer juicy cultural and historical morsels (or a boat trip), while also giving visitors the flexibility to explore at their leisure.

City Sightseeing BUS TOUR
(Map p56; www.citysightseeing.no; adult/child/family Nkr250/125/650; ⌚ first departure 9.30am, last departure 5.25pm mid-May–mid-Sep) Oslo's version of the hop-on, hop-off phenomenon. There are departures every half-hour. Tickets are valid for 24 hours, and cover the overwhelming proportion of city sights, which you can explore at your own pace. The tourist office has a list of bus stops.

Oslo Promenade WALKING TOUR
(Map p56; ☎22 42 70 20; www.guideservice.no; adult/child Nkr150/free, with Oslo Pass free) Oslo Guide Service offers personalised city tours for groups of up to 25 people (Nkr2000 per group), which have to be booked in advance. There's also a 1½-hour evening city walk starting from in front of the Rådhus (p51) at 5.30pm. The guides are knowledgeable and entertaining, making this a good option for getting an insider's view of Oslo.

Båtservice Sightseeing BOAT TOUR
(Map p56; ☎23 35 68 90; www.boatsightseeing.com; Pier 3, Rådhusbrygge; per person Nkr185-590; ⌚Apr-Sep) For a watery view of Oslo and the Oslofjord, Båtservice Sightseeing offers a whole array of tours aboard either a traditional wooden schooner or a more up-to-date motor boat. Some tours are also combined with bus rides.

Festivals & Events

For details on all upcoming events in the city, take a look at www.visitoslo.com.

Inferno Metal Festival MUSIC
(www.infernofestival.net; ⌚early Apr) This festival lets the dark lords of heavy metal loose on the good people of Oslo.

National Constitution Day CULTURAL
(⌚17 May) Oslo's most festive annual event is surely this celebration, when Oslo residents, whose roots spring from all over Norway, descend on the Royal Palace dressed in the finery of their native districts.

Norwegian Wood Festival MUSIC
(www.norwegianwood.no; ⌚Jun) Oslo plays host to dozens of music festivals but this is one of the bigger ones. The 2011 event saw Arcade Fire as one of many performers.

Oslo International Jazz Festival MUSIC
(www.oslojazz.no; ⌚mid-Aug) Jazz and Oslo's long summer evenings go well together. This festival brings big names to the city.

Oslo Opera Festival PERFORMING ARTS
(www.operafestival.no; ⌚Oct) Live opera fills the concert halls – and even the streets – of Oslo throughout October.

Oslo World Music Festival MUSIC
(www.osloworldmusicfestival.no; ⌚late Oct-early Nov) It's not just the West that can make music. The rest of the planet's diverse rhythms are showcased at this world-music festival, which also includes lots of child-friendly events.

Sleeping

Oslo has plenty of accommodation, including a growing number of small B&Bs, which offer more character than the chain hotels. However, compared to many other parts of Europe, most hotels tend to be rather bland and – yes, you guessed it – prices are very high.

Central Oslo & Around

★**Oslo Vandrerhjem Central** HOSTEL €
(Map p56; ☎23 10 08 00; www.hihostels.no; Kongens gate 7; dm/tw/f Nkr395/835/1495;) New and slickly run, this utterly immaculate hostel has plain and functional rooms, a big sociable lounge area, good internet access, lots of travel info and a very central location. All up, Oslo's new youth hostel is great news for budget travellers.

PS: Hotell DESIGN HOTEL €
(Map p52; ☎23 15 65 00; www.pshotell.no; Maridalsveien 13c; tw/tr/ste Nkr680/850/1250;) Located in the heart of the trendy new Vulkan development, a 25-minute walk northeast of the city centre, the PS: Hotell is an industrial-chic space with cool, grey-toned rooms that make the most of the tiny space allotted to them. Considering the price, this is a really good deal.

Anker Hostel HOSTEL €
(Map p56; ☎22 99 72 00; www.ankerhostel.no; Storgata 55; dm Nkr230-250, s & tw Nkr620-640;)

This huge traveller-savvy hostel boasts an international atmosphere, rather sterile rooms, a laundry, luggage room, kitchens (some rooms also contain kitchens) and a small bar. Breakfast costs an extra Nkr60, linen Nkr70 and parking Nkr230 per 24 hours. The location isn't very scenic, but it's convenient, with Grünerløkka and the city centre only a five-minute walk away.

⭐**Ellingsens Pensjonat**　PENSION €€
(Map p52; ☎22 60 03 59; www.ellingsenspensjonat. no; Holtegata 25; s/d from Nkr600/990, without bathroom s/d Nkr550/800, apt s/d Nkr700/1200; 🖘) Located in a quiet, pleasant neighbourhood, this homey pension offers one of the best deals in the capital. The building dates from 1890 and many of the original features (high ceilings, rose designs) remain. Rooms are bright, airy and beautifully decorated, with fridges and kettles, and there's a small garden to lounge about in on sunny days.

It's very popular, so book ahead.

⭐**Hotel Folketeateret**　HOTEL €€
(Map p56; ☎22 00 57 00; www.choiceno; Storgata 21-23; s/d half board from Nkr900/1250; 🖘) The rooms here are smart, large, decorated in deep reds and cool blacks (which might not appeal to everyone), and have more character than most Oslo hotels. Outside stands a giant statue of a woman contorted into a crazy yoga position. Yoga or not, what really makes this place stand out is that a set dinner is included.

⭐**Grand Central**　HOTEL €€
(Map p56; ☎22 98 28 00; www.choice.no; Jernanetorget 1; d from Nkr1050; 🖘) Every trainspotter's dream hotel. This hotel is built out of part of the former train station (which is being converted into a new shopping and cultural centre, Østbanehallen) and has a trainload of character with graffiti-covered rooms and a position that almost overlooks the Opera House.

Thon Hotel Astoria　HOTEL €€
(Map p56; ☎24 14 55 50; www.thonhotels.com; Dronningens gate 21; s/d from Nkr645/800; 🖘) This might be marketed as a Thon 'budget' hotel, but if it weren't for the slightly smaller-than-normal bathroom and the lack of a minibar or pay TV, there would be nothing to distinguish this hotel from some much more expensive options. It's well positioned close to the train station, but the only nearby parking is on the street.

Do note that single rooms can be truly microscopic in dimension; single travellers may prefer to splash out on a double room.

Anker Hotel　HOTEL €€
(Map p56; ☎22 99 75 00; www.anker-hotel.no; Storgata 55; s/d from Nkr690/890; 🖘) This busy place could be described as a 'budget business hotel'. The plain and simple rooms, which have everything you need in a hotel room and nothing more, are a perfect compromise between a hostel and an upper-crust hotel. There's a huge breakfast spread.

Hotell Bondeheimen　HOTEL €€
(Map p56; ☎23 21 41 00; www.bondeheimen.com; Rosenkrantz gate 8; s/d from Nkr1140/1340; 🖘) 🌱 This century-old hotel, which has spacious, colourful (if rather IKEA) furnishings, started life as a boarding house for rural folk coming down to the big city and was owned by an organisation promoting Norwegian culture. Today those 'poor' rural folk have to pay like the rest of us, but the owners, and their work, continues.

P-Hotel　HOTEL €€
(Map p56; ☎23 31 80 00; www.p-hotels.com; Grensen 19; s & d Nkr795-995; 🖘) In addition to offering some of the best prices in central Oslo, the P-Hotel has comfortable rooms with decent bathrooms, wooden furnishings and, for Oslo, space in relative abundance. Breakfast is put in a bag and delivered to your door. There are tea- and coffee-making facilities in the rooms. This hotel couldn't be much more central.

Cochs Pensjonat　PENSION €€
(Map p56; ☎23 33 24 00; www.cochspensjonat.no; Parkveien 25; s/d with kitchenette from Nkr610/840, without bathroom Nkr510/720; 🖘) Opened as a guesthouse for bachelors in the 1920s, Cochs has sparsely furnished, clean rooms, some of which have kitchenettes. It's ideally located behind the Royal Palace. The rooms at the back overlooking the Slottsparken are especially spacious. There is a luggage room. The hotel offers a discounted breakfast buffet at a coffee shop around the corner from Nkr42.

⭐**Thief**　BOUTIQUE HOTEL €€€
(Map p52; ☎24 00 40 00; www.thethief.com; Landgangen 1; d from Nkr2890; 🖘🌊) Part of the new waterfront development, the Thief is a world-class hotel (albeit one with a strange name) overlooking the Astrup Fearnley Museet. The hotel's decoration is inspired by

the next-door art: there are moving human images in the elevators, gold knitting clocks that don't tell the time, and swish rooms with piles of cushions.

Food and service are both all you would expect of such a place.

Saga Hotel Oslo BOUTIQUE HOTEL €€€
(Map p52; ☑ 22 55 44 90; www.sagahoteloslo. no; Eilert Sundts gate 39; s/d from Nkr1295/1695; 🛜) In a grand old building in a quiet neighbourhood, this stylish 46-room hotel is that rare thing in Oslo – a hotel that dares to be arty and even a little adventurous. There are leafy wall patterns, purple reception lighting and black-and-white photographic art. Downstairs is a basement restaurant serving superb sushi dishes.

Grims Grenka BOUTIQUE HOTEL €€€
(Map p56; ☑ 23 10 72 00; www.firsthotels.no; Kongens gate 5; s/d from Nkr1445/1645; P✳🛜) Oslo's answer to the exclusive, cosmopolitan experience offered by boutique hotels in London and New York, Grims Grenka has minimalist, modern rooms, a hipster rooftop bar, an Asian-fusion restaurant and is, without doubt, one of the most exciting hotels in Oslo.

Grand Hotel HISTORIC HOTEL €€€
(Map p56; ☑ 23 21 20 00; www.grand.no; Karl Johans gate 31; s/d from Nkr1395/1495; P🛜🏊) Brimming with period character, the regal Grand Hotel has long been considered the benchmark of true elegance in Oslo. The rooms are beautifully appointed and classy without being overdone; there is a range of rooms designed and decorated soley with the female traveller in mind. If you book early enough, some fantastic bargains are available.

Greater Oslo

Bogstad Camping CAMPGROUND €
(☑ 22 51 08 00; www.bogstadcamping.no; Ankerveien 117; tent with/without car from Nkr270/185, cabins Nkr500-1290; ☺year-round; P) Located at the edge of the Nordmarka, Bogstad Camping is an ideal base for enjoying the Oslo outdoors. It can get very busy, but as it's also very large it copes well with crowds. The facilities include showers and communal kitchen, and there is a nearby kiosk and restaurant. It's 9km north of the city centre. To get here, take bus 32 from Oslo S (about 30 minutes).

ⓘ BED & BREAKFAST IN THE CITY

One of the cheapest ways to stay in Oslo, and one that promises a much more personable stay than anything a hotel can offer, is to take a room in one of the city's handful of B&Bs. **B&B Norway** (www.bbnorway.com) is an online source of information that lists many of Norway's better-established B&Bs. The tourist office can also point you towards some options (but only if you visit in person).

Oslo Vandrerhjem Haraldsheim HOSTEL €
(☑ 22 22 29 65; www.haraldsheim.no; Haraldsheimveien 4; incl breakfast dm with/without bathroom Nkr280/255, s/d Nkr510/690, with shared bathroom Nkr455/610; @🛜) A pleasant, if hard to find, hostel 4km from the city centre. It has 24-hour reception and 268 beds, mostly in clean four-bed dorms. There are kitchen and laundry facilities. Linen costs Nkr50. Take tram 12, 15 or 17, or bus 31 or 32 to Sinsenkrysset, then walk five minutes uphill.

Holmenkollen Park Hotel Rica HISTORIC HOTEL €€
(☑ 22 92 20 00; www.holmenkollenparkhotel.no; Kongeveien 26; s/d from Nkr1105/1355; P🛜🏊) Founded in 1891 as a sanatorium by Dr Ingebrigt Christian Lund, this castlelike hotel offers luxury, history, great views and, all things considered, a very reasonable price. If that weren't enough, you also get a vast breakfast buffet, complete with organic produce.

✕ Eating

In the past, going to a restaurant in Oslo meant parting with great wads of cash for very little that could be called good food. Luckily, this has changed, and though costs are still high, today there are plenty of places to choose from. If you're after a healthy meal that won't break the bank, the secret is to think Asian and African. Oslo is full of decent Indian, Thai, Vietnamese and Ethiopian restaurants where a proper meal normally costs about half that of a standard Norwegian restaurant.

For the ultimate snack try a *polse* (hot dog) in a *lumpe* (potato cake) for around Nkr20 or a waffle with sour cream and strawberry jam.

Central Oslo

Taste of the Far East ASIAN €

(Map p56; ☎ 22 20 56 28; Bernt Ankersgate 6b; mains Nkr80-120; ☺ 1pm-midnight) As the name suggests, it's light and healthy Thai and Vietnamese curries, soups and noodles at this popular restaurant that offers low prices and high tastes.

Ruffino Ristorante ITALIAN €€

(Map p56; ☎ 22 55 32 80; www.ruffino.no; Arbins gate 1; mains Nkr189; ☺ 4-11pm Mon-Sat) There's no shortage of places in Oslo in which to eat pizza and pasta but only really one in which to eat Italian cuisine. With assured, authentic, but good-value Italian food, this place (which sits opposite the beautiful Slottsparken) has gained a loyal following among locals and visitors in the know.

Rust INTERNATIONAL €€

(Map p56; ☎ 23 62 65 05; www.rustoslo.com; Hegehaugsveien 22; tapas Nkr40-80, mains Nkr129-195; ☺ 11am-1am Mon-Sat, noon-midnight Sun) On a small side street lined with cafes and restaurants, Rust is bright, colourful and 100% modern Oslo. It has plenty of outdoor seating and loads of blankets for when it gets cold. Good for a quiet cocktail, hearty salads or some creative tapas late into the night.

Gate of India INDIAN €€

(Map p52; ☎ 22 69 09 33; www.gateofindia.no; Bogstadveien 66a; lunch specials Nkr149, mains Nkr150-200; ☺ 3-10pm Mon, 3-11pm Tue-Sat, 2-10pm Sun) Upstairs across from the Majorstuen T-bane station, Gate of India is a little pricey, but for scrumptious subcontinental flavours in a fairly refined atmosphere, it's hard to beat. The service is slow.

Café Sara INTERNATIONAL €€

(Map p56; ☎ 22 03 40 00; www.cafesara.no; Hausmanns gate 29; mains Nkr120-180; ☺ 11am-3.30am Mon-Sat, 1pm-3.30am Sun) Despite the light and airy name, this is a dark but warm English-style pub serving a hearty mix of Norwegian dishes as well as pizzas, Turkish and Tex-Mex. The house special is a meat stew with corn, rice and potatoes – perfect for a cold winter's night.

Café Skansen MEDITERRANEAN €€

(Map p56; ☎ 24 20 13 11; www.cafeskansen.no; Rådhusgata 32; mains Nkr110-230; ☺ 11am-midnight Mon-Fri, noon-midnight Sat, noon-11pm Sun) One of the wave of sophisticated cafes and restaurants currently taking Oslo by storm. As in many such places, this one looks south to the Mediterranean for style and taste – and on sunny summer days its outdoor terrace does indeed feel very far from the popular images of a frozen Norway.

★ Hos Thea NORWEGIAN €€€

(Map p52; ☎ 22 44 68 74; www.hosthea.no; Gabelsgata 11; mains Nkr295-330, menus from Nkr495; ☺ 5-10pm Mon-Thu & Sun, to 10.30pm Fri & Sat) Krone for krone, this place, with its creative dishes such as locally caught lobster ravioli with an apple and curry sauce or duck in rosehip sauce, is arguably the best place to eat in Oslo.

What's so refreshing about a place with such good food is that the atmosphere is totally casual, the dining room is intimate and the staff are delightfully friendly.

★ Fauna NORWEGIAN €€€

(Map p52; ☎ 41 67 45 43; www.restaurantfauna.no; Solligata 2; menus from Nkr750; ☺ from 6pm Tue-Thu, from 5.45pm Fri & Sat) A stand-out choice in Oslo; the Fauna is all hip, modern elegance with its large, open kitchen, massive, well-stocked bar and a menu that turns stodgy old Norwegian food into culinary art that's good enough to have been blessed with a Michelin star. Unlike some other Norwegian restaurants of this class it's quite a relaxed place to eat.

Feinschmecker NORWEGIAN €€€

(Map p52; ☎ 22 12 93 80; www.feinschmecker.no; Balchens gate; mains from Nkr345, set menus Nkr895-1295; ☺ 5-9pm Mon-Sat) This sublime restaurant, with its artistic, delicately presented Norwegian gourmet dishes, is regarded as one of the best in town and if you have the impression that eating in Norway is all about burgers, then one meal here will quickly change your mind. It's a fairly large and formal place. Book ahead.

Plah THAI €€€

(Map p56; ☎ 22 56 43 00; www.plah.no; Hegdehaugsveien 22; 5-/9-course menu Nkr545/625; ☺ 5pm-12.30am Mon-Sat) Light and inventive Thai-inspired cuisine is the hallmark of this well-regarded, very cool, intimate restaurant on a quiet pedestrianised side alley close to the Royal Palace. The place is split into two parts: a restaurant, and a bar serving Southeast Asian street-food-style tapas.

Theatercafeen TRADITIONAL €€€

(Map p56; ☎ 22 82 40 50; Stortingsgata 24/26; mains Nkr180-250) A favourite with Norwe-

---

ⓘ ATTENTION SELF-CATERERS & HOME DRINKERS

Anyone aged over 18 can buy beer at Oslo supermarkets until 8pm from Monday to Friday and 6pm on Saturday. For wine or spirits, you'll have to be at least 20 years old and visit the **Vinmonopolet** (Map p56; Oslo City Shopping Centre; ⊙ 10am-5pm Mon-Wed, 10am-6pm Thu, 9am-6pm Fri, 10am-2pm Sat). There are a number of other branches throughout the city.

The Grønland district and the backstreets east of Storgata are brimming with inexpensive ethnic supermarkets where you'll find otherwise unavailable items such as fresh herbs and African, Asian and Middle Eastern ingredients. One such place is the excellent **Nor Brothers** (Map p56; Storgata 34; ⊙ 8am-10pm Mon-Sat), which also has a fruit and veg section that surpasses any of the big supermarkets for quality and price. **Grønland Bazaar** (Map p56; Tøyengata 2) is a Middle Eastern–themed shopping centre.

---

gian families during Christmas and on 17 May, the Theatercafeen, located directly across from the Nationaltheatret, presents Norwegian classics in posh Viennese surroundings. Much of the food is inspired by the wild and stormy seas surrounding Norway, and the cold, clear rivers – favourites such as Arctic char or halibut with asparagus and mushrooms feature.

Grand Café NORWEGIAN €€€
(Map p56; ☎ 23 21 20 18; www.grand.no; Karl Johans gate 31; mains Nkr235-335) At 11am sharp, Henrik Ibsen would leave his apartment and walk to Grand Café for a lunch of herring, beer and one shot of aquavit (alcoholic drink made from potatoes and caraway liquor). His table is still here. Don't worry, though, there's more than herring on the menu. Take your pick from reindeer, Arctic char and mussels and chips.

✖ Aker Brygge

Aker Brygge, the old shipyard turned trendy shopping complex west of the main harbour, has been recently revamped and now has dozens of eateries and waterside restaurants that are among the most popular in Oslo.

If the weather is nice, the local meal of choice is peel-and-eat shrimp, eaten dockside with a fresh baguette, mayonnaise and just a touch of lemon. **Fishermen's Coop** (Map p56; Rådhusbrygge 3/4; shrimp per kg Nkr150; ⊙ 7am-5pm Tue-Sat), during summer, is a good place to buy shrimp.

People & Coffee INTERNATIONAL €
(Map p56; Rådhusgata 21; mains Nkr59-140, lunch specials Nkr129; ⊙ 7am-6pm) Much more than a mere coffee shop, this friendly place could be called a 'world food' centre with loads of dishes from Latin America, Africa and Asia

popping up alongside carrot cakes, soups and coffees. Its lunch specials are one of the cheaper ways to eat in Oslo at lunchtime.

Solsiden Seafood SEAFOOD €€€
(Map p56; ☎ 22 33 36 30; www.solsiden.no; Søndre Akershus Kai 34; mains Nkr295-315; ⊙ 4.30-10pm Mon-Sat, to 9pm Sun) Solsiden means 'sunny side' in Norwegian, which explains why this place is so popular among sun-craving locals. Located inside a grey warehouse, and often overlooked by massive cruise ships, on the opposite side of Pipervika from Aker Brygge, Solsiden serves up some of the city's best seafood and has an ideal view over the fjord.

Bølgen & Moi SEAFOOD €€€
(Map p52; ☎ 22 44 10 20; www.bolgenogmoi.no; Tjuvholmen Allé 5; mains Nkr189-356, menus from Nkr565; ⊙ noon-10pm Mon-Sat, 3-9pm Sun) Part of a small chain, Bølgen & Moi is cool, jazzy and serves decent seafood from a prime position overlooking the docks. It's as popular a place to just kick back on a summer evening with a drink as it is a place to eat.

✖ Around Oslo S & Grønland

The area east and north of the main train station has traditionally been the place for cheap Asian and African dishes, and offers a very different dining experience to central and western Oslo. Sadly though, in the past couple of years a number of classic Ethiopian restaurants have closed down.

★ Punjab Tandoori INDIAN €
(Map p56; ☎ 22 17 20 86; www.punjabtandoori. no; Grønlandsleiret 24; lunch special Nkr69, mains Nkr80-110; ⊙ 11am-11pm Mon-Sat, noon-10pm Sun) Full of the richness and flavours of the north of the subcontinent, this simple canteen-style affair serves spot-on curries

MATHALLEN OSLO

One of the most exciting developments from Oslo's current makeover is the **Mathallen Oslo** (Map p52; www.mathal-lenoslo.no; Maridalsveien 17; ⊙noon-6pm Tue-Sat, to 5pm Sun). It's a seriously hip, post-industrial-like food court dedicated to showcasing the very best of Norwegian regional cuisine, as well as foods from elsewhere. There are dozens of delis, cafes and miniature restaurants crammed into this space and the surrounding buildings, and the place buzzes throughout the day. Eating here is a casual affair where strangers find themselves eating and chatting together. Prices are generally low and quality high.

that would stand out in India let alone Oslo. It's a real neighbourhood institution for the local Asian community and Norwegians in the know, and is as authentic an Indian restaurant as you'll get anywhere in Europe.

Teddy's Soft Bar   AMERICAN €
(Map p56; ☑22 17 36 00; Brugata 3a; light meals from Nkr83; ⊙11am-3am Mon-Sat) The jukebox in the corner gives Teddy's Soft Bar a flavour of 1950s USA. It's something of a local institution that has scarcely changed in decades. Its burgers go well with that other 1950s America favourite – milkshakes. It's as much a place for a beer as a meal.

Süd Øst   INTERNATIONAL €€
(Map p56; ☑23 35 30 70; www.sudost.no; Trond-heimsveien 5; menus from Nkr295, mains Nkr150; ⊙11am-midnight Tue-Thu, to 1am Fri-Mon) This fashionable restaurant, with its large outdoor terrace overlooking the river for summer sun seekers, heaves with people eager to lap up some Southeast Asian fusion flavours. Booking ahead is a wise idea.

✘ Grünerløkka Area

Oslo's Greenwich Village, while always lively and frequented by a well-dressed, youthful crowd, is especially pleasant in the summer when life spills out onto the pavements from the numerous cafes, bars and restaurants around Olaf Ryes plass.

★ Kasbah   MIDDLE EASTERN €
(Map p52; ☑21 94 90 99; www.thekasbah.no; King-sogate 1b; mains Nkr90-100, mezes from Nkr42; ⊙11am-1am) Graze on mezes or tuck into a more substantial lunch, including such tummy pleasers as homemade felafels and a veggie coucous soup, at this totally chilled Norwegian-run, Middle East–flavoured restaurant bursting with colour.

Kolonihagen Grünerløkkha   NORWEGIAN €
(Map p56; ☑95 96 83 52; www.kolonihagen.no; Korsgata 25; mains Nkr110-140; ⊙11am-8pm Mon-Thu & Sun, to 10pm Fri & Sat) There's an old farmhouse feel to this tucked-away little place with its incredibly friendly staff, exacting attention to detail and low prices (it's Oslo so this last statement is relative!). At lunchtime the food is mainly wholesome open sandwiches and such, while in the evening there's some fairly imaginative Norwegian dishes.

Bistro Brocante   FRENCH €€
(Map p52; ☑22 35 68 71; www.bistrobrocante. no; Thorvald Meyers gate 40; lunch specials Nkr59-129, starters Nkr96-102, mains Nkr192-199; ⊙11am-midnight Mon-Sat, noon-midnight Sun) This informal French-inspired cafe serves simple French snacks and typical bistro dishes such as salads, pork chops with onion compote, and coq au vin. The outdoor tables are at a premium in summer.

Fru Hagen   CAFE €€
(Map p52; ☑45 49 19 04; www.fruhagen.no; Thorvald Meyers gate 40; mains Nkr159-189; ⊙11am-midnight Mon & Tue, to 1am Wed, to 2am Thu, to 3am Fri & Sat, noon-11am Sun) The low-key and always full Fru Hagen (Mrs Garden) serves snacks, light meals and appealing mains such as local sausage with mushrooms and onion. Its location facing Olaf Ryes plass also makes it good for people-watching.

Villa Paradiso   PIZZA €€
(Map p52; ☑22 35 40 60; www.villaparadiso.no; Olaf Ryes plass 8; pizzas Nkr130-170; ⊙8am-10pm) Overlooking a little park, with summertime alfresco dining next to an old Italian car, this place is rated by many as serving some of the best pizzas in the capital – no minor feat in a city obsessed with pizza.

Hotel Havana   SPANISH €
(Map p52; ☑23 23 03 23; www.hotelhavana. no; Thorvald Meyers gate 38; mains Nkr80-120; ⊙10am-midnight Mon-Wed & Sun, to 1am Thu, to

2am Fri & Sat) With blue-and-white Andalucian tiles this little place models itself on a Spanish bar. The food is likewise Spanish but with a Norwegian twist, such as a lump of mayonnaise piled atop a paella. There's also a small selection of tapas and big jugs of fresh juice.

Mucho Mas MEXICAN €€
(Map p52; ☎ 22 37 16 09; www.muchomas.no; Thorvald Meyers gate 36; mains from Nkr145; ⊙noon-midnight Mon-Thu, to 3am Fri & Sat; 🖋) What it lacks in Mexican authenticity, Mucho Mas more than makes up for in cheese and portion size. The full Tex-Mex repertoire is on offer, including tacos, nachos and burritos (which are enormous); all dishes are offered in meat or vegetarian versions. Well-priced beer helps put out the fire.

★Markveien Mat & Vinhus NORWEGIAN €€€
(Map p56; ☎ 22 37 22 97; Torvbakkgt 12; mains Nkr240-290, 3 courses Nkr495; ⊙4pm-1.30am Tue-Sun) With a hint of truffle oil or a dash of dill, the cooks at Markveien make Norwegian cooking unforgettable. The restaurant focuses on using local seafood and meat, as well as organic produce, to create its delectable dishes. You shouldn't miss the house specials of either lamb or crayfish.

Dr Kneipp's Vinbar NORWEGIAN €€€
(Map p56; ☎ 22 37 22 97; www.markveien.no; Torvbakkgt 12; mains Nkr195-249; ⊙4pm-1am Mon-Sun) If you're not in the mood for the formal dining room of its sister establishment, Markveien Mat & Vinhus, slide into one of the dark wooden booths at Dr Kneipp's next door for finger food with a strong Spanish and Italian flavour or a sumptuous dessert (the cheesecake is legendary), not to mention an amazing 400-strong wine list.

Greater Oslo

Smia Galleri NORWEGIAN €€€
(☎ 22 19 59 20; Opplandsgata 19; mains Nkr185-230; ⊙2-10pm Tue-Fri, noon-10pm Sat, noon-9pm Sun) Smia Galleri is one of those places Oslo residents are so fond of they almost hate to share it. The leafy patio is perfect on summer afternoons and there's jazz on Thursday evenings. If the restaurant has it, try the rhubarb crumble with wild-strawberry sorbet.

It takes about 15 minutes to get here: from Oslo S, take bus 37 towards Helsfyr T-bane station and get off at Vålerenga.

Drinking & Entertainment

The tourist office's free monthly brochure *What's On in Oslo* lists current concerts, theatre and special events, but the best publication for night owls is the free *Streetwise*, published annually in English by Use-It (p76).

Bars & Clubs

Going out in one of the world's most expensive cities requires a bit of skill, but high prices certainly don't keep the locals at home. Quite the opposite: Oslo is more vibrant, busy and nonchalantly proud of its up-and-coming status than ever. And the manageable size of the city makes it easy to figure out where to be on any given night.

Note that many Oslo nightspots have an unwritten dress code that expects patrons to be relatively well turned out – at the very least, don't show up in grubby gear and hiking boots. For most bars and clubs that serve beer and wine, you must be over 18 years of age, but many places, especially those that serve spirits, impose a higher age limit. On weekends, most Oslo nightspots remain open until at least 3am.

Beer prices for half-litres typically range from Nkr50 to Nkr75, but for those travellers watching their kroner, some places (usually grim and inhabited by wary elbow-on-the-bar locals) charge as little as Nkr35.

DON'T MISS

THE HOUSE OF LITERATURE

If you like books, you really shouldn't miss Oslo's shrine to the printed word, **Litteraturhuset** (House of Literature; Map p56; ☎ 22 95 55 30; www.litteraturhuset.no; Wergelandsveien 29; ⊙10am-12.30am Mon-Thu, 10am-2am Fri & Sat, noon-8pm Sun). The promotion of literature is at the core of everything it does – there are frequent workshops, talks and debates. Perhaps of equal interest is the in-house **cafe** (Map p56; mains Nkr245; ⊙10am-12.30pm Mon & Tue, 10am-3.30pm Wed-Sat, noon-8pm Sun). It serves pasta, salads and main courses such as steak and chips, which are tasty enough to attract the odd princess from the neighbouring Royal Palace. There's also a well-stocked bookshop, a bar and frequent screenings of art-house films.

CAFES

Fact: unaided by Starbucks, Norwegians drink more coffee per capita (9.9kg per year) than any other nationality bar the Finns. And while most coffee drinking happens at home, preferably alongside waffles, in Oslo there is a good selection of coffee bars. Most cafes offer toothsome open-faced sandwiches to snack on, topped with *gulost* (yellow cheese) or mayonnaise and shrimps. *Boller* (raisin rolls) and *skolebrød* (pastry with vanilla cream filling) are also popular.

Tim Wendleboe (Map p52; ☎40 00 40 62; www.timwendelboe.no; Grüners gate 1; ✆8.30am-6pm Mon-Fri, 11am-5pm Sat & Sun) Most of the space in this tiny cafe, known city-wide for producing maybe the most authentic Italian-style espresso in a city addicted to the bean, is given over to a giant coffee-bean grinder and roaster.

Kaffebrenneriet (Map p56; www.kaffebrenneriet.no; Universtetsgata 1; ✆7am-7pm Mon-Fri, 9am-6pm Sat & Sun) Opposite the National Gallery, this relaxed cafe has dozens of types of coffee (including packets to take away), cakes, yoghurts and other tasty snacks. All of which make it a great place to refuel before an assault on the National Gallery.

Zagros Café (Map p56; Storgata 34; ✆10am-6pm Mon-Sat, noon-8pm Sun) Kick back on a sofa and argue with yourself about which of the sweet and rich honey-coated Indian or Middle Eastern cakes on sale will go best with your strong Italian coffee.

Stockfleths (Map p56; www.stockfleths.as; Lille Grensen; ✆7am-6pm Mon-Fri, 10am-5pm Sat) Founded in 1895, the award-winning Stockfleths is one of Oslo's oldest coffee shops. It also serves thick slices of wholegrain bread with brown cheese, a favourite Norwegian snack.

Åpent Bakerei (Map p52; ☎22 04 96 67; Inkognito terasse 1; ✆7.30am-5pm Mon-Fri, 8am-3pm Sat) A neighbourhood cafe that serves coffee in deep, cream-coloured bowls and has unbeatable breads and pastries. A freshly baked roll topped with homemade *røre syltetøy* (stirred jam) and enjoyed on the bakery's patio makes for one of Oslo's best, and least expensive, breakfasts.

The city's best neighbourhood bar scene is along Thorvald Meyers gate and the surrounding streets in Grünerløkka. The Youngstorget area has some of the most popular places close to the city centre and the new developments around Aker Brygge have brought more after-dark life to the waterfront, while the Grønland neighbourhood has a more alternative feel.

★ Fuglen COCKTAIL BAR
(Map p56; www.fuglen.com; Universitetsgaten 2; ✆7.30am-10pm Mon & Tue, 7.30am-1am Wed & Thu, 7.30am-3am Fri, 11am-3am Sat, 11am-10pm Sun) By day this is a renowned coffee bar, but by night it transforms itself into what is hands down the hippest cocktail bar in town. And if you like the retro decorations and furnishings, then why not take some home with you – all the furnishings are for sale!

Tea Lounge BAR
(Map p52; Thorvald Meyers gate 33b; ✆11am-1am Mon-Wed, 11am-3am Thu-Sat, noon-1am Sun) During the bright and cheerful daylight hours, this split-personality bar is a teashop with a small range of brews and a chilled-out soundtrack, but in the dark of night it transforms itself into a hip bar, with a list of cocktails to suit.

Bar Boca BAR
(Map p52; Thorvald Meyers gate 30; ✆noon-1am Sun-Tue, 11am-2pm Wed & Thu, 11am-3am Fri & Sat) Squeeze into what is quite possibly the smallest bar in Oslo and you'll find that you have slid back in time to the 1960s. It's retro cool and has a cocktail selection as great as its atmosphere.

Fisk Og Vilt Club CLUB
(Map p56; Pløens gate 1; ✆8pm-3.30am Mon-Sat) DJs rock the crowd in the covered backyard of this bar-club, which boasts an impressive selection of beers and cocktails. It's a popular central spot, and on a Monday night it's really the only place worth considering.

Palace Grill BAR
(Map p52; Solligata 2; ✆6-10pm Mon-Sat) The well-heeled crowd of Oslo West can be found sipping cocktails at this fabulously over-the-

top bar covered with black and silver graffiti, and snakes, dolls and old phones preserved in bottles lining the shelves.

Villa
CLUB

(Map p56; www.thevilla.no; Møllergata 23; ⊙11pm-3am Fri & Sat) With arguably the best sound system in the city, this is a die-hard house- and electro-music club. In addition to Friday and Saturday, it's also open on some Thursdays.

Dattera Til Hagen
BAR

(Map p56; www.dattera.no; Grønland 10; ⊙11am-1am Mon-Wed, 11am-2am Thu, 11am-3.30am Fri & Sat, noon-midnight Sun) The trippy, flower-power back garden of this bar is especially busy in the summer. DJs and live music often fill the courtyard with sound.

Live Music

Oslo has a thriving live-music scene – it's said that the city hosts around 5000 gigs a year. Keep your ear to the ground in summer to hear about outdoor concerts at Vigeland Park – a weird and wonderful venue.

The city's largest concert halls, **Oslo Spektrum** (Map p56; www.oslospektrum.no; Sonja Henies plass 2) and **Rockefeller Music Hall** (Map p56; www.rockefeller.no; Torggata 16), once a bathhouse, host a wide range of artists and events.

★Blå
JAZZ

(Map p56; www.blaaoslo.no; Brenneriveien 9c; admission Nkr100-180) It would be a pity to leave Oslo without checking out Blå, which features on a global list of 100 great jazz clubs compiled by the savvy editors at the US jazz magazine *Down Beat*. As one editor put it, 'To get in this list means that it's quite the club'.

Sometimes it veers into other musical styles such as salsa, and when there's no live music, DJs get the crowds moving.

Mono
LIVE MUSIC

(Map p56; www.cafemono.no; Pløens gate 4; ⊙11pm-3.30am) An upbeat place, Mono is the alternative club of choice with the cool and beautiful of Oslo. It's known for booking the best up-and-coming indie bands.

Gloria Flames
LIVE MUSIC

(Map p56; www.gloriaflames.no; Grønland 18) Gloria Flames is a popular rock bar with frequent gigs (including some big-name performers), and a roof-terrace bar during daylight hours.

Theatre

You can catch a world-class opera or ballet performance at the Oslo Opera House (p47).

Nationaltheatret
THEATRE

(National Theatre; Map p56; www.nationaltheatret.no; Stortingsgata 15; tickets Nkr160-400) Norway's showcase theatre, with its lavish rococo hall, was constructed specifically as a venue for the works of Norwegian playwright Henrik Ibsen, whose works are still performed here.

Cinema

Saga Kino
CINEMA

(Map p56; ☑22 83 23 75; www.oslokino.no; Stortingsgata 28) The six-screen Saga Kino cinema shows first-run movies, including Hollywood fare, in their original language; the entrance is on Olav V's gate.

Filmens Hus
CINEMA

(Map p56; ☑22 47 45 00; www.nfi.no; Dronningens gate 16) Filmens Hus screens old classics and international festival winners.

🔒 Shopping

Oslo excels in upmarket shopping and there are many fine shops on Grensen and Karl Johans gate. For art, try the galleries on Frognerveien; for exclusive boutiques head to Hegdehaugsveien or Skovveien; and for funky shoes or T-shirts go no further than Grünerløkka.

Oslo City Shopping Centre (Map p56; www.oslocity.no; Stenersgata) and the more glamorous **Glasmagasinet Department Store** (Map p56; www.glasmagasi net.no; Stortorvet 9) are good for mainstream shopping.

★Chillout Travel Centre
BOOKS

(Map p56; ☑22 35 42 00; www.chillout.no; Markveien 55; ⊙10am-7pm Mon-Sat, to 5pm Sun) This is our kind of shop: good coffee, tasty dishes from around the world (dhal from India, snacks from Italy and cakes from where else but Norway), loads of travel essentials such as bags and shoes, and a travel bookshop bursting with travel literature and guidebooks in Norwegian and English including Lonely Planet guides.

Nomaden
BOOKS

(Map p56; www.nomaden.no; Uranienborgveien 4; ⊙10am-6pm Mon-Fri, to 4pm Sat) This is a classic travel bookshop where the shelves are bursting with guides, maps and travel literature that will have you dreaming of your next holiday in no time.

Vestkanttorget Flea Market   MARKET
(Map p52; Amaldus Nilsens plass; ⊙10am-4pm Sat) If you're happy with pot luck and sifting through heaps of junk, take a chance here. It's at the plaza that intersects Professor Dahls gate, a block east of Vigeland Park, and it's a more than pleasant way to pass a Saturday morning.

Norli   BOOKS
(Map p56; www.norli.no; Universitetsgata 20-24; ⊙10am-7pm Mon-Sat) The largest bookshop in Norway stocks a good range of foreign-language titles as well as numerous Lonely Planet guidebooks.

Hassan og Den Dama   CLOTHING, JEWELLERY
(Map p52; www.hassanogdendama.no; Skovveien 4; ⊙10am-6pm Mon-Fri, to 2pm Sat) One of many boutiques on Skovveien, this shop has clothing, shoes and jewellery produced by Scandinavian and international designers.

Norway Designs   CLOTHING, JEWELLERY
(Map p56; www.norwaydesigns.no; Stortingsgata 28; ⊙10am-6pm Mon-Wed & Fri, to 7pm Thu, to 4pm Sat) Features designer clothing and beautiful glassware, stationery and watches within a stone's throw of the Nationaltheatret.

ⓘ Information

EMERGENCY
Ambulance (⊉113)
Fire (⊉110)
Police (⊉112)

LAUNDRY
A Snarvask (Thorvald Meyers gate 18; ⊙10am-8pm Mon-Fri, 8am-3pm Sat)
Billig Vask & Rens (Ullevålsveien 15; ⊙8am-9pm Mon-Fri, to 3pm Sat)

LEFT LUGGAGE
Oslo S and the bus station have various sizes of lockers. Those under the age of 26 can also leave luggage for free at the Use-It centre.

MEDICAL SERVICES
If you're pressed for time (and not worried about the expense), the Oslo Kommunale Legevakten clinic has a list of private doctors it recommends.
Jernbanetorget Apotek (Fred Olsens gate; ⊙24 hr) A 24-hour pharmacy opposite Oslo S.
Oslo Kommunale Legevakten (Oslo Emergency Clinic; ⊉22 93 22 93; Storgata 40; ⊙24hr) Casualty and emergency medical clinic.

POST
Main post office (Map p56; ⊉23 14 90 00; cnr Prinsens gate & Kirkegata) As well as this main office, you'll also find convenient post office-branches at Solli plass (Map p52), Oslo Sentralstasjon (Oslo S) and on Grensen (Map p56).

TOURIST INFORMATION
Den Norske Turistforening Tourist Information Centre (DNT, Norwegian Mountain Touring Club; Map p56; www.turistforeningen.no; Storget 3; ⊙10am-5pm Mon-Wed & Fri, to 6pm Thu, to 3pm Sat) Provides information, maps and brochures on hiking in Norway and sells memberships, which include discounted rates on the use of mountain huts along the main hiking routes. You can also book some specific huts and pick up keys. It also sells hiking gear.
Oslo Tourist Office (Map p56; ⊉81 53 05 55; www.visitoslo.com; Fridtjof Nansens plass 5; ⊙9am-6pm May-Sep, to 4pm Oct-Apr) The main tourist office is located just north of the Rådhus and can provide masses of information. Look out for its useful *Oslo Guide* or the monthly *What's On in Oslo* (both are available at all tourist offices in and around the city, as well as at many sights and hotels). Sells the Oslo Pass (p50).
Use-It (Map p56; ⊉24 14 98 20; www.use-it. no; Møllergata 3, Oslo; ⊙10am-6pm Mon-Fri, noon-5pm Sat Jul-early Aug, 11am-5pm Mon-Fri, noon-5pm Sat rest of year) The exceptionally helpful and savvy Ungdomsinformasjonen (Youth Information Office, better known as Use-It) is aimed at, but not restricted to, backpackers under the age of 26. It makes (free) bookings for inexpensive or private accommodation and provides information on anything from current events to hitching possibilities.

ⓘ Getting There & Away

AIR
Oslo Gardermoen International Airport (www.osl.no) has a motorway and high-speed rail link to the city centre.

Numerous domestic flights also go in and out of Gardermoen.

KLM, Widerøe, SAS Braathens, Ryanair and other airlines also operate 'Oslo' services to/from Torp International Airport, some 123km southwest of Oslo, and Rygge Airport, around 60km southeast of the centre.

BOAT
Ferries operated by **DFDS Seaways** (www.dfdsseaways.com; Vippetangen 2) connect Oslo daily with Denmark from the Vippetangen Quay (Map p52) off Skippergata. Bus 60 stops within a couple of minutes' walk of the terminal.

In the summer **Color Line Ferries** (Map p52; www.colorline.no; Color Line Terminalen, Hjortnes) runs daily to/from Kiel (Germany); boats dock at Hjortneskaia, west of the central harbour. Take tram 13 from Oslo S, bus 33 or the Color Line bus, which leaves from platform 7 of the central bus terminal one hour before boat departures.

BUS

Long-distance buses arrive and depart from the **Galleri Oslo Bus Terminal** (Map p56; 23 00 24 00; Schweigaards gate 8); the train and bus stations are linked via a convenient overhead walkway for easy connections.

Nor-Way Bussekspress (81 54 44 44; www. nor-way.no) has the biggest range of services. International services also depart from the bus terminal.

CAR & MOTORCYCLE

The main highways into the city are the E6 from the north and south, and the E18 from the southeast and west. Each time you enter Oslo, you must pass through (at least) one of 19 toll stations and pay Nkr31.

TRAIN

All trains arrive and depart from Oslo S located in the city centre. It has **reservation desks** (6.30am-11pm) and an **information desk** (81 50 08 88) that can provide details on routes and timetables throughout the country.

Norges Statsbaner (Norwegian State Railways, NSB; www.nsb.no) has frequent train services around Oslofjord (eg Drammen, Skien, Moss, Fredrikstad and Halden). Other major destinations include Stavanger via Kristiansand, Bergen via Voss, Røros via Hamar, and Trondheim via Hamar and Lillehammer.

ⓘ Getting Around

Oslo has an efficient public-transport system with an extensive network of buses, trams, underground trains (T-bane) and ferries. In addition to single-trip tickets, one-day and transferable eight-trip tickets are also available. Children aged four to 16 and seniors over 67 years of age pay half price on all fares.

The Oslo Pass (p50) includes access to all public-transport options within the city, with the exception of late-night buses and trams, and most of the ferries around Oslofjord including Ferry 91 to Bygdøy.

Trafikanten (177; www.ruter.no; Jernbanetorget; 7am-8pm Mon-Fri, 8am-6pm Sat & Sun) is located below Oslo S tower and provides free schedules and a public-transport map, *Sporveiskart Oslo*.

TO/FROM OSLO GARDERMOEN INTERNATIONAL AIRPORT

Flybussen (www.flybussen.no) is the airport shuttle to Gardermoen International Airport, 50km north of Oslo. It departs from the bus terminal at Galleri Oslo, as well as a few other stops in the city every 20 minutes from 4am to around 10pm. Times vary a little depending on the day of the week; see website for a full schedule. The trip costs Nkr160/250 one way/return (valid one month) for an adult and Nkr80/160 for a child. The journey takes about 40 minutes. **Flybussekspressen** (www.flybussekspressen. no) connects Gardermoen with Majorstuen T-bane station (Nkr205) and other places, one to four times hourly. Buses run from the city to the airport from around 4am until 8.30pm.

FlyToget (www.flytoget.no) rail services leave Gardermoen airport for Oslo S (adult/child Nkr170/85, 19 minutes) every 10 minutes between 4.40am and midnight. Trains carry on to the Nationaltheatret and stops south of there, terminating at Drammen. In total contrast to Norwegian road-traffic speeds, this train pelts along at 210km/h, apparently making it the fastest airport train in the world. In addition, most northbound NSB intercity and local trains stop at Gardermoen (Nkr90, from 26 minutes, hourly but fewer on Saturday).

TO/FROM TORP AIRPORT

To get to/from Torp Airport in Sandefjord, 123km southwest of Oslo, take the **Torp-Expressen** (www.torpekspressen.no; adult/child Nkr240/120; 1½ hours) bus between Galleri Oslo bus terminal and the airport. Buses leave Oslo around 3½ hours before check-in closes and they leave Torp around 35 minutes after a flight arrives, but they will wait if a plane is late arriving. NSB (p77) trains run roughly hourly between Oslo S and Torp station (Nkr252). A shuttle bus meets the trains and takes passengers to the airport (the fee is included in the price of the train ticket).

TO/FROM RYGGE AIRPORT

To get to/from Oslo's newest airport, Rygge, in Moss, 60km southeast of Oslo, take the **Rygge-Expressen** (www.ryggeekspressen. no) bus between Galleri Oslo bus terminal and the airport (adult/child Nkr160/80, one hour). Departures from Oslo leave three hours before scheduled flights, and leave from Rygge 35 minutes after flights arrive. Trains also run from Oslo S (Nkr156, 50 minutes) to the airport roughly hourly.

BOAT

Ferries to the Oslofjord islands sail from Vippetangen Quay.

DON'T MISS

OSLOFJORD'S DON'T-MISS EXPERIENCES

➡ Take the ferry down the Oslofjord past Oscarsborg fortress, imagining the fateful shots that sank the German warship *Blücher* on 9 April 1940.

➡ Step into the 1700s, complete with cannons and duels, during a historical re-enactment in the Gamlebyen (p80) at Fredrikstad.

➡ Gasp for breath after a spring dip in the Oslofjord during a visit to the Hvaler Skerries (p82).

Boat 62 connects Oslo with Drøbak (Nkr90, 1½ hours, 10am weekdays, 10am and 3pm weekends) and other Oslofjord stops en route: Ildjernet, Langåra and Håøya (which is a holiday spot offering fine swimming and camping). It departs from **Aker Brygge pier** (Map p56).

BUS & TRAM

Bus and tram lines lace the city and extend into the suburbs. There's no central local bus station, but most buses converge at Jernbanetorget in front of Oslo S. Most westbound buses, including those to Bygdøy and Vigeland Park, also stop immediately south of the Nationaltheatret.

The frequency of service drops dramatically at night, but on weekends, night buses N12, N14 and N18 follow the tram routes until 4am or later; there are also weekend night buses (201 to 218).

Tickets for trips in zone 1 (most of the city centre) cost adult/child Nkr30/15 if bought from a sales point in advance (ticket machine, 7-Eleven, Narvesen and Trafikanten) or adult/child Nkr50/25 if bought on the bus or tram. Oslo Pass (p50) holders can travel for free on all daytime lines in the city centre.

CAR & MOTORCYCLE

Oslo has its share of one-way streets, which can complicate city driving a bit, but the streets are rarely as congested as in most other European cities.

Metered street parking, identified by a solid blue sign with a white 'P', can be found throughout the city. Payment is usually required from 8am to 5pm Monday to Friday, and until 3pm Saturday. At other times, parking is free unless otherwise posted. The city centre also has 16 multistorey car parks, including those at Oslo City and Aker Brygge shopping centres. Parking fees in a public carpark cost between Nkr230

and Nkr260 per 24-hour period, depending on the carpark.

Note that the Oslo Pass (p50) includes parking at all municipal car parks; instructions for display come with the pass.

TAXI

There are taxi stands at Oslo S, shopping centres and city squares, but any taxi with a lit sign is available for hire. Otherwise, phone **Norgestaxi** (☑ 08000; www.norgestaxi.no) or **Oslo Taxi** (☑ 02323; www.oslotaxi.no), but note that the meter starts running at the point of dispatch! Oslo taxis accept major credit cards.

T-BANE

The six-line Tunnelbanen underground system, better known as the T-bane, is faster and extends further from the city centre than most city bus lines. All lines pass through the Nationaltheatret, Stortinget and Jernbanetorget (for Oslo S) stations. Tickets for trips in zone 1 (most of the city centre) cost adult/child Nkr30/15 if bought from a sales point in advance (ticket machine, 7-Eleven, Narvesen and Trafikanten).

AROUND OSLO

Drøbak

POP 1746

Once Oslo's winter harbour, Drøbak is a cosy little village by the water's edge, home to enough clapboard timber buildings to warrant a day trip from the capital.

Although just strolling the village streets is enough entertainment for most, you shouldn't miss the imposing **Oscarsborg fortress**, which lies on an offshore island and dates back to the 1600s. It was the Oscarsborg batteries that sank the German warship *Blücher* on 9 April 1940, an act that saved the king and the Norwegian government from being captured. The fort museum was renovated in 2005, and open-air concerts and complete operas are held here during the summer. There is even a hotel, spa and restaurant on the island if you want to extend your stay. **Ferries** (www.oscarsborgfestning.no; adult/child Nkr70/50) to the island depart every five minutes or so from the harbour year-round (in winter, when demand is lighter, ferries will be less frequent).

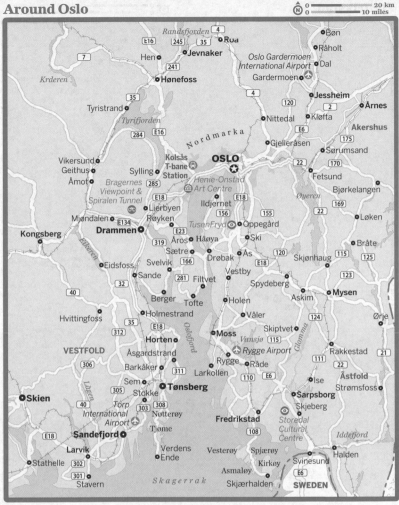

The hourly **bus 541** (Map p56) travels between Oslo and Drøbak. Alternatively, in July you can travel by boat.

ØSTFOLD

The Østfold region, the detached slice of Norway to the east of Oslofjord, is a mix of forest, pastoral farmland and small seaside villages that carry great historical significance. It's an area that's popular with holidaying Norwegians, but most foreign visitors make the mistake of simply rushing through in transit between Oslo and Sweden.

Fredrikstad

POP 106,758

Once an important trading centre between mainland Europe and western Scandinavia, Fredrikstad is home to one of the best-preserved, and prettiest, fortress towns in Scandinavia: the Gamlebyen (Old Town), with the modern waterfront district just across the water.

Fredrikstad

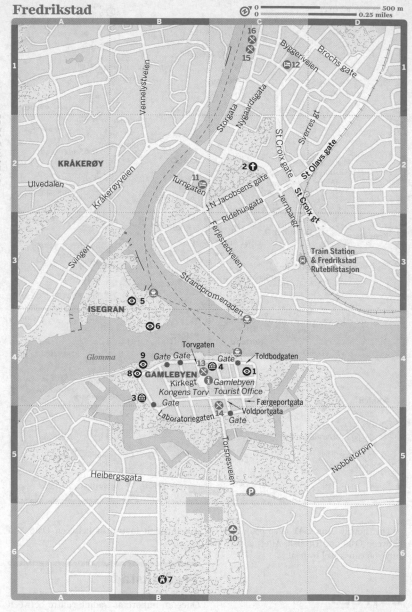

KRÅKERØY

Ulvedalen

ISEGRAN

Glomma

GAMLEBYEN

Kongens Torv

Gamlebyen
Tourist Office

Train Station
& Fredrikstad
Rutebilstasjon

Heibergsgata

⊙ Sights

Fredrikstad also has a **cathedral** (1880), which contains stained-glass work by Emanuel Vigeland; bizarrely, the steeple contains a lighthouse, which still functions at night.

★Gamlebyen   OLD TOWN

The timbered houses, moats, gates and drawbridge of the Fredrikstad Gamlebyen are simply enchanting. The perimeter walls, once defended by 200 cannons, now consist of grassy embankments that

Fredrikstad

⊙ Sights
1 Balaklava..C4
2 Cathedral..C2
3 Fredrikstad Museum.........................B4
4 Hvalfanger (Whaling) Museum.........C4
5 Isegran..B3
6 Isegran Ruins.....................................B4
7 Kongsten Festning............................B6
8 Old Convict Prison............................B4
9 Stone Storehouse.............................B4

⨁ Sleeping
10 Fredrikstad Motell & Camping..........C6
11 Hotel Victoria....................................B2
12 Quality Hotel Fredrikstad.................C1

⊗ Eating
13 Lille Frederik.....................................B4
14 Major-Stuen.......................................C4
15 Pizzanini..C1
16 Restaurant La Riveria.......................C1

make for a very pleasant stroll. The narrow, cobbled streets have been similarly preserved and are still lined with picturesque 17th-century buildings, many of which remain occupied today.

The town was first built in 1663; as a primary trade outlet connecting southern Norway with mainland Europe, but being vulnerable to waterborne assaults, the Old Town became a military enclave.

Among the finest old buildings in town are the old **convict prison** (Salveriet; 1731); the **stone storehouse** (1674–91), the oldest building in Gamlebyen and now a ceramics showroom; and **Balaklava** (1783), a historic building.

From mid-June to the end of August, the Gamlebyen tourist office runs one-hour **guided tours** (adult/child Nkr95/20). They leave from the tourist office at noon and 2pm.

Fredrikstad Museum   MUSEUM
(www.ostfoldmuseet.no; Tøihusgaten 41; combined ticket with Isegran adult/child Nkr50/20; ⊘ noon-4pm mid-Jun–late Aug, noon-3pm rest of year) The Fredrikstad Museum is housed in a building dating back to 1776 and is well worth a browse. The downstairs area houses temporary exhibitions, while upstairs you'll find scale models of the Old Town and an interesting collection of relics from three centuries of Fredrikstad's civilian, military and industrial activities. Also on the top floor is a military museum.

Isegran   ISLAND
(www.isegran.no; combined ticket with Fredrikstad Museum adult/child Nkr50/20; ⊘ noon-4pm Fri-Sun mid-Jun–late Aug) Norse sagas mention the 13th-century fortress of Isegran, an islet in the Glomma that became a further line of defence against Sweden in the mid-17th century. The **ruins** of a stone (originally wood) tower remain visible at the eastern end of the island. It's also the site of a small **museum** on local boat building (from the time when boats were lovingly handcrafted from wood).

By road or on foot, access is from Rv108, about 600m south of Fredrikstad city centre.

Hvalfanger (Whaling) Museum   MUSEUM
(Toldbodgaten 37; admission Nkr10; ⊘ noon-4pm Jun-Aug) This small museum is run by proud old men only too keen to show you around the old photos, the formidable whaling guns once used in the Antarctic, and the even more formidable penis of a blue whale. No English is spoken and all labels are in Norwegian.

Kongsten Festning   FORT
(Kongsten Fort) On what was once called 'Gallows Hill' stands the flower-festooned Kongsten Festning. Dating from 1685, it once served as a lookout and warning post for the troops at nearby Gamlebyen. Although it can get overrun on summer weekends, this otherwise lonely and appealingly unkempt spot is a fun place at which to scramble around the turrets, embankments, walls and stockade, or just sit in the sun and soak up the quiet.

✶✶ Festivals & Events

Glomma Festival   MUSIC, FOOD
(www.glommafestivalen.no) The Glomma Festival runs in late June or early July. It's dedicated to culinary delights and musical performances, ritual duels, a 'bathtub regatta' for creative vessels, and a veteran-sailing-ship exhibition. It's a very popular festival, so book ahead for accommodation.

⨯ Sleeping

Fredrikstad Motell & Camping CAMPGROUND €
(☑ 69 32 03 15; www.fredrikstadmotel.no; Torsnesveien 16-18, Sarpsborg; tent with/without car Nkr200/150, motel s/d Nkr450/550, cabins from Nkr850; ℗ �), This multifaceted but largely uninspiring place, in the grounds of Kongsten Fort, is nonetheless good for its proximity to the Old Town. The beds might be big enough for a troll but a human will struggle to fit into them. From the centre, take any bus (eg 362) headed for Torsnes.

Quality Hotel Fredrikstad
HOTEL €€

(☑ 69 39 30 00; www.qualityinn.com; Nygata 2-6, New Town; s/d from Nkr1200/1300; ☎) The business traveller's choice has supersmart, if rather functional, rooms enlivened by photographic art. Service is spot on and it couldn't be any more central.

Hotel Victoria
HISTORIC HOTEL €€

(☑ 69 38 58 36; www.hotelvictoria.no; Turngaten 3, New Town; s/d Nkr1195/1320; ☎) The common areas of this century-old hotel are full of period trimmings and there are sturdy, old-fashioned rooms, some of which have views to the trees and the flowers of the neighbouring park. The staff are exceptionally helpful and friendly.

✕ Eating

The Old Town has a handful of cafes and restaurants. In the New Town, the Fredrikstad waterfront between Storgata and the water is lined with all manner of restaurants and bars, most with pleasant outdoor terraces ideal for a summer's afternoon or evening

Lille Frederik
INTERNATIONAL €

(Torvgaten, Gamlebyen; mains around Nkr80-109; ⊙ 11am-10pm Mon-Fri, 10am-10pm Sat, noon-10pm Sun) For burgers, snacks and coffee, cosy Lille Frederik is just the place. It's hugely popular in summer, when snackers descend on the outdoor tables like seagulls, and queues can be long. Steak and chips for Nkr109 is a good deal.

Major-Stuen
NORWEGIAN €€

(☑ 69 32 15 55; Voldportgata 73, Gamlebyen; mains Nkr149-159; ⊙ noon-8pm Mon-Thu, to 9pm Fri & Sat, to 7pm Sun) This fine place specialises in Norwegian dishes cooked in the sort of slow, old-fashioned manner that guarantees a good meal. There's a formal indoor dining room or an informal garden area out the back.

Restaurant La Riveria
SEAFOOD €€

(☑ 69 33 86 88; Storgata 13, Engelsviken, New Town; lunch special Nkr105, mains Nkr125-249; ⊙ 11am-10pm Mon-Thu, 11am-11pm Fri & Sat, noon-10pm Sun) This red clapboard building has a summer terrace, a waterfront setting and fair-priced seafood dishes (the lunch specials are great value). It also serves Tex-Mex and pasta dishes.

Pizzanini
INTERNATIONAL €€

(☑ 69 30 03 00; Storgata 5, New Town; pizzas Nkr109-299; pastas Nkr169; ⊙ noon-1am Sun-Thu, to 2am Fri & Sat) When other restaurants stand empty, this place always buzzes, due in part to its young vibe and extensive, well-priced menu. It's as popular a spot for a drink as it is a meal.

ℹ Information

Gamlebyen Tourist Office (☑ 69 30 46 00; www.visitoslofjord.no; Kongens Torv; ⊙ 9am-5pm Mon-Fri, 10am-4pm Sat, 11am-4pm Sun Jul-Aug, 9am-4.30pm rest of year) Helpful little office tucked into the old town.

ℹ Getting There & Away

Intercity buses arrive and depart from the Fredrikstad Rutebilstasjon at the train station. Nor-Way's Oslofjordekspress has one to seven daily services between Oslo and Fredrikstad (Nkr235, two hours), with most buses continuing on to Hvaler; there are also regular **Flybussekspressen** (www.flybussekspressen.no) services from Fredrikstad to Oslo Gardermoen International Airport (Nkr295, 2¼ hours, every hour or two).

Fredrikstad lies on the **NSB** (www.nsb.no) rail line between Oslo and Göteborg, Sweden. Trains to/from Oslo (Nkr205, one hour) run about 10 times daily, and also go to Sarpsborg and Halden, but note that southbound international trains require a mandatory seat reservation.

Drivers should follow the E6 south out of Oslo. Just after Råde, turn south on the 110 and follow it to Fredrikstad.

ℹ Getting Around

To cross the Glomma to Gamlebyen, you can either trek over the high and hulking Glomma bridge or take the ferry (free; two minutes), which shuttles across the river Glomma to the main gate of Gamlebyen regularly between around 5.30am and midnight (exact times depend on the day).

Around Fredrikstad

Hvaler Skerries

Norwegian holidaymakers and artists love the Hvaler Skerries, an offshore archipelago of 833 forested islands and islets guarding the southern entrance to Oslofjord. The main islands of **Vesterøy**, **Spjærøy**, **Asmaløy** and **Kirkøy** are connected to the mainland by a toll road (Nkr55) and tunnel. Bus 365 (Nkr65) runs all the way from Fredrikstad to Skjærhalden, at the far end of Kirkøy.

Fredrikstad tourist office (p82) can point you in the direction of the numerous sights dotted around the islands. There are a couple of other seasonal tourist offices scattered around the islands.

Above the coastline of **Akerøy island**, accessible only by ferry (taxi boat) from Skjærhalden, clings a well-preserved 17th-century coastal **fortress**, renovated in the 1960s. Admission is free and it's always open.

The mid-11th-century **stone church** (Skjærhalden, Kirkøy; ◷noon-4pm Jul, noon-4pm Sat late Jun & early Aug) on Kirkøy is one of the oldest in Norway. The church hosts a week-long music and arts festival in July.

Tourist offices have lists of fully equipped private houses and chalets in the Hvaler Skerries, which are available for between Nkr450 and Nkr800 per day.

Storedal Cultural Centre

This **cultural centre** (☑69 11 56 50; www. storedal.no; Storedal; adult/child Nkr40/20; ◷10am-4pm Tue-Sun mid-Jun–mid-Aug) is 11km northeast of Fredrikstad. King Magnus the Blind was born here in 1117; he took the throne at 13 years of age and earned his nickname at 18 when he was blinded by an enemy in Bergen. A later owner of the farm, Erling Stordahl, who was also blind, developed a monument to King Magnus, as well as a centre dedicated to the blind and people with other disabilities.

The most intriguing feature is the *Ode til Lyset* (Ode to the Light), a 'sound sculpture' by Arnold Haukeland and Arne Nordheim, which, using photo cells and a computer in the farmhouse, transmutes the slightest fluctuations in natural light into haunting, ever-changing music. To get here, follow Rv110 east for about 9km from Fredrikstad; the centre is 2.1km north of the main road.

Borgarsyssel Museum

This excellent Østfold county **museum** (www.ostfoldmuseet.no; Gamlebygaten 8, Sarpsborg; adult/child Nkr40/20; ◷noon-5pm mid-Jun–mid-Aug) lies in the town of Sarpsborg (14km northeast of Fredrikstad). The open-air display contains 30 period buildings from various parts of the country and includes a vast collection of cultural art and artefacts. It also has a **herb garden**, a **petting zoo** and the **ruins** of King Øystein's St Nikolas church, constructed in 1115 and destroyed by the Swedes in 1567. From Fredrikstad, trains and buses run frequently to Sarpsborg.

Oldtidsveien

People have lived and worked in the Østfold region for thousands of years, and numerous examples of ancient stone works and rock paintings lie along the Oldtidsveien (Old Times Way), the old sunken road between Fredrikstad and Sarpsborg. At Solberg, there are three panels with around 100 figures dating back 3000 years. At Gunnarstorp are several 30m-wide **Bronze Age burial mounds** and several **Iron Age standing stones**. The site at Begby includes well-preserved renditions of ships, men and animals, while Hunn has several **stone circles** and a series of **burial mounds** dating from 500 BC to AD 800. The **rock paintings** at Hornes clearly depict 21 ships complete with oarsmen. The sites are signposted off the E6, just south of Sarpsborg, but they may also be visited on a long day walk or bike ride from Fredrikstad.

Halden

POP 24,410

The soporific border town of Halden, at the end of Iddefjord between steep rocky headlands, possesses a hugely significant history as a cornerstone of Norwegian defence through centuries of Swedish aggression. With a pretty little harbour filled with yachts, a looming fortress rising up behind the town and a sprinkling of decent restaurants, this place makes a worthwhile detour.

History

Halden served as a garrison during the Hannibal Wars from 1643 to 1645. From 1644 it was fortified with a wooden stockade. In the 1658 Roskilde Treaty between Sweden and Denmark, Norway lost its Bohuslän province (and Bohus fortress), and Halden was left exposed as a border outpost requiring heavy defences. When attacks by Swedish forces in 1658, 1659 and 1660 were scarcely repelled, the need for better fortification became apparent, resulting in the fortress, which was begun in 1661.

In the midst of it all, in 1659 and 1716, the Halden resistance resorted to fire to drive out the enemy, a sacrifice honoured with a mention in the Norwegian national anthem, which includes the lines: '...we chose to burn our nation, lest we let it fall'. The fires also serve as a centrepiece for a museum in the fortress on the town's history.

Further attacks from the Swedes continued into the 19th century. In the first few years of the 20th century, Fredriksten Fortress was armed with increasingly powerful modern cannons, turret guns and howitzers. However, this firepower was removed during the 1906 negotiations for the dissolution of the Swedish-Norwegian union and the town nestled into life as a quiet seaside village.

◉ Sights

Fredriksten Fortress & Museums
FORTRESS, MUSEUM

(Fredriksten Festning; www.fredrikstenfestning.com; fortress free, adult/child all museums Nkr60/20, guided tour Nkr70/30; ⊙ fortress 24hr, museums 11am-5pm daily mid-May–Aug, guided tours 2pm year-round) Crowning the hilltop behind Halden is the 1661 Fredriksten Fortress, which has resisted six Swedish sieges and never been captured.

On 28 July 1660 King Fredrik III of Denmark issued a declaration ordering a more sturdy fortification above Halden. The pentagonal citadel (as well as the adjoining Gyldenløve Fort to the east) was constructed across two parallel hills from 1661 to 1671, and augmented between 1682 and 1701. Its crowning event came on 11 December 1718, when the war-mongering Swede King Karl XII was shot dead on the site (a monument now marks the spot).

The fortress covers a large area, much of which is grassy expanses and tumble-down walls, but there are a couple of interesting museums, a restored cobbled street and great views. The whole place is brought entertainingly to life through the guided tours.

The museums in the castle grounds cover various facets of the fortress' history. Downhill from the main entrance, the War Museum contains military artefacts and a variety of information on Halden's experiences of war from 1660 onwards, including details about the Norwegian independence movement in 1905. A tunnel leads up into Prince Christian's Bastion – the main vantage point for the fortress' defenders. A broader sweep of Halden's history is outlined in the Byen Brenner Museum ('City in Flames' Museum) about halfway down the main thoroughfare. Displays in the Gamle Kommandantbolig (Commandant's Residence) cover the history of trade and relations with

neighbouring Sweden. The building itself was constructed between 1754 and 1758 and damaged by fire in 1826. After renovation it was used as a powder laboratory, armoury and barracks. Note the Fredrik V monogram over the doorway.

Perhaps the most interesting sites are the brewery, which once produced up to 3000L of beer a day, and the bakery ovens, which baked bread for up to 5000 soldiers. There's also a multimedia presentation and shop at the Infosenter, just inside the main entrance of the fortress.

There are many intriguing old buildings dotted around the fortress, but even better are the views over Halden.

Guided tours of the fortress and the buildings on the grounds are in Norwegian or English. At other times you can take an audio tour (Nkr50). There are also self-guided ghost tours, in which you're almost guaranteed to see the fortress' famous 'Lady in White'...

On Tuesday and Wednesday evenings in season various dance and musical shows are staged in the fortress grounds. The Wednesday night show is actually part of a national TV show, *Allsangpå Grensen* (Sing Along).

To reach the fortress from the town, a half-overgrown cobbled footpath climbs from the top of Festningsgata in Sørhalden (a neighbourhood of 19th-century sea captains' cottages) up the unkempt lilac-covered slopes. The road for cars leads up from the same street.

Rød Herregård
HISTORIC BUILDING

(Herregårdsveien; tours adult/child Nkr60/20; ⊙ tours noon, 1pm & 2pm Mon-Sat, noon, 1pm, 2pm & 3pm Sun mid-Jun–mid-Aug, noon, 1pm & 2pm Sun May–mid-Jun & mid-Aug–Sep) Dating from at least 1690, Rød Herregård manor has fine interiors, which include notable collections of both weapons and art, as well as the mounted heads of many specimens of local wildlife. The formal gardens are some of the most pleasant in Norway. It's 1.5km northwest of the town centre and is well signposted.

⌂ Sleeping

Fredriksten Camping
CAMPGROUND €

(☑ 69 18 40 32; Fredriksten Festning; tent with car Nkr200, 4-/5-bed cabins Nkr450/750; ℗) A great location amid the trees and adjacent to the fortress makes this well-run place a winner. It also offers minigolf and, after the fortress closes and the crowds disappear, a quiet green spot to pitch a tent. There's an on-site restaurant selling various none-too-healthy fried things.

Thon Hotel Halden
HOTEL €€

(☎69 21 33 00; www.thonhotels.no; Langbrygga 1; s/d Nkr1225/1425; ☎) You could step straight off your million-euro yacht and into this plush hotel overlooking the waterfront. Oh, you didn't come by luxury yacht? Well, never mind, at least you can content yourself relaxing in this bright and cheery hotel with friendly service.

Grand Hotell
HISTORIC HOTEL €€

(☎69 18 72 00; www.grandhotell.net; Jernbanetorget 1; r from Nkr1290; P ☎) The Grand Hotell, opposite the train station, is the oldest hotel in town and has a slightly forced old-world feel, but it's otherwise a very comfortable base.

✖ Eating

Around Gjesthavn (Guest Harbour) you'll find several pleasant restaurants with outdoor seating.

Kongens Brygge
PIZZA €€

(☎69 17 80 60; Gjesthavn; mains Nkr125-185, pizzas Nkr145-255; ☺1-11pm Sun-Tue & Thu, 1pm-2.30am Wed, noon-2.30am Fri & Sat) Right on the waterfront, this place has a cruisy atmosphere and a wonderful pontoon terrace that's open in summer. The pizzas are expensive, but come in quite-generous portions and are bound to fill hungry travellers. There are several similar places nearby.

ⓘ Information

The Halden **tourist office** (☎69 19 09 80; www.visithalden.com; Torget 2; ☺9am-4.30pm

Mon-Fri, 9am-noon Sat & Sun mid-Jun–mid-Aug, 9am-3.30pm Mon-Fri rest of year), just off Torget, has some useful information.

ⓘ Getting There & Away

The long-distance bus terminal sits right on the harbour.

Trains between Oslo and Halden (Nkr260, 1¾ hours) via Fredrikstad run hourly from Monday to Friday and every second hour on weekends. An average of four trains daily continue on to Göteborg and Malmö in Sweden.

Halden Canal (Haldenkanalen)

East and north of Halden, a canal system connects the town with Göteborg, Sweden, for all but one short (1.8km) dry section. The highlight is the Brekke Locks, a system of four locks between Femsjøen and Aspern (on the Halden–Strømsfoss run), which raise and lower the boats a total of 26.6m.

The **M/S Strømsfoss** (☎90 60 63 21; www.turisten.no; adult/child Nkr310/200) follows the Haldenkanalen between Tistedal (just east of Halden) and Strømsfoss. The boat leaves Strømsfoss at 10.45am and Tistedal at 3.15pm on Thursday and Saturday. The journey takes around six hours. To reach the town of Tistedal from Halden, take bus 103 or 106 (Nkr32, 18 minutes, twice hourly except late Saturday afternoon and Sunday). From Strømsfoss back to Halden a special ferry bus meets the boat and drives you back (Nkr98).

Southern Norway

Best Places to Eat

➡ Måltid (p101)
➡ Smag & Behag (p97)
➡ Sanden (p92)
➡ Villa Marina (p101)
➡ Provianten (p104)

Best Places to Stay

➡ Farris Bad (p91)
➡ Lillesand Hotel Norge (p97)
➡ Rjukan Hytteby & Kro (p115)
➡ Lampeland Hotell (p109)

Why Go?

Come summer, the southern coastline draws Norwegian holidaymakers in droves. With a string of pristine coastal villages of whitewashed timber beside an island-studded sea, it's not difficult to see why. For travellers, the 'Norwegian Riviera' offers a chance to experience a totally different destination from that of the fjords and high plateaus of the tourist brochures, one that is at once cosmopolitan and essentially Norwegian.

Venture inland and the scenery turns ever more dramatic. Deep in the region's interior is Rjukan, gateway to some of Norway's most scenic high country – the Hardangervidda National Park and the spectacularly formed mountain of Gausta. Elsewhere, scattered among a landscape smothered in forest and decorated in dark lakes filled with beavers, you'll discover idyllic, remote villages, wooden stave churches and a rich traditional culture.

When to Go
Kristiansand

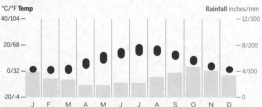

Feb–Mar Prime season for ice-climbing, skiing and dog-sledding in Rjukan.

Jul For south-coast beach towns at their most lively.

Aug–Sep Inland trails beckon as the autumn colours begin to appear.

THE COAST

You probably didn't come to Norway for the beaches, but if you did, expect to be accompanied by masses of local tourists drawn by the lure of a paddle and picturesque islands. The towns along the coast are gorgeous, but *way* overpriced in peak season.

Tønsberg

POP 41,485

Tønsberg is the oldest town in Norway, although so distant are its origins that few interesting remnants remain. There are nonetheless a few Viking-era ruins and a decrepit castle that make the town worth a brief detour as you head along the coast.

◉ Sights

Tønsberg Castle FORTRESS
(Castrum Tunsbergis; ⊙ tower noon-5pm mid-Jun–mid-Aug, shorter hours rest of year) FREE Tønsberg Castle, spread across the hill behind the town, was the largest fortress in Norway in the 13th century. In 1503 the Swedes destroyed what they could, but nonetheless, the modern (1888), 17m-high **Slottsfjellstårnet tower** provides a good viewpoint over the ruins. Parts of the 600m-long outer wall remain intact, while the extant medieval stone foundations include **King Magnus Lagabøte's keep**, the 1191 **Church of St Michael**, the **hall of King Håkon Håkonsson** and various **guard towers**. The park is always open.

Vestfold County Museum MUSEUM
(Vestfold Fylkesmuseum; www.vfm.no; Farmannsveien 30; adult/child Nkr60/40, Tue free; ⊙11am-4pm mid-May–mid-Sep, shorter hours rest of year) At the foot of **Slottsfjellet** (Castle Rock) at the northern end of town, a five-minute walk northwest of the train station, this museum's highlights include displays on the excavation of the impressive *Oseberg* Viking ship (now shown in Oslo's Viking Ship Museum), a collection of historic period-furnished farm buildings, and a section on Tønsberg's whaling history.

⌖ Sleeping

Tønsberg Vandrerhjem HOSTEL €
(☑33 31 21 75; tonsberg@hihostels.no; Dronning Blancasgata 22; dm Nkr350, s/d with shared bathroom Nkr750/850, d with bathroom Nkr895, q Nkr1600; P�$) This exceptionally well-run and friendly hostel is well equipped, clean and tidy, and just a five-minute walk from the train station. The common areas would be the envy of many a fancy hotel. A good breakfast is served. The reception area is shut between noon and 3pm.

Thon Hotel Brygga BUSINESS HOTEL €€
(☑33 34 49 00; www.thonhotels.no; Nedre Langgate 40; d Nkr1115; @$) Inside a traditional wooden warehouse, this modern waterfront hotel has pleasant, if smallish, rooms and great breakfasts; it's popular with car-tripping families.

Quality Hotel Tønsberg BUSINESS HOTEL €€€
(☑33 00 41 00; www.nordicchoicehotels.com; Ollebukta 3; d Nkr1480; P�$≋) Big chain hotel with neat, stylish rooms and lots of public space by the waterfront. The rooftop pool and deck is a bonus when the weather's good. Parking is a steep Nkr189 per day.

✕ Eating

Tønsberg has dozens of decent restaurants, with the best atmosphere along the water.

Restaurant Havariet INTERNATIONAL €€
(☑33 35 83 90; havariet.no; Nedre Langgate 30e; mains Nkr110-325; ⊙11am-1am) Arguably the most popular along the waterfront, this place offers solid pub grub in a warm, inviting interior. It has good-value lunch deals and plenty of marine life on the menu, including some tasty, if sometimes overburdened, salads.

Roar I Bva SEAFOOD €€
(roaribua.com; Nedre Langgate; sandwiches Nkr80-99, mains Nkr150-199; ⊙10am-6pm) This cute wooden shack is half fishmonger and half seafood cafe. However you choose to class it, the well-priced fish is so fresh it might well flop off your plate and back into the sea. If you're looking for picnic provisions, grab a slab of its smoked salmon to take away.

❶ Information

Tourist Office (☑48 06 33 33; www.visit-tonsberg.com; Storgaten 38; ⊙9am-4.30pm Mon-Fri, 10am-2pm Sat mid-Jun–early Aug, 9am-2pm Mon-Fri rest of year) Just off the main square.

❶ Getting There & Around

The **Tønsberg Rutebilstasjon** (☑33 30 01 00; Jernbanegaten) is a block south of the train station. Nor-Way Bussekspress buses run to/from Kristiansand (Nkr425, 4½ hours, one to two daily) via most coastal towns en route, including

Southern Norway Highlights

1 Strike out on foot across the haunting wilderness of the **Hardangervidda Plateau** (p116), home to Europe's largest herd of wild reindeer.

2 Board a slow boat down the **Telemark Canal** (p110) to Dalen.

3 Climb to the summit of **Gausta** (p113), Norway's most beautiful mountain.

4 Take the quiet, beautiful **coastal road** (p106) between Flekkefjord and Egersund.

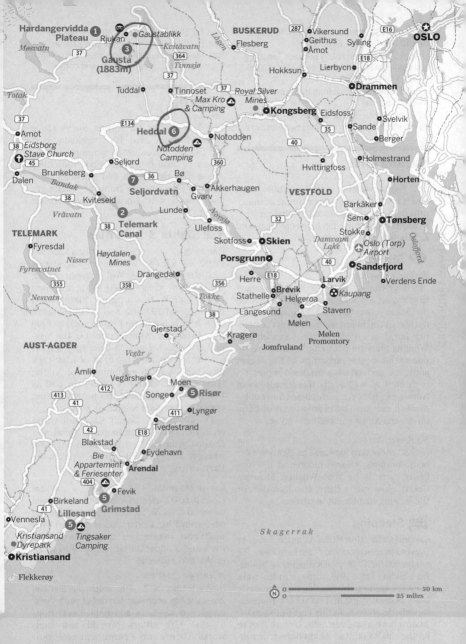

Hardangervidda ❶ **Plateau**
Møsvatn
Rjukan ⊙ •*Gaustablikk*
❸ *Kvitåvatn*
Gausta
(1883m)
Tuddal ⊙
•Tinnoset
❷ *Tinnsjø*
BUSKERUD ⟨287⟩ •Vikersund
Flesberg •Geithus Sylling ⟨E16⟩
•Åmot
Hokksun ⟨E18⟩
Lågen Lierbycn•
Drammen
Totak
•Amot
⟨38⟩ *Eidsborg*
Stave Church
⟨45⟩
•Brunkeberg
Bandak
•Dalen
⟨38⟩ •Kviteseid
Royal Silver
Mines
Max Kro ⛺
& Camping
Heddal ❻
Notodden
Camping
•Notodden
•Kongsberg Eidsfoss
⟨35⟩ •Sande •Svelvik
•Berger
•Holmestrand
Hvittingfoss
•Horten
⟨37⟩
⟨E134⟩
⟨360⟩
⟨40⟩
❼ ⟨36⟩ •Bø
Seljordvatn
•Seljord
Vråvatn
TELEMARK
•Fyresdal
Nisser *Høydalen*
Mines
⟨38⟩
Gvarv
•Akkerhaugen
•Lunde
Norsjø
•Ulefoss
⟨32⟩
VESTFOLD
Barkåker•
Sem• •**Tønsberg**
Stokke•
Damvann
Lake
Oslo (Torp)
Airport
•Sandefjord
Skotfoss •**Skien**
Porsgrunn
⟨355⟩
⟨358⟩
Fyresvatn
•Drangedal
Tokke
⟨356⟩
•Herre ⟨E18⟩
Stathelle• •**Brevik**
Langesund Helgeroa•
⟨38⟩
•Mølen
Larvik
⊗*Kaupang*
•Stavern
⟨40⟩
Verdens Ende
AUST-AGDER
Vegår
•Gjerstad
Kragerø•
Jomfruland
Mølen
Promontory
•Åmli
•Vegårshei
•Moen
Songe• ❺ •**Risør**
⟨413⟩
⟨412⟩
⟨41⟩
⟨411⟩ •Lyngør
⟨42⟩ •Tvedestrand
⟨E18⟩
Blakstad
Bie
Appartement
& Feriesenter •**Arendal**
⟨404⟩ ⛺
•Eydehavn
•Fevik
•Birkeland
⟨41⟩
Lillesand
❺ ⛺
Kristiansand
Dyrepark
Tingsaker
Camping
•**Kristiansand**
Flekkerøy
Grimstad
S k a g e r r a k
OSLO

⊕ 0 _____ 50 km
Ⓝ 0 _____ 25 miles

❺ Stroll the narrow streets of the 'white towns', **Grimstad**, (p96), **Lillesand** (p97) and **Risør** (p93).

❻ Admire the exquisite roof lines and paintings in the stave church at **Heddal** (p111).

❼ Scour the surface of **Seljordvatn** (p115) in search of Selma the Serpent.

Larvik (Nkr130, one hour, two daily). Nettbuss runs to Oslo (Nkr199, 1½ hours) .

Intercity trains run hourly between Tønsberg and Oslo (Nkr225, 1½ hours) or south to Larvik (Nkr103, 34 minutes).

Bike rental is available from the tourist office for Nkr75 per day.

Drivers of their own vehicles will be stung by automatic tolls for entering the town precincts.

Sandefjord

POP 44,950

This former whaling capital is a busy town and is home to one of only a couple of museums in the world dedicated to whaling.

Most buses running between Oslo and Kristiansand stop in Sandefjord.

◉ Sights

Whaling Museum   MUSEUM
(Hvalfangst-museet; ☑94 79 33 41; www.hval-fangstmuseet.no; Museumsgaten 39; adult/child Nkr55/30; ☺10am-5pm late Jun-Aug, shorter hours rest of year) You might not agree with the practice, but there's no denying that Sandefjord's Whaling Museum is a well-presented exhibition of this most controversial of Norwegian activities, and offers a balanced report on both sides. As well as charting the history of Norwegian whaling, with photos and equipment, it contains information and displays on general Arctic and marine wildlife.

Southern Actor   SHIP
(☺9.30am-5pm late Jun-Aug) The 1950s whaleboat *Southern Actor* is moored at the harbour; entry is by your Whaling Museum ticket; while you're there, also look out for the striking monument to whalers.

🛏 Sleeping

Clarion Collection Hotel Atlantic   HOTEL €€
(www.nordicchoicehotels.no; Jernbanealleen 33; s/d Nkr990/1090; ⓟ🛜) Occupying a beautiful building from 1914, three minutes' walk from the station, this Clarion boutique-style hotel is great value and one of the more atmospheric choices on this part of the coast. Rooms have a luxe aesthetic, though they're on the small side, and a light dinner, or supper as they call it, is complimentary every night from 6pm.

❶ Information

Tourist office (☑33 46 05 90; www.visitsan-defjord.com; Thor Dahls gate 7; ☺9am-5.30pm

Mon-Fri, 10am-5pm Sat, 12.30-5pm Sun Jul-Aug, 9am-4pm Mon-Fri rest of year) The excellent Sandefjord tourist office is just back from the waterfront. There's free tea and coffee.

Larvik

POP 41,400

Larvik is one of the largest towns along Norway's south coast. It's a workaday port but has the region's most glamorous hotel, a new cultural centre and good museums. Along with that, you'll find Norway's most accessible excavations from the Viking era and Bøkeskogen, Norway's largest beech forest.

◉ Sights & Activities

Kaupang   ARCHAEOLOGICAL SITE
(☑90 62 27 44; www.kaupangprosjektet.no; adult/child Nkr50/free, Wed activities Nkr70; ☺10am-4pm mid-Jun–mid-Aug) Kaupang, 5km east of Larvik, was a former Viking town built around AD 800 and occupied until 960. It is believed that up to 1000 people once lived here. Although most of the original artefacts are now in Oslo, the custodians of the site make the most of what they have with a small exhibition, four Viking tents and knowledgable guides dressed as Vikings who can show you nearby Viking graves and explain Kaupang's past.

On Wednesday (family day) and weekends, they cook Viking soup and bread, and fire up the forge. The guides can also tell you where to find other Viking cemeteries in the Larvik area.

Larvik Museum   MUSEUM
(☑48 10 66 00; www.larvikmuseum.no; adult/child combined ticket Nkr50/10; ☺noon-4pm Tue-Sun late Jun–mid-Aug, shorter hours rest of year) This multi-part museum is spread across the town and is under the auspices of the broader Vestfold Museene.

➡ Verkensgården

(Nedre Fritzøegate 2; ☺noon-4pm Tue-Sun end Jun–early Aug, noon-4pm Sun rest of year) Verkensgården has tools and implements from a local 17th-century sawmill and ironworks. There's also a permanent geological exhibition documenting the evolution of blue larvikite, a beautiful, locally quarried 500-million-year-old type of granite.

➡ Larvik Maritime Museum

(Skottebrygga and Jærbuen; Kirkestredet 5) A 1730 brick structure immediately east of the harbour is home to maritime art and a number of impressive model ships. Colin Archer, the famous Norwegian naval architect and shipbuilder, was from Larvik and his beautiful skate, *Jærbuen II,* dating to 1898, is also usually docked here.

➡ **Herregården Manor House**
(☑48 10 66 00; Herregårdsbakken; ⊘noon-4pm Jun–mid-Sep) The classic baroque timber Herregården manor house was constructed in 1677 as the home of the Norwegian governor-general, Ulrik Frederik Gyldenløve, the Duke of Larvik. As the illegitimate son of King Frederik IV of Denmark, Gyldenløve was given a dukedom and packed off to Norwegian obscurity. It's furnished in 17th- and 18th-century style.

Bølgen CULTURAL CENTRE
(Kulturhus; www.kulturhusbolgen.no; Sanden 2; ⊘5-9pm Wed-Thu, 1-5pm Sat & Sun) The town's impressive wave-shaped cultural centre houses a gallery that has an interesting curatorial calendar of contemporary Norwegian artists, concert halls and cinema (screening original films), as well as the town's best cafe and bar, Sanden (p92).

Bøkeskogen FOREST
Its name means 'beech forest', and this sublime patch of green overlooking Larvik is Norway's largest and the world's most northerly beech tree forest. It is criss-crossed with walking trails, from 2.6km to 10km in length. There are stunning views over Lake Farris from its northwestern apex.

🛏 Sleeping

Lysko Gjestegaard GUESTHOUSE €€
(☑97 74 44 90; www.lysko-it.no; Kirkestredet 10; s/d from Nkr840/1050; ℗ 🛜) This quiet guesthouse occupies a lovely old timbered house opposite the Maritime Museum at the eastern end of the harbour. The rooms themselves are crammed with character via hand-decorated furniture and liberally applied colour on the walls and ceilings. There's a kitchen for guest use and an attached antique shop. Prices don't include breakfast.

★ **Farris Bad** HOTEL €€€
(☑33 19 60 00; www.farrisbad.no; Fritzøe Brygge 2) Along from the newly redeveloped dock precinct, built next to, and over, the town's nicest sandy beach, this full-service spa hotel has luxurious rooms, many with views straight out to sea, and lavishly decorated public spaces. Outside high season, there are good deals here, and with spa entry complimentary for guests, it can work out a real bargain.

The spa is up there with Europe's best, with entrance (Monday to Thursday/Friday to Sunday/evening Nkr495/595/325) allowing access to an impressive collection of pools, steam rooms and saunas, a tantalising staircase down into the sea, lounges with stunning sea views and a women's-only sauna. There's 'obligatory textile-free' time on Wednesday nights and Sunday afternoons, which includes some *interesting* sauna rituals. The hotel's restaurant has a beachside terrace and does a generous lunchtime seafood buffet (Nkr350) in summer.

🍴 Eating

There are a few good eating-out choices in Larvik, including the Farris Bad restaurant, though most locals head to Stavern's beachside places.

SOUTHERN NORWAY LARVIK

THOR HEYERDAHL

Larvik's favourite son was the intrepid and controversial Thor Heyerdahl (1914–2002), a quirky scientist, anthropologist and explorer who spent his lifetime trying to prove that the world's oceans were vast highways that were essential to understanding ancient civilisations – a novel idea in the hallowed halls of scientific research.

In 1947 he sailed 6000km in a balsa-wood raft, the *Kon-Tiki,* from Peru to Polynesia to prove that the South Pacific may have been settled by migrants from South America rather than Asia. His theories were supported by discoveries of similar fauna and cultural artefacts in Polynesia and South America, and by the fact that Pacific Ocean currents run east to west.

The film of his journey won an Oscar in 1951 for best documentary and his medal-winning bravery in resisting the Nazis only added to his legend. His book describing the expedition sold an astonishing 60 million copies worldwide. The actual *Kon-Tiki* ship is on display at the Kon-Tiki Museum (p63) in Oslo.

★ **Sanden** CAFE, BAR €
(www.bolgenkulturhus.no/sanden; Bølgen, Sanden 2; burgers Nkr98-119, mains Nkr145-185; ⊙noon-8pm Tue-Sat, to 4pm Sun, later for concerts) A bastion of cosmopolitan cool in Larvik, Sanden's soaring waterfront space makes you want to settle in for hours. Coffee here is the best for miles around, with Oslo's Solberg & Hansen beans, and there's a burger menu that goes from basic to inspired ('Carla' has coriander and chilli mayo, 'Barbara' caramelised onion). It's open late as a bar for events; check ahead.

Georg Marius Larsen
Fisk Delikatese FISH SHOP €€
(⊘33 18 17 44; Dronningensgt 43; dishes Nkr170; ⊙9am-4.30pm Mon-Fri, to 2.30pm Sat) An authentic fish deli that sells hot fish cakes, salads, preprepared meals such as seafood gratins, and fresh seafood.

❶ Information

Tourist office (⊘33 69 71 00; www.visitlarvik. no; Bølgen, Sanden 2; ⊙1-8pm) This helpful tourist office is located inside the swish new Bølgen cultural centre on the waterfront.

❶ Getting There & Away

Nor-Way Bussekspress buses pass through Larvik en route between Seljord (Nkr280, 2¼ hours, up to three times daily) and Tønsberg (Nkr115, one hour). For other destinations along the coast, you may need to change at Tønsberg or Arendal. Local trains run hourly between Oslo S (Central Station) and Larvik (Nkr249 to Nkr311, two hours). The train and bus stations are side by side on Storgata.

Around Larvik

The low-lying Brunelanes Peninsula southwest of Larvik has a few pleasant towns, all packed in summer with local holidaymakers.

Stavern

POP 5600

Stavern, just south of Larvik, is set around a stunning fold of coastline; the ocean is full of granite outcrops, creating a maze of icy waterways. The village itself is almost as pretty as the natural beauty surrounding it. Its pedestrian streets are lined with cafes, small private galleries and creamy white houses, and it serves as Larvik's social club most summer nights. Highlights include the mid-18th-century fort **Fredriksvern Verft**,

which is surrounded by block houses that once formed part of the fortress defences.

Stavern is the start of the beautiful, and very popular, 33km-long Kyststien Coastal Walk to Ødegården on the western coast of Brunelanes. The Stavern tourist office has route maps.

🛏 Sleeping

Hotel Wassilioff HISTORIC HOTEL €€
(⊘33 11 36 00; www.wassilioff.no; Havnegata 1; s/d Nkr1195/1400; P⟐) In operation since 1844, the Hotel Wassilioff knows about keeping guests happy and, thanks to touches such as old sepia photos of Norwegian royalty and vintage dining chairs, it has character in abundance. Rooms are a little less exciting than common areas. Its location next to parkland and a pocket-sized beach is delightful.

❶ Information

Tourist office (⊘91 12 32 22; Kongens gate 2; ⊙10am-4pm Wed-Sat, 1-4pm Sun mid-Jun–early Aug)

❶ Getting There & Away

To get to and from Larvik (Nkr36, 15 minutes, hourly), use bus 1.

Mølen

The Mølen Promontory is something of a geological oddity. It forms the end of the ice-age **Ra moraine** (rock and silt pushed ahead of the glacier and deposited as a new landform), which extends from the lake Farrisvatn (which the moraine dammed) to the southwestern end of Brunelanes. The 230 stone cairns and heaps of boulders, which are laid out in parallel rows, are Iron Age burial mounds.

Damvann

Some 20km north of Larvik is the beautiful, haunting lake of Damvann, surrounded by forests. Legend claims it to be the home of a witch called Huldra, who is of such exquisite beauty that any man who looks upon her is doomed. Access is difficult without a car; the nearest bus stop is at Kvelde (6km from the lake) on Numendalslågen Rd.

Kragerø

POP 10,510

One of the favourite summer retreats for Norwegians, Kragerø has narrow streets and whitewashed houses climbing up from the water's edge. Kragerø has long served as a retreat for Norwegian artists, and Edvard Munch spent a few restorative fishing holidays here, calling Kragerø 'the pearl of the coastal towns'. A statue of Munch stands on the spot where he painted a winter sun over the sea.

Sights & Activities

There's not much to see here; the offshore island of Jomfruland is Kragerø's most popular attraction. For a great view over the town and its *skerries* (islets), climb from Kragerø Stadium to the lookout point on **Steinmann Hill**.

Berg-Kragerø Museum MUSEUM
(Lovisenbergveien 45; adult/child Nkr50/free; ⊙11am-5pm Tue-Sun mid-Jun–mid-Aug) On the shore of Hellefjord, 3km from the centre, this museum consists of a 120-hectare estate with a country residence dating from 1803. There are gardens, walking tracks and a gallery for visiting art and history exhibits.

Seal Watching WILDLIFE WATCHING
(www.fjordbat.no; adult/child Nkr250/200; ⊙10.45am Tue, 3.25pm Fri, 11.10am Sat, 11.45am & 7.45pm Sun) M/S *Kragerø*, the same boat that runs ferry services to Jomfruland, offers a seal-watching package where you get return boat rides to Jomfruland, wildlife fact sheets and a take-home pair of binoculars. Seals are seen on around 50% of ferry crossings.

Sleeping & Eating

The tourist office can recommend private apartments to rent.

Kragerø Sportell Apartments APARTMENTS, HOTEL €
(☑35 98 57 00; www.kragerosportell.no; Lovisenbergveien 20; d/apt Nkr750/1280; 🅿@🛜) A former youth hostel, now privately owned, this place is an excellent deal with modern and comfortable, if plain, rooms and lovely waterfront apartments that sleep up to four and have their own kitchens. Breakfast is included in room rates but not if you're staying in an apartment. To get here, follow the signs to the village of Kalstadkilen.

Victoria Hotel HISTORIC HOTEL €€
(☑35 98 75 25; www.victoria-kragero.no; PA Heuchtsgata 31; s/d Nkr1100/1250; 🛜) The rooms in the grand old Victoria all differ from one another and are the best in town. Some have little kitchenettes, while others have balconies overlooking the wharf. It's well run and nicely idiosyncratic.

ℹ Information

Tourist office (☑35 98 23 88; www.visit-kragero.no; Tovgaten 1; ⊙9am-6pm Mon-Sat, 9am-3pm Sun Jul–mid-Aug, 9am-4pm Mon-Fri May-Jun & mid-Aug–Sep) The exceptionally helpful tourist office is at the bus station.

ℹ Getting There & Away

Buses run up to five times daily to Oslo (Nkr340, 3½ hours) and Kristiansand (Nkr290, 2½ hours), although you may have to change in Tangen on the E18. Trains from Oslo or Kristiansand stop at Neslandsvatn, where most are met by a bus to Kragerø.

Risør

POP 6900

Snaking around the base of cliffs and hills and overlooking a moody ocean, the white-on-white town of Risør is one of southern Norway's prettiest. The focus of the town falls on the U-shaped harbour full of colourful fishing boats and private yachts, and surrounded by historic houses dating from 1650 to 1890.

Sights & Activities

Risør Saltwater Aquarium AQUARIUM
(Saltvannsakvariet; www.risorakvarium.no; Dampskipsbrygga; adult/child mid-Jun–mid-Sep Nkr100/80, rest of year Nkr30/20; ⊙11am-6pm Jul, noon-4pm Jun & Aug, shorter hours rest of year) The interesting Risør Saltwater Aquarium, on the quay in front of the Risør Hotel, is a small showcase of saltwater fish, crustaceans and shellfish common to Norway's south coast. Highlights include baby lobsters, the colourful cuckoo wrasse and the *underwater post office*. Yes, you read that correctly.

Festivals & Events

To get summer rolling, the town hosts a number of festivals.

Risør Chamber Music Festival MUSIC
Held in the last week of June, this festival has a growing cast of local and international performers in attendance.

Risør Wooden Boat Festival SPORTS
Held over the first weekend in August, this festival (known as Trebåtfestival) has boat races, concerts and kids' activities. Finding accommodation at this time can be difficult.

🛏 Sleeping

Sorlandet Feriesenter CAMPGROUND €
(☑90 02 61 68; www.sorlandet-feriesenter.no; Sandnes; campsites Nkr260, cabins Nkr600-1800; 🛉) This delightful waterside campsite, on the peninsula south of Risør, has a range of very well-equipped cabins alongside lots of trees under which you can plonk a tent. Children will love all the activities and facilities on offer (boat rides, playgrounds, 'elephant' showers, giant bouncing balloons and so on).

Det Lille Hotell APARTMENTS €€€
(☑37 15 14 95; www.detlillehotel.no; apt per night Nkr1400-2200; P 🛜) Superb-value, self-catering suites and apartments are dotted around town under the umbrella host. Most are in delightfully restored homes with period furnishings – ideal if you plan to spend a week here. Daily rates are cheaper outside the peak summer season, and booking for a week reduces costs significantly.

Risør Hotel HOTEL €€€
(☑37 14 80 00; www.risorhotel.no; Tangengata 16; s/d from Nkr1395/1595; P 🛜) The only official hotel accommodation in the town centre, with a beautiful location and oh-yes harbour views, the Risør rests a little on its laurels. Rooms are comfortable, if staid; those with views don't cost any more, so ask if one's available. It's opposite the aquarium, 500m west of the harbour.

🍴 Eating

Around, and just back from, the harbour you'll find several moderately priced cafes and restaurants.

Kast Loss SEAFOOD €€€
(☑37 15 03 71; Strandgata 23; mains from Nkr215; ☺4-10pm Mon-Fri, 11am-midnight Sat, 1-10pm Sun) Seafood is, not surprisingly, a big deal here, and locals rate Kast Loss as about the best-value restaurant in town. It also serves up good pizzas (Nkr170).

ℹ Information

Tourist office (☑37 15 22 70; www.risor.no; Kragsgata 3; ☺10am-6pm mid-Jun–mid-Aug, 11am-3pm Mon-Fri, noon-2pm Sat rest of year) The tourist office is 50m west of the harbour.

ℹ Getting There & Away

Nettbuss buses to Oslo (Nkr319, 3¼ hours) connect at Vinterkjær with local buses to/from Risør (Nkr30, 40 minutes). It also has a direct service to Kristiansand (Nkr249, 1¾ hours). The nearest train station is at Gjerstad, but you'll need your own car to get there (thus somewhat defeating the point of train travel!).

Around Risør

The *skerries* just offshore are a popular excursion from Risør. The southernmost island of **Stangholmen**, with a pretty lighthouse dating from 1855, is the most popular. This may be due to the fact that it's the only one of the islands with a restaurant, **Stangholmen Fyr Restaurant & Bar** (☑37 15 24 50; www.stangholmen.no; mains Nkr310), which is in the lighthouse.

To get to Stangholmen take one of the twice-hourly summertime boats (return Nkr65, from 10am to 1am mid-June to mid-August) from the harbour in Risør. Note that they don't go during bad weather.

Arendal

POP 40,100

Arendal, one of the larger south-coast towns, has an undeniable buzz throughout summer, with the outdoor restaurants and bars around the harbour (known as Pollen) filling up with holidaymakers, and a full calendar of festivals. Large enough to have an array of amenities but not too big to overwhelm, it's a nice place to spend a few days. The matchbox-sized old district of Tyholmen, which features many timbered houses, adds considerable charm, while those seeking greater communion with the sea than a harbourside cafe can set off to the offshore islands of Merdø, Tromøy and Hisøy.

👁 Sights

Tyholmen NEIGHBOURHOOD
Rising up behind the Gjestehavn (Guest Harbour) is the old harbourside Tyholmen district, home to beautiful 17th- to 19th-century timber buildings featuring neoclassical, rococo and baroque influences. Tyholmen was once separated from the mainland by a canal, which was filled in after the great sailing era. Look out for the **rådhus** (town hall), a striking wooden building dating from 1815.

Bomuldsfabriken Kunsthall GALLERY
(www.bomuldsfabriken.no; Oddenveien 5; ☺noon-4pm Tue-Fri) **FREE** This highly regarded con-

temporary art gallery is a 10-minute walk from the town centre on the northern edge of Arendal. One of the largest galleries in southern Norway, its temporary exhibitions are housed in a stunning example of Norwegian industrial architecture, a former cotton factory from the late 19th century.

✯✯ Festivals & Events

There's always something going on in Arendal, with open-air concerts by the water quite common on weekends.

Hove Festival MUSIC
(www.hovefestivalen.no) Music festival drawing big international acts to the island of Tromøy. Headliners in 2014 included M.I.A, Disclosure and Earl Sweatshirt.

Canal Street Jazz & Blues Festival MUSIC
(www.canalstreet.no) World-class jazz and blues, with surprise acts such as Patti Smith.

🛏 Sleeping

Arendal has a good sprinkling of midrange hotels, but those on a tight budget will need to head out of town.

Clarion Tyholmen Hotel HISTORIC HOTEL €€€
(☑37 07 68 00; www.choice.no; Teaterplassen 2; s/d Nkr1520/1720; ❊☜) Undoubtedly Arendal's best hotel, the Clarion combines a prime waterfront position with attractive-enough rooms in a restored old building that seeks to emulate Tyholmen's old-world ambience. The corner suites offer magnificent sea views.

Thon Hotel Arendal HOTEL €€€
(☑37 05 21 50; www.thonhotels.no; Friergangen 1; s/d Nkr1345/1545; ❊☜) It might not have waterfront views, but this typical Thon is just 50m from the water's edge. Bland on the exterior, the rooms are modern, large and comfortable. There's a public pay carpark nearby.

✗ Eating & Drinking

There's no need to stray too far from the harbour; indeed you may find yourself spending much of your day and evening by the water.

Café Victor CAFE €
(www.cafevictor.no; Kirkengaten 5; light meals Nkr74-139; ⊙10am-midnight Jun-Aug, 10am-5pm Mon-Thu, 10am-11pm Fri, 10am-7pm Sat Sep-May) Café Victor, with its prime waterfront position and interesting antique ceiling, is a nice place for lunch, with good coffee and gener-

ous open sandwiches. Or if you happen to be here on a Friday night, stop by for its cheese menu.

Blom Restaurant SEAFOOD €€€
(☑37 00 14 14; www.blomrestaurant.no; Langbrygge 5; mains Nkr289-299; ⊙4-10pm Mon-Sat, 3-8pm Sun) The most upmarket of the Pollen harbour crowd, Blom provides a respite from the boozy vibe that sometimes wins at the other waterside bars. Dishes such as grilled scallops and smoked mackerel salad are tasty.

Madam Reiersen NORWEGIAN, INTERNATIONAL €€€
(☑37 02 19 00; madamreiersen.no; Nedre Tyholmsvei 3; lunch mains Nkr99-159, dinner mains Nkr219-260; ⊙11am-2am Mon-Sat, 2pm-2am Sun) A happy, kooky, bright space along the Pollen harbour that morphs into a pub and live-music venue depending on the night. The menu reads like so many others – mussels, fish soup, spare ribs, roast fish, pasta – but the saucing is subtle and the fish and meat are top quality.

No.9 Kaffe & Platebar CAFE
(☑37 02 77 92; www.no9.no; Langbrygge 9; ⊙10am-5pm Mon-Sat, open later for events) No.9 is the work of Espen Larsen, a local jazz musician who sells a range of (mostly jazz) CDs and plays them while you sip your coffee or snack on a pastry.

ℹ Information

Tourist office (☑37 00 55 44; www.arendal.com; Sam Eydes plass; ⊙9am-5pm Mon-Fri, 11am-4pm Sat Jul–mid-Aug, 10am-3pm Mon-Fri mid-Aug–Jun) Note that outside the high season, hours can be erratic. Even if the office is shut, someone will be on hand to answer phone calls.

ℹ Getting There & Away

M/S Merdø (www.skilsoferga.no; adult/child one way Nkr35/25) sails from Arendal (Pollen) to Merdø twice hourly from early July to mid-August. It leaves hourly between 11am and 4pm on weekends year-round from Merdø and returns on the half-hour.

There are also ferries to Hisøy (adult/child Nkr35/20).

Nor-Way Bussekspress buses to Kristiansand (Nkr220, 1½ hours, up to nine daily) and Nessbuss services to Oslo (Nkr350, four hours) call in at the Arendal Rutebilstasjon, a block west of Pollen harbour. Local Timekspressen buses connect Arendal with Grimstad (Nkr76, 30 minutes, half-hourly) and Risør (Nkr127, 1¼ hours, hourly).

Around Arendal

The 260-hectare island of **Merdø**, just off Arendal, has been inhabited since the 16th century. One nice maritime peculiarity is that the island bears the remnants of vegetable species introduced in the ballast of early sailing vessels.

The favoured bathing sites are on **Tromøy**, **Spornes**, **Hisøy** and **Hove**. For Spornes, take the bus marked 'Tromøy Vest/Øst'; it's a 15-minute walk from the stop. Alternatively, take a bike on the M/S *Skilsø* ferry (adult/child Nkr25/18, 10 minutes), which sails frequently between Arendal and the western end of Tromøy. Tromøy also has some enjoyable and easy-to-follow **walking trails**. The Arendal tourist office (p95) can give route suggestions.

On the islets of **Store** and **Lille Torungene** rise two grand lighthouses that have guided ships into Arendal since 1844. They're visible from the coasts of both Hisøy and Tromøy.

Grimstad

POP 19.500

Grimstad is at its most lovely in the pedestrianised streets that lie inland from the waterfront; these are some of the most atmospheric on the Skagerrak coast. Grimstad has a number of interesting calling cards: it was home to playwright Henrik Ibsen and has a good museum; it is the sunniest spot in Norway, with an average of 266 hours of sunshine per month in June and July; and the town also has an unmistakably young vibe, thanks to its large student population.

◉ Sights

★ Ibsenhuset Museum   MUSEUM

(www.gbm.no; Henrik Ibsens gate 14; adult/child Nkr80/free; ⊙11am-4pm Mon-Sat, noon-4pm Sun Jun–mid-Sep, closed mid-Sep–May) Norway's favourite playwright, Henrik Ibsen, washed up in Grimstad in January 1844. The house where he worked as a pharmacist's apprentice, and where he lived and first cultivated his interest in writing, has been converted into the Ibsenhuset Museum. It contains a re-created pharmacy and many of the writer's belongings, and is one of southern Norway's most interesting museums. The young staff here are wonderful, their tours full of fascinating detail and the odd spot of salacious gossip.

Grimstad Maritime Museum   MUSEUM

(Sjøfartsmuseet; www.gbm.no; Hasseldalen; adult/child Nkr50/free; ⊙11am-4pm Mon-Sat, noon-5pm Sun Jul) This spectacularly sited, but rarely open, museum in the office of the 1842 Hasseldalen shipyard provides a glimpse into Grimstad's history during 'the days of the white sails' when the town was one of the shipbuilding capitals of Europe.

★ Festivals & Events

Sørlandet Boat Show   SPORTS

(www.baadmessen.no) Floating boat show held in May.

Ikkjevel   MUSIC

(ikkjevel.no) Supercool, local indie and electronic festival in mid-June.

🛏 Sleeping

For camping, there are at least six nearby campsites that are on the tourist office's website, while **Grimstad Hytteutleie** (☑37 25 10 65; www.grimstad-hytteutleie.no; Grooseveien 103) can book holiday cabins in the area.

Bie Appartement
& Feriesenter   CAMPGROUND €

(☑37 04 03 96; www.bieapart.no; off Arendalsveien; campsites Nkr200, cabins/apt from Nkr650/1390; [P][⛺]) The nearest camping option to Grimstad is this friendly, well-equipped site 800m northeast of the centre along Arendalsveien. As well as big, grassy pitches it has a range of huts and some seriously kitted-out apartments.

Cafe Ibsen B&B   B&B €€

(☑90 91 29 31; www.cafeibsen.no; Løkkestredet 7; s/d Nkr600/900) This is a great central B&B option, run by the friendly owners of Café Ibsen. There are six simple, but character-filled rooms in a historic house, all with private bathrooms.

Rica Hotel Grimstad   HISTORIC HOTEL €€

(☑37 25 25 25; www.rica.no; Kirkegata 3; s/d Nkr1145/1345; [P][✳][☎]) At the town's heart, this historic hotel spans a number of converted and conjoined timber houses, with an atmospheric breakfast room and basement restaurant. Rooms here can be absolutely delightful, if a little staid, but make sure you're not allocated one of the dark, stuffy and very noisy internal rooms overlooking the lobby.

Grimstad Vertshus & Kro
HOTEL €€
(✆37 04 25 00; www.grimstad-vertshus.no; Grimstadtunet; s/d Nkr795/950; P🌐) This friendly, cosy place is a fair hike from town, but given the shortage of midrange places on the coast, its simple rooms are good value.

✗ Eating & Drinking

Café Ibsen
CAFE €
(✆37 27 57 63; Henrik Ibsens gate 12; sandwiches Nkr89; ⊙10am-4pm Mon-Sat, noon-4pm Sun) Come here for homemade pastries, slabs of cake, quiches and big sandwiches. It's in a lovely rambling space opposite the Ibsenhuset Museum.

★Smag & Behag
CAFE, DELI €€
(www.smag-behag.no; Storgaten 14; mains Nkr115-165; ⊙10am-10pm Mon-Sat) We concur with this upmarket deli-cafe's name: 'taste and enjoy'. Come for lunch or a casual dinner and sample the region's best produce (which is also available from the deli counter) and a carefully selected wine list. A summer salad of beets and 40°cured salmon is a riot of colour, an open sandwich of pulled beef and coleslaw is a revelation.

Apotekergården
SEAFOOD €€
(✆37 04 50 25; Skolegata 3; mains Nkr160-260, pizzas Nkr125; ⊙noon-midnight) The Apotekergården is a fun, busy restaurant with a cast of regulars who wouldn't eat anywhere else. It can be difficult to get a table out on the terrace in summer, especially as the night wears on. If so, head up the old wooden stairs for a beer and a game of shuttleboard.

Galleri
BAR
(Storgaten 28; ⊙5-7pm Sun-Thu, 3pm-2am Fri & Sat) The centre of Grimstad's nightlife has DJs, jam sessions, quiz nights and a crowd that seems to spring from Grimstad's woodwork on the most unlikely of nights.

❶ Information

Guest Harbour (Gjestehavn; ✆37 25 01 69; www.grimstadgjestehavn.no) Public toilets, showers and a laundry (all open to landlubbers).
Tourist office (www.visitgrimstad.com; Storgata 1a, Sorenskrivergården; ⊙9am-6pm Mon-Fri, 10am-4pm Sat mid-Jun–mid-Aug, 8.30am-4pm Mon-Fri Sep-May) Down on the waterfront inside the big white timber building. Staff run guided tours of the town every Wednesday and Friday in July at 1pm (adult/child Nkr100/free).

❶ Getting There & Away
The Grimstad Rutebilstasjon is on Storgata at the harbour, though some buses only stop up at the highway, rather than coming into town. Nor-Way Bussekspress buses between Oslo (Nkr400, 4½ hours) and Kristiansand (Nkr220, one hour) call at Grimstad three to five times daily. Nettbuss' Timekspressen buses run to/from Arendal once or twice hourly (Nkr73, 30 minutes).

Lillesand
POP 9465
Between Kristiansand and Arendal, lovely Lillesand has a pedestrian-only whitewashed village centre full of second-hand shops and cafes, along with a stunning circular harbour.

🛏 Sleeping

Tingsaker Camping
CAMPGROUND €
(✆37 27 04 21; www.tingsakercamping.no; campsites Nkr230, cabins per week Nkr11,000; P🌐) This crowded but well-equipped campsite, on the shore 1km east of Lillesand centre, is a typical seaside holiday resort with camping, caravans and a range of pricey cabins.

★Lillesand Hotel Norge
HISTORIC HOTEL €€€
(✆37 27 01 44; www.hotelnorge.no; Strandgata 3; s/d Nkr1390/1690; P🌐) This boutique hotel has been thoughtfully renovated to reflect its original 1837 splendour and overflows with period touches, particularly in the public areas. The rooms, which aren't quite as ornate, include ones dedicated to King Alfonso XIII of Spain and author Knut Hamsun, both of whom stayed here.

Features include an antiquarian library, an atmospheric lounge area (complete with stained-glass windows), a superb restaurant (lunch mains Nkr175, dinner menus Nkr285 to Nkr495) and a fragrant garden courtyard. In summer the hotel hosts a concert series, with everything from classical performances to big-name Norwegian stars.

✗ Eating

★Kafe Strandhaven
CAFE €
(www.kafestrandhaven.com; Strandgata 10; mains Nkr99-179; ⊙10am-10pm Jul & Aug, 10.30am-5pm Mon-Thu & Sat, to 11.30pm Fri, noon-5pm Sun rest of year) In the heart of the village, with garden tables that lead down to the harbour,

this is the kind of village cafe that can transform a destination. It's decorated in a stylish mashup of vintage and Nordic modern furniture, and friendly young staff serve up wraps, salads, soups, burgers and, later, wine. And the luscious house-made cakes are as good as they look.

Sjøbua   CAFE €€
(Strandgate 8; mains 179-189; ⊙10am-2.30am Jul & Aug, 10am-midnight Mon-Thu & Sun, to 2.30am Fri & Sat rest of year) Part takeaway kiosk, part waterside restaurant, part kick-on bar; come here for fish and chips in an unbeatable location.

Beddingen   SEAFOOD €€€
(☑37 27 24 22; Havnegata 3; lunch specials Nkr99, dinner mains Nkr276-295; ⊙10am-11pm, bar to 2am Jul & Aug, 11am-11pm Mon-Sat, 1-7pm Sun rest of year) This is a traditional Norwegian seaside restaurant, doing big-night-out holiday meals for families. Along with fantastically fresh fish and seafood, there's a full steak menu as well as, surprisingly, the occasional taco buffet.

ⓘ Information

Tourist Office (☑37 40 19 10; ⊙9am-6pm Mon-Fri, 10am-4pm Sat, noon-4pm Sun mid-Jun–mid-Aug) In the town hall in summer.

ⓘ Getting There & Away

The most pleasant way to reach Lillesand in summer is by the **M/S Øya** (www.blindleia. no; adult/child one way Nkr290/140, return Nkr460/240) boat from Kristiansand. There's also an hourly Nettbuss to Kristiansand (Nkr78).

Kristiansand

POP 85,681

Kristiansand, Norway's fifth-largest city, calls itself 'Norway's No 1 Holiday Resort'. That can be a bit misleading: sun-starved Norwegians do flock here in the summer, and there's a petite town beach and flash marina, but it tends to serve more as a gateway to the villages of Norway's southern coast and the inland region of Setesdalen. What Kristiansand does offer in spades, though, is a lively cultural and shopping scene, some excellent restaurants and very healthy nightlife. In addition, anyone travelling with children will more than likely find themselves cajoled into visiting the town's outstanding children's park and zoo.

◉ Sights

★**Kristiansand Dyrepark**   ZOO
(www.dyreparken.com; adult/child high season incl all activities from Nkr549/489; ⊙10am-7pm mid-Jun–mid-Aug, to 3pm mid-Aug–mid-Jun) Off the E18, 10km east of Kristiansand, Dyrepark is probably *the* favourite holiday destination for Norwegian kids. The former zoo is several parks rolled into one. There's a **fun fair** that includes rides such as the pirate-ship cruise, Captain Sabretooth's Treasure Trove and enchanted houses. **Kardamomme By** (Cardamom Town) is a fantasy village based on the children's stories of Thorbjørn Egner. There's a **water park** with heated pools and water slides. The biggest attraction, though, is still the **zoo** itself.

It houses a large number of species, including red pandas, a crocodile house, lions and tigers and an African savannah filled with giraffe, zebra and others. For non-Norwegians, the highlight is the **Nordisk Vilmark** (Northern Wilderness), where visitors are transported through the habitat of moose, wolves, lynx and wolverines on elevated boardwalks.

★**Sørlandets Kunstmuseum**   GALLERY
(SKMU; ☑38 07 49 00; Skippergata 24b; adult/child Nkr60/free; ⊙11am-5pm Tue-Sat, noon-4pm Sun) This exceptional regional art museum focuses on both fine and craft-based practices, and the collection includes some particularly strong contemporary work from local, Norwegian and Nordic artists. There is a bright, beautifully designed, pleasingly sophisticated children's wing. For anyone interested in Norwegian ceramics, the 44 works by local Kari Christensen will prove a treat.

Posebyen   NEIGHBOURHOOD
The Kristiansand Posebyen takes in most of the 14 blocks at the northern end of the town's characteristic *kvadraturen* (square grid pattern of streets). It's worth taking a slow stroll around this pretty quarter, the name of which was given by French soldiers who came to *reposer* here (it's French for 'relax').

A scale model (with buildings around 1m high) of the city as it appeared when designed by Christian IV is on view at **Vest-Agder Folk Museum**. The annual Kristiansand guide, published by the tourist office, includes a good section called 'A Stroll through Posebyen' to guide your wandering. The most well-preserved buildings include **Bentsens Hus** (Kronprinsens gate 59), which dates to 1855; the **former post office** (Kronprinsens gate 45), dating to 1695; and **Gyldenløves gate 56** (1802).

Kristiansand Kunsthall GALLERY
(www.kristiansandkunsthall.no; 4th fl Rådhusgata 11; ⏲noon-4pm Tue-Sun) FREE Shows change seasonally, but are usually high-concept, challenging surveys well worth a browse. It's a stunning space, with a rare elevated town outlook. It hosts key events during the annual Punkt festival.

Kristiansand Cathedral CATHEDRAL
(Domkirke; Kirkegata; tower adult/child Nkr20/10; ⏲11am-2pm Mon-Sat) FREE Built in 1884 in late Gothic style, the Kristiansand Cathedral, with seating for 1800 people, is Norway's third-largest church.

Christiansholm Fortress FORTRESS
(Kristiansand Festning; ⏲grounds 9am-9pm mid-May–mid-Sep) FREE Strandpromenaden's hulking centrepiece is the distinctive Christiansholm Fortress. Built by royal decree between 1662 and 1672 to keep watch over the strategic Skagerrak Straits and protect the city from pirates and rambunctious Swedes, the construction featured walls up to 5m thick and an armoury buried within a concentric inner wall. It was connected to the mainland by a bridge over a moat (filled in during the 19th century) deep enough to accommodate tall ships.

Agder Natural History Museum & Botanic Gardens GARDENS
(naturmuseum.no; Gimleveien 23; adult/child Nkr70/free; ⏲11am-5pm mid-Jun–mid-Aug, 10am-3pm Tue-Fri, noon-4pm Sun rest of year) The winding paths through the 50-hectare park at Gimle Estate lead through a botanic garden that contains greenhouses with the largest collection of cacti in Norway. The estate house has 19th-century period interiors and extraordinary teethlike columns at the front, and there's also a historic rose garden dating from 1850. It's just over 1km from the centre, across the Oddernes bridge.

Kristiansand Museum MUSEUM
(Vest-Agder Fylkesmuseet; www.vestagdermuseet.no; Vigeveien 22b; adult/child Nkr70/free; ⏲10am-5pm Tue-Fri, noon-5pm Sat-Mon mid-Jun–Aug, 9am-2pm Mon-Fri rest of year) This open-air folk museum, 4km east of town on the E18, houses a collection of 40 farmsteads and hamlets from the Setesdalen region and Kristiansand itself. In summer there are lots of kids' activities, including some nice hands-on historical re-creations. Eastbound buses M1, M2 and M3 from Henrik Wergeland gate pass the museum.

Baneheia & Ravnedalen PARK
Baneheia and Ravnedalen, both north of the city centre, offer greenery and a network of lakeside hiking and skiing tracks for those keen to escape the city for a while. Both parks were created between 1870 and 1880. Over a total 30-year period, the planting of 150,000 coniferous trees transformed the area into a recreational green belt.

Odderøya PARK
This island, a rocky outcrop just by the fish market and connected by a bridge, is one of the city's wonderful green spaces. There are some delightful places for a walk, a swim or a picnic; it's also home to artists' studios and Vaktbua (p102) cafe and bar.

🏃 Activities

One Ocean Dive Center DIVING
(📞38 09 95 55; www.oneocean.no; Dvergsnesveien 571; 1/2 dives with equipment from Nkr950/1300) A professional centre that runs dives to wrecks, including a downed plane and even a mine sweeper. It's 8km east of Kristiansand.

Setesdalsbanen RAILWAY
(www.vestagdermuseet.no/setesdalsbanen; adult/child return Nkr120/60; ⏲departures 11.30am, 1.20pm & 3.10pm Sun mid-Jun–Aug) The 78km-long narrow-gauge railway between Kristiansand and Byglandsfjord linked Setesdalen with the coast from 1896 to 1962. It was used to transport nickel from the Evje mines, among other things. Steam- or diesel-powered locomotives still travel the last 6km between Grovane (2km north of Vennesla) and Røyknes, a 25-minute journey one way. Norges Statsbaner (NSB; Norwegian State Railways) trains run from Kristiansand to Vennesla (Nkr44, 12 minutes, four daily).

🎊 Festivals

Punkt MUSIC
(punktfestival.no) Edgy electronic festival in September specialising in live remixes; Brian Eno, Laurie Anderson and David Sylvian were past guests.

🛏 Sleeping

Kristiansand can be expensive for what you get, which may be nothing unless you book early for summer, especially once the July school-holiday period begins. If you

Kristiansand

N 0 ————————— 500 m
0 ————————— 0.25 miles

Ravnedalen (575m); Agder Nature
Museum & Botanic Gardens (1.1km);
Kristiansand Museum (4.1km);
Kristiansand Dyrepark (9.1km)

Nordik Walk · Baneheia

Ravnedalen

Café Generalen
(1.3km)

Agder
Taxis

Train
Station · Bus Station

Colour Line
Terminal
(International Ferries)

Quay 6 (M/S
Øya to
Lillesand)

Odderøya
(350m)

Sørlandets
Kunstmuseum

Town
Square

Kristiansand
og Oppland
Turistforening

Tourist
Office

Yacht
Harbour

Gjestehavn

Lundsbrua

Kristiansand

◉ Top Sights
1 Sørlandets Kunstmuseum B2

◉ Sights
2 Bentsens Hus B1
3 Bystrand Beach D3
4 Christiansholm Fortress D3
5 Former Post Office C1
6 Gyldenløves Gate 56 .... C2
7 Kristiansand Cathedral B3
8 Kristiansand Kunsthall B3
9 Posebyen B1

🛏 Sleeping
10 Clarion Hotel Ernst B3
11 Scandic Kristiansand Bystranda D2
12 Sjøgløtt Hotell D2
13 Thon Hotel Wergeland B3
14 Yess Hotel A2

✕ Eating
15 Bølgen & Moi B4
16 Drom Me Plass En B2
17 Fish Market B4
18 Kick Malt & Mat B3
19 Måltid B3
20 Sjøhuset C4
21 Snadderkiosken D2
22 Villa Marina C4

🍸 Drinking & Nightlife
23 Cuba Life B3
24 Frk Larsen B3
25 Håndverkeren B2
Kick ....(see 18)
Mean Bean ....(see 1)
26 Vaktbua C4
27 will.i.juice B2

are driving, there are a number of chain
hotels around the entrance to Kristiansand
Dyrepark, 10km east of town.

Roligheden Camping   CAMPGROUND €
(☎ 38 09 67 22; www.roligheden.no; Framnesveien;
campsites Nkr220, large cabins Nkr2200; ☺ May-

Sep) Tent campers are in luck at this well-run campsite situated at a popular beach 3km east of the centre. Take bus 15 from the centre.

★ **Sjøgløtt Hotell**　　　　HOTEL €€
(⌂38 70 15 66; www.sjoglott.no; Østre Strandgate 25; s/d Nkr895/975; ☎) This low-key 15-room hotel in a historic building is run by a lovely young couple. The rooms are, admittedly, small, but have big windows and are well designed, and include extras unusual at this price, such as Nespresso machines. Breakfast, afternoon-tea-time waffles and evening pizza and wine are served in an atmospheric basement or relax in the sun in its cute courtyard.

Scandic Kristiansand Bystranda　HOTEL €€
(⌂21 61 50 00; www.scandic-hotels.com; Østre Strandgate 76; s/d Nkr1290/1390; P@) This brand-new beachside place is big and brash, but very beautifully designed. It has a warm, textured and relaxed kind of style, and has all the facilities and extras you can expect in a hotel of this size. It's a wonderful spot for families with its beach, park and poolside position.

Yess Hotel　　　　　HOTEL €€
(⌂38 70 15 70; www.yesshotel.no; Tordenskjolds gate 12; s/d Nkr748/848; P❋☎) This good-value, 'back-to-basics' hotel chain steps in when B&Bs are in short supply. It does have a corporate sunniness that can be grating, but rooms are pleasant, with wall-to-wall photographs of trees, comfortable beds and pristine bathrooms.

Thon Hotel Wergeland　　HOTEL €€
(⌂38 17 20 40; www.thonhotels.no; Kirkegata 15; s/d Nkr1040/1385; ☎) It doesn't get any more central than this attractive hotel right next to the cathedral. It's all very smart and modern within, although a grand stairwell and a few other lovely old features remind you of the building's history. Rooms have dark hardwood floors and Nespresso machines.

Clarion Hotel Ernst　　HOTEL €€€
(⌂38 12 86 00; www.clarionernst.com; Rådhusgata 2; s/d Nkr1580/1750; P@) This Clarion is in one of the town's most stately buildings. Inside it has been done out in an urban, contemporary style with huge, pearl-string lampshades, gold and silver thronelike chairs, purple lighting and massive jet black bedheads.

✗ Eating

In summer everyone ends up at the small, remodelled harbour around the fish market, where you'll find fresh seafood, beer and ice cream. There are, however, a huge number of options in the city grid too.

Drom Me Plass En　　BAKERY, CAFE €
(Skippergata 26; sandwiches, salads & soups Nkr99-119; ⊙7am-6pm Mon-Sat, 10am-5pm Sun) This big, bustling bakery has lots of tables inside and on the pretty footpath. Locals flock here every morning for a great range of freshly baked *boller* (raisin rolls) and loaves of bread, or pop in later for chicken salads, tuna melts and big soups.

Snadderkiosken　　　FAST FOOD €
(Østre Strandgate 78a; dishes Nkr89-115; ⊙8.30am-11.30pm Mon-Fri, 11.30am-1.30am Sat & Sun) We don't normally go out of our way to recommend fast-food kiosks, but Snadderkiosken is one of the best of its kind, plus it also feels apt for a seaside town. Just behind the beach, this lovely, tiled, 1920s-style kiosk serves up hearty meatballs and mashed potatoes or grilled chicken with rice and salad to beachgoers and late-night wanderers.

★ **Villa Marina**　　　　ITALIAN €€
(⌂38 12 07 21; mat-uteliv.no/villa-marina; Østre Strandgate 2a; pizzas Nkr109-192, mains Nkr229-269; ⊙noon-10.30pm Mon-Sat, 1-9pm Sun) Taking the Norwegian Riviera notion to its natural conclusion, you can spend a few sunny hours here and fancy yourself by the Med – superyachts all around and an Aperol spritz (Aperol and *prosecco*, Nkr96) in hand. Pizzas, made under the direction of a Neopolitan *pizzaiolo*, are the best on the coast; modern Italian mains are similarly spot on.

The look is contemporary rustic Italian tempered by Nordic restraint – quite lovely.

★ **Måltid**　　　　NORWEGIAN €€€
(⌂47 83 30 00; www.maltid.no; Tollbodgata 2b; 1-9 courses Nkr395-920; ⊙5-9.45pm Tue-Sat) We advise booking well ahead to secure a table at this unassuming, elegant Kristiansand shopfront. It's been hailed Norway's 'fifth best restaurant' and offers top-notch neo-Nordic dining with extreme attention to detail and the best local produce.

Dishes closely follow the seasons, but expect descriptions that read something like 'Norwegian oysters with kohlrabi and dill and sea herbs/fried cabbage with juice of vegetables and butter/common nettle'.

Wines, many from Burgundy, and beers from Grimstad's Nøgne Ø are skillfully matched course by course. Tip: if you've not planned ahead, it's always worth popping in to see if there's space at the bar.

Sjøhuset
SEAFOOD €€€

(☑38 02 62 60; www.sjohuset.no; Markens gate; dining room mains Nkr315-425, outside mains Nkr199-349, 3-/4-/5-course set menus Nkr535/615/695; ⊘11am-11pm) Along the waterfront next to the yacht harbour, the woody, maritime fantasia of a formal dining room specialises in seafood set menus, or you can sit out on the covered deck and have a 500g bucket of the freshest prawns with bread and butter, *moule frites* (mussels and fries) or fish soup.

Bølgen & Moi
SEAFOOD €€€

(☑38 17 83 00; www.bolgenogmoi.no; Sjølystveien 1a; mains Nkr225-340, 3-/4-/5-course set menu Nkr545/595/645; ⊘3pm-midnight Mon-Sat) The fish-market harbour's upmarket choice, Bølgen & Moi does a rich fish and shellfish soup, excellent *moule frites*, a tasty range of fish and steaks, as well as set menus and seafood platters. In summer the outdoor tables are packed and can get raucous once the kitchen closes (blankets provided, if required).

Kick Malt & Mat
BRITISH €€€

(☑38 02 83 30; www.kickcafe.no/gastropuben; Dronningensgate 8; mains Nkr230-280; ⊘3pm-midnight) Not to be confused with the nightclub it secrets out the back, this is a dark, clubby pub styled on the British gastropub, with a menu of hearty local dishes and Anglophile roasts. It is, as you'd hope, serious about its beer, with 29 rotating beers on tap, including local legend Nøgne Ø.

🍷 Drinking & Nightlife

Drinking coffee in the sun is a key Kristiansand pastime and there's a number of cafes that use local roasts and serve above-average espresso. The city comes alive on weekend nights, although everything closes down at 2.30am sharp.

⭐ Mean Bean
CAFE

(Kunstmuseet; Skippergata 24; ⊘8am-5pm Mon-Fri, 11am-5pm Sat, noon-4pm Sun) Owner Steinar Svenning roasts coffee for Mean Bean and its sibling, Cuba Life, under the Mean Bean name. This wonderful high-ceilinged space has, naturally, fabulous coffee but the

friendly staff here also serve up roast beef, salmon or roast vegetable open sandwiches, fresh strawberry smoothies in summer, and moreish sweets such as homemade Snickers slices.

Cuba Life
CAFE

(Tollbodgata 6; ⊘8am-4pm Mon-Fri, 9am-6pm Sat, 10am-4pm Sun) Great little hole-in-the-wall cafe with excellent espresso and filter coffee, plus a whole range of coffee beans and chocolate to take away.

Vaktbua
CAFE, BAR

(Odderøya; ⊘noon-3.30pm Tue, Thu & Sun, to 10pm Wed, to 2.30am Fri & Sat) In a beautiful island spot, this is Kristiansand's bastion of alternative culture, and where you'll find the city's most interesting locals. Head here for all-organic cake and coffee. For a range of performances, after parties and club nights come weekend evenings.

will.i.juice
JUICE BAR

(Gyldenløves gate 11; smoothies & juices Nkr65; ⊘8am-6pm Mon-Sat, 10am-5pm Sun Jun-Aug, 9am-6pm Mon-Fri, 11am-4pm Sat Sep-May) Huge range of freshly pressed juices and smoothies you can take away or sit and sip in the bright space. The protein mocca with almonds, coconut, cocoa and banana is a good way to start an active day.

Frk Larsen
BAR

(Markens gate 5; ⊘11am-midnight Mon-Wed, 11am-3am Thu-Sat, noon-midnight Sun) A great all-day drinking hole in Kristiansand, with a mellow ambience by day and late-night music for the crowds on weekend nights. The cocktail bar opens at 8pm, but the sofas are just as attractive for a midday coffee en route to the foreshore.

Håndverkeren
PUB

(Rådhusgata 15; ⊘3pm-2am) This rowdy, regular public house is set in a stunning building that looks like it's lifted straight out of New England. There's a big selection of local beers (it even does gluten-free on tap), and atmospheric billiards and shuffleboard rooms.

Café Generalen
CAFE

(☑38 09 07 91; Ravnedalsveien 34; ⊘noon-9pm Mon-Sat, to 6pm Sun Jun-Aug, to 6pm daily Sep-May) Up in the green spaces of Ravnedalen, this cute cafe hosts a range of special nights and concerts, as well as being known for its burger menu.

Kick NIGHTCLUB
(www.kickcafe.no; Dronningens gate 8; ⊙11pm-
2.30am Sat, live music from 9pm) Out the back
of the gastropub of the same name, this is
the town disco, a full-service nightclub with
big DJ booth, massive lighting rigs and an
endless bar area (it has capacity for up to
700 happy punters). Kick also hosts occasional live music and big-city DJs on Friday
nights.

ℹ Information

Kristiansand og Oppland Turistforening
(☑38 02 52 63; www.kot.no; Kirkegata 15;
⊙10am-4pm Mon-Wed & Fri, to 5pm Thu) Maps
and information on hiking, huts and organised
mountain tours in southern Norway.
Tourist office (☑38 12 13 14; www.visitkrs.no;
Rådhusgata 6; ⊙8am-6.15pm Mon-Fri, 10am-
6pm Sat, noon-6pm Sun Jul-Aug, 8am-3.30pm
Mon-Fri rest of year)

ℹ Getting There & Away

BOAT
Ferries to Denmark and Sweden leave from the
Colour Line Terminal.

BUS
There's a bus information office and left-luggage
facilities inside the bus station. Note, most local
buses, including those to Lillesand, Grimstad
and Arendal leave from central Henrik Werge-
lands gate, rather than the bus station.

CAR & MOTORCYCLE
With a vehicle, access to the E18, north of the
centre, is via Vestre Strandgate; when arriving
you'll most likely find yourself along Festningsgata. Once in Kristiansand, you'll notice it's
possibly the most traffic-light blighted town
in the whole of Norway. There's street parking
outside the pedestrianised centre.

TRAIN
There are up to four trains daily to Oslo (Nkr299
to Nkr677, 4½ hours) and up to five to Stavanger
(Nkr249 to Nkr474, 3¼ hours).

ℹ Getting Around

Unlike many Norwegian towns, Kristiansand is
flat and the downtown area is easily negotiable
on foot. The **Agder Taxis** (☑38 00 20 00) booth
just outside the bus station is the best bet for
the airport.

Around Kristiansand

In summer, Kristiansand's archipelago of
offshore *skerries* becomes a popular destination for sea-and-sun adventure. The most
popular island, **Bragdøya**, lies close to the
mainland and is, charmingly, home to a
preservation workshop for wooden boats,
which you can borrow for free, gentle forest
walks and several beautiful bathing sites. In
the distance, you'll see the classic lighthouse
Grønningen Fyr.

Ferries for Bragdøya leave from Kristiansand's Quay 6, twice to four times daily
in summer. Ask at the Kristiansand tourist
office for exact schedules, as well as those for
other offshore islands.

M/S Øya (p98) sails a three-hour return
route to and from Lillesand every morning at
10am, except Sunday, from late June to early
August. It departs Quay 6.

Mandal
POP 14,200

Norway's southernmost town, Mandal, is famous for its 800m-long beach,
Sjøsanden. About 1km from the centre and
backed by forests, the Copacabana it ain't,
but it is Norway's finest stretch of sand.
Just don't rely on a Mediterranean climate
to go with it.

◉ Sights

Mandal Museum MUSEUM
(Vestagdermuseet; www.vestagdermuseet.no; Store
Elvegata 5/6; adult/child Nkr70/free; ⊙11am-5pm
Mon-Fri, noon-5pm Sat & Sun mid-Jun–mid-Aug)

BUSES FROM KRISTIANSAND

DESTINATION	DEPARTURES (DAILY)	COST (NKR)	DURATION (HR)
Arendal	up to 9	220	1½
Bergen	1	680	12
Evje	7-8	160	1
Flekkefjord	2-4	250	2
Oslo	up to 9	400	5½
Stavanger	2-4	390	4½

Displays of historical maritime and fishing artefacts and works by local artists are pleasant enough, but this museum is elevated above the mundane by impressive exhibits of works by Mandal's favourite son, Gustav Vigeland. His childhood home, **Vigeland House**, is also part of the museum.

🎭 Festivals

Shellfish Festival   FOOD
(www.skalldyrfestivalen.no) Fresh seafood everywhere and a range of musical performances held in the second week of August.

🛏 Sleeping & Eating

Accommodation in Mandal can be on the expensive side.

Hald Pensjonat   GUESTHOUSE €
(☑38 26 01 00; haldpensjonat.no; d/q Nkr400/500; P🛜) This traditional-style guesthouse has wackily ornate public spaces and a lovely garden. Basic, hostel-style rooms make it one of the few budget options on the coast. Rates do not include a Nkr100 per person linen charge.

Sjøsanden Feriesenter   CAMPGROUND €
(☑38 26 10 94; www.sjosanden-feriesenter.no; Sjøsandveien 1; campsites Nkr220, d Nkr750, 2- to 4-person apt Nkr900-1050, 2-bed cabin Nkr1250; P🛜🏊) Just a few metres away from the beach, this well-run place distinguishes itself from the other campsites in the vicinity. It even has its own water slide. There are motel rooms as well as your usual camping huts and self-catering apartments.

Kjøbmandsgaarden Hotel   HISTORIC HOTEL €€
(☑38 26 12 76; www.kjobmandsgaarden.no; Store Elvegate 57; s/d Nkr899/1099; 🛜) In the heart of the icy-white Old Town streets, this listed, very pretty timber hotel has rather stuffy rooms with decent, recently updated bathrooms. The downstairs restaurant is one of the most popular places in town to eat.

★Provianten   ITALIAN €€
(☑48 27 88 88; www.provianten.no; Store Elvegate 43; mains Nkr199-259, pizzas Nkr139-185) In Norway's southernmost town it seems fitting to eat somewhere on the waterfront with a Mediterranean bent. Yes, Provianten serves genuine wood-fired pizzas, as well as oven-prepared tasty Norwegian dishes, but it's so much more. Possibly the most ambitious place for miles, staff brew their own beer as well as distilling aquavit and schnapps on site.

ℹ Information

Tourist office (☑38 27 83 00; www.region-mandal.com; Bryggegaten 10; ⊙9am-6pm Mon-Fri, 10am-4pm Sat & Sun Jun-Aug, 9am-4pm Mon-Fri Sep-May) The tourist office is situated on the waterfront.

ℹ Getting There & Away

The Mandal Rutebilstasjon lies north of the river, just a short walk from the historic district. The Nor-Way Bussekspress coastal route between Stavanger (Nkr390, 3½ hours) and Kristiansand (Nkr110, 45 minutes) passes through Mandal two to four times daily.

Lindesnes

Why go north when you can go south? At the almost 'polar' opposite to Nordkapp (some 2518km away) is Lindesnes, the southernmost point in Norway (latitude 57° 58' 95" N). Lindesnes (literally 'arching land peninsula') provides an occasional glimpse of the power that nature can unleash between the Skagerrak and the North Sea. On calm days, the series of intricate rocky coves that twist and turn their way around this snake-like coastline are incredibly enticing.

◉ Sights

Lindesnes Fyr   LIGHTHOUSE
(www.lindesnesfyr.no; adult/child Nkr60/free; ⊙10am-8pm late Jun-early Aug, shorter hours rest of year) Rising above the cape is the evocative Lindesnes Fyr, a classic lighthouse. In two of the buildings you'll pass as you climb to the cape, there are exhibitions on the history of the lighthouse, while the visitors centre next to the gate has an informative video. The first lighthouse on the site (and the first in Norway) was fired up in 1655 using coal and tallow candles to warn ships off the rocks. The current electrical version, built in 1915, is visible up to 19.5 nautical miles out to sea.

🛏 Sleeping

Lindesnes Camping og Hytteutleie   CAMPGROUND €
(☑38 25 88 74; www.lindesnescamping.no; Lillehavn; campsites Nkr215, cabins Nkr260-1500; P🛜) Set beside a tiny cove and surrounded by interesting granite outcrops, this campsite, with excellent modern facilities, is on the shore 3.5km northeast of Lindesnes Fyr. There's a small kiosk and kitchen facilities, and you can also organise boat hire.

Lindesnes Havhotel
HOTEL €€
(s/d Nkr1045/1295, 2-bed apt Nkr1450; P 🖥 🕱) This big, stylish resort-style place draws Norwegian families. It may be a little soulless on the outside, but it is supremely comfortable, has great facilities and can be a bargain. Views are wonderful and there are complimentary bicycles.

⊙ Getting There & Away

Buses from Mandal (Nkr78, one hour) travel to the lighthouse via Spangereid on Monday, Wednesday and Friday.

Flekkefjord
POP 8920

Flekkefjord is an enjoyable, quiet place with a pretty, historic centre. The town's history dates back to 1660 when it rivalled Kristiansand. It's 'famous' for having virtually no tidal variation, with typically less than 10cm between high and low tides.

⊙ Sights

The **Hollenderbyen** (Dutch Town) district with its narrow streets and old timber buildings is richly atmospheric.

Flekkefjord Church
CHURCH
(Kirkegaten; ⊙ 11am-1pm Mon-Sat Jul) One building that stands out of the uniform streetscape is the unusual octagonal log-built Flekkefjord church, which was consecrated in 1833. Designed by architect H Linstow (he of the Royal Palace in Oslo), the octagonal theme continues throughout, with the columns, steeple and baptismal font all conforming to the eight-sided shape.

Flekkefjord Museum
MUSEUM
(www.vestagdermuseet.no; Dr Kraftsgata 15; adult/child Nkr50/free; ⊙ 11am-5pm Mon-Fri, noon-5pm Sat & Sun mid-Jun–Aug) Flekkefjord Museum is housed in a home dating from 1724. The 19th-century interiors, mostly the bequest of one local woman, illustrate how a high-bourgeois home of the time would have been furnished.

⊨ Sleeping

Egenes Camping
CAMPGROUND €
(✉ 38 32 01 48; www.egenescamping.no; campsites Nkr240, cabins Nkr550-1250; 🌐) This spectacularly located campsite is beside Seluravatnet (Selura Lake), 1km off the E39 and 5km east of Flekkefjord. There's boat and canoe hire, a climbing wall, minigolf, fishing and other activities on offer here, which make it a great choice for those travelling with children.

★ Grand Hotell
HISTORIC HOTEL €€
(✉ 38 32 23 55; www.grand-hotell.no; Anders Beersgt 9; s/d from Nkr1095/1295; P 🕱) The Grand Hotell sits perfectly in this old town. Housed in a delightful castlelike timber building, rooms have been smartly updated but retain a historic character with hand-printed wallpaper, velvet sofas and festoon drapes. It's subtly done, but if you don't fancy the period look, there's a number of straightforward modern rooms too. The restaurant and pub are charming.

Maritim Fjordhotell
HOTEL €€
(✉ 38 32 58 00; www.fjordhotellene.no; Sundegaten 9; s/d Nkr949/1199) Flekkefjord's largest hotel has an absolute waterfront position, stylish rooms, a sunny terrace bar and a decent restaurant (mains from Nkr149), although the exterior architecture is about as brutal as it can be.

✗ Eating

Pizza Inn
PIZZA €€
(✉ 38 32 22 22; Elvegata 22; pizzas/pasta from Nkr179/229, mains Nkr140-215) This pleasant, publike harbourside restaurant has breezy outdoor tables at which to pass a summer's afternoon or cosy booths for a winter's evening. The service is good, as is the food, which is not all of the pizza variety. The prawn salad (Nkr119) contains a good proportion of the Atlantic Ocean's prawns.

Fiskebrygga
INTERNATIONAL €€
(✉ 38 32 04 90; Elvegata 9; mains Nkr149-210; ⊙ 10am-4pm Mon, Tue & Sat, to 6pm Wed & Fri, to 7pm Thu) Possibly the nicest place in Flekkefjord for a light meal, this cafe-style restaurant next to the tourist office serves fish and chips, marinated spare ribs, delicious cakes and ice cream. It has a certain urban sensibility that's welcome in quiet little Flekkefjord. During the summer you might be in luck and catch one of its concerts, too.

⊙ Information

Tourist Office (✉ 38 32 69 95; www.regionlister.com; Elvegata 3; ⊙ 10am-6pm Mon-Fri, 10am-4pm Sat mid-Jun–mid-Aug, plus 11am-4pm Sun Jul, 9am-4pm Mon-Fri rest of year) Ask for the *A Tour of Flekkefjord* pamphlet.

DON'T MISS

HERE WERE VIKINGS

From the 8th to the 11th centuries, Norway's coastline was the domain of Vikings, but the cape at Lindesnes, where the waters of the Skagerrak and the North Sea collide, proved a challenge even to these formidable seafarers. Their solution? In a spirit of creative engineering that Norway's road builders would later emulate when faced with daunting geographic forms, the Vikings carved a canal across the Lindesnes Peninsula at Spangereid (once a home port of Viking chieftains) to avoid the dangerous seas of the cape. In summer 2007 a replica canal was opened to re-create the Viking detour.

❶ Getting There & Away

The Nor-Way Bussekspress bus between Kristiansand (Nkr250, two hours) and Stavanger (Nkr250, two hours) passes through Flekkefjord.

Flekkefjord to Egersund

If you have your own vehicle, forsake the E39 and take the coastal road Rv44 to Egersund – it's one of southern Norway's most beautiful drives. The road swerves through barren, boulder-blotched hills with a few forested sections, lakes and moorlands, before descending to Jøssingfjord, around 32km west of Flekkefjord, with its breathtaking, perpendicular rock scenery and fine waterfall. Two 17th-century houses, known as Helleren, are nestled under an overhanging cliff and were definitely not built for the claustrophobic. Despite the danger of falling rocks, the overhang did provide protection from the harsh Norwegian climate. The houses are open year-round.

Some 30km southeast of Egersund and 2.5km south of Hauge i Dalane, Sogndalstrand should not be missed for its picturesque timber homes and warehouses that jut out over the river. The houses, which date from the 17th and 18th centuries, feature on the covers of tourist brochures across the region and they're well worth seeking out. It's a quiet, beautiful place. If the small village wins your heart, consider staying at Sogndalstrand Kultur Hotell (☑51 47 72 55; www.sogndalstrand-kulturhotell. no; s/d Nkr1190/1490), an unusual, authentic historic hotel that occupies nine houses and sits right on the river. It also has an excellent restaurant.

For more information on scenic lighthouses and other attractions along this route, and the entire coastal road from Kristiansand to Haugesund, visit the excellent www.nordsjovegen.no.

Egersund

POP 9502

One of the prettiest towns along this western stretch of coastline, Egersund is a serene place strewn with old timber houses that tell the story of its long history. Intriguing rune stones found in nearby Møgedal are among the oldest written forms found in southern Norway.

◉ Sights

★**Egersund Fayancemuseum**　　MUSEUM
(Egersund Pottery Museum; www.dalanefolke.museum.no; ⊙11am-5pm mid-Jun–Aug, 11am-3pm Wed-Fri, 11am-5pm Fri & Sat rest of year) A walkable 1.5km northeast of Egersund centre, this well-designed museum (squirrelled away in an unprepossessing shopping centre), houses the wares of Egersund Fayance, the ceramic and porcelain firm that sustained the district from 1847 to 1979. The collection is organised chronologically, so is a fascinating encapsulation of 19th- and 20th-century design trends, ranging from early monumental pieces to the utilitarian stoneware that has now become highly collectable. The museum sells decorative prints of original patterns and some reproductions.

Dalane Folk Museum　　MUSEUM
(www.dalanefolke.museum.no; Slettebø; adult/child Nkr40/20; ⊙11am-5pm mid-Jun–mid-Aug, shorter hours rest of year) The 'folk' part of the Dalane Folk Museum features eight historic timber homes at Slettebø, 3.5km north of town just off the Rv42.

Egersund Kirke　　CHURCH
(Torget; ⊙11am-4pm Mon-Sat, 12.30-3pm Sun mid-Jun–mid-Aug) There has been a church in Egersund since at least 1292. The cute, current manifestation dates back to the 1620s. The carved altarpiece, a depiction of the baptism and crucifixion of Christ by Stavanger carpenter Thomas Christophersen and

painted by artist Peter Reimers, dates back to 1607; the baptismal font is from 1583. The cross-shaped design, intimate balconies and wonderfully decorated pew doors are all worth lingering over.

Historic Buildings

Some 92 homes, nearly two-thirds of the original town, were gutted by fire in 1843, after which Egersund was reconstructed with wide streets to thwart the spread of future fires. Most buildings in the Old Town date from this period. **Strandgaten**, a street of timber houses constructed after 1843, is well worth a stroll.

Skrivergården was built in 1846 as the home of the local magistrate Christian Feyer. The small town park opposite served as his private garden. **Strandgaten 43** is arguably more beautiful and has what's known as a 'gossip mirror', which allowed the inhabitants to keep an eye on the street. The **Bilstadhuset** still has its original timberwork and includes a sailmaker's loft upstairs. None of the houses are open to the public, but the tourist office hands out a leaflet, *Strolling in Egersund*, which has a map and informative commentary.

🛏 Sleeping

Steinsnes Camping   CAMPGROUND €
(🖉51 49 41 36; www.steinsnescamping.no; Tengs; campsites Nkr180, cabins Nkr325-1500; P🖧) Egersund's most convenient campsite is 3km north of town alongside a rushing stream; buses heading for Hellvik will get you there. As a very Norwegian touch, it sells salmon-fishing permits.

Grand Hotell   HISTORIC HOTEL €€€
(🖉51 49 60 60; www.grand-egersund.no; Johan Feyersgate 3; s/d from Nkr1560/1790; P🖧) The Grand Hotell is a lovely 19th-century dame with stylish, renovated rooms, although you pay more for those in the picturesque original wing. The corner rooms (eg 307 in the old wing and 224 in the newer section) are the best on offer. In summer significant discounts are available. It also has a good restaurant.

ℹ Information

Kulturkontonet (Strandgaten 58; ⊘8am-3pm Mon-Fri) Open year-round, the Kulturkontonet can help with basic tourist information. The building itself is worth checking out, even if you don't need any help.

Tourist office (🖉51 46 82 33; www.eigersund. kommune.no; Jernbaneveien 2; ⊘10am-6pm Mon-Fri, to 4pm Sat & Sun Jun-Aug) The tourist office is fine for local information, but it's only open in summer.

ℹ Getting There & Away

Trains to/from Kristiansand (Nkr249 to Nkr336, two hours) run four times daily, and there are eight daily services to/from Stavanger (Nkr164, one hour).

THE INTERIOR

Inland from Norway's southern coast, quiet mountain valleys such as Setesdalen and the magnificent peak of Gausta, close to Rjukan, are wonderful places. Another highlight is the lake-studded Telemark region, connected by a canal with pretty Seljord – home to the Nessie-esque Selma the Serpent.

Kongsberg

POP 25,900

Surrounded by dark and dense forests and with cascading rapids running through the heart of town, Kongsberg is one of the most agreeable towns in southern Norway. In addition to the pretty setting there's plenty of cultural interest in the form of the fascinating Royal Silver Mines, a host of low-key museums, a pretty clapboard old quarter and one of Norway's best jazz festivals.

History

The history of Kongsberg begins and ends with silver, which was discovered by two children with an ox in 1623 in the nearby Numedal Valley. Their father attempted to sell the windfall, but the king's soldiers got wind of it and the family was arrested and forced to disclose the site of their discovery. Kongsberg was founded a year later and in the resulting silver rush it briefly became the second-largest town in Norway, with 8000 inhabitants including 4000 miners. Between 1623 and 1957, 1.35 million kg of pure threadlike 'wire' silver (one of the world's purest forms of silver) was produced for the royal coffers. Kongsberg is still home to the national mint, but the last mine closed in 1957.

◉ Sights & Activities

Royal Silver Mines
MINE

(☑91 91 32 00; norsk-bergverksmuseum.no/ omvisning; adult/child Nkr150/90; ⊘tours hourly 11am-4pm Jul–mid-Aug, shorter hours mid-May–Jun, Sep & Oct) The profusion of silver mines in Kongsberg's hinterland is known collectively as Sølvgruvene. The easiest way to visit is with the tours that leave from the signposted Kongsgruvene, 700m from Saggrenda (8km south of Kongsberg along the road to Notodden). The admission price includes a bus ride from outside Kongsberg's tourist office.

Ride a 2.3km rail along the *stoll*, a tunnel painstakingly chipped through the mountain to drain water from the mines. The main shaft of the largest mine plunges 1070m into the mountain, down to 550m below sea level.

Constructed without machinery or dynamite – the rock was removed by heating it with fire, then throwing water on the rock to crack it – the tunnel moved forward at 7cm per day and took 73 years (from 1782 to 1855) to complete.

Inside, visitors are guided around equipment used in the extraction of silver, including an ingenious creaking and grinding lift and work area on 65 wet and slippery ladders. Bring warm clothing as the underground temperatures can be a chilly 6°C.

Travellers with disabilites and children under three are not allowed to enter the mines for safety reasons (it's also not recommend for under fives).

Other activities organised in and around the mine include learning how to mint your own coins (sadly though we're yet to find a bank willing to accept the ones we made) and a crash course in digging a mine in your own garden. With advance reservation you can join a rope-and-torch tour (☑91 91 32 00; per group Nkr10,000), which begins with a 1km walk through Crown Prince Fredrik's tunnel. You must then abseil by torchlight 112m down into the mine, after what is hopefully not a 'crash' course in abseiling.

Norwegian Mining Museum
MUSEUM

(Norsk Bergverks-museum; norsk-bergverksmuseum.no; Hyttegata 3; adult/child Nkr80/40; ⊘10am-5pm mid-May–Aug, noon-4pm Tue-Sun Sep–mid-May) Set in a smelter dating from 1844 (the old furnaces survive in the basement), this museum tells Kongsberg's story with relics, models and mineral displays. In the same building, other sections include the Royal Mint, which was moved from Akershus Fortress in Oslo to the source of the silver in 1686, as well as a skiing museum (Kongsberg is home to one of the world's oldest ski-jumping competitions) and an arms and industry museum. All are included in the same ticket.

Lågdal Folk Museum
MUSEUM

(Lågdalsmuseet; www.laagdalsmuseet.no; Tillisch-bakken 8-10; adult/child mid-Jun–mid-Aug Nkr50/20; ⊘10am-4pm mid-Jun–mid-Aug, 11am-3pm mid-Aug–mid-Jun) This folk museum, a 10-minute walk southeast of the train station, houses a collection of 32 period farmhouses around which sheep, goats and pigs frolic. Inside the main building is a WWII resistance museum and a re-creation of 19th-century and early-20th-century Kongsberg, complete with interesting descriptions of each shop and its former owner (much of which is written in Norwegian only). In summer there are guided tours on the hour from 11am to 3pm.

Kongsberg Kirke
CHURCH

(Kirketorget; adult/child Nkr35/10; ⊘10am-4pm Mon-Fri, 10am-1pm Sat, 2-4pm Sun mid-May–mid-Aug, shorter hours rest of year) Norway's largest baroque church, in the Old Town west of the river, officially opened in 1761. The rococo-style interior features ornate chandeliers and an unusual altar that combines the altarpiece, high pulpit and organ pipes on a single wall. In August there are organ recitals held here at 7pm on Wednesdays and noon on Sundays.

Knutefjell
HIKING, SKIING

Kongsberg's best hiking and cross-country skiing is found in the green, forested Knutefjell, immediately west of the town. The Kongsberg tourist office sells the map *Kultur-og Turkart Knutefjell* (Nkr120), which details the hiking and skiing tracks.

✵ Festivals

Kongsberg Jazz Festival
MUSIC

(www.kongsberg-jazzfestival.no) Norway's second-largest jazz festival is held over four days in early July and draws numerous avant-garde international and Norwegian performers. A percentage of profits goes towards humanitarian projects.

Kongsberg

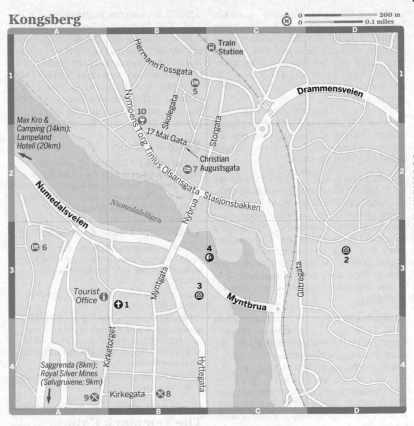

Kongsberg

◎ Sights
1 Kongsberg Kirke	B3
2 Lågdal Folk Museum	D3
3 Norwegian Mining Museum	B3
Royal Mint	(see 3)
4 Waterfall	C3

🛏 Sleeping
5 Gyldenløve Hotell	B1
6 Kongsberg Vandrerhjem	A3

7 Quality Hotel Grand	B2

✖ Eating
8 Fuji Sushi	B4
9 Restaurant Opsahlgården & Christians Kjeller	A4

⊙ Drinking & Nightlife
10 Jonas B. Gundersen Jazzkjøkken	B1

🛏 Sleeping

Kongsberg Vandrerhjem HOSTEL €
(☑ 32 73 20 24; www.kongsberg-vandrerhjem.
no; Vinjesgata 1; dm/s/d from Nkr350/750/970;
P @ ☎) Kongsberg's youth hostel bridges
the gap between budget and midrange with
small but smart and comfortable rooms in a
quiet but accessible part of town. There's a
kitchen available for use of guests.

Max Kro & Camping CAMPGROUND €
(☑ 32 76 44 05; Jondalen; campsites Nkr210, 4-/6-
bed cabins Nkr450/680) The nearest campsite
to town is this low-key site 14km northwest
of Kongsberg along the Rv37. To get here use
the Kongsberg–Rjukan bus. It has nine huts.

★ Lampeland Hotell BOUTIQUE HOTEL €€
(☑ 32 76 09 00; www.lampeland.no; Rv40; s/d from
Nkr995/1290; P ☎) 🌱 From the outside this

might look like a typical roadside motel but Lampeland Hotell, 20km north of Kongsberg on the Geilo road, has plenty of charm. The common areas are decorated using subtle, deep tones and the cosy velvet sofas are perfect for curling up with a book on a cold day. Rooms are simple with a few luxurious elements.

There's a decent restaurant that serves traditional Norwegian mains at lunch and dinner (Nkr155 to Nkr305), though the evening service can finish early – check ahead if arriving after 8pm.

Quality Hotel Grand   BUSINESS HOTEL €€€
(☑32 77 28 00; www.nordicchoicehotels.no; Christian Augustsgata 2; s/d Nkr1380/1580; P🛜🖥️) Many of the swish, spacious rooms here have memorable river views. It calls itself a 'boutique business hotel' and it has enough going for it in terms of decor and facilities to earn both titles (including a pool, sauna and on-site restaurant). All that said, it is almost impossible to get a booking here, it's so popular.

Gyldenløve Hotell   BUSINESS HOTEL €€€
(☑32 86 58 00; www.gyldenlove.no; Hermann Fossgata 1; s/d Nkr1685/1885; P@🛜) It's the giant black-and-white photographs of the town and its environs that first grab the eye on entering one of the rooms at this well-managed hotel. There are enough other nice details to take it from being a regular chain hotel to an appealing, if rather over-priced, option.

✖️ Eating & Drinking

⭐Fuji Sushi   SUSHI €
(☑32 73 12 00; Myntgata 15; sushi plates Nkr90-145, noodles Nkr99; ⊘noon-9pm Mon-Sat, 1-9pm Sun) The menu here is a light and healthy escape from the rigours of burgers and hot dogs. The owners will happily pack your sushi up for you to take away for a riverside picnic.

Restaurant Opsahlgården & Christians Kjeller   NORWEGIAN €€
(☑32 76 45 00; Kirkegata 10; mains Nkr308-338; ⊘restaurant 3-10pm Mon-Fri, cafe 3-10pm Mon-Fri & 2-10pm Sat) This upmarket, rather old-fashioned restaurant surprises with the odd spot-on dish and is complemented by a pleasant pub-cum-cafe where casual meals are available. In the warmer months music in the courtyard is a regular occurrence. Note that the opening hours are a little 'flexible'!

Jonas B. Gundersen Jazzkjøkken   BAR, CAFE
(☑32 72 88 00; Nymoens Torg 10; ⊘2-10pm Sun & Mon, 2-11pm Tue-Thu, 2pm-midnight Fri, noon-midnight Sat) This 'jazz kitchen' chain has a few outlets around southern Norway. This one is a cosy place for a drink or to hear whoever's playing on the weekend. It has a pizza, *piadina* and bruschetta menu (Nkr149 to Nkr234). Some locals say the pizza is the best in town; the coffee is decent too.

ℹ️ Information

Tourist office (☑32 29 90 50; www.kongsberg.no; Kirketorget 4; ⊘9am-6pm Mon-Fri, 10am-2pm Sat late-Jun–mid-Aug, shorter hours rest of year) This excellent tourist office has helpful staff and lots of resources.

ℹ️ Getting There & Around

Several bus companies operate near-hourly buses between Kongsberg and Oslo (Nkr200, 1½ hours), as well as to Notodden (Nkr90, 35 minutes).

Hourly trains connect Kongsberg with Oslo (Nkr189, 1½ hours).

If you're driving your own car and park in the town's supermarket car park, make sure you take a (free) ticket otherwise you'll get nailed with a hefty fine (yes, we talk from experience – bitter experience).

The tourist office hires out bicycles for a cost of Nkr185 a day.

The Telemark Canal

The 105km-long Telemark Canal system, a series of lakes and canals that connect Skien and Dalen, with a minor branch from Lunde to Notodden, lifts and lowers boats a total of 72m in 18 locks. The canal was built for the timber trade between 1887 and 1892 by up to 400 workers. Today, taking a slow boat along the canals is one of the highlights of a visit to southern Norway. For useful information, check out www.visittelemark.com.

Notodden
POP 12,200
Unless you're here for the hugely popular **Blues Festival** (www.bluesfest.no) in early August, drive straight past industrial Notodden until you reach the marvellous, imposing Heddal Stave Church, about 5km northwest of town on the E134. Otherwise, the only reason to pause in town is the Notodden **tourist office** (☑35 01 50 00; www.notodden.kommune.no; Teatergate 3; ⊘8am-3pm Mon-Fri).

◉ Sights

★ **Heddal Stave Church** CHURCH
(www.heddalstavkirke.no; Heddal; adult/child Nkr70/
free, entry to grounds free; ⏱ 9am-6pm Mon-Sat
mid-Jun–mid-Aug, 10am-5pm May–mid-Jun & mid-
Aug–Sep) This fairytale church is the largest
and one of the most beautiful of Norway's
28 remaining stave churches. It's constructed
around 12 large and six smaller Norwegian
pine support pillars, all topped by fearsome
visages, and has four carved entrance portals.
Of special interest are the lovely 1668 'rose'
paintings, a runic inscription in the outer pas-
sageway and the 17th-century 'Bishop's chair'.

Its ornate carvings relate the pagan tale of
the Viking Sigurd the Dragon-slayer, which
has been reworked into a Christian para-
ble involving Jesus Christ and the devil. The
church, heavily restored in the 1950s, is dated
to 1242, but parts of the chancel are from as
early as 1147. The altarpiece originally dates
from 1667 but was restored in 1908, and the
exterior bell tower was added in 1850.

From Notodden, bus 301 goes right by;
otherwise take any bus for Seljord or Bon-
dal. You could also walk from town in half
an hour, along the busy road and past slowly
rusting factories. The church is sometimes
closed for weddings.

🛏 Sleeping

Notodden Camping CAMPGROUND €
(☏ 35 01 33 10; www.notoddencamping.com; Resh-
jemveien; campsites Nkr180, cabins Nkr450-1550)
This is an acceptable riverside site 3km west
along the E134, then 200m south on Resh-
jemveien. You'll be lucky to find a square
inch of space at festival time. Take a bus
from the centre in the direction of Seljord.

❶ Getting There & Away

Timekspressen buses run between Kongsberg
and Notodden (Nkr90, 35 minutes) once or twice
an hour.

Akkerhaugen

POP 375

The attractive waterside village of Akkerhaugen sits on the northern fringes of the
pretty Norsjø lake, itself a branch of the Telemark Canal system. The village is a popular
place from which to begin or end a half-day
Telemark Canal boat journey.

The **Norsjø Ferieland** (☏ 35 95 84 30; www.
norsjo-ferieland.no; campsites Nkr270, caravan sites
Nkr340, cabins Nkr1200-1900; 🅿 🛜 ♨) is a superb

waterside campsite with an impressive array
of facilities and activities, including a private
beach, minigolf, wakeboarding and waterskiing, boat and canoe rental, nature trails, a restaurant and children's activities. The setting is
a delight and the cabins are well appointed.

If you're planning to take a boat from Lunde back to Akkerhaugen, a bus leaves from
the campsite daily; check for seasonal times.

Skien

POP 63,955

Industrial Skien mostly serves as a setting-off
point along the Telemark Canal, but if you're
a fan of Ibsen or Norwegian ceramics, there's
some extra interest here for you.

◉ Sights

Henrik Ibsenmuseet MUSEUM
(www.telemarkmuseum.no; Venstøphøgda; adult/
child Nkr70/30; ⏱ 11am-7pm mid-May–Aug) Author, playwright and so-called 'Father of
Modern Drama' Henrik Ibsen was born in
Skien on 20 March 1828. In 1835 the family
fell on hard times and moved out to the farm
Venstøp, 5km north of Skien, where they
stayed for seven years. The 1815 farmhouse
has now been converted into the excellent
Henrik Ibsenmuseet. There are some terrific audiovisual displays in the former barn,
while guides, some of whom are Ibsen actors, show you around the family home.

Ask about Ibsen theatre performances
here or at the tourist office.

Porsgrund Porselænsfabrikk FACTORY
(☏ 41 04 07 65; www.porsgrund.com; Porselensveien
6, Porsgrunn; ⏱ tours 9am-3pm Mon-Fri, shop 9am-
8pm Mon-Fri, 9am-6pm Sat) In Porsgrunn, just
south of Skien, is one of Norway's best-known
and longest-running porcelain factories. You
can book a tour to see artisans painting the
famous 'straw' pattern, done with the finest
of brushes, or visit the factory outlet shop.

🛏 Sleeping

Kilden Gård B&B €
(Aashammeren 55; d with shared bathroom Nkr700;
🅿 🛜) In a beautiful riverside spot, 8km
north of town, this traditional B&B in a family home offers a friendly welcome and prettily decorated rooms. It's a particularly good
choice if you're here in winter for the skiing.

Thon Hotel Høyers BUSINESS HOTEL €€
(☏ 35 90 58 00; www.thonhotels.no; Kongensgate
6; d Nkr1340; 🅿 🛜) Right next to the harbour,

DON'T MISS

A SLOW BOAT THROUGH TELEMARK

Every day from June to mid-August, a variety of different boats, mostly old-fashioned steamers, chug along the canals of Telemark. Although full-day trips are available, for most people a half-day package is sufficient. One particularly good route involves catching the boat (adult/child Nkr450/225, 3¾ hours, daily at 10am) from Akkerhaugen, 24km south of Notodden, from where you travel to Lunde. A bus takes you back to your starting point at Akkerhaugen. The trip can also be done in reverse by leaving your car for free at the Norsjø Hotell in Akkerhaugen and taking the bus to Lunde (it stops at the hotel), from where you catch the boat and sail serenely back to Akkerhaugen.

For a full-day trip you can make the leisurely 10-hour journey between Skien and Dalen (adult/child Nkr975/488; late June to mid-August). Boats leave Skien around 8am and arrive in Dalen a little after 6pm, from where you can catch a special 'canalbus' back to Skien. It's also possible to jump off (or board) in Lunde, the halfway point, as well as various other combinations.

For seasonal departure times, boat details and to book, contact **Visit Telemark** (☑ 35 90 00 30; www.visittelemark.com).

A great way to see the canal is by canoe, kayak or bicycle. Ferries will transport your boat/bicycle for Nkr250/150.

---

this family-run place is set inside a grand building and has spacious, modern rooms and stately traditional public spaces. Free filter coffee is the norm for most Norwegian hotels, but there is a lobby Nespresso machine here.

✦ Festivals

Smieøyafestivalen   MUSIC
(smieoyafestivalen.no) In late August, this two-day festival draws names like Wyclef Jean and a good selection of Norwegian talent.

❶ Information

Tourist office (☑ 35 90 55 20; www.visitgrenland.no; Nedre Hjellegate 18; ⊙9am-7pm Mon-Fri, 11am-4pm Sat & Sun mid-Jun–mid-Aug, 8.30am-4pm Mon-Fri rest of year) Has information on hiking trails and cycling routes.

❶ Getting There & Away

Nor-Way Bussekspress buses run from Skien to Rjukan (Nkr273, 3¼ hours) once or twice daily. NSB trains run every hour or two to Larvik (Nkr91, 45 minutes) and Oslo (Nkr199 to Nkr300, three hours).

Dalen
POP 800

Surrounded by steep forested hills and settled comfortably beside a lazy lake busy with beavers, pretty little Dalen is a jumping-off point for ferries along the Øst Telemark Canal system.

◉ Sights

Eidsborg Stave Church   CHURCH
(guided tour adult/child Nkr70/35; ⊙10am-6pm Jun-Aug, shorter hours rest of year) High above town on the Rv45 to Høydalsmo, the quaint, 13th-century Eidsborg Stave Church, dedicated to St Nicolas, has but a single nave and is in particularly good shape. The grounds are open year-round, and a caretaker can usually open the church if it's locked.

⊨ Sleeping

Buøy Camping   CAMPGROUND €
(☑ 35 07 75 87; www.buoycamping.com; campsites Nkr225, cabins Nkr590-1500; ⊙May-Sep; P@🛜🅿) Surrounded on all sides by water, this attractive, well-run campsite has plenty of activities for children, lots of shady pitches for tents and quaint Little Red Riding Hood–style wooden cabins that are just as cute inside as they are out. There's a restaurant here and bike rental is available for Nkr150 per day.

Campers aren't the only ones who like this place; the waters around the campsite are home to several beaver families whom you'll almost certainly get to meet if you go on a dusk walk along the river.

Dalen Bed & Breakfast   B&B €€
(☑ 35 07 70 80; www.dalenbb.com; d Nkr1195-1750; P🛜) This family-run venture is a good option: breakfast is excellent, and staff dole out free maps pointing you to the area's best moose- and beaver-spotting sites.

Dalen Hotel
HISTORIC HOTEL €€€

(📞 35 07 90 00; www.dalenhotel.no; s/d Nkr1600/2200; 🅿 🛜) The ornate Dalen Hotel, with its faint resonance of a stave church, and a Wild West ambience inside, first opened in 1894. Although looted by the Nazis in WWII, it remains an authentic place with public areas a riot of antiques and moose heads. Room 17 is said to be haunted.

The restaurant serves suitably old-fashioned Norwegian country cooking (mains from Nkr210).

ℹ️ Information

Tourist office (📞 35 07 70 65; www.visitdalen. com; ⊘ 9am-7pm Mon-Fri, 10am-5pm Sat & Sun May-Aug, closed Sep-Apr; 🛜) The tourist office in the village centre has free coffee.

ℹ️ Getting There & Away

To get to Oslo by bus (Nkr520, 4½ hours) involves a change in nearby Amot on the E134.

Rjukan

POP 5900

Sitting in the shadow of what is arguably Norway's most beautiful peak, Gausta (1883m), Rjukan is a picturesque introduction to the Norwegian high country as well as southern Norway's activities centre par excellence.

The town stretches like elastic for 6km along the floor of the steep-sided Vestfjorddalen and while the centre, which consists of a couple of blocks of pastel-painted wooden buildings, is attractive, the remainder stands in utter contrast to its majestic setting.

If you're here from late September to March, you'll notice the winter gloom is no more, with the town's valley floor illuminated by 'concentrated solar power', that is; three giant remote-controlled mirrors that track and reflect the much needed sunshine from the mountain above.

History

This hydroelectric-company town was founded in 1907 and at its peak the industry supported 10,000 residents. In the early days, the administrators' homes occupied the highest slopes, where the sun shone the longest; below them were the homes of office workers and in the valley's dark depths dwelt the labourers. The builders of the Mår Kraftverk hydroelectric plant on the eastern limits of town clearly had an eye for records: its daunting wooden stairway consists of 3975 steps (it's one of the world's longest wooden stairways and is open to very fit visitors).

⊙ Sights

★ Norwegian Industrial Workers Museum
MUSEUM

(Norsk Industriarbeidermuseet Vemork; www.visit-vemork.com; adult/child Nkr80/50; ⊘ 10am-6pm mid-Jun–mid-Aug, to 4pm mid-Aug–Sep & May-mid-Jun, noon-3pm rest of year) This museum, 7km west of Rjukan, is in the Vemork power station, which was the world's largest when completed in 1911. These days it honours the Socialist Workers' Party, which reached the height of its Norwegian activities here in the 1950s. There's an interesting exhibition about the race in the 1930s and '40s to make an atom bomb, plus a fabulous miniature power station in the main hall.

Travellers with disabilities and seniors over 65 are permitted to drive up to the entrance; everyone else must park at the swinging bridge. In summer a bus runs up from the carpark to the entrance. Otherwise, it's a 15-minute, 700m climb on foot.

Krossobanen
CABLE CAR

(www.krossobanen.no; 1 way/return adult Nkr50/100, child Nkr20/40, bike Nkr50/100; ⊘ 9am-8pm mid-Jun–Aug, 10am-4pm Sun-Thu, to 8pm Fri & Sat rest of year) The Krossobanen cable car was constructed in 1928 by Norsk Hydro for its employees. It now whisks tourists up to Gvepseborg (886m) for a view over the deep, dark recesses. The best panoramas are from the viewing platform atop the cable-car station. It also operates as the trailhead for a host of hiking and cycling trails.

★ Gaustabanen Cable Railway
SCENIC RAILWAY

(www.gaustabanen.no; 1-way/return adult Nkr250/350, child Nkr125/175; ⊘ 10am-5pm late Jun–mid-Oct) Gaustabanen runs 860m deep into the core of Gausta before a different train climbs an incredible 1040m, alongside 3500 steps at a 40-degree angle, to 1800m, just below the Gaustahytte, not far from the summit. It was built by NATO in 1958 at a cost of US$1 million to ensure it could access its radio tower in any weather. Taking the railway is an incredible experience, although it's not for the claustrophobic. The base station is 10km southeast of Rjukan.

Rjukanfossen
WATERFALL

Believed to be the highest waterfall in the world in the 18th century (Angel Falls

HIKING & CYCLING FROM RJUKAN

Rjukan makes a superb base from which to strike out into the surrounding wilderness on foot or by mountain bike. To get an idea of what's possible, visit the tourist office (p116) to pick up the free *Rjukan – og Tinn,* which has a number of route suggestions.

Gausta

The most obvious goal for peak baggers is the hike to the summit of beautiful Gausta (1883m), from where you can see a remarkable one-sixth of Norway on a clear day. The popular, and easy, two- to three-hour, 4km hiking track leads from the trailhead of Stavsro (15km southeast of Rjukan) up to Den Norske Turistforening's (DNT; Norwegian Mountain Touring Club) Gaustahytta (1830m), next to the rather ugly NATO radio tower. The summit is reached by walking along the rocky ridge for a further half-hour. A 13km road link, but unfortunately no public transport, runs from the far eastern end of Rjukan to Stavsro (altitude 1173m) at lake Heddersvann. Taxis (☎ 35 09 14 00) charge around Nkr450 one way. Allow all day for the hike, which leaves plenty of time for exploring the summit. The tourist office distributes a map of the Fv651, but the *Turkart Gausta Området* is a better option and is available for Nkr50.

More-difficult, three- to four-hour routes to the summit also run from Rjukan itself and from the Norwegian Industrial Workers Museum.

If you can't make the hike, the Gaustabanen service (p113) takes you almost to Gaustahytta.

Hardangervidda

For something a little wilder, but bleaker, the Hardangervidda Plateau, the biggest mountain plateau in Europe and home to Europe's largest herd of wild reindeer, rises up to the north of Rjukan and offers a wealth of fantastic hikes that vary from easy two- to three-hour strolls to longer day hikes and multiday challenges. From Gvepseborg, the summit of the Krossobanen cable car (p113), the most rewarding day hike is the five-hour (without stops) round trip to the Helberghytta DNT Hut. The route has good waymarking and although it can be very boggy in sections, it's easily achievable for any moderately fit walker. The first section winds up from the cable-car platform through a forest of stumpy, twisted trees before emerging onto the gently undulating plateau. The scenery, which takes in icy-cold lakes, snow-streaked hills, barren moorland and views back over towards Mt Gausta, is supremely impressive.

For something more challenging, an eight- to nine-hour route, which can also be used by cyclists, leads from the cable-car platform past the Helberghytta DNT Hut (following the route described previously) and onward to Kalhovd Turisthytte. From there you can either catch a bus or hike nine hours down to Mogen Turisthytte, where you can catch the Møsvatn ferry (Nkr255) back to Skinnarbu, west of Rjukan on Rv37; ferry timetables are available from the Rjukan tourist office. Serious hikers can also strike out north from Kalhovd, deep into the high Hardangervidda.

Alternatively, you can follow the marked route that begins above Rjukan Fjellstue, around 10km west of Rjukan and just north of the Rv37. This historic track follows the Sabotørruta (Saboteurs' Route), the path taken by the members of the Norwegian Resistance during WWII. From late June until mid-August, the tourist office organises three-hour guided hikes along this route (Nkr200; noon Tuesday, Thursday and Sunday).

The best hiking map to use for this part of the plateau is Telemark Turistforening's *Hardangervidda Sør-Øst,* at a scale of 1:60,000. It's available from the tourist office for Nkr98.

---

in Venezuela now has that claim), the 104m-high Rjukanfossen is still a spectacular sight, even if most of the water has been diverted to drive the Vemork power station. To get the best view, take the Rv37 heading west and park just before the tunnel 9.5km west of town; a 200m walk leads to a fine viewpoint.

Tinn Museum   MUSEUM
(tinn.visitvemork.no; Sam Eydesgt 299; adult/child Nkr40/20; ⊙ 11am-7pm mid-Jun–mid-Aug, shorter

hours rest of year) This peaceful, open-air folk museum, at the eastern end of town, traces rural Norwegian architecture from the 11th century to the early 1900s.

 Activities

You can rug up against the winter cold and take a horse-drawn sleigh ride through a forested, magical winter wonderland or strike out across the bleak Hardangervidda Plateau on the back of a sleigh pulled by a team of **husky dogs**. The tourist office (p116) can put you in touch with local tour operators running either of these winter-only activities.

Ice-Climbing
ADVENTURE SPORTS

If the idea of hauling yourself up a giant vertical icicle that looks as if it's going to crack and send you tumbling to an early grave sounds like fun, then Rjukan is the place for you. It is fast becoming known as *the* place for ice-climbing. There are more than 150 routes in the immediate area of the town.

The tourist office can suggest guides and **Climb Inn** (www.climb-inn.com) puts together climbing packages including guides, equipment rental, accommodation and food.

Bungee Jumping
ADVENTURE SPORTS

(☑ 99 51 31 40; www.telemark-opplevelser.no; per session Nkr790; ☺ mid-May–Sep, exact times vary) Described as Norway's highest land-based bungee jump, this 84m plunge into the canyon from the bridge leading to the Norwegian Industrial Workers Museum is Rjukan's biggest adrenalin rush. Book through the tourist office.

Skiing
SKIING

The whole area around Rjukan is pockmarked with excellent ski runs. The tourist office (p116) has a wealth of information and its *Gaustablikk Skisenter* brochure provides the definitive guide to all things white and powdery. The main ski area is the **Gaustablikk Ski Centre**. One-day adult/child passes cost Nkr370/290.

Moose Safari
WILDLIFE WATCHING

(☑ 35 06 26 30; www.visitrauland.com; adult/child Nkr350/250; ☺ book by 4pm for dusk departure, 28 Jun-23 Aug) You can get up close and personal to the largest member of the deer family in Europe on one of the moose safaris organised through the tourist office in the village of Rauland (on the Rt37 southwest of Rjukan), or head out in your own car with a downloadable map.

🛏 Sleeping

Rjukan's town centre has a few places to stay, but there are more choices up in the Gaustablikk area.

🛏 Rjukan & West

Krokan Turisthytte
CABINS €

(☑ 92 26 94 36; krokan.turistforeningen.no; near Rv37; cabins Nkr500) Around 10km west of Rjukan, this historic place was built in 1869

as the first hut of Den Norske Turistforening (DNT). You're housed in museumlike 16th-century log cabins and it serves traditional meals. Phone ahead as there's not always someone here.

★ Rjukan Hytteby & Kro
CABINS €€

(☑ 35 09 01 22; www.rjukan-hytteby.no; Brogata 9; large cabins Nkr895-1400, small cabins with linen s/d Nkr950/1095; ☎) Easily the best choice in town, Rjukan Hytteby & Kro sits in a pretty spot on the river bank and has carefully decorated, very well-equipped huts that sweetly emulate the early-20th-century hydroelectric workers' cabins. The owner is exceptionally helpful. It's a pleasant 20-minute walk along the river bank to the town centre.

Rjukan Gjestegård
HOSTEL €€

(☑ 35 08 06 50; www.rjukangjestegard.no; Birkelandsgata 2; dm Nkr235, s/d without bathroom Nkr385/580, d Nkr990; P @) This central guesthouse occupies the buildings of the old youth hostel and is something of a travellers' centre. Despite its bleak exterior, the rooms here are simple and fine enough; there's a guest kitchen; and the location is good if you want to be in town. Breakfast costs Nkr80.

Rauland Høgfjellshotell
LODGE €€€

(☑ 35 06 31 00; www.rauland.no; Rv37; s/d Nkr945/1650; ☺ Jun-Apr; P ☎ ☀) Around 45km west of Rjukan, this excellent mountain hotel promises sweeping views, hints of traditional Telemark decoration, an indoor swimming pool and an excellent spa centre. It's booked out well in advance in winter (and is nearly double the price) as it opens onto hundreds of kilometres of ski runs.

🛏 Gaustablikk

A couple of places beside the beautiful lake Kvitåvatn, off the Fv651 and 10km from town, provide a front-row view of Gausta and easy access to the Skipsfjell/Gaustablikk ski area; you'll need a car for access.

In the busy winter season, **Gausta Booking** (☑ 45 48 51 51; www.gaustatoppenbooking.com) can help track down a spare hut.

Rjukan Vandrerhjem
HOSTEL €

(☑ 35 09 20 40; www.kvitaavatn.dk; dm Nkr225, s/d Nkr625/750, with shared bathroom Nkr400/500,) This youth hostel offers simple accommodation in a cosy pine lodge with six bunks per room in huts. At time of writing, 10 new rooms were expected to be available from 2015, all with balconies, great views of Gaustatoppen, four beds, a work place and private bathroom. Note that the reception is only staffed from 8.30am to 10.30am and 4pm to 7pm.

Gaustablikk Høyfjellshotell LODGE €€€
(☎35 09 14 22; www.gaustablikk.no; s/d from Nkr1075/1590; 🅿🛜) With a prime location overlooking the lake and mountain, this lodge is one of Norway's better mountain hotels. Rooms are modern and many have lovely views of Gausta, while the evening buffet dinner (Nkr385) is a lavish affair. Geared towards a winter skiing crowd (prices rise considerably in winter and advance reservations are necessary), it's also a great place in summer.

✖ Eating

Kinokafeen INTERNATIONAL €€
(☎40 85 60 48; Storstulgate 1; mains Nkr120-179) Kinokafeen, at the cinema, has a pleasing art-deco style and its outdoor tables (summer only!) and fading interior make it the most memorable place to eat in the town centre.

Gaustablikk Høyfjellshotell NORWEGIAN €€€
(☎35 09 14 22; lunch specials from Nkr99, dinner buffet Nkr385) Even if you're not staying here, this mountain hotel's enormous buffet is worth the trip up the mountain and not just for the food – the views are stupendous.

ℹ Information

Tourist office (☎35 08 05 50; www.visitrjukan.com; Torget 2) The tourist office in Rjukan is possibly the best in Telemark, with loads of information and knowledgable staff.

ℹ Getting There & Around

Buses connect Rjukan with Oslo (Nkr390, 3½ hours) via Notodden (Nkr146, 1¼ hours; where you need to change buses) roughly every other hour between 5.30am and 3.30pm. These buses also stop in Kongsberg (Nkr295, two hours).

Rjukan's linear distances will seem intimidating, but the local Bybuss runs from Vemork to the eastern end of the valley. Bike hire from Rjukan Gjestegård (p115) costs Nkr200 per day.

Tuddal

Lying beside a deep blue lake surrounded by snow- and forest-dappled peaks, the handful of colourful wooden houses that make up the tiny mountain village of Tuddal have a setting that is hard to top. There's nothing much to do here except relish the peace and quiet and maybe embark on a gentle ramble or two.

The village sits at the foot of a bleak and spectacular summer-only mountain road between Rjukan and the E134 Notodden–Seljord road. Halfway along this mountain road is a summer tourist-office booth that has maps and route descriptions detailing a number of excellent hikes.

Seljord

POP 2944

Lakeside Seljord is known mainly as the home of Selma the Serpent, the Nessie-type monster that inhabits the depths of the lake Seljordvatn. Other creatures of legend call the nearby hills home and hikers can also seek out the feuding troll women, Ljose-Signe, Glima and Tårån. Personally we haven't seen them but locals assured us that they're there. Seljord was also the inspiration for some of Norway's best-known folk legends, including Asbjørnsen and Moe's *The Three Billy Goats Gruff*, known the world over.

⊙ Sights

Seljord Church CHURCH
(⊙11am-5pm mid-Jun–mid-Aug) This charming Romanesque church was built in the 12th century in honour of St Olav; it looks as if someone built a stave church and then changed their mind and tried to build a house around it. In the grounds, between the church and the churchyard wall, are two impressions reputedly made by two mountain trolls who were so upset by the encroachment of Christianity that they pummelled the site with boulders.

✳ Festivals & Events

Dyrsku'n Festival AGRICULTURAL
On the second weekend of September, Seljord holds the Dyrsku'n Festival, which started in 1866 and is now Norway's largest traditional market and cattle show, attracting 60,000 visitors, almost as many cows and not all that many monsters.

🛏 Sleeping & Eating

Seljord Camping og Badeplass CAMPGROUND €
(☎35 05 04 71; www.seljordcamping.no; tent sites Nkr200, cabins Nkr500-1400) There are soft

grassy pitches beside the lake and cabins that range from the superbasic to the truly luxurious. The camp also serves as the dock for monster boats on Seljordvatn and has a telescope to help you spot Selma. Kayaks and canoes can also be rented here for Nkr40 per hour.

★ **Seljord Hotell**　　　　HISTORIC HOTEL **€€**
(☑35 06 40 00; www.seljordhotel.no; s/d Nkr990/1250; P@奈) This lovely old wooden hotel, which dates back to 1858, started life as a ladies' college, but on running out of potential 'ladies', it became a hotel. Rooms have period touches and are individually named, each with its own story. It, unusually, has the same rates all year. The restaurant (mains Nkr215 to Nkr310) is Seljord's best, with local fish and game dishes.

❶ Information

Tourist office (☑35 06 59 88; www.seljordportalen.no; ☺10am-6pm Mon-Fri mid-Jun–mid-Aug, shorter hours rest of year) Lots of local information, and staff revel in good troll stories.

❶ Getting There & Away

Nor-Way Bussekspress (Haukelickspressen) buses connect Seljord with Notodden (Nkr160, 1¼ hours) and Oslo (Nkr390, 3¼ hours) up to four times daily.

Setesdalen

The forested hillsides and lake-filled mountain valleys of Setesdalen, one of Norway's most traditional and conservative regions, remain little frequented by travellers, although the area has recently begun to lure a new generation of outdoor enthusiasts.

Evje

POP 3300

The riverside town of Evje, surrounded by forests and rolling hills, serves as the southern gateway to Setesdalen. It's famous among geologists for the variety of rocks – a mineral park and the chance to prospect for your own rocks are among Evje's primary attractions. This town is also a first-class base for white-water rafting and other activities.

❍ Sights

Evje Og Hornnes Museum　　　MUSEUM
(www.setesdalsmuseet.no; adult/child Nkr35/free; ☺11am-5pm Jul-early Aug, by appointment rest of

year) Budding geologists will find plenty to get excited about in Evje. This small museum, 2km west of town and across the river in Fennefoss, displays more than a hundred different types of minerals found in the nearby hills, as well as exhibits on local nickel mining and rural life in Setesdalen.

Setesdal Mineral Park　　　　　PARK
(www.mineralparken.no; Hornnes; adult/child Nkr140/90; ☺10am-6pm Jul–mid-Aug, shorter hours rest of year) For displays of local and worldwide minerals, this well-run park is every rock collector's dream come true, with a wonderful world of colour and quartz, and many items for sale. It's about 10km south of Evje.

🏃 Activities

TrollActiv　　　　　　ADVENTURE SPORTS
(☑37 93 11 77; www.troll-mountain.no; ☺9am-8pm Apr-Oct) Around 6km north of Evje, this is the town's centre of high-energy thrills. White-water rafting (per person from Nkr470) is its forte, but it organises all manner of activities, including overnight kayaking trips (from Nkr1950), mountain-bike tours (Nkr420) and nightly beaver and elk safaris (adult/child Nkr350/300). Other high-thrill activities include riverboarding, rock climbing, river kayaking, paintballing, waterskiing and fishing safaris.

🛏 Sleeping & Eating

★ **TrollActiv**　　　　　　HOSTEL **€**
(☑37 93 11 77; www.troll-mountain.no; Evje Vandrerhjem; d from Nkr530, tents/tepees per person Nkr70/100, cabins Nkr400-630; P@) This energetic activities centre doubles as Evje's youth hostel, 6km north of town. It's exceptionally well run and the place to be if you're planning any one of the many activities on offer. Accommodation varies from sleeping in your own tent, kipping in a *lavvo* (tepee) or stretching out in comfort in a cabin or comfortable double room.

Odden Camping　　　　CAMPGROUND **€**
(☑37 93 06 03; www.oddencamping.setesdal.com; campsites Nkr280, 2- to 8-bed huts Nkr375-1375) This large campsite is extremely well run and can be found in a postcard setting by the water just 200m south of town. It can become crowded in summer.

Revsnes Hotell　　　　　HOTEL **€€**
(☑37 93 46 50; www.revsneshotell.no; Byglandsfjord; s/d from Nkr890/1100; P奈) The

SETESDALSMUSEET

A fine collection of **folk museums** (www.setesdalsmuseet.no; adult/child/family Nkr20/free/40) along Rv9 breaks up your journey through Setesdalen.

Setesdalsmuseet (www.setesdalsmuseet.no; ☉11am-5pm, outdoors area Jun–mid-Aug) Coming from the south, Rysstad's main Setesdalsmuseet is a fine, refurbished exhibition space displaying period interiors and cultural artefacts, including displays of regional dress.

Rygnestadtunet (www.setesdalsmuseet.no; ☉11am-5pm Jul-8 Aug, shorter hours rest of year) Around 9km northwest of Valle, this farm has a unique three-storey storehouse dating to 1590, and an extraordinary collection of 15th-century painted textiles. Local legend has its owner as Evil Åsmund, a mercenary who brought back looted weapons and artwork from his travels, including a 14th-century painting of St George rescuing a grateful damsel from the clutches of a dragon and a whole set of paintings depicting the Ten Commandments. Staff may be dressed in traditional costume.

good-value Revsnes is 12km north of town and set on the banks of lush lake Byglands-fjorden. The rooms are large and modern, and most have wonderful big windows overlooking the water. It's a family-run place and you'll be made to feel welcome.

Pernille Cafeteria　　FAST FOOD €
(☎37 93 00 69; mains Nkr99-149; ☉8am-6pm Mon-Fri, 8am-4.30pm Sat, 10am-6pm Sun) Right in the heart of Evje, this upstairs place is popular with locals although the menu is not Norway's most inspirational. Expect burgers, and eggs and bacon alongside a few Norwegian staples.

ⓘ Information

Information Centre (☎37 93 14 00; www.setesdal.com; ☉11am-6pm Mon-Thu, to 7pm Fri, to 3.30pm Sat mid-Jun–mid-Aug, 10am-noon Mon-Fri rest of year) The information centre occupies the same old log building as the bus terminal. Ask here about permits for mineral prospecting.

ⓘ Getting There & Away

Nor-Way Bussekspress buses travel to Kristiansand (Nkr160, one hour) seven to eight times daily. Heading north from Evje, car drivers will be stung with an ever-rising toll.

Hovden

POP 450

Watching over the northern end of Setesdalen, Hovden is a winter ski resort and low-key summer hiking base.

🏃 Activities

Chairlift　　CHAIRLIFT
(adult/child Nkr90/60; ☉11am-2pm Jul & Aug, 9.30am-3.30pm Dec-Apr, shorter hours rest of

year) In summer, for fine views you can reach the summit of **Mt Nos** (1176m) by taking this chairlift. From the summit a number of hiking trails, ranging from an hour or two's easy ramble to an overnight slog, snake out across the high moorland plateau. The tourist office can provide more information.

🛏 Sleeping

Hovden Resort　　HISTORIC HOTEL €€
(Hovden Høyfjellshotell & Hovdestøylen; ☎37 93 88 00; hovdenresort.com; s/d from Nkr1100/1445, apt Nkr985; P🛜🎿♿) Located at the top end of the town, this hotel and lodge is Hovden's finest accomodation option. Rooms are tasteful and there's a host of resort amenities, including its own ski slope, indoor pool, sauna, a children's playroom chock-full of toys and the best restaurant in the area.

Hovden Fjellstoge & Vandrerhjem　　HOSTEL €€
(☎37 93 95 43; www.vandrerhjem.no/hovden; dm/s/d Nkr250/750/980; P🛜) Housed in a traditional-style wooden building with a grass roof, this jolly hostel has something to please everyone, from rooms with fairy-tale wooden bunk beds to cute cabins. There's virtually an entire zoo of stuffed local wildlife here, including a wolf and a reindeer. It's about 3.5km north of the centre.

Hovden Høyfjellsenter　　CABINS €€
(☎37 93 95 01; www.hovdenhoyfjellsenter.no; cabins Nkr950-1650; P) No-fuss large and comfortable cabins with well-equipped kitchens.

Central Norway

HIGHEST ELEV GALDHØPIGGEN 2469M

Best Places to Experience Nature

➜ Musk Ox Safari (p136)

➜ Finse (p150)

➜ Besseggen Ridge (p149)

➜ Elk Safari (p137)

➜ Hardangervidda National Park (p148)

➜ Elgåhogna Hike (p134)

Best Places to Stay

➜ Finse 1222 (p151)

➜ Erzscheidergården (p132)

➜ Elvesæter Hotell (p147)

➜ Turatgrø Hotel (p147)

➜ Kongsvold Fjeldstue (p138)

Why Go?

Bleak tundra and dramatic mountain massifs at seemingly every turn, charming villages, stave churches, fascinating wildlife and arguably Norway's best hiking and white-water rafting – with so much going for it, central Norway more than matches the fjords.

Here on the roof of Norway, trails snake their way past glaciers, waterfalls and snowbound peaks in more than a dozen national parks. Jotunheimen National Park is one of Europe's premier hiking destinations, and is bisected by one of Norway's most beautiful drives. But Rondane, Dovrefjell-Sunndalsfjella and the desolately beautiful Hardangervidda are also superb. Within the parks' boundaries you may find wild reindeer, elk and musk ox. At the gateway to the parks, Unesco World Heritage–listed Røros, a centuries-old mining town of timber houses and turf-roofed cottages, and Lom with its beautiful stave church, are two of inland Norway's most attractive villages.

When to Go

Røros

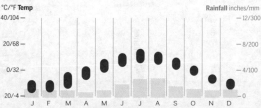

Feb The Rørosmartnan (Røros Market) and skiing at Trysil. Be prepared to be *very* cold.

May & Jun Generally fine weather without the crowds of midsummer.

Jul & Aug Hiking trails are passable, rafting is in full swing and wildlife safaris are possible.

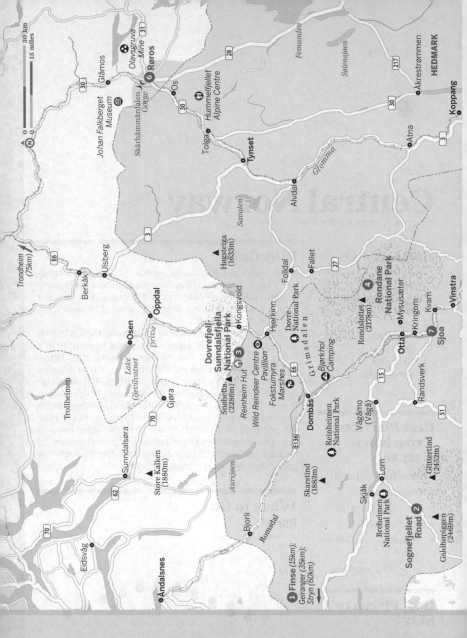

Central Norway Highlights

1 Creep gingerly across the massive Hardangerjøkulen icecap on a guided glacier walk from **Finse** (p150), central Norway's Arctic dream *par excellence*.

2 Trek along the highest trails in Norway in the endlessly beautiful **Jotunheimen National Park** (p145), or drive over **Sognefjellet Road** (p145).

3 Search for the prehistoric musk ox in **Dovrefjell-Sunndalsfjella National Park** (p138).

4 Explore **Rondane National Park** (p139), Norway's oldest national park and one of its most beautiful.

1 Finse (15km); Geiranger (35km); Stryn (60km)

Sognefjellet Road 2

4 Rondane National Park

Dovrefjell-Sunndalsfjella National Park 3

6 Røros

7 Sjoa

30 km
15 miles

Trondheim (75km)

HEDMARK

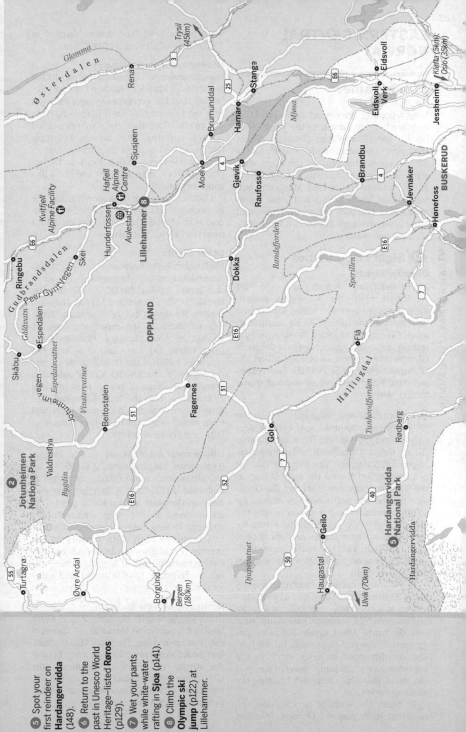

5 Spot your first reindeer on **Hardangervidda** (148).

6 Return to the past in Unesco World Heritage-listed **Røros** (p129).

7 Wet your pants while white-water rafting in **Sjoa** (p141).

8 Climb the **Olympic ski jump** (p122) at Lillehammer.

EASTERN CENTRAL NORWAY

Lillehammer

POP 27,051

Long a popular Norwegian ski resort, Lillehammer became known to the world after hosting the 1994 Winter Olympics. These Olympics, overwhelmingly considered a great success, still provide the town with some of its most interesting sights. Lying at the northern end of Lake Mjøsa and surrounded by farms, forests and small settlements, it's a laid-back place with year-round attractions, although in winter it becomes a ski town par excellence.

◉ Sights & Activities

Olympic Sights

After Lillehammer won its bid for the 1994 Winter Olympics, the Norwegian government ploughed over two billion kroner into the town's infrastructure. In an example to other Olympic host cities, most amenities remain in use and visitors can tour the main Olympic sites over a large area called the Olympiaparken (☑ 61 05 42 00; www.olympiaparken.no; ☺ 9am-6pm mid-Jun–mid-Aug, shorter hours Oct-May).

★Lygårdsbakkene Ski Jump   SKI JUMP
(☺ 9am-7pm early Jul–mid-Aug, to 4pm late May–early Jul & mid-Aug–late Sep) The main ski jump (K120) drops 136m with a landing-slope angle of 37.5 degrees. The speed at take-off is a brisk 86km/h, and the longest leap at the Olympics was 104m. During the Olympics, the site was surrounded by seating for 50,000 spectators and it was here that the opening ceremony was held; the tower for the Olympic flame stands near the foot of the jump. There's also a smaller jump (K90) alongside, where you'll often see athletes honing their skills.

The ski-jump chairlift (adult/child one-way Nkr35/30, return Nkr55/50; ☺ 9am-7pm early Jul–mid-Aug, to 4pm late May–early Jul & mid-Aug–late Sep) ascends to a stunning panoramic view over the town. Alternatively, for those undaunted by the 952 steps, walk up for free. The chairlift price includes entry to the Lygårdsbakkene ski-jump tower. Here you can stand atop the ramp and imagine the prejump nerves.

To reach the summit by car, take the road that leads past the Olympic Museum north out of town. The turn-off (signed as 'Lygårdsbakkene') comes after 2.8km.

Norwegian Olympic Museum   MUSEUM
(www.ol.museum.no; Olympiaparken; adult/child Nkr110/55; ☺ 10am-5pm Jun-Aug, 11am-4pm Tue-Sun Sep-May) The excellent Olympic museum is at the Håkons Hall ice-hockey venue. On the ground floor there is a well-presented display covering the ancient Olympic Games, as well as all of the Olympic Games of the modern era, with a focus on the exploits of Norwegian athletes and the Lillehammer games.

Upstairs, you can look down upon the ice-hockey arena, which is circled by corridors with displays and video presentations from the Lillehammer games.

Other Sights

Maihaugen Folk Museum   MUSEUM
(www.maihaugen.no; Maihaugveien 1; adult/child/family Jun-Aug Nkr150/75/375, Sep-May Nkr110/55/275; ☺ 10am-5pm Jun-Aug, 11am-4pm Tue-Sun Sep-May) One of Norway's finest folk museums is the expansive, open-air Maihaugen Folk Museum. Rebuilt like a small village, the collection of around 180 buildings includes the transplanted Garmo stave church, traditional Gudbrandsdalen homes and shops, a postal museum and 27 buildings from the farm Bjørnstad. The three main sections encompass rural and town architecture, with a further section on 20th-century architecture.

Lillehammer Art Museum   MUSEUM
(Lillehammer Kunstmuseum; ☑ 61 05 44 60; www.lillehammerartmuseum.com; Stortorget 2; adult/child Nkr100/free; ☺ 11am-5pm daily mid-Jun–Aug, 11am-4pm Tue-Sun rest of year) This art museum is not only architecturally striking, it also covers Norwegian visual arts from the early 19th century to the present. Highlights of the permanent collection include some of Norway's finest artists (including Edvard Munch) and some local painters.

Norwegian Vehicle Museum   MUSEUM
(Norsk Kjøretøyhistorisk Museum; ☑ 61 25 61 65; Lilletorget 1; adult/child Nkr50/30; ☺ 10am-6pm daily mid-Jun–mid-Aug, 11am-3pm Mon-Fri, 11am-4pm Sat & Sun rest of yr) Tucked away behind the stream in central Lillehammer, the Norwegian Vehicle Museum is for car buffs, featuring everything from sleighs to vintage cars and motorcycles.

✨ Festivals & Events

Lillehammer Jazz Festival MUSIC
(☑81 53 31 33; www.dolajazz.no) Lillehammer Jazz Festival is held over four days in October; tickets go on sale from 1 July each year.

🛏 Sleeping

★Lillehammer Vandrerhjem HOSTEL €
(☑61 26 00 24; www.stasjonen.no; 1st fl, Railway Station; dm/s/d/f from Nkr340/745/890/1200; P🛜) If you've never stayed in a youth hostel, this one above the train station is the place to break the habit of a lifetime. The rooms are simple but come with a bathroom, bed linen and free wireless internet. There's a spick-and-span communal kitchen, but the downstairs cafe is pretty terrible (hot-dog soup anyone?!). Free parking.

Øvergaard B&B €
(☑61 25 99 99; www.oevergaard.net; Jernbanegata 24; s/d with shared bathroom Nkr395/690; P🛜) Just above the centre of town, this friendly B&B has simple rooms with plenty of family character in quiet surrounds. It's a well-run place and about as cheap as you'll get in Norway. Breakfast is Nkr65. It's an equally short walk to both the town centre and the Olympic sites.

Gjeste Bu GUESTHOUSE €
(☑61 25 43 21; www.gjestebu.no; Gamleveien 110; s Nkr310-900, d Nkr450-1200; apt Nkr640-1730; 🛜🍴) Part hostel, part guesthouse and with the feel of a mountain cabin, this friendly place has a range of accommodation, shared kitchen facilities, and apartments that are ideal if you'll be in town for a while. Breakfast costs extra, as does bed linen (Nkr60). If you understand its pricing system, let us know.

Lillehammer Camping CAMPGROUND €
(☑61 25 33 33; www.lillehammer-camping.no; Dampsagveien 47; tent & 2 people Nkr155, caravan sites from Nkr260, cabins Nkr475-1030; 🌣year-round; 🛜) Camping is available here on the shores of the lake. It's a typical urban site with cooking and laundry facilities, water-sports equipment, children's play areas, a Viking camp and cable TV.

Clarion Collection Hotel Hammer HOTEL €€
(☑61 26 73 73; www.clarionhotel.com; Stortorget 108b; s/d incl breakfast & dinner from Nkr1220/1320; 🛜) In an architecturally pleasing mustard yellow building, this hotel is considered the town's foremost address. The service is fast and efficient, and the inclusion of a dinner buffet in the price makes it very tempting for couples. For people travelling solo there are better-value options.

Mølla Hotell HOTEL €€
(☑61 05 70 80; www.mollahotell.no; Elvegata 12; s/d from Nkr990/1290; P🛜) Although you wouldn't know it from the lurid yellow exterior, this hotel was built from the shell of an old mill. Fully refurbished with good-quality, but slightly dated rooms, the hotel has mill memorabilia in the public areas, and flat-screen TVs and comfy beds in the rooms. The rooftop bar has fine views and the architecture is distinguished.

✗ Eating

Øverlie Café INTERNATIONAL €
(☑61 25 03 61; Stortorget 50; mains Nkr90-160; 🌣11am-11pm) Filling, inexpensive meals (with Turkish dishes the mainstays) are the order of the day at this pleasant pavement-side cafe. It also does pizzas, salads, ice cream and good coffee.

Café Opus CAFE €
(Stortorget 63; baguettes from Nkr59; 🌣9am-6pm Mon-Fri, 9am 4pm Sat, 11am-4pm Sun) Hugely popular for its baguettes, rolls and cakes (and for its outdoor tables in summer), Café Opus gets the simple things right – tasty food, friendly service and smart-casual decor.

Blåmann INTERNATIONAL €€
(☑61 26 22 03; www.blaamann.com; Lilletorget 1; lunch mains & light meals Nkr109-189, dinner mains Nkr169-259; 🌣noon-11pm Mon-Sat, to 9pm Sun) This recommended spot has a clean-lined interior and a trendy menu that ranges from kangaroo fillet to Mexican dishes to reindeer. The decor is classy, yet the atmosphere is casual.

Nikkers INTERNATIONAL €€
(www.nikkers.no; Elvegata; mains Nkr150-200; 🌣11am-11pm) Right by Lillehammer's bubbling brook, this is a dark, warm and cosy pub where a moose has apparently walked through the wall (look outside for the full effect). It attracts masses of locals, and whether you have a craving for salad, coffee, a burger or even reindeer stew, this place delivers.

🍸 Drinking & Nightlife

Bars are an integral part of the Lillehammer experience, especially during the ski season. Nikkers and Blåmann also double as bars.

Lillehammer

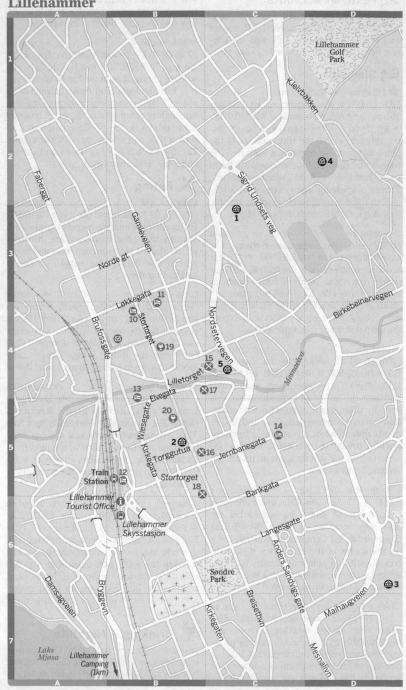

Lillehammer Golf Park

Lillehammer Tourist Office

Train Station

Lillehammer Skysstasjon

Søndre Park

Lake Mjøsa

Lillehammer Camping (1km)

0 — 400 m
0 — 0.2 miles

Olympiaparken

Lillehammer

One-Hand Clapping   COFFEE

(Stortorget 80; ⊙9.10am-5pm Mon-Wed & Fri, to 6pm Thu, to 3.30pm Sat) This very cool little coffee shop has superb coffee, as well as croissants and chocolate cake to die for. It's the sort of place to linger over a good book as you inhale the blends from around the world. It also has an extensive range of teas.

Haakons Pub   PUB

(Stortorget 93; ⊙1pm-3am Mon-Thu, noon-3am Fri & Sat) During the day this is the preserve of elbow-on-the-bar locals; when the sun sets, it kicks into action, becoming a crowded and agreeable place to drink. It can get a little raucous during the ski season.

ℹ Information

Lillehammer Tourist Office (www.lillehammer. com; Lillehammer Skysstasjon; ⊙8am-6pm Mon-Fri, 10am-4pm Sat & Sun mid-Jun–mid-Aug, 8am-4pm Mon-Fri, 10am-2pm Sat rest of year) Inside the train station.

❶ Getting There & Away

Lillehammer Skysstasjon (☑177) is the main transport terminal for buses, trains and taxis.

BUS

Lavprisekspressen bus services run to/from Oslo (Nkr440, three hours, three to four daily) via Oslo's Gardermoen airport (Nkr319, 2¼ hours). Nor-Way Bussekspress runs to Bergen (Nkr615, nine hours, two daily).

TRAIN

Trains run to/from Oslo (Nkr383, 2¼ hours, 11 to 17 daily) and Trondheim (from Nkr705, 4¼ to seven hours, four to six daily).

Around Lillehammer

Hunderfossen

Some 15km north of Lillehammer, just off the E6, Hunderfossen has a handful of attractions worth coming out of your way for.

❍ Sights & Activities

Hunderfossen hosted some of the events of the 1994 Winter Olympics and, as in Lillehammer, some of these can now be enjoyed by all of us.

Olympic Bobsled Run ADVENTURE SPORTS
(☑61 05 42 00; www.olympiaparken.no; adult/child Nkr240/170; ☺10.30am-4pm daily Jul-early Aug, weekends May-Jun & mid-Aug–mid-Sep, 3-8pm Wed, 11am-4pm Sat & Sun rest of yr) In Hunderfossen, you can careen down the Olympic Bobsled Run aboard a wheel bob under the guidance of a professional bobsled pilot. Wheel bobs take five passengers and hit a top speed of 100km/h. The real thing, **taxibobs**, take four passengers, reach an exhilarating 130km/h and you won't have much time to get nervous – you're down the mountain in 70 seconds. Bookings are advisable during winter.

**Norwegian Museum
of Road History** MUSEUM
(Norsk Vegmuseum; ☑61 28 52 50; www.vegmuseum.no; ☺10am-5pm mid-Jun–mid-Aug, 10am-3pm Tue-Sun rest of yr) FREE The Norwegian Museum of Road History tells the story of Norway's battle to forge roads through its challenging geography. Up the hill and part of the same complex, the **Fjellsprengnings-museet** (Rock-blasting Museum) is a 240m-long tunnel that gives you a real insight into the difficulties of building a tun-

nel through the Norwegian mountains. The walk, guided with lighting, models and video commentary, takes around 30 minutes.

Hunderfossen Familiepark AMSEMENT PARK
(☑61 27 55 30; www.hunderfossen.no; adult/child Nkr375/320; ☺10am-6pm late Jun–mid-Aug, hours vary early Jun & mid-Aug–early-Sep, closed mid-Sep–mid-May) The Hunderfossen Familiepark, one of Norway's best parks for children, has water rides, 3D presentations, fairy-tale palaces and wandering trolls. The latest attraction is a huge roller-coaster. If your child is under 90cm tall, he or she gets in free.

❶ Getting There & Away

In summer there are frequent buses from the Lillehammer Skysstasjon. In winter the service is more erratic. A considerable uphill walk is involved to reach the bobsled run.

Olympic Ski Slopes

Lillehammer has two Olympic ski slopes: **Hafjell Alpine Centre** (☑61 27 47 00; www.hafjell.no), 15km north of town, hosted the downhill events, while **Kvitfjell Alpine Facility** (☑61 28 36 30; www.kvitfjell.no), 50km north of town, was used for cross-country. Both offer public skiing between late November and late April and they're connected by bus with Lillehammer Skysstasjon.

Hamar

POP 26,000

This medium-sized town would never win a beauty contest, but it does possess a surprising number of attractions that are worth a detour on your way between Oslo and the north. The showpiece **Viking Ship Sports Arena** (Vikingskipet; ☑62 51 75 00; www.hoa.no; Åkersvikaveien 1; admission Nkr40; ☺8am-8pm Mon-Fri, to 5pm Sat & Sun 1st-17th Aug, to 3pm Mon-Fri rest of year) dates from the 1994 Winter Olympics in Lillehammer, when Hamar hosted a number of events, but there are also some good museums.

❍ Sights

**Hedmark Museum
& Glass Cathedral** MUSEUM
(Hedmarkmuseet; ☑62 54 27 00; www.domkirkeodden.no; Strandveien 100; adult/child Nkr100/50; ☺10am-5pm daily mid-Jun–mid-Aug, 10am-4pm Tue-Sun mid-May–mid-Jun & end Aug) West of town (1.5km), this extensive open-air museum includes 18th- and 19th-century build-

ings, a local folk-history exhibit featuring the creepy Devil's Finger (a finger cast in pewter of unknown origin, but which is said to have caused a number of deaths when it was removed from the church), the ruins of the castle, and the extraordinary showcase 'glass cathedral' (Domkirkeodden), which dominated Hamar until 1567, when it was sacked by the Swedes.

The grounds themselves are free to visit and open all the time, and you can also peer through the glass-house-like structure that surrounds the ruined cathedral but to get inside this or any of the other museum exhibit buildings you'll need a ticket.

It's a pleasant walk or cycle from town along the lake shore to the museum.

Norwegian Railway Museum MUSEUM
(Norsk Jernbanemuseum; ☑ 62 51 31 60; www.norsk-jernbanemuseum.no; Strandveien 163; adult/child Nkr90/55; ☉ 10am-5pm Jul–mid-Aug, 11am-5pm Tue-Sat, 11am-4pm Sun rest of year) Established in 1896 to honour Norway's railway history, this open-air railway museum lies on the Mjøsa shore around 3km west of the centre. In addition to lovely historic stations, engine sheds, rail coaches and steam locomotives, you'll learn about the extraordinary engineering feats required to carve the railways through Norway's rugged terrain.

🎊 Festivals & Events

Hamar Beer Festival BEER
(Hamar Ølfestival; ☉ early Jun) Beer and music.

Middle Ages Festival CULTURAL
(www.middelalderfesti val.no; ☉ 2nd weekend in Jun) Locals in period costume; Gregorian chants in the glass cathedral.

Hamar Music Festival MUSIC
(www.musicfest.no; ☉ late Jun) Local and international acts.

🛏️ Sleeping & Eating

Scandic Hamar HOTEL €€
(☑ 21 61 40 00; www.scandichotels.com; Vangsveien 121; s/d from Nkr789/1020; P🅿️🕾) With sleek-lined Scandinavian design, a gymnasium and a reasonably priced restaurant (mains around Nkr150), Scandic Hamar could just be Hamar's best address – if you don't mind the five-minute walk to the town centre.

Quality Inn Astoria BUSINESS HOTEL €€
(☑ 62 70 70 00; www.choicehotels.no; Torggata 23; s/d from Nkr745/1045; 🕾) Overlooking the town's main square, this is the most obvious

place to rest up for the night. Although the rooms lack sparkle they are a good size, very comfortable and good value by Norwegian standards.

Vikingskipet Motell og Vandrerhjem HOTEL, HOSTEL €€
(☑ 62 52 60 60; www.vikingskipet.no; Åkersvikavegen 24; dm/s/d Nkr410/745/880, 2-/4-bed apt Nkr1290/1560; P🅿️🕾🐕) This excellent choice is a short way out of town and has a range of accommodation choices. The hostel wing has tidy dorms, while the simple double rooms have a cabin-style feel. There are also terrific self-contained apartments.

Kai & Mattis Café INTERNATIONAL €€
(☑ 62 53 01 45; Torgatta 53; mains Nkr150; ☉ 11am-6pm) If you've ever wondered what an art-deco boudoir looked like (don't pretend you haven't!), then this place, with its burgundy red walls and over-the-top decorations, will probably give you a fair idea. Boudoir or not, the meals are good: as well as the sandwich and burger staples, it does meals such as chicken curry pie.

ℹ️ Information

Hamar Regional Tourist Office (☑ 40 03 60 36; www.hamarregionen.no; Grønnegata 52; ☉ 9am-5pm Mon-Fri, 10am-5pm Sat & Sun mid-Jun–mid-Aug, 9am-4pm Mon-Fri rest of year) On the main square in the town centre,

---

WORLD'S OLDEST PADDLE STEAMER

Skibladner (☑ 61 14 40 80; www.skibladner.no; Hamar-Lillehammer 1-way/return Nkr220/320, under 12yr free), the world's oldest paddle steamer, is a wonderfully relaxing way to explore Lake Mjøsa. First built in Sweden in 1856, the boat was refitted and lengthened to 165ft (50m) in 1888. From late June until mid-August, the Skibladner plies the lake between Hamar, Gjøvik and Lillehammer. Most travellers opt for the route between Hamar and Lillehammer (3½ hours) on Tuesday, Thursday and Saturday. The boat leaves Hamar at 11.15am, arrives in Lillehammer at 3pm and returns straight away. If, as most people do, you only travel one way, then it's easy enough to hop on a train back to your starting point. There's also an on-board restaurant (lunch menu Nkr 335).

this office rents bicycles for Nkr100 per day and can supply cycling-route maps that take you through pretty farming countryside.

ℹ️ Getting There & Away

BUS

Lavprisekspressen buses go to Oslo (Nkr319) and Trondheim (Nkr499) once or twice a day.

TRAIN

Trains go to Oslo (Nkr268, 1¼ hours, once or twice hourly), Røros (Nkr543, 3¼ hours, up to four daily), and Trondheim (Nkr780, five hours, four or five daily) via Lillehammer (Nkr133, 45 minutes).

Elverum

POP 14,000

With a name like Elverum, you might expect a whiff of magic, but in reality this is a nondescript town set amid the vast and lush green timberlands of southern Hedmark county. Its excellent forestry museum is the main reason to stop here en route to elsewhere.

⊙ Sights

Norsk Skog Museum MUSEUM
(Norwegian Forestry Museum; ☑ 62 40 90 00; www.skogmus.no; Rv20; adult/child Nkr110/50, incl Glomdal Museum Nkr150/80; ⊘10am-5pm

mid-Jun–mid-Aug, 10am-4pm rest of year) This museum, 1km south of central Elverum, covers the multifarious uses and enjoyments of Norwegian forests. It includes a nature information centre, a children's workshop, geological and meteorological exhibits, wood carvings, an aquarium, nature dioramas with all manner of stuffed native wildlife (including a mammoth), a pretty little botanical garden and a 20,000-volume reference library.

If you're going to visit this museum and the Glomdal Museum, buy the joint ticket because it works out cheaper by Nkr10.

Glomdal Museum MUSEUM
(☑ 62 41 91 00; www.glomdal.museum.no; adult/child Nkr100/50, incl Norsk Skog Museum Nkr130/80; ⊘10am-5pm mid-Jun–mid-Aug, 10am-4pm rest of year) This collection of 90 historic buildings from the Glomma valley is one of the better examples of Norway's numerous 'folk' museums. It's 2km west of the town centre

🛏 Sleeping & Eating

Elverum Camping CAMPGROUND €
(☑ 62 41 67 16; www.elverumcamping.no; Halvdans Gransvei 6; tent sites Nkr200, cabins without water Nkr400, 2-/4-person cabins Nkr500/700) This decent place is in a green setting just south of the Norsk Skog Museum.

Solvårs Bed'n Breakfast B&B €
(☑ 99 61 20 26; www.elverumbb.com; Barbara Ringsvei 14; s/d from Nkr350/700; 🛜) A simple but friendly guesthouse, Solvårs Bed'n Breakfast lies 2km south of the Norsk Skog Museum; take the small turn-off on the left marked 'Bed'n Breakfast', 1km after leaving the museum. It's offers a more personal touch than most hotels, and there are lovely meals available on request.

Forstmann NORWEGIAN €€
(☑ 62 41 69 10; mains from Nkr185-265; ⊘10am-5pm Mon-Thu, 10am-9pm Fri & Sat, 11am-6pm Sun mid-Jun–mid-Aug) The fish-and-game restaurant at the Norsk Skog Museum serves traditional Norwegian cooking and has views over the swishing river waters.

ℹ️ Information

Tourist office (☑ 40 02 88 80; www.visitelverum.com; ⊘10am-5pm late-Jun–mid-Aug, 10am-4pm Mon-Fri rest of year) At the Norwegian Forestry Museum.

ⓘ Getting There & Away

The Nor-Way Bussekspress 'Trysil Ekspressen' runs between Oslo (Nkr190, 2½ hours) and Trysil (Nkr101, 1¼ hours) via Elverum seven times daily.

Trysil

POP 6763

Surrounded by forested hillsides close to the Swedish border, and overlooked by Norway's largest collection of ski slopes, little Trysil is well worth a detour, with year-round activities taking you into the wilderness.

Although Trysil lives and breathes winter skiing, for the rest of the year you can do just about anything to keep active, from canoeing and canyoning to horse riding, as well as the more sedate pastime of fishing. The tourist office (☑ 62 45 10 00; www.trysil. com; Storveien 3; ☉ 9am-8pm Mon-Fri, 9am-6pm Sat & Sun mid-Jun–mid-Aug, shorter hours rest of year) can organise any of these activities for you.

Perhaps the most rewarding activity in summer is cycling. There are at least six cycle routes: the shortest 6km, the longest 38km. Route maps are available from the tourist office. Bikes can be hired from most hotels and campsites for around Nkr200 per day.

🛏 Sleeping

Trysil Hyttegrend　　　　CABINS €€

(☑ 90 13 27 61; www.trysilhytte.com; Ørånset; 4-bed huts with/without bathroom Nkr810/450; P🛜) By the water's edge, 2.5km south of town, this excellent site has many drawcards including wireless internet, a wood-fired sauna, plenty of activities, a playground for children and a perfect riverside setting. All cabins have cooking facilities.

★ Radisson Blu Resort　　　HOTEL €€€

(☑ 62 44 90 00; www.trysil.radissonblu.com; Hotellveien 1; summer s/d from Nkr890/990, winter d from Nkr1990; P🛜🏊♨) One of the few Trysil hotels to open year-round, this is Trysil's most luxurious accommodation and outside the winter ski season (when prices are high) it's a first-rate bargain with huge, impeccable rooms in a large building at the edge of a ski slope. It also has an impressive pool complex. The resort also has Trysil's best restaurant (mains Nkr150 to Nkr236). It's signed just off the Elverum road south of town.

ⓘ Getting There & Away

The Nor-Way Bussekspress 'Trysil Ekspressen' connects Trysil with Oslo (Nkr361, four hours), via Elverum (Nkr101, 1¼ hours), seven times daily.

NORTHERN CENTRAL NORWAY

Røros

POP 5576

Røros, a charming Unesco World Heritage–listed site set in a small hollow of stunted forests and bleak fells, is one of Norway's most beautiful villages. The Norwegian writer Johan Falkberget described Røros as 'a place of whispering history', and this historic copper-mining town has wonderfully preserved, colourful wooden houses that climb the hillside, as well as fascinating relics of the town's mining past. Røros has become a retreat for artists, who lend even more character to this enchanted place.

Røros is one of the coldest places in Norway – the temperature once dropped to a mighty bracing -50.4°C.

History

According to local legend, in 1644 Olsen Åsen shot a reindeer at Storvola (Storwartz), 13km from Røros. The enraged creature pawed at the ground, revealing a glint of copper ore. In the same year Røros Kobberverk was established, followed two years later by a royal charter that granted it exclusive rights to all minerals, forest products and waterways (and local labour) within 40km of the original discovery.

The mining company located its headquarters at Røros due to the abundant wood (fuel) and the rapids along the river Hyttelva, which provided hydroelectric power. The use of fire in breaking up the rock in the mines was a perilous business and cost Røros dearly. Røros first burnt to the ground during the Gyldenløve conflict with the Swedes between 1678 and 1679, and the smelter was damaged by fire again in 1953. In 1977, after 333 years of operation, the company went bankrupt.

◉ Sights

Røros' historic district, characterised by the striking log architecture of its 80 protected

Røros

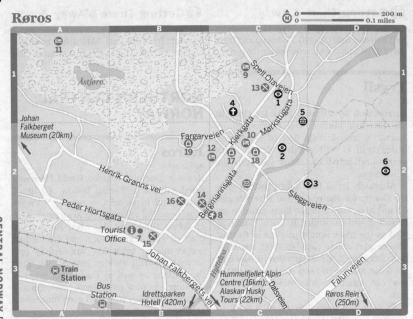

buildings, takes in the entire central area. The two main streets, **Bergmannsgata** and **Kjerkgata**, are lined with historical homes and buildings, all under preservation orders. The entire area is like an architectural museum of old Norway. For one of the loveliest turf-roofed homes you'll see, head up to the top of Kjerkgata to the house signposted as **Harald Sohlsbergs Plass 59**.

If Røros looks familiar, that's because several films have been made here, including Røros author Johan Falkberget's classic *An-Magrit*, starring Jane Fonda. Flanderborg gate starred in some of Astrid Lindgren's *Pippi Longstocking* classics and Røros even stood in for Siberia in *A Day in the Life of Ivan Denisovich*.

Røros Kirke
CHURCH
(Kjerkgata; adult/child Nkr40/free; ☺ 10am-4pm Mon-Sat, 12.30-2.30pm Sun mid-Jun–mid-Aug, 11am-1pm Mon-Sat early Jun & mid-Aug–mid-Sep, 11am-1pm Sat rest of year) Røros' Lutheran church is one of Norway's most distinctive, not to mention one of the largest, with a seating capacity of 1640. The first church on the site was constructed in 1650, but it had fallen into disrepair by the mid-18th century and from 1780 a new baroque-style church (the one you see today) was built just behind the original at a cost of 23,000

riksdaler (at the time, miners earned about 50 *riksdaler* per year).

The posh King's Gallery at the back, identified by both royal and mining-company logos, has never hosted a king; visiting royals have always opted to sit among the people. Unusually, the pulpit sits over the altarpiece, while the organ (1742) is the oldest Norwegian-built organ still functioning.

Until 1865 the building was owned by the mining company and this is reflected in the church art. By the altar you'll see the grizzled Hans Olsen Åsen among other company dignitaries. There are also paintings of the author Johan Falkberget and the original 1650 church.

For five weeks from early July to early August, the church hosts **organ recitals** (6-6.45pm Mon-Sat, mid-Jul–9 Aug), sometimes accompanied by orchestral musicians from across Europe.

Smelthytta
MUSEUM
(www.rorosmuseet.no; Malmplassen; adult/student/child incl guided tour in summer Nkr80/70/free; ☺ 10am-6pm mid-Jun–mid-Aug, 11am-4pm Mon-Fri, 11am-3pm Sat & Sun early Jun & mid-Aug–mid-Sep, shorter hours rest of year, guided tours during summer in Norwegian 11am or 3.30pm, in English 12.30pm) Housed in old smelting works, which were central to Røros' *raison*

Røros

CENTRAL NORWAY RØROS

d'être until 1953, this museum is a town highlight. The building was reconstructed in 1988 according to the original 17th-century plan. Inside you'll discover a large balance used for weighing ore, some well-illustrated early mining statistics, and brilliant working models of the mines and the water- and horse-powered smelting processes. Displays of copper smelting are held at 3pm Tuesday to Friday from early July to early August.

Outside the museum entrance spreads the large open area known as the **Malmplassen (Ore Place)**, where loads of ore were dumped and weighed on the large wooden scale. Just across the stream from the museum are the protected **Slegghaugen** (slag heaps), from which there are lovely views over town. Off the southwestern corner of the slag heaps, the historic smelting district with its tiny turf-roofed **miners' cottages**, particularly along **Sleggveien**, is one of Røros' prettiest corners.

🏃 Activities

Canoeing, horse riding and, in winter, sleigh rides and ice fishing are possible in Røros. The tourist office has a full list of operators.

Røros Sport   CYCLING
(📞72 41 12 18; Bergmannsgata 13; ⊙9am-6pm Mon-Sat) In summer Røros Sport rents mountain bikes for Nkr175/300/385 for one/ two/three days.

Alaskan Husky Tours   DOG-SLEDDING
(📞62 49 87 66; www.huskytour.no; Os; dog-sledding winter/summer adult from Nkr1400/1100, child Nkr700/550) 🖉 Organises winter dog-sledding

tours that last from a few hours to a few days. It also operates summer tours on wheel-sleds. Located some distance outside Røros; you can book through the tourist office.

Røros Husky   DOG-SLEDDING
(📞91 51 52 28; www.roroshusky.no) Organises winter dog-sledding tours of varying lengths. It's located about 10km north of Røros, but bookings can be made via the tourist office.

Røros Rein   SLEIGH RIDING
(📞97 97 49 66; www.rorosrein.no; Hagaveien 17) 🖉 Organises a winter program that includes sleigh rides, getting up close and personal with reindeer, and a traditional Sami meal in a Sami hut.

Hummelfjellet Alpine Centre   SKIING
(www.hummelfjell.no) Has two lifts and six slopes. Located 16km south of Røros.

---

❶ COMBINED TICKETS & WEBSITES

Although separated by 13km, the Smelthytta and Olavsgruva Mine (p134) form part of the **Røros Museum** (Røros Museet; 📞72 40 61 70; www.rorosmuseet. no), a catch-all name for most of the village's museums, and it works out cheaper to buy a combined ticket (adult/child/student & senior Nkr150/ free/120) if you plan to visit both sites.

In addition to the main museum website, www.worldheritageroros.no is an excellent resource about Røros' historical sites.

Ålen Ski Centre
SKIING

(☑72 41 55 55; www.aalenskisenter.no) Boasts two lifts and four slopes. Located 34km northwest of town.

Wilderness Life
WILDLIFE-WATCHING

(☑98 48 21 30; www.wildernesslife.no; Tylldalen) Runs courses in the art of wildlife tracking and bush survival. It's located outside of Røros.

☞ Tours

Guided Walking Tours
WALKING

(adult/child Nkr80/free; ⊙ tours 10.30am, 12.30pm, 2.30pm Mon-Sat, 11.30am & 1pm Sun mid-Jun–mid-Aug, 11am Mon-Sat early Jun & mid-Aug–mid-Sep) Run by the tourist office, these walking tours take you through the historic town centre. English tours are at 12.30pm Monday to Saturday and 1pm Sunday. The office also runs children's tours (Nkr60; in Norwegian only) at noon on Tuesdays and Thursdays throughout July and the first week of August.

✳ Festivals & Events

Fermund Race
SPORTS

(www.femundlopet.no) One of Europe's longest dog-sled races starts and ends in Røros in the first week of February.

Rørosmartnan (Røros Market)
CULTURAL

This is the biggest winter event. It began in 1644 as a rendezvous for hunters who ventured into town to sell their products to miners and buy supplies. Thanks to a royal decree issued in 1853 stipulating that a grand market be held annually from the penultimate Tuesday of February to the following Saturday, it continues today. Nowadays it's celebrated with cultural programs, street markets and live entertainment.

Winter Chamber Music Festival
MUSIC

(www.vinterfestspill.no) Concerts held in Røros Kirke in the first week of March.

Elden
PERFORMING ARTS

(www.elden-roros.no) In late July and early August, Røros stages a nightly three-hour rock opera that recounts the invasion of Trøndelag by Sweden in 1718, covering the occupation of Røros and the subsequent death of thousands of soldiers on their frozen trek homewards to Sweden. It's enacted on the slag heaps in the upper part of town.

🛏 Sleeping

The tourist office keeps a list of summer cabins and guesthouses, some within walking distance of town.

Vertshuset Røros
HISTORIC HOTEL €€

(☑72 41 93 50; www.vertshusetroros.no; Kjerkgata 34; s/d from Nkr1185/1540, 2-/4-bed apt Nkr1690/2140; ⊛) Located in a historic 17th-century building on the main pedestrian thoroughfare, the Vertshuset Røros is a wonderful choice. The all-wood rooms are generously sized and have numerous period touches, such as wooden beds with columns – arguably the most comfortable beds in town.

Do be aware though that during busy periods staff may book you a room at the 'sister' hotel, the Røros Hotel, a very different kind of place, without telling you.

Frøyas Hus
B&B €€

(☑72 41 10 10; www.froyashus.no; Mørkstugata 4; s/d Nkr850/950; ⊛) With only two rooms, this gorgeous place has an intimacy you won't find elsewhere. Rooms are small and have scarcely changed in over 300 years – it's rustic in the best sense of the word. Throw in friendly service, a lovely courtyard cafe and public areas strewn with local antiques and curiosities, and it's all perfectly integrated into the Røros experience.

Røros Hotell
HOTEL €€

(☑72 40 80 00; www.roroshotell.no; An Magritveien 10; s/d from Nkr950/1400; 🅿@⊛🕿 ▦ ♿) This 167-room colossus at the top end of town is popular with tour groups and has well-appointed rooms. Styled as a mountain hotel, it has a touch more character than most larger hotels, at least in the public areas, but far less than the smaller Røros hotels.

Be aware that during very busy periods staff put people in the overflow accommodation over the road – rooms here are little more than sheds (and they don't voluntarily reduce the rates). Avoid these if possible.

Idrettsparken Hotell
HOTEL €€

(☑72 41 10 89; www.idrettsparken.no; Øra 25; cabins from Nkr550, hotel r from Nkr900; 🅿) The family-run Idrettsparken Hotell, 500m south of the train station, has a range of options for most budgets and although it's not the most inspiring of places, the price is about right.

★ Erzscheidergården
GUESTHOUSE €€€

(☑72 41 11 94; www.erzscheidergaarden.no; Spell Olaveien 6; s/d from Nkr1245/1590; 🅿⊛) This appealing, very cosy 24-room guesthouse is up the hill from the town centre and behind the church. The wood-panelled rooms are loaded with personality, the atmosphere is Norwegian-family-warmth and the breakfasts were described by one reader as 'the best homemade breakfast buffet in Norway'. We're inclined to agree.

✗ Eating

There are many small coffee shops (some of which are attached to crafts and souvenir shops) that serve snacks and some light meals.

Opening hours will be much reduced in winter.

Frøyas Hus CAFE €
(Mørkstugata 4; snacks Nkr50-100; ⊙10am-5pm) A blissed-out garden courtyard cafe serving good waffles and *rømmegrøt*, a traditional slightly sour porridge eaten with cured ham in the evening.

Galleri Thomasgården CAFE €
(☑48 21 90 08; Kjerkgata 48; snacks Nkr50-100; ⊙11am-5pm Mon-Wed, Fri & Sat, 11am-11pm Thu, noon-5pm Sun) Half cafe, half art gallery – perfectly complete place for coffee and cake.

Trygstad Bakeri BAKERY €
(☑72 41 10 29; www.trygstadbakeri.no; Kjerkgata 12; snacks Nkr 30-80; ⊙8.30am-7pm Mon-Fri, 9am-4pm Sat, noon-5pm Sun) This stand-out cafe and bakery will treat you to the town's most popular coffee and baked goodies.

Kaffestugu Cafeteria NORWEGIAN €€
(www.kaffestuggu.no; Bergmannsgata 18; mains Nkr88-225; ⊙9am-9pm daily mid-Jun–mid-Aug, 10am-6pm Mon-Fri & 10am-5pm Sat & Sun rest of year) This historic place offers a good range of coffee, pastries, snacks and light meals, as well as some more substantial main dishes such as reindeer steak. Its lunchtime specials are a little heavy on the potatoes, but the food in general is enduringly popular.

Peder Hiort Mathus INTERNATIONAL €€
(☑72 40 60 80; www.bergstadenshotel.no/peder hiort_mathus; Bergmannsgata 1; mains from Nkr120-170, barbecue buffet Nkr249; ⊙2-10pm Mon-Thu, 2-11pm Fri, 11am-11pm Sat, noon-10pm Sun) With old photos of Røros and traditional decor, you might expect this to be a bastion of traditional cooking, but it's mostly about pizza. Of more interest is its garden barbecue buffet (from 5pm Thursday to Sunday in summer,

weather permitting). Its outdoor tables have views up this historic street.

★Vertshuset Røros NORWEGIAN €€€
(☑72 41 93 50; Kjerkgata 34; lunch mains Nkr 100-185, set menu from Nkr385; ⊙10am-9.30pm) Lunch dishes here include fairly standard soup, sandwiches and burgers, but from 4pm onwards the food is exquisite – the tenderest fillets of reindeer or elk, as well as Arctic char and desserts such as 'blue cheese and pear marinated in cinnamon, walnuts in honey and balsamico'. In short, it's one of the region's finest eating experiences. Book ahead.

🔒 Shopping

Bergmannsgata and Kjerkgata are lined with small craft shops.

Galleri Thomasgården CERAMICS
(☑48 21 90 08; Kjerkgata 48; ⊙11am-5pm Mon-Wed, Fri & Sat, 11am-11pm Thu, noon-5pm Sun) At the worthwhile Galleri Thomasgården, potter Torgeir Henriksen creates rustic stoneware and porcelain. You will also find the wonderful nature-inspired wood carvings of Henry Solli. The player piano is one of only two in Norway and dates back to 1929.

Hartzgården Sølvsmie JEWELLERY
(Kjerkgata 35; ⊙10am-6pm Mon-Fri, 10am-4pm Sat, noon-5pm Sun summer, shorter hours rest of year) At this silversmith's shop you'll find locally handcrafted silver jewellery with an emphasis on Viking themes, as well as a small historical-jewellery exhibit.

Per Sverre Dahl Modellør CERAMICS
(☑72 41 19 89; www.persverredahl.no; Mørkstugata 5; ⊙10am-4pm Mon-Sat summer, shorter hours rest of year) Per Sverre creates ceramic sculptures and wall decorations, which range across themes as diverse as trolls and modern saxophone-bearing musicians.

Potteriet Røros CERAMICS
(☑72 41 17 10; www.potteriet-roros.no; Fargarveien 4; ⊙9am-5pm Mon-Fri, 10am-4pm Sat & Sun Jul, 10am-4pm Mon-Fri, 11am-5pm Sat rest of year) Here you'll find pottery based on traditional designs from all over Trøndelag, along with some creative modern interpretations. The pottery workshop next door is open to the public and staff are always happy to explain the history behind each design (morning is the best time to catch them at work).

ⓘ Information

Tourist office (📞 72 41 00 00; www.roros. no; Peder Hiortsgata 2; ⏰ 9am-6pm Mon-Sat, 10am-4pm Sun mid-Jun–mid-Aug, 9am-3.30pm Mon-Fri, 10am-4pm Sat rest of year) The tourist office has loads of good info on things to see and do in and around the town but walkers wanting to explore the surrounding moorland peaks will find them of little use in regards to route suggestions.

ⓘ Getting There & Away

AIR

Røros has two daily **Widerøe** (www.wideroe.no) flights to/from Oslo except Saturday. Fares can be as low as Nkr599.

BUS

There are two daily buses from Røros to Trondheim (Nkr286, four hours).

TRAIN

Røros lies on the eastern railway line between Oslo (from Nkr249, five hours, six daily) and Trondheim (from Nkr249, 2½ hours).

Around Røros

Olavsgruva Mine

The **Olavsgruva mine** (📞 72 40 61 70; www.rorosmuseet.no; adult/child/senior & student Nkr100/free/80; ⏰ guided tours 10.30am, noon, 2pm, 3.30pm & 5pm mid-Jun–mid-Aug, 1pm & 3pm Mon-Sat, noon Sun early Jun & mid-Aug–mid-Sep, shorter hours rest of year) is 13km north of Røros. The moderately interesting museum exhibition is far surpassed by **mine tours** passing through the historic Nyberget mine, which dates from the 1650s. The modern Olavsgruva mine beyond it was begun in 1936. The ground can get muddy and the temperature in the mine is 5°C year round; bring a jacket (unless its midwinter outside in which case you may be tempted to don a T-shirt!) and good footwear. There's no public transport to the mine. Cheaper combined tickets with Smelthytta (p130) are also available.

Johan Falkberget Museum

The works of Røros' favourite son, author Johan Falkberget (1879–1967), have been translated into 19 languages and cover 300 years of the region's mining history. His most famous work, *An-Magrit,* which was made into a film starring Jane Fonda, tells the story of a peasant girl who transported copper ore in the Røros mining district. The **museum** (www.falkberget.no; Ratvolden; adult/child Nkr80/free; ⏰ guided tours 1pm Tue & Thu-Sun Jul-early Aug, by appointment rest of year) is at Ratvolden, beside Lake Rugelsjø 20km north of Røros. To get there, take a local train to Rugeldalen station, where a small walking track leads to the museum.

Femundsmarka National Park

The national park (573 sq km) that stretches east of Femunden, Norway's second-largest lake, to the Swedish border was formed in 1971 to protect the lake, forests, marshes and mountain peaks of the area. Sadly overlooked by foreign tourists, the park has been named one of the best three hiking areas in Norway by the Norwegian hiking association.

The park has long been a source of falcons for use in the European and Asian sport of falconry, and several places in the park are known as Falkfangerhøgda, which means 'falcon hunters' height'. If you're lucky, you may also see wild reindeer grazing in the heights (as well as easily seen domestic ones) and, in summer, a herd of around 30 musk oxen roams the area along the Røa and Mugga Rivers (in winter they migrate to the Funäsdalen area). It's thought that this group split off from an older herd in the Dovrefjell area and wandered all the way here. There are also a handful of exceedingly rare brown bears, as well as even rarer lynx and, occasionally, wolves drifting by from other areas.

On the eastern shore of the lake is the tiny village of Elgå, which is the main base for the park. It has campsites (with cabins) and a park information centre.

🏃 Activities

This is excellent hiking country and the very helpful national park information centre in Elgå can provide route suggestions and maps.

One especially fine, and fairly easy, hike is the 3½-hour, 10.5km-return hike up Mt Elgåhogna (1403m). From Elgå, the main village (and only real road access point into the park) head south for 4km to a small farm building on the left. A hundred metres further south is a small parking area where the trail begins. The walk is well marked with red dots painted onto rocks and trees. It starts off passing though stunted woodland before emerging onto a barren tundrascape which climbs moderately upwards. The last part to the summit is steeper and involves a little scrambling over rocks. All the time the views back down westward over the lake get steadily better, but this walk saves its best for last – a view from the summit over Sweden and across endless barren sub-Arctic moorland and tundra.

🛏 Sleeping

On the western side of the lake the two main sleeping options are **Johnsgård Turistsenter** (☑62 45 99 25; www.johnsgard.no; cabins Nkr240-745, camping Nkr180), 9km west of Buvika; and **Langen Gjestegård** (☑72 41 37 18; www.langen-gjestegaard.com; s/d from Nkr300/600, cabins Nkr350-1000), a cosy turf-roofed farmhouse near the lake.

ℹ Getting There & Away

The historic ferry **M/S Fæmund II** (☑96 39 20 17; www.femund.no) sails daily at 9am between mid-June and mid-August from Synnervika (also spelt Søndervika), on the northern shore of Lake Femunden, to Elgå (adult/child one way Nkr240/120, 6½ hours return). From mid-June to late August, buses leave Røros train station for Synnervika 45 minutes before the boat's departure. Buses for Røros later meet the boat at Synnervika.

Oppdal

POP 6603

Oppdal is a quintessential feeder town for the Norwegian wilderness: there's nothing much to detain you in town, but the surrounding countryside is beautiful with loads of activities on offer.

🛏 Sleeping

If you are unable to find a bed, contact Oppdal Booking or the tourist office for help.

Oppdal Gjestetun　　　HOTEL, APARTMENTS €€
(☑98 69 33 00; www.oppdalbooking.no; Olav Skasliens vei 6; s/d Nkr715/755; P🖥) The exterior doesn't exactly draw you towards it, but the spacious, equipped apartments at this simple place offer fab value for money. Unusually for Norway, prices don't include breakfast.

Skifer Hotel　　　BUSINESS HOTEL €€
(☑73 60 50 80; www.skiferhotel.no; Olav Skasliens vei 9; d from Nkr1250; P🖥) This new place in the town centre offers Oppdal's best rooms, with smart, dark-grey accents and business-standard facilities. Some rooms have mountain views. Others have views over the main road. We needn't tell you which ones to ask for!

🍴 Eating

Møllen Restaurant
& Pizzeria　　　INTERNATIONAL €€
(☑72 42 18 00; Dovreveien 2; pizzas from Nkr139, mains from Nkr230; ⊙1-11pm Mon-Sat, to 10pm Sun) In the town centre alongside the E6, this jack-of-all-trades kind of place has a huge menu spanning everything from pasta to fish to steak and, just in case you haven't eaten one in a while, pizzas and burgers. It's a good choice if you feel like a sit-down meal, but with a reasonable price tag.

ℹ Information

Oppdal Booking (☑72 40 08 00; www.oppdal-booking.no; Olav Skasliens vei 10; ⊙9am-6pm mid-May–Oct) An efficient one-stop shop for reserving activities and accommodation; booking fees apply.
Tourist Office (☑72 40 04 70; www.oppdal.com; ⊙9am-4pm Mon-Fri, 10am-1.30pm Sat & Sun mid-Jun–mid-Aug, 9am-4pm Mon-Fri rest of year) A small office inside the train station.

ℹ Getting There & Away

BUS

Nor-Way Bussekspress runs between Bergen (Nkr783, 12½ hours) and Trondheim (Nkr260, two hours) daily. Lavprisekspressen buses also pass through once or twice daily en route between Oslo and Trondheim.

TRAIN

Trains run to Oslo (Nkr399 to Nkr549, five hours, four daily) and Trondheim (Nkr213, 1½ hours, four daily).

Trollheimen

The small Trollheimen range, with a variety of trails through gentle mountains and lake-studded upland regions, is most readily accessed from Oppdal. From Oppdal take the westbound 70 road for 15km to the village of Albu, where a toll road (Nkr50 by car), signed Gjevilvasshytta, leads 8.8km to **Osen**, a small collection of lakeside cabins and the main entrance point to the wilderness region. You could walk the toll road but at weekends it's quite busy with cars and the walk wouldn't be much fun. The best map to use for the park is Statens Kartverk's

Turkart Trollheimen (1:75,000), which is available at the tourist office in Oppdal.

A straightforward hiking destination in Trollheimen is the hut and historic farm at **Vassendsetra**. From Osen (the outlet of the river Gjevilvatnet), 3km north of the main road to Sunndalsøra, you can take the boat *Trollheimen II* all the way to Vassendsetra (Nkr175 return). From July to mid-August it leaves from Osen daily at noon and from Vassendsetra at 3.30pm.

Alternatively, it is possible to drive or hike (although this isn't the most exciting of walks) 6km along the road from Osen to the 19th-century Den Norske Turistforening (DNT) hut, **Gjevilvasshytta** (☑ Oslo 40 00 18 68; www.tt.no; incl breakfast, dinner &

bed DNT members/nonmembers Nkr745/1060), one of Norway's most beautiful mountain lodges. This places dates back to 1819 and is very well organised with beds in small dorms or twin rooms. It's open year round but is unstaffed in the winter. From there, follow the lakeshore trail for another 12km until you come to **Vassendsetra** (☑ Oslo 40 00 18 68; www.tt.no; DNT members/nonmembers Nkr350/500; ⊙ year-round) an unstaffed but otherwise comfortable mountain lodge. Bring your own food.

The popular and highly rewarding three-day 'Trekanten' hut tour follows the impressive Gjevilvasshytta–Trollheimshytta–Jøldalshytta–Gjevilvasshytta route; contact Oppdal Booking (p135) for details.

OPPDAL ACTIVITIES

White-Water Rafting

The nearby, wild and white Driva promises excellent rafting runs from May to October. The outdoor-adventure company **Opplev Oppdal** (☑ 72 40 41 80; www.opplevoppdal. no; Olav Skasliens vei 10; ⊙ rafting early Jun–mid-Aug) organises trips, from relatively tame Class I–II trips to full-day Class III–IV trips that provide substantial thrills. Prices range from Nkr750 to Nkr850 per person per day; the company also organises family trips (Nkr1850 for seven people).

Musk Ox & Elk Safaris

To track down the prehistoric musk ox, take one of the four- to six-hour **musk ox safaris** (☑ 72 40 08 00; adult/child Nkr325/225; ⊙ 9am mid-Jun–mid-Aug, by appointment rest of year) organised by Oppdal Booking (p135). Tours leave from outside the tourist office at 9am and you need your own transport (although with advance notice it can organise transport for you). For those who want a more personalised and up-close encounter, private day or overnight musk ox safaris are also available year-round.

Oppdal Booking also organises three-hour **elk safaris** (☑ 72 40 08 00; per person Nkr350). Tours depart at twilight (between 7.30pm and 11pm). The meeting point is outside the tourist office.

Advance bookings are required for both safaris.

Skiing & Snowboarding

The three-part Oppdal Skisenter climbs the slopes from Hovden, Stølen and Vangslia, all within easy reach of town. The smaller Ådalen ski area nearby has two lifts. Vangslia is generally the easiest, with a couple of beginners' runs; Stølen offers intermediate skiing and Hovden has three challenging advanced runs. The season runs from late November to late April. Ski passes for adults/children start at Nkr370/300 for one day.

Other Activities

Oppdal Booking also arranges the following activities:

Cable-Car Ride (adult/child Nkr100/70; ⊙ 11am-5pm Jul–Aug, 11am-5pm Sat & Sun rest of year) Gondola rides up Skjørstadhovden (1125m) to Hovden Skisenter for fine views.

Guided Mountain Hikes (adult/child Nkr265/135; ⊙ 10am Jun-Sep) Four- to six-hour treks; advance booking and your own transport is required.

Bikes and child trailers can be hired from **Savanah AS** (www.oppdalbooking.no; Olav Skasliens vei 10; per day bike hire/trailer hire Nkr175/175; ⊙ 11am-5pm May-Oct), which is located within the Oppdal Booking office. It can recommend cycling routes for all levels of stamina.

Dombås

POP 1200

Dombås, a popular adventure and winter-sports centre, comprises little more than a couple of petrol stations and a shopping complex, and is far outdone in the beauty stakes by its surroundings. It does make a convenient break for travellers between the highland national parks and the western fjords, though. That said, there's more choice of activities to the north in Oppdal, while Sjoa is the region's best location for rafting. The Rauma Railway from Dombås to Åndalsnes is one of Norway's most beautiful train rides.

🏃 Activities

Activities in the surrounding national parks can be arranged through the tourist office from mid-June through to mid-August.

Elk Safari   WILDLIFE-WATCHING
(☑ 45 67 19 95; adult/child Nkr200/100) This evening tour departs from the tourist office at 7pm from mid-June to mid-August; advance bookings not required.

Musk Ox Safari   WILDLIFE-WATCHING
(☑ 45 67 19 95; adult/child Nkr350/150; ⊘ mid-Jun–mid-Aug) This four- to five-hour tour departs daily at 8.30am from the tourist office. No advance booking is necessary.

Bjorli Skisenter   SKIING
(☑ 61 24 55 77; www.bjorliskisenter.no) From early autumn until Easter, downhill skiing is possible at Bjorli Skisenter, which has 11 runs, six lifts and a dedicated children's area.

Dombås Skisenter   SKIING
(www.trolltun.no) Closer to town, Dombås Skisenter also offers skiing from October to May, although with artificial snow for much of the season; day lift tickets cost Nkr250.

🛏 Sleeping

Bjørkhol Camping   CAMPGROUND €
(☑ 61 24 13 31; www.bjorkhol.no; Bjørkhol; tent/caravan sites Nkr130/160, 2-/4-bed cabins with shared bathroom from Nkr350/450, 2-bed cabins with bathroom Nkr650-800) One of Norway's best-value, friendliest campsites is 6km south of Dombås. The facilities are in excellent condition and a bus runs several times daily from Dombås. It is, however, situated fairly close to the main road.

Trolltun Gjestegård & Dombås Vandrerhjem   HOSTEL, GUESTHOUSE €€
(☑ 61 24 09 60; www.trolltun.no; campsites Nkr110, hostel dm/s/d Nkr325/850/1050, cabins from Nkr995; P🔊📶) This good-value place is 1.5km northeast of town, up the hill from the E6. The setting is lovely, the rooms are tidy and the meals are reasonably priced (two-course dinner Nkr85). You're ideally located for winter skiing and summer hiking with Dovrefjell-Sunndalsfjella National Park on your doorstep. Part of the Fjordpass network.

Dovrefjell Hotell   HOTEL €€
(☑ 61 24 10 05; www.dovrefjellhotell.no; Svenskebakken; s/d Nkr795/950; P🔊❄) This place in the countryside, 2km northwest of Dombås off the E136, is a bit uninspired but the price is about right and the swimming pool is a welcome bonus.

🍴 Eating

Napoli Restaurant & Pizzeria   INTERNATIONAL €€
(Kyrkjevegen 5; mains & pizzas Nkr120-180; ⊘ 1-11pm Mon-Sat, 1-10pm Sun) The most exciting place to eat in Dombås, but don't get too excited – it's still the standard Norwegian mix of pizzas and burgers. It's next to the Statoil petrol station in the town centre.

ℹ Information

Tourist Office & Dovrefjell National Park Centre (Dovrefjell Nasjonalparksenter; ☑ 61 24 14 44; www.rondane-dovrefjell.no; Sentralplassen; ⊘ 2-7pm Mon, 11am-2pm Tue, Fri & Sat) Small displays on nearby national parks and plenty of information on activities.

ℹ Getting There & Away

BUS
Nor-Way Bussekspress buses between Bergen (Nkr723, 11¼ hours) and Trondheim (Nkr380, 3¼ hours) call in daily in both directions. Cheaper Lavprisekspressen buses also pass through en route between Oslo (from Nkr449) and Trondheim (from Nkr319).

TRAIN
Dombås lies on the railway line between Oslo (Nkr249 to Nkr659, 4¼ hours, four daily) and Trondheim (Nkr249 to Nkr431, 2½ hours). It is also the starting point for the spectacular **Rauma Railway** (Raumabanen; www.nsb.no; Nkr230), which runs from Romsdalen to Åndalsnes (1½ hours, four daily).

Dovrefjell-Sunndalsfjella National Park

Bleak, cold and dramatic, the hauntingly beautiful Dovrefjell-Sunndalsfjella National Park is a high, bitter-cold plateau of gently undulating mountains buried under a thick blanket of snow for much of the year. These mountains peak with Snøhetta (2286m), and the park provides a suitably Arctic-like habitat for Arctic foxes, reindeer, wolverines and, the park's flagship animal, musk oxen, which are easily seen during a summertime musk-oxen safari.

The Knutshøene massif (1690m) section of the park, east of the E6, protects Europe's most diverse intact alpine ecosystem.

◉ Sights & Activities

Most non-Norwegians visit the park as part of a daylong musk-ox safari. However, Dovrefjell-Sunndalsfjella offers numerous wonderful walking trails many of which are clearly signed. Ask in local tourist offices for route suggestions. Serious hikers will fare best with the Statens Kartverk map *Dovrefjell* (1:100,000). However, it doesn't include the Knutshøene section; for that, you need Statens Kartverk's *Einunna 1519-I* and *Folldal 1519-II* topographic sheets. The park's highest mountain, Snøhetta, can be ascended by hikers from Snøheim (allow six hours) but it should only be attempted by experienced walkers with equipment suitable for extreme weather. While walking independently in the park you might well encounter musk oxen. Though generally fairly docile they can be dangerous and half-a-tonne of monster-sized sheep ploughing into you at up to 60km/h will make an awful mess. Do not approach closer than 300m and if one starts snorting then that might be a warning to you to back off. Move away in a sideways and backwards direction (musk oxen have poor eyesight and if you move directly backwards they cannot always tell that you're retreating). Never get between a mother and her calf.

For a totally different look at the park, the Fokstumyra marshes are home to an astonishing array of bird life. Approximately 87 species nest in the area and 162 species in total have been observed. Among the species found here are the red-breasted merganser, long-tailed duck, black-throated diver, whimbrel, wood sandpiper and short-eared owl. For a more extensive list, pick up the brochure *Fokstumyra Nature Reserve* from the Dombås tourist office (p137).

Many of these species can be viewed from the 7km-long marked trail near the Dombås end of the reserve; note that from May to July, visitors are restricted to this trail to prevent the disturbance of nesting birds.

Norwegian Wild Reindeer Centre Pavilion
VIEWPOINT

Commonly known as Snøhetta (which is in fact the name of the park's largest mountain, as well as the architectural firm who designed the pavilion), this arresting building of rippled timber and mirrored glass was commissioned to serve as an educational centre and observation point. It's open to the public and offers astounding views over the valley to Mt Snøhetta.

It's a gentle 1.5km walk from the car park (the trail is suitable for pushchairs and wheelchairs – just). The turn-off for the pavilion is well signed off the E6 by Hjerkinn.

🛏 Sleeping & Eating

The original DNT Snøheim hut was, thankfully, judged to be too near the army's Hjerkinn firing range and was replaced by the new self-service Reinheim hut, 5km north and at 1341m, in Stroplsjødalen. DNT also maintains several other self-service huts in the adjacent Skrymtheimen region; keys are available from the Dombås tourist office.

★ **Kongsvold Fjeldstue**
LODGE €€

(☑ 72 40 43 40; www.kongsvold.no; Kongsvold; s/d from Nkr795/1185, with shared bathroom Nkr675/995; 🅿 🛜) This charming and historic place of intriguing early-18th-century timber buildings is 13km north of Hjerkinn on the E6. Every room is different although all are warm and cosy. Locals will drive kilometres to come and enjoy the excellent evening meals (set menus Nkr485 to Nkr895) and every other person driving past seems to stop for coffee and waffles in the cafe.

Park information, maps, meals and accommodation are available here and there's a small museum dedicated to the park. Musk oxen safaris can also be organised from here (adult/child NKr350/275). It's 500m from tiny Kongsvold station (trains stop only on request).

Hjerkinn Fjellstue
LODGE €€

(☑ 61 21 51 00; www.hjerkinn.no; Hjerkinn; s/d from Nkr950/1290, 4-person apt Nkr1450;

P 🤖 🛜 🚿) This relaxed inn is about 1.5km northeast of Hjerkinn on Rv29. It has a warm welcome, spotless rooms, lots of information on the park and children will love all the horses that surround the hotel. You will also find a restaurant, a campsite and horse-riding expeditions (half-/full day Nkr700/900).

ℹ Information

For more information, including on tours into the park, see the national park centre (p137) in Dombås.

ℹ Getting There & Away

There's no public transport into the park. Trains run from Dombås to Hjerkinn (Nkr96, 30 minutes).

Otta

POP 1677

Set deep in Gudbrandsdalen, Otta occupies a strategic position at the confluence of the Otta and Lågen Rivers. Otta's main attraction is as the gateway to Rondane National Park.

🛏 Sleeping & Eating

Otta Camping   CAMPGROUND €
(☑ 47 36 75 01; www.ottacamping.no; Ottadalen; tent & car/caravan sites for 2 people Nkr170/170, plus electricity Nkr40, 4-bed cabins Nkr350-500; ☉ May–mid-Oct; 🛜 🚿) The riverside Otta Camping is convenient and popular; cross the Otta bridge from the centre, turn right and continue about 1km upstream.

Norlandia Otta Hotell   HOTEL €€
(☑ 61 21 08 00; www.ottahotell.no; Ola Dahlsgate 7; d Nkr1195; 🛜) A rather uninspiring hotel in a modern block that will suffice for a night if you get stuck in Otta.

Pillarguri Kafé   CAFE, RESTAURANT €€
(☑ 61 23 01 04; www.pillargurcafe.no; Stortorget 7; snacks & light meals Nkr70-145, mains Nkr175-260; ☉ 8am-8pm Mon-Thu & Sun, to 10pm Fri, to 2am Sat) In business for over a century, the Pillarguri promises a varied menu, with sandwiches, pasta, salads and a handful of hearty Norwegian dishes. The outdoor tables are the place to be on a summer's afternoon.

ℹ Information

Rondane National Park Centre (☑ 61 24 14 44; Johan Nygårdgata 17a; ☉ 10am-4pm Mon-Fri) Although focused on Rondane, there are displays on other nearby national parks, as well as an extensive library.

Tourist office (☑ 61 24 14 44; www.visitrondane.com; Otta Skysstasjon; ☉ 8am-4pm Mon-Fri mid-Jun–mid-Aug, shorter hours rest of year) The small tourist office is located inside the train station.

ℹ Getting There & Away

Nor-Way Bussekspress has buses to/from Trondheim (Nk445, four hours, up to five daily) and Bergen (Nkr688, five to six hours). Lavprisekspressen buses (from Nkr439) also pass through en route to Trondheim once or twice daily.

Trains run to Oslo (Nkr586, 3½ hours) and Trondheim (Nkr515, three hours, four daily). To get to Bergen change trains in Oslo.

Rondane National Park

Henrik Ibsen described the landscapes that now make up the 963-sq-km (www.nasjonalparkriket.no) as 'palace piled upon palace'. It was created in 1962 as Norway's first national park to protect the fabulous Rondane massif, regarded by many as the finest alpine hiking country in Norway. Ancient reindeer-trapping sites and burial mounds suggest that the area has been inhabited for thousands of years. Much of the park's glaciated and lichen-coated landscape lies above 1400m and 10 rough and stony peaks rise to over 2000m, including Rondslottet (2178m), the highest, and Storronden (2138m). Rondane's range of wildlife includes 28 mammal species and 124 bird species, and the park is now one of the last refuges of the wild reindeer.

If you're driving, the 87km-long Rv27 between Folldal and the E6 (5km north of Ringebu) is a stunningly beautiful route that runs along the Rondane range. This is a designated **National Tourist Route** (www.turistveg.no).

🏃 Activities

The hiking season runs only in July and August. The most accessible route into the park is from the Spranghaugen car park, about 13km uphill along a good road from Otta and via the toll road (Nkr20). From there, it's a straightforward 6.2km (1½ hour) hike to **Rondvassbu**, where there's a popular, staffed DNT hut. From Rondvassbu, it's a five-hour return climb to the summit

Rondane National Park

of **Storronden**. Alternatively, head for the spectacular view from the more difficult summit of **Vinjeronden** (2044m), then tackle the narrow ridge leading to the neighbouring peak, **Rondslottet** (about six hours return from Rondvassbu).

The best maps to use are Statens Kartverk's *Rondane* (1:100,000; Nkr99) and *Rondane Sør* (1:50,000).

Bicycle Hire   CYCLING
(Spranghaugen car park; per day bike/child bike Nkr100/50) An automatic bicycle-rental place is located inside the Spranghaugen car park. Bikes can be used only on the trail to Rondvassbu.

🛏 Sleeping & Eating

Camping is permitted anywhere in the national park except at Rondvassbu, where you're restricted to the designated area. There are DNT huts throughout the park.

Mysusæter Fjellstue   HUTS €
(📞 41 40 99 30; www.mysuseter.com; Mysusæter; d per person with/without bathroom Nkr600/400) A basic roof over your head and equally basic meals are available.

**Rondane Spa
Høyfjellshotell**   LODGE €€
(📞 61 20 90 90; www.rondane.no; Mysusæter; s/d Nkr395/790, 4-person cabins Nkr1450; 🅿🛜) A comfortable upmarket option with good spa facilities, including pedicures for worn-out feet and pine-tinged rooms that are unusually good value. The restaurant serves hearty Norwegian and international fare (set dinner menu Nkr200). It's roughly halfway between Otta and the Spranghaugen car park.

ℹ Getting There & Around

In summer, buses run twice daily between Otta and Mysusæter, from where it's a further 4km to the Spranghaugen car park.

From Rondvassbu, the ferry *Rondegubben* crosses the lake Rondvatnet to Nordvika (adult/child Nkr120/60, 30 minutes) three times daily from early July to late August.

Other National Parks

As if the Rondane, Dovrefjell-Sunndalsfjella and Jotunheimen National Parks weren't enough, there are three further national parks in the same area.

Breheimen National Park

One of Norway's newest national parks, Breheimen opened in 2009 and covers 1691 sq km. It's wedged between the Jotunheimen and Jostedalsbreen National Parks and has some of the best hiking in the southern half of Norway. However, walking here is not for the inexperienced. Trail markings are harder to follow than in some more trodden parks and all the DNT huts are unstaffed. This is the place for an off-the-beaten-track adventure. For more information, visit the Lom tourist office (p144).

Dovre National Park

Immediately north of Rondane National park, this 289-sq-km **park** (www.nasjonalparkriket.no) was established in 2003 and is famous for having almost every Norwegian flora type within its borders. The park's highest point is Fokstuhøe (1716m). For more information, visit the Dombås tourist office (p137).

Reinheimen National Park

Founded in 2006, this 1969-sq-km park stretches from Lom in the southeast to Åndalsnes in the northwest. It's a varied and relatively unexplored park, steep and mountainous in the west with a more gentle Alpine plateau in the east. It's home to wild reindeer, wolverines and golden eagles. For more information, visit the Lom tourist office (p144).

Sjoa

The tiny settlement of Sjoa, 10km south of Otta, is little more than a couple of buildings overlooking a pretty stretch of river. It would have little to detain you were it not for the fact that it's arguably the white-water-rafting capital of Norway.

Activities

The white-water rafting season runs from the middle of May until early October. Excursions range from sedate Class I runs (ideal for families) up to thrilling Class Vs. A note of warning: white-water rafting can be dangerous. There were four fatalities on one day alone in 2010 and another nine in the 20 years proceeding that.

Prices start from Nkr775 for a 3½-hour trip; there are also five-hour trips (from Nkr1050) through to multiday trips (from Nkr2900). A shorter, family-friendly rafting trip is also available (Nkr650). These prices are approximate and depend on the company you use, but most charge, and offer, roughly the same.

In addition to rafting, most operators also organise riverboarding (from Nkr990), low-level rock climbing (from Nkr490), canyoning (from Nkr820), caving (from Nkr690) and hiking.

Go Rafting   RAFTING
(☑61 23 50 00; www.gorafting.no) About 8km west of Sjoa along Rv257.

Heidal Rafting   RAFTING
(☑61 23 60 37; www.heidalrafting.no) Just 1km west of E6 along Rv257.

Sjoa Rafting   RAFTING
(☑90 07 10 00; www.sjoarafting.com; Nedre Heidal) Some 7.5km upstream from Sjoa along Rv257. Also offers accommodation.

Sjoa Rafting Senter NWR   RAFTING
(☑47 66 06 80; www.sjoaraftingsenter.no; Varphaugen Gård) About 3km upstream from Sjoa along Rv257.

Villmarken Kaller   RAFTING
(☑90 52 57 03; www.villmarken-kaller.no) About 20km upstream from Sjoa along Rv257.

Sjoa Kajakksenter   KAYAKING
(☑90 06 62 22; www.kajakksenteret.no; Nedre Heidal) Around 8km west of Sjoa along Rv257; this place runs kayaking trips and courses.

Sleeping

Most of activities operators also have accommodation, with huts, camping and a few double rooms.

Sjoa Camping   CAMPGROUND €
(☑99 52 99 51; www.sjoa.no; campsites Nkr150, 1- to 5-bed huts per person Nkr290-450; ⊗Jun-Aug)

Sjoa Camping, down by the river bank, is a pleasant grassy site with a front-row seat for some of the minor rapids. Cabins are very simple but have basic cooking equipment and a bargain price. There's lots of tent-friendly soft grass.

Sjoa Vandrerhjem HOSTEL €
(☑ 61 23 62 00; www.heidalrafting.no; dm Nkr340, s/d/family Nkr770/975/1040; ☺ mid-May–mid-Sep; P ☎) This atmospheric hillside hostel is run by Heidal Rafting (p141). Rooms are simple, but of a high quality; dinner costs Nkr150 and is served in the wonderful 1747 log farmhouse building. To get there cross the bridge over the river near the campsite and follow the signs for Heidal Rafting for around 1km.

❶ Getting There & Away

Nor-Way Bussekspress bus routes link Sjoa with Bergen and Trondheim.

Ringebu

POP 4540

The southernmost small community of Gudbrandsdalen (the narrow river valley that stretches for 200km between Lake Mjøsa and Dombås), Ringebu is worth a detour for its lovely stave church.

◉ Sights

Ringebu Stave Church CHURCH
(Ringebu Stavkyrkje; www.stavechurch.no; adult/child Nkr50/30; ☺ 8am-6pm Jul, 9am-5pm late May-Aug) A church has existed on this site since the arrival of Christianity in the 11th century. The current version, which remains the local parish church, dates from around 1220, but was restored in the 17th century when the distinctive red tower was attached. Inside, there's a statue of St Laurence dating from around 1250, as well as some crude runic inscriptions.

Entrance to the grounds themselves are free and the gate is open year-round. The church is around 2km south of town, signposted off the E6. It hosts occasional concerts of Norwegian folk music in summer.

Ringebu Samlingene NOTABLE BUILDING
(☑ 61 28 27 00; Vekkomsvegen 433; adult/child Nkr50/30, joint ticket with stave church adult/child Nkr80/40; ☺ 10am-5pm Jun-Aug) Some 300m uphill to the east of the Stave Church are the buildings from 1743 Ringebu Samlingene, which served as the vicarage until

1991. Guided tours are available and there's a cafe within the grounds.

❶ Information

Tourist office (☑ 61 28 47 00; www.ringebu. com; ☺ 8am-6pm Mon-Thu, 8am-8pm Fri, 10am-1pm Sat, 5-8pm Sun mid-Jun–mid-Aug, 8am-3.30pm Mon-Fri rest of year) The small tourist office is inside the train station.

❶ Getting There & Away

Lavprisekspressen buses to Oslo (Nkr299; 3½ hours) and Trondheim (Nkr439; five hours) pass through one or two times a day.

Trains go to Oslo (Nkr299 to Nkr488, 3¼ hours, four daily) and Trondheim (Nkr299 to Nkr603, 3¾ hours, four daily)

WESTERN CENTRAL NORWAY

Lom

POP 2410

If you were to set up a town as a travellers' gateway, you'd put it somewhere like Lom, in the heart of some of Norway's most spectacular mountain scenery. Rapids cascade through the village centre, houses in dark wood climb the steep hills, and roads out of town lead to Geiranger (74km) at the edge of Norway's famous fjords, via the staggering Sognefjellet Rd which winds across the top of the Jotunheimen National Park. Aside from its location, Lom's main attraction is a lovely stave church.

◉ Sights

Lom Stavkyrkje CHURCH
(adult/child Nkr55/20; ☺ 9am-7pm 9 Jun–mid-Aug, 9am-5pm late Aug, 10am-4pm mid-May–8Jun & Sep) This delightful Norman-style stave church, in the centre of town on a rise by the water, is one of Norway's finest. Still the functioning local church, it was constructed in 1170, extended in 1634 and given its current cruciform shape with the addition of two naves in 1663.

Guided tours explain the interior paintings and Jakop Sæterdalen's chancel arch and pulpit (from 1793). At night, the church is lit to fairy-tale effect. Entry to the grounds, which are open year-round, is free.

Lom Stavkyrkje Museum MUSEUM
(☑ 61 21 19 33; www.gbdmuseum.no; admission Nkr10; ⊙9am-8pm mid-Jun–mid-Aug, 9am-4pm May–mid-Jun & mid-Aug–Christmas, 10am-3pm Jan-Apr) In the souvenir shop next to the stave church, there's a small museum about the stave church.

Fossheim Steinsenter MUSEUM
(Stone & Mineral Museum; ☑ 61 21 14 60; www. fossheimsteinsenter.no; ⊙10am-7pm Mon-Sat, 10am-6pm Sun mid-Jun–mid-Aug, 10am-4pm May & mid-Aug–Sep) FREE The fascinating Fossheim Steinsenter combines an impressive selection of rare and beautiful rocks, minerals, fossils, gems and jewellery for sale, and a large museum of geological specimens from all over Norway and the world; don't miss the downstairs fossil exhibition. The knowledgable owners of the centre are especially proud of the Norwegian national stone, thulite. It was discovered in 1820 and is now quarried in Lom; the reddish colour is derived from traces of manganese.

Norsk Fjellmuseum MUSEUM
(Norwegian Mountain Museum; ☑ 61 21 16 00; www. fjell.museum.no; adult/child 12-16yrs Nkr70/40; ⊙9am-6pm Mon-Fri, to 4pm Sat, to 3pm Sun mid-Jun–mid-Aug, to 4pm Mon-Sat & 3pm Sun mid-May–Jun & mid-Aug–early Sep) Acting as the visitors centre for Jotunheimen National Park, this worthwhile museum contains mountaineering memorabilia, and exhibits on natural history (the woolly mammoth is a highlight) and cultural and industrial activity in the Norwegian mountains. There's also an excellent 10-minute mountain slide show and, upstairs, a scale model of the park.

Lom Bygdamuseum MUSEUM
(Lom Folk Museum; ☑ 47 45 15 23; www.gudbrandsdalsmusea.no; adult/child Nkr20/free; ⊙11am-4pm Tue-Sun Jul–mid-Aug) Behind Norsk Fjellmuseum, this museum is a collection of 19th-century farm buildings, several *stabbur* (elevated store houses), an old hut (it's claimed that St Olav slept here) and a summer mountain dairy.

🏃 Activities

The tourist office has details of hikes, glacier walks and ice-climbing in Jotunheimen National Park.

Hiking
Although most of the serious trekking takes place in neighbouring Jotunheimen National Park, there are several hiking trails closer to town. Many of these are passable much later into the winter than those in the high, snowbound mountains; ask the tourist office for maps, directions and its terrific *Walks in Lom* pamphlet, which has a map and detailed route descriptions.

The three most popular hikes:

➡ **Lomseggen** (1289m) Five-hour return hike past the century-old stone cottage called Smithbue, with some excellent views of Ottadalen, Bøverdalen and Norway's highest peak, Galdhøpiggen (2469m), en route.

➡ **Tronoberget** Three-hour return hike up the mountain that lies west across the river from Lom, with excellent views of the peaks of Reinheimen National Park.

➡ **Soleggen & Læshø** (1204m) Five-hour return hike above Lom with views of the Rondane, Dovrefjell, Reinheimen, Breheimen and Jotunheimen massifs.

White-Water Rafting & Other Activities
If Sjoa is too much of a scene, white-water rafting is possible from Skjåk, 18km upstream from Lom.

Lom & Skjåk Adventure ADVENTURE SPORTS
(☑ 47 26 16 72; www.lsadventure.no) Activities centre 10 minutes' drive northwest of Lom along the E15. Lom & Skjåk Adventure arranges white-water rafting, climbing, kayaking, caving, canyoning, hiking and riverboarding.

Naturopplevingar HIKING, SKIING
(☑ 61 21 11 55; www.naturopplevingar.no) No white-water rafting, but ski tours, hiking and climbing.

🛏 Sleeping & Eating

Accommodation prices in Lom are generally a little higher than elsewhere in central Norway.

Nordal Turistsenter Camping CAMPING €
(☑ 61 21 93 00; www.nordalturistsenter.no; campsites Nkr225, cabins with/without bathroom Nkr835/475; ⊙May-Oct; 🛜) Unusually this campsite, which is run under the Nordal Turistsenter banner, is slap in the centre of town. This means fairly small pitches and a lack of rural peace, but it does allow you to walk to the town's various sights.

Fossheim Turisthotell HOTEL €€
(☑ 61 21 95 00; www.fossheimhotel.no; hotel s/d Nkr1150/1590, hotel annex s/d Nkr995/1295, cabins

Nkr1650; P🌐) This historic family hotel at the eastern end of town has all-wood rooms in the main hotel building (we especially like rooms 401 and 402 for the balconies and views). There are also luxurious log cabins with modern interiors and simpler, cheaper rooms (some with good views) in the adjacent annexe; although annexe rooms have dreadful sound insulation.

Nordal Turistsenter
HOTEL €€

(📞61 21 93 00; www.nordalturistsenter.no; s/d/f Nkr990/1310/1830; ⊙Apr–mid-Dec; 🌐) A busy, rambling place in the centre of town, the Nordal Turistsenter has comfy rooms with thick sheepskin rugs on the floor. It also has a cosy pub and a casual cafeteria-style restaurant that serves simple meals (from Nkr175).

Fossberg Hotell
HOTEL €€

(📞61 21 22 50; www.fossberg.no; s/d Nkr1040/1440; P🌐🍽) An appealing enough, though rather overpriced, place in the centre of town with tidy, pine-clad rooms. It also has a range of cabins and apartments, and a popular cafeteria where the food is nothing to write home about, but the outdoor tables are a pleasant place to do so.

Kuba–Kafe Isbar
CAFE €€

(light meals & mains Nkr65-155; ⊙10am-11pm mid-Jun–mid-Aug, shorter hours rest of year) In the centre of town, this informal cafe is probably the best place in Lom for a quick, no-frills meal. Aside from the usual snacks and fast-food choices, it does a small selection of traditional Norwegian dishes, such as sour-cream porridge and smoked roasted reindeer meat.

Fossheim Turisthotell Restaurant
NORWEGIAN €€€

(📞61 21 95 00; www.fossheimhotel.no; Fossheim Turisthotell; set dinner menu from Nkr380; ⊙1-3.30pm & 7-10pm) The traditional Norwegian food at the restaurant of the Fossheim Turisthotell is the best in town, and although it constitutes a memorable meal for Norway, it wouldn't really stand out anywhere in southern Europe. Specialities include wild trout, reindeer, elk and ptarmigan.

🛍 Shopping

Brimi Bue
FOOD

(www.brimibue.no; Fossheim Turisthotell; ⊙10am-4.30pm Mon-Fri, to 3pm Sat Jun-Sep) The small Brimi Bue, next to the Fossheim Turisthotell,

has cookbooks, organic foods and kitchenware.

ℹ Information

Tourist office (📞61 21 29 90; www.visitjotunheimen.com; ⊙9am-4pm Mon-Sat, 9am-3pm Sun Jul–mid-Aug, 9am-4pm Mon-Sat mid-Aug–early Sep; 🌐) The helpful Lom tourist office, in the Norsk Fjellmuseum, dispenses advice and brochures. It also provides free wi-fi access.

ℹ Getting There & Away

Three daily Nordfjordekspressen bus services run from Oslo to Lom (Nkr509, 6½ hours). There are local buses to/from Otta (Nkr129, 1½ hours, six daily). There's also a daily bus through the Jotunheimen National Park to Sogndal (Nkr250, 3½ hours, two daily) from late June to the end of August. You'll probably never go on a more impressive bus ride.

Around Lom

East of Lom, just off the Rv15, a couple of sites pay homage to Arne Brimi, perhaps Norway's best-loved celebrity chef.

🛏 Sleeping

Brimisæter
FARMSTAY €

(📞91 13 75 58; www.brimi-seter.no; dm Nkr350, d from Nkr1000; P🌐♿) This former summer mountain dairy has a simple but lovely rural family ambience and plenty of animals that kids will love. Accommodation is in a mixture of dorms with beds arranged in a long line half built into the wall, and private rooms. Good meals are available.

Brimi-Fjellstugu
LODGE €€

(📞61 23 98 12; www.brimiland.no; r per person from Nkr600, dinner menus Nkr395-525) 🌱 Owned by celebrity chef Arne Brimi, this delightful mountain hotel offers high levels of comfort in a stirring mountain setting. Meals are prepared by the man himself. This means you'll be in for a real culinary treat.

Vågå Gardshotell
HOTEL €€

(www.gardshotell.kulturgardar.no; per person from Nkr650) These converted 19th-century farm buildings located just off the Rv15 between Lom and Vågå are a wonderful alternative to hotels, and make a great place to base yourself if you'll be in the area for more than a night.

Jotunheimen National Park

This is it. This is the big one. The high peaks and glaciers of the 1151-sq-km Jotunheimen National Park, whose name means the 'Home of the Giants', make for Norway's best-loved, busiest and, arguably, most spectacular wilderness destination. Seemingly hundreds of hiking routes lead through ravine-like valleys past deep lakes, plunging waterfalls and 60 glaciers to the tops of all the peaks in Norway over 2300m; these include Galdhøpiggen (the highest peak in northern Europe at 2469m), Glittertind (2452m) and Store Skagastølstind (2403m). By one count, there are more than 275 summits above 2000m inside the park.

For park information, contact Lom tourist office (p144).

◎ Sights & Activities

★ Sognefjellet Road   SCENIC DRIVE
(www.turistveg.no) Town councillors of the world: you may have built a lot of roads in your time – many of them are probably very useful – but chances are none of them are as spectacular as this one. Snaking through Jotunheimen National Park (and providing access to most of the trailheads), the stunningly scenic Sognefjellet Rd (Rv55) connects Lustrafjorden with Lom, and is billed as 'the road over the roof of Norway'. With little doubt it's one of Norway's most beautiful drives.

Constructed in 1939 by unemployed youths, the road rises to a height of 1434m, making it the highest mountain road in northern Europe. It is one of Norway's 18 'National Tourist Routes'.

Access from the southwest is via multiple hairpin bends climbing up beyond the treeline to Turtagrø, with a stirring view of the Skagastølstindane mountains on your right. If you're coming from Lom, the ascent is more gradual, following beautiful Bøverdalen, the valley of the Bøvra River, with its lakes, glacial rivers, grass-roofed huts and patches of pine forest. The road summit on Sognefjell offers superb views.

The snow sometimes doesn't melt until early July, although the road is usually open from May to September. The road can get very narrow and snow is often piled metres high on either side. Ample camping and other accommodation options line the road.

Although this road is mainly traversed by motorised transport, the Sognefjellet Rd has legendary status among cyclists and frequently appears on lists of the world's most spectacular cycle routes. It's a serious undertaking that requires high levels of fitness and perfect brakes.

From mid-June to late August, a daily bus runs between Lom and Sogndal (Nkr250, 3½ hours) via Sognefjellet Rd.

Mímisbrunnr Klimapark & Istunnel   TUNNEL
(www.mimisbrunnr.no; adult/child Nkr300/150; ⊙ guided tours 10.30am & 2pm late Jun–late Aug, weekends only late Aug–mid-Sep) Close to the Galdhøpiggen Summer Ski Centre, this 70m-long ice tunnel has an exhibition on the region's natural history and climate change. Buy your tickets online at least 24 hours before your planned visit or from the Lom tourist office (p144) or Juvasshytta (☑61 21 15 50; www.juvasshytta.no; per person Nkr380-500).

Turtagrø to Øvre Årdal   SCENIC DRIVE
The 33km toll mountain road between Turtagrø and the industrial town of Øvre Årdal is one of Norway's most scenic short drives. Open from late May to October, it runs above the treeline through wild and lonely country. From late June to late August, the route is served by two daily buses. The vehicle toll (Nkr75) is collected by a gatekeeper at the pass (1315m).

Randsverk to Fagernes   SCENIC DRIVE
Between Randsverk and Fagernes, the Rv51 climbs through the hilly and forested Sjodalen country onto a vast upland with far-ranging views of peaks and glaciers; it's used by hikers heading for Jotunheimen's eastern reaches. En route it passes the DNT hut at Gjendesheim, the launching point for the popular day hike along the Besseggen ridge.

From mid-June to early September, two daily buses run between Otta and Gol, via Vågå, Randsverk, Gjendesheim, Valdresflya and Fagernes. You'll have to change at Gjendesheim. From Fagernes, the trip to Gjendesheim takes two hours and costs Nkr126.

Jotunheimvegen   SCENIC DRIVE
Branching off the Rv51 at Bygdin, the 45km-long Jotunheimvegen to Skåbu is quiet and picturesque. It's usually open from mid-June until October, depending on the weather,

Jotunheimen National Park

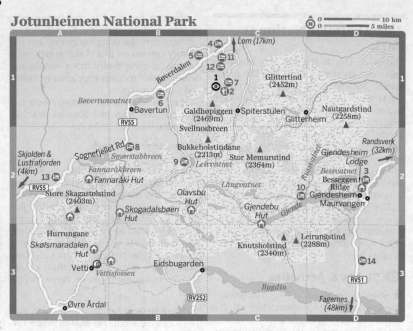

Jotunheimen National Park

and you pay a Nkr100 toll; motorcycles travel for free. There's no public transport along the route but there are campsites at Beitostølen and Skåbu. The route also links up with Peer Gynt Vegen (p128).

Galdhøpiggen Summer Ski Centre
SKIING

(📞 61 21 17 50; www.gpss.no; ski/snowboard rental Nkr300/300, adult/child day lift pass Nkr370/300) This ski centre, at 1850m on the icy heights of Norway's highest mountain, is a stunning spot for summer skiing. From Galdesand on the Rv55, follow the Galdhøpiggen road (Nkr100 toll) to its end at 1841m. The main season runs from June to mid-November. Apart from the skiing opportunities, this road takes you to the highest point reachable by road in Norway.

🛏 Sleeping & Eating

DNT maintains staffed huts along most of the routes and there's also a choice of private lodges by the main roads. The majority of accommodation is to be found along the Sognefjellet Rd. On the Rv51, options are more limited to campsites, although there are some lodges in the vicinity of Gjendesheim, which are handy for an early start on the Besseggen ridge. Most open from May to September.

Krossbu Turiststasjon LODGE €
(☑61 21 29 22; www.krossbu.no; dm from Nkr390, s Nkr490, d from Nkr900; P 🛜) Excellent-value, cosy wood-lined rooms look out over a landscape of inspiring bleakness. Meals are available. Dozens of impressive walks start from here including a guided glacier walk (Nkr500 per person, minimum four people).

Bøverdalen Vandrerhjem HOSTEL €
(☑61 21 20 64; www.hihostels.no; Bøverdalen; dm Nkr180, s/d/f with shared bathroom Nkr300/500/600, cabins Nkr600; P 🛜) This fine riverside hostel has a small cafe, tidy rooms, good cabins and delightful surrounds to enjoy once the day trippers have returned home. It's popular so be sure to book ahead in summer. Breakfast costs adult/child Nkr85/55.

Gjendesheim Lodge HUT €
(☑61 23 89 10; www.gjendesheim.no; Gjendesheim; dm adult/child Nkr210/105, r 4-6 beds adult/child Nkr300/150, r 1-3 beds adult/child Nkr350/175; 🛜) At the trailhead to the Besseggen trek, on the eastern side of the park, this highly organised place has good-quality accommodation and meals. It's very popular so book ahead.

Valdresflya Vandrerhjem HOSTEL €
(☑90 12 23 51; Valdresflya; dm Nkr280) Fifteen minutes' drive south from Gjendesheim, this rather uninspiring hostel in a bitterly cold moorland setting prides itself on being the highest in northern Europe (1389m). There's no guest kitchen, but breakfast costs Nkr80 and meals around Nkr100.

A number of walks start from here ranging from a child-friendly 3km round-trip hike up Fisketjernnuten (1527m) to far more challenging treks.

★Elvesæter Hotell HOTEL €€
(☑61 21 99 00; www.ton.no; Bøverdalen; s/d from Nkr850/1150; P 🛜) 🏊 Run by the sixth generation of the Elvesæter family, this gorgeous hotel has pretty rooms and lovely architecture. It's high on novelty value as it's adjacent to the Sagasøyla, a 32m-high carved wooden pillar tracing Norwegian history from unification in 872 to the 1814 constitution. Decent set three-course dinners are Nkr325. A great Jotunheimen base.

Storhaugen HOTEL €€
(www.storhaugengard.no; Bøverdalen; cabins Nkr700-3000; P 🛜🅿) At their traditional farm, the Slettede family offers an array

of different accommodation options in modern, fully equipped cabins and apartments with views of both the Jotunheimen heights and Bøverdalen. Children will love the farm animals. It's all great value, but they don't provide meals so you'll need to come prepared.

At Galdesand, turn south on the Galdhøpiggen road and continue 1.5km to the signposted turn-off for Storhaugen.

Jotunheimen Fjellstue LODGE €€
(☑61 21 29 18; www.jotunheimen-fjellstue.no; s/d from Nkr1045/1390) From the outside this modern mountain lodge is hugely outdone by its breathtaking surrounds, but inside are light and airy rooms that are better than many in the area. There's a busy in-house restaurant and cafe.

Bessheim LODGE €€
(☑61 23 89 13; www.bessheim.no; r per person Mon-Fri/Sat & Sun Nkr560/690, cabins Nkr450-1575, bedding Nkr100; P 🛜) This superslick and organised mountain lodge, just 3km east of Gjendesheim, is the best place to stay in the vicinity of the Besseggen ridge. Three-course set dinners cost Nkr335. Book ahead in summer.

★Turtagrø Hotel LODGE €€€
(☑57 68 08 00; www.turtagro.no; Fortun; campsites Nkr125, dm from Nkr550, annexe tw Nkr770, s/d Nkr1850/2760, tower ste per person Nkr1595; P 🛜) This historic hiking and mountaineering centre is a friendly yet laid-back base for exploring Jotunheimen and Hurrungane, whatever your budget. The main building has wonderful views and supremely comfortable rooms. The hotel also conducts weeklong climbing courses and guided day trips (hiking, climbing and skiing) and there's a great bar full of historic Norwegian mountaineering photos.

The dining room serves hearty meals (three-course meal Nkr450).

Røisheim Hotel HISTORIC HOTEL €€€
(☑61 21 20 31; www.roisheim.no; Bøverdalen; d from Nkr1500; P 🛜) 🏊 This charming place combines architecturally stunning buildings that date back to 1858 with modern comforts, although there are no TVs. Some rooms have wonderful baths made out of old barrels. Apart from the charming accommodation, the appeal lies in the meals, which are prepared by Ingrid Hov Lunde, one of the country's best-loved chefs.

HIKING IN JOTUNHEIMEN

Jotunheimen's hiking possibilities are practically endless and all are spectacular. The best maps are Statens Kartverk's *Jotunheimen Aust* and *Jotunheimen Vest* (1:50,000; Nkr99 each). The tourist office (p144) in Lom can offer advice, route descriptions and guided hikes through the park, while **Top of Norway** (www.ton.no), which is based at the Elvesæter Hotel (p147) and Leirvassbu Lodge, organises guided hikes, as well as glacier walks, rock climbing, ice-climbing and caving from around Nkr500 per person.

Krossbu

Krossbu Turiststasjon (p147), near the head of Bøverdalen, lies at the outset of a tangle of hiking routes, including a short day trip to the Smørstabbreen glacier.

Galdhøpiggen

With its dramatic cirques, arêtes and glaciers, Galdhøpiggen is a fairly tough, eight-hour day hike (1470m of ascent) from Spiterstulen, where the toll road begins. Although the trail is well marked, you'll need a map and compass.

Øvre Årdal

From Øvre Årdal, head 12km northeast up the Utladalen valley to the farm Vetti, from where hiking tracks lead to Vettisfossen, Norway's highest free-falling waterfall (275m), and to the unstaffed hut at **Skølsmaradalen**. This is an alternative access route, via upper Utladalen, to longer hikes in Jotunheimen.

Hurrungane

The fabulous Hurrungane massif rises darkly above the westernmost end of the park. Although some of these prominent peaks are accessible to experienced mountaineers and, in some cases, skilled scramblers, most hikers head eastwards from Turtagrø Hotel (p147). From the hotel, a four-hour hike will take you to Norway's highest Den Norske Turistforening (DNT) hut, **Fannaråki**, on the summit of Fannaråken (2068m). While the hut itself is your typical DNT deal (ie clean and basic), the views are some of the best from accommodation anywhere in Norway, taking in a representative sample of the Hurrungane massif and the glacier country to the west; to reach the hut, ask for directions at the hotel. An alternative to returning to the hotel is to descend the eastern slope along the well-marked track to Keisarpasset and thence back to Ekrehytta. To launch into a multiday trip, you can also descend Gjertvassdalen to **Skogadalsbøen hut**, then choose from one of many routes eastwards through Jotunheimen.

Leirvassbu Lodge LODGE €€€
(☎ 61 21 12 10; www.leirvassbu.no; s/d without bath Nkr895/1540, s/d with bath Nkr1100/1900; 🅿 🛜) Leirvassbu, a typical mountain lodge at 1400m and beside Leirvatnet lake, is a good hiking base. Guided glacier walks on Smørstabbreen are available. Despite its large capacity, and slightly optimistic prices, it can get crowded. The toll on the access road is a wallet-lightening Nkr100 per car.

HARDANGERVIDDA

The desolate and beautiful Hardangervidda plateau, part of the 3430-sq-km **Hardangervidda National Park**, Norway's largest, ranges across an otherworldly tundra landscape that's the southernmost refuge of the Arctic fox (the natural population of which has increased through reintroduction programs) and home to Norway's largest herd of wild reindeer. Long a trade and travel route connecting eastern and western Norway, it's now crossed by the main railway and road routes between Oslo and Bergen.

Reindeer numbers have dropped in recent years, from a high of 19,000 in 1998 to around 7000. This fall in numbers is, however, part of a program of resource management by the park's authorities, as a ban on hunting until recently meant that herd numbers became too large and reindeer body weights began to fall dangerously due to a lack of sufficient fodder.

Apart from Finse and Geilo, Hardangervidda National Park is accessible from

Besseggen

No discussion of hiking in Jotunheimen would be complete without mention of Besseggen ridge, the most popular hike in Norway. Indeed, some travellers find it *too* popular, with at least 30,000 hikers walking it in the three months a year that it's passable. However, it's popular for a very good reason and if you don't mind sacrificing solitude for one of Norway's most spectacular treks, you won't regret it. Henrik Ibsen wrote of Besseggen: 'It cuts along with an edge like a scythe for miles and miles...And scars and glaciers sheer down the precipice to the glassy lakes, 1600ft below on either side.' One of Peer Gynt's mishaps was a plunge down to the lake on the back of a reindeer.

The day hike between **Memurubu Lodge** and Gjendesheim (p147) takes about six hours and climbs to a high point of 1743m. Most people do it in this direction but there's nothing to stop you doing it in reverse, except that if you're planning on returning to the trek start point, and your car, then you need to time your walk well in order to get the last ferry back (4.30pm). From the carpark (Nkr100) at Gjendesheim hop on the **M/S Gjende** (www.gjende.no) ferry that plies Gjende lake to Memurubu (adult/child Nkr120/60, 30 minutes, departures Gjendesheim–Memurubu 7.45am, 8am, 9.30am, 10.30am and 2.25pm, departures Memurubu–Gjendesheim 8.45am, 8.55am, 10am, 10.55am and 4.35pm). Note that at busy times (which is most of the July to August period) long queues can form for the ferry and the boats operate a near continuous service.

From Memurubu follow the signs steeply uphill. After much huffing and puffing you emerge on a flatter plateau. The trail is very obvious and it would be hard to get lost. The route winds past Bjørnbøltjørn, a small glacial lake, and offers amazing views down to the much larger, turquoise Gjende lake, which gains its extraordinary colour thanks to the 20,000 tonnes of glacial silt dumped into it each year by the Memuru River. After an undulating couple of hours you reach the steepest part of the climb up onto the Besseggen ridge proper. From afar this looks very narrow and precarious, and although you do have to do quite a lot of scrambling and have a head for heights, it's actually not as hard, or narrow, as it seems from a distance. Once up onto the ridge the route climbs gently through scree slopes to the summit of the Veslefjellet plateau before a fairly tame walk back down to Gjendesheim.

The walk is accessible to anyone of reasonable fitness. We have seen lots of families with small children doing it, although you will have to carry them up parts of it and the climb up the Besseggen ridge becomes somewhat trickier with a young child clinging to you.

Rjukan and Eidfjord; there's an excellent national park centre at the latter.

Geilo

POP 2363

At Geilo (pronounced yei-lo), midway between Oslo and Bergen, you can practically step off the train onto a ski lift. In summer there's plenty of fine hiking in the area. A popular nearby destination is the expansive plateau-like mountain called Hallingskarvet, frosted with several small glaciers. Apart from hiking across the Hardangervidda, it's possible to go glacier trekking on Hardangerjøkulen (1862m), horse-riding, white-water rafting, riverboarding and go on elk safaris. For more information on these and other activities, contact the tourist office.

🛏 Sleeping & Eating

Geilo has dozens of accommodation choices, most of which are geared towards the adventure and outdoor-activity crowds. The tourist office has a full list.

⭐ **Ro Hotell & Kro**　　　　HOTEL €
(📋 32 09 08 99; www.rohotell.no; Geilovegen 55; s/d Nkr730/950, with shared bathroom Nkr470/670; 📶) At first glance this cheap place next door to the train station doesn't look promising, but its large and spotless rooms, good sound insulation, comfy chairs and desk, helpful staff and fast wi-fi that reaches all the rooms add up to as good a value as Norway gets.

Øen Turistsenter & Geilo Vandrerhjem HOSTEL €
(☎ 32 08 70 60; www.oenturist.no; Lienvegen 137; dm Nkr290, huts Nkr495-900, bed sheets Nkr95; P 🛜) A kilometre or so east of the town centre along the Rv7, this hostel has tidy cabins and dorms but little atmosphere. Its roadside location isn't ideal.

Dr Holms Hotel HOTEL €€€
(☎ 32 09 57 00; www.drholms.no; s/d from Nkr995/1490; P 🛜🏊) This huge, white, wood-panelled hotel, which lords it over the train station, styles itself as a mountain lodge and has been a reliable source of a good night's sleep for over a hundred years. Rooms are divided into those in the old section, which have the most character, and those in the new annexe.

Prices during the winter ski season are much higher than those quoted here.

★**Halling-Stuene** NORWEGIAN €€€
(☎ 32 09 12 50; www.hallingstuene.no; Geilovegen 56; mains Nkr200-380; ⊗1-10pm Mon-Fri & Sun, to 11pm Sat) This is the town's stand-out restaurant and it offers high-quality, traditional Norwegian food that's been simmered, boiled and fired with love by celebrity-chef Frode Aga.

ℹ️ Information

Geilo Tourist Office (☎ 32 09 59 00; www.geilo.no; Vesleslåttveien 13; ⊗ 8.30am-6pm Mon-Fri, 9am-5pm Sat, 11am-5pm Sun) The tourist office can book activities and accommodation, and suggest hiking routes.

ℹ️ Getting There & Away

Most visitors arrive on the train between Oslo (Nkr508, 3½ hours, five daily) and Bergen (Nkr460, three hours).

Finse

Finse, which lies at 1222m near the Hardangerjøkulen icecap, is accessible only by train, bike or foot, and is *the* place in central Norway for a wild, Arctic-like wilderness experience. Its bleak and remote lakeside setting is addictive, whether seen sparkling under blue skies with a fresh coat of snow or on a cold, grey day when the winds lash across the tundra and glaciers.

You only need walk a few minutes away from the tiny train station to find total silence, but if you prefer your rest time to be more adrenalin-filled then the countryside surrounding Finse offers nordic skiing in winter and hiking in summer, not to mention what could be Norway's steepest mountain-bike ride.

🏃 Activities

Finse is the starting point for some exceptional treks, including the popular four-hour trek to the Blåisen glacier tip of

---

HIKING THE HARDANGERVIDDA

Trekking through the western Hardangervidda is possible only in July and August – for the rest of the time, snow and the possibility of sudden changes in weather conditions make setting out hazardous; new snow is a possibility at any time of year. Before exploring the park, visit the outstanding Hardangervidda Natursenter (p187), which sells maps. This centre can offer advice on hiking routes, and has a wonderful exhibition on the park. Hikers and skiers will find the Turkart series (Nkr149 to Nkr279), at a scale of 1:100,000, to be the maps of choice. You should also pick up **Hardangervidda Hytteringen** (www.hardangerviddanett.no), which gives a rundown on mountain huts. The Bergen Turlag DNT office (p171) is another good source of information.

There are numerous trailheads, among them the waterfalls at Vøringfoss, Finse or Geilo. Some of our favourite routes:

➡ **Finse to Vøringfoss** (two days) The steepest hiking country in Hardangervidda, skirting the Hardangerjøkulen glacier and overnighting in Rembesdalsseter; you could also make the four- to five-hour (one-way) detour to Kjeåsen Farm (p187).

➡ **Vøringfoss to Kinsarvik via Harteigen** (three days) To the picturesque mountain of Harteigen with its panoramic views of Hardangervidda, then down the monk's stairway to Kinsarvik.

➡ **Halne to Dyranut via Rauhelleren** (two days) Trails lead south off the Rv7. There's a strong chance hikers will encounter reindeer herds.

RALLARVEGEN

The Rallarvegen, or Navvies' Rd, was constructed as a supply route for Oslo–Bergen railway workers (the railway opened on 27 November 1909). Nowadays, this 83km route of asphalt and gravel extends from Haugastøl through Finse and all the way down to Flåm, and is open only to bicycle and foot traffic; the distance from Finse to Flåm is 56km. Following this route down to Flåm means that you get the best of the stunning scenery of the Flåmsbana railway, with the additional benefit of being able to stop whenever you like to enjoy the view. The popular stretch between Vatnahalsen and Flåm descends 865m in 29km. Brakes on bikes usually have to be changed after just one descent

Cyclists and hikers will find optimum conditions between mid-July and mid-September. To rent bikes (Nkr595 to Nkr900 depending on the date and type of bike) ready for the Rallarvegen challenge, contact **Finse 1222** (☑ 56 52 71 00; www.finse1222. no); bikes must be booked before arriving in Finse due to high demand in summer, and prices include the return bike transportation fee on the train.

Hardangerjøkulen. It's a stunning walk, but no matter how tempting it looks do *not* ever attempt to walk on the glacier unless on a guided glacier walk led by an expert. Adding interest to your hike is the fact that scenes set on the planet Hof in *The Empire Strikes Back* were filmed around the glacier.

It's also possible to walk around the glacier and down to Vøringfoss. The wonderful three- or four-day Finse–Aurland trek follows Aurlandsdalen down to Aurlandsfjorden and has a series of DNT and private mountain huts a day's walk apart.

Glacier Walk　　　　WALKING
(☑ 99 33 12 22; www.joklagutane.no; per person Nkr550) Well-run, highly exhilarating glacier walks lasting roughly seven hours (with around two hours spent actually on the glacier) take you onto the edge of the ice-sheet to peer down into crevices and possibly clamber into an ice-cave, as well as climb right up onto the vast domed icecap summit. Tours leave from the train station at 11.30am. Book in advance.

No matter what the temperature is like elsewhere in Finse you can be certain it will be bitterly cold on the ice sheet. Bring lots of warm, waterproof layers and gloves, hat and sunglasses. If you have children under about 12 years old with you, it's better to organise a private hike because many children find the long walk, the cold and the general fear of the ice a bit much.

🛏 Sleeping & Eating

There are only two places to stay and nowhere to eat outside of the dining rooms of these hotels. Many people wild camp near the lake shore.

Finsehytta　　　　LODGE €
(☑ 56 52 67 32; www.finsehytta.turistforeningen.no; dm Nkr210-350; ☺ mid-Mar–late Sep; 🖎) Most budget travellers stay at the staffed DNT hut, Finsehytta, which has decent dorms, some of which sleep only two or three people making it a fine choice for couples and families. A set three-course dinner costs Nkr350.

★ Finse 1222　　　　LODGE €€€
(☑ 56 52 71 00; www.finse1222.no; full board s/d from Nkr1750/2800; 🖎) The exceptionally pleasant Finse 1222, right by the tiny train station, has modern, tidy, well-insulated rooms, many of which have outrageous views over the lake and glacier. Parts of the lodge are actually built out of old trains. Finse 1222 is also the starting point and best source of information for many of the activities in the region.

Set meals, which are so full of flavour and imagination that they have to be ranked among Norway's finest eating experiences, are taken in a dining room with huge floor-to-ceiling windows and views over the Arctic landscape.

❶ Getting There & Away

Five daily trains run between Oslo (from Nkr593, 4½ hours) and Bergen (from Nkr368, 2½ hours) via Finse.

Bergen & the Southwestern Fjords

HIGHEST ELEV 1654M

Best Places to Eat

➜ Lysverket (p166)

➜ Colonialen Litteraturhuset (p165)

➜ Renaa Matbaren (p202)

➜ Pingvinen (p165)

➜ Bien (p166)

Best Places to Stay

➜ Hotel Park (p162)

➜ Stalheim Hotel (p184)

➜ Utne Hotel (p190)

➜ Patina (p183)

➜ Sandven Hotel (p185)

Why Go?

If you could visit only one region of Norway and hope to grasp the essence of the country's appeal, this would be our choice.

Cool, cultured Bergen is one of the world's most beautiful cities, with its streets of white-washed timber cottages climbing steep hillsides up from busy Vågen Harbour. It's a destination in itself but also the ideal starting point for a journey into splendid Hardangerfjord, with its gorgeous fjord-side villages, or the vast Sognefjorden network. En route to the latter, Voss is Norway's destination of choice for thrill-seekers.

Down south, boom-town Stavanger is a diverting staging post for Lysefjord, home to two of Norway's most recognisable images, impossibly high above the ice-blue waters of the fjord: Preikestolen (Pulpit Rock) and Kjeragbolten.

When to Go
Bergen

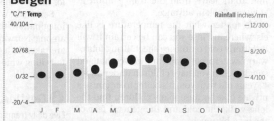

Jun Bergen International Festival and Voss' Veko for extreme sports and music.

May Hardangerfjord's fruit farms spring into a riot of blossom.

Jul & Aug Perfect for hiking to Pulpit Rock.

BERGEN

POP 258,496

Surrounded by seven hills and seven fjords, Bergen is an utterly beguiling city. The beautiful Unesco World Heritage–listed Bryggen is its centrepiece, and nature, be that mountains, fjords or sea, is never far away. But you'll also discover a dynamic cultural life, one that a city 10 times its size would be proud of. Dive into its booming local food and coffee scene, fascinating art collections and excellent music venues.

History

During the 12th and 13th centuries, Bergen was Norway's capital and the country's most important city. By the 13th century, the city states of Germany allied themselves into trading leagues, most significantly the Hanseatic League with its centre in Lübeck. At its zenith, the league had over 150 member cities and was northern Europe's most powerful economic entity; the sheltered harbour of Bryggen drew the Hanseatic League's traders in droves. They established their first office here around 1360, transforming Bryggen into one of the league's four major headquarters abroad, accommodating up to 2000 mostly German resident traders who imported grain and exported dried fish, among other products.

For over 400 years, Bryggen was dominated by this tight-knit community of German merchants, who weren't permitted to mix with or marry Norwegians. By the 15th century, competition from Dutch and English shipping companies, internal disputes and, especially, the Black Death (which wiped out 70% of Bergen's population) ensured the Hanseatic League's decline.

By the early 17th century Bergen was nonetheless the trading hub of Scandinavia again, and Norway's most populous city with 15,000 people. During the 17th and 18th centuries, many Hanseatic traders opted to take Norwegian nationality and join the local community. Bryggen remained an important maritime trading centre until 1899, when the Hanseatic League's Bergen offices finally closed.

Sights

Making time just to wander Bergen's historic neighbourhoods is a must. Beyond Bryggen, the most picturesque are the quiet streets climbing the hill behind the Fløibanen funicular station, Nordnes (the peninsula that runs northwest of the centre, including along the southern shore of the main harbour) and Sandviken (the area north of Håkonshallen).

Central Bergen

★ Bryggen   *The iconic row*   HISTORIC SITE

(Map p160) Bergen's oldest quarter runs along the eastern shore of Vågen Harbour (the name simply translates to 'wharf') in long, parallel and often leaning rows of gabled buildings with stacked-stone or wooden foundations and reconstructed rough-plank construction. It's enchanting, no doubt about it, but can be exhausting if you hit a cruise ship and bus tour crush.

The current 58 buildings (25% of the original, although some claim there are now 61) cover 13,000 sq metres and date from after the 1702 fire, although the building pattern is from the 12th century. The archaeological excavations suggest that the quay was once 140m further inland than its present location.

In the early 14th century, there were about 30 wooden buildings, each usually shared by several *stuer* (trading firms). They rose two or three stories above the wharf and combined business premises with living quarters and **warehouses** (Map p160). Each building had a crane for loading and unloading ships, as well as a *schøtstue* (large assembly room) where employees met and ate.

The wooden alleyways of Bryggen have become a haven for artists and craftspeople, and there are bijou shops and boutiques at every turn. The atmosphere of an intimate waterfront community remains intact, and losing yourself in Bryggen is one of Bergen's pleasures.

➜ Hanseatisk Museum & Schøtstuene

(Map p160; www.museumvest.no; Finnegårdsgaten 1a & Øvregaten 50; adult/child Nkr70/free; ⊙9am-6pm Jul-Aug, 11am-2pm Tue-Sat, to 4pm Sun Sep-May) This interesting museum provides a window into the world of Hanseatic traders. Housed in a rough-timber building dating to 1704, it starkly reveals the contrast between the austere living and working conditions of the merchant sailors and apprentices, and the comfortable lifestyle of the trade partners.

Highlights include the manager's office, private liquor cabinet and summer bedroom; the apprentices' quarters, where *↑we did not do this* beds were shared by two men; the fish storage room, and the *fiskeskrue* (fish press), which pressed and processed over a million pounds (450,000kg) of fish a month.

An essential complement to the Hanseatic Museum, **Schøtstuene** (Map p160; Øvregaten 50) is a reconstruction of one of the original assembly halls where the fraternity of Hanseatic merchants once met for their business meetings and beer guzzling.

➤ **Bryggens Museum**

(Map p160; www.bymuseet.no; Dreggsallmenning 3; adult/child Nkr70/free; ⊙10am-4pm mid-May-Aug, shorter hours rest of year) This archaeological museum was built on the site of Bergen's first settlement, and the 800-year-old foundations unearthed during construction have been incorporated into the exhibits, which include medieval tools, pottery, skulls and runes. The permanent exhibition documenting Bergen circa 1300 is particularly fascinating.

➤ **Theta Museum**

(Map p160; Enhjørningsgården; adult/child Nkr20/10; ⊙2-4pm Tue, Sat & Sun Jun-Aug) This excellent one-room reconstruction of a clandestine Resistance headquarters, uncovered by the Nazis in 1942, is now Norway's tiniest museum. Fittingly, finding it is still a challenge. It's behind the Enhjørningen restaurant; pass through the alley and up the stairs to the 3rd floor.

KODE GALLERY

(☑55 56 80 00; kodebergen.no; adult/child Nkr100/free, students free Thu) Bergen's art museums are collected under the umbrella institution KODE and together form one of the largest art and design collections in Scandinavia. Four separate, and architecturally unique, buildings line up along the Lille Lungegård lake, each with its own specialist focus.

KODE is also home to one of the city's best restaurants and bars, Lysverket (p166), and a lovely cafe, Smakverket (p167). A single ticket allows entry to all four KODEs for two days, as well as a 30% discount at the Edvard Grieg Museum Troldhaugen.

➤ **KODE 1**

(Map p156; Nordahl Bruns gate 9) This bombastic 1897 edifice houses a large collection of design pieces and domestic objects, from majestic rococo cupboards to kitchenware by Alessi and chairs by Arne Jacobsen. Don't miss Ole Bull's beautiful Gasparo da Salo violin from 1562, with carved decoration by Benvenuto Cellini, or the dramatically displayed permanent exhibition of local silver on the 2nd floor.

➤ **KODE 2**

(Map p156; Rasmus Meyers allé 3) Hosts several temporary exhibitions every year, as well as a contemporary art collection with a focus on Norwegian and Scandinavian artists from the 1980s onwards. Cafe Smakverket (p167) and a great gallery shop are at street level.

➤ ★**KODE 3**

(Map p156; Rasmus Meyers allé 7) The Rasmus Meyer Collection's **Edvard Munch** hoard is among the world's best. Far less trafficked than Olso's Munch Museum and National Gallery, the rooms are beautifully hung and fabulously intimate: an apt place to really spend some time contemplating the artist's key works. This includes several pieces from his Frieze of Life, a series of paintings depicting various aspects of the psyche – *Jealousy, Melancholy, Women in Three Stages, Evening on Karl Johan* and *By the Death Bed.*

Works from 18th- and 19th-century Norwegian painters such as JC Dahl, Harriet Backer, Erik Werenskiold and Gerhard Munthe are interesting as well as atmospheric, as are the complete rooms of strange and wonderful historical interiors from the Bergen area.

Rasmus Meyer, a local businessman and philanthropist, was among the first significant collectors of Munch's art, securing major works from all of his artistic periods. The 1924 building was designed by Ole Landmark and purpose-built to house Meyer's extraordinary gift.

Guided tours in English of the Munch rooms take place at noon on Saturdays and Sundays in July and August, and are free with your entrance ticket.

➤ **KODE 4**

(Map p156; Rasmus Meyers allé 9) Converted into a museum in 2003, this austerely beautiful functionalist building from the 1930s was the head office of Bergen's electrical power company. It's home to a large permanent collection of European modernist works including the odd Klee, Picasso and Miro, and there is a gallery dedicated to the Norwegian landscape painter Nikolai Astrup.

Astrup's neo-Romantic, almost naive, paintings, drawings and woodcuts depict the fjords, fields and mountains of his home region of Jølster, as well as traditional life there at the beginning of the 20th century. Viewing

BERGEN & THE SOUTHWESTERN FJORDS BERGEN

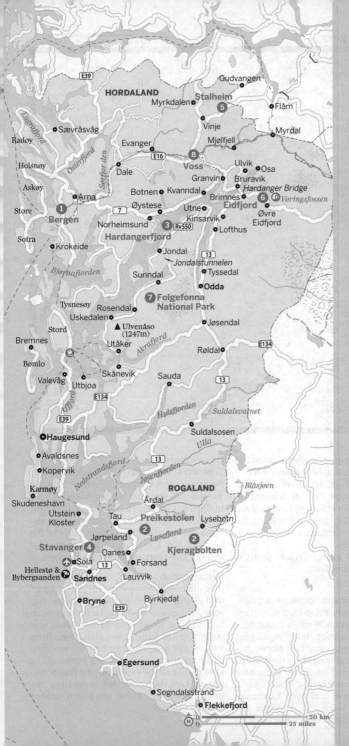

Bergen & the South-western Fjords Highlights

❶ Stroll historic **Bryggen** (p153) in Bergen, a Unesco World Heritage site.

❷ Climb to **Preikestolen** (p205) or **Kjeragbolten** (p205) overlooking Lysefjord.

❸ Relax on a slow boat up **Hardangerfjord** (p184) from Bergen to tranquil Ulvik.

❹ Savour a local ale at the dockside bars in **Stavanger** (p203).

❺ Wake up to the best view in Norway at the **Stalheim Hotel** (p184).

❻ Climb up (or through) the mountain from Eidfjord to **Kjeåsen Farm** (p187).

❼ Go for a glacier walk atop the icecap in **Folgefonna National Park** (p192).

❽ Parasail, para-bungee or kayak through the fjords from **Voss** (p172).

Central Bergen

his work makes for an evocative background to your own exploration of Norway's west.

For those with little art lovers on board, **KunstLab** is Norway's first art museum especially designed for children; here kids are encouraged to explore artworks by Gauguin, Miro, Picasso and Slettemark through play and experimentation.

Restaurant and bar Lysverket (p166) is located on the ground floor.

Bergen Kunsthall
GALLERY

(Map p156; www.kunsthall.no; Rasmus Meyers allé 5; adult/child Nkr50/free, from 5pm Thu free; ⊙11am-5pm Tue-Sun, to 8pm Thu) Bergen's major contemporary art institution hosts significant exhibitions of international and Norwegian artists, often with a single artist's work utilising the entire space. The cleanly glamorous 1930s architecture is worth a look in itself. The attached venue and bar, Landmark (p168), also hosts video and electronic art, concerts, film, performances and lectures.

Rosenkrantztårnet
TOWER

(Rosenkrantz Tower; Map p160; www.bymuseet.no; Bergenhus; adult/child Nkr60/free; ⊙9am-4pm mid-May-Aug, noon-3pm Sun Sep-mid-May) Built in the 1560s by Bergen governor Erik Rosenkrantz, this tower was a residence and defence post. It also incorporates parts of the keep (1273) of King Magnus the Lawmender and the 1520s fortress of Jørgen Hansson.

Håkonshallen
HISTORIC BUILDING

(Map p160; www.bymuseet.no; Bergenhus; adult/child Nkr60/free; ⊙10am-4pm mid-May-Aug, noon-3pm Sep-mid-May) This large ceremonial hall, adjacent to the Rosenkrantz Tower, was constructed by King Håkon Håkonsson from 1247–61 and completed for his son's wedding and coronation. The roof was blown off in 1944 thanks to the explosion of a Dutch munitions boat, but extensive restoration has been carried out. There are hourly guided tours in summer.

Central Bergen

Mariakirken ✈ CHURCH
(Map p160; Dreggen) This stone church, with its Romanesque entrance and twin towers, dates from the early 12th century and is Bergen's oldest building. The interior features 15th-century frescoes and a splendid baroque pulpit donated by Hanseatic merchants in 1676.

Leprosy Museum MUSEUM
(Lepramuseet; Map p156; St George's Hospital, Kong Oscars gate 59; adult/child Nkr70/free; ⊙11am-3pm mid-May–Aug) Although most of the buildings at St George's Hospital date from the 19th century, in medieval times the site was also a leprosarium. Far more palatable that it sounds, exhibits here detail Norway's contributions to leprosy research, including the work of Dr Armauer Hansen, who discovered the leprosy bacillus in Bergen in 1873 and gave his name to the modern name for leprosy.

Bergen Museum MUSEUM
(www.uib.no/bergenmuseum; adult/student & child combined ticket Nkr50/free; ⊙10am-4pm Tue-Fri, 11am-4pm Sat & Sun Jun-Aug) Comprising two collections at separate sites, the Cultural History Collection (Kultur-Historik Samlinger; Map p156; Haakon Sheteligs plass 10) takes in Viking weaponry, medieval altars, folk art, period furnishings, and Inuit and Aleut culture, and there are displays cover everything from Henrik Ibsen to Egyptian mummies. At time of research, the **Natural History Collection** (Naturhistorisk Samlinger; Map p156; ☏55 58 29 20; Muséplass 3) was scheduled to be closed until 2018.

Sjøfartsmuseet MUSEUM
(Map p156; www.bsj.uib.no; Haakon Sheteligs plass 15; adult/student & child Nkr50/free; ⊙10am-4pm Mon-Fri, from 11am Sat & Sun Jun-Aug, 11am-3pm Sep-May) Bergen's Maritime Museum features models of ships from Viking times to the present. Exhibits trace Norway's rich maritime history.

Bergen Akvariet AQUARIUM
(www.akvariet.no; Nordnesbakken 4; adult/child Nkr250/150; ⊙10am-6pm) At the end of the pretty Nordnes Peninsula, this aquarium has a big outdoor tank with seals and penguins, plus 70 indoor ones, along with snakes, crocodiles and a shark tunnel. There are penguin and seal feedings throughout the day. On foot, you can get there from Torget in 20 minutes; alternatively, take the Vågen ferry or bus 11.

Bergen Cathedral CATHEDRAL

(Domkirke; Map p160; ☎55 31 58 75; Domkirke-plass 1; admission free; ⊙11am-4pm Mon-Fri mid-Jun–mid-Aug, 11am-12.30pm Tue-Fri rest of year) Bergen's cathedral, also known as St Olav's Church, features stonemasonry in the entrance hall that was carved by the same stonemasons as those who adorned Westminster Abbey's chapter house in London. From mid-June until the end of August, there are free organ recitals (p170) on Sunday and Thursday.

◎ Greater Bergen

★ Edvard Grieg Museum MUSEUM

(Troldhaugen; griegmuseum.no; Troldhaug-vegen 65, Paradis-Bergen; adult/child Nkr90/free; ⊙9am-6pm May-Sep, 10am-4pm Oct-Apr) Composer Edvard Grieg and his wife Nina Hagerup spent summers at this charming Swiss-style wooden villa from 1885 until Grieg's death in 1907. Surrounded by fragrant, tumbling gardens and occupying a semi-rural setting on a peninsula by coastal Nordåsvatnet lake, south of Bergen, it's a truly lovely place to visit. Apart from the Grieg's original home, there is a modern exhibition centre, a 200-seat concert hall and perhaps the most compelling feature of them all, a tiny, lake-side **Composer's Hut**. Here the composer was always guaranteed silence, if not his muse.

From June to mid-September there is a daily **bus tour** (adult/child/student & senior Nkr250/100/200) departing from the tourist office (p171) at 11.30am that includes transport, entrance and a short piano concert; it's wise to pre-purchase tickets. Also see the website or visit the tourist office for details of summer recitals; there is a free shuttle bus for evening performances. The best public transport access is via a city centre tram to Nesttun (two-hour ticket Nkr36), alighting at the stop 'Hop'; from there it's a 20-minute signed walk.

Harald Sæverud Museum MUSEUM

(Siljustøl; siljustolmuseum.no; Siljustølveien 50, Råda; adult/child Nkr60/free; ⊙noon-4pm Sun late Jun–mid-Aug) Composer Harald Sæverud and his wife Marie lived in this simple timber home, 3km south of Troldhaugen. It was constructed in the 1930s of natural stone and untreated wood aiming to create unity with the environment. To get here, take bus 30 from platform 20 at the bus terminal.

Ole Bull Museum MUSEUM

(Museet Lysøen; www.lysoen.no; adult/child incl guided tour Nkr40/10; ⊙11am-4pm mid-May–Aug, Sun only Sep) This beautiful estate, on the island of the same name, was built in 1873 as the summer residence of Norway's 'first superstar', violinist Ole Bull. This extravagant, fantastical 'Little Alhambra', designed by Bull and Conrad Fredrik von der Lippe, took much of its inspiration from the architecture of Moorish Granada and integrated not only intricate frets and trellises, but also onion domes, garden paths, Italian marble columns and a high-ceilinged music hall made of Norwegian pine.

The grounds are criss-crossed with 13km of leisurely walks and there's a small cafe. There's a passenger ferry (adult/child Nkr60/30, eight minutes, hourly 11am to 3pm) from Buena Quay to the island; Skyss buses run an infrequent service to Buena from Bergin bus station.

Damsgård MANOR

(www.bymuseet.no; Alleen 29, Laksevåg; adult/child Nkr60/free; ⊙noon-4pm Jun-Aug, tours at noon & 2pm) The 1770 Damsgård manor, 3km west of town, may well be Norway's (if not Europe's) finest example of 18th-century rococo timber architecture. The building's superbly over-the-top garden includes sculptures, ponds and plant specimens that were common 200 years ago. To get here, take bus 19 from the centre.

Fantoft Stave Church CHURCH

(Fantoft Stavkirke; Paradis; adult/child/student Nkr40/15/25; ⊙10.30am-6pm mid-May–mid-Sep) This stave church, in the leafy southern suburb of Paradis, was built in Sognefjord around 1150 and moved here in 1883. In fact, a reconstruction, as the original fell victim to an early '90s black metal/neopagan church burning. The adjacent **cross**, originally from Sola in Rogaland, dates from 1050.

From Bergen, take the tram to Fantoft (two-hour ticket Nkr36).

Activities

Fløibanen Funicular CABLE CAR

(Map p160; www.floibanen.no; Vetrlidsalmenning 21; adult/child return Nkr85/43; ⊙7.30am-11pm Mon-Fri, 8am-11pm Sat & Sun) For an unbeatable view of the city, ride the 26-degree Fløibanen funicular to the top of Mt Fløyen (320m), with departures every 15 minutes. From the top, well-marked hiking tracks lead into the forest; the possibilities are mapped out on the free *Walking Map of Mount Fløyen,* which are available from the Bergen tourist office (p171).

Track 2 makes a 1.6km loop near Skomakerdiket lake, while Track 1 offers a 5km loop over hills, through forests and past several lakes. For a delightful 40-minute walk back to the city from Fløyen, follow Track 4 clockwise and connect with Track 6, which switchbacks down to the harbour.

Ulriken643
CABLE CAR

(www.ulriken643.no; adult/child return Nkr150/80, with bus Nkr250/140; ⏰9am-9pm May-Sep, 9am-5pm Tue-Sun Oct-Apr) Bergen's cable car ascends to the radio tower and cafe atop Mt Ulriken (642m), offering a fine panoramic view of the city and surrounding fjords and mountains. An antique shuttle bus to the cable-car lower station leaves every half-hour from the Torget fish market from 9am to 9pm mid-May to September. Otherwise, it's a 45-minute walk from the centre or a short bus ride (bus 2, 31, 50).

For locals, a perfect day out is taking the cable car up and then following the marked trail north (four to six hours) to the top of the Fløibanen funicular.

Nordnes Sjøbad
SWIMMING

(Public Swimming Pool; ☑53 03 91 90; Nordnesparken; adult/child Nkr65/30; ⏰7am-7pm Jun-Aug) Much loved by locals of all ages, this heated public pool right on the harbour is a beautifully scenic spot to catch some sun and have a picnic.

Tours

Bergen Fjord Sightseeing
BOAT TOURS

(White Lady; ☑55 25 90 00; www.rodne.no; harbour tour adult/child/family Nkr150/80/350, fjord cruise Nkr 500/300/1250) A vintage ferry operates one-hour harbour tours offering good views of Bryggen and the surrounding hills or four-hour fjord tours to Osterfjord, north of Bergen. Boats depart from the waterfront next to the fish market (daily June to August, 2.30pm for the fjord, 11.30am or 1pm for the harbour).

City Sightseeing Bergen
BUS TOUR

(www.citysightseeingbergen.com; adult/child/family Nkr150/100/400; ⏰half-hourly 9am-4.30pm May-Sep) This daily summer sightseeing bus does the usual hop-on, hop-off city circuit from Gamle Bergen to the aquarium, with commentary in eight languages.

FJORD TOURS FROM BERGEN

There are dozens of tours of the fjords from Bergen; the tourist office (p171) has a full list and you can buy tickets there or purchase them online. Most offer discounts if you have a Bergen Card (p170). For a good overview, pick up the *Round Trips – Fjord Tours & Excursions* brochure from the tourist office, which includes tours offered by a range of private companies. The following are the most comprehensive round trips on offer.

Fjord Tours (☑81 56 82 22; www.fjordtours.com) Fjord Tours has mastered the art of making the most of limited time with a series of tours into the fjords. Its popular and year-round **Norway in a Nutshell** tour is a great way to see far more than you thought possible in a single day.

The day ticket (adult/child Nkr1145/585) from Bergen combines a morning train to Voss, a bus to the Stalheim Hotel and then on to Gudvangen, from where a ferry takes you up the spectacular Nærøyfjord to Flåm, joining the stunning mountain railway to Myrdal, and then taking a train back to Bergen in time for a late dinner (or for Nkr1550/790 per adult/child you can continue on to Oslo to arrive at around 10pm).

From May to September, Fjord Tours also runs a range of train-bus-boat round-trips from Bergen, including the 10-hour **Hardangerfjord in a Nutshell** (adult/child Nkr1180/490), which goes via Voss, Ulvik, Eidfjord and Norheimsund, and **Sognefjord in a Nutshell** (adult/child Nkr1340/670), which explores more of Sognefjord by boat. It also has four-day tours (adult/child Nkr5560/3460) that include Oslo, Sognefjorden, Geiranger and Ålesund.

Rødne Fjord Cruise (Map p160; ☑51 89 52 70; www.rodne.no; ⏰May-Aug) Rødne Fjord Cruise runs a seven-hour round-trip tour (adult/child Nkr725/325) to Rosendal that leaves Bergen at 9am, spending 3½ hours in Rosendal, including lunch and a guided tour of Baroniet Rosendal, and returns to Bergen at 4.15pm.

Bryggen & Vågen Harbour

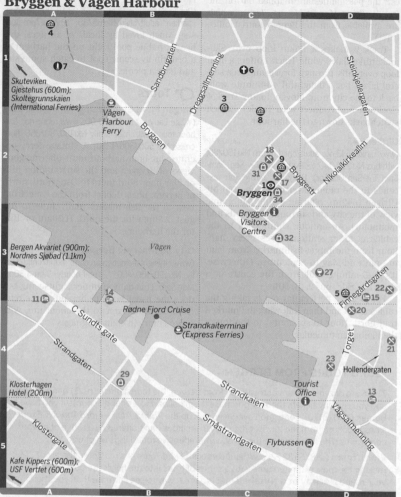

Fonnafly HELICOPTER TOUR
(☎ 55 34 60 00; www.fonnafly.no) This national group will put together a custom sightseeing trip; the views over the fjords are once-in-a-lifetime stuff. Prices start at Nkr4000 for three passengers.

Guided Tours of Bryggen WALKING
(Map p160; ☎ 55 58 80 30; adult/child Nkr120/free; ☻ tours at 11am, in English noon Jun-Aug) ✐ The Bryggens Museum (p154) offers excellent walking tours through the timeless alleys of Bryggen. Tours last 90 minutes and leave from the museum. The commentary includes descriptions of life during Bergen's trading heyday. The ticket includes admission to Bryggens Museum, Schøtstuene and the Hanseatic Museum (plus re-entry later the same day).

✸ Festivals & Events

For a full list of events on offer, see the website www.visitbergen.com.

Night Jazz Festival MUSIC
(www.nattjazz.no) May jazz festival that is popular with Bergen's large student population.

Bergenfest　　　　　　　MUSIC
(www.bergenfest.no) International music festival in June.

Bergen International Festival　　CULTURAL
(www.fib.no) Held over 14 days in late May, this is the big cultural festival of the year, with dance, music, theatre and visual arts shows throughout the city.

Bergen Food Festival　　　　FOOD
(www.matfest.no) September showcase of local food producers (including whale meat).

Bergen International Film Festival　　FILM
(www.biff.no) Early October.

🛏 Sleeping

Bergen has good hotels, but *always* book before arriving in town; the city fills up fast in summer and for festivals, but also sells out for hard-to-anticipate events and conferences year-round.

The tourist office has an accommodation booking service both online and on site.

Marken Gjestehus　　　　　HOSTEL €
(Map p156; ☑ 55 31 44 04; www.marken-gjestehus.com; Kong Oscars gate 45; dm Nkr240, s/d Nkr705/810, with shared bathroom Nkr525/610) Midway between the harbour and the train station, this hostel-within-a-hotel has simple, modern rooms. White walls and wooden floors lend a sense of light and space, bright chairs and wall decals are cheery, and the communal areas are more stylish than you'd expect for the price.

Skiven Gjestehus　　　　　B&B €
(Map p156; www.skiven.no; Skivebakken 17; s/d shared bathroom Nkr450/650; 🖥) Basic and bright rooms occupy the ground floor of this traditional house in a peaceful, elevated neighbourhood that's close to everything. Good-quality beds and down duvets, a heated bathroom floor and guest kitchen make it very good value.

Citybox　　　　　　　　　HOSTEL €
(Map p156; ☑ 55 31 25 00; www.citybox.no; Nygårdsgaten 31; s/d/f Nkr650/950/1550, without bathroom Nkr550/750; 🖥) The Citybox mini-chain began in Bergen and is one of the best of the hostel–budget hotel hybrids. Colour-splashed modern rooms make use of the original historic features and are blissfully high-ceilinged; the extra-large family rooms are very generous in size and have small kitchen areas. Communal spaces, including a shared laundry room, can be hectic, but staff are friendly and helpful.

Bergen Vandrerhjem YMCA　　HOSTEL €
(Map p160; ☑ 55 60 60 55; www.bergenhostel.no; Nedre Korskirkealmenning 4; dm Nkr195-320, s/d Nkr600/950) Gone are the days when staying in a hostel meant a long hike into town: this friendly place could be Norway's most central budget choice. While it's a standard hostel – same-sex or mixed dorms, large kitchen facilities etc – the terrace is extraordinary and staff are great. Bookings are essential

Bryggen & Vågen Harbour

year-round and, unusually, bed linen is included in the price.

Lone Camping CAMPGROUND €
(☑55 39 29 60; www.lonecamping.no; Hardangerveien 697, Haukeland; campsites Nkr250, cabins Nkr570-1300) This lakeside campsite 20km from town, between Espeland and Haukeland, is accessible by public transport; bus 900 runs to/from town (Nkr53, 30 minutes).

Bratland Camping CAMPGROUND €
(☑55 10 13 38; www.bratlandcamping.no; Bratlandsveien 6, Haukeland; campsites Nkr240, cabins Nkr450-1350) Accessible on bus 900 (Nkr53, 30 minutes), this well-equipped site is 24km south of Bergen.

★**Hotel Park** HISTORIC HOTEL €€
(Map p156; ☑55 54 44 00; hotelpark.no; Harald Hårfagresgate 35; s/d Nkr1190/1390; ☎) This hotel is managed by the daughters of the longtime owner and its mix of family treasures, design flair, fresh ideas and friendliness make for a very special place indeed. Spread across two 19th-century stone buildings in a quiet, stately street, it offers elegant rooms, each different, but all furnished with an appealing combination of antiques and contemporary comforts.

Corner rooms are particularly gorgeous, filled with light and with nicely vignetted views of city rooftops and Mt Fløyen. Complimentary afternoon tea includes their signature brownies – ask for the recipe. It's a 15-minute walk from the city centre and close to the good cafes, bars and restaurants that are frequented by the university crowd.

Skansen Pensjonat GUESTHOUSE €€
(Map p160; ☑55 31 90 80; www.skansen-pensjonat.no; Vetrlidsalmenning 29; s/d/apt Nkr550/900/1100; ☎) This cute-as-a-button seven-room place has an unbeatable location high up behind the lower funicular station and warm, welcoming owners and staff. The house retains a traditional feel and scale, rooms are light and airy (if far from fancy), and the 'balcony room' has one of the best views in Bergen.

Grand Hotel Terminus HISTORIC HOTEL €€
(Map p156; ☑55 21 25 00; www.ght.no; Zander Kaaesgate 6; s/d Nkr1050/1395; ☎) This historic hotel from 1928 harks back to the glory days of rail travel and has requisite elaborate, baronial lobby and resident ghost story. Suites aside, the rooms are small, though beautifully decorated. Under the care of the Augustin Hotel family, there's an attention

to detail and modern energy that do its great old bones justice.

Klosterhagen Hotel
HOTEL €€

(☑53 00 22 00; www.klosterhagenhotell.no; Strangehagen 2; s/d Nkr995/1400; 🛜) Nordnes makes a great Bergen base, and this small, smart hotel is in a key position, surrounded by the pretty rowhouses and parkland that the neighbourhood's known for, and within walking distance of either harbour. Rooms are decorated in rich, bright tones with big original window frames, bathrooms are small but modern, and there's a nice courtyard garden.

Kindly, single bookings are upgraded to double on availability. Another nice touch: the hotel is run along altruistic lines, offering training programs for disadvantaged people.

Steens Hotell
HISTORIC HOTEL €€

(Map p156; ☑55 30 88 88; www.steenshotel.no; Parkveien 22; s/d Nkr1000/1350) This lovely 19th-century building is brimming with period detail, from the gentle curve of the stairway to the grand dining room with its stunning stained-glass windows. Rooms are more straightforward, but well-sized, and higher ones come with pretty tree-top outlooks. Staff are welcoming and, bonus, it has Bergen's cheapest parking (Nkr50).

Skuteviken Gjestehus
GUESTHOUSE €€

(☑93 46 71 63; www.skutevikenguesthouse.com; Skutevikens Smalgang 11; d Nkr1100, attic r Nkr1200; 🛜) This authentic timber guesthouse, set on a small cobbled street in Sandviken, is decorated with white wicker furniture, lace cushions and a few modern touches. The rooms are more like apartments and the owners are charming.

Basic Hotel Victoria
HOTEL €€

(Map p160; ☑55 31 50 30; basichotels.no; Kong Oscars gate 29; s/d Nkr995/1095; 🛜) You know the drill at these Scandinavian budget chains: smart, smallish, comfortable rooms without frills such as daily room cleaning or human check-in.

Clarion Collection Hotel No.13
BOUTIQUE HOTEL €€€

(Map p156; ☑55 36 13 09; Torgallmenningen 13; d/ste Nkr2000/3500; ✳🛜) With 34 rooms this city-centre place retains the relaxed, personal feel of a boutique hotel, while delivering the services of a larger chain. Glamorous, sexy rooms have black-stained floorboards,

CITY CABIN

Tubakuba, Bergen's most unique accommodation option, also happens to be free. This forest cabin was built by architecture students using experimental wood-moulding techniques. It's Norwegian design exemplified: pared back, purposeful, organic and sensual. Designed to help families with young children get back into nature, the cabin has no water or electricity but provides the shelter and warmth that a tent can't.

It's an easy walk here south-east of the Fløibanen funicular top station, and the site has the spectacular cliffside views you might imagine. Tubakuba is available in July and August for stays of one night only. Bookings can be made via the **Bergen Kommune office** (☑55 56 62 09; www.bergen.kommune. no), where you also 'check-in' and pick up the keys.

huge TVs and lots of space, even at standard level. There's a show-stopper of a top-floor suite, with a king bed set beneath a large curved ceiling window.

In warmer weather, **No13**, the dramatically decorated and highly regarded lobby restaurant and bar, is open to the square, and guests can take their complimentary evening meal there or in a cosy basement. If you're not staying, its Nkr200 neo-Nordic lunch specials are a great deal.

Clarion Hotel Admiral
HOTEL €€€

(Map p160; ☑55 23 64 00; www.clarionadmiral.no; C Sundts gate 9; s/d from Nkr1000/1400; ✳🛜) With sweeping views across the water to Bryggen from the balconies of its harbour-facing rooms, this stylish hotel promises waking up to the most iconic view in Bergen. Its recent interior remodel gives it one of the city's most fashionable lobbies and rooms that are both contemporary but also moodily redolent of the historic location.

Augustin Hotel
HOTEL €€€

(Map p160; ☑55 30 40 00; www.augustin.no; C Sundts gate 22; s/d Nkr1485/1665; 🛜) 🌱 As Bergen's oldest family-run hotel, the Augustin is renowned for the warmth of its welcome and its ecological awareness. Rooms are not huge but are light, airy and elegantly furnished, especially in the new wing. Compli-

Bergen Region

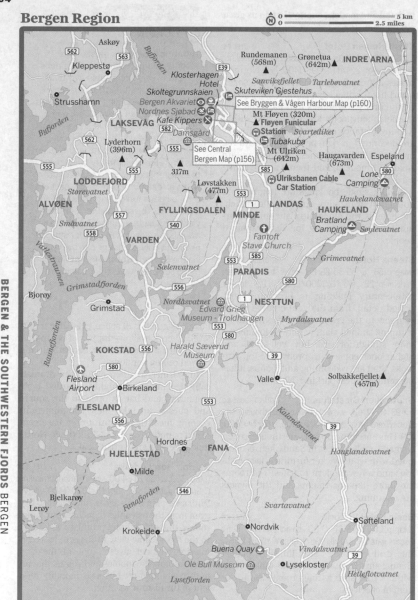

mentary lobby waffles in the afternoon and Altona (p169), the much-loved wine bar, add to the appeal.

There's easy access to the harbour and city, but it is also nicely nestled below a strip of local shops and cafes.

Det Hanseatiske Hotel HISTORIC HOTEL €€€
(Map p160; ☎55 30 48 00; www.dethanseatiske-hotell.no; Finnegårdsgaten 2; d from Nkr1900; ❄️🌐) This is the only hotel to be housed in one of Bryggen's original timber buildings. Spread over two buildings and connected by

a glassed-in walkway, extraordinary architectural features from Bryggen's days as a Hanseatic port mix with luxe contemporary fittings. It's undeniably atmospheric, though some rooms get the mix right better than others.

🍴 Eating

Bergen's culinary scene is a diverse one, taking in a small but internationally acknowledged local food movement, lots of casual places catering to the city's student population, and quite a few bastions of west coast tradition. As might be expected, the fish and seafood are something special.

Torget Fish Market   SEAFOOD €

(Map p160; www.torgetibergen.no; Torget; ⊙7am-7pm Jun-Aug, to 4pm Mon-Sat Sep-May) For atmosphere, it's hard to beat the fish market. Right alongside the harbour and a stone's throw from Bryggen, you'll find everything from salmon to calamari, fish and chips, fish cakes, prawn baguettes, seafood salads, local caviar and, sometimes, reindeer and elk.

Kjøttbasarell   FOOD MARKET €

(Map p160; cnr Torget & Kong Oscars gate; ⊙10am-5pm Mon-Wed & Fri, 10am-6pm Thu, 9am-4pm Sat) This lovely old food market has cheeses, meats, jams and all sorts of gourmet items.

Pingvinen   NORWEGIAN €

(Map p156; www.pingvinen.no; Vaskerelven 14; daily specials Nkr119, mains Nkr159-249; ⊙1pm-3am Sun-Fri, noon-3am Sat) Devoted to Norwegian home cooking, and with a delightfully informal ambience, Pingvinen is *everyone* in Bergen's old favourite. They come for meals their mothers and grandparents used to cook, and although the menu changes regularly, there'll be one or more of the following: fish-cake sandwiches, reindeer, fish pie, whale, salmon, lamb shank and *raspeballer* (aka *komle*), west-coast potato dumplings. The kitchen usually closes around 9pm, whereafter there are snacks and kicking on – it does double duty as a popular late-night bar.

Royal Gourmetburger og Gin   BURGERS €

(Map p156; ☎56 90 12 33; royalburger.no; Neumanns gate 2a; burgers Nkr104-129; ⊙3pm-midnight Sun-Thu, to 1am Fri & Sat) Big call, but we declare these to be Bergen's best burgers. This convivial, stylishly-tiled corner bar with big windows that overlook the pedestrianised street has a cracking playlist and draws the city's winsome 20- and 30-somethings early *and* late. Oh, and did we mention there's gin?

SEASIDE SEAFOOD

Plan ahead to experience **Cornelius Sjømat Restaurant** (☎56 33 48 80; www.cornelius-restaurant.no; Måseskjæret 18, Holman; 3-/5-course menus incl transport Nkr845/995), an island restaurant just beyond Bergen. Here they smoke their own salmon, harvest herbs from a kitchen garden and gather fresh seaweed daily. Their saltwater tanks hold lobsters, crab, crayfish, scallops, mussels, sea urchins and oysters, and this is what ends up on your platter. Boat transport leaves Bryggen at 6pm nightly – reserve when booking a table.

The G&T menu starts at Tanqueray and Tonic (Nkr99), but then takes this mixed-drink staple to places we'd never dreamt of. Particularly memorable: the gin, geranium and coriander (Nkr119).

Bastant Bryggen   CAFE €

(Map p160; ☎40 07 22 47; Jacobsfjorden 4, Bryggestredet; soups Nkr99-129, sandwiches Nkr119, soup & half sandwich Nkr155; ⊙11am-5pm) Cuddle in or take away at this super-popular all-organic cafe in the heart of Bryggen's tiny alleyways. Daily soups always include a vegan, vegetarian and meat option, and sandwiches are hearty. There's homemade lemonade and strawberry frappes in summer, killer hot chocolates when it's cold and excellent coffee year-round. **Bastant Stølegaten** (Stølegaten 8a, Sandviken; ⊙11am-11pm) in Sandviken is roomier and open late.

Pølse Kiosk   SAUSAGES €

(Map p160; Kong Oscars gate 1; hot dogs from Nkr55; ⊙10am-2am) If you've been travelling around Norway for a while, you may be heartily sick of hot dogs bought from petrol stations. But this place has *real* sausages (including wild game, reindeer, lamb and chilli) and a better-than-average range of sauces.

Colonialen Litteraturhuset   NORWEGIAN €€

(Map p160; 55 90 16 00; Østre skostredet 5-7; lunch Nkr145-175, dinner Nkr175-235; ⊙9-11am Mon-Fri, cafe 11am-9pm, brasserie 4-10pm Mon-Sat) This airy, open-plan space is subtly divided into two distinct venues by a bustling kitchen: one side for all-day breakfasting, snacking, lunching and drinking, the other an elegantly informal 'brassierie' where well-to-do

Bergeners come for thoughtful dishes such as mackerel with apples, turnips, peas and horseradish. Staff know their wine, too.

Breakfast and lunch dishes at the cafe are similarly fresh and beautifully presented, plus their *boller* (raisin rolls), baked by Colonialen's bakery at Kranen, vie for best in town. You can also pick up bread by the loaf here.

Bien
BISTRO €€

(☑55 59 11 00; bienbar.no; Fjøsangerveien 30, Kronstad; lunch Nkr109-149, dinner Nkr179-275; ⏰11am-2.30am Mon-Sat) Easily accessible by tram to Danemarks pass, and handy if you're driving in or out of town, this restaurant and bar is a true local's haunt. The 1930s shop fittings at this former pharmacy remain entirely intact and are stunning. The menu is short and comforting: famous ragu Bolognese, fish or meat done simply, but with flair and excellent produce.

★ Lysverket
NORWEGIAN €€€

(Map p156; ☑55 60 31 00; lysverket.no; KODE 4, Rasmus Meyers allé 9; 1/2/3 lunch courses Nkr205/295/320, 3/5/9 dinner courses Nkr595/745/995, bar dishes from Nkr75-195; ⏰noon-1am Tue-Thu, noon-3am Fri & Sat, 1-5pm Sun) Lysverket poetically translates as 'light plant', though the name has a down-to-earth explanation: this building once housed the city power company. The food itself is an intriguing combination of the everyday and the poetic, with chef Christopher Haatuft using seafood caught right on Bergen's doorstep and familiar seasonal vegetables in surprising combinations of colour, texture and flavour.

The elegant dining room, with its industrial brass pendant lamps, smoked oak chairs and tables, and big banquettes in grey felt and wild black-sheep fleece, suits a long evening of degustation dining, though the large windows and lake view also make lunch a treat (lunch is excellent value). The kitchen offers bar snacks from 3pm – good drinking fare such as fish and chips, pork-belly tacos, sourdough and mackerel butter. After dinner service, there's a crush for cocktails as the city's best DJs, as well as the occasional international star, play until late.

Sky:Skraperen
NORWEGIAN €€€

(☑55 32 04 04; www.skyskraperen.no; Ulrikens topp; mains Nkr159-230, 4-course set menus with aperitif Nkr643; ⏰9am-9pm May-Sep, 10am-4pm Oct-Apr) You can drop in for a sausage sandwich (Nkr39) or a fish soup (Nkr95) at this mountain-top restaurant any time dur-

ing the day, though we suggest making an evening of it. The set dinner menu follows the seasons and showcases west-coast produce. Dishes pop with fresh, clean flavours and are prettily presented. Book at least one day ahead.

Colonialen Restaurant
NORWEGIAN €€€

(Map p156; ☑55 90 16 00; www.colonialen.no/restaurant; Kong Oscars gate 44; 7/12 courses Nkr950/1350, mains Nkr435; ⏰Mon-Sat 6-11pm) Okay, there's zip view and it's in a less-than-glamorous locale, but we can't imagine a Michelin is far off for this Bergen fine diner. Tasting menus emphasise seafood, but can be tailored to meat or vegetable preferences. Bold flavours are teased from amazing produce and whimsical, but far from fey, combinations take your senses on a wonderful west-coast journey.

Staff are delightful, from the chefs shouting 'hei' as you walk in the door, to the careful, unpretentious way in which dishes and wines are described by waiters and sommeliers. Wine pairings (an additional Nkr950/1250), many of them rare or naturally produced, are generous, if absurdly expensive for non-Norwegians.

Hanne på Høyden
NORWEGIAN €€€

(Map p156; ☑55 32 34 32; hannepaahoeyden. wordpress.com; Fosswinckels gate 18; 3/4/6 courses Nkr585/665/845) 🌱 It's easy to love this 19th-century shopfront restaurant, with pots of herbs lining the entrance lane and vegetables sprouting in the courtyard. Set menus make the best use of local produce, be it line-caught seafood or organic meat from the Hardanger. Dishes are innovative but also deeply infused with Norwegian tradition; think flavour not fuss.

Restaurant 1877
NORWEGIAN €€€

(Map p160; ☑92 87 18 77; www.restaurant1877.no; Kjøttbasaren, Vetrlidsallmenningen 2; 3-/5-course set menus Nkr565/695) This fine dining room in a historic harbourside building is hushed and elegant but far from stuffy, with young, passionate staff who are knowledgeable but warmly informal. Decide on either three or five courses, and then choose from a divinely simple list: shellfish, fish, meat, cheese, dessert. What will follow, a sequence of thoughtful and hyperlocal dishes, changes daily.

Bryggen Tracteursted
NORWEGIAN €€€

(Map p160; Bryggestredet 2, Bryggen; lunch mains Nkr185-215, dinner mains Nkr285-385;

⊘11am-10pm May-Sep) Housed in a 1708 building that ranges across the former stables, kitchen (note the stone floor, which meant that it was the only Bryggen building allowed to have a fire) and Bergen's only extant *schøtstuene* (dining hall), this restaurant serves traditional Norwegian dishes that change regularly; it's pubby and informal by day, traditionally upmarket by night.

Potetkjelleren   NORWEGIAN €€€
(Map p160; ☑55 32 00 70; Kong Oscars gate 1a; mains Nkr315-335, 3- to 6-course menus Nkr565-750; ⊘4-10pm Mon-Sat) The 'Potato Cellar' is one of Bergen's classic restaurants, with a monthly menu based around seasonal ingredients and Norwegian traditions. The wine list is carefully selected.

Wesselstuen   NORWEGIAN €€€
(Map p156; ☑55 55 49 49; Øvre Ole Bulls plass 6; lunch mains Nkr119-159, dinner mains Nkr289-309; ⊘lunch & dinner) Bergen's oldest restaurant evokes the wood-panelled dining halls of Bergen's past and is well known for its traditional dishes such as sirloin of reindeer (Nkr309) and *klippfisk* (bacalao) with split peas and bacon (Nkr289)

🍷 Drinking & Nightlife

Coffee is taken seriously in Bergen, with the best cafes using small-batch local roasts, top-of-the-line technology and gun baristas. Bergen also has a great bar scene and locals are enthusiastic drinking companions. Most of them favour the places in the centre or southwest of Øvre Ole Bulls plass. Big, multilevel nightclubs cluster around here too; they are easy to spot, often fabulously trashy, and only admit those over 24.

★ Blom   CAFE
(Map p156; John Lunds plass 1; ⊘8.30am-5pm Mon-Fri, 11am-5pm Sat & Sun) This cafe is known for its excellent coffee (this is where off-duty baristas come for a pour-over) and attracts a fashionable, young crowd. It's a simple, warm place, with sweet service, lots of room to pull out your laptop, big sandwiches and more-ish homemade muesli slices, brownies and fruit crumbles.

Smakverket   CAFE
(Map p156; KODE 2, Rasmus Meyers allé 3; ⊘11am-5pm) This moody, perpetually busy, gallery cafe serves good coffee and snacks all day, but also has a menu of smart lunch dishes

and good wine by the glass if you're after something more substantial.

Krog og Krinkel   CAFE
(Map p160; Lille Øvregaten 14; ⊘11am-7pm Mon-Sat, noon-5pm Sun) Street-side tables line up along the cobbles in the warm weather, or you can venture down into the cosy, comfortable basement filled with painted vintage furniture, and, yes, books. The coffee is good and they make all their own *boller* and cakes on site, including a *suksesskake* (almond meringue cake with custard topping; Nkr45) that will have you hooked at first bite.

Kafemisjonen   CAFE
(Map p160; Øvre Korskirkealmenning 5; ⊘7.30am-6pm Mon-Fri, 10am-6pm Sat & Sun) One of Norway's coffee greats, Kafemisjonen pleases with its espresso and airy, subtly glamorous shopfront that pairs early 20th-century blue velvet and steel chairs with richly, evocative tile work. If you've had your fill of *boller* and brownies, come here for Bergen's best croissants.

Det Lille Kaffekompaniet   CAFE
(Map p160; Nedre Fjellsmug 2; ⊘10am-8pm Mon-Fri, 10am-6pm Sat & Sun) This was one of Bergen's first third-wave coffee places and retains a super local feel. Everyone overflows onto the neighbouring stairs when the sun's out and you're not sure which table belongs to who.

Kaffebrenneri   CAFE
(kaffebrenneri.de.gpu.no; Thormøhlensgate 45, Møhlenpris; ⊘8am-7pm Mon-Fri, from noon Sat & Sun) 🚲 Out in Møhlenpris, in an old shipyard, this independent coffee roastery has an on-site cafe with outside seating and fresh, organic sandwiches and cakes. If you're headed out of town and want a bag of ground beans to go, their 'Snop' blend is the business.

Also part of the offering, **Dumpster Pizza** does great thin-crust pizzas in a wood oven, using vegetables that are from local farmers and otherwise would go to waste.

Nobel Bopel   CAFE, BAR
(Map p156; Welhavens gate 64, Møhlenpris; ⊘11.30am-6pm Thu-Sun) 🚲 This corner cafe sits in one of studenty Møhlenpris' impressively grand streets. Big brunches are the thing: on Sundays they're washed down with glasses of sparkling wine or microbrews from Flåm or Florø. A super-relaxed vibe

LOCAL KNOWLEDGE

EIRIK GLAMBEK BØE

Eirik Glambek Bøe, one half of **Kings of Convenience**, the internationally acclaimed indie folk duo whose 2001 album *Quiet is the New Loud* came to define the Bergen Wave sound, continues to live and work in his hometown. Here are his suggestions for a perfect Bergen day.

Breakfast pastries Bergen claims to be the home of *kanelboller* (cinnamon buns). I have no idea if there's any truth to it, but several places serve really good ones: try Det Lille Kaffekompaniet (p167).

Coffee run We were proud of our lack of Starbucks here, due to the strong, local coffee scene. Now you'll have to pass by a few to find the local shops: Kaffemisjonen, Blom (p167) and Kaffebrenneri (p167) are my favourites.

City lunch No.13's (p163) restaurant offers neo-Nordic gourmet lunches for low-budget travellers. And the sandwiches at Smakverket (p167) are very good.

Afternoon tea and nature Bergen has mountains and seaside within walking distance. If the weather is bad, you can drink your tea indoors at Sky:Skraperen (p166) restaurant at the top of Mt Ulriken, or at Kafe Kippers (p169) by the seaside at Nordnes.

West-coast flavours There has been something of a revolution in terms of good, local food here lately. Lysverket's (p166) mackerel ceviche with rhubarb is just one dish I could mention. But so many places are really good: Colonialen (p166), Hanne på Høyden (p166), Cornelius (p165), Restaurant 1877 (p166), Bien (p166), Bastant (p165), **Dr Wiesener** (✐416 25 969; Nye Sandviksveien 17a; ⊙1pm-1am Sun-Mon, to 2am Fri & Sat).

Cocktails Have a quiet drink at Altona (p169) or Grand Hotel Terminus (p162), or a more lively one at Legal (p169), Lysverket (p166) or Ujevnt (p169; its aqua sours are an idiosyncratic signature).

Live music So many venues. Find a local with your taste in clothes and ask him or her: 'What's on tonight?'

Club night Landmark (p168), Østre (p170) and Café Opera (p169) are all places where you are likely to find a DJ and people dancing. One Friday every month, you can come to my own Klubb Kavalér (for dates, check the Facebook page). It's in a beautiful old ballroom called Fensal; a 20-piece big band is invited to try and recreate what New York must have felt like when the Glenn Miller Orchestra used to play. Expect partner dance.

belies the thoughtfulness behind everything here. Interiors are all from recycled finds and the food is organic and sourced from small, local suppliers.

Landmark
CAFE, BAR

(Map p156; Bergen Kunsthalle, Rasmus Meyers allé 5; ⊙cafe 11am-5pm Tue-Sun, bar 7pm-1am Tue-Thu, to 3.30am Fri & Sat) This large, airy room was named after the architect Ole Landmark. It is a beautiful example of 1930s Norwegian design, and the venue really multitasks: it's a day-time cafe, a lecture and screening hall, a live-performance space, a bar and also the venue for Bergen's best club nights. The place is a favourite with the city's large creative scene – you'll find them refreshingly unpretentious and ready to *really* kick on.

Garage
LIVE MUSIC

(Map p156; www.garage.no; Christies gate 14; ⊙3pm-3am Mon-Sat, 5pm-3am Sun) Garage has taken on an almost mythical quality for music lovers across Europe. They do have the odd jazz and acoustic act, but this is a rock and metal venue at heart, with well-known Norwegian and international acts drawn to the cavernous basement. Stop by for their Sunday jam sessions in summer.

Apollon
BAR

(Map p156; Nygårdsgaten 2a; ⊙10am-12.30am Mon-Sat, from noon Sun) One of Norway's oldest independent record stores (vintage: early '80s) is also one of Bergen's happiest little bars. Flip through their excellent selection of new and secondhand indie, metal, folk, garage and psychedelia, then watch Bergen's hip kids go by from the window stools. Good selection of local beer on tap.

Legal BAR
(Map p156; cnr Nygårdsgaten & Christies gate; ⊘2pm-1.30am Sun-Thu, 2pm-2.30am Fri & Sat) Possibly Bergen's best student bar, this laid-back, hipster-embracing place is friendly and fun. There's Tuesday grill nights, sausages whenever and DJs upstairs who know their audience's tastes very well indeed.

Don Pippo WINE BAR
(Map p156; ☑55 31 30 33; Christies gate 11, enter from Gamle Nygårdsveien lane) This fabulous European-style charmer draws a bubbly, sophisticated crowd. Staff open different bottles for wine-by-the-glass choices each day and the Italian selections are particularly strong. Mop up the vino with platters of local and imported meats and cheese (Nkr135) or hearty sourdough sandwiches (Nkr89). And, just because this is Norway, after all, there's a pancake buffet on Sundays.

Ujevnt WINE BAR
(Map p156; ujevnt.no; Christiesgate 5-7; ⊘3pm-2.30am Mon-Sat, from 6pm Sun) You might find yourself in this moody little bar one afternoon, nursing a pint of the excellent Voss Bryggeri nut brown ale on tap, but it's hard not to stay around and have them mix you up a cocktail once the music's turned up and the beautiful people arrive.

Café Opera CAFE, CLUB
(Map p156; Engen 18; ⊘11am-3am Mon-Sat, noon-12.15am Sun) By day, Café Opera has a literary-cafe feel, though on the weekends, there's also a rota of DJs and a crowd that likes to pump up the jams. When the sun's out, its outside tables are some of the nicest in town to while a way a few hours.

Fincken CLUB
(Map p156; Nygårdsgaten 2a; ⊘7pm-1.30am Wed & Thu, 8pm-2.30am Fri & Sat) A welcoming gay club that has huge weekend nights with house, pop, pure disco and Latino beats keeping the mixed crowd happy. You need to be over 20 on weekends.

Kafe Kippers BAR
(USF; Georgernes Verft 12; ⊘11am-12.30am Mon-Fri, noon-12.30am Sat & Sun) There's a popular restaurant here, but we love Kippers most for a late afternoon glass or two of wine or a cup of tea. When the sun shines, its waterside tables overlooking the sparkling harbour, docks and far hills are highly coveted;

otherwise, the big windows inside are great for a moody view in the rain.

Altona Vinbar WINE BAR
(Map p160; C Sundts gate 22; ⊘6pm-12.30am Mon-Thu, to 1.30am Fri & Sat) Set in a warren of vaulted underground rooms that date from the 16th century, Altona's huge, carefully selected wine list, soft lighting and murmured conversation make it Bergen's most romantic bar (particularly appealing when the weather's cold and wet). The bar menu tends towards tasty comfort food, such as Norwegian lamb burgers (Nkr175).

Terminus Bar WHISKY BAR
(Map p156; Zander Kaaesgate 6, Grand Terminus Hotel; ⊘5pm-midnight) Consistently voted one of the word's best whisky bars, this grand old bar in the Grand Hotel Terminus is the perfect place for a quiet dram. It promises over 500 different tastes, and the oldest whisky dates back to 1960. The 1928 room looks gorgeous both before and after you've sampled a few.

Una Bryggeri BREWERY
(Map p160; Bryggen 7; ⊘11am-1am Sun-Thu, to 2.30am Fri & Sat) Right in the heart of Bryggen, this stylish but informal brewery is a welcome newcomer. There are Norwegian microbrews on tap, including their own; bar staff love their product and are happy to provide tips and tastes to make sure you're happy. Besides ale, they serve good pub-food standards at reasonable prices (for the location) and upstairs there's a dedicated restaurant area.

Henrik PUB
(Map p156; Engen 10; ⊘4pm-12.30am Sun-Fri, from 2pm Sat) Unusually, this petit pub is upstairs but, rest assured, it's the 'brownest' of the brown – well known and loved for its beer selection. Last count there were 56 beers on tap. Our pick? Shh, it's the out-of-towner, Nøgne Ø from south coast Grimstad.

Naboen BAR
(Map p156; Neumanns gate 20; ⊘5pm-1.30am Sun-Thu, 5pm-2.30am Fri & Sat) Basement pub with a good indie soundtrack and big, serious selection of beer. There's also a popular Swedish restaurant upstairs if you need sustenance.

☆ Entertainment

Bergen has something for everyone, from high culture to late-night live-music venues. Check out www.bergenlive.com for major acts on tour. Grieghallen is often the venue.

Hulen LIVE MUSIC
(Map p156; www.hulen.no; Olaf Ryes vei 48; ⊘9pm-3am Thu-Sat mid-Aug–mid-Jun) A veteran of 1968, this is the oldest rock club in northern Europe and one of the classic indie stages of the world. Come here to hear the best up-and-coming west-coast bands, or catch an international act. Hulen means 'cave' and the venue is indeed underground, in a converted bomb shelter.

Østre LIVE MUSIC
(Map p160; www.oestre.no; Østre Skostredet 3) This venue hosts cutting-edge Norwegian electronic artists, along with respected international acts. There are often three or more gigs a week; see the website for its calendar.

Café Sanaa LIVE MUSIC
(Map p156; www.sanaa.no; Marken 31; ⊘8pm-3am Fri & Sat) This little shopfront cafe just up from the lake spills over onto the cobblestones and draws a fun, alternative crowd with live music and, later, resident DJs who might be pumping out West African beats, tango, blues or jazz.

Kafe Kippers/USF Vertfet JAZZ
(USF; ☑55 31 00 60; www.bergenjazzforum.com; Georgernes Verft 12; admission Nkr170; ⊘10pm Fri Sep-May) Check the website for the latest concerts.

Logen LIVE MUSIC
(Map p156; logen-teater.no; Øvre Ole Bulls plass 6; ⊘6pm-2am Mon-Thu, 6pm-3am Fri & Sat, Sun for performances) Part of the Logen theatre, this 3rd-floor bar has a loyal local following for its concerts (Nkr75 to Nkr100) on most Sunday and Monday nights from September to June. For much of the summer, it's a peaceful place for a drink.

ⓘ **BERGEN CARD**

The **Bergen Card** (www.visitbergen. com/bergencard; adult/child 24hr pass Nkr200/75, 48hr Nkr260/100) gives you free travel on local buses; free entrance to some museums, with discounted entry to the rest; free or discounted return trips on the Fløibanen funicular, depending on the time of year; free guided tours of Bergen; and discounts on city and boat sightseeing tours, concerts and cultural performances. It's available from the tourist office, some hotels, the bus terminal and online.

Classical Music Concerts
Bergen has a busy program of concerts throughout summer, many of them focusing on Bergen's favourite son, composer Edvard Grieg. Most take place at evocative open-air venues such as the Grieg Museum (p158), the Sæverud Museum (p158), atop Mt Fløyen and in the park adjacent to Håkonshallen. For details, schedules and ticket sales, see the tourist office; for some classical concert series, the Bergen Card (p170) offers significant discounts.

Bergen Cathedral CLASSICAL MUSIC
(Map p160; ⊘Sun & Thu mid-Jun–late Aug) Free organ recitals.

Grieghallen CLASSICAL MUSIC
(Map p156; ☑55 21 61 50; www.grieghallen.no; Edvard Griegs plass; ⊘Aug-Jun) Performances by the respected Bergen Philharmonic Orchestra.

🔒 **Shopping**

★**Aksdal i Muren** CLOTHING
(Map p160; www.aksdalimuren.no; Østre Muralmenning 23) This enticing shop in a historic landmark building has been ensuring the good people of Bergen are warm and dry since 1883. The city's best selection of rainwear includes cult Swedish labels such as Didriksons, big names like Helle Hansen and Barbour, but also local gems such as Blæst by Lillebøe. We can't think of a better Bergen souvenir than a stripey sou'wester.

Antonio Stasi Classic Cameras CAMERAS
(Map p160; www.antoniostasi.com; Lille Øvregaten 4) Expat Italian Antonio Stasi's shop is both a homage to the golden age of analog photography and something of a drop-in centre for local hipsters, whom he documents in Polaroid photographs. Come in and chat cameras, darkroom techniques or just browse his highly covetable stock of Leica, Contax, Rolleiflex and classic Polaroids.

Bergen Steinsenter GEMS
(Map p160; www.bergen-steinsenter.no; Bredsgården, Bryggen; ⊘11am-4pm Tue-Fri, noon-3pm Sat Jun–mid-Sep, shorter hours rest of year) Satisfy your inner troll at this eccentric gem and crystal merchant, which stocks some stunning geological specimens from around Norway and further afield.

Røst SOUVENIRS
(Map p160; www.butikkenrost.no; Bryggen 15; ⊘10am-10.30pm Jul-Aug, to 6pm Sep-Jun) Short

BUSES FROM BERGEN

DESTINATION	DEPARTURES (DAILY)	COST (NKR)	DURATION (HR)
Ålesund	2	686	10
Oslo	3	680	11
Stavanger	6	550	5½
Stryn	3	538	6½
Trondheim	1	848	14½

on souvenir-buying time and want something a bit more upmarket than a troll doll? This bright boutique right in the centre of Bryggen has a large range of well-designed Norwegian and Scandinavian objects and homewares, as well as local fashion for women, children and babies.

Schau Design FURNITURE
(Map p160; Lille Øvregaten 5; ☺noon-5pm Tue-Fri, to 3.30pm Sat) Nice selection of reasonably priced Scandinavian mid-century objects and furniture, with lots of packable options such as lamps, vases and kitchenware.

Pepper CLOTHING
(Map p156; pepper-bergen.blogspot.no; Christies gate 9) If you are overcome with the urge to get the artfully informal 'Bergen look', this is the city's best-curated fashion retailer. There's a solid selection of Swedish stars such as Filippa K and Acne, Denmark's stylish but sturdy menswear Norse Projects and haute-casual French labels A.P.C. and Maison Kitsune.

Svala & Udd CRAFT
(Map p160; Jacobsfjorden, Bryggen; ☺noon-7pm mid-May–mid-Aug, shorter hours rest of year) At one of Bryggen's many artisan shops, Maria Udd handcrafts interesting skirts, scarves and gloves in felt and fleece, while Svala has a range of bold silver jewellery.

❶ Information

DANGERS & ANNOYANCES

Although Bergen is generally a very safe city, pickpockets are known to operate around the fish market and Bryggen areas.

EMERGENCIES
Ambulance (☑113)
Police (☑112)

TOURIST INFORMATION
Bergen Turlag DNT Office (Map p156; ☑55 33 58 10; www.bergen-turlag.no; Tverrgaten 4; ☺10am-4pm Mon-Wed & Fri, to 6pm Thu, to 3pm Sat) Maps and information on hiking and hut accommodation throughout western Norway.

Bryggen Visitors Centre (Map p160; Jacobsfjorden, Bryggen; ☺9am-5pm mid-May–mid-Sep)
Tourist Office (Map p160; ☑55 55 20 00; www.visitbergen.com; Vågsallmenningen 1; ☺8.30am-10pm Jun-Aug, 9am-8pm May & Sep, 9am-4pm Mon-Sat Oct-Apr) One of the best and busiest in the country, Bergen's tourist office distributes the free and worthwhile *Bergen Guide* booklet, as well as a huge stock of information on the entire region. It also sells rail tickets. If booking or making an enquiry, come early or be prepared to queue.

WEBSITES
Lonely Planet (www.lonelyplanet.com/norway/bergen-and-the-western-fjords) Planning advice, author recommendations, traveller reviews and insider tips.

❶ Getting There & Away

AIR
Bergen airport is at Flesland, about 19km southwest of the centre.
Norwegian (www.norwegian.com) Flights to Oslo and Tromsø.
SAS (www.sas.no) Oslo and Stavanger.
Widerøe (www.wideroe.no) Oslo, Haugesund, Stavanger and many coastal destinations as far as Tromsø.

BOAT
International ferries to/from Bergen dock at Skoltegrunnskaien northwest of the Rosenkrantz tower, while the Hurtigruten coastal ferry leaves from the Hurtigruteterminalen, southwest of the centre, at 8pm daily from mid-April to mid-September, and from 10.30pm the rest of the year.

A number of operators have express boats.
Norled Bergen (☑51 86 87 00; www.norled.no; Kong Christian Frederiks plass 3) offers at least one daily ferry from Bergen to Sogndal (Nkr645; five hours), with some services going on to Flåm (Nkr750; 5½ hours).

BUS
The Bergen **bus terminal** (Map p156) is located on Vestre Strømkaien.

TRAIN

The spectacular train journey between Bergen and Oslo (Nkr349 to Nkr829, 6½ to eight hours, five daily) runs through the heart of Norway. Other destinations include Voss (Nkr189, one hour, hourly) and Myrdal (Nkr286, 2¼ hours, up to nine daily) for connections to the Flåmsbana railway.

ⓘ Getting Around

TO/FROM THE AIRPORT

Flybussen (Map p160; www.flybussen.no; one way/return adult Nkr90/160, child Nkr50/80) Runs up to four times hourly between the airport, the Radisson SAS Royal Hotel, the main bus terminal and opposite the tourist office on Vågsallmenningen.

BICYCLE

Sykkelbutikken (www.sykkelbutikken.no; Kong Oscars gate 81; touring bikes per day/week Nkr200/800; ⊙10am-8pm Mon-Fri, 10am-4pm Sat) Bicycle hire near the train station.

BUS & TRAM

Skyss (🖉177; www.skyss.no) Skyss operates buses and light-rail trams throughout Bergen, its suburbs and into Hordaland. Single tickets can be used on both buses and light rail. Beyond the centre, prices are based on distance (Zone 1 to 2, Nkr29 to Nkr41); 10-trip tickets are good value if you're visiting the composers' museums (Zone 1 to 2, Nkr255). Purchase at the machines at every tram stop. Bergen Card (p170) holders are entitled to free travel within Bergen.

CAR & MOTORCYCLE

Metered parking limited to 30 minutes or two hours applies all over central Bergen. The largest and cheapest (Nkr130 per 24 hours) indoor car park is the 24-hour Bygarasjen at the bus terminal; elsewhere you'll pay upwards of Nkr200. The tourist office has two brochures covering where to park in Bergen.

BOAT

Vågen Harbour Ferry (Beffen; Map p160; 🖉55 56 04 00; adult/child Nkr20/10; ⊙every 10 min 7.30-4pm Mon-Fri year-round, 11am-4pm Sat May-Aug) From late May to late August, the Vågen Harbour Ferry runs between the Torget fish market and Tollbodhopen at Nordnes (near the Bergen Aquarium).

VOSS

POP 13,902

Voss sits on a sparkling lake not far from the fjords and this position has earned it a world-renowned reputation as Norway's adventure capital. The town itself is far from pretty: everyone is here for white-water rafting, bungee jumping and just about anything you can do from a parasail, most of it out in the fjords.

◉ Sights & Activities

Vangskyrkja & St Olav's Cross   CHURCH
(Uttrågata; adult/child Nkr20/free; ⊙10am-4pm Mon-Sat, 2-4pm Sun Jun-Aug, shorter hours rest of year) Voss' stone church occupies the site of an ancient pagan temple. A Gothic-style stone church was built here in the mid-13th century and although the original stone altar and unique wooden spire remain, the Lutheran Reformation of 1536 saw the removal of many original features. The 1923 stained-glass window commemorates the 900th anniversary of Christianity in Voss. Miraculously, the building escaped destruction during the intense German bombing of Voss in 1940.

In a field about 150m southeast of the tourist office stands a weathered stone cross erected by King Olav Haraldsson den Heilige (St Olav) in 1023 to commemorate the local conversion to Christianity.

Voss Folkemuseum   MUSEUM
(www.hardangerogvossmuseum.no; Mølstervegen 143; adult/child Nkr70/free; ⊙10am-5pm mid-May–Aug, 10am-3pm Mon-Fri Sep-Apr) This museum consists of a number of historic farms and homes, with the showpiece a hilltop farm at Mølster, high above Voss. The collection of 16 farm buildings here were once typical of the region and date from 1600 to 1870. Tours are on the hour, every hour.

**Prestegardsmoen Recreational
& Nature Reserve**   HIKING
The Prestegardsmoen Recreational and Nature Reserve extends south from Voss Camping in a series of hiking tracks through elm, birch and pine forests with hundreds of species of plants and birds.

Hangursbahnen   CABLE CAR
(www.vossresort.no; adult/child Nkr100/60; ⊙10am-5pm Jun-Aug) This cable car whisks you to Mt Hangur (660m), high above Voss, for stunning panoramic views over the town and the surrounding mountains. There's a restaurant at the top as well as walking paths.

⬡ Tours

Although normally done from Oslo or Bergen, the **Norway in a Nutshell tour** (adult/child Nkr775/400) can also be done from Voss. It involves rail trips from Voss to Myrd-

(Continued on page 181)

VEGAR ABELSNES PHOTOGRAPHY/GETTY IMAGES ©

Spectacular Norway

Few countries can match the sheer, jaw-dropping beauty of Norway. It begins, like so many Norwegian journeys, with the fjords, but the otherworldly rock formations of the Lofoten Islands, and the ice-bound ramparts of Svalbard are every bit as beautiful. And there's no better way to explore it all than taking to the great outdoors.

Contents

Above Rocky beach at Vestvågøy (p297)

DAVE STAMBOULIS TRAVEL PHOTOGRAPHY/GETTY IMAGES ©

1. Geirangerfjord (p236) **2.** Pulpit Rock (p205) in Lysefjord
3. Hardangerfjord (p184) **4.** Nærøyfjord (p213)

2

NO_LIMIT_PICTURES/GETTY IMAGES ©

Fjords

The fjords of Norway rank among the most dramatic landforms on earth. To travel to Norway and not draw near to one of its signature fjords is to miss an essential element in Norway's enduring appeal.

If Norway's fjords were an art collection, Unesco World Heritage–listed Geirangerfjord would be its masterpiece. Yes, it gets overwhelmed by tour buses and cruise ships in summer, but they're there for a very good reason and their presence only slightly diminishes the experience. Also inscribed on the World Heritage list, Nærøyfjord is similarly popular yet unrelentingly breathtaking. It's merely one of many tributary arms of Sognefjorden, which, at 203km long and 1308m deep, is the world's second-longest and Norway's deepest fjord.

Hardangerfjord is another extensive fjord network sheltering charming villages that promise front-row seats from which to contemplate the beauty at every turn, while away to the south, Lysefjord is long and boasts some of Norway's best views. And that's just the beginning...

4

TOP MAINLAND FJORDS

➡ **Geirangerfjord** The king of Norwegian fjords.

➡ **Sognefjorden** A vast fjord network.

➡ **Hardangerfjord** Rolling hills and lovely villages.

➡ **Lysefjord** Plunging cliffs, cruises and death-defying lookout points.

➡ **Nærøyfjord** One of Norway's narrowest and prettiest fjords.

➡ **Eidfjord** The most spectacular branch of Hardangerfjord.

➡ **Trollfjord** An astonishingly steep fjord on Lofoten.

➡ **Vestfjorden** Sheltered bays and pretty villages separate Lofoten from the mainland.

176

DAVE STAMBOULIS TRAVEL PHOTOGRAPHY/GETTY IMAGES ©

1. Bungee jumping, Lyngenfjord (p322) **2.** Hiking, Jotunheimen (p148) **3.** Kayaking, Sjoa (p141) **4.** Cross-country skiing, Trondheim (p254)

Activities

Norwegians are experts at combining an appreciation of the country's wild beauty with a true sense of adventure. There's a seemingly endless list of summer activities, but winter is a wonderful time for heading out into the snow.

Hiking (Summer)

The right to wander at will in Norway has been inscribed in law for centuries and there's world-class hiking throughout the country. The best trails traverse glaciers or climb through the high country that, by some estimates, covers 90% of Norway.

Extreme Sports (Summer)

Voss, with its mountainous, fjord-strewn hinterland, is Norway's thrill-seeking capital. It's the perfect place to take to the air strapped into a parasail or hurtle towards the earth on a bungee-rope.

Snow Sports (Winter)

Slip through the snow on a sled pulled by huskies. Speed across the ice astride a snowmobile. Or join the Norwegians in their national pastime of skiing downhill or cross-country. Whichever you choose, winter is a terrific time to visit.

White-Water Rafting (Summer)

Norway's steep slopes and icy, scenic rivers create an ideal environment for veteran and beginner rafters alike. Central Norway is rafting's true Norwegian home, but the cascading waters around Sjoa offer the widest range of experiences.

Cycling (Summer)

Cyclists in search of seriously challenging but seriously beautiful routes will find their spiritual home in Norway. Longer routes abound, but there isn't a more exhilarating descent than the one from Finse down to Flåm.

1. Vesterålen (p303) 2. Austvågøy (p290) 3. Flakstadøy (p298)
4. Reconstructed Viking ship, Vestvågøy (p297)

Lofoten

It is the fjords that have forever marked Norway as a land of singular natural splendour, but the surreal beauty of the Lofoten Islands is a worthy rival. For sheer drama, this magical archipelago (which in summer is bathed in the crystal-clear light of the north) could well be Norway's most beautiful corner.

Moskenesøy

Tolkienesque landscapes and glacier-carved landforms lend Moskenesøy a supernatural beauty that is truly special. The village of Å is the island's soul, while Reinefjord is particularly scenic.

Flakstadøy

Isolated, wind-blown crags along the southern shore are the most eye-catching feature of Flakstadøy, but the old-world beauty of Nusfjord and the utter improbability of white-sand beaches at Ramberg and Flakstad also deserve attention.

Austvågøy

Most people's entry point into the Lofoten, Austvågøy is a gentle introduction to the islands' charm. The Raftsund strait and the dizzyingly narrow Trollfjord provide the backdrop, while the villages of Kabelvåg and Henningsvær offer perfect bases.

Vestvågøy

Many travellers rush across Vestvågøy on their way deeper into the Lofoten, but the Lofotr Viking Museum captures the spirit of more epic times and the walk from Unstad to Eggum is magnificent.

Værøy

Intimate little Værøy, occupying Lofoten's southern reaches, is Moskenesøy's rival for the title of Lofoten's most picturesque island. The combination of vast colonies of seabirds, soaring ridgelines and remote, tiny villages is glorious.

Polar bear on Svalbard ice

Svalbard

The Svalbard archipelago – as close to the North Pole as it is to mainland Norway, and the world's most accessible slice of the polar north – is one of the natural world's grand epics.

STAND-OUT SVALBARD

➡ **Midnight-sun hiking** Trek deep into the interior or close to Longyearbyen.

➡ **Pyramiden** Take a summer boat trip or winter snowmobile expedition past the Nordenskjöldbreen glacier to this former Russian mining settlement.

➡ **Dog-sledding** The perfect way to experience the silence of Spitsbergen.

➡ **Polar bears** Spot the Arctic's most soulful presence, but hopefully from afar.

➡ **Magdalenefjord** A serious contender for the title of Norway's most beautiful fjord.

Arguably Europe's last and most extensive great wilderness area, Svalbard has all the elements for an Arctic idyll. Here you'll find more polar bears than people, as well as a roll-call of Arctic wildlife that includes walruses, reindeer, Arctic foxes and a stunning collection of bird species. They roam a landscape that, for the most part, remains ice-bound throughout the year – an astonishing 60% of Svalbard is covered by glaciers. Splendidly uninhabited fjords, formidable peaks never traversed by a human and the echoes of the great sagas of polar exploration are all part of the mix. Whether experienced in the strange blue half-light of the Arctic night (late October to mid-February) or the midnight sun (mid-April to mid-August), Svalbard is quite simply unforgettable.

(Continued from page 172)

al and from there to Flåm, then the boat to Gudvangen and the bus back to Voss or vice versa. Book through the tourist office, **NSB** (☑ 56 52 80 07; www.nsb.no) at the train station or online directly with **Fjord Tours** (☑ 81 56 82 22; www.fjordtours.com).

Ask also at the tourist office for details on day excursions to Ulvik and Eidfjord on Hardangerfjord.

✨ Festivals

Vossajazz   MUSIC
(www.vossajazz.no) An innovative jazz, folk and world-music festival held annually in late March/early April.

Extreme Sports Festival   SPORT
(Veko; www.ekstremsportveko.com) A week-long festival at the end of June that combines all manner of extreme sports (skydiving, paragliding and base jumping) with local and international music acts.

Sheep's Head Food Festival   FOOD
(www.smalahovesleppet.no; ☺ late Sep) Celebrating the local delicacy with plenty of sheep's heads to go round, as well as entertainment.

🛏 Sleeping

Voss Camping   CAMPGROUND €
(☑ 56 51 15 97; www.vosscamping.no; Prestegardsalléen 40; campsites Nkr170, cabins from Nkr600; ☺ Easter-Sep; P@) Lakeside and centrally located, Voss Camping offers basic facilities and a rather rowdy summer scene.

Tvinde Camping   CAMPGROUND €
(Tvinde; ☑ 56 51 69 19; www.tvinde.no; campsites Nkr240, cabins from Nkr570; ☺ year-round; P☎) A scenic site beside a waterfall about 12km north of town. Access is on the Voss–Gudvangen bus (20 minutes).

Voss Vandrerhjem   HOSTEL €
(☑ 56 51 20 17; www.vosshostel.com; Evangervegen 68; dm/s/d from Nkr235/695/1150; P@) This modern hostel offers decent rooms with en suite and fine views; ask for a top-floor, lakeside room. Bicycles can be hired and there's a free sauna.

Fleischer's Hotel   HISTORIC HOTEL €€
(☑ 56 52 05 00; www.fleischers.no; Evangervegen; s/d from Nkr1290/1790; P☎☒) Fleischer's Hotel, which opened in its current

form in 1889, has a quaint historic charm. Rooms tend towards old-fashioned rather than authentic, but some have lake views, there's a swimming pool (with children's pool) and a lavish dining hall. Celebrity guests who once stayed here include Edvard Grieg, in 1901.

Fleischer's Appartement   APARTMENTS €€
(☑ 56 52 05 00; www.fleischers.no; Evangervegen 13; 2-/4-bed apt Nkr1200/2100; P) This lakeside annexe of Fleischer's Hotel offers well-equipped self-catering units in an almost comically brutal '60s building.

🍴 Eating & Drinking

★ **Tre Brør Café & Bar**   CAFE €
(www.vosscafe.no; Vangsgata 28; sandwiches & light meals Nkr85-185; ☺ 10am-3am Tue-Sat, 10am-11pm Sun & Mon; ☎) This casual cafe in one of Voss' few original buildings is a long-time favourite with both travellers and locals. The recent addition of a basement bar means the fun continues until late most nights. Upstairs, there's a selection of snacky staples – organic beef burgers, soups, wraps – and a changing daily special, often with an Asian twist.

Beer is care of Voss Bryggeri, one of Norway's best, and there are live acts or DJ sets downstairs most nights.

Ringheim Kafé   NORWEGIAN €€
(www.ringheimkafe.no; Vangsgata 32; mains Nkr160-220; ☺ lunch) One of numerous cafes lined up along the main Vangsgata thoroughfare, Ringheim has outdoor tables and a cafeteria-style interior. Far from fancy, it serves regional-style dishes, including elk burgers (Nkr165), baked trout (Nkr210) and *hjortekoru* (Nkr180), the local smoked sausage with potato and cabbage stew.

ℹ Information

Tourist office (☑ 40 61 77 00; www.visitvoss. no; Vangsgata 20; ☺ 8am-7pm Mon-Fri, 9am-7pm Sat, noon-7pm Sun Jun-Aug, 8.30am-4pm Mon-Fri Sep-May) Well-stocked tourist office that also offers a booking service for various activities.

ℹ Getting There & Away

BUS
Buses stop at the train station, west of the centre. Frequent bus services connect Voss with Bergen (Nkr163, two hours), Flåm (Nkr143, 1¼ hours) and Sogndal (Nkr299, three hours), via Gudvangen and Aurland.

TRAIN

The **Norges Statsbaner** (Norwegian State Railways, NSB; ☑ 56 52 80 00) rail services to/from Bergen (Nkr189, one hour, hourly) and Oslo (Nkr349 to Nkr829, 5½ to six hours, five daily) connect at Myrdal (Nkr117, 50 minutes) with the scenic line down to Flåm.

AROUND VOSS

Evangar

This tiny village, just off the highway around 12km west of Voss, has a delightful toy-town feel, with a tight grid of restored

VOSS ACTIVITIES

If slow boats up the fjords seem like a pretty tame response to extraordinary Norwegian landscapes, Voss may be your antidote.

To book activities, contact individual operators or get in touch with the tourist office (p181).

Paragliding, Parasailing & Bungee Jumping

Nordic Ventures (☑ 56 51 00 17; www.nordicventures.com; ☺ Apr–mid-Oct) is one of the most professional operators of its kind in Norway, offering tandem paragliding flights (Nkr1500), parasailing (solo/dual flights Nkr575/950) and even 180m-high, 115km/h bungee jumps (Nkr1800) from a parasail! It claims to offer the highest bungee jump in Europe. As its motto says: 'Be brave. Even if you're not, pretend to be. No one can tell the difference'.

Kayak Fjord Expeditions

If you do one activity in Voss (or anywhere in the fjords), make it this one. The guided kayak tours offered by Nordic Ventures are the perfect way to experience Hardangerfjord, stunning Nærøyfjord and beyond without hurry or crowds. The tours come in a range of options.

One day (nine-hour) tours cost Nkr995 (including lunch and transport to/from the fjord), while the two-day version costs Nkr2295 and allows you to camp on the shores of the fjord. But our favourite is the three-day kayaking and hiking expedition (Nkr3295), which explores the fjords in kayaks and then takes you high above them for unrivalled views.

Nordic Ventures rents out kayaks (one/two/three days Nkr550/925/1295) if you'd rather branch out on your own.

White-Water Rafting

Voss Rafting Senter (☑ 56 51 05 25; www.vossrafting.no) specialises in white-water rafting (Nkr1150) with some gentler, more family-friendly options (from Nkr630). Rafters (and riverboarders) can choose between three very different rivers: the Stranda (Class III to IV), Raundalen (Class III to V) and Vosso (Class II). The company's motto is: 'We guarantee to wet your pants'.

Skiing

The ski season in Voss usually lasts from early December until April. The winter action focuses on the cable-car route up Mt Hangur from Voss, where there's a winter ski school. Those with vehicles can opt for Bavallen, 5km north of the centre, which is used for international downhill competitions. On the plateau and up the Raundalen Valley at Mjølfjell, you'll also find excellent cross-country skiing.

Other Activities

Voss Rafting Senter organises **canyoning** (Nkr1150), **waterfall abseiling** (from Nkr990), **riverboarding** (Nkr1150), **fishing** (from Nkr630) and **hiking** (from Nkr530). For additional guided-hiking options, contact **Vossafjell** (☑ 99 15 15 00; www.vossafjell.no).

Voss tourist office can also provide details of **cycling routes** and **self-guided hikes**, and sells fishing permits.

wooden houses and gorgeous setting by a lake. There's absolutely zip to do here besides relax or maybe go for a languid row, but it makes a blissfully peaceful alternative to Voss during its high-season frenzy.

★**Patina**   GUESTHOUSE €€
(☑90 95 73 88; www.evanger.net; Knute Nelson gata 17; 2-bed apt Nkr1000; ☺cafe & shop 11am-5pm Tue-Sat Jul–mid-Aug, 11am-5pm Sat Sep-Jun) A labour of love dreamt up by three local women, Patina is part guesthouse, part cafe and part vintage shop. There's one large, family-sized apartment overlooking the lake available for daily/weekly stays (and sometimes a smaller one); its winning decor shows off the trio's excellent eye for evocative, whimsical design pieces. Most of the objects and furniture are also for sale.

The charming cafe serves up beautiful homemade cakes and over-stuffed sandwiches and the shop is full of amazing finds, most of it sourced directly from friends and neighbours. Guests can borrow a (vintage, naturally) row boat for exploring Lake Evangervatnet.

Evangerista   GUESTHOUSE €
(☑92 24 81 16; www.evangerista.no; Knute Nelson gata 15; dm/d/q with shared bathroom Nkr200/600/1000) This bright, bohemian guesthouse offers two double rooms, a four-bed room, and a family room with bunks, daubed in jewel-like hues and decorated with Indian and vintage textiles. Mona, the friendly owner, serves a breakfast of organic bread, homemade muesli and coffee (Nkr100) daily, and will also make lunches (Nkr100) and dinner (Nkr150) to order.

Myrkdalen

This ski resort has only been in operation for a decade or so but has recently added a luxurious year-round hotel. The season runs from mid-November to mid-April and experiences 5m snow falls on average. During summer there's great hiking with several marked high mountain trails starting at the hotel, a program of nature-based kids' activities as well as easy access to Voss' roll call of outdoor pursuits.

**Myrkdalen Cabins
& Apartments**   APARTMENTS €€
(☑56 52 30 60; www.myrkdalenhotel.no; studio Nkr800, 3-bed Nkr1200) These black-timber, turf-topped, self-catering cabins and apart-

ments form a sprawling village beneath the ski runs. Inside they show an attention to detail and flair: all have flat-screen TVs and dishwashers, most have a fireplace, and some have laundry facilities and saunas too.

Myrkdalen Hotel   HOTEL €€€
(☑56 52 30 40; www.myrkdalenhotel.no; s/d Nkr1095/1495) The resort revolves around this large, stylish hotel and it provides a large range of facilities and dining spaces for guests who often spend a week or more here. Rooms are decorated in a super-smart Norwegian contemporary style, with light wood, greys and pops of colour; there's a large range of room sizes and layouts to suit different needs.

Eating options include fine dining in winter, along with a year-round casual restaurant, fondue station, two bars and a cafe.

Stalheim

POP 200

High above the valley, Stalheim is a place of extraordinary natural beauty with an interesting, lively past. Between 1647 and 1909, Stalheim was a stopping-off point for travellers on the Royal Mail route between Copenhagen, Christiania (Oslo) and Bergen. A road was built for horses and carriages in 1780. The mailmen and their weary steeds rested in Stalheim and changed to fresh horses after climbing up the valley and through the Stalheimskleiva gorge, flanked by the thundering Stalheim and Sivle waterfalls.

Although a modern road winds up through two tunnels from the valley floor, the **old mail road** (Stalheimskleiva) climbs up at an astonishing 18% gradient. As tour buses, improbably, use this road, it's a one-way road: you can drive down, but not up.

◉ Sights

Everyone comes here for the view from the Stalheim Hotel garden. If you're not staying at the hotel, the **terrace** (☺9.30am-6pm mid-May–Sep) **FREE** has a breathtaking outlook straight down Nærøydalen.

Stalheim Folkemuseum   MUSEUM
(☑56 52 01 22; Stalheim; adult/child Nkr60/free; ☺on request) This folk museum, near the Stalheim Hotel, has exhibits of traditional crafts and rustic objects as well as 30 log buildings laid out as a traditional farm. It

only opens if there are 10 or more visitors; ask at the hotel for details.

Activities

There are at least two rewarding half-day hikes that begin at Stalheim.

Husmannsplassen Nåli
HIKE

This cotter's farm, along the ledge from Stalheim high above Nærøydalen, was occupied until 1930. The route here (two hours return) is not for the faint-hearted. The path beneath the cliff wall is extremely narrow in parts and there is nothing between you and the valley floor far below; don't even think of walking here after rain.

As long as you don't suffer from vertigo, it's one of Norway's most beautiful walks. Ask for directions from the reception of the Stalheim Hotel.

Brekkedalen
HIKE

This three-hour return hike leads up into the valley above Stalheim. Locals in the know claim it's the region's prettiest walk, and the views are certainly magnificent. It's a relatively easy way to leave behind the crowds and have this stunning high country all to yourself. The tourist office in Voss has route descriptions, or ask at Stalheim Hotel for directions.

🛏 Sleeping

Stalheim Fjord og Fjellhytter
MOUNTAIN HUT ₵

(✆56 51 28 47; www.stalheim.no; 4- to 6-person cabins per night/week from Nkr750/5500) These cabins are large and comfortable and have the views you're here for.

Stalheimsøy Gard
FARMHOUSE ₵₵

(✆56 52 00 22; www.stalheimsoy.no; 6-bed apt per night/week Nkr1365/8400, 12-bed apt Nkr2100/13,230) This farmhouse with two family-sized apartments is in the valley far below.

★Stalheim Hotel
HISTORIC HOTEL ₵₵₵

(✆56 52 01 22; www.stalheim.com; s/d/superior from Nkr1160/1750/2150; ⊘mid-May–mid-Sep; P@🛜) Arguably Norway's most spectacularly sited hotel, this large '60s place has simple, spacious rooms, around half of which have glorious views (room 324, in particular, once featured in Conde Nast Traveler's 'best rooms with a view'). The stunning lounge, lobby and dining hall are filled with a truly exceptional collection of Norwegian mid-century design and historical paintings.

Despite the onslaught of tour groups during the day, the friendly staff and elegant owner maintain a sense of calm. The buffets at lunch (Nkr250) and dinner (Nkr450) are lavish, or there is an a la carte menu (mains Nkr245); meals work out cheaper on half-board rates.

ℹ Getting There & Away

To reach Stalheim from Voss, take any bus (Nkr101, one hour, four to 11 daily) towards the towns of Gudvangen and Aurland, but you may have to hike 1.3km up from the main road unless you can persuade the bus driver to make the short detour.

Myrdal

Between the towns of Voss and Finse, Myrdal is the junction of the Oslo–Bergen railway and the spectacularly steep Flåmsbana railway; it's also a famous stop on the Norway in a Nutshell tour. From here, the dramatic Flåmsbana line twists 20km down to Flåm on Aurlandsfjorden, an arm of Sognefjorden.

HARDANGERFJORD

Running from the Atlantic to the steep wall of central Norway's Hardangervidda Plateau, Hardangerfjord is classic Norwegian fjord country. There are many beautiful corners, although our picks would take in Eidfjord, Ulvik and Utne, while Folgefonna National Park offers glacier walks and top-level hiking. You can easily explore Hardangerfjord from Bergen; www.hardangerfjord.com is a good resource.

Norheimsund

POP 2224

Tranquil Norheimsund serves as the gateway to Hardangerfjord. There are more beautiful places further into the fjord network, but it's a pretty little town nonetheless. Ferries from here head to Eidfjord, making it a useful staging post if you're travelling on public transport.

◎ Sights

Steinsdalsfossen
WATERFALL

Just 1km west of Norheimsund along Rv7, this 50m-high waterfall is a far cry from Norway's highest, but it does offer the chance to walk behind the water. It can get overcrowded with tour buses in summer; inexplicably, this is one of the most visited natural sites in Norway.

Hardanger Fartøyvernsenter MUSEUM
(☑47 47 98 39; www.fartoyvern.no; adult/child Nkr90/50; ⊙10am-5pm early May-early Sep) ✦ This engaging museum keeps alive the local boat-building tradition and is home to old wooden boats, exhibitions on restoration procedures and rope-making, as well as temporary exhibitions. Children can try their hand at building a boat and other maritime skills. The museum also offers three daily 2.5-hour cruises on the fjord in a restored cutter (mid-June to mid-August; adult/child Nkr330/165).

🛏 Sleeping

Oddland Camping CAMPGROUND €
(☑56 55 16 86; www.oddlandcamping.no; small/family cabins Nkr650/1250; ⊙small cabins Apr-Oct, family cabins year-round; 🛜) This well-equipped, family-run camp by the lake has good fjord views and simple cabins. There's access to a new bike and walking track, and there are bikes for hire.

★ Sandven Hotel HISTORIC HOTEL €€
(☑56 55 20 88; www.sandvenhotel.no; s/d from Nkr1090/1390; 🅿🛜) Located right on the waterfront in the centre of Norheimsund, the atmospheric Sandven Hotel dates from 1857 and has loads of charm, expansive balconies and excellent views from the fjord-facing rooms. Its public spaces are lavish but unusually light with white-painted floorboards and pale oak boiserie.

Along with the grand dining spaces, there's also a pleasant fjord-side cafe and clubby bar that offers an excellent beer selection. And, yes, it has the requisite celeb room, the Crown Prince suite, where the future king of Norway once stayed.

❶ Information

Tourist office (☑56 55 31 84; www.visitkvam.no; ⊙10am-6pm Jun–Aug, to 4pm Mon-Fri May & Sep) The main tourist office for Norheimsund and Øystese is located at Steinsdalsfossen.

❶ Getting There & Away

Of the up to five daily buses between Bergen (Nkr137) and Norheimsund, the 7.30am bus connects with the 8.50am ferry that travels from Norheimsund to Eidfjord (one-way Nkr265). From Voss, most services require a change in Arna.

Øystese
POP 1881

Just around the shoreline from Norheimsund, Øystese has an exceptional art museum, the kind you just don't expect to find in a small fjord-side village. Interesting detours abound, including the constant lure of Hardangerfjord's famed fruit farms.

◉ Sights

Kunsthuset Kabuso GALLERY
(www.kabuso.no; adult/child incl admission to Ingebrigt Vik Museum Nkr60/free; ⊙10am-5pm Tue-Sun Jun-Aug, shorter hours rest of year) The Kunsthuset Kabuso runs a fascinating program that features big-name contemporary artists (Damien Hirst, Matthew Barney and James Turrell have all exhibited here in the past) during most of the year, with summer shows that focus on Norwegian identity and traditional, often local, work.

The museum also has a range of concerts right across the musical spectrum year-round (Nkr180 to Nkr250); the small theatre has fantastic acoustics.

Ingebrigt Vik Museum MUSEUM
(www.kabuso.no; adult/child incl admission to Kunsthuset Kabuso Nkr60/free; ⊙10am-5pm Tue-Sun Jun-Aug, shorter hours rest of year) Under the direction of the Kunsthuset Kabuso, this permanent collection of the work of Ingebrigt Vik (1867–1927), one of Norway's best-loved sculptors, is housed in a beautiful and unusual early modernist pavillion designed by Torgeir Alvsaker. Vik was born in Øystese, and although he spent most of his working life in Paris, he returned to the fjords in his last years. Pieces in bronze, plaster and marble are on display.

Steinstø Fruktgard FARM
(www.steinsto.no; Steinstø; ⊙11am-5pm Sun-Fri, 11am-4pm Sat mid-Jun–mid-Oct) ✦ A high summer pilgrimage to this farm, a short distance east of Øystese, rewards with ripe strawberries in June and a bounty of raspberries, cherries, plums and apples in July. A cafe serves great apple juice and a rustic apple cake, as well as *lefse* (flat bread) and waffles. If you come on Sunday afternoon there is a homey late lunch (mains Nkr165).

Tours can be arranged for groups, but it's often possible to tag along.

BERGEN & THE SOUTHWESTERN FJORDS ØYSTESE

🛏 Sleeping

Hardangerfjord Hotel   HOTEL €€€
(📞56 55 63 00; www.hardangerfjord-hotell.no; s/d
from Nkr1330/1950; 🅿🛜❄) This large modern hotel on the fjord has views across the
water to mountains crowned by the Folgefonna icecap. Rooms have been renovated
and are comfortable, if on the bland side. It
has a restaurant, heated swimming pool and
minigolf, and can arrange other activities.

ℹ Getting There & Away

There are at least five daily buses between
Øystese and Bergen (Nkr135, 1¾ hours) via
Norheimsund.

Ulvik

POP 1129

Located in the innermost reaches of
Hardangerfjord at the heart of Norway's
apple-growing region, Ulvik is framed by
mountains and affords wonderful views up
the fjord. You're in the heart of stunning fjord
country dotted with farmsteads and almost
too many cycling and hiking opportunities in
the surrounding hills. The town is bathed in
silence once the tourist boats disappear.

⊙ Sights & Activities

The tourist office can point you in the direction of hikes in the surrounding area,
including a 5km trail that takes you past
four fruit farms in the hills above town;
one of these, the **Hardanger Saft og Sud-
erfabrikk** (Hardanger Juice & Cider Factory; www.
hardangersider.no), also produces apple cider.
Visits to the farms are possible for groups,
but ask the tourist office if you can tag along
on a tour that's already going.

🛏 Sleeping & Eating

Ulvik Fjord Hotel   HOTEL, CAMPGROUND €€
(📞56 52 61 70; www.ulvikfjord.no; tent/caravan sites
Nkr180/220, 4-person cabins from Nkr600, d from
Nkr985; 🅿🛜) At the entrance to town, this
well-run guesthouse offers very comfortable
rooms, some of which have balconies overlooking a bubbling stream. The main buidling
is across the road from the water, but the
campsites and huts are right by the fjord.

Doktergarden   B&B €€
(📞90 76 70 98; www.doktergarden.no; d Nkr1000;
🅿🛜) You'll need to book ahead at this
charming old timber farmhouse, perched on
a rise about 2km east of the village centre,

as Bjørnar and Bjørg operate it on an 'as
needs' basis. The rooms, most with shared
bathroom, are bright, comfortable and have
fjord views; the airy garden is a sun trap too.

Brakanes Hotel   HOTEL €€€
(📞56 52 61 05; www.brakanes-hotel.no; s/d
Nkr1185/1685, with fjord views Nkr1385/1885;
🅿🛜❄) This large modern hotel has a
front-row seat to some of the best views in
Hardangerfjord, none finer than those from
the balconies in its fjord-facing rooms. All
rooms are traditional, as are the public spaces, although the lounge and casual dining
area have had a recent stylish makeover.

The soaring glass frontage from these
areas also has intoxicating views, to say the
least. The restaurant has buffet (Nkr450) and
a la carte dinner service (mains Nkr280), but
we'd opt for lunch, where peace reigns and
lunch specials (Nkr155) offer hearty, homey
dishes such as local lamb sausages and potato gratin or salmon and asparagus.

Drøs Bakeri & Cafe   CAFE €€
(📞91 62 57 71; Tyssevike 36; ⊙noon-9pm Mon-
Thu, noon-2am Fri & Sat, noon-6pm Sun late Jun-
late Aug, Fri & Sat Sep-May) A friendly, bustling
cafe with a menu of easy, international dishes (from Nkr150), coffee and cake. It morphs
into a surprisingly raucous bar on weekend
nights. There's a great selection of French
and Italian wines that can be enjoyed during
either of its moods.

ℹ Information

Ulvik Tourist Office (📞56 52 62 80; www.har-
dangerfjord.com; Tyssevike 15; ⊙10am-4pm Jul
& Aug, shorter hours rest of year) The tourist
office has walking maps and bicycle hire (half/
full day Nkr150/200) and can arrange fishing
licences and waterskiing (from Nkr200).

ℹ Getting There & Away

Buses run three to five times daily between Voss
and Ulvik (Nkr126, 1¼ hours).

Eidfjord

POP 950

Eidfjord is one of the most beautifully sited towns in this part of Norway, dwarfed by
sheer mountains and cascading waterfalls.
Eidfjord's beauty does, however, come at a
price. Although it's only accessible by ferry
or spiral tunnels, in summer cruise ships arrive on an almost daily basis, and the town
can get overwhelmed.

⊙ Sights

Viking Burial Mounds
ARCHAEOLOGICAL SITE

(Hæreid; adult/child Nkr90/40, Troll Train Nkr90/40; ⊙Troll Train hourly 10am-5.30pm Jun-Aug) The 350 Viking burial mounds found here make this the largest Iron Age site in western Norway, dating from AD 400 to 1000. The tourist office can point you in their direction and supply a basic map with a marked 90-minute walking trail.

Another way to reach these mounds is with the Troll Train – a Noddy train bus thingy – that travels up to the Hæreid Plateau, where the most accessible graves are. These run only when cruise ships are docked; tickets can be purchased at the tourist office.

Kjeåsen Farm
FARM

Kjeåsen Farm, 6km northeast of Eidfjord and close to the treeline, 530m above the valley floor, should not be missed. Now one of Norway's top scenic locations, the wonderfully remote farm buildings are still inhabited by a woman who has lived alone here for more than 40 years – alone, that is, apart from the busloads of tourists who visit the farm every day in summer.

According to some accounts, there has been a farm here for 400 years, although vehicle access was only possible with the construction of the road in 1975. This road goes through a one-way tunnel, driving up on the hour, down on the half-hour; although the tunnel is open 24 hours, the latest you should drive up to the farm is 5pm, so as to respect the privacy of Kjeåsen's inhabitant.

It's possible to climb up to the farm on foot (four hours return), but it's steep and quite perilous, involving at least one rope-bridge; the path begins in Sæ in Simadal with parking by Sima Power Plantask – ask the tourist office for directions. If Kjeåsen Farm has piqued your curiosity, the booklet *Kjeåsen in Eidfjord*, by Per A Holst, tells the history of the farm and its inhabitants; it's available for Nkr20 from the Eidfjord tourist office.

Skytjefossen
WATERFALL

Plunging almost 300m off the Hardangervidda Plateau to the valley floor below, these falls, 12km north of Eidfjord in the Simadalen valley, are among the highest in Norway. To reach the trailhead, drive as far as Tveit and park just after the last house. The hike to the falls and back takes 1½ hours.

Hardangervidda Natursenter
MUSEUM

(www.hardangerviddanatursenter.no; Øvre Eidfjord; adult/child/family Nkr120/60/280; ⊙9am-8pm mid-Jun–mid-Aug, 10am-6pm Apr–mid-Jun & mid-Aug–Oct) The exceptional Hardangervidda Natursenter is a fantastic introduction to one of Norway's most beautiful national parks, and is located 6.5km southeast of Eidfjord in Øvre Eidfjord. As well as providing detailed trekking maps and advice on trails and skiing, the centre screens a 20-minute film with dramatic panoramic footage of the park: if you can't visit its inner depths on foot, this is the next best thing.

There are also interactive displays, informative explanations of the region's natural history, fish tanks of mountain species, and interesting geology exhibits.

⚡ Activities

In addition to hiking up to Kjeåsen Farm and trekking in the Hardangervidda National Park, a range of other activities are available. Boat rental is possible (half/full day for a medium-sized motor boat Nkr300/500); ask at the tourist office (p188), Vik Pensjonat (p188) or Eidfjord Fjell og Fjord Hotel (p188).

Flat Earth
ADVENTURE SPORTS

(☑ 47 60 68 47; www.flatearth.no; adult incl crampons & ice axes Nkr700) One of the best activities operators in Norway's fjord country, Flat Earth arranges sea/river kayaking (three/six hours Nkr450/850), white-water rafting (Nkr480, three hours), climbing (Nkr250, three hours), downhill mountain-biking (half/full day Nkr150/200) and glacier hikes (Nkr740, full day).

Its headquarters are close to the Hardangervidda Natursenter (p187) in Øvre Eidfjord, 6.5km southeast of Eidfjord. It also rents out sea kayaks (Nkr200, full day), canoes (Nkr140 first hour, Nkr40 each hour after) and mountain bikes (half/full day Nkr150/200).

🛏 Sleeping & Eating

★Eidfjord Gjestegiveri
GUESTHOUSE €

(☑53 66 53 46; www.ovre-eidfjord.com; Øvre Eidfjord; huts Nkr480, s/d without bathroom Nkr690/980; ⊙May-Aug; 🅿) This delightful guesthouse run by Dutch owners Eric and Inge has a homely feel with just five sweetly furnished double rooms and one single, upstairs in a beautifully maintained building built in 1896. There are six cute camping huts that are self-catering and use facilities in the main house's basement.

Breakfasts are good (the secret's in the homemade bread) and there's a pancake cafe, which has around 20 varieties of fantastic, filling, sweet and salty Dutch pancakes, with toppings that range from mountain trout to Hardanger apple compote. It also has a good range of dried meals for hikers heading out into the wilds. It's 6.5km from central Eidfjord, and is close to the Hardangervidda Natursenter.

Sæbø Camping
CAMPGROUND €
(☑ 53 66 59 27; www.saebocamping.com; Øvre Eidfjord; tent & caravan sites Nkr210, cabins Nkr470-1110; ☺ mid-May–mid-Sep; ☞) This spacious and well-equipped lakeside campsite has a pretty location in Måbødalen, just 500m from the Hardangervidda Natursenter. The owners promise freshly baked bread in the mornings and there are canoes for hire.

Vik Pensjonat
GUESTHOUSE €€
(☑ 53 66 51 62; www.vikpensjonat.com; Eidfjord; s/d with shared bathroom Nkr500/880, d/f with private bathroom Nkr1100/1580, cabins Nkr800-1150; ℗) This appealing place in the centre of Eidfjord, not far from the water's edge, is set in a lovely renovated old home. It offers a friendly welcome and cosy rooms. Rooms with balconies are sought after, but the modern six-person cabin on the riverbank is also outstanding.

The attached cafe is one of the better places to eat in town, with reasonable prices (mains Nkr165 to Nkr210) and everything from soups and sandwiches to main dishes such as mountain trout.

Eidfjord Fjell og Fjord Hotel
HOTEL €€
(☑ 53 66 52 64; www.effh.no; Eidfjord; d Nkr1390, s/d with fjord view Nkr1150/1570) This modern, brightly decorated hotel on an elevated ledge overlooking town has a stylish lounge and dining room. The rooms, apart from the new *kunst* (art) ones, are yet to be given the same makeover, but are still comfortable and many have decent views of the fjord. The garden terrace with its sweeping outlook is a fine place to end the day.

ℹ Information

Eidfjord tourist office (☑ 53 67 34 00; www.visiteidfjord.no; Simadalsvegen 3; ☺ 9am-7pm Mon-Fri, 10am-6pm Sat & Sun mid-Jun–mid-Aug, 10am-5pm Mon-Fri mid-Aug–mid-Jun)

ℹ Getting There & Away

BUS

Up to five buses run daily between Eidfjord and Odda (1¾ hours) and some continue on to Geilo. In summer, a minibus service (Nkr100) operates between Tinnhølen lake/Trondsbu and the main Rv7 Eidfjord–Geilo road; it's a convenient entry/exit point for hiking on the Hardangervidda Plateau.

CAR

The spectacular, and often very windy, Hardanger Bridge (the longest tunnel-to-tunnel suspension bridge in the world), joins Bruravik and Brimnes, just west of Eidford along the Rv7/13.

Around Eidfjord

Eidfjord is a gateway to the **Hardangervidda Plateau**, the largest mountain plateau in northern Europe and the site of one of Norway's largest national parks. From Eidfjord, the Rv7 twists up through Måbødalen, taking in a number of corkscrewing tunnels, before climbing up onto the plateau.

Vøringsfossen
WATERFALL
At the summit after a steep 20km drive, and where Hardangervidda begins, is the stunning, 182m-high Vøringfoss Waterfall. There are actually numerous waterfalls here, which together are called Vøringsfossen. They plunge over the plateau's rim and down into the canyon, some with a vertiginous drop of 145m. The best views are from the lookout next to the Fossli Hotel (parking Nkr40) or from a number of lookouts reached from the Vøringsfossen Cafeteria back down the valley on the Rv7.

This is one of Norway's most popular natural attractions, with an endless stream of tour buses in summer (the record is 43 buses at any one time). Public buses between Geilo and Odda pass right by the falls.

Fossli Hotel
HISTORIC HOTEL €€
(☑ 53 66 57 77; www.fossli-hotel.com; s/d Nkr890/1290; ☺ May-Sep; ℗) If you fancy falling asleep to the roar of cascading water, the Fossli Hotel is set just back from the precipice. The views from this historic hotel are stunning and though rooms might be a little faded, they have character and modern parquet floors. Best of all, staying overnight means enjoying the falls once the crowds disappear down the mountain.

The hotel is run by Erik, a quiet and engaging host with a treasure-trove of stories from the Hardangervidda region, whose great-grandfather built the hotel in the 1890s. Edvard Grieg composed his Opus 66 in the hotel. The hotel is well signposted 1.3km off the Rv7. The hotel's restaurant (mains Nkr190 to Nkr270) serves fine Norwegian dishes, such as lamb, baked salmon and wild deer, and there's a waffle cafe downstairs.

Kinsarvik & Lofthus

POP 3382

The towns of Kinsarvik and nearby Lofthus rest peacefully on the shore of Sørfjorden, an offshoot of Hardangerfjord in the heart of a region known as Ullensvang, home to an estimated half a million fruit trees.

Kinsarvik wasn't always so serene – it was home to up to 300 Vikings from the 8th to 11th centuries. The small U-shaped patch of greenery opposite the Kinsarvik tourist office is all that remains of the former Viking port. Kinsarvik offers an appealing access trail past the four cooling Husedalen waterfalls, along what's known as the Monk's Stairway, and onto the network of tracks through the wild forest of Hardangervidda National Park.

If driving here from the north side of the fjord, you'll get to use the recently completed **Hardanger Bridge**, the longest tunnel-to-tunnel suspension bridge in the world.

◉ Sights

Kinsarvik Stone Church　　　　CHURCH
(Kinsarvik) Built in around 1180, this is one of Norway's oldest stone churches. It was restored in the 1960s; the walls still bear traces of lime-and-chalk paintings depicting Michael the Archangel weighing souls while the devil tries to tip the scales. According to local legend, the church was built by Scottish invaders on the site of an earlier stave church.

Grieg's Hut　　　　HISTORIC BUIDLING
(Lofthus; ⊙ 24hr) The one-time retreat of Norwegian composer Edvard Grieg is in the garden of Hotel Ullensvang.

Lofthus Stone Church　　　　CHURCH
(Lofthus; ⊙ 10am-7pm late May–mid-Aug) This stone church dates back to 1250 (although the tower was added in the 1880s) and has some fine stained-glass windows. It's surrounded by an atmospheric cemetery containing some graves from the Middle Ages.

🛏 Sleeping & Eating

Kinsarvik Camping　　　　CAMPGROUND €
(✍ 53 66 32 90; www.kinsarvikcamping.no; Kinsarvik; sites Nkr245, 4- to 8-bed cabins Nkr595-1595; ⊛) This simple, friendly place is right by the water's edge; if you've kids in tow, Mikkelparken's waterslides and other activities are 500m away.

Lofthus Camping　　　　CAMPGROUND €
(✍ 53 66 13 64; www.lofthuscamping.com; Lofthus; tent or caravan sites Nkr230, 2-/4-bed cabins Nkr485/595; ⊛) A well-equipped fjord-side campsite with front-row views, Lofthus Camping has a heated indoor pool and can arrange boat rental. Cabins are traditional and super cute.

Dreiarstovo　　　　COTTAGE €€
(✍ 53 66 39 17; www.ringoy-camping.no; Ringøy Camping, Ringøy; 6-bed house from Nkr950; ⊙ May-Sep; P ��) Part of a prettily-sited camping ground in the village of Ringøy, northeast of Kinsarvik, this renovated 19th-century crofters' cottage sits a little way up the hill. Furnishings are of simple pine and it has a kitchen, a washing machine and heated floors in the bathroom.

Ullensvang Gjesteheim　　　　GUESTHOUSE €€
(✍ 53 66 12 36; www.ullensvang-gjesteheim.no; Ullensvang; s/d/f with shared bathroom from Nkr490/990/1450; ⊙ May–mid-Sep; P ⓦ) Kristin and Tor will make you feel right at home in this renovated 16th-century farmhouse just off the Rv13. The rooms are simple, but there's a warm feeling about this place. The downstairs restaurant serves a small traditional menu (mains Nkr149 to Nkr210) as well as a large selection of Thai dishes (Nkr125 to Nkr155) and Thai takeaway (mains Nkr115).

Hotel Ullensvang　　　　HISTORIC HOTEL €€€
(✍ 53 67 00 00; www.hotel-ullensvang.no; Lofthus; s/d Nkr1345/1970, d with fjord views from Nkr2370; P ⓦ ⊛) This enormous, luxurious place dates back to 1846, although it's now essentially a modern resort hotel. It has terrific views, supremely comfortable rooms and a good restaurant (lunch/dinner Nkr295/525). There's almost nothing you can't do here: it has a sauna, swimming pool, gym, golf simulator, tennis and squash courts, and boat rental.

It's also a great jumping-off point for activities, including summer skiing, glacier walking and 'Queen Sonja's Panoramic Hiking Trail', a six-hour route that can be done either on foot or skis. It's right on the fjord, between Lofthus and Ullensvang.

ℹ Information

Kinsarvik tourist office (☑ 53 66 31 12; www.visitullensvang.no; Kinsarvik Brygge, Kinsarvik; ☺ 9am-6.30pm Mon-Fri, 10am-5.30pm Sat mid-Jun–mid-Aug, shorter hours rest of year)
Lofthus tourist office (☑ 45 78 58 22; www.visitullensvang.no; Rv13, Loftus ; ☺ 11am-7pm mid-Jun–mid-Aug)

ℹ Getting There & Away

BOAT

Every couple of hours a ferry connects Kinsarvik with Utne (per person/vehicle Nkr31/81, 40 minutes) before continuing on to Kvanndal (Nkr41/122, one hour). There's also a daily tourist boat (passenger only) in summer to Eidfjord, Ulvik and Norheimsund, although it's more for sightseeing than getting anywhere in a hurry – it stops for three hours in Eidfjord.

BUS

Buses run between Odda (one hour) and Eidfjord (one hour) around five times a day and pass through Kinsarvik and Lofthus.

Utne

One of the most picturesque villages you'll find in Hardangerfjord, Utne is famous for its fruit-growing and its pristine traditional streets. It's also the jumping-off point for one of the region's most enchanting drives.

◉ Sights

Hardanger Folk Museum   MUSEUM
(www.hardangerogvossmuseum.no; adult/child Nkr75/free; ☺ 10am-5pm May-Aug, to 3pm Mon-Fri Sep-Apr) This excellent open-air museum is a repository for the cultural heritage of the Hardanger region. Wander through its collection of historic homes, boats, shops, outhouses and a school, and explore exhibitions that document the exquisite local folk costume and embroidery, wedding rituals, the famed Hardanger fiddle and fiddle-making, fishing and orchard keeping. There's also a cafe with home-baked cakes.

🛏 Sleeping & Eating

Hardanger Gjestegård   GUESTHOUSE €€
(☑ 53 66 67 10; www.hardanger-gjestegard.no; Alsåker; d from Nkr750) This beautifully located guesthouse, 10km west of Utne on Fv550, is in a pretty 1898 building right on the water. Its character-filled rooms are decorated with handpainted traditional furniture and it offers good weekly rates.

★ **Utne Hotel**   HISTORIC HOTEL €€€
(☑ 53 66 64 00; www.utnehotel.no; Utne; s/d annex Nkr1290/1690, historic main bldg Nkr1490/1890; ℗) ❂ The historic wooden Utne Hotel was built in 1722 after the Great Nordic War, giving it claim to the title of Norway's oldest hotel, and has an interesting lineage of female hoteliers. Rooms have a simple elegance that harks back to another time, although bathrooms are smart and modern.

The public spaces retain the scale of the 18th-century, with cosy low-ceilings, winding stairs and beautiful woodwork all setting off a wonderful collection of antiques, including local textile work and paintings. Staying on a half-pension basis (Nkr525) is recommended. The hotel's fabulous decor makes it worth a look even if you're not staying, and it has the best (and sometimes only) restaurant in town.

ℹ Getting There & Away

Ferries run between Utne, Kinsarvik (per person/vehicle Nkr31/81, 40 minutes) and Kvanndal (Nkr15/39, 20 minutes) at least six times a day.

Odda

POP 7006

Despite the promising location at the far end of Hardangerfjord, Odda is, in fact, an industrial, iron-smelting town. That said, it serves as a gateway to Folgefonna National Park, home to the Folgefonn glacier, and has a host of activities on offer.

◉ Sights

Trolltunga   VIEWPOINT
Norway's specialises in extraordinary rock platforms offering both panoramic views and postcard-perfect photo opportunities. Up there with the best of them is Trolltunga, a narrow finger of rock that hangs out over the void high above the lake Ringedalsvatnet. To reach it, drive north of Odda to Tyssedal, then northeast to Skjeggedal, from where Trolltunga is an eight- to 10-hour return hike away. En route, watch out for the **Tyssestrengene waterfall** (646m).

If you continue on a little beyond Trolltunga, you reach another fine vantage point, **Preikestolen** (Pulpit Rock), a smaller version of the lookout of the same name above Lysefjord, near Stavanger.

Norwegian Museum for Hydroelectric Power and Industry
MUSEUM

(Tyssedal Hydroelectric Power Station; ☑ 53 65 00 60; www.nvim.no; Naustbakken 7, Tyssedal; adult/child Nkr90/free, tours by arrangment; ⊘ 10am–5pm mid-May–Aug, 10am-5pm Mon-Fri Sep–mid-May) Designed by Thorvald Astrup, a 20th-century architect known for industrial projects inspired by both Italian cathedrals and the burgeoning functionalist movement, the Tysso 1 plant was constructed between 1906 and 1918. It is one of the country's most significant industrial heritage sites, protected under historic monument legislation, and it is indeed beautiful. There are tours and exhibitions as well as visits to the nearby Ringedal dam and a group of preserved workers' housing in Odda.

If you have reasonable fitness levels and appropriate shoes, you can climb the footpath used by the workers to reach the beginning of the pipeline at Lilletopp, 400m above the power station. There is also a small intake dam, the dam-watchers house, water tunnels and the huge waterpipes, not to mention spectacular views of the Sørfjord. **Opplev Odda** (☑ 90 82 45 72; www.opplevodda.com) take guided climbs (Nkr750, including museum entrance) along via ferrata that replicate the experience of the workers who built the plant.

🏃 Activities

For hikes of up to six hours around town, pick up the helpful brochure *Hikes in Odda*, or the more detailed *Hiking and Biking – Odda, Røldal, Seljestad, Tyssedal* from the tourist office.

Flat Earth
HIKING

(☑ 47 60 68 47; www.flatearth.no) Flat Earth runs guided hikes up the lovely Buer valley followed by a glacier walk on the Buer arm of Folgefonna (adult Nkr750, including crampons and ice axes). This is one of the best places to do a glacier walk: you're onto the ice straight away without wading through snow first. The round-trip from Odda takes a full day.

You will need to make your own arrangements to get to the starting point, at Buer, 8km west of Odda. The hikes are suitable

WORTH A TRIP

JONDAL DRIVE

While there are no heart-in-mouth hairpin bends, dramatic high passes or deep, dark fjords to stir the soul, the gentle drive along the **Rv550** from Utne to Jondal is one of Norway's most delightful, especially in late spring or early summer. The road hugs the fjord the whole way, passing through orchards and by fisherman's shacks and tiny beaches. There's plenty of 'come hither' rocky outcrops for picnics, lolls in the sun or a paddle. In Hereiane, smooth rock rises straight up from the fjord to the peaks above and a small service building made entirely from natural stone sits on a brilliant yellow plinth. The ferry from Jondal takes you back to Norheimsund, but, before you depart, make time for a waffle at the boat-shed kiosk and a wander around the town's Swiss-style cottages. Or continue on to Rosendal or Odda via the Jondalstunnelen.

for anyone in good physical condition with warm clothing and sturdy footwear.

🛏 Sleeping & Eating

Odda Camping
CAMPGROUND €

(☑ 41 32 16 10; www.oddacamping.no; Odda; tent/caravan sites Nkr140/150, 4-bed cabins Nkr690-890; ⊘ mid-May–Aug) The most convenient camping is on the shores of Sandvinvatnet lake, a 20-minute uphill walk south of the town centre.

Tyssedal Hotel
HOTEL €€

(☑ 53 64 00 00; www.tyssedalhotel.no; Tyssedal; s/d Nkr995/1295; P 🛜) The Jugendstil-era Tyssedal Hotel has terrific rooms with parquet floors and stylish fittings. Norwegian ghosts seem to have a penchant for hotels: Eidfjord artist Nils Bergslien 'visits' the ground and 3rd floors. His earthly legacy, some fantastic fairy-tale and Hardangerfjord landscape paintings, also grace the hotel.

The **restaurant** (lunch Nkr79-99, dinner Nkr229-299) is Odda's best.

Trolltunga Hotel
GUESTHOUSE €€

(☑ 55 09 28 00; www.trolltungahotel.no; Vasstun 1, Odda; s/d Nkr990/1300, with shared bathroom Nkr710/905; P 🛜) There are 27 recently refurbished rooms at this personal, welcoming hotel close to Odda Camping at the far southern end of town. The rooms are modern, if a little spartan, and some have magnificent lake views.

ⓘ Information

Tourist Office (☎ 53 65 40 05; www.visitodda. com; ⏱ 9am-7pm mid-Jun–mid-Aug, shorter hours May & Sep)

ⓘ Getting There & Away

Between Odda and Jondal, Skyss buses operate one to three times daily (Nkr69, 45 minutes). Buses also run to/from Bergen, Geilo and Oslo.

Around Odda

Røldal

The pretty town of Røldal, 22km southeast of Odda, has the popular **Røldal Skisenter** (www.roldal.no; ⏱ Dec-Apr), a winter ski station that offers ultra-deep snow and a long season for downhill, cross-country and backcountry skiers. There's also a 13th-century **stave church**, where, according to local legend, the wooden cross sweats every midsummer's eve; the sweat is said to have healing powers, and was an important place of pilgrimage in the Middle Ages.

Folgefonna National Park

Established in 2005, this 545-sq-km national park encompasses mainland Norway's third-largest icefield. The Folgefonn icecap covers 168 sq km and the ice is up to 400m thick in places. It's a dramatic, beautiful place, with glaciers snaking down the heights of nearby valleys.

🏃 Activities

The most popular way to explore Folgefonna is on a glacier hike, either from Odda (p191) or Jondal.

For an excellent online guide to hiking on the fringes of Folgefonna, visit www.visit sunnhordland.no and look for the 'Fancy a Walk?' page, where there are links to route descriptions and downloadable maps.

Folgefonni Breførarlag   HIKING
(☎ 55 29 89 21; www.folgefonni-breforarlag.no; Jondal; ⏱ mid-Jun–mid-Aug, on request rest of year) The highly professional Folgefonni Breførarlag has a range of glacier hikes that set out in summer from the Fonna Glacier Ski Resort and hike onto the glaciers. The advan-

tage of doing the walk here is the promise of exceptional views, although you do have to hike across the snow to reach the glacier.

Tours range from three-hour hikes across the icecap (Nkr500) to three- to six-hour 'Blue-Ice' trips to Juklavassbreen (from Nkr650). The minimum age for participants is 12.

Fonna Glacier Ski Resort   SKIING
(☎ 46 17 20 11; www.folgefonn.no; ⏱ 9am-4pm May-Oct) It's possible to do summer skiing, snowboarding and sledding from May until October, although the season can finish earlier. You can visit the resort by public transport from Bergen, Jondal or Norheimsund; see the resort website for details.

ⓘ Information

Folgefonna National Park Centre (☎ 53 48 42 80; folgefonna.info/en/welcome-folgefonna-national-park; Skålakaien, Rosendal; ⏱ 10am-7pm Jun-Aug) An excellent resource on the park, this centre in Rosendal has exhibits, a boat-building museum and a 20-minute film about the formation of Folgefonna and its geology.

Jondal Tourist Office (☎ 53 66 85 31; www. visitjondal.no; ⏱ 9.30am-4pm Jun, 9.30am-6pm Jul & Aug)

ⓘ Getting There & Away

The national park is accessible from Odda and Jondal, which are connected by semiregular buses.

Rosendal

POP 944

Separated from the rest of Hardangerfjord by high mountains and the Folgefonna National Park, Rosendal sits picturesquely by the fjord with a close backdrop of high hills. Access to the national park is easier from Odda and Jondal, but Rosendal has a good national park centre and is a worthwhile destination in its own right.

◉ Sights & Activities

The tourist office (p193) can advise on hiking, climbing, boat rental (per day/week Nkr400/1220 plus petrol) and horse riding, and it has a useful *Cycling Trips in Sunnhordland* brochure for longer cycling excursions around the region.

Baroniet Rosendal   HISTORIC BUILDING
(☎ 53 48 29 99; www.baroniet.no; Rosendal; adult/child Nkr75/10; ⏱ 10am-6pm Jul, variable hours May,

BERGEN & THE SOUTHWESTERN FJORDS AROUND ODDA

Jun & Aug) Norway's only baronial mansion dates back to 1665 and sits on a gentle rise above the town. The period interiors include a collection of tapestries, an intact library and beautiful examples of Meissen and Royal Danish porcelain. Outside there is a stunning Renaissance rose garden. The Baroniet hosts excellent weekend concerts by eminent Norwegian musicians from mid-May to early September, and performances of Shakespeare by British actors, usually in late July.

You can also sleep here, in the farm annexe; dinners in the garden greenhouse can be booked with concert and other event tickets.

Steinparken
PARK

Signposted off the road running to Baroniet Rosendal, this intriguing little open-air gallery has rock monoliths from the Folgefonna region, which have been sculpted and smoothed to stunning effect to show the region's geological diversity; some of it is the work of contemporary artist Bård Breivik. A path runs from an antique sawmill up through the park. Carved tables are a good choice for a picnic lunch.

Rødne Fjord Cruise
BOAT TOUR

(☑51 89 52 70; www.rodne.no; adult/child Nkr380/200) This company offers a 3½-hour sightseeing cruise of Hardangerfjord, as well as trips to Rosendal from Bergen.

✵ Festivals

Rosendal Mat & Kunstfestival
FOOD

(Rosendal Food & Art Festival; www.rosendalmatogkunstfestival.no; ☺early–mid-Jul) A local arts and food festival and market, held in even-numbered years.

🛏 Sleeping & Eating

Sundal Camping
CAMPGROUND €

(☑53 48 41 86; www.sundalcamping.no; tent sites Nkr130, cabins Nkr450-700) The nearest campsite to Rosendal is the reasonable Sundal Camping, in Sundal, 28km northeast of Rosendal.

★ Rosendal Turisthotell
GUESTHOUSE €€

(☑/fax 53 47 36 66; www.rosendalturisthotell.no; Skålagato 17, Rosendal; s/d with shared bathroom Nkr800/980; P🐾) This lovely designer guesthouse opposite the quay dates from 1887, but a recent overhaul has given it a fresh, contemporary look inside. The 14 light-filled rooms pair antique beds and whitewashed floor boards with rustic Norwegian textiles. Yes, bathrooms are shared, but these, too, are super-stylish – a cut above your average corridor facilities.

Baroniet Rosendal
FARMHOUSE €€

(☑53 48 29 99; www.baroniet.no; Rosendal; s/d with shared bathroom Nkr700/980; ☺May-Aug; P) Just outside the grounds of the Baroniet Rosendal, this rambling farmhouse has attractive rooms with wrought-iron bedsteads and shared bathrooms. Dinner is available and is served in the farmhouse's large kitchen; the three-course menu (Nkr490) changes daily and utilises fruit, vegetables and herbs from the garden.

Martha Meidell
NORWEGIAN €€

(Rosendal Touristhotel; lunch dishes Nkr168-185, mains Nkr255-275; ☺lunch 1-6pm, dinner 7-10pm) Rosendal Touristhotell's restaurant-cafe is the smartest in town, with a simple but nicely considered menu of traditional dishes such as baked trout or 48-hour braised beef, made from local produce. Lunches are lighter, say brisket rolls or hot smoked salmon, and the kids menu must be the country's most gourmet, with venison meatballs (Nkr95) or fish *quenelles* (Nkr85).

On Friday and Saturday nights, the basement wine bar **Gjesten** opens until 1am.

Snikkeriet
RESTAURANT €€

(www.snikkeriet.no; mains Nkr150-210; ☺noon-10pm Sun-Thu, noon-1am Fri & Sat Easter-Aug) Snikkeriet is known for its well-priced homecooked Norwegian meals, including fjord trout and local sausages. The first time we walked into this place, we found the owner playing guitar and singing to an empty bar. We almost walked out, but we're glad we didn't; she was warming up for the hugely popular Friday night (9pm) live jam session.

This is a local institution, as musicians from all over the region come to play rock, blues or jazz.

🛈 Information

Rosendal Tourist Office & Folgefonna National Park Centre (☑53 48 42 80; www.visitsunnhordland.no; Skålakaien; ☺10am-7pm Jun-Aug, 10am-3pm May & Sep)

🛈 Getting There & Away

BOAT

Rødne Fjord Cruise (☑51 89 52 70; www.rodne.no; adult/child return Nkr725/325) runs a daily return service with lunch and tour from Bergen.

BUS

Buses run three to seven times daily between Rosendal and Odda via Sunndal.

CAR & MOTORCYCLE

Rosendal can be reached via an 11km-long road tunnel (car Nkr85, free midnight to 6am) under the icefield from Odda; Rosendal is 32km along the coast from the tunnel entrance/exit. There is also a tunnel connection from Jondal. If you're heading south towards Haugesund or Stavanger, the E39 is the fastest route and includes the Rannavik–Skjersholmane ferry. However, the route via the Utåker–Skånevik ferry is cheaper.

Around Rosendal

Sunndal

At Sunndal, 4km west of the tunnel, take the road up the Sunndal valley (drivable for 1km), then walk 2km on a good track to lake Bondhusvatnet, where there's a wonderful view of the glacier **Bondhusbreen**. This is also a trail head for some fine hikes.

Uskedalen

In Uskedalen, 14km west of Rosendal, there's an extraordinary rock-slab mountain, Ulvenåso (1247m), offering some of the best **rock climbing** in Norway; contact the tourist office in Rosendal (p193) for details.

Møsevatnet

One of the prettiest (and quietest) roads in this part of Norway climbs up to the dam at Møsevatnet, from where there are good views to one of the glacier arms of the Folgefonna icecap. Take the Rv48 south of Rosendal and turn off to the southwest at Dimmelsvik; the road is signposted to Fjellhaugen, Matre and Åkra. From the road junction that signposts Matre and Åkra to the right, follow the signs left to Blådal and the winter-only Fjellhaugen Skisenter; later, ignore the signs to the ski centre. From this road junction, road climbs up through some glorious wooded, rocky hills, studded with lakes and dams.

HAUGELANDET & RYFYLKE

North and east of Stavanger lies a region of low-lying hills and coastal inlets and islands that are reminiscent of the northern Scottish isles. Happy Haugesund is the regional capital.

Haugesund

POP 34,620

The North Sea port of Haugesund lies beyond the well-trodden west coast routes. That's a shame, because it's both a great jumping-off point to the rich cultural sites and stunning beaches of Karmøy island, just to the south, as well as being a rollicking, well-to-do town that knows a good time when it sees it. In fact, there appears to be more bars than people and the shopping is some of the country's best. Plus if you've a penchant for boats, of all persuasions, you're in luck.

The region carries huge historical significance for Norwegians. It was in the nearby Hafrsfjord that the decisive battle took place in 872 and Norway was first unified. As such, the area bills itself as 'Norway's Birthplace'.

Ryanair flies direct, so this may be your entry point into Norway. Note that hotels cater to industry not travellers, with little in the way of boutique or budget options; that said, you can often score some great last-minute deals at the big chains.

◎ Sights

Haraldshaugen   MONUMENT
(Haraldshaugvegen) The burial site of Viking King Harald Hårfagre, who died of plague at Avaldsnes on nearby Karmøy, is 1.5km north of Haugesund. The obelisk, erected in 1872, commemorates the decisive 872 battle.

Rådhus   HISTORICAL BUILDING
(Town Hall) Haugesund has retained many of its historical buildings and this impressive salmon-tinted, neoclassical pile is a highlight.

Marilyn Monroe Memorial   MONUMENT
Bizarrely, Haugesund claims to be the ancestral home of Marilyn Monroe, whose father, a local baker, emigrated to the USA. This monument on the quay, next to the Rica Maritim Hotel, is suitably coquettish, if not a great likeness. It commemorates the 30th anniversary of her death.

☞ Tours

The tourist office (p196) organises a comprehensive range of tours, from a guided walk around the town hall, to coastal boat trips to view historic lighthouses and visit remote island communities.

✨ Festivals

Silda Jazz MUSIC
(Haugesund International Jazz Festival; www.silda-jazz.no; ☺ early–mid-Aug) Well-respected music festival with international jazz, soul, folk and indie acts.

Norwegian International Film Festival FILM
(www.filmweb.no/filmfestivalen; ☺ mid–late Aug) Norway's major film festival, considered to be the Nordic Cannes.

🛏 Sleeping

Strandgaten Gjestgiveri GUESTHOUSE €€
(☑ 52 71 52 55; www.gjestgiveri.net; Strandgata 81; s/d Nkr600/865; 🛜) A tidy, old-school guesthouse in an old townhouse in the centre of Haugesund. Rooms are basic but all have a TV and fridge.

Rica Maritim Hotel HOTEL €€
(☑ 52 86 30 00; www.hotelmaritim.no; Åsbygaten 3; s Nkr850-1100, d Nkr1250-1800; P🛜) This large, luxurious hotel has a perfect waterfront location (a two-minute walk along the quay from the main action) and most of the well-designed rooms have great views and neat glassed-in balconies that can be sealed if the sun is out but the wind is high. Its restaurants and bars line up along its sun-drenched waterfront terrace.

Scandic Haugesund HOTEL €€
(☑ 21 61 41 00; www.scandichotels.com; Kirkegata 166; s/d from Nkr670/870; P🛜) Big and busy, this business-oriented hotel quietens down in summer and offers characteristic Scandic rooms: contemporary and comfortable, with good bathrooms. Despite the size and pace, staff are friendly and down to earth.

⭐**First Hotel
Hendersons City** BOUTIQUE HOTEL €€
(☑ 47 27 18 80; www.nordicchoicehotels.com; Strandgata 161; s/d Nkr1160/1300) One street up from the waterfront, in a grand, turn-of-the-century stone building, this is Haugesund's most glamorous hotel. Rooms come in a variety of shapes and sizes: architecturally interesting and super spacious, as well as standard, if luxurious, business-traveller-oriented rooms. Views over city rooftops to the surrounding islands from the top-floor mansard rooms are worth upgrading for.

Public spaces are decked with chandeliers and velvet sofas and, along with the requisite groaning breakfast buffet, there is a complimentary supper buffet, as well as an all-day drinks and cake service.

🍴 Eating & Drinking

Haugesund's waterfront promenade, Smedasundet, is almost entirely given over to restaurants, giving the area an agreeable hum whenever the weather's remotely warm. There's also a number of more intimate places tucked away in the grid running up from the water; these tend to have a better gender balance than those down the hill. Although the town has its fare share of dedicated drinking holes, any Haugesund restaurant worth its salt also morphs into a bar as the night wears on.

Lothes Mat & Vinhus RESTAURANT €€€
(☑ 52 71 22 01; www.lothesmat.no; Skippergata 4; mains Nkr195-349; ☺ 11am-1.30am) With its lovely outdoor terrace overlooking the waterfront, and period wood architecture, this long-standing Haugesund landmark is one of the town's most popular dining options. It also has a more casual space, the sprawling kitschy **Matbar**, where you can grab a burger (Nkr180) or plates of local small goods and feta (Nkr90).

To Glass RESTAURANT €€€
(☑ 52 70 74 00; www.toglass.no; Strandgata 169; tapas per person from Nkr290, mains Nkr310-339; ☺ 3-11pm Mon-Fri, to midnight Sat) This cosy, cosseted upstairs place is particularly atmospheric. Come for after-work tapas, bistro dishes such as carpaccio and grilled scampi or burgers that are definitely a cut above.

⭐**RootDown** CLUB
(www.rootdown.no; Strandgaten 116; ☺ 4pm-midnight Sat Jun-Aug) This shopfront space, decked out with some stunning mid-century pieces and overlooked by a photomural of a classic Volvo, hosts events that tie in with the town's festivals, regular club nights, exhibitions, DJ courses and is generally party-central for Haugesund's cool kids. Don't worry: they're friendly.

Skapåbar WINE BAR
(☺ 11am-10pm Mon-Thu, to 1.30am Fri & Sat, 6-10pm Sun) A busy basement bar, cafe and vintage shop that's a great spot to meet locals while sampling a huge selection of microbrewed beer. Snack on open sandwiches (Nkr115) made from fresh, organic ingredients. If you

need something heartier as the night wears on, dishes from To Glass upstairs will be obligingly delivered to your bar stool.

Totalen
CAFE

(Haraldsgata 173; ⊕9am-5pm Mon-Fri, 10.30am-4pm Sat) This cafe has the town's best coffee, with beans from Jacu and delicious scones and biscuits. The interesting shopfront space is, in fact, an old theatre that is used by the Pionerkirken for Sunday services.

🛍 Shopping

Amundsen Spesial
FOOD

(Skippergata 5) A good choice for gourmet picnic supplies if you're daytripping, with a wow-factor cheese selection that includes the best local products as well as good French, Italian and Spanish choices. It also specialises in nuts and chocolate.

Crush Concept
HOMEWARES, CLOTHING

(Strandgarten 186) Hauguesund punches above its weight in terms of retail, but even so, this shop is a standout. They stock an incredible collection of cult Scandinavian labels, as well as fabulous picks from Paris and Milan. Similarly, their home range features great innovative designers as well as classic lines.

ℹ Information

Haugesund Tourist Office (☑52 01 08 30; www.visithaugesund.no/; Strandgata 171; ⊕9am-5pm Mon-Fri, 10am-3pm Sat & Sun mid-Jun–Aug, 10am-4.30pm Mon-Fri Sep-May)

ℹ Getting There & Away

AIR

SAS (www.sas.no) flies regularly to Haugesund from Bergen and Oslo; **Widerøe** (www.wideroe. no) has flights from Bergen, while **Norwegian** (www.norwegian.com) also serves the Haugesund–Oslo route.

BOAT

Kolumbus (☑81 50 01 82; www.kolumbus. no) Kolumbus ferries run from Stavanger to Haugesund and back three times daily (Nkr357, 1¾ hours).

BUS

Nor-Way Bussekspress buses connect Haugesund with Stavanger (Nkr220, 2¼ hours, up to six daily) and Bergen (Nkr350, 3½ hours) almost hourly on weekdays and every second hour on weekends. Bus4You by **Nettbuss** (www. nettbuss.no) does the run to Stavanger (Nkr199) and Bergen (Nkr329) too.

ℹ Getting Around

Haugesund airport (☑52 85 79 00) is 13km southwest of the city. The **airport bus** (www. flybussen.no/haugesund; one-way adult/child Nkr70/40) has services to coincide with all SAS and Norwegian flights, but not the Widerøe ones. For Ryanair flights, the service is operated by **Kystbussen** (www.kyst bussen.no), which connects with bus services to Bergen and Stavanger.

Karmøy Island

Low-lying Karmøy island is blessed with natural beauty: besides a number of exquisite pale sand beaches, it crams in forests, open marshes, heather uplands and lakes. Culturally it's no slouch either, with a number of significant historical sites, pretty wooden villages and, in early June, a spirited **Viking Festival** (www.vikingfestivalen.no).

⊙ Sights

Skudeneshavn
HISTORIC SITE

The wonderful Skudeneshavn, 37km south of Haugesund, got very rich on the herring trade in the 19th century and is known for its 'empire-style' wooden houses, winding main street Søragadå and pretty gardens. There's a number of year-round cafes and a **tourist office** (☑52 85 80 00; www.visitskudeneshavn.no; Kaigata5, Torget; ⊕10am-4pm Mon-Sat, noon-4pm Sun Jun-Aug) next to the quay.

St Olav's Church
CHURCH

(www.visitkarmoy.no; Avaldsnes; ⊕1pm-3.30pm Sun-Tue Jun-Aug) King Håkon Håkonsson's huge stone church, about 5km south of Haugesund, was dedicated to St Olav in 1250 and has helped guide sailors through the strait of Karmsund for more than 750 years. The adjacent 7.2m spire, known as the **Virgin Mary's Needle**, leans perilously towards the church wall, and legend suggests that when it actually touches the wall the Day of Judgment is at hand – it was close but still free-standing when we were there.

Nordvegen Historiesenter
MUSEUM

(www.vikinggarden.no; Avaldsnes; adult/child Nkr100/50; ⊕10am-4pm Mon-Fri, 11am-3pm Sat, noon-5pm Sun Jun-Aug, shorter hours rest of year) Down a short path from the carpark for St Olav's Church, this history centre recreates the story of Harald Fair-Hair and other monarchs of the newly unified Nordvegen from the 10th century onwards. Also nearby, on a tiny forested island is a reconstructed **Viking farm** (Avaldsnes; adult/child Nkr100/50, with Nordvegen ticket Nkr50/25; ⊙noon-4.30pm late Jun–mid-Aug) – it's great for kids, with staff in period dress.

Karmøy Fiskerimuseum MUSEUM
(www.fiskerimuseum.net; Vedavågen; adult/child Nkr30/10; ⊙11am-4pm Mon-Fri, 2-6pm Sun Jun–mid-Aug) In Vedavågen, on the island's west coast, this museum explores the region's modern fishing industry and also has a saltwater aquarium. Designed by Snøhetta, of Oslo Opera House fame, it's worth the trip here for the architecture alone.

Visnes Grubeområde MUSEUM
(www.visitkarmoy.no; Visnes; adult/child Nkr60/15; ⊙11am-5pm Mon-Fri, noon-5pm Sun Jun–mid-Aug) Copper from this mine at Visnes, 4km west of Avaldsnes, was used to build the *Statue of Liberty* in New York and the operations here were the largest and most modern in northern Europe. The museum showcases operations at the copper mine back to 1865, along with access to the extensive parkland that the mine's progressive French manager and engineer originally created for workers' recreation.

🛌 Sleeping

Norneshuset B&B €€
(📞90 05 90 07; www.norneshuset.no; Nordnes 7, Skudeneshavn; s/d Nkr990/1190) This B&B has character-filled rooms right by the harbour and very friendly service; it's located in a former warehouse that was shipped from Riga, Latvia, in the 1830s.

❶ Getting There & Away

To reach Avaldsnes from central Haugesund, catch bus 8, 9 or 10 (Nkr42) from next to the post office. Bus 10 continues further south to Skudeneshavn (Nkr65, 1¼ hours). There are semiregular car ferries from Skudeneshavn to Mekjarvik (for Stavanger) and the Haugesund–Stavanger passenger ferry stops into Kopervik.

STAVANGER & LYSEFJORD

Tucked away in Norway's southwest, the oil-rich city of Stavanger guarantees a good night out and has some excellent museums. It also serves as the gateway to Lysefjord, the southernmost of Norway's signature fjords and home to one of its most recognis-

able vantage points – Preikestolen (Pulpit Rock).

Stavanger

POP 124,936

No, Stavanger can't compete with Bergen on looks, but it's a far from unlovely city, with original dockside warehouses and pretty 18th-century streets climbing up from a bustling harbour. And while it retains something of its small-town roots – an enchanting feeling of light and space, for one – if you want to see the fruits of Norway's oil boom, Stavanger is a good place to start. Most nights, especially in summer, the city's waterfront comes alive in the best tradition of port cities, and you can eat well here, if not cheaply.

◉ Sights & Activities

★**Gamle Stavanger** NEIGHBOURHOOD
Gamle (Old) Stavanger, above the western shore of the harbour, is a delight. The Old Town's cobblestone walkways pass between rows of late-18th-century whitewashed wooden houses, all immaculately kept and adorned with cheerful, well-tended flowerboxes. It well rewards an hour or two of ambling.

★**Norsk Oljemuseum** MUSEUM
(Oil Museum; www.norskolje.museum.no; Kjeringholmen; adult/child/family Nkr100/50/250; ⊙10am-7pm daily Jun-Aug, to 4pm Mon-Sat, to 6pm Sun Sep-May) You could spend hours in this state-of-the-art, beautifully designed museum, one of Norway's best. Focusing on oil exploration in the North Sea, from discovery in 1969 until the present, it's filled with high-tech interactive displays and authentic reconstructions.

Highlights include the world's largest drill bit, simulated rig working environments, documentary films on a North Sea dive crew's work day, and a vast hall of amazing oil platform models.

There is also an exhibition recreating millions of years of natural history and an interactive display that teases out energy and climate policy dilemmas.

The museum nicely balances the technical side of oil exploration and extraction while honouring those whose working lives have been spent in the industry. The latter is done through fascinating archival material that highlights significant moments in the history of Norwegian oil including coverage of the Alexander L Kielland tragedy in 1980, when 123 oil workers were killed, and the 1972 decision by Norway's parliament that Statoil should be based in Stavanger.

You *will* spend longer here than you planned, especially if you have kids.

Stavanger Domkirke
CHURCH

(Haakon VII's gate; Nkr30; ☺11am-7pm Jun-Aug, 11am-4pm Mon-Sat Sep-May) This beautiful church is an impressive but understated medieval stone cathedral dating from approximately 1125; it was extensively renovated following a fire in 1272 and contains traces of Gothic, baroque, Romanesque and Anglo Norman influences. Despite restoration in the 1860s and 1940, and the stripping of some features during the Reformation, the cathedral is, by some accounts, Norway's oldest medieval cathedral still in its original form.

Its interior, with wonderful stone columns, tapestries, elaborate baroque pulpit and stained-glass window depicting the main events of the Christian calendar, is moving.

Stavanger Museum
MUSEUM

(✆51 84 27 00; www.museumstavanger.no; ☺11am-4pm daily mid-May–Aug, Tue-Sun rest of year) The large 11-part museum, with its sites scattered around Stavanger, could easily fill a sightseeing day or more. Entrance to all parts is by one-day ticket (adult/child Nkr70/40), or there is a four-day MUSTpass (adult/family Nkr100/250). Museums include the **Norwegian Printing Museum**, the **Norwegian School Museum** and the Medical Museum.

➡ Canning Museum

(Øvre Strandgate 88a) Don't miss this museum housed in an old cannery, as it's one of Stavanger's most appealing. Before oil, there were sardines, and Stavanger was once home to more than half of Norway's canning factories. By 1922 the city's canneries provided 50% of the town's employment. Guides are on hand to answer your questions or crank up some of the old machines.

You'll get the lowdown on canning brisling and fish balls: the exhibits take you through the whole 12-stage process from salting through to threading, smoking, decapitating and packing. On the first Sunday of every month (and Tuesday and Thursday from mid-June to mid-August), the fires are lit and you can sample smoked sardines straight from the ovens. An adjoining build-ing houses a cafe and touchingly restored workers cottages furnished in 1920s (downstairs) and 1960s (upstairs) styles.

➡ Stavanger Maritime Museum

(Sjøfartsmuseet; Nedre Strandgate 17-19) This worthwhile museum, spread over two warehouses dating from around 1800, covers 200 years of Stavanger's maritime history. There's a large collection of model boats, sailing vessels, a wind-up foghorn and reconstructions of a late-19th-century sailmaker's workshop and merchant's living quarters. Exhibitions examine the history of shipwrecks and rescue operations over 400 years. The museum also owns two historic sailing vessels: the 1848 *Anna of Sand* and the 1896 *Wyvern,* both of which can be visited when in port.

➡ Stavanger Bymuseum

(Musègata 16) Features at this city museum include evidence of Stone Age habitation, the medieval bishopric, the herring years and the development of the city into a modern oil capital. Stavanger of the 1880s is described in a series of tableaux focusing on local author Alexander L Kielland. Also in the same building is the **Norwegian Natural History Museum** (☺11am-4pm mid-Jun–mid-Aug, Tue-Sun rest of year).

➡ Ledaal

(Eiganesveien 45) The empire-style Ledaal was constructed between 1799 and 1803 for wealthy merchant shipowner Gabriel Schanche Kielland. Recently restored, and featuring unusual antique furniture, it serves as the local royal residence and summer home.

➡ Breidablikk

(Eiganesveien 40a) This opulent manor was constructed for the merchant shipowner Lars Berentsen. Its authentic late-19th-century interiors include old farming implements, books and decorative objects.

➡ Stavanger Kunstmuseum

(Henrik Ibsensgate 55) This museum, 2.5km south of the town centre, displays Norwegian art from the 18th century to the present, including the haunting *Gamle Furutrær* and other landscape paintings by Stavanger's own Lars Hertervig (1830–1902). A nine-sided annexe houses the largest assemblage of mid-20th-century Norwegian art, including works by Harald Dal, Kai Fjell, Arne Ekeland and others.

→ Norwegian Museum of Childhood

(Norsk Barnemuseum; www.norskbarne.museum. no; off Laugmsgata) Kids do seem to like it at this part-museum, part-indoor-playground space, which has a range of activity-based exhibits centred on the themes of landscape, labyrinth, curiosity and theatre.

Arkeologisk Museum
MUSEUM

(☑51 84 60 00; am.uis.no; Peder Klows gate 30a; adult/child Nkr50/20; ⊙10am-5pm Mon-Fri, 11am-4pm Sat & Sun Jun-Aug, 11am-4pm Wed-Sat, to 8pm Tue Sep-May) This well-presented museum traces 11,000 years of human history, including the Viking Age. Exhibits include skeletons, tools, a runestone and a description of the symbiosis between prehistoric humans and their environment. There's a full program of activities for kids (eg treasure hunts and wandering Vikings) in summer.

Jernaldergarden
MUSEUM

(www.jernaldergarden.no; Ullandhaugvn 3, Ullandhaug; adult/child incl entry to Arkeologisk Museum Nkr100/50; ⊙11am-4pm daily mid-Jun–mid-Aug, 11am-4pm Sun May–mid-Jun & mid-Aug–Oct) This reconstruction of a 1500-year-old Iron Age farm, 4km south of the centre, features various activities, staff in period dress and food preparation on Sunday. Take bus 5a or 5b towards Sandnes to Ullandhaug (Nkr36, 15 minutes) from next to the Radisson Hotel on Breiavann lake.

☞ Tours

Siddisvandring
WALKING TOUR

(per person Nkr100; ⊙daily 2pm, mid-Jun–Aug) The name of these tourist office–run summer walking tours translates to 'stroll with a local'. A great concept, it makes for a casual, chatty hour of exploring.

Guide Companiet
WALKING TOUR

(☑51 85 09 20; www.guidecompaniet.no; 2hr tour adult Nkr170) Guide Companiet tours leave from outside the tourist office and cover the cathedral, old Stavanger and the listed wharf houses.

✵ Festivals & Events

Stavanger Vinfest
WINE

(www.stavangervinfest.no; ⊙mid-Apr) A weeklong wine celebration at the city's best restaurants.

May Jazz Festival
MUSIC

(www.maijazz.no; ⊙early May) Serious jazz acts, with at least a couple of international legends each year.

Gladmat
FOOD

(www.gladmat.no; ⊙late Jul) Reportedly Scandinavia's largest food festival.

International Chamber Music Festival
MUSIC

(www.icmf.no; ⊙early Aug) Well-respected classical-music festival, with unusual venues and interesting programming.

NuArt
VISUAL ARTS

(⊙early Sep) International street-art festival with exhibitions, tours and live events.

NuMusic
MUSIC

(www.numusic.no; ⊙early Sep) Long-running electronic music festival with big names and interesting, intimate venues.

🛌 Sleeping

This is an oil city and prices soar on weekdays, plus it's not uncommon for every bed in town to be occupied. That said, prices drop and availability returns on weekends and during high summer. Do, however, be sure to avoid the end of August in even-numbered years, when the Offshore Northern Seas Foundation (ONS) show takes over the entire town.

The tourist office website has a full list of small B&Bs in and around Stavanger, though these too are utilised by conference goers – book ahead when you can.

★ Thompsons B&B
B&B €

(☑51 52 13 29; www.thompsonsbedandbreakfast. com; Muségata 79; s/d with shared bathroom Nkr400/500; ℗) Housed in a 19th-century villa in a peaceful residential area, this four-bed B&B has a home-away-from-home vibe engendered by the warm and welcoming owner, Sissel Thompson. Rooms are cosy and comfortable, and traditional Norwegian breakfast, taken around the downstairs dining table, is generous.

Sissel has a wealth of city tips and can help you plan an itinerary for the surrounding coast and countryside.

Comfort Hotel Square
HOTEL €

(☑51 56 80 00; www.nordicchoicehotels.no; Løkkeveien 41; d from Nkr749; ✱🛜) In a wavy wooden building up behind Gamle Stavanger, this option from the Nordic Choice Comfort

Stavanger

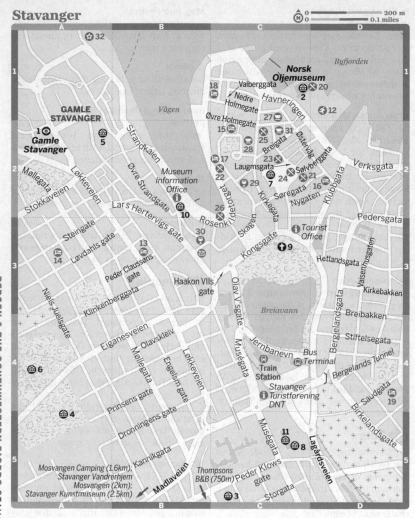

line does the hip boutique thing (think exposed concrete walls, creative lighting and wall-sized photos) with chain convenience, facilities and value. Weekend rates are particularly good value (under half the weekday price) and the elevated location is a good one.

Skansen Hotel
HOTEL, GUESTHOUSE €
(☏ 51 93 85 00; www.skansenhotel.no; Skansegata 7; d Mon-Thu Nkr995, Fri-Sun Nkr770) Earmarked to be transformed into a Smarthotel in 2016, this hotel is the only budget option in the city centre. Rooms are spartan but clean and there are a few extras that please,

such as tea- and coffee-making facilities and complimentary Norwegian sweets. There's also a beer garden out the back and a locals' favourite watering hole, B.brormann B.bar (p203), downstairs.

With no on-site reception, check in is done at the nearby Victoria Hotel.

Mosvangen Camping
CAMPGROUND €
(☏ 51 53 29 71; www.stavangercamping.no; Tjensvoll 1b; campsites Nkr230, caravan or camper Nkr290, huts Nkr450-750; ☉ Apr-Sep) During nesting season around Mosvangen lake, campers are treated to almost incessant

Stavanger

birdsong amid the green and agreeable surroundings, 3km south of town on the road to Ullandhaugveien.

Stavanger Vandrerhjem Mosvangen
HOSTEL €
(☎51 54 36 36; stavanger.hostel@vandrerhjem.no; Henrik Ibsensgate 19; dm/s/d without bathroom Nkr220/345/565; ⊙mid-May–mid-Sep) Stavanger's pleasant and simple lakeside hostel, 3km southwest of the city centre, charges Nkr60 for breakfast. It opens only in the summer months.

Take bus 78 or 79 (Nkr36) from opposite the cathedral to Ullandhaugveien.

★Darby's Inn
B&B €€
(☎47 62 52 48; www.darbysbb.com; Kong Oscars Gate 18; s/d from Nkr1180/1290; P❄🛜) The two front rooms at this understated, oppulent B&B might be Stavanger's nicest, even without a sea view. Traditional interiors in this historic house combine dark wood with antique furniture, paintings, Persian rugs and a baby grand in the lounge and dining room. The large guest rooms are simpler but still have luxury linen, plump cushions and suitably heavy curtains.

A terrace, underground parking and an attentive host, Wenche Darby, complete the picture, and it's also super-convenient to the airport bus.

Stavanger B&B
B&B €€
(☎51 56 25 00; www.stavangerbedandbreakfast.no; Vikedalsgata 1a; s/d Nkr790/890, with shared toilet Nkr690/790; P🛜) This low-key place offers simple, bright rooms with TV, a shower and a smile from the friendly owners. Packed lunches are available for a small fee and free coffee, tea and waffles are served nightly.

Havly Hotel
HOTEL €€
(www.havly-hotell.no; Valberggata 1; s/d Nkr1030/1390; 🛜) This smaller business place occupies a great spot in a central but quiet street. The building is unusually high-'60s in style, though rooms are decorated in a standard

STAVANGER FOR CHILDREN

Older children will enjoy the Norsk Oljemuseum (p197), while younger visitors could spend an entire day playing in the Museum of Childhood (p199). The Arkeologisk Museum (p199) sometimes has Viking-themed activities in summer, while children of all ages will enjoy Geoparken (Norsk Oljemuseum), a playground fashioned from oil-exploration equipment at the Norsk Oljemuseum. And don't miss the beautiful stretches of sand at Sola, Hellestø and Bybergsanden.

CITY BEACHES

A 20-minute drive south of Stavanger, a number of soft-sand beaches stretch down the coast. Backed by sea-grass spiked dunes and dotted with wooden holiday shacks, they are all incredibly atmospheric, if often on the fresh side. Sola sits right near the airport, and has parking and a kiosk, plus the historic **Sola Strand Hotel** (☑51 94 30 00; Sola Strand Hotel; Axel Lunds veg 27, Sola). Further along, Hellestø and Bybergsanden form a gorgeous peaceful continuum: perfect for bracing walks whatever the weather, or a shallows frolic in summer.

clubby, midrange business manner. Staff are friendly and there's a set high-summer discount rate from June to August.

Skagen Brygge Hotel HOTEL €€€
(☑51 85 00 00; www.skagenbryggehotell.no; Skagenkaien 30; s/d from Nkr1890/1990; ❄ 🛜) This large, waterfront Clarion Collection flagship is quietly luxurious and rooms at the front have the best views in town (unusually, this includes some single rooms). There's a gym, free afternoon waffles and the waterfront lounge is delightful. Prices halve come the weekend.

Myhregaarden Hotel BOUTIQUE HOTEL €€€
(☑51 86 80 00; www.myhregaardenhotel.no; Nygaten 24; s/d Nkr1995/2195; ❄ 🛜) The Myhregaarden sits in a completely refurbished early-20th-century building and retains some original features. The contemporary refit, however, is dominant: the large rooms are business-luxe in style with lots of black and purple. All but five rooms have fireplaces, and those without have original wooden beams.

There's no real lobby or facilities but it's right in the thick of city shopping, eating and bar-hopping.

🍴 Eating

Stavanger has a large choice of restaurants, including some tasty Thai and Indian, but also what we suspect is the most expensive eating-out scene in Norway.

★**Renaa Matbaren** INTERNATIONAL €€
(Breitorget 6, enter from Bakkegata; small dishes Nrk135-189, mains Nkr195-335; ⏰11am-1am Mon-Sat, 1-10pm Sun) Yes, that's a proper Tracey

Emin on the far wall and an actual Anthony Gormley in the middle of the room. This perpetually bustling bistro is testament to just how cashed-up and cultured this North Sea port is. You'd be happy to be here just for the buzz, but the food is fabulous too.

With a menu that ranges across Europe, the open kitchen turns out an excellent *vitello tonnato* and a very credible *cassoulet* as well as a number of coal grill specials. Produce is often local: butter is sourced from Røros, beef from the nearby Jæren valley.

Renaa Xpress
Sølvberget NORWEGIAN €€
(Stavanger Kulturhus; www.restaurantrenaa.no; Sølvberggata 2; lunch dishes Nkr69-98, pizza Nkr160-200; ⏰10am-midnight Mon-Sat) This newcomer has quickly won its way into the heart of Stavangerites and is all things to everybody at all hours of the day. Grab a morning coffee as the *kanelboller* come out of the oven, line up for the daily soup deal (Nkr160) or huge salad (Nkr69 to Nkr98) at lunch, or come later for wood-fired wild-yeast pizza.

The margherita passes the authentic pizza litmus test with flying colours, or try the flat bread special of bacon, pecorino and rosemary. It does get very busy during the day, so if you're just after coffee, pop through the Kulturhus to the little Renaa Xpress across the street.

Thai Cuisine THAI €€
(thaicuisine.no; Kirkegata 41; lunch mains Nkr110-160, dinner mains Nkr230-295) Norwegian Thai often outshines that found elsewhere in Europe and here's a fine example. There's a full menu of Thai standards; dishes have an authentic mix of dry spicing, fresh herbs and chilli. Service is effortless and the dining room fills a bright shopfront space with big windows overlooking a cobbled corner just up from the water.

Bølgen & Moi NORWEGIAN €€
(Kjerringholmen, Norsk Oljemuseum; lunch dishes Nkr179-225, 3-/4-/5-course set menus Nkr535/595/695; ⏰11am-4pm Mon, noon-9.30pm Tue-Sat, noon-5pm Sun) This stylish Stavanger outpost of the national restaurant group is attached to the Oljemuseum. There's pizza, burgers and salads available at both lunch and dinner, as well as a nicely inventive set menu in the evening.

NB Sørensen's
Damskibsexpedition NORWEGIAN €€
(☑51 84 38 00; Skagen 26; mains Nkr125-329; ⏰11am-1.30am Mon-Sat, 1-10pm Sun) Our pick

of the waterfront restaurant row, this large maritime-themed place serves everything from confit duck (Nkr310) to roast Atlantic makerel (Nkr290). It really hits its straps when it comes to hearty mains, which may not be elegant but use top-quality produce.

Snackier dishes, such as chorizo tortilla or pork platters, are good value. The atmospheric indoor dining area is ideal when the weather turns; locals swear that the food and service is better upstairs.

Emilio's Tapas Bar   SPANISH €€
(Sølvberggata 13; tapas Nkr50-220, lunch mains Nkr105-175; ☺ lunch & dinner daily Jun-Aug, Mon-Sat Sep-May) This old-school tapas bar with friendly service creates traditional Iberian tapas. The lunch-time selection of six tapas (Nkr175) is good value. They also have a small selection of Spanish wines and beers.

Renaa Restauranten   NORWEGIAN €€€
(☑ 51 55 11 11; www.restaurantrenaa.no; Breitorget 6, entrance from Bakkegata; tasting menus Nkr995; ☺ 6pm-late Tue-Sat) A rambling basement is home to Stavanger's most highly respected restaurant and seduces from the get-go with a darkly glamorous, earthy and intimate dining room. A set tasting menu is responsive to place and the seasons; for most of the year it highlights locally caught fish and seafood, though in autumn and winter game comes into its own.

Torget Fish Market   FISH MARKET €€€
(Rosenkildetorget; mains Nkr269; ☺ market 9am-4.30pm Mon-Sat, restaurant 11am-9pm Mon-Wed, 11am-midnight Thu-Sat) With just a tiny wet market, this place is not a patch on the Bergen version. The prime waterfront restaurant, however, does a good changing menu of entrees such as tuna tataki (Nkr169) and has a super fresh catch of the day. It's also a favoured after-work watering hole.

🍷 Drinking & Nightlife

We can only scratch the surface of Stavanger's surfeit of places to drink, dance and stay out late; the waterfront bar strip is loud, brash and perpetually busy, especially in the warmer months, and is definitely not hard to find.

★ Bøker & Børst   CAFE, BAR
(Øvre Holmegate 32; ☺ 10am-2am) There are many little cafes beckoning in the lanes climbing the hillside west of the oil museum, but our favourite is book-clad Bøker & Børst, with its bohemian decor, good coffee and Stavanger's most interesting crowd, day or night.

Renaa Xpress   CAFE
(Breitorget 6, enter from Steinkargata) Not to be confused with Renaa Xpress Sølvberget, this little cafe sits at the back of the glass-roofed arcade, up the stairs from the other two Renaa outfits. It's a great spot to soak up the sun in the company of Stavanger's stylish mums and babes with great coffee and brownies.

Sjokoladepiken   CAFE
(www.sjokoladepiken.no; Øvre Holmegate 27; ☺ 10am-10pm Mon-Thu, 10am-midnight Fri & Sat, 11.30am-9pm Sun) When the wind whips up off the North Sea and thoughts turn to hot chocolate, this cosy place delivers. They also serve coffee, wine and beer and sell a range of artisan chocolate and patisserie-style cakes.

B.brormann B.bar   BAR
(Skansegata 7; ☺ 6pm-2am Mon-Thu, 4pm-2am Fri & Sat) One of Stavanger's best-loved bars, this low-key shopfront place draws a discerning over-30s crowd and, later, local hospitality staff for post-shift beers and gun-mixed cocktails (Nkr120).

GNU   BAR
(www.gnubar.no; Nedre Strandgate 23; ☺ 6pm-2am Sat-Thu, from 3pm Fri) A classic rock-n-roll bar that has both street cred and quiet style. Take your Pilsner upstairs for brilliant views of the harbour or pull up a downstairs bar stool and get in the jukebox queue. Friday night happy hour (4pm to 7pm) features delicious local spicy sausages on potato cakes; weekend DJs play crowd-pleasing ecclectic sets.

Cardinal   PUB
(Skagen 21; ☺ 3pm-1.30am Sun-Wed, from noon Thu-Sat) If you're after a big, comfortable, convivial pub, Cardinal will please. An older crowd convene here to sample what's claimed to be Norway's biggest selection of beers, some 600 or so, with 22 of those on tap.

Checkpoint Charlie   NIGHTCLUB
(☑ 51 53 22 45; www.checkpoint.no; Nedre Strandgate 5; ☺ 8pm-2am) This venue has been around for 30-odd years, making it older than most of the current regulars. Still, everyone in Stavanger ends up here at some point and has a Checkpoint story to tell. The website lists upcoming local and international live acts (indie to straight-out rock and roll) and club nights.

TRAINS FROM STAVANGER

DESTINATION	DEPARTURES (PER DAY)	COST (NKR)	DURATION (HR)
Egersund	4	164	1¼
Kristiansand	5	474	3
Oslo	up to 5	929	8

Café Sting   CAFE
(☑ 51 89 32 84; Valbergjet 3; ⊘ noon-11pm Mon-Thu, to 1.30am Fri & Sat, 2-11pm Sun) Up the hill and a world away from the harbour, the whitewashed old house that's home to this interesting venue overlooks an elevated little park. Part cafe, part bar, part cultural space there's a nice mix of exhibitions, live jazz and weekend club nights, and a variety of nooks and crannies from which to enjoy them.

☆ Entertainment

Stavanger Konserthus   CLASSICAL MUSIC
(www.stavanger-konserthus.no; Nedre Strandgate 89b) Stavanger has a thriving cultural scene. Check out the Stavanger Konserthus program online or at the tourst office; there are occasional free classical concerts.

❶ Information

Museum Information Office (Nedre Strandgate 21; tour free with entrance ticket to Maritime Museum; ⊘ 10am-4pm Jun-Aug, tour 11am in English, 1pm in Norwegian Jul–mid-Aug) Information on most of the city's museums.

Stavanger Turistforening DNT (off Muségata; ⊘ 10am-4pm Mon-Wed & Fri, to 6pm Thu, to 3pm Sat) Information on hiking and mountain huts.

Tourist Office (☑ 51 85 92 00; www.regionstavanger.com; Domkirkeplassen 3; ⊘ 9am-8pm Jun-Aug, to 4pm Mon-Fri, to 2pm Sat Sep-May) Local information and advice on Lysefjord and Preikestolen.

❶ Getting There & Away

AIR

Stavanger airport (☑ 51 65 80 00) is at Sola, 14km south of the city centre. As well as international airlines, there are a number of domestic-airline services.

Norwegian (www.norwegian.com) Flights to Oslo, Bergen and Trondheim.

SAS (www.sas.no) Oslo and Bergen.

Widerøe (www.wideroe.no) Bergen, Kristiansand and Sandefjord.

BOAT

International ferries and boat tours of Lysefjord are available from Stavanger.

Kolumbus (p196) ferries run from Stavanger to Haugesund and back three times daily (Nkr357, 1¾ hours).

M/S Lysebotn (☑ 91 65 28 00; www.kolumbus.no) Car-and-passenger ferries from Stavanger to Lysebotn (adult/child/car Nkr173/87/356).

BUS

Most services to Oslo change at Kristiansand.

CAR & MOTORCYCLE

Driving between Bergen and Stavanger along the direct E39 can be expensive once you factor in ferries, road tolls and city tolls. In all, you'll end up paying around Nkr600.

TRAIN

Most train services to Oslo change at Kristiansand.

❶ Getting Around

Between early morning and mid-to-late evening, **Flybussen** (☑ 51 52 26 00; www.flybussen.no/stavanger) runs every half-hour between the bus terminal and the airport at Sola (one way/return Nkr110/160).

Lysefjord

All along 42km Lysefjord (Light Fjord), the granite glows with an ethereal light and even on dull days it's offset by almost-luminous mist. This is the favourite fjord of many vis-

BUSES FROM STAVANGER

DESTINATION	DEPARTURES (PER DAY)	COST (NKR)	DURATION (HR)
Bergen	13	440	5½
Haugesund	16	220	2
Kristiansand	3	390	4½
Oslo	3	820	9½

VISITING LYSEFJORD

The most spectacular aspect of visiting Lysefjord is the two-hour hike up to Preikestolen (Pulpit Rock), although a ferry along Lysefjord is an alternative. For general information on the region, check out www.lysefjordeninfo.no and www.visitlysefjorden.no.

Pulpit Rock by Public Transport

From May to mid-September, five to seven ferries a day run from Stavanger's Fiskespiren Quay to Tau, where the ferries are met by a bus, which runs between the Tau pier and the Preikestolhytta Vandrerhjem. From there, the two-hour trail leads up to Preikestolen. The last bus from Preikestolhytta to Tau leaves at 7.55pm. **Tide Reiser** (www.tidereiser. no) offers all-inclusive round-trip tickets (adult/child Nkr250/125); there are timetables online or at the tourist office. You can buy tickets at the tourist office, online or at Fiskespiren Quay.

Pulpit Rock by Car

If you've got your own vehicle, you can take the car ferry (adult/child/car Nkr42/21/125, 40 minutes, up to 24 departures daily) from Stavanger's Fiskespiren Quay to Tau. From the pier in Tau, a well-signed road (Rv13) leads 19km to Preikestolhytta Vandrerhjem (take the signed turn-off after 13km). It costs Nkr70/35 per car/motorcycle to park here.

An alternative route from Stavanger involves driving to Lauvvik (via Sandnes along Rv13), from where a ferry crosses to Oanes (10 minutes, departures almost every half-hour).

Either way, the trip between Stavanger and the trailhead takes around 1½ hours.

Boat Tours to Lysefjord

Two companies offer three-hour boat cruises from Stavanger to the waters below Preikestolen on Lysefjord and back.

Rødne Fjord Cruise (☑ 51 89 52 70; www.rodne.no; Skagenkaien 35-37, Stavanger; adult/senior & student/child/family Nkr450/350/280/1150; ⊙ departures 10am & 2pm Sun-Fri, noon Sat Jul & Aug, noon daily May, Jun & Sep, noon Fri-Sun Oct-Apr)

Tide Reiser (☑ 51 86 87 88; www.tidereiser.no; adult/senior & student/child Nkr360/280/250; ⊙ departures noon late May-late Aug, noon Sat Sep-late May)

Round Trips to Kjeragbolten

From mid-May to late August Tide Reiser also runs 13½-hour bus-boat-hike return trips to Kjeragbolten (Nkr490), which can otherwise be difficult to reach. It includes a five-hour return hike.

itors, and there's no doubt that it has a captivating beauty. Whether you cruise from Stavanger, hike up to Preikestolen (604m), or drive the switchback road down to Lysebotn, it's one of Norway's finest destinations.

Preikestolen

The sight of people perched without fear on the edge of this extraordinary granite rock formation is one of Norway's emblematic images. Preikestolen (Pulpit Rock), with astonishingly uniform cliffs on three sides plunging 604m to the fjord below, is a freak of nature, which, despite the alarming crack where it joins the mountains, is likely to be around for a few more centuries. Looking down can be daunting, but you won't regret the magical view directly up Lysefjord. It's quite simply a remarkable place, a vantage point unrivalled anywhere in the world.

As with many of Norway's natural attractions, there are no fences or barriers of any kind. While the rock receives over 200,000 visitors a year, there has only been one accidental fatality, in 2013. That said, do take all due care even if other people seemingly don't. For those with vertigo, even watching other people dangling limbs over the abyss can make the heart skip a beat. Rocky trails lead up the mountains behind, offering more wonderful views.

The two-hour, 3.8km trail up to Preikestolen leaves from Preikestolhytta Vandrerhjem. It begins along a steep but well-marked route, then climbs past a series of alternating steep and boggy sections to the final climb across granite slabs and along some windy and exposed cliffs to Preikestolen itself. The steepest sections are at the beginning and in the middle parts of the trail and can be challenging for the unfit.

The area also offers several other fabulous walks – the **Vatnerindane ridge circuit** (two hours), **Ulvaskog** (three hours), the **Refsvatnet circuit** (three hours), the summit of **Moslifjellet** (three hours) and even a two-day hike all the way to **Lysebotn** – all of which are accessible from the Preikestolhytta car park. For more information on possible routes and DNT huts along the trails, visit the Stavanger Turistforening DNT (p204) before setting out from Stavanger.

🛏 Sleeping & Eating

★ Preikestolen Fjellstue   LODGE €

(📞51 74 20 74; www.preikestolenfjellstue.no; Jørpeland; hostel dm/s/d/q Nkr300/520/760/1360, lodge s/d Nkr1125/1495, water camp adult/child/family Nkr500/375/1575) Completely overhauled in recent years, this DNT mountain lodge and hostel at the Preikestolen trailhead means Preikestolen finally has accommodation worthy of its natural splendour. There is a range of accommodation for all budgets, including a well-kept hostel (with breakfast and linen included in the price), stylishly simple lodge rooms and family cottages.

In summer you can even stay in a hammock slung on a roofed dock by the lakeside at their B&B Basecamp's 'water camp'. Canoe or walk there along Refsvatn lake – canoe rental is included in the price and it can be used throughout your stay. Hot breakfasts are prepared on the campfire.

Preikestolen Camping   CAMPGROUND €

(📞48 19 39 50; www.preikestolencamping.com; Jørpeland; tent sites Nkr280; ⊙Apr-Oct, gates open 7am-10pm) The closest campsite to Preikestolen (5km, or 1km off the Rv13) is surrounded by forest, is well run and has good facilities, including a shop-restaurant. They offer helicopter sightseeing on Mondays and Thursdays at 6pm (Nkr500 per person).

❶ Information

Lysefjordsenteret (📞51 70 31 23; www.lysefjordsenteret.no; Oanes; salmon farm adult/child Nkr60/30; ⊙11am-8pm Jun-Aug, 11am-5pm Sep-May) In a fabulous setting north of the ferry terminal at Oanes, with tourist information, salmon farm, restaurant and geological and folk-history exhibits.

Lysebotn

The ferry ride from Stavanger takes you to the fjord head at Lysebotn, where a narrow and much-photographed road corkscrews spectacularly 1000m up towards Sirdal in 27 hairpin bends. From Lysebotn, the road twists up the mountain, from where you can continue on into the Setesdalen region and to Oslo.

🏃 Activities

After Preikestolen, the most popular Lysefjord walk leads to **Kjeragbolten**, an enormous oval-shaped boulder, or 'chockstone', lodged between two rock faces about 2m apart. The 10km, five-hour return hike involves a strenuous 700m ascent from the Øygardsstølen Café car park (parking Nkr30), near the highest hairpin bend above Lysebotn.

The route trudges up and over three ridges and, in places, steep muddy slopes can make the going quite rough. Once you're at Kjeragbolten, actually reaching the boulder requires some tricky manoeuvring, including traversing an exposed ledge on a 1000m-high vertical cliff! From there, you can step (or crawl) directly onto the boulder for one of Norway's most astonishing views. The photo of you perched on the rock is sure to impress all of your Instagram followers.

If this doesn't provide sufficient thrills, then base jumping from Kjeragbolten could just be Norway's craziest activity; check out the website of the **Stavanger Base Club** (www.basekjerag.com).

🛏 Sleeping & Eating

Lysefjorden Tourist Cabin   HOSTEL

(📞94 82 66 02; booking@lysefjordenturisthytte.no; Lysebotn; r per person Nkr325; ⊙Jun-Aug) Fifty metres from the quay is the former Lyse canteen. Stavanger Hiking Association now offers rooms with shower and toilet, or cheaper accommodation in dormitories. An attached cafe and lounge is open for breakfast, lunch and dinner and is licensed for beer and wine. Bed linen and towels can be hired.

Øygardsstølen Café   CAFE €

(snacks & light meals Nkr79-189; ⊙9.30am-8pm mid-Jun–mid-Sep) For views at this end of Lysefjord, whether you come to eat or just gawp, you can't beat the 'eagle's nest', perched atop the cliff overlooking the hairpin twists down to Lysebotn.

The Western Fjords

Best Places to Eat

➡ Maki (p244)

➡ Anno (p244)

➡ Restaurant Arven (p211)

➡ Sødahl-Huset (p234)

Best Places to Stay

➡ Juvet Landscape Hotel (p235)

➡ Hotel Aak (p234)

➡ Villa Norangdal (p239)

➡ Hotel Brosundet (p243)

➡ Flåm Camping & Hostel (p211)

➡ Eplet (p219)

Why Go?

Scoured and gouged by glaciers, ancient and modern, western Norway's deep, sea-drowned valleys are pincered by steep, rugged terrain. It's a landscape that is so utterly unique and so profoundly beautiful that it is one of the most desirable destinations in the world.

Although overshadowed by the sublime fjords, the coastline is nonetheless extraordinary, blasted by an often ferocious ocean and backed closely by deep green mountain peaks.

Ferries are a way of life in the west. These reliable workhorses make navigating the insane geography possible but are also an enjoyable part of your journey, offering staggering, otherwise inaccessible, panoramas.

This is great hiking country, whether wild walking, following one of the many signed trails or lumbering along in a guided glacier-walking group. And if, after so much fresh air, you crave some small-town sophistication, the bijou art nouveau settlement of Ålesund has that in spades.

When to Go
Ålesund

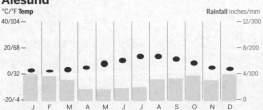

Early Jul Norsk Fjellfestival in stunning Åndalsnes, a folk and outdoor celebration.

Mid-Jul Molde parties all week long during Moldejazz.

Late Aug Savour Ålesund's seafood haul during the town's Norwegian Food Festival.

The Western Fjords Highlights

1 Cruise between Geiranger and Hellesylt in the embrace of the towering cliffs of **Geirangerfjord** (p236).

2 Ride the dramatic **Flåmsbana railway** (p210) between wild Hardangervidda and Flåm.

3 Take the otherworldy **Trollstigen road** (p232) between Åndalsnes and Valldal.

4 Get your boots damp on a tiny icy tongue of the vast **Jostedalsbreen icecap** (p222).

5 Immerse yourself in the Jugendstil era in architecturally unique **Ålesund** (p240).

ATLANTIC OCEAN

Dyrnesvågen
Smøla
Grip

Kristiansund
E39
Kvernes
Bremsnes
Averøya
Kvenvik
Atlanterhavsveien **6**
Vevang
Sylte
Bud
Atukra
Smøge
Ona
Molde
Langfjorden
Romsdalfjorden

MØRE OG ROMSDAL
Isfjorden
Romsdalshorn (1550m)
Andalsnes
Trollvegen
RV63
Trollstigen Route **3**
E136
Romsdal
Raumabanen Railway
Zakariasdammen
Dømbås (55km)
E136
Bjorli

Spjelkavik
Blindheim
Valderøy
Giske
Godøy
Ålesund **5**
Runde
Gurskøy

Stordal
Sykkylven
Stranda
60
Øye
665
Langstøylvatnet

Linge
Valldal
Eidsdal
Tafjord
Ørnevegen
Geirangerfjord **1**
Geiranger

E39
E136

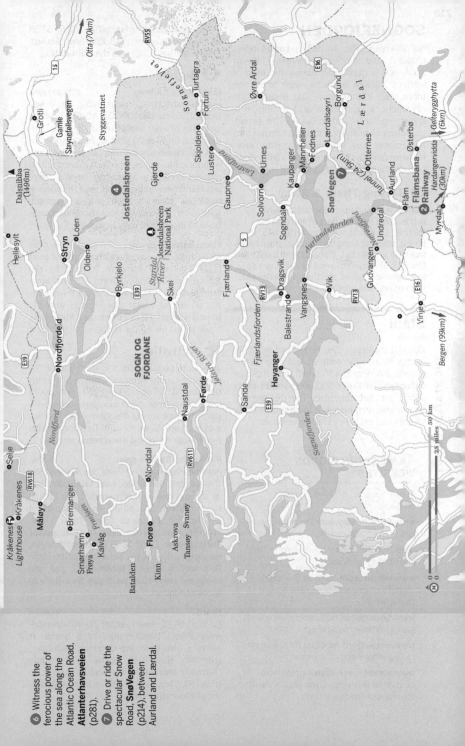

6 Witness the ferocious power of the sea along the Atlantic Ocean Road, **Atlanterhavsveien** (p281).

7 Drive or ride the spectacular Snow Road, **SnøVegen** (p214), between Aurland and Lærdal.

SOGNEFJORDEN

Sognefjorden, the world's second-longest (203km) and Norway's deepest (1308m) fjord, cuts a deep slash across the map of western Norway. In places, sheer walls rise more than 1000m above the water, while elsewhere a gentler shoreline supports farms, orchards and villages. The broad, main waterway is impressive, but cruise into its narrower arms, such as the deep and lovely Nærøyfjord to Gudvangen, for idyllic views of abrupt cliff faces and cascading waterfalls.

ℹ Getting There & Away

Norled (www.norled.no) operates a daily express boat between Bergen and both Flåm (Nkr750, 5½ hours) and Sogndal (Nkr645, 4¾ hours), stopping along the way at 10 small towns including Vik (Nkr510, 3½ hours) and Balestrand (Nkr545, 3¾ hours). Several local ferries also link Sognefjord towns, and there's an extensive, if infrequent, bus network.

Flåm

POP 450

Flåm, at the head of Aurlandsfjorden, sits in a truly spectacular setting. As a stop on the popular Norway in a Nutshell tour, this tiny village receives over 500,000 visitors every year. It's a charming place, but this piece of heaven can turn hellish if too many of those visitors end up here at the same time.

ℹ WESTERN FJORDS WEBSITES

These websites will help in your planning.

www.fjordnorway.com Detailed coverage of the fjords region.

www.nordfjord.no Equally comprehensive about Nordfjord.

www.visitmr.com Møre og Romsdal region's official website with a host of useful links.

www.fjordkysten.no Covers the region's northern coastline.

www.sognefjord.no Great for the whole of Sognefjord and its environs.

www.stavechurch.com A great introduction to stave churches, plus in-depth coverage of the major ones.

The seasonal **tourist office** (☑57 63 33 13; www.visitflam.com; ☉8.30am-8pm Jun-Aug, 8.30am-4pm May & Sep) is in the train station.

◉ Sights

Flåmsbana Railway SCENIC RAILWAY
(www.flaamsbana.no; adult/child one way Nkr300/150, return Nkr400/300) A 20km-long engineering wonder hauls itself up 864m of altitude gain through 20 tunnels. At a gradient of 1:18, it's the world's steepest railway that runs without cable or rack wheels. It takes a full 45 minutes to climb to Myrdal on the bleak, treeless Hardangervidda plateau, past thundering waterfalls (there's a photo stop at awesome Kjosfossen). The railway runs year-round, with up to 10 departures daily in summer.

Flåmsbana Museum MUSEUM
(☉9am-7pm May-Sep, shorter hours rest of year) **FREE** This little museum is right by the Flåmsbana Railway platform. It's not, however, just about railways: there are fascinating photos of construction gangs and life in and around Flåm before cars and buses made it this far up the fjords.

🏃 Activities

To simply pedal along the shoreline or for something more strenuous, rent a bike from the tourist office (Nkr50/250 per hour/day). The tourist office also has six easy-to-interpret free sheets describing local walks, varying from 45 minutes to five hours, with routes superimposed upon aerial photos.

Riding the Rallarvegen CYCLING
(www.rallarvegen.com) Cyclists can descend the Rallarvegen, the service road originally used by the navvies who constructed the Flåmsbana railway, for 83km from Haugastøl (1000m) or an easier 56km from Finse. You can rent bicycles from the **Haugastøl Turistsenter** (☑32 08 75 64; Haugastølvegen, Haugastøl; 2-day bike hire incl return transport from Flåm weekday/weekend Nkr480/580) and the company also offers packages that include accommodation.

Njord KAYAKING
(☑91 31 66 28; www.njord.as) Njord operates from Flåm's handkerchief of a beach. It offers a two-hour sea-kayaking induction (Nkr350), three-hour gentle fjord paddle (Nkr550) and four-hour paddle and hike trips (Nkr710), plus multiday kayaking, hiking and camping trips.

Fjord Safari ADVENTURE
(www.fjordsafari.com; adult/child 1½hr trips Nkr480/290, 3hr Nkr690/420) Bounce along in a Zodiac/RIB inflatable to see more of the fjord in less time. The team supplies full-length waterproof kit – you'll need it for this exhilarating scoot across the waters. Trips, with stops, last from 1½ hours (adult/child Nkr510/310) to three hours (adult/child Nkr610/380).

**Flåm Marina
og Apartement Boat Hire** BOAT HIRE
(☑57 63 35 55) If you'd like to paddle your own canoe, row or simply sit back at the tiller, Flåm Marina og Apartement, a five-minute walk from the jetty, hires out rowing boats and canoes and motorboats.

🛌 Sleeping

**★Flåm Camping
& Hostel** HOSTEL, CAMPGROUND €
(☑57 63 21 21; www.flaam-camping.no; car/caravan sites Nkr215/220, dm/s/tw/q Nkr300/500/865/1255, with shared bathroom Nkr230/390/650/950; ⊙Mar–Oct; 🛜) Family-run and built on the site of their old family farm, there's a lot of love gone into every aspect of this operation. Rooms, from dorms to ensuite doubles, are spread across the lush site, each with a stylish simplicity of their own. Campsites are idyllically located too. In a gorgeous spot a few minutes' walk from the station.

It has been consistently judged by Hostelling International as one of the best in Norway and the world.

Flåm Marina og Apartement APARTMENTS €€
(☑57 63 35 55; www.flammarina.no; apt Nkr1198) This modern block, right at the water's edge, offers a magnificent outlook down the length of the fjord from the terrace of its small bar-cafe (dishes Nkr110 to Nkr185), open to all. Its 10 self-catering apartments, comfortable for two, can sleep up to five (Nkr300 extra per bed); living spaces have fjord views but bedrooms are tucked away.

Heimly Pensjonat GUESTHOUSE €€
(☑57 63 23 00; www.heimly.no; s/d Nkr795/1195; 🛜) Overlooking the water on the fringe of the village and away from all the port hubbub, this 1930s home has basic rooms. The more expensive ones have magnificent views right down the fjord.

Fretheim Hotel HOTEL €€€
(☑57 63 63 00; www.fretheim-hotel.no; s/d Nkr1195/2190; 🅿@🛜) A haunt of fly-fishing English aristocracy in the 19th century, the vast, 122-room Fretheim, despite its size, manages to be intimate and welcoming. In the original 1870s building, 17 rooms have been restored to their historic selves, although with full modern comfort, while the American wings are straight-up contemporary luxe.

The hotel will arrange and advise on walking and bike trips. Exertions over, the 3rd-floor bar in the tower does a great range of beers and is a pleasant place to enjoy the view (but for the very best panorama, climb the spiral staircase to the glass-floored eyrie at the top).

Flåmsbrygga HOTEL €€€
(☑57 63 20 50; www.flamsbrygga.no; s/d Nkr1390/1790) All but two of the rustic, woody rooms in this modern dockside place have a balcony, making for some superb fjord vistas. It's a busy location, but super handy to everything, including the attached pub and restaurant, Ægir Bryggeri.

🍴 Eating & Drinking

Restaurant Arven RESTAURANT €€€
(☑57 63 63 00; Fretheim Hotel; set menu/buffet Nkr545/464) At the Fretheim Hotel's restaurant, chefs salt and smoke their own meat and there's an 'ecological and local' menu, sourced from the region's agricultural college. You can also sample locally raised lamb, reindeer and goat kid, grilled in the barbecue hut.

Ægir Bryggeri BREW PUB
(www.flamsbrygga.no/bryggeri; ⊙noon-10pm May–mid-Sep, from 6pm rest of year) Looking for all the world like a stave church, Ægir Brewery, all appealing woodwork and flagstones, offers six different kinds of draught beer, all brewed on the spot. It also does a tasty, creative take on Norwegian comfort food as well as burgers and pizzas (Nkr160 to Nkr210).

ℹ Getting There & Away

BOAT
From Flåm, boats head out to towns around Sognefjorden. The most scenic trip from Flåm is the passenger ferry up Nærøyfjord to Gudvangen (one way/return Nkr295/400). It leaves Flåm at 3.10pm year-round and up to five times daily between May and September. You can also hop aboard in Aurland. At Gudvangen, a connecting

BUSES FROM FLÅM

DESTINATION	PRICE (NKR)	DURATION	FREQUENCY (DAILY)
Gudvangen	52	20min	4-8
Aurland	36	15min	4-8
Sogndal	184	1¾hr	2-6
Lærdalsøyri	95	45min	2-6
Bergen	330	3hr	2-6

bus takes you on to Voss, where you can pick up the train for Bergen or Oslo. The tourist office sells all ferry tickets, plus the Flåm to Voss ferry-bus combination. From Flåm-Bergen, there's at least one daily express boat (Nkr695, 5½ hours) via Balestrand (Nkr265, 1½ hours).

TRAIN
Flåm is the only Sognefjorden village with a rail link, via the magnificent Flåmsbana railway. There are train connections to Oslo and Bergen at Myrdal.

Aurland

POP 777

Peaceful Aurland is much less hectic than its neighbour, Flåm, a mere 10km south along the fjord. These days it's renowned as one end of Lærdalstunnel (24.5km), the world's longest road tunnel. This essential link in the E16 highway connects Oslo and Bergen; before its completion traffic had to ferry-hop between Lærdal and Gudvangen. It's a fast alternative to the sinuous and seasonal 45km-long SnøVegen. Your choice: speed and convenience, or a hair-raising, view-feast on the ascent and descent, and an eerily serene, waterfall and lake-strewn high mountain plateau in the middle.

It also marks the end of the spectacular Aurlandsdalen hiking route.

🏃 Activities

The Aurland and Lærdal tourist offices have produced six walker-friendly sheets of local walks, where the route is superimposed upon an aerial photo.

Flåm to Aurland Hike   HIKE
For consistently outstanding views and near solitude, hike the 12km trail that mainly follows the old road between Aurland and Flåm, passing by Otternes. Until 1919 and the construction of the coast road, it was the only means of land communication between the two villages. Allow around three hours.

Geiteryggen to Aurland Hike   HIKE
The classic trek down Aurlandsdalen from Geiteryggen to Aurland follows a stream from source to sea as you tramp one of the oldest trading routes between eastern and western Norway. From mid-July, you can start this four-day walk in Finse, on the Oslo–Bergen rail line, with overnight stops at Geiterygghytta, Steinbergdalen and Østerbø.

The final section, usually open between early June and late September, from Østerbø (820m) to Vassbygdi (95m) is the most scenic and makes for a hugely enjoyable day hike (allow six to seven hours). Buses run twice daily between Aurland and both Vassbygdi (15 minutes) and Østerbø (one hour).

🛏 Sleeping & Eating

Lunde Gard & Camping   CAMPGROUND €
(☑ 99 70 47 01; www.lunde-camping.no; campsites Nkr240, cabins with outdoor bathroom Nkr600, with bathroom Nkr1050, 3-bed apt Nkr820; ☺ May-Sep; 🐾) This small campsite nestles agreeably beside a river, 1.2km up a side valley. Kitchen and toilet facilities are impeccable.

Vangsgaarden   HOTEL €€
(☑ 57 63 35 80; www.vangsgaarden.no; d/f Nkr1100/1350, 4-bed cabins Nkr1250 (linen per person Nkr65); 🐾) Four 18th-century buildings along with six cabins down at sea level and the **Duehuset (Dovecot) Cafe & Pub** (mains from Nkr129; ☺ 3-11pm Jun-Aug) make up this friendly prime waterfront place. Some rooms are furnished in antique style, others are simpler. It's atmospheric – the dining room, for example, could be your grandmother's parlour – and the gardens are pretty.

Aurland Fjordhotell   HOTEL €€
(☑ 57 63 35 05; www.aurland-fjordhotel.com; s/d from Nkr920/1240) At this 30-room, family-owned hotel, most rooms have fjord

views and balcony. It's old-fashioned, but both comfortable and friendly.

Aurlandskafeen CAFE €
(mains Nkr110-170; ⊙10am-9pm) A typical small-town Norwegian cafe but with a neat little terrace overlooking the rippling river where it flows into Aurlandsfjord, plus all-day beer and wine.

ⓘ Information

Aurland Tourist Office (☑57 63 33 13; www.alr.no; ⊙9am-5pm Mon-Fri, 10am-5.30pm Sat & Sun Jun-Aug, shorter hours rest of year) The tourist office is beside the village church.

ⓘ Getting There & Away

Buses run up to eight times daily between Aurland and Flåm (Nkr36, 15 minutes) and up to six times daily between Aurland and Lærdal (Nkr83, 30 minutes). Express buses to/from Bergen (Nkr300, three hours) call in up to six times daily.

Watch out for the speed cameras in Lærdalstunnelen – all 24.5km of them.

Undredal

POP 112

Undredal, tucked midway between Flåm and Gudvangen, is a truly lovely little village, its pleasures enhanced – and its traditional quality sustained – because you need to make that bit of extra effort to get there. However, it has recently been added as a brief stop to some boat tours and its former tranquillity is at risk.

Undredal's local claim to fame is its cheeses. Well, not exactly fame, as you'll only find them in a few specialised cheese shops and delicatessens within Norway. Around 500 goats freely roam the surrounding grassy slopes and between them they provide the milk for around 10 tonnes of cheese per year (work it out: that's a hugely impressive yield per nipple). Farmers from the valley supply the village's two remaining dairies – once there were 10 – which still produce the firm yellow Undredal cheese and its brown, slightly sweet variant, made from the boiled and concentrated whey. You can pick up a hunk of each at the village shop; it's the light-blue building beside the shore.

Undredal is 6.5km north of the E16 down a narrow, steeply threading road (until its construction in 1988, the only access was by sea). If travelling by bus, get off at the eastern end of the 11km tunnel that leads

to Gudvangen. Best of all, take the bus out, walk down the spectacular valley along the lightly trafficked road and return by boat (press the switch beside the yellow blinking lamp on the cafe wall beside the jetty to alert the next passing ferry).

◉ Sights

Undredal Church CHURCH
(adult/child Nkr30/free; ⊙noon-5pm mid-May–mid-Sep) Originally built as a stave church in 1147 and seating 40, this barrel-vaulted village church is the smallest still-operational house of worship in mainland Scandinavia. Look up at the roof with its charmingly naive roof paintings of angels, Christ on the cross and other biblical figures, surrounded by stylised stars.

Gudvangen & Nærøyfjord

Nærøyfjord, its 17km length a Unesco World Heritage Site, lies west of Flåm. Beside the deep blue fjord, only 250m across at its narrowest point, are towering 1200m-high cliffs, isolated farms, and waterfalls plummeting from the heights. It can easily be visited as a day excursion from Flåm.

Kjelsfossen waterfall tumbles from the southern wall of Nærøydalen valley,

SNØVEGEN

The 45km **Snow Road** (☉ Jun–mid-Oct), officially signed **Aurlandsvegen**, climbs from sea level, twisting precipitously to the desolate, boulder-strewn high plateau that separates Aurland and Lærdalsøyri (Lærdal). This heart-stopping drive – strictly for summertime as snow banks line the road and tarns are still deep-frozen even in late June – has been designated as a National Tourist Route, so get there before the coaches catch on. Even if you don't opt for the whole route, drive the first 8km from Aurland to the magnificent **Stegastein observation point**. Projecting out over the fjord way below, the biomorphic pine-clad structure is striking to look at, not to mention designed to push you just a little out of your comfort zone, rather like Norway itself.

above Gudvangen village. Notice too the **avalanche protection scheme** above Gudvangen. The powerful avalanches here typically provide a force of 12 tonnes per square metre, move at 50m a second and, local legend reckons, can bowl a herd of goats right across the fjord!

The approach by boat is wondrous but Gudvangen itself, like a mini Flåm only more constricted, can disappoint when overwhelmed with boat and coach traffic.

🛏 Sleeping

Gudvangen Camping　CAMPGROUND €€
(☎993 80 803; www.visitgudvangen.com; campsites Nkr120, 2-/4-person cabins with outdoor bathroom Nkr420/480, with bathroom Nkr820/1290; ☉mid-Apr–mid-Sep) On the right side of the E16, just over 1km from the ferry port, this is a well-equipped campground at the base of sheer cliffs.

Vang Camping　CAMPGROUND €€
(☎57 63 39 26; www.vang-camping.no; campsites Nkr100, cabins with outdoor bathroom Nkr300-500, with bathroom Nkr950-1200; ☉May–mid-Sep) On the left side of the E16, around 1km out of Gudvangen, these cabins and campsites nestle between the road and the river.

ⓘ Getting There & Away

Scenic ferries between Gudvangen and Flåm (one way/return Nkr295/400) via Aurland run

up to five times daily in summer. A car ferry runs three times daily to/from Lærdal (car and driver/passenger Nkr665/280, three hours) via Kaupanger (Nkr630/280).

Up to eight buses daily run to/from Flåm (Nkr52, 20 minutes) and Aurland (Nkr65, 30 minutes).

Lærdalsøyri (Lærdal)

POP 2200

The village of Lærdalsøyri, usually called Lærdal, is where the lovely green dale of the same name – whose fertile lower reaches produce the juiciest of cherries – meets the fjord. A quiet place nowadays, it was once a busy port, where produce from the surrounding area was loaded on Bergen-bound boats. A fire swept through streets in the town's southwest in early 2014, and while devastating for those who lost homes and were injured, has not affected the town's charm for visitors.

◉ Sights & Activities

The historic centre (Gamle Lærdalsøyri) makes for pleasant strolling through its well-preserved 18th- and 19th-century heart. There are well over a hundred lovingly maintained homes, warehouses and fisherfolk's shacks to explore here. The tourist office has a free town map that describes the best of them and sets out a walking route.

There's free **fishing** in the fjord, and the upper reaches of the Lærdal river are good for trout (day permits are available from the tourist office or nearest campsite).

For **hiking**, pick up the tourist office's free leaflet of walks in the area. It also sells a much more detailed local map (Nkr139) at a scale of 1:50,000.

Norsk Villaks Senter　AQUARIUM
(www.norsk-villakssenter.no; adult/child Nkr90/60; ☉10am-6pm end-Jun–mid-Sep) You can watch wild salmon and sea trout through viewing windows, see an excellent 20-minute film about the salmon's lifecycle, try to tie flies to increase the odds of you hooking one of your own and do a little virtual casting.

Lærdal Sport og Rekreasjon　OUTDOOR ACTIVITIES
(☎57 66 66 95; www.laerdalsport.com; Lærdal Ferie-og Fritidspark, Grandavegen; ☉May-Sep 8am-10pm, Oct-Apr by appointment) There's a good

range of bikes for hire here (from Nkr45/125 per hour/day). They also arrange guided hiking and biking trips ranging from three hours to full days (bike tours from Nkr230, hiking from Nkr75).

🛏 Sleeping & Eating

Sanden Pensjonat
GUESTHOUSE €

(☑ 57 66 64 04; www.sandenpensjonat.no; Øyragata 9; s/d Nkr850/950, with shared bathroom Nkr550/490, apt Nkr1300) Used as a guesthouse for almost 100 years, this charming historic house was restored and returned to its original use by owners Jon and Hallvard in 1994. It retains the simplicity and cosy scale of its era, but is furnished with care and a clever eye for detail. For families or small groups, they also have a nearby apartment.

Lærdal Ferie og Fritidspark
CAMPGROUND, MOTEL €

(☑ 57 66 66 95; www.laerdalferiepark. com; campsites Nkr250, 2-/3-/4-bed cabins Nkr995/1095/1195, motel s/d Nkr500/595; 🛜) This campsite, almost at the water's edge, has sweeping views of the fjord. Its 'motel' has communal self-catering facilities, plus a common room with a terrace and broad picture window that give a magnificent panorama of the fjord.

Lindstrøm Hotell
HOTEL €€

(☑ 57 66 69 00; www.lindstroemhotel.no; s/d Nkr900/1200; ⊙ Apr-Oct; 🅿 @ 🛜) This central fifth-generation family-run hotel is divided between a beautiful Swiss-style gabled building in a garden and the main '60s block across the road. The latter, a charming warren of lounges and libraries, filled with splendid original mid-century Scandinavian design and some Norwegian baroque for good measure, has neat rooms that follow suit. The 19th-century ones are stylish too.

Their pale floorboards and bright walls contrast nicely with beautiful antique iron beds. There are cosy armchairs and big windows overlooking the garden. The restaurant serves a nightly buffet (Nkr365).

Laksen
PUB €€

(☑ 57 66 86 20; lunch dishes Nkr190, dinner mains Nkr210-275; ⊙ 11am-9.30pm Jul & Aug) The informal Laksen Pub & Restaurant at the Wild Salmon Centre offers substantial meals. It dispenses tempting snacks and sandwiches during the daytime, then morphs into a restaurant from 6pm to 9pm.

ℹ️ Information

The **tourist office** (☑ 57 66 67 71; www.alr. no; Øyraplassen 7; ⊙ 10am-6pm Jul & Aug) occupies a lovely old clapboard house, once the town's bank, set back from the main street. It has a neat little photo exhibition on early Lærdal and a free internet point.

ℹ️ Getting There & Away

If you're driving south, you have the choice between the world's longest road tunnel, linking Aurland and Lærdal (mercifully, it's toll free), or, in summer, climbing up and over the mountain, following the Snøvegen. Express buses run to/ from Bergen (Nkr385, 3¾ hours) two to six times daily via the tunnel.

Three daily car ferries run to/from Gudvangen (car and driver/passenger Nkr620/265, three hours) via Kaupanger (Nkr605/245).

Vik
POP 2731

Vik has two splendid small **churches** (combined entry adult/child Nkr80/70; each owing their existence and present form to the 19th-century architect Peter Blix (who designed, among much else, many of the stations on the Oslo–Bergen railway line).

◉ Sights

Hopperstad Stave Church   CHURCH (adult/child Nkr60/50; ⊙ 10am-5pm late May-late Sep) On the southern outskirts of the village of Vik is this splendid stave church, about 1km from the centre. Built in 1130 and Norway's second oldest, it escaped demolition by a whisker in the late 19th century. Inside, the original canopy paintings of the elaborately carved baldaquin have preserved their

---

> ### NORWAY IN A NUTSHELL
>
> Although most visitors do the classic Norway in a Nutshell tour from either Oslo or Bergen, you also can do a mini version (adult/child Nkr775/400).
>
> This circular route from Flåm – boat to Gudvangen, bus to Voss, train to Myrdal, then train again down the spectacular Flåmsbana railway to Flåm – is truly the kernel within the nutshell and takes in all the most dramatic elements. The Gudvangen boat leaves Flåm at 9am and the Flåmsbana train brings you home at 4.55pm.

freshness of colour. A combined ticket for the Hove stone church, 1km to the south, is Nkr80/70.

Hove Stone Church
CHURCH

(adult/child Nkr50/40; ⊙ 11am-4pm end Jun–mid-Aug) The region's oldest stone building, dating to the late 12th century, this church retains its original form beneath Peter Blix's elaborate makeover. This includes the abstract wall painting of nave and chancel, the wooden figures from Norse legend in the roof beams and the external gables.

Balestrand

POP 1337

Balestrand sits facing an impressive stretch of fjord, at its rear an impressive mountain backdrop. It has been a tranquil, small-scale holiday resort ever since the 19th century, and can sometimes out-twee itself.

◉ Sights

Norwegian Museum of Travel & Tourism
MUSEUM

(Norsk Reiselivsmuseum; ☎ 57 69 14 57; reiselivsmuseum.no) This new museum is housed in a beautiful piece of architecture that reflects the surrounding rocky landscape.

Church of St Olav
CHURCH

This charming wooden church (1897), in the style of a traditional stave church, was built at the instigation of English expat Margaret Green, who married a local hotel-owner. It's just up the hill; should you find it closed, the owner of Midtnes Hotel has the key.

Viking Age Barrows
ARCHAEOLOGICAL SITES

Less than 1km south along the fjord, excavation of this pair of barrows revealed remnants of a boat, two skeletons, jewellery and several weapons. One mound is topped by a statue of legendary King Bele, erected by Germany's Kaiser Wilhelm II. Obsessed with Nordic mythology, he regularly spent his holidays here prior to WWI (a similar monument, also funded by the Kaiser and honouring Fridtjof, the lover of King Bele's daughter, peers across the fjord from Vangsnes).

Sognefjord Aquarium
AQUARIUM

(adult/child Nkr70/35; ⊙ 10am-7pm May-Sep) View the 15-minute audiovisual presentation then tour the 24 aquariums in which lurk saltwater creatures from Sognefjord, large, small and very small. The entry price includes an hour of canoe or rowing-boat hire.

🏃 Activities

The tourist office's free pamphlet *Outdoor Activities in Balestrand* has plenty of suggestions for hiking, ranging from easy to demanding. It also stocks *Balestrand Turkart* (Nkr70), a good walking map at 1:50,000 with trails marked up.

Njord
KAYAKING

(☎ 91 32 66 28; www.kajakk.com) Njord explores the fjord off Balestrand in a range of guided sea-kayak tours, lasting from three hours (Nkr600) and including multinight trips. Reserve at the tourist office.

🛏 Sleeping

Sjøtun Camping
CAMPGROUND €

(☎ 95 06 72 61; www.sjotun.com; campsite Nkr210, 4-/6-bed cabins with outdoor bathroom Nkr300/400; ⊙ Jun–mid-Sep) At this green campsite, a 15-minute walk south along the fjord, you can pitch a tent on soft grass amid apple trees or rent a sweet cabin at a very reasonable price.

Vandrerhjem Kringsjå
HOSTEL €

(☎ 57 69 13 03; www.kringsja.no; Laerargata 9; dm Nkr290, s/d/f with bathroom Nkr690/890/990, all incl breakfast; ⊙ mid-Jun–mid-Aug) Uphill from the dock, Balestrand's family-run HI-affiliated hostel is nowadays an outdoor activities centre during the school year. It started life as a hotel, and this shows; it's a fine lodge-style place with comfortable rooms and decent self-catering facilities.

Balestrand Hotell
HOTEL €€

(☎ 57 69 11 38; www.balestrand.com; s/d Nkr850/1340; ⊙ mid-May–mid-Sep) This summertime-only, family-run hotel, is a friendly, jolly, intimate place that eschews the tour groups that fill so many beds elsewhere in town. It's well worth paying more for inspirational views over the fjord.

Midtnes Hotel
HOTEL €€

(☎ 57 69 42 40; www.midtnes.no; s Nkr790, d Nkr850-1290; P 🐾) Beside St Olav's church, this 32-room family-run place, has a breakfast room with great views of the water, an attractive terrace and a lawn that extends down to a jetty, where a rowing boat, free for guests, is moored. Breakfast, with three kinds of pickled herring, hams, prawns and more, is a meal in itself.

Kvikne's Hotel
HOTEL €€€

(☎ 57 69 42 00; www.kviknes.no; s/d from Nkr1110/1720; ⊙ May-Sep; P @) The dreamy pale-yellow, timber exterior of Kvikne's Hotel belies the more-is-more late-19th-century Norwegiana aesthetic in its lounges and dining halls. Of its 190 rooms, all but 25 are in the newer building, erected in the 1960s. They're comfortable to a fault, but a little dated for the price.

Balholm Bar og Bistro serves snacks and light meals and you can take your drinks into the salon where there's plenty to look at outside and in. The hotel is on a point just south of the ferry landing.

✖ Eating

Pilgrim
CAFE €

(☑ 915 62 842; www.detgylnehus.no; meals Nkr90-185) Near the tourist office, this kooky-as-anything little place is integrated into Det Gylne Hus (Golden House), an equally eccentric art gallery. The food, by contrast, is simple, traditional stuff: locally caught sea trout, elk patties, reindeer sausage or meatballs. If it's sunny, the terrace, with freshly cut flowers adorning the tables, is just the spot.

Ciderhuset
NORWEGIAN €€

(☑ 98 47 77 65; www.ciderhuset.no; Sjøtunsvegen 32; mains Nkr140-250; ⊘ 4-10pm late-Jun–mid-Aug) 🍴 Within a fruit farm that produces organic juices, jams, bottled fruits, cider and cider brandy, this happy restaurant fuses Nordic and Mediterranean culinary traditions. They use local produce wherever possible; even the dinnerware is fired by a local potter. Dine on the first-floor terrace or inside the cosy glass house, where fresh herbs and cherry tomatoes climb the panes.

Do savour one of the desserts of organic fruit from their orchards, enhanced by a dollop of equally organic, locally made ice cream. Signs for Ciderhuset run off Sjøtunsvegen, which runs inland from Villavegen.

ℹ Information

Tourist office (☑ 99 23 15 00; www.visitbalestrand.no; ⊘ 10am-5.30pm Jun-Aug, 10am-5pm Mon-Fri May & Sep) This tourist office, run by an extremely knowledgable and helpful local, is opposite the ferry quay. It hires out bicycles for Nkr70/170/270 per hour/half-day/full day.

ℹ Getting There & Away

Express boats run to/from Bergen (Nkr545, 3¾ hours, twice daily) and Sogndal (Nkr240, 45 minutes, once daily).

WORTH A TRIP

BORGUND STAVE CHURCH

Some 30km southeast of Lærdalsøyri along the E16, the 12th-century **Borgund Stave Church** (adult/child Nkr80/60; ⊘ 8am-8pm May-Sep, 10am-5pm Oct-Apr) was raised beside one of the major trade routes between eastern and western Norway. Dedicated to St Andrew, it's one of the best known, most photographed and certainly the best preserved of Norway's stave churches. Its simple, inky interior and sublimely rustic alter are deeply moving. Beside it is the only free-standing medieval wooden bell tower remaining in Norway.

Buy your ticket at the visitors centre, where an exhibition (included in the price of your admission) on this peculiarly Norwegian phenomenon as well as recent early Viking finds from a nearby archaeological dig are evocatively displayed. There's also a nice two-hour circular hike on ancient paths and tracks that starts and ends at the church.

From June to August, a daily ferry (Nkr240/390 one way/return, 1½ hours, twice daily) follows the narrow Fjærlandsfjorden to Fjærland, gateway to the glacial wonderlands of Jostedalsbreen.

Express buses link Balestrand and Sogndal (Nkr128, one hour, three daily).

The scenic Gaularfjellsvegen (Rv13) is an exciting drive to Førde, on Førdefjord, negotiating hairpin bends and skirting Norway's greatest concentration of roadside waterfalls.

Sogndal

POP 7050

Sogndal, though not the area's prettiest town, has a nice community and makes a good base for a trio of magnificent day drives: Jostedalen and Nigardsbreen, Urnes, and Lustrafjord and the spectacular Sognefjellet circuit.

◉ Sights & Activities

Sogn Folkmuseum
MUSEUM

(www.dhs.museum.no; Kaupanger; adult/child Nkr70/30; ⊘ 10am-3pm May & Sep, to 5pm Jun-Aug, 10am-3pm Mon-Fri Oct-Apr) This extensive open-air folk museum is between Sogndal and Kaupanger, beside the Rv5. More than 30 buildings, including farms, a schoolhouse and a mill, have been brought from their original sites and embedded in the surrounding woods. Each is well documented in Norwegian and English. There are three short, themed walking trails with informative panels (reception has English translation sheets).

Children can pet the animals, build their own log cabin and indulge in other backwoods activities, plus there are gorgeous picnic spots.

Sogn Fjordmuseum   MUSEUM
(Kaupanger; ⊙ 10am-3pm or 5pm May-Sep) Part of the much larger Sogn Folkmuseum, also on the Rv5, this museum has a collection of 19th- and 20th-century fishing and freight boats and equipment, and some striking old photos, illustrating in particular the coastal trade in timber for then-booming Bergen's needs.

Stave Church   CHURCH
(Kaupanger; adult/child Nkr60/50; ⊙ 10am-5pm Jun-Aug) The area's main attraction was raised in 1184. It impresses from within by its sheer height, although much of what you see dates from a fundamental renovation in the 17th century. Wall paintings in the nave feature musical annotation, while vine and flower motifs entwine around the chancel. The Celtic-style chancel arch is unique.

🛏 Sleeping & Eating

Kjørnes Camping   CAMPGROUND €
(☑ 57 67 45 80; www.kjornes.no; campsites Nkr240, 2-/5-bed cabins Nkr900/1350, with outdoor bathroom Nkr410/580, apt Nkr800; 🛜) This large, well-maintained campground, where the young owners have expanded and improved facilities, enjoys a gorgeous fjordside setting. Choose a large cabin with fjordside terrace and heated floors; there's a few that allow you to be almost alone with the forest at your back and the fjord before you.

Kjørnes Camping is 3km from Sogndal, off the Rv5, in the direction of Lærdal.

Sogndal Vandrerhjem   HOSTEL €
(☑ 57 62 75 75; www.hihostels.no/sogndal; Helgheimsvegen 9-10; dm/s/d with shared bathroom Nkr310/410/620, d with bathroom Nkr755; ⊙ mid-Jun–mid-Aug) This well-equipped, summertime-only HI-affiliated hostel, near the bridge that carries the Rv5, functions as a boarding school during the rest of the year.

Loftesnes Pensjonat   GUESTHOUSE €€
(☑ 57 67 87 00; Fjøravegen; s/d Nkr650/850) This small, central place above the China House restaurant, and run by the restaurant's own-

ers, is great value. Nine of its 12 rooms have a bathroom and there are self-catering facilities and a rooftop terrace.

★ Sogndal Lodge & Guiding   HOSTEL €€
(☑ 57 62 99 88; www.sogndallodge.no; Almenningen 10; 2-/3-/4-bed r with shared bathroom Nkr850/1260/1600, whole house Nkr3600) This 12-bed lodge is sparkling new, with rooms that are Scando-simple in style, plus nice vintage finds to lend character. It may be right in the middle of the village but, with owners Sigrid and Sander's local guiding expertise, serves as a direct gateway into the surrounding landscape.

You can organise kayaking, climbing, glacier walks and skiing, or longer trips involving all of the above through the lodge. They also do an interesting culinary tour, exploring the area's traditional food producers. There's also rental of kayaks, bikes and paddleboards.

Hofslund Fjord Hotel   HOTEL €€
(☑ 57 62 76 00; www.hofslund-hotel.no; s/d Nkr1095/1395; 🅿@🛜🐾) This venerable 100-bed hotel, approaching its first century, has been run by the same family for four generations. It enjoys a wonderful location; most rooms have a balcony and view of the fjord and a neat lawn sweeps down to the water.

The outdoor pool's heated and there are a couple of rowing boats and fishing gear, loaned free to guests. The restaurant has a nightly buffet (Nkr295) that's good value and open to all-comers.

Galleri Krydder Kaffe   CAFE €
(www.gallerikrydder.no; Parvegen 6; salads Nkr80-110, sandwiches, Nkr80-95; ⊙ 11am-7pm Mon-Fri, 11am-5pm Sat & Sun) Good espresso coffee's guaranteed at this friendly cafe attached to an art gallery – most of the town passes through for a double shot at some time of the day. There's a trampoline and swings next door and a big terrace to eat salads, sandwiches and super-size brownies.

❶ Information

Tourist office (☑ 91 13 64 03; www.sognefjord. no; Hovevegen 2; ⊙ 10am-10pm Mon-Sat, from 11am Sun mid-Jun–Aug, limited hours May & Sep) Sogndal's seasonal tourist office, a five-minute walk east of the bus station and at the back of a convenience store, can book accommodation. It has a huge stock of hiking maps and local guides, rents bike (Nkr70 per day) and issues one-week fishing permits (Nkr150).

ℹ Getting There & Away

Sogndal has Sognefjord's only airport, which has two daily flights to/from Bergen and three to/from Oslo.

Express passenger boats connect Sogndal with Balestrand (Nkr175, 45 minutes, daily) and Bergen (Nkr645, 4½ hours, twice daily).

Bus destinations include Kaupanger (Nkr32, 20 minutes, up to 12 per day), Fjærland (Nkr73, 30 minutes, up to six per day), Balestrand (Nkr94, 1¼ hours, three per day).

Twice-daily buses (mid-June to late August) head northeast past Jotunheimen National Park to Lom (3¼ hours) and Otta (4¼ hours).

Solvorn & Around

Diminutive Solvorn is everything you'd want a fjord-side village to be: spectacularly sited, fetchingly pretty, quiet as a mouse but with warm, welcoming locals. It's all that *and* in striking distance of some of the region's best hiking, biking and paddling.

There are two very different, but equally appealing, accommodation options here, making it a wonderful place to base yourself for at least a few days.

🏃 Activities

FjordSeal   KAYAKING

(☑ 95 77 41 96; www.fjordseal.com; adult/child Nkr550/400; ⊗ tours 9.30am daily May-Sep)

For a delightful four hours of peaceful paddling on smooth-as-silk Lustrafjord, and the chance to cruise among a colony of seals, sign on with one of the daily guided kayak tours of FjordSeal, based at Marifjøra, just off the Rv55, 17km north of Svolvorn.

Mollandsmorki Circuit   MOUNTAIN BIKING

This 25km circuit from Solvorn travels a combination of sealed, gravel and finally dirt roads, with stunning views for much of the distance. It's not easygoing, with some sections of dirt rugged enough to require you to get off and push, but it's incredibly rewarding. Some say, despite its modest distance, even more so than Rallarvegen (p210) cycle route.

🛏 Sleeping

★ Eplet   HOSTEL €

(☑ 41 64 94 69; www.eplet.net; camping per person Nkr100, dm Nkr200, s/d Nkr500/600; ⊗ May-Sep; @ 🛜) Among a bountiful apple orchard and circled by raspberry canes and blueberry bushes, this special hostel is set in terraced gardens, in two rustic wooden buildings, along with some garden campsites. From its windows there are magnificent views of Lustrafjord (they seem even nicer from a hammock in the garden). Rooms are sweetly furnished with local touches.

THE SOGNEFJELLET CIRCUIT

A spectacular circular, day-long driving route, the Sognefjellet circuit runs beside one of Norway's loveliest fjords, climbs a sizeable chunk of the magnificent **Sognefjellet National Tourist Route**, meanders along a lonely, lightly travelled single-lane road that threads across the heights, then plunges in a knuckle-clenching descent, once more to fjord level. The trip can't be done by public transport and cyclists will need to be very fit, and attempt it over a few days.

From Sogndal, head out on the Rv55 to the northeast as it hugs, for the most part, lovely Lustrafjord all the way to Skjolden at the head of the waters. About 5km beyond this tiny settlement, the road starts to seriously twist and climb. You're following an ancient highway where for centuries, when it was no more than a rough track, fish and salt would be hauled up from the coast to be exchanged for iron, butter and hides from communities deep inland.

At wind-battered Turtagrø you can continue along the Rv55, which runs through Jotunheimen National Park, up and over northern Europe's highest road pass (1434m) and on to Lom.

To return to Sogndal, turn right to leave the Rv55 and head for Årdal. The narrow road, known as **Tindevegen** (Route of the Peaks) keeps climbing, just above the treeline, until the pass (1315m) and a toll booth (Nkr75 per vehicle). Then it's a plunge down through woods of spindly birch to the emerald-green waters of Årdalsvatnet and the undistinguished village of Øvre Årdal. From here, the Rv53 takes you, via the ferry between Fodnes and Mannheller, back to Sogndal.

Everything you'd expect in terms of self-catering facilities are provided, as well as a small organic juice factory, a croquet course, lambs to pet and free bikes to borrow. Eplet is run by Agnethe and Trond Henrik: Trond is an environmental geologist, seasoned traveller, climber and serious long-distance cyclist. They can let you in on the best cycle routes and walking trails around, including the extraordinary Molden hike.

★ **Walaker Hotell** HOTEL €€€
(☏ 57 68 20 80; www.walaker.com; d Nkr2250-2700; ☻ May-Sep; @ ☎) This venerable, incredibly atmospheric place, sitting right beside the fjord, is Norway's oldest family hotel. In the hands of nine generations of the Nitters, back to 1640, you'll probably be greeted by Ole Henrik, the current owner, himself. Spread between three buildings, the main one has evocatively decorated (but unfussy) historical rooms with antique wallpaper, and two have claw-foot baths.

The Tingstova wing, the oldest, has four beautiful historical rooms, with stunning hand painted furniture. Standard rooms, in the '60s annex, are comfortable but unremarkable. Not least of the hotel's pleasures is its lovely lawn and garden of lilac, roses, apple and cherry trees, which is available to all.

Urnes

Urnes Stave Church CHURCH
(adult/child Nkr80/45; ☻ 10.30am-5.45pm May-Sep) Norway's oldest preserved place of worship is a Unesco World Heritage Site. Directly across the fjord from Solvorn, it gazes out over Lustrafjord. The original church was built around 1070, while most of today's structure was built a century later. Highlights are elaborate wooden carvings – animals locked in struggle, stylised intertwined bodies and abstract motifs – on the north wall, all recycled from the original church, and the simple crucifixion carving, set above the chancel wall.

Ticket prices include an interesting 45-minute tour in English. Be aware that it's a 20-minute uphill walk from the ferry to the church: don't dawdle, as the guided tour waits for no one. It's also worth noting that, your visit over, you won't have time to catch the very next ferry, so relax a while at Urnes Gard cafe, just below the church.

If you want to stay or catch something to eat, try **Urnes Gard** (www.urnes.no; s/d Nkr400/700, cabins & apt 3-night minimum

Nkr2500, linen extra; ☻ 10.30am-5.30pm Jun-Sep). Once farm stables, the accommodation here is lovely, with a cabin, apartment or B&B options. All are decorated in a modern, rustic style: simple, earthy and warm. The cabin is particularly atmospheric. The cafe sells punnets of fruit fresh from the fields, home cakes and its own juices – strawberry, raspberry, gooseberry and blueberry.

❶ Getting There & Away

A car and passenger ferry (adult/child/car Nkr33/17/90, 20 minutes) shuttles hourly from 9am to 4.50pm between Solvorn and Urnes; most drivers prefer to leave their vehicles on the Solvorn bank.

Skjolden

POP 500

Skjolden is at the northern limit of Lustrafjord. In Fjordstova, its main building, you'll find most that matters tucked under one roof: the tourist office, a cafe, a swimming pool, a climbing wall and even a shooting gallery. The bit of industrial-looking junk on display outside is a turbine from the Norsk hydropower station.

East of Skjolden, the Rv55 at first runs beside the lovely turquoise glacial lake **Eidsvatnet**. **Mørkridsdalen**, the valley that runs north of the village, makes for some excellent hiking.

The village was home to Austrian philosopher Ludwig Wittgenstein between 1913 and 1914. The fjords obviously worked their magic – it was one of the most productive years of his life.

▨ Sleeping

Vassbakken Kro & Camping CAMPGROUND
(☏ 57 68 61 88; www.vassbakken.com; car/caravan site Nkr120/140 plus per person Nkr25, cabins with outdoor bathroom Nkr480, cabins with bathroom Nkr850; ☻ May–mid-Sep) Along the Rv55, 3km from Skjolden, this smallish campsite is set beneath a surging waterfall. There's a popular cafe-restaurant here and all rooms in its HI-affiliated **hostel** (☏ 57 68 61 88; www.hihostels.no/skjolden; dm 250, s/dNkr545/755, all incl breakfast) come with a bathroom.

❶ Information

Tourist office (☏ 99 23 15 00; www.sognefjord.no; ☻ 11am-7pm mid-Jun–mid-Aug; ☎) You can hire bicycles (Nkr75/120 per half/full day) and kayaks (Nkr75/140 per half/full day) from here, which can also supply you with a brochure (Nkr20) on signed walks in the area.

❶ Getting There & Away

Bus 153 connects Skjolden with Sogndal (Nkr130, 1½ hours) three to five times daily.

If you're heading north on Rv55, check your fuel gauge; Skjolden's petrol stations are the last for 77km.

JOSTEDALSBREEN

For years mighty Jostedalsbreen, mainland Europe's largest icecap, crept countercurrent, slowly advancing while most glaciers elsewhere in the world were retreating. Now Jostedalsbreen itself has succumbed and is also withdrawing.

It's still a powerful player, though, eroding an estimated 400,000 tonnes of rock each year. With an area of 487 sq km and in places 600m thick, Jostedalsbreen rules over the highlands of Sogn og Fjordane county. The main icecap and several outliers are protected as the Jostedalsbreen National Park.

The best hiking map for the region is Statens Kartverk's *Jostedalsbreen Turkart* at 1:100,000. The free *Jostedalsbreen Glacier Walks* brochure, available at tourist offices and many other venues, gives a comprehensive list of glacier walks, their levels and guiding companies.

Fjærland

POP 310

The village of Fjærland, also called Mundal, at the head of scenic Fjærlandsfjorden, pulls in as many as 300,000 visitors each year. Most come to experience its pair of particularly accessible glacial tongues, Supphellebreen and Bøyabreen. Others come to be bookworms. This tiny place, known as the **Book Town of Norway** (www.bokbyen.no), is a bibliophile's dream, with a dozen shops selling a wide range of used books, mostly in Norwegian, but with lots in English and other European languages.

The village virtually hibernates from October onwards, then leaps to life in early May, when the ferry runs again.

◎ Sights

Supphellebreen   GLACIER

You can drive to within 300m of the Supphellebreen glacier, then walk right up and touch the ice. Ice blocks from here were used as podiums at the 1994 Winter Olympics in Lillehammer.

Bøyabreen   GLACIER

At blue, creaking Bøyabreen, more spectacular than Supphellebreen to the east over the hill, you might happen upon glacial calving as a hunk tumbles into the melt-water lagoon beneath the glacier tongue.

★**Norwegian Glacier Museum**   MUSEUM

(Norsk Bremuseum; ☑57 69 32 88; www.bre. museum.no; adult/child Nkr120/60; ⊙9am-7pm Jun-Aug, 10am-4pm Apr-May, Sep & Oct) For the story on flowing ice and how it has sculpted the Norwegian landscape, visit this well executed museum, 3km inland from the Fjærland ferry jetty. You can learn how fjords are formed, see a 20-minute audio-visual presentation on Jostedalsbreen, touch 1000-year-old ice, wind your way through a tunnel that penetrates the mock ice and even see the tusk of a Siberian woolly mammoth who met an icy demise 30,000 years ago.

🏃 Activities

Kayaking

Fjærland Kayak & Glacier   KAYAKING

(☑92 85 46 74; www.kayakandglacier.com; Sandaneset; ⊙May-Aug 10am-4pm, or by appointment) At the small fjord-side shack, you can hire a kayak, canoe, motor or rowing boat or join one of its daily guided kayaking trips, ranging from 2½ hours (Nkr420) to a full day (Nkr950).

Walking

The tourist office's free sheet, *Escape the Asphalt,* lists 12 marked walking routes, varying from 30 minutes to three hours. For greater detail, supplement this with *Turkart Fjærland* (Nkr80) at 1:50,000, which comes complete with route descriptions and trails indicated; pull on your boots and you're away. Most walks follow routes the local shepherds would have used until quite recently to lead their flocks to higher summer pastures.

🛏 Sleeping & Eating

Bøyum Camping   CAMPGROUND €

(☑57 69 32 52; www.boyumcamping.no; campsites Nkr190, dm Nkr200, d without bathroom Nkr315-400, 4-/8-bed cabins Nkr890/1100; ⊙May-Sep) Beside the Glacier Museum and 3km from the Fjærland ferry landing, Bøyum Camping

LUSTER STOP

Luster, on Lusterfjord's northern bank between Solvorn and Skjolden, makes for a diverting pit stop, with both divine and more earthly sustenance on offer.

Lustrabui (www.lustrabui.no; Luster; ⊙7am-5pm Mon-Fri, to 3pm Sat) The two local ladies behind this traditional bakery trained with Bakeriet i Lom's Morten Schakenda, who is considered Norway's best baker. All natural sour dough is made by hand, with minimal ingredients, although it's the sweet goods that people drive miles for. There are tables to enjoy your *skillingsbollar* (sweet buns) and cinnamon swirls on the spot. They do espresso too.

Dale Kyrkje (Luster; ⊙10am-8pm) Spectacular wooden stave churches get all the attention around here, but this little gem of a medieval parish church, built of stone, shouldn't be overlooked. Constructed around 1250, it's mainly Gothic in style with a wooden tower and elaborately painted western entrance (the work of a typically near-anonymous ecclesiastical artist known simply as 'Nils the Painter') that were added in the early 1600s. The crucifix above the chancel arch and fine multicoloured pulpit are from the church's earliest days.

The naive 16th-century paintings in the chancel were revealed only in the 1950s, when the whitewash was removed.

has something for all pockets and sleeping preferences, not to mention a great view of the Bøyabreen glacier at the head of the valley.

★**Hotel Mundal** HOTEL €€€
(☑57 69 31 01; www.hotelmundal.no; s/d Nkr850/1200, water-view s/d Nkr1200/2100; ⊙May-Sep; P@) Run by the same family ever since it was built in 1891, this beautiful hotel retains much of its period interior: original local furniture with the odd bit of Viennese Thonet, paintings, rugs, leather armchairs made by local craftsmen and a 'modern' remodel of a 1920s parlour. Rooms are traditional, but pretty and light.

For Nkr500 extra, you can sleep the night in the tower's one suite, complete with wraparound views of fjord and glacier – as did US ex-vice president Walter Mondale, whose family came from Mundal, and the present Queen of Norway (not, as the charming receptionist explains, on the same occasion). The restaurant serves carefully prepared traditional four-course Norwegian dinners (Nkr360). Non-guests need to book by 6pm. On one wall of its Mikkel Kaffe, a mountaineering theme, there's a giant, evocative 1898 map of Sognefjorden.

Brævasshytta Cafeteria CAFE €
(⊙8am-8pm May-Sep) Do visit the Brævasshytta, built into the moraine of Bøyabreen glacier's latest major advance, even if it's only for a cup of coffee. With the glacier right

there and in your face, it's like you're in an Imax cinema, only it's real.

ℹ Information

Tourist office (☑57 69 32 33; www.fjaerland. org; ⊙10am-6pm Jun-Aug, to 4pm Sep-May) Fjærland's exceptionally friendly tourist office is within the Bok & Bilde bookshop on the main street, 300m from the ferry point. It displays a full list of accommodation options, together with prices, on the main door and rents bikes (half/full day Nkr40/160). Also ask about ferry and bus trips to Balestrand that take in the glacier and musuem.

ℹ Getting There & Away

A car ferry (Nkr275/360 one way/return, 1¼ hours) runs twice daily between Balestrand and Fjærland in July and August (in May, June and September there's a daily passenger ferry).

Buses bypass the village and stop on the Rv5 near the glacier museum. Three to six run daily to/from Sogndal (Nkr73, 30 minutes) and Stryn (Nkr200, two hours).

Jostedalen & Nigardsbreen

The Jostedalen valley pokes due north from Lustrafjord's Gaupne. This slim finger sits between two national parks: long established Jostedalsbreen on the west side and, to its east, Breheimen National Park. It's a spectacular drive as the road runs beside the

Jostedalsbreen National Park

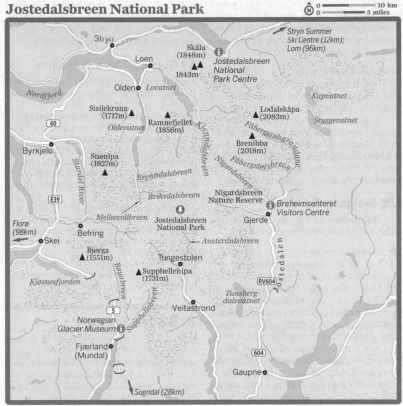

milky turquoise river, tumbling beneath the eastern flank of the Nigardsbreen glacier.

Of the Jostedalsbreen glacier tongues visible from below, Nigardsbreen is the most dramatic and easy to approach, and also offers the best glacier walks.

If you're an experienced walker and fancy communing alone with (but not on) the ice, continue further up the road past the braided glacial streams at Fåbergstølsgrandane to the dam that creates the big glacial lake, Styggevatnet. Along the way you'll find several scenic glacial tongues and valleys offering excellent wild hiking.

◉ Sights

Breheimsenteret Visitors Centre　MUSEUM
(☑57 68 32 50; www.jostedal.com; adult/child Nkr60/free; ⊙9am-6pm mid-Jun–Aug, 10am-5pm May–mid-Jun & Sep) Jostedal's visitor centre has a small museum of geological displays, a shop and a cafe with spectacular views

down the valley to the winding blue glacial tongue. Their website collects together all the tour and activities operators.

🏃 Activities

You can book directly or at the visitors centre for each of these outfits.

Ice Troll　GLACIER TOURS
(☑97 01 43 70; www.icetroll.com; 6hr excursions Nkr750, overnight Nkr1500) Andy – from New Zealand and with a decade of guiding experience on Nigardsbreen – and his team offer truly original glacier visits, where kayaks are used to get to isolated spots.

Most are suitable for first-timers as well as the more experienced, or there's a motorboat option for young families. All kayaking and glacier hiking equipment supplied, and they also do longer overnight and two-day sorties.

Riverpig   RAFTING

(www.riverpig.no; rafting Nkr800; ☉ Jun-Sep)
Riverpig offers white-water rafting on the
Jostedalen river (Nkr800) and, for the truly
hardy, riverboarding (Nkr1300).

Jostedalen Breførarlag   GLACIER TOURS

(☑ 57 68 31 11; www.bfl.no; tours from Nkr260-
760) Leads several guided glacier walks on
Nigardsbreen. The easiest is the family walk
to the glacier snout and briefly along its
tongue (around one hour on the ice, adult/
child Nkr260/130). Fees for the two-hour
(Nkr460), three-hour (Nkr525) and five-
hour (Nkr760) walks on the ice include the
brief boat trip across Nigardsvatnet lake.

🛏 Sleeping & Eating

Two fascinating and friendly sisters run the
valley's most tempting sleeping options.

★ Jostedal Camping   CAMPGROUND €

(☑ 57 68 39 14; www.jostedalcamping.no; car/
caravan sites Nkr180/190, cabins Nkr390-1300;
🛜) Astrid, after many years travelling and
working overseas, returned to her home village and with her partner runs this bucolic,
well kept campsite, right beside the Jostedal
river. Facilities are impeccable, with a beautiful new terrace, communal kitchen, lounge
and dining space with floor to ceiling windows overlooking the river's rapid course.

All cabins are neat, clean and cosy, but the
three-bedroom is particularly swish. Astrid
has researched a range of local walks and is
happy to provide itinerary suggestions. In
winter, this is an excellent starting point for
off-piste skiing.

Jostedal Hotel   HOTEL €€

(☑ 57 68 31 19; www.jostedalhotel.no; s Nkr820, d
Nkr1070, f Nkr1320; @) 🌐 Just 2.5km south
of the Breheimsenteret visitors centre, this
friendly hotel has been run by the same
family for three generations and is currently
under Laila's care. Newly renovated rooms
are very comfortable, light and have very
pretty views. There are also family rooms
(Nkr1360) with self-catering facilities that
can accommodate up to five guests.

> ### ⓘ MISSING THE BOAT
>
> Should you be unfortunate enough to
> miss the last ferry shuttle back over
> Nigardsvatnet, there's always a rowing
> boat left at the landing point for the use
> of the tardy.

Even if you're not staying, you can enjoy
the valley outlook from the cafe or come for
dinner. Meat, milk and vegetables for the
restaurant come from the family farm.

ⓘ Getting There & Around

If you're driving, leave the Rv55 Sognefjellet Rd
at Gaupne and head north up Jostedal along the
Rv604.

From mid-June to mid-September, **Josted-
alsbrebussen** (No 160; Glacier Bus; www.
jostedal.com/brebussen; adult/child
Nkr136/68) runs from Sogndal (with connections from Flåm, Balestrand and Lærdal) via
Solvorn to the foot of the Nigardsbreen glacier,
leaving at 8.45am and setting out on the return
journey at 4.50pm.

From the Breheimsenteret visitors centre, a
3.5km-long toll road (Nkr35 per vehicle), or a
pleasant walk with interpretive panels, leads to
the car park at Nigardsvatnet, the lagoon at the
glacial snout. From mid-June to August, a ferry
(Nkr48 return, 10am to 6pm) shuttles over the
lagoon. From the landing, it's a sturdy walk over
rocks to the glacier face itself.

Briksdalsbreen

From the small town of Olden at the eastern
end of Nordfjord, a scenic road leads 23km
along Oldedalen past Brenndalsbreen, and
from there on to the twin glacial tongues of
Melkevollbreen and Briksdalsbreen. More
easily accessible, Briksdalsbreen attracts
hordes of tour buses. It's a temperamental
glacier; in 1997 the tongue licked to its furthest point for around 70 years, then retreated by around 500m. In 2005, the reaches
where glacier walkers would clamber and
stride cracked and splintered. So for the
moment, there are no guided hikes on Briksdalsbreen, but capricious as she is, this may
change.

It's about a 5km-return walk to the Briksdal glacier face, either up the steepish path
or along the longer, gentler cart track. Alas,
the traditional pony-carts that plied the
route for over 100 years no longer transport visitors, but Oldedalen Skyss (☑ 57
87 68 05; www.oldedalen-skysslag.com) has 'troll
cars', vehicles like giant golfing carts (Nkr195
per person). From their turnaround point,
there's still a 15-minute hike on a rough path
to see the ice. To breathe up close in the glacier's face, take a guided trip in an inflatable
dinghy. Dinghies (adult/child Nkr250/125),
operated by Briksdal Adventure (p225), depart approximately hourly in summer. We

strongly recommend advance reservation for both troll cars and dinghies as places are often snapped up by tour groups.

🛏 Sleeping & Eating

Melkevoll Bretun CAMPGROUND €€
(📞57 87 38 64; www.melkevoll.no; campsites Nkr170, cabins Nkr700-800, with outdoor bathroom Nkr350; ⊗May-Sep) There's no bad positions here. Look south and the Melkevollbreen glacier is sticking its tongue out towards you, spin west and the long, slim Volefossen waterfall cascades, turn north and the long reach of Oldevatnet lake shimmers, while eastwards, the Briksdalsbreen glacier blocks the horizon.

While the larger cabins are very well equipped, the far more basic camping huts here are cute as buttons with folky '70s touches that look like they've been styled for a hipster magazine. There's a gorgeous green campsite with stacks of space between pitches, or see if you can nab a rock bed and reindeer skin in the 'stone-age cave' (Nkr125).

Briksdalsbre Fjellstove LODGE €€
(📞57 87 68 00; www.briksdalsbre.no; s/d Nkr890/1190, 4-bed cabins Nkr980) This cosy mountain lodge has six comfortable rooms, cabins and a cafe-restaurant serving delicacies such as trout (Nkr200) and reindeer (Nkr260).

ℹ Getting There & Away

Between June and August, buses leave Stryn for Briksdal (Nkr75, one hour) once or twice daily, calling by Loen and Olden.

Kjenndalsbreen & Bødalsbreen

The **Kjenndalsbreen** glacier is a delightful 21km run up Lodalen, a parallel valley to Oldendalen, from the Nordfjord village of Loen. The least visited of the four best-known glacial tongues, it vies with Nigardsbreen for the most beautiful approach as you track parallel to the intensely turquoise glacial lake of Lovatnet. After paying a road toll (Nkr40), there's a lovely little spot where you can snack and hire a bike, canoe or rowing boat, before undertaking the final 5km to the glacier viewing point. You may not find yourself alone but you'll be in far less company than at Briksdalsbreen, just over the mountain.

Bødalsbreen, up a short side valley to the east, provides a couple of good hiking possibilities.

🛏 Sleeping

Sande Camping CAMPGROUND €
(📞57 87 45 90; www.sande-camping.no; Loen; campsites Nkr225, 2-/4-bed cabins Nkr450/600, apt Nkr950) You could spend an active day or two in the lovely environs of Sande Camping, near the northern end of Lovatnet. There's also a free sauna and, for hire, rowing boats, canoes and bikes. Its small cafe-restaurant serves fresh fish from the lake or you can try your luck and dangle your own line (rods per day Nkr70).

The apartments are strangely urban for the location, though the cabins remain reliably retro.

🏃 Activities

Briksdal Adventure ADVENTURE TOURS
(📞info 57 87 68 00; www.briksdal-adventure.com; ⊗May-Sep) Briksdal Adventure, also known as Briksdal Breføring, is based at Briksdalsbre Fjellstove, the end of the blacktop road, the next glacial tongue north of Briksdalsbreen. There are daily five- to six-hour guided glacier hikes (Nkr600). Walks leave at 10am and your crampons crunch the ice for about half the total time.

NORDFJORD TO THE COAST

For most travellers the 100km-long Nordfjord is but a stepping stone between Sognefjorden and Geirangerfjorden. These two popular fjords are linked by a road that winds around the head of Nordfjord past the villages of Byrkjelo, Olden and Loen to the larger town of Stryn.

Stryn, Olden and Loen are not so much destinations in themselves, but each makes a good base for Briksdalsbreen and Kjenndalsbreen glaciers.

Olden

POP 498

Olden serves as a gateway to Briksdalsbreen. For walks in and around the valley, pick up the map *Olden og Oldendalen* (Nkr50; 1:50,000), which indicates and describes 15 signed trails.

🛏 Sleeping

There are several campsites along the route to Briksdalsbreen and many of them occupy stunningly pretty sites.

Olden Fjordhotel   HOTEL €€€
(☑ 57 87 04 00; www.olden-hotel.no; s Nkr930-1170, d Nkr1260-1670, all incl breakfast; s/d Nkr1200/1750; ⊙ May–mid-Sep) It may be big and bustling, but the welcome is warm and most of the rooms have fjord views and nearly all have balconies.

ℹ Information

Tourist office (☑ 57 87 31 26; www.nordfjord. no; ⊙ 10am-4pm mid-Jun–mid-Aug) Next door to the fjord-side supermarket; they have a free map with suggested walks.

Loen

POP 398

Loen, at the mouth of dramatic Lodalen valley, is, like nearby Olden, a gateway to the glaciers. From this tiny village, a road leads to the spectacular Bødalen and Kjenndalen glacial tongues.

Like Olden, it makes a good base for hikers. Arm yourself with *Walking in Loen & Lodalen* (Nkr50; 1:50,000), which describes 20 day walks. One great, though strenuous, hike leads to the Skålatårnet tower, atop the 1848m-high summit of Skåla. The route begins at a signed car park 2.5km east of Loen. Allow seven to eight hours – considerably more than the course record of under one hour 10 minutes for La Sportiva Skaala annual uphill race.

🛏 Sleeping & Eating

Lo-Vik Camping   CAMPGROUND €
(☑ 57 87 76 19; www.lo-vik.no; campsite Nkr220, 4-bed cabins with outdoor bathroom Nkr495, with bathroom Nkr695-1290; ⊙ May-Sep) This campsite is in the centre of town; find yourself a spot at the northern end beside the fjord, where there's a peaceful green area that's well away from traffic noise.

Hotel Alexandra   HOTEL €€€
(☑ 57 87 50 00; www.alexandra.no; s/d incl breakfast from Nkr1670/2540; P@🛜) Loen's undisputed centre of action is a full-service resort and dominates tourism in the valley. It offers two restaurants, two cafes, bars, a nightclub, swimming pools (both indoor and open), a spa and fitness centre, a tennis court and marina. Run as a family hotel

since 1884, it's managed nowadays by the fifth generation. Summer family deals are good.

Hotel Loenfjord   HOTEL €€€
(☑ 57 87 50 00; www.loenfjord.no; s/d incl breakfast from Nkr1210/1640; ⊙ Jun-Sep, Fri-Sun only Oct-May; P@🛜) The Loenfjord offers waterside accommodation that's a little less expensive than the Alexandra, to which it belongs. It's altogether gentler on the eye, less crowded and offers bicycle and rowing-boat hire.

Stryn

POP 2300

The small town of Stryn, de facto capital of upper Nordfjord, is a modern regional hub. It does sprawl, but retains some of its original wooden houses along the river and, in any case, its 'real' vibe is nicely energising if you've been in the wild for a while.

🛏 Sleeping

Stryn Camping   CAMPGROUND €
(☑ 57 87 11 36; www.stryn-camping.no; Bøavegen 6; campsites Nkr180/260, 4-bed cabins with outdoor bathroom Nkr350, 3-/6-bed cabins with bathroom Nkr750/1050; ⊙ year-round) The facilities are well maintained and the welcome friendly at neat Stryn Camping. It's at the eastern end of town, just two blocks uphill from the main street.

Stryn Vertshus B&B   B&B €€
(☑ 57 87 05 30; www.strynvertshus.no; s/d Nkr750/1250; 🛜) Stryn's favourite cafe has five simple rooms upstairs and Fred and Anne couldn't be more welcoming. The original house's hundred-year-old bones add charm, plus they all have en suites.

Visnes Hotel   HOTEL €€€
(☑ 57 87 10 87; www.visneshotel.no; Prestestegen 1; s Nkr900, d Nkr1495; ⊙ mid-May–Sep; P🛜) The Visnes, run by the same family for six generations, occupies two magnificent listed properties, each with its own character. Most rooms are in the larger building, constructed in 1850. It's furnished in period style but with a rustic restraint. The more expensive rooms have stunning fjord views and there are also a couple of large family rooms (Nkr1950).

To feel like royalty, request a room in the smaller 1890 'dragon style' building that was occupied by King Rama V of Siam during his 1908 tour, or the one where King Oscar of

Sweden and Norway rested his head in 1913. The restaurant, in the hotel's larger building, serves traditional dishes made from local produce.

🍴 Eating & Drinking

★ Stryn Vertshus   CAFE, RESTAURANT €€
(📞57 87 05 30; www.strynvertshus.no; Tonningsgata 19; mains Nkr180-230; ⊙9am-1am Mon-Thu, to 2am Fri & Sat, 11am-8pm Sun) Both inside and on its flower-bedecked terrace, this happy village hub serves the town's best coffee (they use Italian Illy beans, and there is a varied legion of European baristas), tasty lunchtime burgers and salads (both Nkr130) and tapas platters (Nkr210), steaks (Nkr180) and pasta (Nkr160).

Bryggja   FISH RESTAURANT €€
(📞90 16 81 34; www.bryggja.info; Perhusvegen 11; mains Nkr170-310; ⊙6pm-midnight mid-Jun–Aug, from 4pm Sun) Dine on the tiny outside terrace to make the most of the gorgeous riverside location. If it rains, the staff simply pulls over the sail-shaped cover. Fish is done simply, as are desserts like a good chocolate fondant. The nautical interior is an intimate space (there are only 30 seats; it's wise to book).

Base Camp   BAR
(1st fl Tonningsgata 31; ⊙10pm-2.30am Sat) On the main street, Stryn's most popular bar gets its disco on as the night progresses.

ℹ Getting There & Away

Express bus destinations include the following:
➡ Måløy (Nkr240, two hours, three daily)
➡ Ålesund (Nkr255, 3¾ hours, one to four daily) via Hellesylt (Nkr105, one hour), from where the ferry runs to Geiranger

➡ Bergen (Nkr538, 6¾ hours, three daily) via Loen (Nkr52, 10 minutes) and Olden (Nkr59, 15 minutes)

Florø
POP 8450

Florø, Norway's westernmost town, is a pleasant if sleepy settlement whose coat of arms features, appropriately, three herrings rampant.

Nowadays, wealth comes from the oil industry. The large Fjord Base, just northeast of town, serves the giant Snorreankeret offshore oil field. Florø is also enriched by fish farming and shipbuilding – the herring, the town's original raison d'être, plays a somewhat diminished role.

For a scenic overview, it's an easy 10-minute climb up the Storåsen hill from the Florø Ungdomsskule on Havrenesveien.

A group of several offshore islands is easily accessible by local ferry and makes for an atmospheric day trip to a number of significant historical sites from which to take in their incredible natural beauty.

◉ Sights

On and around Strandgata, Florø's main street, the most significant 19th-century timbered houses are well signed and documented in both Norwegian and English.

Sogn og Fjordane Kystmuseet   MUSEUM
(📞57 74 22 33; kyst.museum.no; Brendøyvegen; adult/child Nkr60/30; ⊙11am-6pm Mon-Fri, noon-4pm Sat & Sun Jun-Aug, 10am-3pm Mon-Fri, noon-3pm Sat & Sun Sep-May) The first museum building is dedicated to fishing, including a model 1900 fishing family's home and exhibits on

---

THE LOVATNET DISASTERS

Ascending Lodalen, you'll see what appear to be islands that nearly split the lake into two. These are in fact giant rocks that were dislodged from Ramnefjell and crashed down into the lake in three separate calamities. In 1905, when the resulting giant wave swept away 63 people – only nine of whom were ever found – *Lodalen,* the lake steamer, was deposited 400m inland. In 1936, an estimated 1 million cubic metres of rock crashed down, its wave killing 72 and lifting the steamer even higher. The third, in 1950, left a bigger scar on the mountain, but fortunately claimed no lives.

A path signed Pilgrimssti (Pilgrim's Path; indicated by blue markers), descends steeply through birchwood to a simple wooden cross that marks the site of a memorial to the victims of the 1905 disaster – itself swept away in the 1936 cataclysm. It can be found 100m before the toll road signs to Kjenndalsbreen. On the way, besides a series of edifying biblical tracts, you can spot the rusting remains of Lodalen, the lake steamer beached this far inland after being carried on the waves of disasters one and two. Allow 35 to 45 minutes for this out-and-back walk.

THE WORLD'S LONGEST HERRING TABLE

On the third Friday in June, a herring table 400m long is erected in the heart of Florø. Just imagine a standard 400m running track, straightened out and laden with plates of herring, potatoes, bread and drinks, all free of charge, and you've got the scene. Then, once the table's cleared away, the festivities continue all weekend.

the foundation of the island as a small herring trading post barely 150 years ago. A second houses a collection of typical coastal boats. The **Snorreankeret** display – in a building that has the shape of the original oil platform that first pumped the country's oil – illustrates the exploration and exploitation of the North Sea oil and gas fields.

 Activities

Boating
Florø Rorbu (☎57 74 81 00; www.florbu.com; Krokane Kai) hires motor boats (Nkr200 to Nkr400 per day) and sea kayaks (Nkr200 per day), while **Krokane Camping** (☎57 75 22 50; www.krocamp.no) rents out rowing boats (Nkr100 per day) and motor boats (from Nkr200/300 per three hours/day).

Hiking & Cycling
The tourist office sells a useful booklet, *Cycling in Flora* (Nkr10), and has map sheets on local hikes.

☞ Tours
Between June and August, the tourist office runs a number of tempting guided tours. Pick up its leaflet of summer venues.

🛏 Sleeping
Florø Rorbu   APARTMENTS €
(☎91 39 28 88; www.florbu.com; Krokane Kai; apt Nkr650-1000) These excellent, family-owned, fully furnished flats are right beside a tiny inlet and have their own moorings (you can hire a boat or kayak and putter around the fjord).

Krokane Camping   CAMPGROUND €
(☎57 75 22 50; www.krocamp.no; campsites Nkr150, 2-/4-bed cabins Nkr450/550, 5-/6-bed cabins Nkr675/975, all with bathroom; ☎) Krokane Camping occupies a wooded site on a peninsula 2.5km east of town. The shoreside

meadow, though a trek to the toilets, is a tent camper's delight.

Quality Hotel Florø   HOTEL €€
(☎57 75 75 75; www.nordicchoicehotels.no; Hamnegata 11; s/d from Nkr1100/1400; P@☎) On the quayside, right beside the marina and constructed in the style of a dockside warehouse (the present banqueting area is a former fish store), this is Florø's best accommodation. Rooms with sea views cost no extra and a couple have 'boat beds', made of recycled rowing boats. Bryggekanten, its restaurant, sources most of its food locally and warrants a visit in its own right.

✖ Eating & Drinking
Bistro To Kokker   CAFE €
(☎57 75 22 33; Strandgata 33; dishes Nkr106-130; ⊙9am-10pm) Come here for well-priced fare and large portions rather than atmosphere. There's squid, salmon, monkfish and other seafood served with cream sauce and mash, as well as fish and chips, burgers, good salads and pizzas. The special dish of the day goes for a song (Nkr97).

Hjørnevikbua   PUB, RESTAURANT €€
(☎57 74 01 22; www.tokokker.as; Strandgata 23; lunch dishes Nkr65-169, dinner mains Nkr255-285) The restaurant on the 2nd floor of Hjørnevikbua, with its ship-like interior, serves lunch that includes mean fish soups, then some rather ambitious evening meals, mostly featuring halibut, cod or salmon. You can also eat outdoors on its moored barge.

🍷 Drinking & Entertainment
Shamrock   PUB
(Strandgata 58) One of a couple of pubs where the young folk of Florø head to down a beer, nibble on a snack or let their hair down at the Saturday-night disco. It also shows all major football matches.

ℹ Information
Tourist office (☎57 74 30 00; www.fjordkysten.no; Strandgata 30; ⊙9am-6pm Mon-Fri, 10am-4pm Sat, 11am-3pm Sun Jun-Aug)

ℹ Getting There & Away
Widerøe flies here up to four times daily from Oslo and Bergen and four times a week from Stavanger.

Florø is the first stop on the Hurtigruten coastal ferry as it heads north from Bergen.

GAMLE STRYNEFJELLSVEGEN: A DRIVING TOUR FROM STRYN

This spectacular 130km route takes a comfortable four hours. Head eastwards from Stryn along the **Rv15** as it runs alongside the river that descends from Lake Strynevatnet, then follows the lake shore itself. It's an inspirational ride with mountain views as impressive as anywhere in the country.

After 20km, stop to visit the **Jostedalsbreen National Park Centre** (Jostedalsbreen Nasjonalparksenter; www.jostedalsbre.no; adult/child Nkr80/40; ☺10am-4pm or 6pm May–mid-Sep) in the village of **Oppstryn**. There's a worthwhile and informative 10-minute film about the glacier plus exhibits illustrating avalanches and rock falls and a variety of stuffed wildlife. Outside, enjoy its unique garden with more than 300 species of endemic vegetation, each labelled in Norwegian, English and French. A cluster of picnic tables offers a spectacular vista over the lake.

At an interpretive panel and sign 17km beyond the National Park Centre, turn right to take the **Rv258**. It took a team of local and immigrant Swedish navvies more than 10 years to lay the **Gamle Strynefjellsvegen** (old Stryn mountain road) over the mountain. The road, considered a masterpiece of civil engineering at the time, opened to traffic in 1894. For more than 80 years, it was the principal east-to-west route in this part of the country. Until well into the 1950s, a team of some 200 workers, armed only with spades, would keep it clear in winter, digging through several miles of metres-high snow.

The climb to the high plateau is spectacular, enhanced by thin threads of water tumbling from the heights and a trio of roaring roadside torrents carrying glacial melt. There are several stopping points as you ascend this narrow strip. Savour, in particular, the viewing platform above Videfossen, where the water churns beneath you.

Some 9km along the Gamle Strynefjellsvegen, you reach **Stryn Summer Ski Centre** (Stryn Sommerskisenter; www.stryn.no/sommerski), a bleak place outside the short season. But from late May until some time in July, it offers Norway's most extensive summer skiing; most of those photos of bikini-clad skiers you see around were snapped right here.

The steep ascent behind you, continue along a good-quality unsurfaced single-track road that runs above a necklace of milky turquoise tarns overlooked by bare, boulder-strewn rock. Here on this upland plateau, the sparse vegetation hugs the ground close.

After crossing the watershed 10km beyond the ski centre, there begins a much more gentle descent to rejoin the Rv15. Turn left for a fast, smooth, two-lane run beside **Lake Breidalsvatn** before diving into the first of three long tunnels that will bring you back to the National Park Centre and onward, retracing your steps back to Stryn.

After the completion of these three linked tunnels in 1978, the old road was overshadowed by its younger alternative: 12 speedy kilometres along a wide road against 27km of winding single track – there was no comparison. But the Gamle Strynefjellsvegen always drew travellers with time on their hands and lovers of wild scenery. Now, freshly designated a National Tourist Route, it again enjoys a share of a new, if softer, limelight.

The Gamle Strynefjellsvegen is normally free of snow from June to October. Electronic signs along the Rv15 indicate if the 'Strynfjellet' (its official name) is indeed open.

Express boats call in twice daily on the run between Bergen (Nkr630, 3½ hours) and Måløy (Nkr255, one hour).

If you're driving, the most scenic way north to Måløy by road is via Bremanger island.

Offshore Islands Around Florø

Local ferries leaving from Florø's **Fugleskjærskaia Quay** connect the mainland to several small islands, each making for a stimulating off-the-beaten-track day trip. The tourist office can reserve ferries and also advise on island accommodation.

Askrova has a prehistoric Troll Cave, whose deepest depths have never been explored. On the island of **Batalden**, check out the gallery and small museum at Batalden Havbu. You can overnight in their sensitively restored cottage B&B.

Kinn has a beautifully restored 12th-century church, believed to have been built by British Celts sheltering from religious

WORTH A TRIP

KALVÅG

If you're travelling between Florø and Måløy via Bremanger island, do make the 5km detour from the ferry landing point at Smørhamn to the small, sensitively preserved fishing village of Kalvåg. Nowadays it's picture-postcard pretty and there's just one giant fish-processing factory on its outskirts that operates when the herring and mackerel shoals come near. But at its peak Kalvåg had over 50 herring salt houses that employed a seasonal workforce of around 10,000. You can still visit a couple of them; ask at the quayside **tourist office** (☑ 48 14 04 88; www.fordkysten.no; ☺ 10am-6pm Mon-Fri, 10am-4pm Sat, noon-4pm Sun Jul–mid-Aug, 10am-4pm Mon-Fri rest of year). To while away the time between ferries, scoff a plate of shrimps, split some crab claws or down a beer, brewed specially for the restaurant, on the dockside terrace of **Knutholmen** (☑ 57 79 69 00; www.knutholmen.no; mains Nkr298-319, seafood platters Nkr595; ☺ 8am-midnight) with the fishing boats right before you.

persecution. On the second or third weekend in June, it's the site of the Kinnespelet pageant, which celebrates the history of the church on the island. Climbers and hikers will savour the dramatic landscapes, particularly the Kinnaklova cleft.

On **Svanøy**, enjoy the hiking and pass by the small deer centre.

At 233m, the highest point on Tansøy offers great panoramic views over the surrounding archipelago.

Måløy

POP 3500

The little fishing town of Måløy, at the mouth of Nordfjord, lies on Vågsøy island. Nestling beneath a pair of rounded hills, for all the world like a pair of giant breasts, it's linked to the mainland by the graceful S-curve Måløybrua bridge. Commercial boats ply up and down and it's a refreshingly real, working town.

Vågsøy island and neighbouring Selje are laced with sea-view hiking routes (pick up the 1:50,000 walking map *Outdoor Pursuits: Selje & Vågsøy Communes*).

A short drive for about 10km west of town brings you to the bizarre rock **Kannesteinen**, rising from the sea like the tail of a whale.

🛏 Sleeping

Steinvik Camping CAMPGROUND €
(☑ 57 85 10 70; www.steinvik-camping.no; campsites Nkr200, cabins Nkr400-900, apt Nkr500-750; ☺ year round) The nearest campsite to Måløy has spectacular views over the busy sea lane and a particularly cosy common room with sofas and armchairs. To get there, cross the bridge to the east bank, turn right after 2km beside a school and follow the track downhill for 1.2km. No credit cards.

Torget Hotell HOTEL €€
(☑ 95 33 31 33; www.torgethotell.no; Gate 1 49; s/d Nkr1090/1190; P ⬆) This modern, and unexpectedly stylish, hotel is friendly and informal. It occupies what was once an old caning factory: half of its 17 rooms have balconies and look directly across the waterfront and far mountains. There's a great open loft space on the top floor where you can drink tea and watch boats dock from floor to ceiling mansard windows.

✗ Eating

You'll find a cluster of three good places to eat and drink very near the express boat jetty.

Snorre Sjømat CAFE, MARKET €
(Havfruen; ☑ 57 85 23 36; ☺ 10am-4.30pm Mon-Fri, 10am-2pm Sat) This dockside place is both a wet fish shop ('Born to fish, forced to work' says the plaque on the wall) and small cafe, serving fish cakes with mash (Nkr90), salmon and shrimp sandwiches (Nkr45), various stockfish dishes and, of course, cod and chips (Nkr130).

Din & Min CAFE €
(☑ 57 85 18 75; Gate 1 44) 'Yours and Mine' is a busy little cafe and late night drinking hole. And small's the word; sip a coffee or something stronger or nibble a snack within the confines of its agreeably woody interior. In warmer weather climb to the upstairs terrace, where you'll have the harbour spread before you.

Kraftstasjonen FISH €€
(☑ 57 85 12 60; Gate 1; dinner mains Nkr250-350; ☺ 11am-10pm Mon-Thu, 11am-1am Fri & Sat) Rita and Arne Andal offer the freshest of fish. Come for cod, halibut and monkfish

prepared a variety of ways, plus one of the international style starters. Rita's fish soup (Nkr140) is tasty too. On weekends, live acts sometimes take up on the little elevated stage after dinner.

❶ Information

Tourist office (☑ 57 84 50 77; Gate 1; ⊙ 9am-5pm Mon-Fri, 10am-4pm Sat & Sun Jul, 10am-4pm Mon-Sat Jun & Aug)

❶ Getting There & Away

The express boat to and from Bergen (Nkr790, 4½ hours) to Selje (Nkr83, 25 minutes) puts in at Måløy. The Hurtigruten coastal ferry also calls in.

Nettbus express runs three times daily to/from Oslo (Nkr620, 11 hours) via Stryn (Nkr180, two hours).

Selje & Selja Island

POP 700

Few visitors make it to **Selje** and therein lies the charm of this village on the western edge of Norway, with its strand of pristine, white beach. **Vestkapp**, 32km by road from Selje, isn't Norway's westernmost point despite the name, but it still provides superb sea views. You can surf the point break at **Ervik** or the more reliable beach one at **Hoddevik**.

◉ Sights

Selja monastery   HISTORIC SITE
The haunting ruins of Selja monastery and the church of St Sunniva on Selja Island date from the 11th and 12th centuries respectively: this has been a place of pilgrimage for over 1000 years. A 40m-high tower is still intact and can be climbed for a splendid panorama. From mid-June to mid-August, the tourist office arranges two-hour guided tours, including boat transport (adult/child Nkr200/100), departing at 10am and 1.15pm.

⌂ Sleeping

Doktorgarden   B&B €€
(☑ 90 92 97 71; www.doktorgarden-selje.no; d with shared bathroom Nkr1090; ⊙ Easter-Oct) Up the hill from the port, you can wake here to sea views and the aroma of freshly baked cakes. Four big, carefully decorated rooms occupy the second floor of this lovely old house up the hill from the harbour. They share a large, spotless bathroom and guest kitchen. Downstairs, Anna, Torkjell and Karin also have a basement gallery, excellent little bookshop

and bright **cafe** (⊙ 9am-6pm Jun-Aug, Sat & Sun 10am-3pm rest of year).

Selje Hotel   HOTEL, SPA €€€
(☑ 57 85 88 80; www.selje hotel.no; s/d Nkr975/1700) The Selje Hotel is right beside the beach, a '60s wood and shaped-stone pile. Its rooms are expensive in season, but super comfortable and there's a spa. There's a nice retro charm to it all.

❶ Information

Tourist office (☑ 57 85 66 06; www.nordfjord. no; ⊙ 9am-6pm mid-Jun–mid-Aug, shorter hours rest of year) Selje's tourist office, at the harbour, keeps a list of cabins and apartments in the area and can give you directions to local artisans and food producers, as well as suggesting walking trails and beaches. They are also incredibly knowledgable about the region's rich cultural heritage, from its pilgrim routes to its WWII tunnels and fortifications.

❶ Getting There & Away

From Måløy, you have two stunningly attractive ways of reaching Selje – the splendid fjord-side drive along the Rv618, or aboard the twice-daily Nordfjord express boat (Nkr83, 25 minutes).

Local buses run between Måløy and Selje (Nkr106, one hour) six times daily on weekdays and once on Sunday.

THE NORTHERN FJORDS

More islet-strewn coastline and ever more deeply incised fjords await as you push further northwards into the region of Møre og Romsdal.

Stunning Geirangerfjord, a Unesco World Heritage Site, a must on most tours and a favourite anchorage for cruise ships, staggers beneath its summer influx.

Stray from this tour mecca though and you'll find the waterways and roads less crowded and the scenery just as arresting.

The architecturally unique port of Ålesund deserves at least a wander, and the drive over the Trollstigen pass is one of the world's most spectacular.

Åndalsnes

POP 2244

There are two equally dramatic ways to approach Åndalsnes: by road through the Trollstigen pass or along Romsdalen as you ride the spectacularly scenic Raumabanen.

THE ROLLING ROAD TO KRÅKENES LIGHTHOUSE

This 42km round trip can be comfortably driven in a couple of hours, including stops. Take the Rv617 from Måløy, then follow signs for Kråkenes Fyr (Kråkenes Lighthouse). On the way there or back, it's worth the short, signed detour to visit **Refviksanden**, a 1.4km reach of white sand, voted Norway's finest beach in a 2010 online poll.

The road rolls over treeless, windswept grassland, runs past a long line of twirling windmills (step outside your car and you'll understand why they're sited right here) and offers staggering views of steep cliffs.

Kråkenes Lighthouse (krakenesfyr.com; ste Nkr3950, d Nkr3150, with shared bathroom Nkr2100, minimum 3 nights), at the very end of the road, perches precariously on a rock shoulder. Sunny or stormy, it's a romantic spot with stunning views of the cliffs and pounding ocean. It's possible to stay in its B&B or bridal suite.

The rail route down from Dombås ploughs through a deeply cut glacial valley flanked by sheer walls and plummeting waterfalls. Badly bombed during WWII, the modern town, nestled beside Romsdalfjord might be nondescript, but the locals are delightful and the surrounding landscapes are absolutely magnificent.

◉ Sights

Trollveggen   CLIFF
From Dombås, the E136 and rail line drop in parallel northwest down to Romsdalen (you might have a sense of déjà vu if you've seen *Harry Potter and the Half-Blood Prince*, in which the valley features). Near Åndalsnes, dramatic Trollveggen (Troll Wall), first conquered in 1958 by a joint Norwegian and English team, rears skywards. The highest vertical mountain wall in Europe, its ragged and often cloud-shrouded summit, 1800m from the valley floor, is considered the ultimate challenge among mountaineers.

Trollstigen   SCENIC DRIVE
(www.trollstigen.net; ⊘ Jun-Sep) South of Åndalsnes, the Troll's Ladder is a thriller of a climb or descent. Recently declared a National Tourist Route, it was completed in 1936 after eight years of labour. To add an extra daredevil element to its 11 hairpin bends and a 1:12 gradient, much of it is effectively single lane. Several dramatic waterfalls, including the thundering 180m-high **Stigfossen**, slice down its flanks.

At the top, a visitors centre has been built from concrete, rusted steel and glass, to both withstand the extreme terrain and to mimic its many textures. Leading from here are dramatic viewing platforms that jut out here and there over the abyss and offer panoramas of the snaking road and the lush

valley below, as well as a perpetual waterfall soundtrack. Around you as you descend are the open reaches of Reinheimen National Park, established in 2006 and Norway's third largest, where wild reindeer still crop the mosses and soft grass.

The pass is usually cleared and open from late May to mid-October; early in the season it's an impressive trip through a popular cross-country ski field, between high walls of snow.

Raumabanen   SCENIC RAILWAY
Trains run daily year-round along this spectacular route, meeting the main line, after 114km, at Dombås. There's also a tourist train (adult/child return Nkr460/230, one child per adult travels free) with on-board commentary that runs twice daily from June to August from Åndalsnes' lakeside station up to Bjorli, at 600m. Book at the station or tourist office.

🏃 Activities

Hiking

The pamphlet *Geiranger Trollstigen* (Nkr30) describes seven signed hiking trails in the Trollstigen area. You'll need to supplement this with the map *Romsdals-Fjella* at 1:80,000. The tourist office carries both. The tourist office can arrange mountain walks of four to six hours with a qualified guide.

★ Aksla/Nesaksla   HIKING
(www.romsdal.com) An excellent half-day day hike begins right in town, along Romsdalsvegen, 50m north of the roundabout before the Esso petrol station. It takes around an hour to 90 minutes to reach the summit of Nesaksla (715m), the prominent peak that rises above Åndalsnes. The ascent rewards with the most astonishing views of

the Romsdal Alps, the Rauma river and the Romsdal fjord.

Utilising a series of steel walkways, the initial stage of the walk is easy enough to be done in ballet flats. After Nebba, the first viewing point, the marked path onward to the summit of Nesaksla (715m), gets a little more tricky but includes handrails in the steeper section and did not seem to phase your average Norwegian toddler. The most spectacular section is Romsdalstrappa, a series of natural stone stairs (built by a team of Nepalese sherpas) leading to a 6.5m-long metal grid that juts into thin air (calling it a 'viewing platform' just doesn't seem to do it justice).

This trail can also be the start for walking Romsdalseggen, and you can walk from both directions, from Åndalsnes to Vengedalen or from Vengedalen and back to Åndalsnes. From July to September, a bus (Nkr125, including map and trail information) leaves Åndalsnes for Vengedalen every mornning at 9.30am, making for an easy way to do the walk in reverse. You can buy tickets from the tourist office, hotels and campsites. Wear at least sturdy trainers and bring plenty of water.

Other spin-off hikes from here include the straightforward ascent of the summit of Høgnosa (991m) and a trek on to Åkesfjellet (1215m). Alternatively, traverse along the marked route 5km eastward and descend to Isfjorden village, at the head of Isfjord.

Kløvstien   HIKING
Beginning in Isterdalen, on the RV63, the Kløvstien path's initial valley section is good for a gentle, forrested walk, or, for something more challenging, continue up to the steeper section along Stigfossen.

Climbing
The best local climbs are the less extreme sections of the 1500m-high rock route on Trollveggen and the 1550m-high Romsdalshorn, but there are a wealth of others. Serious climbers should buy *Klatring i Romsdal* (Nkr300), which includes rock-and ice-climbing information in both Norwegian and English.

Skiing
Romsdalen is considered among the best skiing areas in the country, with the rewards of untouched powder and continuous views of fjords and wild peaks awaiting those who are up to its ski up/ski down challenges.

Kirketaket (1439m) is one of the Romsdalen 'classics' and takes three to five hours to ascend but delivers over 1000 vertical

metres of steep downhill slopes, from where you can ski right down to the fjord. Spring and early summer skiing is possible once the Trollstigen road opens as well.

See www.romsdal.com and www.kirketaket.com for more information. For ski guiding see www.skiromsdal.no or contact **Hotel Aak**, who can also organise ski guides.

Fishing

John Kofoed Fishing Trips   FISHING
(📱97 17 94 42; www.rauma-jakt-fiskesafari.no; adult/child 3-hrs Nkr350/175, plus Nkr 75 per rod) John Kofoed runs three-hour fishing tours on Romsdalsfjorden three times daily in summer. Reserve directly or through the tourist office. There are 68 different fish in the fjord, with the most common catches being coalfish, pollack, cod, haddock, turbot, halibut, whiting, herring and mackerel.

★★ Festivals & Events

Norsk Fjellfestival   OUTDOOR ACTIVITIES
(Norway Mountain Festival; www.norsk-fjellfestival.no) A week-long get together for lovers of the great outdoors with plenty of folk events thrown in. Early July.

Rauma Rock   MUSIC
(www.raumarock.com) Central Norway's largest outdoor rock gathering. Two days in early August.

World Base Race   OUTDOOR ACTIVITIES
(www.worldbaserace.com) 'Organised' base jumping was invented in Åndalsnes; this contest is held in mid-August.

🛏 Sleeping

Åndalsnes Vandrerhjem Setnes   HOSTEL €
(📱71 22 13 82; www.aandalsnesvandrerhjem.no; dm/s/d/f Nkr290/500/710/935; ⊗Mar-Nov; P🅿🛜) This welcoming, HI-affiliated, sod-roofed hostel is 1.5km from Åndalsnes train station on the E136, direction Ålesund. It's a nice garden complex of separate buildings with a great lounge area. A big breakfast buffet is included in summer. The Ålesund bus that meets the train passes right by as does the morning bus to Geiranger via Trollstigen.

Trollstigen Resort   CAMPGROUND €
(📱71 22 68 99; www.trollstigenresort.com; car/caravan sites Nkr190/200, 4-/5-bed cabins from Nkr500/1150; 🛜) Recognisable by the strapping wooden troll at its entrance, this well-kept campsite is 2km along the Rv63 highway

DON'T MISS

SVELE AHOY

Norway is well known for its devotion to the waffle, but the western fjords and coast have a sweet afternoon treat that's all its own. *Svele*, a fat, folded pancake, can be found at cafes and hotels throughout the region, but, traditionally, it's the snack of choice for fjord crossings. Ferries have served *svele* in their cafeterias since the early 1970s and have their own closely guarded recipes. So what, apart from the experience of eating one in the presence of stunning fjord scenery, makes a *svele* unique? A particularly satisfying cake-like texture and flavour come from the addition of an unusual rising agent, salt of hartshorn, along with a measure of tart buttermilk. Plus it's in the toppings. Forget jam, *svele* come with either a sublimely simple smear of butter and sprinkle of sugar between the folds, or stuffed with a slice of *brunost*, the characteristic caramelised brown cheese of the region.

from Åndalsnes, direction Geiranger. The welcome's warm and the location, overlooking the River Rauma and embraced by mountains, is scenic and peaceful. All but one of the cabins have bathrooms and the two-bedders are smartly renovated. Open year-round, it's popular with skiers in winter.

Åndalsnes Camping   CAMPGROUND €
(☑ 71 22 16 29; www.andalsnes-camping.com; car/caravan sites Nkr235, 4-bed cabins with outdoor bathroom Nkr490, 7-bed cabins with bathroom Nkr950; ☎) Less than 2km from Åndalsnes, this friendly campsite enjoys a dramatic setting beside the River Rauma and nestled below the peaks. There's a good cafe and a cosy TV/recreation room, and you can order fresh bread to be picked up each morning. Hire canoes (Nkr50/200 per hour/day) and bikes (Nkr50/200 per hour/day) from reception.

★Hotel Aak   HOTEL €€
(☑ 71 22 71 71; www.hotelaak.no; s/d Nkr995/1400; ☺mid-Jun–Aug, restaurant 4-10pm; P☎) ✐ One of the oldest tourist hotels in Norway is now in the hands of a charming young family. Kristine and Odd Erik Rønning – locals, dedicated travellers, super-experienced climbers, hikers and skiers – have imbued all with a light touch that beautifully en-

capsulates the region's rustic appeal, but is super stylish and switched on to a new generation of traveller.

Modern rooms are simple and spacious, while historic rooms are atmospheric and bold – all have views of mountains and fields, each are equally cosy retreats after an active day. Guests and nonguests can prebook for dinner, from simple suppers (Nkr179) to three-course feasts (Nkr595) in the stunning pine-clad dining room; it's the very picture of *koselig* – you'll be greeted by candles and vases brimming with wildflowers. Dishes are hearty and flavourful, made with great local produce and nicely finessed. Breakfasts, too, show the same attention to detail.

The hotel lies beside the E136, in a quiet corner of the Romsdalen Valley, 4km from town.

Grand Hotel Bellevue   HOTEL €€€
(☑ 71 22 75 00; www.grandhotel.no; Åndalgata 5; s/d Nkr1195/1550, dinner mains Nkr275-325; ☺restaurant dinner only Mon-Sat; P@) This large hotel, up on its own hill, is the town's true centre. After a recent, smart renovation, its busy lobby is now rather glamorous. Most of its 86 rooms have fine views and lots of light. The restaurant is the town's most formal and decorated with a fascinating collection of local paintings, though the food is less remarkable.

From the hotel, you can walk straight into the interconnecting town library, cinema and auditorium, or to the public pool, 110m away.

✖ Eating & Drinking

★Sødahl-Huset   CAFE €
(Romsdalsvegen 8; ☺10am-3pm Mon-Thu, to 11pm Fri & Sat, 2-7pm Sun mid-Jun–mid-Aug, shorter hours rest of year) ✐ The blackboard declares 'local and homemade burgers, coffee, cake, ice cream – served by lovely ladies'. And, yes, it's all true. Owners Mari, Rannveig and Sissel are indeed lovely and the food here is proudly local, from the berry sorbets to the pour-over coffee to the *kraftkar* (local blue cheese) burger.

Even if you're not in the need of sustenence, this social hub also sells the work of local artisans (including the multitalented ladies themselves) and there's an enthralling selection of sheep skins, leather, knits, vintage clothes, jewellery and ceramics to poke around. At night there are beer tastings and live performances.

Kaikanten CAFE, RESTAURANT €€
(mains Nkr150-225; ⊘ 10am-9pm Mon-Thu, to 11pm Fri & Sat, noon-9pm Sun mid-May–Aug) Sit back and relax at the jetty's edge and enjoy a drink and one pretty panorama in this welcoming place. The menu takes in those old Norwegian favourites: *svele* (pancakes), pizza and burgers.

Kjellar'n PUB
(⊘ from 10pm Sat) The Grand Hotel Bellevue's cellar bar, backlit in startlingly citified pink and lime green, is where the town meets on Saturday nights to drink, chat and dance until late.

ℹ Information

Tourist office (✆ 71 22 16 22; www.visitandalsnes.com; ⊘ 9am-8pm Jun-Aug, rest of year 9am-3pm Mon-Fri) At Åndalsnes train station. They rent bikes (hour/day Nkr60/185).

ℹ Getting There & Away

BUS

Buses along the spectacular National Tourist Route to Geiranger (Nkr265, three hours), via Trollstigen, the Linge–Eidsdal ferry and the steep Ørnevegen (Eagle's Way), run twice daily between mid-June and mid-August.

There are also services to Molde (Nkr145, 1½ hours, up to eight daily) and Ålesund (Nkr295, 2¼ hours, four times daily).

TRAIN

Trains to/from Dombås (Nkr230, 1½ hours) run twice daily in synchronisation with Oslo–Trondheim trains. Trains connect in Åndalsnes twice daily with the express bus service to Ålesund via Molde.

Valldal & Around

Valldal is a place that travellers tend to pass through, on the way to or from the famous Trollstigen pass or after the blissful ferry journey from Geiranger. Perched in a nick of Norddalsfjord, its agricultural surrounds lay claim to being Europe's northernmost orchards. Here apples, pears and even cherries thrive and you'll find strawberries in profusion, commemorated in an annual **Strawberry Festival**, usually on the last weekend in July.

☆ Activities

Valldal Naturopplevingar WATER SPORTS
(www.valldal.no) From Valldal you can experience a four-hour white-water rush (Nkr790)

down the Valldøla River or gentler stand-up paddleboarding (Nkr590). This outfit's headquarters is 200m from the tourist office. It also offers kayak hire and a variety of other outdoor activities such as wilderness camping and, in winter, moonlight ski trips.

⌂ Sleeping & Eating

Fjellro Turisthotell HOTEL €€
(✆ 70 25 75 13; www.fjellro.no; Syltegata; s/d incl breakfast Nkr785/1180; ⊘ May-Sep, cafe-restaurant 7-10pm) At cheerful 'Mountain Peace', just near Valldal's church, the welcome is warm and rooms nicely cared for. There's a cafe-restaurant here, too, that specialises in fish, and a pub on the ground floor, open at weekends. At the rear is a tranquil garden with a small playground for children.

★ **Juvet Landscape Hotel** BOUTIQUE HOTEL €€€
(www.juvet.com; Alstad; per person Nkr1450; ⊘ Mar-Sep; ▩) ✎ One of Norway's most exclusive hotels, this remote hideaway combines brave contemporary architecture with a setting so compelling it seems mythological. Forget traditional notions of luxury, instead you have the reinvented cabin, with sublimely simple interiors of dark wood. These allow the landscape outside to glow summer green or winter white through cinematic floor to ceiling windows, eclipsing all else.

Breakfasts and evening meals (Nkr500 per person) take place around a long communal table in the rustic, reimagined barn, with local produce such as venison, reindeer, wild salmon or *bacalao* (salt-cod) the star of the show. Breads and pastries are made by an elderly neighbour. Note that to ensure guests' privacy, casual visits are not allowed.

Jordbærstova CAFE €
(⊘ May-Sep) About 6km up the Åndalsnes road from Valldal, Jordbærstova honours the valley's mighty strawberry. Stop in for a slice of their strawberry cake, a sponge with strawberries, cream and strawberry purée that may sound prosaic enough, but could just send you into a state of rapture. They also do traditional Norwegian buffets at lunch.

🛍 Shopping

Valldal Safteri FOOD
(Syltetøysbutikken; www.baer.no; ⊘ 10am-5pm Tue-Fri, 11am-4pm Sat & Sun mid-Jun–mid-Aug, shorter hours rest of year) This artisan jam producer on the road behind and east of Valldal's church,

has a huge selection of jams and juices, pressed and simmered in the small factory behind the shop and sourced in the main from local farmers.

ⓘ Information

Valldal's **tourist office** (☏ 70 25 77 67; www. visitalesund-geiranger.com; ◷10am-6pm mid-Jun–mid-Aug, rest of year 10am-5pm Mon-Fri) rents bikes (Nkr25/100 per hour/day) and can also arrange motor-boat hire (Nkr85/400 per hour/day).

ⓘ Getting There & Away

Valldal lies on the 'Golden Route' bus service that runs twice daily from mid-June to August between Åndalsnes (Nkr125, 1¾ hours) and Geiranger (Nkr85, 1¼ hours), up and over the spectacular Trollstigen pass. If you're driving, pause at **Gudbrandsjuvet**, 15km up the valley from Valldal, where the river sluices and thrashes through a 5m-wide, 20m-deep canyon.

Equally scenic is the spectacular ferry cruise (adult/child single Nkr240/130, return Nkr370/190, 2¼ hours) that runs twice daily between Valldal and Geiranger from mid-June to mid-August.

Tafjord

In 1934 an enormous chunk of rock, 400m high and 22m long – in all, a whopping 8 million cubic metres – broke loose from the hillside. It crashed into Korsnæsfjord and created a 64m-high tidal wave that washed up to 700m inland and claimed 40 lives in Fjørra and Tafjord.

◉ Sights

Tafjord Power Station Museum MUSEUM
(Kraft og skredsenter; ☏ 70 17 56 00; www.tafjord. net/museum; adult/children Nkr100/60; ◷noon-5pm mid-Jun–early Aug) Within this historic, now-defunct, power station, exhibitions detail the advent of hydroelectric power in the valley, rock slides and avalanches. A long tube slide and indoor climbing wall make it extra fun for kids.

It's also worth taking the road that climbs from the village up to the Zakarias reservoir; after it passes through a bizarre corkscrew tunnel, a couple of kilometres higher up there is a short walking route that drops to the crumbling bridge at the dam's narrow base, where you feel at close range the stresses this 96m-high structure has to tolerate.

Geiranger

POP 250

Scattered cliffside farms, most long abandoned, still cling to the towering, near-sheer walls of twisting, 20km-long emerald-green Geirangerfjord, a Unesco World Heritage Site. Waterfalls – the Seven Sisters, the Suitor, the Bridal Veil and more – sluice and tumble. The one-hour scenic ferry trip along its length between Geiranger and Hellesylt is as much mini-cruise as means of transport – take it even if you've no particular reason to get to the other end.

If you arrive from Hellesylt, Geiranger village, despite its fabulous location at the head of the fjord, comes as a shock to the system as you mingle with the waves of those delivered by bus and ship. Every year Geiranger wilts under the presence of over 600,000 visitors and more than 150 cruise ships.

You'll be overawed for another reason if you drop from the north down the Ørnevegen, the Eagle's Way, as the final, super-spectacular 7km of the Rv63 from Åndalsnes is called. As it twists down the almost sheer slope in 11 hairpin bends, each one gives a yet more impressive glimpse along the narrow fjord.

And whichever way you're coming or going, once the last cruise ship and tour bus of the day pulls out, serenity returns to this tiny port.

◉ Sights

Norsk Fjordsenter MUSEUM
(www.verdsarvfjord.no; adult/child Nkr100/50; ◷10am-6pm) The Norwegian Fjord Centre has tools, artefacts and even whole buildings that have been uprooted and brought here, illustrating the essential themes – the mail packet, avalanches, the building of early roads and the rise of tourism – that have shaped the land and its people. It's located up the hill along the Rv63, just past the Hotel Union (p238).

Flydalsjuvet VIEWPOINT
Somewhere you've seen that classic photo, beloved of brochures, of the overhanging rock Flydalsjuvet, usually with a figure gazing down at a cruise ship in Geirangerfjord. The car park, signposted Flydalsjuvet, about 5km uphill from Geiranger on the Stryn road, offers a great view of the fjord and the

green river valley, but doesn't provide the postcard view down to the last detail.

For that, you'll have to drop about 150m down the hill, then descend a slippery and rather indistinct track to the edge. Your intrepid photo subject will have to scramble down gingerly and with the utmost care to the overhang about 50m further along, or if it's a selfie, we advise care when walking backwards.

Dalsnibba   VIEWPOINT

For the highest and perhaps most stunning of the many stunning views of the Geiranger valley and fjord, take the 5km toll road (Nkr85 per car) that climbs from the Rv63 to the **Dalsnibba lookout** (1500m). A bus (adult/child return Nkr180/90) runs three times daily from Geiranger between mid-June and mid-August.

🏃 Activities

Sea Kayaking

Coastal Odyssey   KAYAKING, HIKING

(☑ 91 11 80 62; www.coastalodyssey.com; sea kayaks per hr/half-day/day Nkr150/450/800, kayaking-hiking trips Nkr800-1250) 🏄 Based at Geiranger Camping (a short walk from the ferry terminal), this much recommended company is run by Jonathan Bendiksen, a Canadian from the Northwest Territories who learnt to kayak almost before he could walk. He rents sea-kayaks and does daily hiking and canoeing trips to four of the finest destinations around the fjord.

These include daily kayaking-with-gentle-hiking trips, lasting five to six hours. As his publicity flyer says with pride, these are 'the only trips available in Geiranger that have no environmental impact'.

Boat Tours

Geiranger Fjordservice   BOAT

(☑ 70 26 30 07; www.geirangerfjord.no) This operation offers 1½-hour sightseeing boat tours (adult/child Nkr 110/45, sailing four times daily June to August). Its kiosk is within the Geiranger tourist office. From mid-June to August, it also operates a smaller, 15-seater boat (Nkr390/190) that scuds deeper and faster into the fjord.

Hiking

Get away from the seething ferry terminal and life's altogether quieter. All around Geiranger there are great signed hiking routes to abandoned farmsteads, waterfalls and vista points. The tourist office's aerial-photographed *Hiking Routes* map (Nkr10) gives ideas for 18 signed walks of between 1.5km and 5km.

A popular longer trek begins with a ride on the Geiranger Fjordservice sightseeing boat. A steep 45-minute ascent from the landing at Skagehola brings you to Skageflå, a precariously perched hillside farm. You can retrace your steps to the landing, where the boat stops (on request; tell the crew on the way out or just wave). To stretch your legs more, continue over the mountain and return to Geiranger via Preikestolen and Homlung.

Cycling

Geiranger Adventure   CYCLING

(☑ 47 37 97 71; www.geiranger-adventure.com; Gågata; adult/child incl transport, bikes, helmet & equipment Nkr450/225) This outfit will drive you up to Djupvasshytta (1038m), from where you can coast for 17 gentle, scenically splendid kilometres by bike down to the fjord; allow a couple of hours. It also rents bikes (Nkr50/200 per hour/day).

🛏 Sleeping

Hotels are often booked out by package tours months in advance.

Geirangerfjorden Feriesenter   CAMPGROUND €

(☑ 95 10 75 27; www.geirangerfjorden.net; Grande; campsites Nkr260, cabins from Nkr850; ⊙ late Apr–mid-Sep) An excellent camping option with well-maintained facilities and particularly pretty, well-decorated cabins. Good longer-stay rates are available.

Grande Hytteutleige
og Camping   CAMPGROUND €

(☑ 70 26 30 68; www.grande-hytteutleige.no; Rv63; campsites Nkr220, 4-bed cabins with outdoor bathroom Nkr430, with bathroom from Nkr980; ⊙ Apr-Oct; @🛜) If camping, take the smaller, northernmost of its two fields for the best views up the fjord. It also hires out sea kayaks and fishing gear and can arrange a boat taxi to the fjord farms, accessible only by sea or on foot.

Geiranger Camping   CAMPGROUND €

(☑ 70 26 31 20; www.geirangercamping.no; campsite Nkr160; ⊙ mid-May–end-Sep; P @ 🛜) A short walk from the ferry terminal, Geiranger Camping is sliced through by a fast-flowing torrent. Though short on shade it's pleasant and handy for an early morning ferry getaway.

★ **Westerås Gard** CABIN €€
(☑ 93 26 44 97; www.geiranger.no/westeras; 2-bed cabins Nkr950, apt Nkr1150; ⊘ May-Sep) This beautiful old working farm, 4km along the Rv63 towards Grotli, sits at the end of a narrow road dizzingly high above the bustle. Stay in one of the two farmhouse apartments, or there are five pine-clad cabins. The barn, dating to 1603, is home to a restaurant, where Arnfinn and Iris serve dishes made with their own produce.

From the farm you can do a 45-minute walk to the Storsæterfossen waterfall, along with many other lovely routes. Around 3km from the centre of Geiranger, you'll reach Hole Bru, where you'll see the sign for the farm road.

Hotel Utsikten HOTEL €€
(☑ 70 26 96 60; www.classicnorway.no/hotell-utsikten; s/d Nkr890/1380; ⊘ May-Sep; ℗ @) 'A temple to lift your spirits' – so observed King Rama V of Siam when he stayed during his grand tour. High on the hill above Geiranger (take Rv63, direction Grotli), the family-owned Utsikten, constructed in 1893, still has stunning views over town and fjord over a century later. Rooms, however, are small and a little more prosaic.

Hotel Union HOTEL €€€
(☑ 70 26 83 00; www.union-hotel.no; s/d Nkr 1600/2200; ⊘ Feb–mid-Dec; ℗ @ 🛜 🏊) The spectacularly situated Union is high on the hill above town. It's got a long history, but today takes the form of a large modern complex that includes a spa with a couple of pools and sauna (day access for non-guests Nkr350). Public areas have the air of luxury you'd expect at the town's best, but rooms are nothing special.

Their gargantuan dinner buffet (Nkr530) is good, and available even if you're not staying. The hotel's **Restaurant Julie** also does a local, seasonal multicourse à la carte menu (one to eight courses Nkr325-815).

✖ Eating & Drinking

Olebuda & Cafe Olé RESTAURANT €
(☑ 70 26 32 30; www.olebuda.no; restaurant mains Nkr120-135; ⊘ cafe 9am-7pm, restaurant from 6pm) Occupying Geiranger's old general store, the pretty upstairs restaurant does a range of international-style dishes and good local standards like poached salmon roulade and house-smoked goat; all fish and meat are local. Downstairs is a colourful, casual

cafe with great carrot cake (Nkr45), all day snacks and good coffee.

Brasserie Posten RESTAURANT €€
(☑ 70 26 13 06; www.brasserieposten.no; lunch Nkr99-124, dinner Nkr168-228; ⊘ noon-11pm) A simple menu of salads, burgers, steaks, fish and pizza is elevated above the norm by a passionate local chef who sources his Heelsylt, organice dairy from Røros and makes the most of fresh herbs and vegetables. The modern Scando interior is bright and atmospheric, but the fjord-side terrace wins.

It's the perfect summer evening spot to enjoy their platters of local cured meats and smoked fish (Nkr189) and a glass of Slogen pale ale.

Geiranger Skysstasjon CAFE
(⊘ 8am-6pm Mon-Sat, from 10am Sun Jun-Aug, shorter hours rest of year) Big picture windows and footpath benches at this lovely black-stained Swiss-style shopfront look over the port action but keep you nicely out of the thick of it. The cafe makes great cappuccinos, using Ålesund's Jacu coffee, and delicious homemade *boller* (raisin rolls) and *svele* (pancakes). It's fully licensed and open some evenings for quiz nights and tapas – ask for upcoming dates.

🛍 Shopping

★ **Geiranger Sjokolade** CHOCOLATE
(geirangersjokolade.no; Holenaustet; ⊘ 10am-8.30pm May-Sep, Nov & Dec) Bengt Dahlberg's scented trail can reach as far as the dock as he handcrafts his wares in a basement of an old boathouse. Follow your nose and pick up a selection of his inspired work, including truffles flavoured with brown cheese or filled with cloudberry, or go for instant gratification in the form of ice cream or hot chocolate.

Out of season, if the shop's closed, pop downstairs and knock.

ℹ Information

Tourist office (☑ 70 26 30 99; www.geiranger. no; ⊘ 9am-6pm mid-May–mid-Sep) Located right beside the pier.

ℹ Getting There & Away

BOAT
The popular, hugely recommended run between Geiranger and Hellesylt (car with driver Nkr320, adult/child single Nkr160/79, return Nkr215/115; one hour) is quite the most spec-

tacular scheduled ferry route in Norway. It has four to eight sailings daily from May to September (every 90 minutes until 6.30pm, June to August).

Almost as scenic is the ferry that runs twice daily between Geiranger and Valldal (adult/child single Nkr240/130, return Nkr370/190, 2¼ hours). A minicruise in itself, it runs from mid-June to mid-August.

From mid-April to mid-October, the Hurtigruten coastal ferry makes a detour from Ålesund (departs 9.30am) to Geiranger (departs 1.30pm) on its northbound run.

BUS

From mid-June to mid-August two buses daily make the spectacular run over Trollstigen to Åndalsnes (Nkr265, three hours) via Valldal (Nkr85, 1½ hours). For Molde, change buses in Åndalsnes; for Ålesund, change at Linge.

Hellesylt

POP 250

The old Viking port of Hellesylt, through which a roaring waterfall cascades, is altogether calmer, if far less breathtaking, than nearby Geiranger.

The **tourist office** (☑94 81 13 32; ⊘10am-5pm mid-Jun–Aug) is in the Peer Gynt Gallery. For hikers, it carries *Tafjardfjella,* a walking map at 1:50,000, and for cyclists, *Hellesylt Mountain Biking Map.*

◉ Sights

Peer Gynt Galleriet   CULTURAL CENTRE
(adult/child Nkr120/60; ⊘11am-7pm Jun-Aug) An only-in-the-fjords extravaganza, bas-relief wood carvings fashioned by local chippy Oddvin Parr illustrate the Peer Gynt legend, along with a 35-minute audio-visual show (three daily in English). There's an attached cafeteria with lovely big windows overlooking the fjord.

⊨ Sleeping & Eating

Hellesylt Vandrerhjem   HOSTEL €€
(☑70 26 51 28; www.hihostels.no/hellesylt; dm Nkr260, s/d with shared bathroom Nkr390/640, d with bathroom Nkr750; ⊘year round; @⊛) This HI-affiliated hostel perches on the hillside overlooking Hellesylt. It's not flash, but in a beautiful spot. If you're arriving by bus, ask the driver to drop you off to save a long slog back up the hill.

Hellesylt Camping   CAMPGROUND €
(☑90 20 68 85; www.hellesyltturistsenter.no; campsites Nk190; ⊛) The absence of shade at this site is more than compensated for by its fjord-side location and proximity to the ferry pier.

❶ Getting There & Away

In summer, some ferries from Geiranger connect with buses to/from Stryn (Nkr115, one hour) and Ålesund (Nkr195, 2¾ hours).

Norangsdalen

Norangsdalen is one of the most inspiring yet little-visited crannies of the northern fjords. This glorious hidden valley connects Hellesylt with the Leknes–Sæbø ferry on the scenic Hjørundfjorden, via the village of Øye.

The boulder-strewn scenery unfolds among towering snowy peaks, ruined farmsteads and haunting mountain lakes. In the upper part of the valley at Urasætra, beside a dark mountain lake, are the ruins of several stone crofters' huts. Further on, you can still see the foundations of one-time farmhouses beneath the surface of the pea-green lake Langstøylvatnet, created in 1908 when a rock slide crashed down the slopes of Keipen.

Hikers and climbers will find plenty of scope in the dramatic peaks of the adjacent Sunnmørsalpane, including the lung-searingly steep scrambling ascent of Slogen (1564m) from Øye and the superb Råna (1586m), a long, tough haul from Urke.

Beside the road about 2km south of Øye, there's a monument to one CW Patchell, an English mountaineer who lost his heart to the valley.

★ Villa Norangdal   HISTORIC HOTEL €€€
(☑70 26 10 84; norangdal.com; s/d Nkr1450/1900; ⊛) This enchanting 'mountainpolitan style' hotel began welcoming guests in 1885. The current owner, a descendent of the hotel's founder, began restoration in 2007, after it lay abandoned for decades. Six rooms are each an homage to a different 20th-century decade, utilising iconic Scandinavian design pieces, including Norwegian gems by Nora Gulbrandsen and Grete Prytz Kittelsen.

Downstairs, the traditionally decorated, atmospheric lounge has a log fire, there's a spectacular dining room and an outdoor jacuzzi. The freeride skiing from outside the door is excellent and in summer kayaking and climbing oppurtunities are close at hand. It's a magical place, in a fairytale location.

Hotel Union Øye
HOTEL €€€

(☑70 06 21 00; www.unionoye.no; r Nkr1850; ☺May-Sep) Constructed in 1891, the Union has attracted mountaineers, writers, artists and royalty for over a century. With period artwork and furnishings, panelled in wood and speaking old-world charm, it's an over-the-top delight. The restaurant serves one- and three-course lunches (Nkr195 and Nkr350) and three- and five-course dinners (Nkr475 and Nkr595).

Runde

POP 100

The squat island of Runde, 67km southwest of Ålesund and connected to the mainland by a bridge, plays host to half a million sea birds of around 230 species, including 100,000 pairs of migrating puffins that arrive in April to breed and stay around until late July. There are also colonies of kittiwakes, gannets, fulmars, storm petrels, razor-billed auks, shags and guillemots, plus about 70 other species that nest here.

You'll see the best bird sites, as well as an offshore seal colony, on a **boat tour** (adult/child Nkr180/90). Three boats – the *Aquila*, the *Casablanca* and the *Rundø* – put out from Runde's small harbour, each two or three times daily.

There's a **tourist office** (☑90 18 34 55; www.rundecentre.no; in Runde Miljøsenter; ☺10am-6pm Jun-Aug, to 4pm May) and cafe within the Runde Miljøsenter.

🛏 Sleeping

Goksöyr Camping
CAMPGROUND €

(☑70 08 59 05; www.goksoyr.no; campsite Nkr180, 2-/4-bed cabins with outdoor bathroom Nkr300/450, 4-bed with bathroom Nkr500; ☺May-Sep) Before the road north peters out, waterside Goksöyr Camping has a range of basic cabins and rooms along with a campsite. The owners, long-term residents on the island, are welcoming and readily dispense information on birdwatching and walking trails.

Runde Miljøsenter
APARTMENTS €€€

(Runde Environmental Centre; ☑70 08 08 00; www. rundecentre.no; r Nkr1500, 5-bed apt Nkr2000; ℗☎) ✈ This international research station, testament to the islands importance in the biology sphere, has accomodation, hosts conferences and training courses, and has an exhibition space.

Ålesund

POP 23,000

The home base for Norway's largest cod-fishing fleet, Ålesund sits on a narrow, fishhook-shaped sea-bound peninsula. Despite its primary source of income, this is no regular Norwegian port. After a devastating fire in 1904, the city was rebuilt in curvaceous Jugendstil – art nouveau – style and today remains Scandinavia's most complete and harmonious example of the era.

◉ Sights & Activities

★Jugendstil Senteret
MUSEUM

(Art Nouveau Centre; ☑70 10 49 70; www.jugendstilsenteret.no; Apotekergata 16; adult/child Nkr75/40; ☺10am-5pm Jun-Aug, 11am-4pm Tue-Sun Sep-May) The city's unique architectural heritage is documented in a former pharmacy, the first listed Jugendstil monument in Ålesund. Apart from the building's own exquisite and almost entirely extant interior, including a sinuous staircase and florid dining room, displays include textiles, ceramics, furniture, posters and other ephemera. Even if you're not a keen aesthete, a 'Time Machine' capsule is great fun, presenting 'From Ashes to Art Nouveau', a 14-minute multimedia story of the rebuilding of Ålesund after the great fire.

Ticket price also covers entry to KUBE, next door.

KUBE
MUSEUM

(Møre and Romsdal County Museum of Art; Apotekergata 16; adult/child Nkr75/40; ☺10am-5pm Jun-Aug, 11am-4pm Tue-Sun Sep-May) Ålesund's primary contemporary art space highlights Norwegian artists, as well as hosting the occasional design and architecture focused show. The old Bank of Norway building's upstairs gallery also has a wonderful view of the harbour.

Ticket price also covers entry to Jugendstil Senteret, next door.

Sunnmøre Museum
MUSEUM

(www.sunnmore.museum.no; Borgundgavlen; adult/child Nkr80/30; ☺10am-4pm Mon-Fri, noon-4pm Sun May-Oct, closed Mon rest of year) Ålesund's celebrated Sunnmøre Museum is 4km east of the centre. Here, at the site of the old Borgundkaupangen trading centre, active from the 11th to 16th centuries, over 50 traditional buildings have been relocated. Ship-lovers will savour the collection of around 40 historic boats, including replicas of Viking-era ships and a commercial trading vessel from around AD 1000. Take bus 613, 618 or 624.

Should your visit coincide with its restricted opening hours, don't overlook – as many visitors often do – its Medieval Age Museum. Displayed around excavations of the old trading centre are well documented artefacts discovered on site and reproductions of medieval illustrations depicting the way of life of the west Norwegian coastal folk who inhabited this thriving community.

Atlanterhavsparken   AQUARIUM
(Atlantic Ocean Park; www.atlanterhavsparken. no; Tueneset; adult/child Nkr155/75; ⊙10am-7pm Sun-Fri, 10am-4pm Sat Jun-Aug, 11am-4pm Tue-Sun Sep-May) At the peninsula's western extreme, 3km from the town centre, this aquarium can consume a whole day. Be introduced to the North Atlantic's teeming undersea world and the astonishing richness of coastal and fjord life. Children can dangle a line for crabs or feed the fish in the touch pool while the enormous 4-million-litre aquarium appeals to everyone. The grounds offer superb coastal scenery and walking trails (look out for WWII bunkers and gun batteries).

In summer, a special bus (adult/child Nkr200/100, including admission) leaves from beside the town hall hourly from 9.55am to 3.55pm, Monday to Saturday.

Aalesunds Museum   MUSEUM
(www.aalesunds.museum.no; Rasmus Rønnebergs gate 16; adult/child Nkr50/30; ⊙9am-4pm Mon-Fri, noon-4pm Sat & Sun) The town museum illustrates the history of sealing, fishing, shipping and industry in the Sunnmøre region, the fire of 1904 and the town's Jugendstil rebirth and the German occupation during WWII. There's also a collection of boats and ships, including the *Uræd* lifeboat (piloted across the Atlantic in 1904 by an intrepid Ole Brude).

Fiskerimuseet   MUSEUM
(Molovegen 10; adult/child Nkr50/10; ⊙9am-4pm Mon-Fri, from noon Sat & Sun mid-May–mid-Sep) The 1861 Holmbua warehouse (one of the very few buildings to survive the 1904 fire) has exhibits on the development of fishing across the centuries and special sections on *klippfisk* (salt-cod) production and the processing of cod-liver oil. Its entrance area recreates an old grocery shop, a delight in itself.

WORTH A TRIP

STORDAL

If you're travelling between Valldal and Ålesund on the Rv650, do make a short stop at Stordal's **Rose Church** (Rose-kyrka; adult/child Nkr30/15; ⊙11am-4pm mid-Jun–mid-Aug). Unassuming from the outside, it was constructed in 1789 on the site of an earlier stave church, elements of which were retained. Inside comes the surprise: the roof, walls and every last pillar are sumptuously painted with scenes from the Bible and portraits of saints in an engagingly naive interpretation of high baroque.

Aksla   VIEWPOINT
The 418 steps up Aksla hill lead to the splendid **Kniven viewpoint** over Ålesund and the surrounding mountains and islands. Follow Lihauggata from the pedestrian shopping street Kongensgata, pass the **Rollon statue**, and begin the 15-minute puff to the top of the hill. There's also a cheat's road to the crest; take Røysegata east from the centre, then follow the Fjellstua signposts up the hill.

Ålesund Church   CHURCH
(Aspegata; ⊙10am-4pm Tue-Sun) Built of solid stone in 1909, Ålesund's parish church has a strikingly wide chancel, every square inch covered in frescos over the wide sweep of its tunnel arch. Notable too are the stained glass windows, especially those in the north aisle with their appropriately nautical theme.

⚲ Tours

Guided Town Walk   WALKING TOUR
(adult/child Nkr100/free; ⊙noon-1.30pm mid-Jun–mid-Aug) To get to know Ålesund's architecture with a knowledgable local, sign on for the tourist office's excellent 1½- to two-hour guided town walk, which runs daily during the summer.

62° Nord   TOURS
(⌨70 11 44 30; www.62.no; Skansekaia) This highly respected operation offers a number of top-end excursions such as wildlife safaris, including one to Runde, fishing trips and cruises through Hjørundfjord. They can take you out in a Zodiac or yacht, and create customised itineraries. See them also for bike and kayak hire.

Ålesund

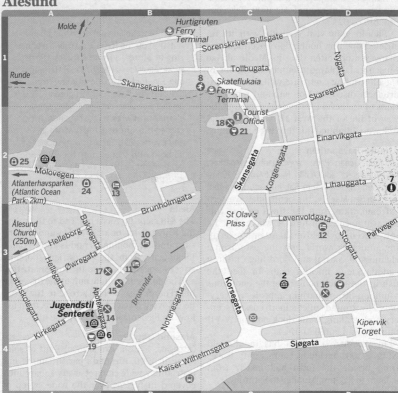

🎆 Festivals & Events

Midsummer Jazz JAZZ
(www.midtsommerjazz.no) Takes place on a weekend in late June.

Ålesund Boat Festival BOATS
(www.batfestivalen.no) A week of watery pleasures in the first half of July.

Jugendfest MUSIC
(www.jugendfest.no) Norwegian and international bands all over town on one weekend in the second half of August.

Norwegian Food Festival FOOD
(www.matfestivalen.no) Last week of August.

🛏 Sleeping

Ålesund Vandrerhjem HOSTEL €
(☑70 11 58 30; www.hihostels.no; Parkgata 14; dm/s/d/apt Nkr285/690/890/1490; ☺year-round; @) In a pretty residential area a few minutes' walk from the port, this attractive build-

ing has big, pristine rooms. There's a large self-catering kitchen and breakfast is included. Most doubles come with bathroom and there are family-sized apartments with their own kitchen and sea views.

Volsdalen Camping CAMPGROUND €
(☑70 12 58 90; www.volsdalencamping.no; Volsdalsberga; campsites Nkr150, 2-/4-bed cabins with outdoor bathroom Nkr550/950, with bathroom Nkr1350; ☺year-round) Above the shore about 2km east of the centre, this particularly friendly campsite is the nearest to town. Mainly for caravans and motorhomes, or for those wanting a cabin, it does have a secluded grassy area for campers at its far end. Take bus 613, 614, 618 or 624.

Scandic Hotel Ålesund HOTEL €€
(☑21 61 45 00; www.scandichotels.com; Molovegen 6; s/d Nkr1060/1255; @☜) The Scandic has a lot going for it, postion being just one. Rooms all have hardwood flooring and the

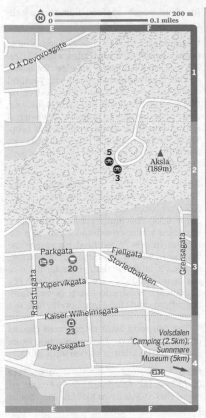

Ålesund

clean, bright Scandic look. While most do have some harbour view, you can't beat the junior suites; they are not large but have stunning round 'lookout' windows that bring the sea seemingly within reach.

Rica Scandinavie Hotel　　　HOTEL €€
(☎70 15 78 00; www.rica.no; Løvenvoldgata 8; s/d Nkr895/1095; P@) Ålesund's oldest hotel, the first to be constructed after the 1904 fire, has beautiful bones indeed. Sadly, its public spaces are rather uncared for and rooms are of your standard bland chain variety. Still, it's central and has great deals.

★Hotel Brosundet　　　HOTEL €€€
(☎70 11 45 00; www.brosundet.no; Apotekergata 5; s/d Nkr1330/1530; d with view Nkr1730; P@🛜) Right on the waterfront and designed by superstar architects Snøhetta, this former warehouse is one of Norway's most charming hotels. Wonderful old beams and exposed brick walls are combined wtih

contemporary comfort and style. Bedroom furnishings are of white oak, bathrooms are set behind smokey glass walls and beds are draped with brown velvet and sheep skins.

Breakfast is served in the elegant, portside Maki restaurant. If simple luxury is not enough, book 'room' 47, once the Molja lighthouse and featuring a round bed.

Clarion Collection Hotel Bryggen HOTEL €€€
(☎70 10 33 00; www.nordicchoicehotels.no; Apotekergata 1-3; s/d from Nkr1380/1580; @) This excellent waterfront option occupies a converted fish warehouse and has a beautiful full-height lobby and lounge area. Rooms have a smart maritime look and the deluxes are super big. Rates include nice extras like a

light evening meal and free waffles throughout the day, along with a guest sauna.

Eating

Ålesund's top-end dining is good, with seafood a highlight. While midrange choices aren't so plentiful, you can't go past a scoop of fresh shrimps procured directly from the fishing boats that moor along the harbour front beside Skansegata.

★ Jacu Coffee Roastery   CAFE
(www.jacu.no; Parkgata 18; sandwiches Nkr99; ⊘9am-3pm Mon-Fri, 10am-2pm Sat) The west coast's most highly respected coffee roastery is head-quartered in this sensitively remodelled industrial space. Drop in for an espresso or a made-to-order filter, breakfast pastries and lunch sandwiches. If you're keen to discover more about the Norwegian coffee scene, you can try one of the tastings and classes. Apart from churning out the best beans, they also host art exhibitions.

Apoteker'n   CAFE
(✆70 10 49 70; Apotekergata 16; sandwiches around Nkr50; ⊘10am-5pm Jun-Aug, 11am-4pm Tue-Sun Sep-May) Within Jugendstil Senteret (p240), this stylish, friendly little place offers excellent coffee and cake. They also do a good lunch menu of sandwiches and salads, made from top quality local produce sourced from Matbuda, a Stranda providore.

Nomaden   CAFE €
(✆97 15 89 85; Apotekergata 10; sandwiches Nkr79; ⊘11am-5pm) Affiliated with antique shop next door, this unpretentious cafe serves sandwiches, big slices of cakes and fresh coffee and has its own changing art exhibition.

Invit   CAFE €€
(✆70 15 66 44; www.invit.no; Apotekergata 9; salads Nkr135, Thu eve seafood buffet Nkr300-450; ⊘8.15am-4.30pm Mon-Fri, 6pm-midnight Thu, 10am-4.30pm Sat) Invit does central Ålesund's best coffee and is its most stylish lunch spot. Daily changing salads are super fresh and inventive, healthy soups are warming and the nutty, fragrant cakes are homemade. If the streetside bar is full, spread out downstairs at one of the beautiful big wooden tables.

Attention to detail is not just in the decor, with even the complimentary water a delight, flavoured with seasonal berries or lemons and limes. If you're in town on a Thursday evening, you're in luck – book in for their weekly seafood buffet and well-chosen glasses of wine.

Lyspunktet   CAFE, RESTAURANT €€
(www.lyspunktet.as; Kipervikgata 1; ⊘10am-10pm Tue-Fri, noon-5pm Sat & Sun) At this great-value place, join the youthful crowd on its deep sofa. There are free refills for coffee and soft drinks, and the west coast pulled pork and coleslaw sandwich is a local favourite, along with its fish soup. There are international cafe standards too, like chili con carne, as well as a 'slice of Sydney' focaccia.

Anno   NORWEGIAN, PIZZA €€€
(✆71 70 70 77; Apotekergata 9B; mains Nkr235-335, pizza Nkr139-189; ⊘11am-11pm Mon-Thu, to 3am Fri & Sat) This upmarket waterfront place attracts a young crowd and caters to a variety of moods. Wood-fired pizzas are the real deal and can be ordered in the lounge, or book a table for their more formal dinner menu. All dishes are described with key ingredient's provinence, such as veal from Sognefjord and fish from, well, just out there.

The fish soup, with its generous chunks of fish and scallops, roe and a subtle foam, is superb. The kitchen is open until 10pm.

Maki   SEAFOOD €€€
(✆70 11 45 00; Apotekergata 5; 5-/7-course set menus Nkr720/850, mains Nkr345) The chef at Hotel Brosundet's portside restaurant earnt his stripes as a ship's cook and his trawler connections means he gets the best seafood along the coast. Dishes have an international slant, though all is kept simple, letting the great produce shine. The street-side bar is a great place for a glass of wine, as is downstairs by the fire.

XL Diner   SEAFOOD €€€
(✆70 12 42 53; Skaregata 1; mains Nkr289-340; ⊘5pm-midnight Mon-Sat) Nothing could be further from a trad greasy diner than this 1st-floor fish restaurant overlooking the harbour. Seductively lit *klippfisk* (salt-cod) line the entrance, so there's no doubt about the house speciality. This quintessentially Norwegian dish is offered in a variety of *bacalao*-loving culinary styles, such as Genovese (with pesto and potato) or Spanish (with 'red' sauce).

There are also local specialities like pan-fried cod tongues with scallops and sour cream (Nkr140), a straight-up fish platter (Nkr340) and steaks (Nkr310).

🍷 Drinking & Nightlife

Milk   BAR
(Skateflua 1B; ⊘ Tue-Thu 3pm-1am, Fri & Sat
to 2.30am) A very stylish big-windowed
bar that is right on the water and open
late. While grown Norwegians are indeed
known to neck a glass of the white stuff,
it's good wines, beer on tap and cocktails
that draw the locals here; the name comes
from the building's former role as a milk
delivery depot.

Piano   BAR
(Kipervikgata 1b; ⊘ 6pm-2am Tue-Thu, 3pm-3am
Fri, noon-3am Sat) A laid-back bar with a steep
rear garden; live bands sometimes use its
flat roof as a stage. There's 28 beers on tap,
the crowd is young and fun, and there are
cosy spots if it's cold outside.

🛍 Shopping

Invit Interior   HOMEWARES
(📋 70 15 66 44; Apotekergata 9; ⊘ 11am-4.25pm
Tue-Sat) Appropriately for such a design-
forward town, this shop displays the very
best of creative modern furniture and Scandinavian kitchenware and home appliances.

Trankokeriet Antikk   ANTIQUES
(📋 70 12 01 00; www.trankokeriet.no; Molovegen 6b;
⊘ 10am-5pm Mon-Sat) This wonderful hotch-
potch antique shop is a collector's dream.
Though there are few bargains, there's an
amazing stock of nautical curiosities, traditional Norwegian crafts, mid-century cer-
maics from Norway's best known designers
as well as things that defy description. The
coffee bar too is an eccentric delight.

Ingrids Glassverksted   GLASSWARE
(www.ingridsglassverksted.no;   Molovegen   15;
⊘ 10am-5pm Mon-Fri, 10am-3pm Sat) You'll find
everything from practical glasses and bowls
to quirky, multicoloured chickens with spiky
cockscombs.

Celsius   GLASS
(www.celsius-glass.com; Kaiser Wilhelmsgata 52;
⊘ 10am-4pm Tue-Sat, to 6pm Thu) 'Luxury for
everyday use' is the motto of this small glass
studio, where each piece is designed to be
stylish yet functional. The kiln is at the front,
the shop at the rear.

ℹ Information

Tourist office (📋 70 15 76 00; www.
visitalesund-geiranger.com; Skaregata 1;
⊘ 8.30am-6pm Jun-Aug, 9am-4pm Mon-Fri

Sep-May) Its booklet *Along the Streets of
Ålesund* (Nkr30) details the town's architectural
highlights in a walking tour.

ℹ Getting There & Away

AIR
Norwegian has direct summertime flights to
Edinburgh and London (Gatwick). Internal
destinations include Bergen (three times daily),
Trondheim (twice daily) and Oslo (up to 10 times
daily).

BOAT
An express boat speeds down the coast daily to
Måløy (3¾ hours).

On its northbound run, the Hurtigruten makes
a popular detour, mid-April to mid-October, to
Geiranger, departing at 9.30am.

BUS
Local buses run to/from Åndalsnes (Nkr295, 2¼
hours, four times daily).

Express buses run to/from Bergen (Nkr686,
9¼ hours, one to three times daily), Hellesylt
(Nkr190, 2¾ hours, up to five daily), Molde
(Nkr155, 1½ hours, hourly), Oslo (Nkr915, 12½
hours, twice daily), Trondheim (Nkr1094, 7½
hours, one to three daily) via Molde (Nkr173,
2¼ hours), and Stryn (Nkr304, 3¾ hours, one
to four daily).

ℹ Getting Around

Ålesund's airport is on Vigra island, connected
to the town by an undersea tunnel. **Flybussen**
(www.flybussen.no; Nkr115, 20 minutes) airport
buses depart from Skateflukaia ferry terminal
and the bus station approximately one hour
before the departure of domestic flights.

Offshore Islands Around Ålesund

With a car, you can take in the four offshore
islands of Valderøy, Vigra, Giske and Godøy
in a pleasant day trip from Ålesund. All offer
excellent short hill or coastal walks.

Godøy

At the furthest, northern extremity of Godøy,
the furthest offshore island from Ålesund, is
the picturesque 1876 **lighthouse** (adult/child
Nkr20/10; ⊘ noon-6pm Jun-Aug) in the fishing
station of **Alnes**. For that end-of-the-world
feeling, climb to the circular balcony via the
five floors of this all-wood structure. Each
displays the canvases of Norwegian artist
and Godøy resident Ørnulf Opdahl.

Giske

Giske was the home of Gange-Rolv (known as Rollon in France, he's also claimed by Vigra), the Viking warrior who besieged Paris. He subsequently founded the Duchy of Normandy in 911 and was an ancestor of England's William the Conqueror. Highlight of the island is its ornate 12th-century **church** (adult/child incl guided tour Nkr20/10; ☺10am-5pm Mon-Sat, 1-7pm Sun mid-Jun–mid-Aug). Built largely of marble, its real jewels are the elaborately carved polychrome altarpiece and pulpit. The island's Makkevika marshes are a prime spot for birdwatching. Nowadays, it's renowned for its annual **free music festival** (www.verdensbestefestival.no), with music of all genres, on the last Saturday in July.

Valderøy

On Valderøy, the **Skjonghellaren caves** have revealed bones of Arctic fox, sea otter and ringed seal, plus evidence of human occupation at least 2000 years ago. In the northwest of the island, they're reached by a breezy 500m walk from the parking spot between cliff and shoreline, then a steep five-minute boulder scramble.

Vigra

Vigra has Ålesund's airport as well as **Blindheimssanden** (also called Blimsand), a long white-sand beach.

Molde

POP 19,900

Molde, hugging the shoreline at the wide mouth of Romsdalsfjorden, is known as the 'Town of Roses' for its fertile soil, rich vegetation and mild climate. But the town's chief claim to fame is its annual jazz festival, held in July.

Modern Molde, though architecturally unexciting, is a pleasantly compact place whose coastal landscapes recall New Zealand or Seattle's Puget Sound. To test the comparison, drive or take the one-hour signed walking trail up to the **Varden overlook**, 400m above the town.

◎ Sights

Romsdalmuseet   MUSEUM
(www.romsdalsmuseet.no; Per Amdamsveg 4; ☺park 8am-10pm) FREE There are nearly 50 old buildings within this open-air museum, shifted here from around the Romsdal region. Among the barns, farms and storehouses, there's a short street of typical town houses and a small reconstructed chapel with adornments rescued from abandoned churches. After rambling around the ample grounds, take a break in **Bygata**, a town house that functions as a summertime cafe. In summer, there are very worthwhile **guided tours** (adult/child Nkr80/free; ☺11am-3pm or 6pm Jun–mid-Aug).

Fiskerimuseet   MUSEUM
(Hertøya; adult/child Nkr80/50; ☺noon-5pm mid-Jun–early Aug) This open-air museum, on the small island of Hjertøya, is a 10-minute boat ride from Molde's Torget terminal. Its cod-liver oil factory, cottages and fishermen's shacks, tiny schoolroom and collection of boats bring to life the coastal fishing cultures around the mouth of Romsdalsfjorden from the mid-19th century onwards. During opening hours, the boat (adult/child return Nkr100/free) runs hourly from Molde between 11am and 5pm; buy tickets from the tourist office.

🛏 Sleeping

The tourist office has a number of private homes on its books, most with self-catering facilities and costing from Nkr500 per person. During the Molde International Jazz Festival, there's a large temporary campsite, Jazzcampen, 3km west of the centre.

Kviltorp Camping   CAMPGROUND €
(☏71 21 17 42; www.kviltorpcamping.no; Fannestrandveien 142; campsites Nkr190, 2-bed cabins Nkr620, 4-bed cabins with shower Nkr950-1020) This fjord-side campsite occupies a potentially noisy spot at the end of the airport runway, but fortunately there's very little air traffic. Cabins are bright and sweetly furnished and available year-round. Bus 214 and the Flybussen pass right by.

Molde Fjordstuer   BOUTIQUE HOTEL €€
(☏71 20 10 60; www.havstuene.no; Julsundvegen 6; s/d Nkr890/1090; P🐾) The welcoming Fjordstuer replicates the squat, solid forms of typical fisherfolk cottages in a modern business hotel. Superior rooms have fjord views and balconies. There are two seafood restaurants onsite to choose from.

Rica Seilet Hotel   HOTEL €€€
(☏71 11 40 00; www.rica.no; Gideonvegen 2; s/d Nkr1195/1445; P@🐾) This soaring hotel juts out into the sound like a huge silver sail. It's undeniably corporate but very pleasant;

rooms have large picture windows and magnificent views. There's lots of boat watching at the waterside lobby bar or lots of cloud and sea from the 15th floor skybar.

Quality Hotel Alexandra
HOTEL €€€
(☑71 20 37 50; www.choice.no; Storgata 1-7; s/d Nkr1280/1440; ℗@☞) Although architecturally less exciting than Molde's waterside Fjordstuer and Seilet hotels, the decor here is pleasing, and most rooms have a balcony and offer water views.

✘ Eating & Drinking

Rød
CAFE €
(☑71 20 30 00; Storgata 19; soups/salads Nkr50-139, mains Nkr139-189; ☺11am-11pm Mon-Thu, to 2am Fri & Sat, 1-9pm Sun) On the ground floor of the town's main student accommodation, expect good value meals all day and some rowdy fun as the night wears on. Daily specials (Nkr145) aim to keep the kids well fed, be that with reindeer stew or a spaghetti carbonara. Note that it's open until 3am right through Moldejazz.

Fole Godt
CAFE, BAKERY €
(☑93 09 13 33; Amtmann Krohgs gate 5; sandwiches & salads Nkr90-110; ☺7.45am-5pm Mon-Sat) Warm and welcoming cafe with a huge range of filled sandwiches, pizza slices, buns and cakes.

Gorvell
NORWEGIAN €€€
(www.xn-grvell-bya.no; Storgata 19; mains Nkr295-315) Beautiful local produce like halibut and crab from Averøya turns up on the menu at Molde's most elegant restaurant, though if you've had your fill of seafood on the coast it has good beef and reindeer too.

Vertshuset
NORWEGIAN €€€
(☑71 20 37 75; Storgata 1-7; restaurant mains Nkr279-319, bistro mains Nkr129-199) Hotel Alexandra's restaurant is all attractive panelled wood and bare brickwork and has a bistro menu of pastas, salads and sandwiches and tempting dinner choices such as fillet of lamb in a red-wine sauce with ginger-glazed vegetables.

Syd
WINE BAR
(www.motsyd.no; Fjordgata 3; ☺from 11.30am Mon-Sat) No, not the name of your host for the night but Norwegian for 'south', the way this wine bar faces. Looking out over the fjord, its terrace offers an inspirational panorama. Wines – reds mainly from Italy, whites from France – have their perfect accompaniment in the proscuitto platters (Nkr125).

❶ Information

Tourist office (☑71 20 10 00; www.visitmolde.com; Torget 4; ☺9am-6pm Mon-Fri, 9am-3pm Sat, noon-5pm Sun mid-Jun–mid-Aug, rest of year 8.30am-4pm Mon-Fri) In Toget, the main square near the express ferry terminal, this office is super well stocked and friendly. Ask for the Nkr95 *Molde Fraena* (1:50,000), the best hiking map of the area.

❶ Getting There & Away

AIR
Molde's shoreside **Årø airport** (☑67 03 23 10) is 5km east of the city centre. Local bus 701 (Nkr35, 10 minutes) from Molde's bus terminal passes by the airport at least hourly. There are up to six planes daily to/from Oslo on SAS and Norwegian; Widerøe has frequent daily fligths to Bergen and a couple a day to Kristiansund and Trondheim.

BOAT
Northbound, the Hurtigruten coastal ferry leaves at 10pm (6.30pm mid-September to mid-April); southbound, it leaves at 9.30pm. Express ferries also operate from Molde. The express-ferry terminal is on Torget, the main square.

BUS
Inland buses run hourly to and from Kristiansund (Nkr195, 1½ hours). Much more attractive and scarcely longer is the coastal run that rolls along the Atlanterhavsveien.

MOLDEJAZZ

Every July, **Moldejazz** (www.moldejazz.no) pulls in up to 100,000 fans and a host of jazz greats. The line-up is primarily Scandinavian though every few years includes international top liners along the lines of Sonny Rollins, Bobby McFerrin and Herbie Hancock.

The town parties all the way from Monday to Saturday. Of over 100 concerts, a good one-third are free, while big events are very reasonably priced at Nkr50 to Nkr600.

Trad jazz belts it out in Perspiration Hall, while the big draws perform outdoors near the Romsdalsmuseet and there are plenty of supporting events, including a daily street parade, from noon onwards in front of the Rådhus.

For this year's events, see the website.

Regular buses run to/from Ålesund (Nkr162, 2¼ hours, hourly) and Åndalsnes (Nkr148, 1½ hours, up to eight daily).

CAR & MOTORCYCLE
Travelling northwards on the Rv64, the Tussen-tunnelen shortcut avoids a dog's leg and lops a good 15 minutes off travel time.

Around Molde

Ona

The beautiful outer islet of Ona, with its bare rocky landscapes and picturesque lighthouse, is still home to an offshore fishing community. It makes a popular day trip from Molde. En route, WWII buffs may want to stop off at **Gossen Krigsminne-samling** (⊙8.30am-3.30pm Mon-Fri Jul–mid-Aug), a former Nazi wartime airstrip built by Russian POWs on the low island of Gossen. The abandoned summer-house village of Bjørnsund also warrants a brief stop.

From Molde, you can visit Ona by public transport in a day. Take the 8am bus 561 to the ferry point at Småge. From here, it's a gorgeous trip by the 9.35am ferry, which stops at three islands en route and docks at Ona at 11.10am. You *could* scurry around and leave by the noon ferry. Better to take the 3.35pm boat from Ona, then the 5.10pm linking bus in Småge to reach Molde at 6.35pm. If you have wheels, leave your vehicle in Småge (it's an encumbrance on the island) and hop on the ferry there.

Bud

The Rv664 coastal route between Molde and Kristiansund is a scenic alternative to the faster E89. En route lies the little fishing village of Bud, huddled around its compact harbour. It's difficult to believe, but in the 16th and 17th centuries Bud was the greatest trading centre between Bergen and Trondheim.

Bus 352 travels regularly between Molde and Bud (one hour; four to seven times daily, except Sunday).

◉ Sights

Ergan Coastal Fort   FORT
(Ergan Kystfort; adult/child Nkr80/35; ⊙10am-6pm Jun-late Aug) Serving as a WWII museum and memorial, this defensive fortification was erected by Nazi forces in 1940. Various armaments and a network of bunkers and soldiers' quarters are dispersed around the hill with the sick bay and store sunk deep inside the mountain.

Draagen Smokehouse   FACTORY
(☑95 86 44 25; ⊙by appointment) Petter Aune set up this operation, where freshly caught Aukra salmon are smoked with pure local wood and herbs, after tiring of the poor quality industrial product. It's one of only a few left in Norway and the resulting salmon does indeed have the elusive 'smakup-plevelse' – a melt-in-your-mouth quality. Come here to see the process, sample and buy.

✖ Eating

Bryggjen i Bud   SEAFOOD €€
(☑71 26 11 11; www.bryggjen.no; mains Nkr150-180; ⊙noon-9pm Mon-Sat, noon-6pm Sun Jul-Aug, noon-6pm Mon-Thu, noon-8pm Fri & Sat rest of year) This unpretentious place attracts people from miles around. 'People weep if they arrive and find it closed,' said the lady in the visitors centre, with perhaps just a touch of exaggeration. They come for coastal comfort food: fish soup, two varieties of fish ball, salted coalfish, and, of course klipfish (Norway's largest klipfish-drying sheds are just up the road).

Averøy

Averøy has all the silence and wild beauty of one of Norway's offshore islands, but the definite advantage of a tunnel connection to Kristiansund along with direct access to the excellent Atlantic Ocean Road. For those road-tripping along the coast, or here to experience the Atlantic Ocean Road, its rocky sea-swept villages make a far more atmospheric base than Kristiansund. The accommodation options mentioned either offer nightly meals or are self-catering.

◉ Sights & Activites

Kvernes Stave Church   CHURCH
(Fv247, Kvernes; adult/child Nkr50/free; ⊙10am-5pm late-Jun–mid-Aug) This beautifully sited stave church dates from the early 14th century, though it was rebuilt in the 17th. Inside are a large 300-year-old votive ship and unusual 15th-century altarpiece, with the Virgin Mary figuring prominently, Catholic to the core. While many such altarpieces were destroyed at the time of the Reformation,

this one luckily survived, although a stylised Lutheran surround was added in 1695. More luck: the church narrowly escaped demolition when the larger one beside it was erected in 1893.

Sveggvika Dive Resort
DIVING
(www.sveggvika.com; guided dives per person from Nkr250) This dive outfit offers easy access to wrecks along with the rich coral and fish life of this part of the west coast. They have the full range of rental equipment and offer PADI courses and accomodation packages.

🛌 Sleeping

★**Sveggvika**   GUESTHOUSE, CABINS €€€
(☑40 01 81 92; www.sveggvika.com; Seivågneset; d Nkr1450; 🐾) Lie in bed and watch the reflection of tiny pink clouds track their way across the still water of the bay or experience a ferocious North Sea storm sweep in – the stylish, if simple, rooms in this converted 1920s *klippfisk* warehouse make you feel part of the coastal landscape whatever the weather. Breakfast and dinners are excellent too.

Håholmen Havstuer   HISTORIC HOTEL €€€
(☑71 51 72 50; www.haholmen.no; Håholmen; d Nkr1900; ☉late-Jun–mid-Aug) This enchanting 'hotel' is in fact a small former fishing village on its own islet just off Averøy. Rooms here are 18th- and 19th-century cottages, mostly for doubles, though there are a couple of multi-bedroomed ones too. Some are more rustic than others, with exposed timber, but all are charming.

Ytterbrugga, its restaurant, serves the freshest of fish.

Parking is on the island of Geitøya, on the Atlanterhavsveien, from where a motor boat makes the five-minute sea journey. It leaves the roadside car park on the hour, between 11am and 9pm, or by appointment.

Skjerneset Bryggecamping   CABINS €
(www.skjerneset.com; Ekkilsøy; campsite Nkr190, 2-bed fishermens cabins Nkr450, 4-bed cottage Nkr820) The coastal cabins here have nice ocean views, along with cute porches to enjoy it from, or there are simple rooms in a former fish warehouse. The owners, themselves former commercial fisherfolk, organise deep-sea trips, or you can hire a boat, with or without motor, and sling your own line (from Nkr480 per day, with skipper Nkr2300 for three hours).

If you don't have any luck out there, it's possible to buy fresh fish to cook at your own cabin.

Kristiansund

POP 24,135

The historic cod-fishing and drying town of Kristiansund still looks below the sea for its wealth. Even though the waters are no longer so bountiful – the huge hauls of yesteryear are now the source of tales as tall as any angler's – cod-processing remains important. A significant amount of the world's klipfish is cured in and around the town, while Mellemværftet, unkempt and chaotic, hangs on as a working boatyard.

Kristiansund also plays a significant role in servicing Norway's North Sea oilfields, with its hotels, bars and restaurants catering to off-duty oil workers (with oil worker wages to spend).

The town ranges over three islands; its port and centre was bombed heavily during WWII and were replaced with little of architectural note.

◉ Sights

Most sights hug the port or are in its grid of streets in the postwar centre. **Gamle Byen**, Kristiansund's old town lives on in a part of the island of Innlandet, with clapboard buildings that date back to the 17th century. The grandiose **Lossiusgården**, at its eastern end, was the distinguished home of an 18th-century merchant. The venerable 300-year-old **Dødeladen Café**, where you can still get a meal and a drink, hosts cultural and musical events. It's a 20-minute walk across the Heinsgata bridge, but the most enjoyable way of getting here is on the stubby Sundbåt ferry from Piren ferry port.

Norsk Klippfiskmuseum   MUSEUM
(www.nordmore.museum.no; Gomalandet; adult/child incl guided tour Nkr70/free; ☉10am-2pm late Jun-early Aug) This museum, in the 1749 Milnbrygga warehouse on Gomalandet peninsula, presents the 300-year history of the dried-cod export industry in Kristiansund. It continues to produce modest quantities of *klippfisk* in the traditional way. From the town centre, take the Sundbåt ferry and ask to be dropped off.

Just north of this museum are two other classic buildings, both normally closed to the public: Hjelkrembrygga, a former *klippfisk* warehouse dating from 1835, and Woldbrygga, a barrel factory constructed in 1875.

Mellemværftet
SHIPYARD

Something of a nautical junkyard, Mellemværftet, free and accessible any time, is best approached on foot along the quayside from the Smia Fiskerestaurant (p251). It's difficult to make out what's what amid the clutter, but it includes the remnants of Kristiansund's 19th-century shipyard, a forge, a workshop and workers' quarters.

Kirkelandet Church
CHURCH

(Langveien 41; ⊘9am-3pm Sun-Fri) Architect Odd Østby's inspirational church was built in 1964 to replace the one destroyed by Nazi bombs. The angular exterior, where copper and concrete alternate, is sober and measured. Inside, all lines direct the eye to the 320 panes of stained glass at the rear of the chancel. Moving upward from the earthy colours at the base, they become paler and, at the top, replicate the 'celestial light of heaven'.

Behind the church lies Vanndamman Park, with plenty of greenery, walking tracks and the eagle's-eyrie Varden watchtower viewpoint.

Petrosenteret
INTERPRETIVE CENTRE

(www.petrosenteret.no; Storkaia 9; adult/child incl guided tour Nkr75/50; ⊘11am-4pm Jun-Aug) Presenting the modern face of Kristiansund industry, this centre portrays, through film, models, an exhaustive guided tour and mind-numbing megastatistics, the impact of oil and gas upon contemporary Norway. There are some nice models, but it's not a patch on the Norsk Oljemuseum in Stavanger.

Festiviteten
OPERA HOUSE

(☏71 58 99 60; www.oik.no; Kong Olav V's gate 1) Constructed in 1914, Kristiansund's monumental theatre, although rather austere from the outside, has an attractive art nouveau interior that's definitely worth a peek for architecture and history buffs (the building is usually open during business hours or call ahead). Norway's oldest opera company resides here, along with the city's opera festival, although these will move to a new waterfront cultural centre by 2017.

🎎 Festivals

Operafestukene
MUSIC

(www.oik.no) A two-week opera festival in early February.

Tahiti Festivalen
MUSIC

(www.tahiti-festivalen.no) A late-June week-long music festival held on Innlandet.

Nordic Light Photo Festival
PHOTOGRAPHY

(www.nle.no) Large fine-art photography festival that attracts big names and up to 70,000 visitors to its exhibitions and workshops, in September.

🛏 Sleeping

Atlanten Camping & Motell
CAMPGROUND, MOTEL €

(☏71 67 11 04; www.atlanten.no; Dalaveien 22; campsites Nkr170, 4-bed cabins with outdoor bathroom Nkr595, with bathroom Nkr995, motel s/d Nkr595/795; ℗🛜) This hostel and campground is an easy 20-minute walk from the centre. It's a friendly place, and the motel has a well-equipped kitchen, TVs in the rooms and a big screen in the lounge for sporting events. Camping facilities have recently been fully renovated and the furnished apartments are a great deal for small groups.

Dala Bergan
CABINS €

(☏71 67 30 25; www.havfiske-kristiansund.no; 2-/12-bed cabins Nkr600/1200) Out along Dalaveien, these cabins are only a 10-minute walk from the centre, although they have a rustic seaside location. All have bathrooms, TVs and, sweetly, sunbathing platforms. Bed linen can be hired.

Thon Hotel Kristiansund
HOTEL €€

(☏71 57 30 00; www.thonhotels.com; Fiskergaten 12; s/d Nkr895/1395; ℗🛜) Located out on Innlandet, this hotel is a good 20-minute walk to the centre, but that could well be a bonus. The rooms in the converted 1915 warehouse combine this chain's usual clean, modern lines with historic beams and big windows. There's a great harbourside terrace attached to the dining room and the views back to the city are fantastic.

Rica Hotel Kristiansund
HOTEL €€€

(☏71 57 12 00; www.rica.no; Storgata 41; ⊘s/d from Nkr1300/1750; ℗@🛜) Recently overhauled, the fjord-side Rica has rooms that overlook the water and your standard chain comforts, including a sauna. It regularly books out and its public areas are often hectic.

🍴 Eating

Dødeladen Café
NORWEGIAN €

(www.dodeladen.no; Innlandet; mains Nkr115-189; ⊘noon-11pm Tue-Thu, to 2am Fri & Sat) Part of

THE ATLANTIC OCEAN ROAD

The eight storm-lashed bridges of Atlanterhavsveien (Atlantic Ocean Road), recently designated a National Tourist Route, buck and twist like sea serpents, connecting 17 islets between Vevang and the island of Averøya. The UK's *Guardian* newspaper once crowned it the 'world's best road trip'. For a highway that is barely 8km long, the weight of expectation may be too great, but it's certainly hugely scenic. During the autumn storms you'll experience nature's wrath at its most dramatic. And in season, look out for whales and seals offshore.

A newly opened rest area and walking path float about the wet marshland of **Eldhusøya**, an island off the southwest of Averøya; the suspended walkway is made of latticework floating above the terrain, secured on poles. There is also a kiosk, information boards, car park and toilets here.

At **Askevågen**, a little over 10km north of Bud, you can venture out onto a beautifully simple glass fronted viewing platform, which not only gives you a 360-degree panoramic view of the archipelago, the ocean and the shore, but a close, if protected, experience of the intense force of the ocean here.

From **Molde**, hit the coast at Bud; from **Kristiansund** and the north, take the new sub-sea road tunnel that connects with Bremsnes.

Whichever your direction, rather than driving the Rv64, which cuts across inland Averøya, choose the quieter, prettier road, signed for Kvernes, that loops around the island's southern coast and takes no longer.

If you're travelling under your own steam, **Eide Auto** (📞 90 77 30 63; www.eideauto.no; Return day ticket adult/child Nkr150/100) buses link Molde and Kristiansund year-round, via the coastal route and Atlanterhavsveien. It's a 2¼ hour round trip, although if you buy the day ticket you can hop on and off at will. During the week there are six departures, two on Saturday and one on Sundays.

Gamle Byen on the city island of Innlandet, this cafe-restaurant-bar dates back to the early 1700s. It serves a menu of west-coast standards including fish soup, *klippfisk* in tomato, burgers, *svele* (pancakes) and waffles. It's also the office of the annual Tahiti Festival, when it comes into its own as the festival after-hours club.

You can get here on the Sundbåten ferry (p252) or take the bus from the centre heading towards Hønebukta.

Sjøstjerna — SEAFOOD €€
(📞 71 67 87 78; www.sjostjerna.no; Skolegata 8; mains Nkr195-279; ⊙ noon-midnight Mon-Sat) The menu here offers traditional fish dinners and its jaunty marine-themed interior is a hoot, although the outlook from its street-side terrace, on a windswept pedestrianised plaza, is grim.

★ **Bryggekanten** — RESTAURANT, BAR €€€
(📞 71 67 61 60; www.fireb.no; Storkaia 1; lunch Nkr159-192, dinner mains Nkr298-310; ⊙ 11.30am-10.30pm Mon-Sat, bar until 2.30am Wed, Fri & Sat) This cheerful brasserie sits right beside the harbour and is convivial both day and night. Burgers, mussels, pizza and bruschetta make for hearty lunches on the terrace, while the

dinner menu allows you to stay snacky or opt for more ambitious choices like smoked Vestfold duck with pear purée or pork with spring cabbage and asparagus.

Smia Fiskerestaurant — SEAFOOD €€€
(📞 71 67 11 70; www.smia.no; Fosnagata 30b; mains Nkr240-295; ⊙ 1pm-midnight) The much-garlanded Smia fish restaurant is in an old forge, adorned from wall to ceiling with blacksmiths tools – plus a couple of whale vertebrae and a hanging split cod. The fish soup (Nkr130) makes a great starter and the *bacalao* gratin does nicely for mains (Nkr249).

🍷 Drinking & Entertainment

Christian's Bar — BAR
(📞 71 57 03 00; Storgata 17) On the 1st floor of Hotell Kristiansund, Christian's Bar is an oddly fascinating place that has the decor of a Williamsburg hipster haunt, but attracts punters that look like they will probably get a little scary as the night wears on.

🛍 Shopping

Klippfiskbutikken — FOOD
(Fosnagata 25; ⊙ 10am-5pm Mon-Fri) Genial Knut Garshol, a member of the international

slow-food ecogastronomy movement, will buttonhole you and enthusiastically proclaim the virtues of klipfish at this splendid temple to the mighty cod. Try his grandmother's recipe for *bacalao*, to eat in or take away.

ℹ Information

Tourist office (☑ 71 58 54 54; www.visitkristiansund.com; Kongens plass 1; ☺ 9am-6pm Mon-Fri, 10am-3pm Sat, 11am-4pm Sun mid-Jun–mid-Aug, 9am-4pm Mon-Fri rest of year) In the centre, back up the hill from the waterfront.

ℹ Getting There & Away

AIR

The town's Kvernberget **airport** (☑ 71 68 30 50) is on Nordlandet island. There are frequent flights daily to/from both Oslo and Bergen.

Buses travel regularly to/from the airport (Nkr60, 15 minutes, up to eight daily) to meet incoming flights.

BOAT

Express boats connect Kristiansund with Trondheim (3½ hours, up to three daily from Nordmørskaia). The Hurtigruten coastal ferry also calls in daily at Holmakaia.

BUS

Inland buses run hourly to Molde (Nkr156, 1½ hours) and on to Ålesund (3¾ hours). The coastal run that rolls along the Atlanterhavsveien is much more impressive and scarcely longer. Northwards, there are up to three buses daily to Trondheim (Nkr400, 4¾ hours).

ℹ Getting Around

The **Sundbåten ferry** (www.sundbaten.no; adult/child Nkr30/15, day ticket Nkr85) claims to be 'the world's oldest public transport system in uninterrupted use'. That's a heavy reputation for these small, squat boats to bear. Whatever the history, it's well worth the ride for its own sake and for the special perspective it gives of the harbour. Boats leave from Piren pier at the foot of Kaibakken hill, linking the town centre and the islands of Innlandet, Nordlandet and Gomelandet. They run every half hour, Monday to Saturday; the full circuit takes 20 minutes.

Around Kristiansund

Grip

Huddled together on a tiny rocky island as though for protection against Atlantic gales, the village of Grip with its pastel-painted houses sits amid an archipelago of 80 islets and skerries. The only elevation is the 47m-tall Bratthårskollen lighthouse on a nearby skerry, built in 1888 and prodding skywards.

In the early 19th century, after a drop in cod hauls and two powerful storms, the village was practically abandoned. But it bounced back, its population swelling during the cod-fishing season when basing yourself on the island saved three hours of hard rowing each way from the mainland. Imagine, as you wander among today's sprinkle of houses, spring fishing seasons, when more than 1000 fisherfolk hunkered down here.

The last permanent inhabitants gave up the fight in 1974. There's a small photographic display with an accompanying sheet in English in one of the storehouses. A summertime cafe serves snacks in what was once the village school (only three pupils were left when its bell rang for the last time in 1972).

The island's **stave church** dates from the late 15th century. Its altarpiece, discarded at the time of the Reformation, was found in a boathouse and restored to its rightful place in the 1930s. The lively frescos in the nave were revealed when later whitewash was stripped off.

From late May to late August, the **M/S Gripexpressen** (www.gripexpressen.no; ☺ late-May–early-August) plies the 14km between Kristiansund's Piren terminal and Grip (40 minutes; adult/child Nkr305/150 return) once or twice daily. Total journey time is 3½ hours, including time ashore. In principle, there's a guided tour included within the fare.

Trøndelag

Best Places to Eat

➡ Vertshuset Tavern (p263)

➡ Baklandet Skydsstasjon (p263)

➡ Ravnkloa Fish Market (p263)

➡ Havfruen (p264)

Best Places to Stay

➡ Britannia Hotel (p261)

➡ Rica Stiklestad Hotel (p267)

➡ Rica Nidelven Hotel (p261)

➡ Pensjonat Jarlen (p261)

Why Go?

Trøndelag, where Norway begins to narrow and head for the Arctic, may be small but it sure packs a lot in. Trondheim is the centrepiece, a beguiling city brimful of historic architecture, including Nidaros Cathedral, Scandinavia's largest medieval structure. But Trondheim's present is as appealing as its past, with buzzing student life and pretty waterfront restaurants and bars. Not far away to the northeast, and an easy detour from the Arctic Highway, atmospheric Stiklestad is famous as the site of the martyrdom of King Olav (St Olav) and lies at the heart of every Norwegian's sense of national identity. Elsewhere in Trøndelag is quintessential Norway, a region of rumpled hills, stippled with ox-blood-coloured farmsteads and ruffled green with wheat and barley. Here, there's always water near at hand, whether sea, lake or incised fjord with fascinating coastal settlements worth lingering over.

When to Go
Trondheim

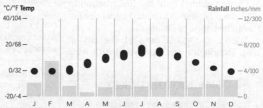

Mid- to late Jun Winter has retreated, and visitors are relatively few.

Last week of Jul Festivities in honour of St Olav in Trondheim and Stiklestad.

Sep Trondheim has a fresh buzz as its student population returns.

TRONDHEIM

POP 182,035

Trondheim, Norway's original capital, is nowadays the country's third-largest city after Oslo and Bergen. With wide streets and a partly pedestrianised heart, it's a simply lovely city with a long history. Fuelled by a large student population, it buzzes with life, has some good cafes and restaurants, and is rich in museums. All the while, boats come and go and seagulls screech overhead. You *can* absorb it in one busy day, but it merits more if you're to slip into its lifestyle.

History

In 997, King Olav Tryggvason moored his longboat alongside a broad sandbank at Nidaros (meaning 'mouth of the River Nid') and established his farm. One plausible theory has it that Leifur Eiríksson (or Leif Ericson as he's usually transcribed in English) visited the king there before setting sail for Iceland and Greenland and possibly becoming the first European to set foot in North America. (If you're from the USA, the Viking staring out to sea near the Hurtigruten quay may seem familiar. That's because he's an exact replica of the Ericson statue in Seattle that commemorates the tens of thousands of Norwegian emigrants to the New World.)

In 1030 another, subsequently more famous, King Olav (Haraldsson) was martyred in battle at Stiklestad, about 90km to the northeast, and canonised. Nidaros became a centre for pilgrims from all over Europe, its bishopric embracing Norway, Orkney, the Isle of Man, the Faroe Islands, Iceland and Greenland. It served as the capital of Norway until 1217, ruling an empire that extended from what is now western Russia to, possibly, the shores of Newfoundland. The cult of St Olav continued until the Reformation in 1537, when Norway was placed under the Lutheran bishopric of Denmark.

After a fire razed most of the city in 1681, Trondheim was redesigned with wide streets. It enjoyed its golden age in the 18th century, when merchants outdid each other in the grandeur of their dwellings. The city's location became key once again in WWII, when German naval forces made it their base for northern Norway, although fortunately the city avoided major damage. Nowadays, Trondheim, with its Norwegian University of Science & Technology and a research institute that employs more than 2000 staff, is the recognised technological capital of Norway.

The epicentre of town is Torvet, the central square (also spelt 'Torget') with its statue of King Olav Tryggvason atop a column that acts as a huge sundial.

Sights

★ Nidaros Domkirke   CATHEDRAL

(www.nidarosdomen.no; Kongsgårdsgata; adult/child/family Nkr70/30/170, tower Nkr30; ⊙9am-7pm Mon-Fri, 9am-2pm Sat, 9am-5pm Sun mid-Jun–mid-Aug, shorter hours rest of year) Nidaros Cathedral is Scandinavia's largest medieval building. Outside, the ornately embellished, altar-like west wall has top-to-bottom statues of biblical characters and Norwegian bishops and kings, sculpted in the early 20th century. Several are copies of medieval originals, housed nowadays in the museum. Within, the cathedral is subtly lit (just see how the vibrantly coloured, modern stained-glass glows, especially in the rose window at the west end), so let your eyes attune to the gloom.

The altar sits over the original grave of St Olav, the Viking king who replaced the Nordic pagan religion with Christianity. The original stone cathedral was built in 1153, when Norway became a separate archbishopric. The current transept and chapter house were constructed between 1130 and 1180 and reveal Anglo-Norman influences (many of the craftsmen were brought in from England), while the Gothic choir and ambulatory were completed in the early 14th century. The nave, repeatedly ravaged by fire across the centuries, is mostly a faithful 19th-century reconstruction.

Down in the crypt is a display of medieval carved tombstones (the majority restored from fragments since many headstones were broken up and carted away to be recycled in domestic buildings). Look for one inscribed in English and dedicated to William Miller, Shipmaster, of Dundee, Scotland, who met his end near Trondheim in the 18th century.

ⓘ COMBINATION TICKET

If you're planning to visit all three sights within the Nidaros Cathedral complex, it's worthwhile purchasing a combined ticket (adult/child/family Nkr140/60/340) that gives access to the cathedral, Archbishop's Palace museum and the crown jewels.

Trøndelag Highlights

① Browse **Nidaros Cathedral** (p254) in Trondheim, at once Norway's most sacred building and one of its most handsome.

② Explore the cultural centre and grounds of **Stiklestad** (p257), where St Olav was martyred.

③ Cross Gamle Bybro into **old Trondheim**, eat at **Baklandet Skydsstasjon** (p263), then wander down to **Solsiden** waterfront for a drink.

④ Hike in the wilderness of **Bymarka** (p251), right in Trondheim's backyard.

⑤ Learn about coastal life at multimedia **Norveg** (p269) in Rørvik.

⑥ Trundle a **trolley** (p268) along the no-longer-active Namsos–Skage railway line.

⑦ Tuck into Norwegian specialities in Trondheim's historic **Vertshuset Tavern** (p263).

You can wander around freely but, between early June and early August, it's worth joining a tour (a 15-minute canter or a more detailed 45-minute visit). Times vary but there are up to four daily in English. Music-lovers may want to time their visit to take in a **recital** on the church's magnificent (and recently restored) organ.

From early June to early August, you can climb the cathedral's **tower** for a great view over the city. There are ascents every half hour from its base in the south transept.

★ **Archbishop's Palace**   MUSEUM
(Kongsgårdsgata; adult/child/family Nkr70/30/170, crown jewels Nkr70/30/170; ☉ 10am-5pm Mon-Fri, 10am-3pm Sat, noon-4pm Sun, shorter hours rest

of year) The 12th-century archbishop's residence (Erkebispegården), commissioned around 1160 and Scandinavia's oldest secular building, is beside the cathedral. In its west wing, Norway's **crown jewels** shimmer. Its **museum** is in the same compound. After visiting the well-displayed statues, gargoyles and carvings from the cathedral, drop to the lower level, where only a selection of the myriad artefacts revealed during the museum's construction in the late 1990s are on show. Also take a look at its enjoyable 15-minute audiovisual program.

National Military Museum   MUSEUM

(Ruskammeret; ☑73 99 52 80; Kongsgårdsgata; ⊙10am-4pm Mon-Sat, noon-4pm Sun mid-May–early Sep) FREE In the same courtyard as the Archbishop's Palace, the National Military Museum is full of antique swords, armour and cannons, and recounts the days from 1700 to 1900, when the palace served as a Danish military installation. On the top floor is the **Hjemmefront** (Home Front) museum, devoted to Trondheim's role in the WWII resistance.

Trondheim Kunstmuseum   GALLERY

(☑73 53 81 80; trondheimkunstmuseum.no; Bispegata 7b; adult/child Nkr80/40; ⊙noon-4pm Tue-Sun) Trondheim's Art Museum, a stone's throw from the cathedral, houses a permanent collection of modern Norwegian and Danish art from 1800 onwards, including a hallway of Munch lithographs. It also runs temporary exhibitions.

Synagogue   SYNAGOGUE

(Arkitekt Christies gate 1b; museum admission Nkr30; ⊙10am-4pm Mon-Fri, noon-3pm Sun mid-Jun–mid-Aug) Trondheim's synagogue claims to be the world's northernmost. It has a small **museum** dedicated to the history of the local Jewish community, which was decimated by the Holocaust.

Museum of Natural History & Archaeology   MUSEUM

(Vitenskapsmuseet; www.vitenskapsmuseet.no; Erling Skakkes gate 47; adult/child Nkr60/free; ⊙10am-4pm Tue-Fri, 11am-4pm Sat & Sun) This museum belongs to the Norwegian University of Science & Technology (NTNU). There's a hotchpotch of exhibits on the natural and human history of the Trondheim area: streetscapes and homes, ecclesiastical history, archaeological excavations and southern Sami culture. More ordered is the small, alluring display in a side building devoted to church

history, and the fascinating everyday artefacts of the medieval section, covering Trondheim's history up to the great fire of 1681.

★ Stiftsgården   PALACE

(www.nkim.no/stiftsgarden; Munkegata 23; adult/child Nkr80/40; ⊙10am-5pm Mon-Sat, noon-5pm Sun Jun–late Aug, 10am-3pm Mon-Wed & Fri & Sat, noon-8pm Thu, noon-4pm Sun Sep–May) Scandinavia's largest wooden palace, the late-baroque Stiftsgården, was constructed as a private residence in the late 18th century, at the height of Trondheim's golden age. It is now the official royal residence in Trondheim. Admission is by tour only, every hour on the hour. The publicly accessible garden around the east side (enter via Dronningens gate) is one of Trondheim's loveliest corners.

Nordenfjeldske Kunstindustrimuseum   GALLERY

(Museum of Decorative Arts; www.nkim.no; Munkegata 5; adult/child Nkr80/40; ⊙10am-5pm Mon-Sat, noon-5pm Sun Jun–late Aug, 10am-3pm Mon-Wed & Fri & Sat, noon-8pm Thu, noon-4pm Sun Sep-May) The permanent collection of this splendid museum exhibits the best of Scandinavian design, including a couple of bijou art-nouveau rooms. A whole floor is devoted to the pioneering works of three acclaimed female artists: the tapestry creations of Hannah Ryggen and Synnøve Anker Aurdal, and the innovative glasswork of Benny Motzfeldt.

Kristiansten Fort   FORTRESS

(Festningsgata; ⊙guided tours noon & 2pm daily Jun-Aug) For a bird's-eye view of the city, climb 10 minutes from the Gamle Bybro to Kristiansten Fort, built after Trondheim's great fire of 1681. During WWII the Nazis used it as a prison and execution ground for members of the Norwegian Resistance. The grounds are open year-round, whenever the flag is raised.

Medieval Church Ruins   ARCHAEOLOGICAL REMAINS

During excavations for the library on Kongens gate, archaeologists found the ruins of a 12th-century church, thought to be **Olavskirken** (⊙10am-7pm Mon-Thu, 10am-6pm Fri, 11am-4pm Sat), now visible beneath the courtyard, together with the skeletons of two adults and a child.

In the basement of nearby Søndre gate 4 are the ruins of the medieval **Gregorius Kirke** (Sparebanken; ⊙8.15am-3pm Mon-Wed & Fri, 8.15am-5pm Thu), discovered during earlier excavations.

TROND-WHAT?

Listen to Trondheimers talk about their city, and you may wonder whether they're all referring to the same place.

Since the late Middle Ages, the city has been called Trondhjem, pronounced 'Trond-yem' and meaning, roughly, 'home of the good life'. But in the early 20th century the fledgling national government was bent on making Norwegian city names more historically Norwegian; just as Christiania reverted to its ancient name of Oslo, on 1 January 1930 Trondhjem was changed back to Nidaros.

Some 20,000 locals took to the streets in protest and by 6 March the government relented – sort of. The compromise was 'Trondheim', the etymologically Danish 'hj' having been duly exorcised.

Nowadays the official pronunciation is 'Trond-haym', but many locals still say 'Trond-yem'. Thanks to the vagaries of the local dialect, still others call it 'Trond-yahm'. Typical of this tolerant city, any of these pronunciations is acceptable, as is the 'Trond-hime' that most English speakers resort to.

Vitensenteret SCIENCE CENTRE
(www.vitensenteret.com; Kongens gate 1; adult/child Nkr75/45; ⏱10am-5pm Mon-Fri, 11am-5pm Sat & Sun late Jun–mid-Aug, 10am-4pm Mon-Fri, 11am-5pm Sat & Sun rest of year) Children especially will enjoy the hands-on experiments at this practical, active centre with over 150 models to choose from.

Modern Art Gallery GALLERY
(☑73 87 36 80; www.modernartgallery.no; Olav Tryggvasons gate 33; ⏱10am-6pm Mon-Fri, 10am-4pm Sat) FREE This small private gallery exhibits the work of modern Norwegian painters; most of what you see is for sale.

Trøndelag Senter for Samtidskunst GALLERY
(Trondelag Centre for Contemporary Art; ☑73 52 49 10; www.samtidskunst.no; Fjordgata 11; ⏱11am-4pm Wed-Fri, noon-4pm Sat & Sun) FREE Run by artists, this gallery space showcases all that's innovative and experimental in the local and national art scene. It won't be to everyone's taste, but it's a restless and endlessly creative exhibition space and it's always worth stopping by to see what's happening. There are free guided tours at 1pm on Sundays.

★Home of Rock MUSEUM
(www.rockheim.no; Brattørkaia 14; adult/child Nkr100/50; ⏱11am-7pm Tue-Fri, 11am-6pm Sat & Sun) This terrific museum is devoted to pop and rock music, mainly Norwegian, from the 1950s until yesterday. It's a dockside temple to R&B, where a huge projecting roof, featuring Norwegian record covers, extends above an equally vast converted warehouse. Within, there's plenty of action and interaction (mix your own hip-hop tape, for example). Home of Rock is on the quayside, very near Pirbadet and the fast-ferry landing stage.

Ringve Music Museum MUSEUM
(www.ringve.no; Lade Allé 60; adult/child/student & senior Nkr100/50/80; ⏱11am-4pm Tue-Sun) The Ringve Museum is Norway's national museum for music and musical instruments. The Russian-born owner was a devoted collector of rare and antique musical instruments, which music students demonstrate. You can also browse the old barn with its rich collection of instruments from around the world. The botanic gardens, set within the surrounding 18th-century estate, are a quiet green setting for a stroll. Take bus 3 or 4 and walk up the hill.

★Sverresborg Trøndelag Folkemuseum MUSEUM, ARCHITECTURE
(www.sverresborg.no; Sverresborg Allé 13; adult/child incl guided tour Nkr125/50; ⏱10am-5pm mid-May–Aug, 11am-3pm Mon-Fri, noon-4pm Sat & Sun rest of year) West of the centre, this folk museum is one of the best of its kind in Norway. The indoor exhibition, Livsbilder (Images of Life), displays artefacts in use over the last 150 years – from clothing to school supplies to bicycles – and has a short multimedia presentation. The rest of the museum, with over 60 period buildings, is open-air, adjoining the ruins of King Sverre's castle and giving fine hilltop views of the city.

Houses, the post office, the dentist and other shops splay around the central market square in the urban section. There are farm buildings from rural Trøndelag, the tiny 12th-century Haltdalen stave church and a

Trondheim

9

Havnegata

19

Pirterminalen Quay

Home of 2 **Rock**

Brattørkaia

Trondheim Sentralstasjon

Intercity Bus Terminal (Rutebilstasjon)

Trondheimfjord

Østre Kanalhavn

Ferries to Munkholmen

Fjordgata

20

16

22
45
Brattørgata

25
51
38
53
54

Vestre Kanalhavn

36

Olav Tryggvasonsgate

52

32

Søndre gate

AtB

10

Thomas Angells gate

30

Tourist Office

Dronningens gate

St Olavs gate

Prinsens gate

Stiftsgården

4

Nordre gate

21

5

14

Kjøpmannsgata

Sandgata

Tordenskiolds gate

24

47

42

18

Kongens gate

6

Torvet

7

Kongens gate

Munkegata

Sverresborg Trøndelag Folkemuseum (1.6km); Vertshuset Tavern (1.7km)

40

33

50

34

Gamle Bybro

11

Erling Skakkes gate

35

13

41

Nidaros Pilgrim Senter

KALVSKINNET

Prinsens gate

17

Bispegata

31

Nidaros 3 **Domkirke**

Gangbrua

Kongsgårdsgata

Archbishop's 1 **Palace**

12

Arkitekt Christies gate

15

Nidelva

Klostergata

Elgeseter Bru

Øvre Bakklandet

Mauritz Hansens gate

Klostergata

Elgesetergate

Christian Frederiks gate

46

couple of small museums devoted to telecommunications (some great old phones) and skiing (with elaborately carved wooden skis).

There are guided tours in Norwegian and English four times daily. Take bus 8 (direction Stavset) from Dronningens gate.

Munkholmen

ISLAND

During Trondheim's early years, the islet of Munkholmen (Monks' Island), 2km offshore, was the town execution ground. Over the centuries it has been the site of a Benedictine monastery, a prison, a fort and, finally, a customs house. Today, it's a popular picnic venue and has the city's best beach. From mid-May to early September, **ferries** (round trip adult/child Nkr80/40) leave at least hourly between 10am and 4pm or 6pm from beside the Ravnkloa Fish Market.

Historic Buildings & Neighbourhoods

From **Gamle Bybro** (Old Town Bridge) there's a superb view of the Bryggen, colourful 18th- and 19th-century riverfront warehouses similar to their better-known counterparts in Bergen. To the east, the one-time working-class neighbourhoods of **Møllenberg** and **Bakklandet** are now gentrified latte-land, all cobbles, car-free alleys, trim houses in pastel shades and gardens scarcely bigger than a towel that burst with flowers. Here, within old warehouses and renovated workers' housing, are some of the city's most colourful places to eat and drink.

The cobblestone streets immediately west of the centre are also lined with mid-19th-century wooden buildings, notably the octagonal 1705 timber church, **Hospitalkirken** (Hospitalsløkka 2-4), in the hospital grounds.

🏃 Activities

The free map, *Friluftsliv i Trondheimsregionen* (Outdoor Life in the Trondheim Region; text in Norwegian), available at the tourist office, shows nearby outdoor recreation areas and walking trails.

Hiking

Two easy strolls within town are the steep, but short, ascent through the traffic-free lanes of Bakklandet to Kristiansten Fort and the riverbank footpaths beside the Nidelva between Bakke Bru and Gangbrua bridges.

West of town spreads the Bymarka, a gorgeous green woodland area laced with wilderness footpaths and ski trails. Take the Gråkallbanen tram, in itself a lovely scenic ride through the leafy suburbs, from the St

TRØNDELAG TRONDHEIM

Trondheim

Olavsgata stop to **Lian**. There you can enjoy excellent views over the city and a good swimming lake, **Lianvannet**.

To the east of Trondheim, **Ladestien** (The Lade Trail) follows the shoreline of the Lade peninsula, beginning only 1km from the town centre.

Kayaking

Trondheim Kajakk KAYAKING
(☑ 48 33 83 18; trondheimkajakk.no; 2hr tour incl rental Nkr300-400) A fine way to get an alternative perspective on Trondheim, these kayak tours paddle from where the Nidelven River meets the fjord and then right through the old town. Prices vary with the number of people.

Skiing

The Vassfjellet mountains, south of town, offer both downhill and cross-country ski-ing. In season, a daily ski bus runs directly from Munkegata to the Vassfjellet Skisenter, only 8km beyond the city limits. The Bymarka also offers good cross-country skiing, as does the Trondheim Skisenter Granåsen, where the brave or foolhardy can launch themselves from the world's largest plastic-surfaced ski jump.

Swimming

Pirbadet SWIMMING POOL
(☑ 73 83 18 00; pirbadet.no; Havnegata 12; adult/child Nkr140/115; ⊙ 6.30am-8pm Mon, Wed & Fri, 10am-8pm Tue & Thu, 10am-6pm Sat & Sun late-Jun–mid-Aug, shorter hours rest of year) On the Pirterminalen quay, Pirbadet is Norway's largest indoor water park with a wealth of liquid pleasures, including a wave pool, sauna and 100m water slide.

☞ Tours

Walking Tours   WALKING TOURS
(tours Nkr170; ⏰2pm daily late Jun–mid-Aug, 2pm
Sat rest of year) Two-hour guided tours in English and Norwegian.

Tripps   BOAT TOURS
(☎95 08 21 44; www.trippsbatservice.no; adult/
child Nkr170/60; ⏰cruises noon & 2.30pm Tue-
Sun Jul–mid-Aug, noon Thu-Sun mid-May–Jun &
mid-Aug–Sep) Tripps runs a 1½-hour cruise
along the estuary of the River Nidelva and
out into the fjord. Departures are from beside the Ravnkloa Fish Market and you buy
your ticket on the boat.

🎉 Festivals & Events

ISFIT   STUDENT
(www.isfit.org; ⏰Feb-Mar) A student-mounted
international youth gathering with participants from over 100 countries. Altogether
more serious in tone and intent than UKA,
but has plenty of concerts and events to
occupy the leisure hours. In February or
March in odd-numbered years.

Kosmorama   FILM
(www.kosmorama.no; ⏰Apr-May) Trondheim's
international film festival occupies an intensive week in late April, often spilling over
into early May.

Nidaros Blues Festival   MUSIC
(www.nidarosbluesfestival.com; ⏰Apr) A who's
who of the international blues scene with
local acts as well.

Olavsfestdagene   CULTURAL
(www.olavsfestdagene.no; ⏰Jul-Aug) In honour
of St Olav and held during the week around
his saint's day, 29 July. There's a medieval
market and a rich program of classical music, folk, pop and jazz.

Trøndelag Food Festival   FOOD
(⏰Jul-Aug) Coincides with Olavsfestdagene.
Stalls selling local fare pack Kongens gate,
east of Torvet.

Pstereo   MUSIC
(pstereo.net; ⏰Aug) Major pop and rock festival over a weekend in late August, with up to
300 performers descending on Trondheim.

UKA   CULTURAL
(www.uka.no; ⏰Oct-Nov) Trondheim's 25,000
university students stage this three-week
celebration, Norway's largest cultural festival. Every other year (in odd-numbered

years) in October and November, it's a continuous party with concerts, plays and other
festivities based at the round, red Studentersamfundet (Student Centre).

🛏 Sleeping

★Pensjonat Jarlen   GUESTHOUSE €
(☎73 51 32 18; www.jarlen.no; Kongens gate 40;
s/d Nkr540/690; 🛜) Price, convenience and
value for money are a winning combination
here. After a recent overhaul, the rooms at
this central spot have a contemporary look
and are outstanding value, although some
bathrooms could do with a fresh look. Some
rooms have polished floorboards, others
carpet, and most have a hot plate and fridge
thrown in.

Flakk Camping   CAMPGROUND €
(☎72 84 39 00; www.flakk-camping.no; car/cara-
van site Nkr220/300, cabins Nkr490-650; ⏰May-
Aug; 🅿) Sitting right beside Trondheimfjord
(there's minimal disturbance from the nearby ferry point), this welcoming campground
is about 10km from the city centre. Take
Rv715 from Trondheim.

Singsaker Sommerhotel   HOTEL €
(☎73 89 32 29; sommerhotell.singsaker.no; Ro-
gertsgata 1; dm/s/d Nkr260/749/889, s/d with
shared bathroom Nkr499/699; ⏰mid-Jun–mid-
Aug; 🅿) On a grassy knoll in a quiet residential neighbourhood, this imposing building
was originally built as a club for occupying
German officers. It represents great value.
Bus 63 from the train station passes by. If
driving, take Klostergata eastwards from the
Studentersamfundet and follow the signs.

Rica Nidelven Hotel   HOTEL €€
(☎73 56 80 00; www.rica.no; Havnegata 1-3; r
Nkr945-1695; 🅿@🛜) A fabulous waterside
location next to Solsiden and within a
five-minute walk of the old part of town,
this stylish hotel has attractive rooms, all
343 of them, and many have river views.
The hotel won the prize for Norway's best
hotel breakfast, which is reason enough to
stay here.

Britannia Hotel   HOTEL €€
(☎73 80 08 00; www.britannia.no; Dronningens
gate 5; s/d from Nkr506/806; 🅿❄@🛜🏊) This
mammoth hotel with nearly 250 rooms was
constructed in 1897 and in 2013 became part
of the Thon Hotel chain. It still exudes old-
world grace from the mellow, wooden pan-
elling of public areas to the magnificent oval
Moorish-revival Palmehaven restaurant –

but one of three places to eat – with its Corinthian pillars and central fountain. Rooms have a graceful, classical charm.

Clarion Collection Hotel
Grand Olav
HOTEL €€

(☑73 80 80 80; www.nordicchoicehotels.no; Kjøpmannsgata 48; r from Nkr1190; @ ☎) The Clarion offers sleek luxurious living above an airy shopping complex and the Olavshallen concert hall. It has 27 different styles among more than 100 rooms, so no guest can complain of a lack of choice.

Radisson Blu Royal Garden Hotel
HOTEL €€

(☑73 80 30 00; www.radissonblu.com; Kjøpmannsgata 73; s/d from Nkr795/995; P ✳ @ ☎ ☎) This first-class, contemporary riverside hotel (you can fish from your window in some rooms) is open and airy from the moment you step into the atrium, where the light streams in through the all-glass walls.

P-Hotel
HOTEL €€

(☑73 80 23 50; www.p-hotels.no; Nordre gate 24; s/d from Nkr595/795; @ ☎) This slick, modern hotel, part of an expanding Norwegian minichain, has 49 spruce rooms, each with a beverage-making kit, that speak of good Scandinavian style. Someone pads by in the early morning and hangs your breakfast bag on the door. There's a washing machine for guest use.

Chesterfield Hotel
HOTEL €€

(☑73 50 37 50; www.bestwestern.no; Søndre gate 26; s/d from Nkr695/895; @ ☎) All 43 rooms at this venerable hotel are spacious. They were decorated and fundamentally renovated, with fresh beds and furniture, in 2006 following a major fire in the adjacent building and they've aged well. Those on the 7th (top) floor have huge skylights with broad city views.

THE PILGRIMS' WAY

Nidaros Cathedral was built on the site of the grave of St Olav, who was canonised and declared a martyr after his death at the Battle of Stiklestad on 29 July 1030. The cult of St Olav quickly grew in popularity and as many as 340 churches were dedicated to the saint in Scandinavia, Britain, Russia, the Baltic states, Poland, Germany and the Netherlands. Pilgrims from all over Europe journeyed to his grave at Nidaros, making it the most popular pilgrimage site in northern Europe. Historically, both rich and poor journeyed from Oslo for up to 25 days, while others braved longer sea voyages from Iceland, Greenland, Orkney and the Faroe Islands. St Olav's grave became the northern compass point for European pilgrims; the other spiritual compass points were Rome in the south, Jerusalem in the east and Santiago de Compostela in the west.

As pilgrims travelled from village to village, their routes became arteries for the spread of the cult of St Olav. The pilgrims' way, with wild mountains, forests and rivers to cross, certainly gave plenty of opportunity to reflect upon the hardships of life's journey towards eternity. Most pilgrims travelled on foot, while the better off journeyed on horseback. Those without means relied on local hospitality; pilgrims were held in high esteem and openly welcomed.

In 1997 the Pilgrims' Way – 926km in all, counting alternative sections – was inaugurated, reviving the ancient pilgrimage route between Oslo and Trondheim. The rugged route, mainly mountain tracks and gravelled roads, has been blazed (look for the logo: the cross of St Olav intertwined with the quatrefoil knot indicating a tourist attraction, which you see everywhere). It follows, wherever practicable, ancient documented trails. Along the trail are signs indicating place names and monuments linked to the life and works of St Olav, as well as ancient burial mounds and other historic monuments.

In Trondheim, the **Nidaros Pilgrim Senter** (☑73 52 50 00; www.pilegrimsgarden.no; Kjøpmannsgata 1; per bed with/without breakfast Nkr400/350; ☒9am-5pm Mon-Fri) is the place to go to get your pilgrim pass stamped and receive the Olavsletter, the certificate stating that you have walked at least 100km of the pilgrimage route. They also offer simple accommodation for pilgrims.

For more information, check pilegrimsleden.no.

The Pilgrim Road to Nidaros – a Trekker's Guidebook by Alison Raju, published by Cicerone Press, is an indispensable, well-written guide if, whether pilgrim or hiker, you're thinking of taking on a stretch.

✕ Eating

Trondheim has plenty of lovely cafes for a light meal, coffee and cake. Some stay open at night and turn into lively pubs. For self-caterers, there's a grand little open-air fruit and veg market on Torvet each morning.

★ Ravnkloa Fish Market SEAFOOD €

(☏73 52 55 21; www.ravnkloa.no; Munkegata; snacks from Nkr45, mains Nkr150-185; ⏲10am-5pm Mon-Fri, 10am-4pm Sat) Everything looks good at this fish market that doubles as a cafe with quayside tables out front. The fish cakes are fabulous and they also do shrimp sandwiches, mussels and a fine fish soup. In addition to seafood, they sell an impressive range of cheeses and other gourmet goods.

Fairytale Cupcakes NORWEGIAN, INTERNATIONAL €

(☏40 05 61 08; www.fairytalecupcakes.no; Thomas Angells gate 10b; light meals from Nk159, 1/4/6 cupcakes Nkr39/150/210; ⏲10am-6pm Mon-Sat) Cupcakes seemed to be such a passing fad that we didn't expect this place to last. But, thankfully, we were wrong. Its survival has everything to do with a perfectly manicured space, some of Trondheim's best *smørbrød* (open sandwiches) and, yes, cupcakes.

Jordbær Pikene CAFE €

(☏73 92 91 80; www.jordbarpikene.no; cnr Erling Skakkes gate & Prinsens gate; mains Nkr129-179; ⏲9am-8pm Mon-Fri, 9am-6pm Sat) 'Strawberry Girls' serves up pasta, salads and sandwiches in an informal, congenial setting. It's good for juices, too. You won't find anything particularly original, but you will enjoy decent, reliable, well-priced cooking.

Café ni Muser CAFE €

(www.nimuser.no; Bispegata 9; light meals & snacks from Nkr79; ⏲11am-11pm) The cafe at the Trondheim Kunstmuseum has inexpensive meals and an arty crowd. On sunny afternoons, the outdoor terrace turns into a beer garden.

Persilleriet VEGETARIAN €

(☏73 60 60 14; persilleriet.no; Erling Skakkes gate 39; lunch from Nkr128; ⏲11am-7pm Mon-Fri, 2-6pm Sat; ✎) This tiny, lunchtime-only box of a place does tasty vegetarian fare, to eat in or take away. The menu changes regularly and the cuisine is eclectic. On any day it may include, for example, elements of Thai, Middle Eastern or Mexican dishes.

★ Baklandet Skydsstasjon NORWEGIAN €€

(☏73 92 10 44; www.skydsstation.no; Øvre Bakklandet 33; mains Nkr138-245; ⏲11am-1am Mon-

Fri, noon-1am Sat & Sun) Within what began life as an 18th-century coaching inn are several cosy rooms with poky angles and listing floors. It's a hyperfriendly place where you can tuck into tasty dishes, such as its renowned fish soup ('the best in all Norway', a couple of diners assured us), or the lunchtime herring buffet (Nkr178) from Thursday to Saturday. Always leave room for a homemade cake.

Søstrene Karlsen NORWEGIAN, INTERNATIONAL €€

(☏73 60 00 25; www.sostrenekarlsen.no; Tmv-kaia 25; lunch mains Nkr135-239, dinner mains Nkr173-358; ⏲11am-midnight Mon-Thu, 11am-2am Fri & Sat, noon-11pm Sun) Despite the irresistible energy of the Solsiden waterfront area, most of the restaurants are of the chain variety – people tend to come here for the atmosphere rather than the quality of the food. Søstrene Karlsen is a cut above the rest and is wildly popular as a result. There's everything from sandwiches to more substantial mains of the usual fish and meat variety.

Bari ITALIAN €€

(☏73 60 60 24; www.bari.no; Munkegata 25; lunch mains from Nkr129, dinner mains Nkr155-215; ⏲11pm-midnight Mon-Thu, 11am-2am Fri & Sat) Eat in the stylish, modern, jazzy interior or choose the small streetside terrace. Bari has a reputation for good Italian fare (pasta and bruschetta), as well as superior burgers.

Frati MEDITERRANEAN €€

(☏73 52 57 33; www.frati.no; 1st fl, Munkegata 25; pasta from Nkr150, pizza from Nkr129, mains Nkr199-290; ⏲3-11pm Mon-Fri, 2-11pm Fri & Sat) Upstairs from Bari and under the same ownership, Frati's decor is all varnished wood, browns and darker hues. There are plenty of pasta choices here, as well as a carefully selected range of antipasto to get you going.

★ Vertshuset Tavern NORWEGIAN €€€

(☏73 87 80 70; www.tavern.no; Sverresborg Allé 11; mains Nkr165-285; ⏲4-9pm Mon, 4-10pm Tue-Fri, 2-10pm Sat, 2-9pm Sun) Once in the heart of Trondheim, this historic (1739) tavern was lifted and transported, every last plank of it, to the Sverresborg Trøndelag Folkemuseum on the outskirts of town. Tuck into its rotating specials of traditional Norwegian fare or just graze on waffles with coffee in one of its 16 tiny rooms, each low-beamed, with sloping floors, candlesticks, cast-iron stoves and lacy tablecloths.

Havfruen
SEAFOOD €€€

(📞73 87 40 70; www.havfruen.no; Kjøpmannsgata 7; 3-/4-/5-course set menus Nkr498/548/598, mains from Nkr275, bar light meals from Nkr90; ⏱6pm-midnight Mon-Sat) This character-filled riverside restaurant, all odd-angled pillars and rickety beams, specialises in the freshest of fish. The quality, reflected in the prices, is excellent, as are the accompanying wines, selected by the resident sommelier. The short menu changes regularly according to what's hauled in from the seas. The attached bar next door is less formal.

To Rom
og Kjøkken
NORWEGIAN €€€

(📞73 56 89 00; www.toromogkjokken.no; Carl Johans gate 5; mains Nkr285-365; ⏱4pm-1am Mon-Thu, 4pm-2am Fri & Sat) At Two Rooms & a Kitchen, service is friendly. The ambience, with original, changing artwork on the walls, is bright and brisk, and dishes range from riesling-poached salmon to pan-fried monkfish. Ingredients are sourced locally, wherever feasible. For a sample of its subtle cuisine with a less formidable price tag, savour its daily bar special (Nkr169).

🍸 Drinking & Nightlife

As a student town, Trondheim offers lots of through-the-night life. The free papers, *Natt & Dag* and *Plan B,* have listings, mostly in Norwegian. Solsiden (Sunnyside) is Trondheim's trendiest leisure zone. A whole wharfside of bars and restaurants nestles beneath smart new apartment blocks, converted warehouses and long-idle cranes.

There's a cluster of nightclubs at the northern end of Nordre gate.

★Den Gode Nabo
PUB

(www.dengodenabo.com; Øvre Bakklandet 66; ⏱4pm-1.30am Sun-Fri, 1pm-1.30am Sat) The Good Neighbour, dark and cavernous within, and nominated more than once as Norway's best pub, enjoys a prime riverside location. Indeed, part of it is on the water; reserve a table on the floating pontoon. There's a reproduction Wurlitzer jukebox; US visitors will find Sam Adams on tap while UK ale connoisseurs can savour Shepherd Neame's Bishop's Finger in the bottle.

★Trondheim Microbryggeri
PUB

(Prinsens gate 39; ⏱5pm-midnight Mon, 3pm-2am Tue-Fri, noon-2am Sat) This splendid home-brew pub deserves a pilgrimage as reverential as anything accorded to St Olav from all committed øl (beer) quaffers. With up to eight of its own brews on tap and good light meals coming from the kitchen, it's a place to linger, nibble and tipple. It's down a short lane, just off Prinsens gate.

Dromedar Kaffebar
CAFE

(Nedre Bakklandet 3; ⏱7am-6pm Mon-Fri, 10am-6pm Sat & Sun) This longstanding local self-service coffee favourite serves what could be Trondheim's best coffee indeed, in all sizes, squeezes and strengths. Inside is cramped so, if the weather permits, relax on the exterior terrace bordering the cobbled street. There's a second **branch** (Nørdre gate 2), similar in style, also with a street-side terrace, that serves equally aromatic coffee, with further branches elsewhere around town.

Bare Blåbær
BAR

(📞73 53 30 32; www.barebb.no; Innherredsveien 16; ⏱11am-1.30am Sun-Thu, 11am-2.30am Fri & Sat) Join the throng that packs both the interior and dockside terrace of this popular place over near the Solsiden waterfront area. It's renowned for its cocktails, shorts and juleps – and for preparing what many believe to be the finest pizzas in town, including the intriguing *chili bollocks* (presumably a wintertime special).

Bruk Bar
BAR

(Prinsens gate 19; ⏱noon-1am Mon-Thu, noon-2am Fri & Sat, 1pm-midnight Sun) Inside, a stuffed elk head gazes benignly down, candles flicker and designer lamps shed light onto the 30-or-so-year-olds who patronise this welcoming joint. The music is eclectic, varying at the whim of bar staff, but guaranteed to be loud.

Løkka
BAR

(Dokkgata 8; ⏱11am-1am Mon-Sat, noon-midnight Sun) Long before its latest makeover, Løkka was a boat repair workshop. It now carries a good range of beers, on draught and in bottle, and also does milkshakes. It's more an early evening venue than a serious late-night drinking den.

Macbeth
BAR

(Søndre gate 22b; ⏱3pm-midnight Sun-Tue, 3pm-1am Wed & Thu, 3pm-2am Fri) Homesick Scots will feel at home, Geordies with nostalgia can weep into their draught Newcastle Brown, and the rest of us can watch big-screen football or car racing. Enjoy a dram or two of its more than a dozen single-malt whiskies...

Studentersamfundet

BAR

(Student Centre; samfundet.no; Elgesetergate 1) During the academic year, this place has 10 lively bars, a cinema and frequent live music, while in summer it's mostly a travellers' crash pad.

☆ Entertainment

Dokkhuset

CULTURAL CENTRE

(www.dokkhuset.no; Dokkparken 4; ⊙ 11am-1am Mon-Thu, 11am-3am Fri & Sat, 1pm-1am Sun) In an artistically converted former pumping station (look through the glass beneath your feet at the old engines), the Dock House is at once auditorium (where if it's the right night you'll hear experimental jazz or chamber music), restaurant and cafe-bar. Sip a drink on the jetty or survey the Trondheim scene from its roof terrace.

Olavshallen

CONCERT HALL

(☑ 73 99 40 50; www.olavshallen.no; Kjøpmannsgata 44) Trondheim's main concert hall is within the Olavskvartalet cultural centre. The home base of the Trondheim Symphony Orchestra, it also features international rock and jazz concerts, mostly between September and May.

Trøndelag Teater

THEATRE

(☑ 73 80 51 00; trondelag-teater.no; Prinsens gate 18-20) Constructed in 1816 and handsomely refurbished, this theatre stages large-scale dance and musical performances and also more intimate theatre.

🛍 Shopping

Moods of Norway

FASHION

(☑ 92 42 57 22; www.moodsofnorway.com; Olav Trygvassonsgate 29; ⊙ 10am-6pm Mon-Wed, Fri & Sat, 10am-7pm Thu) The quirky fashions of this stunning Norwegian success story make a virtue out of eccentricity. Bright colours and harmless fun are recurring themes.

Ting

HOMEWARES

(☑ 45 20 07 00; www.ting.no; Olav Trygvasonsgate 10; ⊙ 10am-6pm Mon-Sat) Modern designer homewares dominate this funky shop – it's all about Scandinavian cool without an outrageous price tag. A couple of doors up, Småting (☑ 47 48 92 88; www.ting.no; Olav Trygvasonsgate 6; ⊙ 10am-6pm Mon-Sat), run by the same people, brings the same creative eye to children's toys.

Husfliden

CLOTHING, HANDICRAFTS

(www.norskflid.no; Olav Trygvasonsgate 18; ⊙ 9am-6pm Mon-Fri, 9am-4pm Sat) Need a bunda for Norwegian national day? Or simply on the lookout for a traditional Norwegian gift? Husfliden is your place.

ℹ Information

Library (Kongens gate; ⊙ 10am-7pm Mon-Thu, 10am-6pm Fri, 11am-4pm Sat) Free internet access. Carries international press.

Tourist office (☑ 73 80 76 60; www.visittrondheim.no; Nordre gate 11; ⊙ 9am-6pm daily mid-Jun–mid-Aug, 9am-6pm Mon-Sat rest of year) In the heart of the city with an accommodation booking service.

ℹ Getting There & Away

AIR

Værnes airport is 32km east of Trondheim. There are flights to all major Norwegian cities, as well as Copenhagen and Stockholm. Norwegian flies to/from London (Gatwick) and KLM covers Amsterdam.

BOAT

Trondheim is a major stop on the Hurtigruten coastal ferry route. Express passenger boats between Trondheim and Kristiansund (3½ hours) depart from the Pirterminalen quay up to three times daily.

BUS

The intercity bus terminal (Rutebilstasjon) adjoins Trondheim Sentralstasjon (train station, also known as Trondheim S).

As the main link between southern and northern Norway, Trondheim is a bus transport crossroads. Nor-Way Bussekspress services run up to three times daily to/from the following:

Ålesund (Nkr587, seven hours, two to three daily)

Bergen (Nkr848, 14½ hours) One overnight bus.

Namsos (Nkr398, 3½ hours) Via Steinkjer (Nkr315, 2¼ hours).

If you're travelling by public transport to Narvik and points north, it's quicker – all is relative – to take the train to Fauske or Bodø (the end of the line), then continue by bus.

TRAIN

There are two to four trains daily to/from Oslo (Nkr899, 6½ hours). Two head north to Bodø (Nkr1059, 9¾ hours) via the following:

Fauske (Nkr1018, 9¼ hours)

Mo i Rana (Nkr847, 7½ hours)

Mosjøen (Nkr763, 5½ hours)

A minipris ticket will considerably undercut these standard prices.

You can also train it to Steinkjer (Nkr217, two hours, hourly).

> **ℹ️ PARKING IN CENTRAL TRONDHEIM**
>
> The city's parking meters in the centre of town can quickly gobble up your holiday money. However, during school summer vacation (ie from mid- to late June to the middle of August), Trondheim Katedralskole lets both cars and campervans park in its playground for Nkr100 per day (7.30am to 9pm). The parking area is open from 8am to 3.30pm from Monday to Saturday (closed Sunday). Check with the tourist office for the latest.

ℹ️ Getting Around

TO/FROM THE AIRPORT

Flybussen (www.flybussen.no; one-way/return Nkr130/220, 35 to 45 minutes) runs every 15 minutes from 4am to 9pm (less frequently at weekends), stopping at major landmarks such as the train station, Studentersamfundet and Britannia Hotel.

Trains run between Trondheim Sentralstasjon and the Værnes airport station (Nkr74, 30 to 40 minutes, half-hourly).

BICYCLE

As befits such a cycle-friendly city, Trondheim has a bike-hire scheme (Nkr50 per day). Pick up a card at the tourist office in return for a refundable deposit of Nkr200 or €25, then borrow a bike from any of the 12 cycle stations around town. You then return the bike to one of the stations, and return the card to the tourist office to claim back your deposit.

Other cycle-friendly measures include clear signing of cycle routes, often traffic-free and shared with pedestrians, a lane of smooth flagstones along cobbled streets that would otherwise uncomfortably judder your and the bike's moving parts – and Trampe, the world's only bike lift, a low-tech piece of engineering to which cyclists heading from the Gamle Bybro up the Brubakken hill to Kristiansten Fort can hitch themselves.

CAR & MOTORCYCLE

If you're driving, be careful not to stray into the right-hand lanes, which are reserved for taxis and buses.

PUBLIC TRANSPORT

The city bus service, run by **AtB** (www.atb.no), has its central transit point (all lines stop at or near it) on the corner of Munkegata and Dronningens gate. Buses and trams cost Nkr30 per ride (Nkr70 for a day card). You'll need the exact change.

Trondheim's tram line, the Gråkalbanen, runs west from St Olavsgata to Lian, in the heart of the Bymarka. Antique trolleys trundle along this route on Saturdays in summer. Transfers are available from city buses.

TAXI

To call a cab, ring **Trønder Taxi** (☎ 07373) or **Norgestaxi** (☎ 08000).

THE ROUTE NORTH

Hell, Norway's most cherished battleground and a string of intriguing coastal settlements occupy northern Trøndelag. Then, at the point where Norway narrows and heads for the Arctic, you've a choice of two routes north from Steinkjer: the more frequented, inland Arctic Highway (E6) or the slower E17 Kystriksveien (Coastal Route). The railway line north to Bodø via Hell and Steinkjer more or less follows the Arctic Highway to Fauske.

Stiklestad

It's difficult to overstate the importance of Stiklestad in Norwegian history. It was here, on 29 July 1030 that the larger and better-equipped forces of local feudal, pagan chieftains defeated a force of barely 100 men led by the Christian King Olav Haraldsson, who had been forced from the Norwegian throne by King Knut (Canute) of Denmark and England.

The Battle of Stiklestad marks Norway's passage between the Viking and medieval eras. Although Olav was killed, the battle is generally lauded as a victory for Christianity in Norway and the slain hero is recalled as a martyr and saint. St Olav developed a following all over northern Europe and his grave in Trondheim's Nidaros Cathedral became a destination for pilgrims from across the continent.

The site, around most of which you can wander for free, is laid out rather like a sprawling theme park, with exhibits on the Battle of Stiklestad, an outdoor folk museum and, predating all, the 12th-century Stiklestad church.

👁 Sights

The **Stiklestad National Cultural Centre** (Stiklestad Nasjonale Kultursenter; www.stiklestad. no; adult/child Nkr160/80; ⏱ 9am-6pm Sep-Jun, 9am-8pm Jul & Aug) is a grandiose wooden structure. Entry entitles you to visit **Stiklestad 1030**, an evocative exhibition about the battle, with dioramas and plenty of shrieks and gurgles on the soundtrack; a 15-minute film on St Olav; a guided tour that includes a visit to the church; and a small WWII resistance museum.

In the grounds there's a collection of over 30 historical buildings (admission free), ranging from humble crofts and artisans workshops to the **Molåna**, a much grander farmhouse and, within it, a small, summertime cafe. In summer, actors in period costume bring several of the buildings to life.

Across the road is lovely Stiklestad **church** (⊙11am-6pm Mon-Sat, 12.30-6pm Sun mid-Jun–mid-Aug), built between 1150 and 1180 above the stone on which the dying St Olav reputedly leaned. The original stone was believed to have healing powers but it was removed during the Reformation and hasn't been seen since.

✹✹ Festivals & Events

Every year during the week leading up to St Olav's Day (29 July) Stiklestad hosts the **St Olav Festival** with a medieval market, lots of wannabe Vikings in costume and a host of other activities. The high point of the festival is an outdoor pageant (held over the last five days) dramatising the conflicts between the king and local farmers and chieftains. Some of Norway's top actors and actresses traditionally take the major roles while locals play minor parts and swell the crowd scenes.

🛏 Sleeping & Eating

Rica Stiklestad Hotel HOTEL €€
(📿74 04 42 00; www.rica.no; r Nkr800-1250; P ❊ ⑳) Inside the Stiklestad National Cultural Centre, this fine addition to the Rica chain has rooms that combine a contemporary look (think dark tones and parquetry floors) with symbolism from the Stiklestad story. There's also a restaurant in the complex.

❶ Getting There & Away

The site of Stiklestad lies 5km east of the E6 on Rv757.

Steinkjer

POP 21.555
Medieval sagas speak of Steinkjer as a major trading centre and indeed it continues to be a crossroads of the two major routes to the north.

There's little here to hold your attention, aside from the town's main attraction, its **Egge Museum** (www.eggemuseum.no; Fylkesmannsgården; adult/child Nkr60/free; ⊙10am-4pm mid-Jun–mid-Aug), an open-air farm complex 2.5km north of town. On the same hilltop site are several Viking burial mounds and stone circles.

🛏 Sleeping & Eating

Føllingstua CAMPGROUND €
(📿74 14 71 90; www.follingstua.com; E6, Følling; car/caravan sites Nkr220/240, cabins Nkr600-1380, s/d with shared bathroom Nkr530/650) Beside the E6, 14km north of Steinkjer, near the Snåsavatnet lake's southwestern end, this lovely, welcoming camping ground may tempt you to linger for a day or two, fish in the lake or rent one of its boats and canoes (Nkr200 per day).

Tingvold Park Hotel HOTEL €€
(📿74 14 11 00; www.tingvoldhotel.no; Gamle Kongeveien 47; s/d from Nkr1070/1270; P @ ⑳) Beside an old Viking burial site, this secluded, good-value option is a member of the Best Western group. Overlooking Steinkjer, it has a pleasant lawn and garden.

Brod & Cirkus RESTAURANT €€€
(📿74 16 21 00; www.brodogcirkus.no; Sannagata 8; mains from Nkr260, 3-course meals Nkr475; ⊙11am-4pm Tue-Fri, from 6pm Wed-Sat) ✐ Meat, fish and shellfish are all sourced locally here at this fine restaurant, and bread and desserts are all created on the premises. It's one block east of main Kongens gate, behind the Statens Hus.

❶ Information

Steinkjer's **tourist office** (📿74 40 17 16; www.visitinnherred.com; Sjøfartsgata 2a; ⊙9am-8pm Mon-Fri, 10am-7pm Sat, noon-7pm Sun mid-Jun–mid-Aug, 9am-4pm Mon-Fri rest of year) is beside the E6, opposite the Amfi shopping centre. From the train station take the foot tunnel. Doubling as the Kystriksveien Info-Center, it can book accommodation in town and along the coastal route. It also rents bikes (per hour/day Nkr60/175).

Around Steinkjer

Leaving Steinkjer, the E6 follows the north shore of the 45km-long, needle-thin lake **Snåsavatnet**, bordered by majestic evergreen forests. You may prefer to take the Rv763 along the quieter southern shore to see the **Bølarein**, a 5000- to 6000-year-old rock carving of a reindeer and several other incised carvings.

Namsos

POP 12,988

Namsos is the first port town of consequence on the northbound coastal route between Trondheim and Bodø; it makes a pleasant overnight stop and has a few interesting diversions.

⊙ Sights

Lysstøperiet   CANDLE FACTORY

(✔74 21 29 00; Finn Christiansens Vei 14; ⊙10am-5pm Mon-Fri, 11am-3pm Sat) FREE Geir Arne Opdahl and Mona Nordfjellmark have converted a former train shed into an artisan-scale candle factory where they fashion around 15 tonnes of prime-quality paraffin wax each year into pumpkins and peppers, boots, cats, flowers, and candles all colours of the rainbow.

Rock City   MUSEUM

(✔95 08 49 39; www.rockcity.no; adult/child Nkr100/50; ⊙5-9pm Sun-Fri, 4.30-6pm Sat) The large white cube under construction is a temple to rock and roll – and homage to the disproportionately large numbers of artists from Namsos who have made it big on the Scandinavian popular-music scene.

Norsk Sagbruksmuseum   MUSEUM

(Norwegian Sawmill Museum; ✔74 27 13 00; sagbruksmuseet.no; Linbergvegen 16, Spillum; adult/child Nkr50/free; ⊙9am-3pm Mon-Fri) If you're interested in wood chopping and chipping, take a guided tour around this tribute to an

important local industry. Over the bridge, 4km east of town, the museum commemorates Norway's first steam-powered sawmill (1853).

Namdalsmuseet   FOLK MUSEUM

(✔74 36 07 90; Kjærlighetstien 1; adult/child Nkr40/free; ⊙noon-4pm Tue-Sun mid-Jun–mid-Aug, 8am-3.30pm Mon-Fri rest of year) Namdal Museum has displays on local history, including the typical wooden sailing boats of the area, and is – hold on to your hat – 'Norway's only museum featuring exhibits of hospital equipment presented in chronological order'. Love it.

🏃 Activities

Bjørumsklumpen   VIEWPOINT

An easy scenic 20-minute walk up Kirkegata from the centre will take you to the lookout atop the prominent loaf-shaped rock (114m) with good views over Namsfjorden, Namsos and its environs. About a third of the way up, a sign identifies a track leading to some impressive WWII Nazi bunkers hewn from solid rock.

Trolley Ride   TROLLEY RIDE

(s Nkr300, up to 4 riders Nkr400) For exercise and for the sake of nostalgia, you can hire a trolley from Namsos Camping and trundle it for 17km along the disused railway line between Namsos and Skage as it follows the gentle River Nansen.

Oasen   SWIMMING

(www.oasen-namsos.no; Jarle Hildrums veg; adult/child Nkr115/50; ⊙9am-8pm Mon-Fri, 10am-4pm Sat & Sun) About 1km east of town and built deep inside the mountain, this swimming hall has three heated pools and a 37m water slide.

🛏 Sleeping & Eating

Namsos Camping   CAMPGROUND €

(✔74 27 53 44; www.namsos-camping.no; tents/caravans Nkr200/250, 4-bed cabins with outdoor bathroom Nkr400-475, with private bathroom Nkr800-1050) This superior campground has a large kitchen and dining room, playground and minigolf. Basic cabins are a bargain and the more expensive ones are well equipped. Alongside is a shallow lake that's ideal for children, who'll also enjoy the go-karts and communing with the squirrels. From Namsos, take Rv17, direction Grong, then follow the airport signs.

GO TO HELL

It may be a cliché but who hasn't been tempted to pull over and snap a photo of themselves under the sign at Hell train station? If you give in to the temptation – and, hell, we have – you'll have the perfect riposte whenever someone tells you to go to hell. I've already been, you can reply, to Hell *and* back... Trondheim's Værnes airport is next door, but clearly naming Trondheim's main portal Hell International Airport was a road too far for the Norwegian authorities. For the record, the town's name means 'prosperity' in Norwegian.

WORTH A TRIP

LEKA

You won't regret taking a short side-trip to the wild and beautiful island of Leka (pop 556); for hikers, the desertlike Wild West landscape is particularly enchanting. This prime habitat for the white-tailed sea eagle (hold on to your little ones; in 1932, a three-year-old girl was snatched away by a particularly cheeky specimen) also has several Viking burial mounds and Stone Age rock paintings.

Bed down at **Leka Motell og Camping** (☑74 39 98 23; www.leka-camp.no; tent/caravan sites Nkr130/230, d/q with bathroom & kitchen Nkr700/900). For comfort, reserve one of its well-equipped, reasonably priced motel rooms. For something different and more spartan, hire a sod-roofed stone hut (Nkr400), sleeping up to four in bunk beds.

Leka is accessed by an hourly ferry from Gutvik, a 20-minute drive from the Rv17 coastal road.

Børstad Hotel
HOTEL **€€**

(☑74 21 80 90; Carl Gulbransons gate 19; s/d Nkr1050/1250; ☏) Bright and friendly, this 19-room hotel has large sunny rooms and a pleasant outdoor garden. There's a cosy lounge, and the huge oak dining table (over a century old and at which breakfast is served) was once used for company board meetings.

Tino's Hotell
HOTEL **€€**

(☑74 21 80 00; www.tinoshotell.no; Verftsgata 5; s/d from Nkr995/1200; ⊙restaurant noon-11pm) Rooms are large and comfortable at this hotel, just a stone's throw from the waterside. Tino, the owner, who is as Italian as they come despite many years in Norway, runs a great **restaurant** (pasta & pizzas from Nkr130, mains Nkr245-280) that serves both international food and fine Italian cuisine (such as 24 varieties of pizza), a continent away from Norway's usual pizza and pasta joints.

Shopping

Aakervik
FOOD

(cnr Havnegata & Herlaugs gate 16; ⊙9am-4.30pm Mon-Sat) This gourmet food shop is a great place to buy wild salmon and other fish, reindeer, roe deer and elk. The interior is a mini-menagerie of stuffed animals and birds eyeing you glassily from all angles; pay your respects to the amiable brown bear.

❶ Information

Tourist Office (☑74 22 66 04; visitnamdalen. com; Havnegata 9; ⊙9am-5pm Mon-Fri, 10am-4pm Sat mid-Jun–mid-Aug) The seasonal tourist office rents bicycles (Nkr50/120 per hour/day) and also provides information about the Kystriksveien.

❶ Getting There & Away

Nor-Way Bussekspress runs twice daily between Namsos and Trondheim (Nkr398, 3½ hours). There are up to eight buses daily to/from Steinkjer (Nkr187, 1½ hours).

Rørvik
POP 498

Tiny Rørvik buzzes when the northbound and southbound Hurtigruten coastal ferries meet each other here every day around 9.30pm. What gets passengers up early from the dinner table is the splendid **Norveg** (☑74 36 07 70; kystmuseetnorveg.no; Strandgata 7; adult/child incl audio guide Nkr80/40; ⊙10am-10pm mid-Jun–Jul, 11am-3pm rest of year & when the Hurtigruten's in port). Architecturally exciting and resembling a sailing ship, it recounts 10,000 years of coastal history through a variety of media, including an accompanying audioguide, available in English. It also runs a well-regarded gourmet restaurant.

A combined ticket (adult/child Nkr150/75), valid for two days, gives admission to Norveg, Berggården (an old trading house once typical of coastal communities) and several other historical buildings.

The swiftest way to travel between Rørvik and Namsos is by express passenger boat (Nkr212, 1½ hours, one to three times daily).

Nordland

Best Places to Eat

➡ Fiskekrogen (p297)

➡ Børsen (p294)

➡ Sjøgato Cafe og Restaurant (p272)

➡ Umami (p311)

Best Places to Stay

➡ Svinøya Rorbuer (p293)

➡ Fru Haugans Hotel (p272)

➡ Norumgården Bed & Breakfast (p280)

➡ Hotel Sandnessjøen (p283)

➡ Hotell Marena (p307)

➡ Vega Havhotell (p283)

Why Go?

For those with a love of all things Arctic, this is where Norway really starts to get interesting. Heading northwards through long, slim Nordland, lush fields give way to lakes and forests, vistas open up, summits sharpen and the treeline descends ever lower on the mountainsides. Above the imaginary curve of the Arctic Circle, travellers get their first taste of the midnight sun in summer, while in winter, the northern lights dance across the night sky.

Linger along the spectacular Kystriksveien Coastal Route. Or travel the inland Arctic Highway, more direct, almost as lovely, yet still lightly trafficked. And then there's Lofoten, where razor-sharp peaks stab at the sky and timeless fishing villages survive. Connected by bridges, the islands are easy to hop around, cycling is possible and hiking is as gentle or as tough as you care to make it.

When to Go
Bodø

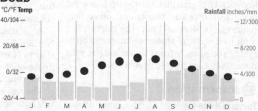

Late Mar Take in Lofoten and then Svolvær's World Cod Fishing Championship.

Mid- to late Jun Activities are in gear and southern European visitors are yet to arrive.

Late Jun Join 2000 walkers for Narvik's mass hike on the last Saturday in June.

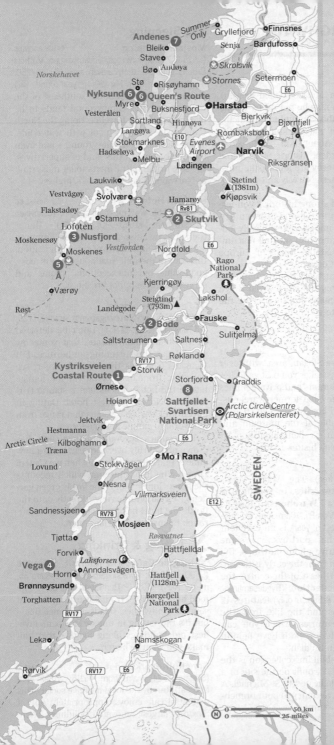

Nordland Highlights

1 Ferry hop and hug the splendid **Kystriksveien Coastal Route** (p281), at least from Sandnessjøen to Storvik.

2 Take the **ferry from Skutvik or Bodø to Lofoten**, one of the world's great ferry trips.

3 Return to the postcard-perfect fishing past of Lofoten in the lovely village of **Nusfjord** (p299).

4 Experience the eider-duck economy and leave the clamour of the modern world behind in Unesco-recognised **Vega** (p282).

5 Linger in the tiny, preserved fishing village of **Å** (p300) in Lofoten.

6 Discover the reborn and isolated village of **Nyksund** (p308), then hike the coastal **Queen's Route** (p305) to Stø in Vesterålen

7 Take to the seas to look for whales from the port of **Andenes** (p306).

8 Get cold feet on one of the glaciers in **Saltfjellet-Svartisen National Park** (p276).

ARCTIC HIGHWAY

Mosjøen

POP 9976

When arriving in Mosjøen (moo-sher-en), along the E6, you may be put off by the industrial face of this aluminium-producing town, especially if you're coming from the north. Don't be. About 1km south, along lake-like Vefsnfjorden, historic Sjøgata and a street or two nearby are among the most charming in northern Norway and well merit a browse.

The town has a strong historical connection with the UK; in the mid-19th century, five Englishmen imported technically advanced steam engines and sawmill machinery and established the North of Europe Land & Mining Company Ltd to provide timber for constructing Britain's burgeoning industrial towns and cities. What was a tiny coastal settlement quickly became the region's first registered town.

◉ Sights

Sjøgata   HISTORIC SITE

A stroll around the Sjøgata area, with over 100 listed buildings, takes you past galleries, coffee shops, restaurants and private homes in attractively renovated former warehouses, workshops and boat sheds. *The History of a Town*, available at the museum and tourist office, is an excellent small booklet that brings Mosjøen's history to life.

Vefsn Museum   MUSEUM

(adult/child Nkr30/free) The Vefsn Museum is split over two sites. In Sjøgata, the **Jakobsensbrygga Warehouse** (Sjøgata 31b; ⊙10am-8pm Mon-Fri, 10am-3pm Sat Jun-Aug, shorter hours rest of year) is an excellent small museum that portrays, via some particularly evocative photo blow-ups, the history of Mosjøen from the early 19th century onwards. Northeast of the centre, the **rural building collection** (Bygdesamlinga; ⊙10am-3pm Tue-Fri & Sun Jul only) features 12 farmhouses, shops and the like from the 18th and 19th centuries, which you can view from the exterior. Both have helpful pamphlet guides in English.

Adjacent to the building collection is the **Dolstad Kirke** (1735), built on the site of a medieval church dedicated to St Michael. A combined ticket gives entry to both branches of Mosjøen's museum.

⊨ Sleeping

Mosjøen Camping   CAMPGROUND €

(⊉75 17 79 00; www.mosjoencamping.no; Mathias Bruuns gata 24; tent/caravan sites Nkr140/250, 4-person cabin from Nkr450; ⊙year-round; ▨) Beside the E6 about 500m southeast of the town centre, this campground tends to be overcrowded with travellers doing the North Cape rush. There's a pool with waterslide, snack bar, children's playground – and even tenpin bowling. In this land of superlatives, the sole urinal in the men's toilet must rank as Norway's, if not the world's, highest.

Mosjøen Hotell   HOTEL €€

(⊉75 17 11 55; www.mosjoenhotell.no; Vollanveien 35; s/d from Nkr620/990; P@⊛) Under the same ownership as Mosjøen Camping and about 100m north of the train station, this run-of-the-mill roadhouse offers cosy, good-value but unexceptional rooms and serves an ample buffet breakfast.

★**Fru Haugans Hotel**   HOTEL €€€

(⊉75 11 41 00; www.fruhaugans.no; Strandgata 39; s/d Nkr1250/1650; @⊛) Don't be deterred by the bland main facade that somehow slipped past the planning authorities. Fru Haugans (she was the original owner; see her stare from her portrait in the lounge beside the hotel's Ellenstuen restaurant) is northern Norway's oldest hotel. Dating in part from 1794, it has rooms that range from old-world to simple and modern.

It occupies several buildings and has grown organically over the years with a new annexe under construction when we visited. Drop by its little museum, which recounts the hotel's long history. The lovely green garden gives panoramic views directly onto the fjord. The hotel has two magnificent restaurants: Ellenstuen and Hagestuen.

✗ Eating & Drinking

★**Sjøgato Cafe og Restaurant**   CAFE €

(⊉90 57 16 39; www.sjogatocafe.no; Sjøgata 35; mains Nkr76-140; ⊙11am-3pm Mon-Sat) The food here is tasty – from a warming chicken soup to sandwiches, salads and omelettes – but it's the setting in one of Mosjøen's loveliest old buildings along Sjøgata that will make you want to linger.

Café Kulturverkstedet   CAFE €

(Sjøgata 22-24; mains from Nkr115; ⊙8am-4pm Mon-Sat) Run by the local heritage society, this delightful cafe enjoys, appropriately, one of Sjøgata's largest renovated buildings. There are books to leaf through and you can sip and nibble in its interconnecting art gallery.

Hagestuen   NORWEGIAN €€
(☑75 11 41 00; mains Nkr190-265) In the Fru Haugans Hotel, tapestry-bedecked Hagestuen offers both à la carte dining and an evening buffet (Nkr300) in summer.

★Ellenstuen   NORWEGIAN €€€
(☑75 11 41 00; mains Nkr255-315; ⊙6-11pm) Ellenstuen, in the Fru Haugans Hotel, is an intimate place that preserves many of the hotel's original fittings. It has a particularly creative menu (if you're in luck, you'll find roasted stag fillet and lightly smoked grouse breast in a raspberry sauce on offer).

Lille Torget   BAR
(☑75 17 04 14; Strandgate 24; snacks from Nkr60; ⊙8am-4pm Mon-Sat) With its decorative interior (take a look at the gorgeous reproduction art nouveau maiden bearing a lamp at her heart) and a terrace opening onto the main square, this place serves great coffee. Rune, its owner, was the 2008 winner of Coffee in Good Spirits, the key event in Norway's annual coffee-making championship (he'll fashion subtle shapes in your foam too).

ⓘ Information
Tourist office (☑75 01 80 00; www.visithelgeland.com; ⊙9am-8pm Mon-Fri, 11am-5pm Sat & Sun late Jun-early Aug, shorter hours rest of year) The tourist office is beside the E6, which bypasses central Mosjøen.

ⓘ Getting There & Away
There are flights to Bodø (via Mo i Rana) and Trondheim.

Buses run from Mosjøen to Brønnøysund (three hours, once or twice daily except Saturday) and Sandnessjøen (1¾ hours, three to five daily). There's also at least one service daily to/from Mo i Rana (1¾ hours) but the train takes less time.

Mosjøen lies on the rail line between Trondheim (Nkr763, 5½ hours, three daily), Fauske (Nkr534, 3½ hours, three daily) and Bodø (Nkr625; 4¼ hours, three daily).

Around Mosjøen

Laksforsen   WATERFALL
About 30km south of Mosjøen and a 600m detour from the E6, the roaring 17m-high Laksforsen waterfall has leaping salmon in season and makes a pleasant picnic spot, although it's a bit of a struggle to reach the shore below the torrent.

Namsskogan
Familiepark   ZOO, AMUSEUMENT PARK
(☑74 33 37 00; www.familieparken.no; Arctic Highway, Trones; adult/child/family Nkr275/250/895; ⊙10am-6pm late Jun–mid-Aug, shorter hours rest of Jun and mid-Aug–Oct, closed Nov-May) A long way from anywhere – it's 40km south of Namsskogan, which is, in turn, 125km south of Mosjøen along the Arctic Highway - the Namsskogan Familiepark is a great way to break up the long journey north. Home to an impressive array of Arctic wildlife – highlights include reindeer, elk, brown bear, wolverine, wolf and Eurasian lynx – it's a spacious, well-run place with plenty of activities for kids, among them trampolines, a flying fox, toboggan and horse riding.

Mo i Rana
POP 25,943
Mo i Rana (just plain Mo to those who know her) is the third-largest city in the north and gateway to the spruce forests, caves and glaciers of the Arctic Circle region. Its friendly reputation is often attributed to its rapid expansion due to the construction of the now-closed steel plant, which in its time employed more than 1000 workers; nearly everyone here once knew how it felt to be a stranger in town.

◉ Sights & Activities
Rana Museum of Natural History   MUSEUM
(☑75 11 01 33; Moholmen; adult/child incl Rana Museum of Cultural History Nkr50/free; ⊙10am-4pm Mon-Fri, 11am-3pm Sat) The Rana Museum of Natural History illustrates the geology, ecology, flora and wildlife of the Arctic Circle

---

WORTH A TRIP

A DETOUR VIA HATTEN

For drivers, a lovely detour that bypasses Mosjøen follows the wild, scenic Villmarksveien route, which runs parallel to the E6 east of the town and approaches the bizarre 1128m peak of Hatten (or Hattfjell). From the end of the nearest road, the hike to the top takes about two hours.

Mo i Rana

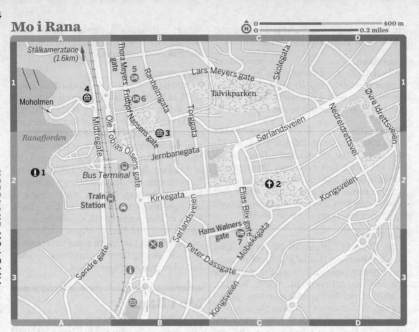

Mo i Rana

◉ Sights
1 Havmannen Statue...............................A2
2 Mo Kirke (Church) C2
3 Rana Museum of Cultural History B2
4 Rana Museum of Natural History A1

🛏 Sleeping
5 Comfort Hotel Ole Tobias B1
6 Meyergården Hotell.............................B1
7 Mo Hotell og Gjestegaard C3

✕ Eating
8 Abelone B3
Søilen..(see 6)

region, and features several hands-on exhibits that will engage children.

Rana Museum of Cultural History MUSEUM
(☎75 11 01 33; Fridtjof Nansens gate 22; adult/child incl Rana Museum of Natural History Nkr50/free; ⊗10am-4pm Mon-Fri, 11am-3pm Sat) The highlight of the Rana Museum of Cultural History is a giant model of old Mo before the steelworks altered its complexion forever.

Mo Kirke (Church) CHURCH
The oldest building in town, Mo's original church was constructed in 1724. With its steeply pitched roof and onion dome, it deserves to be open to visitors during more than the current brief hours, which are, incidentally, anyone's guess. In the graveyard is a monument to Russian prisoners who died in captivity and the gravestones of eight British soldiers, killed in commando raids in May 1940.

Havmannen Statue STATUE
Havmannen (Man of the Sea), a sculpture forever up to his knees in water, turns his back on the town and gazes resolutely out over the fjord. His clean lines and rounded profile are the work of iconic British sculptor Antony Gormley.

🛏 Sleeping

Stålkameratøne HOSTEL €
(☎41 92 62 15; Stålbrakka, Søderlundmyra; dm Nkr250, s/d with shared bathroom Nkr400/600; ⊗mid-Jun–mid-Aug; ℗@🖥) Mo's biggest bargain is just off the first left bend of the E6, heading northwards. This hostel has four plainly furnished single rooms, occupied by students during the school year, an eight-bed dorm and a couple of doubles.

Meyergården Hotell HOTEL €€
(☎75 13 40 00; www.rica.no; Fridtjof Nansens gate 28; r Nkr865-1465; ℗@🖥) An affiliate of the Rica chain, Mo's longest-established hotel

is full of character, with fine rooms, most of them recently refurbished. There are also older style rooms in the original – and much more atmospheric – late-19th-century wing.

Mo Hotell og Gjestegaard   GUESTHOUSE €€
(☑ 75 15 22 11; www.mo-gjestegaard.no; Elias Blix gate 5; s/d Nkr700/900; P ⏶) Up the hill, this pleasant 15-room guesthouse is welcoming and impeccably kept. On the top floor is a pair of large family rooms (Nkr1600), accommodating up to four. It's in a quiet location and has a small garden where you are welcome to sit and relax. It's often fully booked so do reserve in advance.

Comfort Hotel Ole Tobias   HOTEL €€
(☑ 75 12 05 00; www.ole-tobias.no; Thora Meyers gate 2; s/d from Nkr1095/1295; @ ⏶) This railway-themed hotel – the corridor carpets simulate a railway track and each of its 30 rooms has the name of a station – commemorates the local teacher and priest who convinced the government to build the Nordlandsbanen railway connecting Trondheim with Fauske and Bodø. As well as breakfast year-round and free beverages, in summer tariffs include a light evening meal.

✖ Eating

Abelone   RESTAURANT €€
(☑ 75 15 38 88; Ole Tobias Olsens gate 6; mains Nkr175-265; ⏰1-11pm) Abelone is your best dining option outside the hotels. It looks unprepossessing from the street but inside the cosy simulated log cabin makes for a congenial dining environment. Opt for one of its quality meat dishes.

Søilen   RESTAURANT €€€
(☑ 75 13 40 00; Fridtjof Nansens gate 28; mains Nkr215-315; ⏰noon-10pm) The highly regarded Arctic Menu restaurant of Meyergården Hotell gets its meat, dairy products and even honey from local sources. Save room for the caramel pudding with whipped cream.

ℹ Information

Tourist office (☑ 75 13 92 00; www.arctic-circle.no; Ole Tobias Olsens gate 3; ⏰9am-7pm Mon-Fri, 11am-5pm Sat & Sun late Jun-early Aug, shorter hours rest of year) The friendly tourist office has free internet access.

ℹ Getting There & Away

Mo i Rana's Røssvoll airport, 14km northeast of town, has flights to/from Bodø and Trondheim.

You'll enjoy an excellent panorama of the Svartisen icecaps unless it's misty down below.

By bus, options are fairly limited. There are one to three daily services to/from both Sandnessjøen (2¾ hours) and Mosjøen (1¾ hours). At least one bus of **Länstrafiken** (www.tabussen.nu) runs daily between Mo i Rana and Umeå (eight hours) in Sweden.

Most visitors arrive at Mo i Rana's attractive octagonal **train station** (☑ 75 15 01 77), from where trains run to the following destinations:

DESTINATION	DURATION (HR)	FREQUENCY (DAILY)
Bodø	3	4
Fauske	2¼	4
Mosjøen	1½	5
Trondheim	7½	3

ℹ Getting Around

If you're driving, pick up a free visitors' parking permit from the tourist office, which also rents bicycles.

Call if you need a **taxi** (☑ 7550).

Around Mo i Rana

Grønligrotta   CAVE
(☑ 75 13 25 86; www.gronligrotta.no; adult/child Nkr130/90; ⏰tours hourly 10am-6pm mid-Jun–mid-Aug) The most accessible and most visited of the caves around Mo is situated 22km north of town. There's electric lighting (it's the only illuminated tourist cave in Scandinavia). The 30-minute tour takes you along an underground river, through a rock maze, then past a granite block torn off by a glacier and deposited in the cave by the brute force of moving water.

Setergrotta   CAVE
(www.setergrotta.no; Røvassdalen; adult/child Nkr350/300; ⏰tours twice daily early Jun–late Aug) Setergrotta, located 21km north of Mo i Rana and signposted off the E6, is altogether less dragooned and considerably more adventurous than nearby Grønligrotta. Highlights of the two-hour trip include a couple of tight squeezes and a thrilling shuffle between rock walls while straddling a 15m gorge. The operators provide headlamps, hard hats, gumboots and overalls. Cedit cards are not accepted here.

Saltfjellet-Svartisen National Park

The 2102-sq-km Saltfjellet-Svartisen National Park is one of mainland Norway's most dramatic landforms. In the west, it embraces the rugged peaks of the Svartisen icecap, Norway's second-largest glacier, and glacier tongues are visible from the Kystriksveien Coastal Route, north of the ferry crossing of Forøy. To the east, the bleak, high moorlands of the Saltfjellet massif roll to the Swedish border. Charismatic wildlife also inhabit the park, including wolverine, Eurasian lynx, elk and a breeding population of Arctic fox.

The best map for trekking is Statens Kartverk's *Saltfjellet* at 1:100,000.

Northbound travellers on the Hurtigruten coastal ferry can visit the Svartisen glacier as an optional add-on to their journey.

Svartisen

The two Svartisen icecaps, separated by the valley Vesterdalen, straddle the Arctic Circle between Mo i Rana and the Meløy peninsula. At its thickest, the ice is around 600m deep. The average height is about 1500m but some tongues lick down into the valleys and are the lowest-lying glaciers in mainland Europe. You can experience Svartisen from either its eastern or more spectacular western side. Most visitors to either just make a quick hop by boat, but hikers will find more joy approaching from the east.

Østisen, the eastern glacier, is more accessible from Mo. From the end of the Svartisdalen road, 20km up the valley from Mo i Rana's airport, ferries (adult/child return Nkr120/60; ☺mid-Jun–Aug) cross Svartisen lake (Svartisvatnet) four times daily. From the ferry landing, it's a 3km hike to the beginning of the Austerdalsisen glacier tongue. There's a kiosk and campground at the lake.

From the end of the road you can also trek up to the hut on the shore of the mountain lake Pikhaugsvatnet, which is surrounded by peaks and ice. This is an excellent base for day hikes up the Glomdal valley or to the Flatisen glacier.

Saltfjellet

The broad upland plateaus of the Saltfjellet massif transcend the Arctic Circle, connecting the peaks surrounding the Svartisen icecap and the Swedish border. Within this relatively inhospitable wilderness are traces of several ancient Sami fences and sacrificial sites, some dating from as early as the 9th century.

A 15km walk to the east leads to Graddis, near the Swedish border, and the venerable **Graddis Fjellstue og Camping** (☎75 69 43 41; graddis@c2i.net; s/d from Nkr500/680; ☺mid-Jun–mid-Aug). This cosy little guesthouse has been run by the same family since its establishment in 1867. It makes an excellent base to launch yourself into one of Norway's least-tramped hiking areas. Camping is also available, and Methuselah, a 1000-year-old pine tree, is a nearby attraction.

By car, access to Saltfjellet is either along the E6 or the Rv77, which follows the southern slope of the Junkerdalen valley. Rail travellers can disembark at Lønsdal en route between Fauske and Trondheim. Check whether you need to request a stop.

Arctic Circle Centre

Latitude N 66°33' marks the southernmost extent of the midnight sun on the summer solstice and the ragged edge of the polar night on the winter solstice. Where the Arctic Highway between Mo i Rana and Fauske cuts across this imaginary line, in a high, broad valley that remains snowbound for much of the year, the Arctic Circle Centre occupies a lovely natural setting.

Polarsirkelsenteret LANDMARK
(☎75 12 96 96; www.polarsirkelsenteret.no; optional film adult/child Nkr60/30; ☺10am-8pm Jun-Aug, 10am-6pm May & 1st half of Sep) What a missed opportunity: the Polarsirkelsenteret, beside the E6 and surrounded by the bleak moors that roll in from Saltfjellet-Svartisen National Park, is a tourist trap and little more. The only redeeming feature is an audiovisual presentation on the Arctic regions. Outside, and altogether more sober and serious, are the memorials to Slav forced labourers who, during WWII, constructed the Arctic Highway for the occupying Nazi forces and died far from home.

Otherwise, the place exists mostly to stamp postcards with a special Arctic Circle postmark and sell certificates (Nkr99) for visitors to authenticate their crossing the line. Boreal kitsch is flogged here by the basketload. On the plus side, as its website chooses to highlight, it has 'very good lavatory facilities'.

Fauske

POP 9556

Most travellers on the way north end up passing through Fauske – it's the Arctic-Highway gateway for Bodø (for Lofoten), Sulitjelma and Rago National Park. Few linger longer than it takes to fill up on petrol or change buses or trains, but there's enough here to turn your head if you've an hour or two to spare.

◉ Sights

Fauske is known for its fine marble. Its 'Norwegian Rose' stone features in many a monumental building, including the Oslo Rådhus, the UN headquarters in New York and the Emperor's palace in Tokyo. Suitably, its main attraction is the marble-themed **town square**.

Check out also the park-like collection of historic buildings of the Fauske branch of the **Salten Museum** (☑75 50 35 16; nordlandsmuseet.no/fauske_bygdetun; Sjøgata; adult/child Nkr50/10; ⊙11am-5pm mid-Jun–mid-Aug), whose grounds are a lovely spot for a picnic.

⊨ Sleeping & Eating

Campotel   CAMPGROUND €
(☑75 64 39 6675 64 39 66; www.campotel.no; Lundveien; car/caravan sites Nkr175/225, 2-/4-bed cabins Nkr400/500, with bathroom Nkr700/800; ⊙May-Sep) This complex, 3km west of town, has superb views of the fjord and surrounding peaks.

Fauske Hotell   HOTEL €€
(☑75 60 20 00; www.rica.no; Storgata 82; d Nkr890-1140) Fauske's only year-round upmarket choice has cheerful rooms although common areas feel decidedly dated. As you'd expect, marble is a recurring theme and it has a good restaurant which is strong on Arctic dishes.

❶ Information

Tourist office (☑75 50 35 15; Sjøgata; ⊙9am-4pm Mon-Sat, 11am-4pm Sun mid-Jun–mid-Aug) This seasonal office shares its premises with the Salten Museum in the heart of town.

❶ Getting There & Away

BUS
Buses run to/from Bodø (Nkr90, 1½ hours, three to six daily) and Narvik (Nkr280, 5½ hours, two daily).

❶ USEFUL WEBSITES

www.nordnorge.com Official tourist site for the region.

www.177nordland.no Comprehensive listings, together with links, of Nordland bus, boat, ferry, train and plane timetables. Alternatively, phone ☑177 within Nordland or ☑75 77 24 10 beyond.

www.torghatten-nord.no Nordland passenger express and car ferries.

TRAIN
Trains ply the Nordlandsbanen between Trondheim (Nkr1018, 9½ hours) and Bodø (Nkr128, 45 minutes), via Fauske, twice daily and there are additional trains (up to four daily) between Fauske and Bodø. As always, booking online may reap huge savings on the ticket price. To continue further northwards, you've no option but to hop on a bus.

Around Fauske

Saltdal & Museums

Just off the E6 near Saltnes, **Saltdal Historical Village** (adult/child Nkr50/10; ⊙11am-5pm mid-Jun–mid-Aug) is a collection of typical rural and fishing-related buildings. Reception and cafe (try the local speciality, *møsbromlefse*, a sweetish light pancake laced with cream and cheese) are in the Skippergården building.

The moving **Blodveimuseet** (Blood Road Museum; nordlandsmuseet.no/blodveimuseet; adult/child Nkr50/10; ⊙11am-5pm mid-Jun–mid-Aug), in a former German barracks within the museum grounds, is visited by a 30-minute guided tour. It reveals conditions for Slav and Russian forced labourers who forged the road and railway northwards. The prisoners' cemetery, with the remains of some 7000 men, and the nearby graveyard for German soldiers are in Botn, about 3km north.

Sulitjelma

As an interpretive panel just north of Fauske will confirm, you're exactly halfway along the E6. By now, you're probably eager to strangle every slow-moving motorhome driver on its two-lane highway, so it's an appropriate moment to break free from the Arctic Highway for a short while.

It's a gorgeous 40km run along the Rv830, up scenic Langvassdalen to the tiny community of Sulitjelma. It wasn't always such a backwater; in 1860 a Sami herder discovered copper ore in the forested country north of Langvatnet and suddenly the Sulitjelma region was attracting all sorts of opportunists from southern Norway. Large ore deposits were revealed and the Sulitjelma Gruber mining company was founded in 1891. By 1928 the wood-fuelled smelter had taken its toll on the surrounding birch forests, as did high concentrations of carbon dioxide, a by-product of the smelting process. Nowadays, with the furnaces long since cold, the environment is on its way to recovery.

Sights & Activities

Gruvemuseum
MUSEUM
(nordlandsmuseet.no/en/sulitjelma-gruvemuseum; adult/child Nkr50/10; ⊙ 11am-5pm daily mid-Jun–mid-Aug) Alongside the fjord, the Sulitjelma Mining Museum records the area's 100 years of mining history and displays some awesome rusting equipment.

Besøksgruve
MINE
(Sulitjelma Show Mine; ☑ 75 50 35 18; nordlandsmuseet.no/en/sulitjelma-besoksgruve; adult/child Nkr200/50; ⊙ by appointment) A one-hour guided tour of the Besøksgruve includes a 1.5km rail ride deep into the mountain. Advance reservations are essential.

Rago National Park

The small (171-sq-km), scarcely visited Rago National Park is a rugged chunk of forested granite mountain and moorland, riven with deep glacial cracks and capped by great icefields. Rago, together with the large adjoining Swedish parks, Pakjelanta, Sarek and Stora Sjöfjallet, belongs to a wider protected area of 5500 sq km. Wildlife includes not only beavers in the deep Laksåga (aka Nordfjord) river valley, but also wolverines in the higher areas. Along the relatively lush Storskogdalen valley, a series of foaming cascades and spectacular waterfalls tumble.

From the main trailhead at Lakshol, it's a three-hour, 7km walk up the valley to the free Storskogvasshytta and Ragohytta huts, then a stiff climb up and over the ridge into Sweden to connect with the well-established trail system over the border.

Maps to use are *Sisovatnet*, at 1:50,000, or *Sørfold*, at 1:75,000. To reach Lakshol, turn east off the E6 at the Trengsel bridge and continue about 6km to the end of the road.

Narvik
POP 18.705

Narvik has a double personality. On the one hand, its location is spectacular, pincered by islands to the west and mountains in every other direction, while spectacular fjords stretch north and south. At the same time, heavy industry casts a pall of ugliness over the rather scruffy downtown area – the town was founded in 1902 as the port for the coal-mining town of Kiruna in Swedish Lapland and the trans-shipment facility bisecting the city still loads several million tonnes of ore annually from train wagons onto ships.

But Narvik's appeal lies elsewhere, with unique sporting and sightseeing activities offered by its majestic surroundings and the spectacular Ofotbanen Railway to Sweden.

Sights

Ofoten Museum
MUSEUM
(Museum Nord; www.museumnord-narvik.no; Administrasjonsveien 3; adult/concession/child Nkr60/30/free; ⊙ 10am-4pm Mon-Fri, noon-3pm Sat & Sun Jul-early Aug, 10am-3pm Mon-Fri rest of year) The museum tells of Narvik's farming, fishing, railway-building and ore trans-shipment heritage. There's a rolling film about the Ofotbanen Railway and children will enjoy pressing the button that activates the model train. Linger too over the display case of Sami costumes and artefacts, and the collection of historic photos, contrasted with modern shots taken from the same angles. To reach the museum, take the minor road beside the restored building that served as Narvik's post office from 1888 to 1898.

Red Cross War Museum
MUSEUM
(Krigsminnemuseum; ☑ 76 94 44 26; www.war-museum.no; Kongens gate; adult/child Nkr75/25; ⊙ 10am-9pm Mon-Sat, noon-6pm Sun mid-Jun–mid-Aug, 10am-4pm Mon-Sat & noon-4pm Sun rest of year) This small but revealing museum illustrates the military campaigns fought hereabouts in the early years of WWII. The presentation may not be flash but it will still move you. Pick up a folder that explains each of the museum's sections.

Water Spout
FOUNTAIN
No, Narvik can't claim geothermal activity. But locals reckon that its water is the purest in the land. Each day at 1pm and 9pm from May to September, a valve is released and a mighty 75m-high plume of water spurts sky-

HAMSUNSENTERET

Around halfway between the E6 and the ferry crossing to/from the Lofoten Islands at Skutvik, along the Rv81, the **Hamsunsenteret** (☑ 75 50 34 50; www.hamsunsenteret.no; Presteid, Hamarøy; adult/child Nkr100/50; ⊙ 11am-6pm Jun–mid-Aug, 10am-3.30pm Tue-Fri & 11am-5pm Sat & Sun rest of year, closed Jan) is a must for anyone with a vaguely literary bent. The daring architecture of the museum is one of northern Norway's most striking examples of contemporary design, while the museum commemorates the life of Knut Hamsun, who won the Nobel Prize for Literature in 1920. The museum covers his life and work with well-presented displays and helpful staff keen to promote Hamsun's works.

Hamsun moved to Hamarøy with his family at age three and later returned here for a number of his working years as a writer. If you've the time and the inclination, the road from Presteid to Skutvik has a number of Hamsun-related sites signposted, including the school where he studied, as well as some information boards by the roadside about local Hamsun landmarks.

wards. Clearly visible from town, it's even more impressive up close at the viewpoint beside Narvik's hydropower station. To get here, take the road that rises eastwards opposite the Best Western Narvik Hotell.

Main Cemetery   CEMETERY
In this cemetery, beside the E6 on the north side of town, are monuments to the French and Polish troops who fought alongside the Norwegians on land, and the graves of German defenders and British sailors who died at sea.

🏃 Activities

Narvik og Omegns Turistforening   HIKING
(NOT; Narvik Trekking Association; ☑ 91 55 29 08, 40 24 09 87; www.turistforeningen.no/narvik) This is an excellent source of information about hiking. It maintains more than 15 cabins, mostly between Narvik and the Swedish border. Collect keys from the tourist office against a deposit of Nkr100.

★ Narvikfjellet   CABLE CAR
(www.narvikfjellet.no; Mårveien; adult one way/return Nkr100/150, child under 7 free; ⊙ 1-9pm Jun-Aug, shorter hours rest of year) Climbing 656m above town, this cable car offers breathtaking views over the surrounding peaks and fjords – even as far as Lofoten on a clear day. Several marked walking trails radiate from its top station or you can bounce down a signed mountain-bike route. From February to April, it will whisk you up high for trail, off-piste and cross-country skiing with outstanding views. It sometimes stays open later in the height of summer.

Fjord Cruise Narvik   BOAT TRIPS
(☑ 91 39 06 18; www.fremover.no) This outfit mounts summer fishing and sea-eagle viewing trips. From November to mid-January, when the orcas (killer whales) gather to gorge themselves on the winter herring run, it runs trips to their feeding grounds in search of the action. Prices vary with the seasons and the tour.

Narvik Golfklubb   GOLF
(☑ 97 14 60 82; www.narvikgolf.no; all-day/9-hole pass Kkr400/250) The fjord-side journey to this unique golf course at Skjomendalen is wondrous (follow the signs to Skjomdal just before the Skjomen bridge on the E6, about 18km south of town). Sheer, treacherous faces will leave you guessing how there could possibly be a golf course here. Yet nature works wonders, and there's a valley hidden amid the peaks. There's also worthwhile hiking nearby.

✦✦ Festivals & Events

On the last Saturday in June, some 2000 walkers take the train to various stops along the Rallarveien, then hike back to party at Rombaksbotn.

Vinterfestuka   MUSIC, FESTIVAL
(www.vinterfestuka.no; ⊙ Mar) Each year during March, Narvik holds its Vinterfestuka, an action-packed winter week of events, partly in commemoration of the navvies who built the railway.

🛏 Sleeping

★ Spor 1 Gjestegård   HOSTEL, GUESTHOUSE €
(☑ 76 94 60 20; www.spor1.no; Brugata 2a; dm Nkr300, s/d with shared bathroom Nkr500/600;

🏠) Britt Larsen and her partner, both Narvik born and bred and seasoned world travellers, run this delightful place right beside the railway track. It has the facilities of the best of hostels (especially the gleaming, well-equipped guest kitchen) and the comfort and taste of a guesthouse (bright, cheerful fabrics and decor, and soft duvets).

Next door, and run by the same family, is a great pub with outdoor terrace.

Narvik Camping   CAMPGROUND €

(📞76 94 58 10; www.narvikcamping.com; Rombaksveien 75; tent/caravan sites Nkr120/200; 2-bed cabin Nkr350, 4-/6-bed cabin with bathroom Nkr700/850) Sound sleep's not guaranteed for those under canvas at what's otherwise a perfectly adequate campground, overlooking the fjord and E6, 2km northeast of the centre and Narvik's only choice. Trucks rumble along the highway and long wagon trains clank by on the railway, just above.

⭐ Norumgården Bed & Breakfast   B&B €€

(📞76 94 48 57; norumgaarden.narviknett.no; Framnesveien 127; s/d Nkr790/890; ⊘late Jan-Nov; 🏠) This little treasure of a place (it has only four rooms so reservations are essential) offers excellent value. Used as a German officer's mess in WWII (the owner will proudly show you a 1940 bottle of Coca Cola, made under licence in Hamburg), nowadays it brims with antiques and character.

Choose the Heidi room (it's the only one without a shower but the little balcony more than compensates) and you'll be sleeping in the bed once occupied by King Olav. Cross the bridge beside the bus station and head west for about 1km.

Rica Hotel Narvik   HOTEL €€

(📞76 96 14 00; www.rica.no; Kongens gate 33; d Nkr845-1245, dinner mains from Nkr258; ⊘restaurant 6-10.30pm Mon-Sat; 🏠) Towering over the downtown area, this striking glass edifice houses Narvik's most stylish hotel. Rooms are slick and contemporary and those on the upper floors have fabulous views. There's also a fine restaurant and 16th-floor bar.

Breidablikk Gjestehus   GUESTHOUSE €€

(📞76 94 14 18; www.breidablikk.no; Tore Hunds gate 41; dm Nkr350, s Nkr600-1150, d Nkr1195-1750; P@🏠) It's a steep but worthwhile walk from the centre to this pleasant hillside guesthouse with rooms for all budgets and sweeping views over town and fjord. There's a cosy communal lounge and dorms have six beds.

Best Western Narvik Hotell   HOTEL €€

(📞76 96 48 00; www.narvikhotell.no; Skistuaveien 8; s/d from Nkr875/1015; P@🏠) This 90-room tour-group favourite, stretching long and low at the base of the cable car, offers great vistas. Accommodation is in comfortable chalet-type buildings.

🍴 Eating

There's not a whole lot happening in Narvik when it comes to dining. The best bet is actually the restaurant at the dinner-only Rica Hotel Narvik.

Fiskehallen   CAFE €

(📞76 94 36 60; Kongens gate 42; mains Nkr80-150; ⊘9.30am-4.30pm Mon-Fri, 10am-2pm Sat) This tiny cafe, offshoot of the adjacent fish shop, offers tasty ready-to-eat dishes, such as fish cakes and bacalao to eat in or take away.

Rallar'n   BAR, RESTAURANT €€€

(Kongens gate 64; daily specials NKr145, mains Nkr195-325; ⊘1pm-1am) The pub/restaurant of Quality Hotel Grand Royal is all atmospheric low ceilings, bare brick and dark woodwork. Divided into intimate compartments, it offers pizza, pasta and creative mains.

🍷 Drinking & Entertainment

In winter you can tumble out of the cable car into the bar at the Best Western Narvik Hotell, Narvik's leading après-ski venue.

Tøtta Bar   COCKTAIL BAR

(16th fl, Kongens gate 33; ⊘11am-1am Mon-Fri, 11am-2am Sat, 6pm-1am Sun) Encased in glass on the 16th floor of the Rica Hotel Narvik, this classy cocktail bar has fabulous views and is not just for those staying at the hotel.

ⓘ Information

Tourist office (📞76 96 56 00; www.destinationnarvik.com; ⊘10am-7pm Mon-Fri, 10am-3pm Sat & Sun mid-Jun–mid-Aug, 9am-4.30pm Mon-Fri rest of year) At the train station, the tourist office holds Narvik og Omegns Turistforening cabin keys (Nkr100 deposit), has internet access (Nkr60 per hour) and rents bikes (Nkr250 per day).

ⓘ Getting There & Away

AIR

Nearly all flights leave from Harstad-Narvik Evenes airport, 1¼ hours away by road. Narvik's tiny Framneslia airport, about 3km west of the centre, serves only Bodø, Tromsø and Andenes.

BUS

Express buses run northwards to Tromsø (Nkr240, 4¼ hours, three daily) and south to Bodø (Nkr280, 6½ hours, two daily) via Fauske (Nkr280, 5¼ hours). For Lofoten, two Lofotekspressen buses run daily between Narvik and Svolvær (from Nkr250, 4¼ hours) and continue to Å.

Between late June and early September, bus 91 runs twice a day up the E10 to Riksgränsen (45 minutes) in Sweden and on to Abisko and Kiruna (three hours).

TRAIN

Heading for Sweden, there are two daily services between Narvik and Riksgränsen (one hour) on the border, and Kiruna (three hours). Trains continue to Lulea (7¼ hours) via Boden, from where you can pick up connections to Stockholm. The route takes you up the spectacular Ofotbanen Railway and, in Sweden, past Abisko National Park, which offers excellent hiking and lovely Arctic scenery.

ℹ Getting Around

Narvik's Framneslia airport is 3km from the centre. Flybuss runs four to eight times daily between Narvik and Harstad-Narvik Evenes airport (adult/child one way Nkr240/120, adult return Nkr360, 1¼ hours), 79km away.

For a taxi, phone **Narvik Taxi** (☑ 07 550; www.narviktaxi.no).

Ofotbanen Railway & Rallarveien

The spectacular mountain-hugging **Ofotbanen Railway** (☑ 76 92 31 21) trundles beside fjord-side cliffs, birch forests and rocky plateaus as it climbs to the Swedish border. The railway, which opened in 1903, was constructed by migrant labourers at the end of the 19th century to connect Narvik with the iron-ore mines at Kiruna, in Sweden's far north. Currently it transports around 15 million tonnes of iron ore annually and is also a major magnet for visitors.

The train route from Narvik to Riksgränsen, the ski resort just inside Sweden (one way adult/child Nkr130/free, one hour), features some 50 tunnels and snowsheds. Towards the Narvik end of the rail line, you might make out the wreck of the German ship *Georg Thiele* at the edge of the fjord.

You can run the line as a day or half-day trip, leaving Narvik at 10.26am. The 11.39am return train from Riksgränsen allows time for coffee and a quick browse or you can walk a trail in this stunning alpine country and catch the 4.02pm back to Narvik. For the best views, sit on the left side heading from Narvik.

In Sweden, several long-distance trails radiate out from the railway, including the world-renowned Kungsleden, which heads south from Abisko into the heart of Sweden. The **Rallarveien** is a popular hike that parallels the Ofotbanen Railway, following an old navvy (railway worker) trail. Few walkers attempt the entire way between Abisko National Park and the sea, opting instead to begin at Riksgränsen or Bjørnfell, the next station west. It's an undemanding descent as far as Katterat, from where you can take the evening train to Narvik.

For more exertion, drop down to Rombaksbotn at the head of the fjord and site of the main camp when the railway was being built (it's since returned to nature). From here, a boat (adult/child Nkr320/125) runs erratically to Narvik in summer. Check with the tourist office to avoid an unwelcome supplementary 10km trek at the end of the day.

KYSTRIKSVEIEN – THE COASTAL ROUTE

Longer, yes, more expensive, yes (gosh, those ferry tolls mount up). But if you've even a day or two to spare, divert from the Arctic Highway and enjoy the empty roads and solitary splendours of Kystriksveien, the coastal alternative that follows the coast for 650km. If the whole route seems daunting, it's quite possible to cut in or out from Steinkjer, Bodø or, midway, Mosjøen and Mo i Rana. It's one to drive; don't even attempt it by bus or you'll still be waiting when the first snows fall.

Off the coast are around 14,000 islands, some little more than rocks with a few tufts of grass, others, such as Vega, supporting whole communities that for centuries have survived on coastal fishing and subsistence agriculture. The sea was the only highway and the living was harsh year-round – especially between mid-January and Easter, when the menfolk would be absent, working the fishing grounds off Lofoten for cod.

For a budget approach to the notoriously expensive route, visit www.backpacker17.com.

ℹ️ Information

The splendid free *Kystriksveien* (Coastal Route) booklet, distributed by tourist offices and many lodgings along the way, is a mini-Bible. Its website (www.rv17.no) gives even more detail. For greater depth, invest in *The Coastal Road: A Travel Guide to Kystriksveien* (Nkr298) by Olav Breen.

Click on www.rv17.no/sykkel for a recommended 12-day bike-and-ferry journey along the full length of the Kystriksveien. The free brochure *Cycling from Steinkjer to Leka* has detailed maps, and lists highlights and bicycle-friendly accommodation.

Brønnøysund

POP 7700

The small coastal settlement of Brønnøysund is flanked on one side by an archipelago of islets and on the other by rolling farm country.

👁️ Sights

Hildurs Urterarium GARDENS
(www.urterariet.com; Tilrem; adult/child Nkr50/free; ⏱ 10am-5pm mid-Jun–mid-Aug) Around 400 types of herb, 100 varieties of rose and 1000 species of cactus flourish at Hilde's Herb Garden, about 6km north of Brønnøysund; the team also produces its own wine. There are some rustic old farm buildings, a small art gallery and a shop that carries locally grown products. The garden also makes a lovely stop for lunch.

Torghatten MOUNTAIN
A significant local landmark rears up from Torget island, some 15km south of Brønnøysund. The peak, pierced by a hole 160m long, 35m high and 20m wide, is accessed from its base by a good 20-minute walking track. The best perspective of the gap is from the southbound Hurtigruten coastal ferry as it rounds the island.

🚐 Tours

This one's a real winner. The tourist office sells tickets for a spectacular **mini-cruise** on the Hurtigruten. Leaving at 5pm, the coastal ferry passes Torghatten on its way south to Rørvik in Trøndelag – allowing an hour to explore the town and visit its splendid Norveg Centre for Coastal Culture and Industries before you hop aboard the northbound ferry to reach Brønnøysund again at 1am. Prices vary with the seasons and availability.

🛏️ Sleeping & Eating

The Brønnøysund tourist office can book private farm cabins and *rorbuer* (Nkr700 to Nkr1100) accommodating four to eight people.

Torghatten Camping CAMPGROUND €
(☑75 02 54 95; www.visittorghatten.no; tent/caravan sites Nkr120/170, 4-6-bed cabins with bathroom from Nkr950, 6-bed apt from Nkr1100) This lovely option with its small beach beside a constructed lake is great for children. Around 10km southwest of Brønnøysund, it's handy for an ascent of the Torghatten peak.

Galeasen Hotell HOTEL €€
(☑75 00 88 50; www.galeasen.com; Havnegata 32-36; s/d from Nkr950/1250) The 22-room Galeasen sits right beside the quay and runs a small restaurant. Ask for a room in the more recent main building, not the less-attractive annexe, which occupies a converted fish-processing plant.

ℹ️ Information

Tourist office (☑75 01 80 00; www.visithelgeland.com; ⏱ 9am-7pm Mon-Fri, noon-6pm Sat & Sun mid-Jun–mid-Aug, shorter hours Mon-Fri and closed Sat & Sun rest of year) Brønnøysund's tourist office is one block from the Hurtigruten quay. It rents bicycles (Nkr175 per day).

ℹ️ Getting There & Away

Widerøe (www.wideroe.no) flies to Brønnøysund from Trondheim, Oslo and Bergen; the most common approach route passes right over Torghatten and the azure seas that lap around it.

Up to three buses run between Brønnøysund and Sandnessjøen (Nkr275, 3½ hours, daily except Sunday) and to/from Mosjøen (three hours, once or twice daily except Saturday).

Brønnøysund is also a port for the Hurtigruten coastal ferry.

Vega

POP 1223

The island of Vega remains a very Norwegian destination (we were the only non-nationals on our ferry journeys to and from the island). It and the more than 6000 skerries, islets and simply large rocks that form the Vega archipelago are a Unesco World Heritage Site. This distinction comes not for any grand building or monument, nor for the scenery (which is stunning, nevertheless). It's for human endeavour, recognising that the archipelago reflects the way generations of fisherfolk and farmers have, over the past 1500 years, maintained a sustainable living in an inhospitable seascape. This lifestyle is based on the now-unique practice of eider-down harvesting, undertaken mostly by women. For more on these very special ducks and their down, visit the splendid little E-huset museum or click on www.verdensarvvega.no.

◉ Sights

★ E-huset
MUSEUM

(E-house; ☑415 07 364; helgelandmuseum.no; adult/child Nkr50/free; ⊗noon-4pm daily mid-Jun–mid-Aug) In the tiny fishing hamlet of Nes, this delightful, engagingly informative small museum celebrates the eider duck and the way the birds were nurtured as domestic pets, when they returned – each one to its very same nesting box – after their winter migration. The E-house occupies a former trading post, which still retains its original counter and row upon row of goods that your great-grandparents used to buy.

🛏 Sleeping & Eating

Vega Camping
CAMPGROUND €

(☑943 50 080; vegacamping.no; Floa; car/caravan site Nkr150/185, 4-bed cabins Nkr590; ⊗year-round) The close-cropped green grass extending to the still water's edge make this simple campground one of the prettiest in Norway. You can rent a boat or bike (Nkr300/150 per day) or go for a trot at the adjacent horse-riding school.

★ Vega Havhotell
HOTEL €€

(☑75 03 64 00; www.havhotellene.no; Viksås; s/d Nk1190/1390; ⊗closed Oct & Mon Nov-Mar) This isolated getaway, down a dirt track at Vega's secluded northern limit, is tranquillity itself (you won't find a radio or TV in any of its 21 rooms). It's a place to unwind, go for breezy coastal strolls or simply watch the mother eider duck and her chicks pottering in the pool below. It also has an excellent restaurant.

❶ Information

Tourist office (☑75 03 53 88; www.visitvega. no; ⊗9am-7pm Mon-Fri, 9.30am-3.30pm Sat & Sun mid-Jun–mid-Aug, 8.30am-3.30pm rest of year) Vega's tourist office is in Gladstad, the island's largest hamlet.

❶ Getting There & Away

Express boats go to/from both Brønnøysund and Sandnessjøen, while car ferries cross to Vega from the mainland at Horn and Tjøtta.

Sandnessjøen

POP 5900

Quiet little Sandnessjøen is a boom town in waiting – oil has been discovered offshore and big changes are expected here. Until this change comes, this is a slightly scruffy little coastal settlement where life revolves around the fishing port and the pedestrianised Torolv Kveldulvsons gate, one block from the harbour.

The main attractions here are one of the Kystriksveien's most appealing hotels, and the imposing **Syv Søstre** (Seven Sisters) range, south of town.

The Hurtigruten coastal ferry also pulls in twice a day,

🏃 Activities

The tourist office can suggest **walks** in the Syv Søstre range, reached most conveniently via the Rv17 at Breimo or Sørra, about 4km south of town. From there it's a couple of kilometres' walk to the trailhead at the mountains' base. You can also arrange a **taxi** (☑75 04 02 12) to get you to the base. Trails are blazed with red dots and the tourist office can provide simple maps and basic route descriptions, but pack *Alstahaug*, a reliable map at 1:50,000.

Hardy hikers can reach all seven summits (ranging from 910m to 1072m) in a day. Every several years there's a competition that takes in all the peaks – the record is three hours, 54 minutes, although most mortals should count on 15 to 20 hours as a minimum. The climb to Botnkrona (1072m), the highest of the peaks, takes most hikers of reasonable fitness three to four hours one way, while count on two to three hours to climb each of the other peaks (also one way).

Sign your name in the book at each summit, fill in a control card and leave it at the tourist office – in return, you'll receive a diploma in the mail.

🛏 Sleeping

★ Hotel Sandnessjøen
HOTEL €€

(☑40 00 00 91; www.hotel-sandnessjoen.no; Havnegata 4; d from Nkr1080; ℗🛈) This fabulous hotel overlooks the waterfront with stylish rooms with contemporary decor (think bold wallpaper, big mirrors and creative lighting). The breakfast is a cut above the average and a light but excellent evening buffet meal is included in the room rate. Best of all, the service here is more personal than you'll get elsewhere from the chain hotels. Sea-facing rooms cost a little extra.

Rica Hotel Sandnessjøen HOTEL €€
(☑75 06 50 00; www.rica.no; Torolv Kveldulvsons gate 16; d Nkr1025) This large hotel offers all the comfort you'd expect from a member of the Rica chain and a major overhaul and extension was underway at the time of our visit, so things should get even better.

ℹ Information

Tourist office (☑75 04 45 00; www.visithelgeland.com; Skippergata 1; ⊗9am-7pm Mon-Fri, 11am-6pm Sat & Sun mid-Jun–mid-Aug, 10am-3pm Mon-Fri rest of year) The tourist office is in the heart of town and is an excellent resource for the entire Helgeland region.

ℹ Getting There & Away

Widerøe (www.wideroe.no) has direct flights to Oslo, Bodø, Trondheim, Mo i Rana and Mosjøen.

Bus destinations from Sandnessjøen include Brønnøysund (3½ hours, daily except Sunday), Mosjøen (1¾ hours, three to five daily except Saturday) and Mo i Rana (2¾ hours, one to three services daily).

Træna & Lovund

Træna is an archipelago of over 1000 small, flat skerries, five of which are inhabited.

Ferries from the mainland dock on the island of Husøy, which has most of Træna's population and lodgings, but the main sights are on the adjacent island of Sanna. This drop in the ocean is just over 1km long with a miniature mountain range running the length of its spine and culminating at the northern end in the 318m spire, Trænstaven.

Near Sanna's southern end, archaeologists discovered a 9000-year-old cemetery and artefacts (now at the Tromsø Museum) inside the cathedral-like **Kirkehelleren Cave**.

Prolific bird colonies roost on the steep-sided island of **Lovund**, which rises 623m above the sea. Every 14 April the island (home to barely 250 people) celebrates Lundkommardag, the day 200,000 puffins return to the island to nest until mid-August.

Express passenger boats connecting Sandnessjøen and Træna run daily.

Sandnessjøen to Storvik

Superlatives come thick and fast along this stretch of coastline, and if you do only one segment of the coastal highway, make it the length between Sandnessjøen and the improbable sandy beach at Storvik, 100km south of Bodø. Much of this route is a National Tourist Route, a designation awarded only to the most scenic of Norway's scenic roads. With three ferry crossings and ample reasons to stop and stare, it's a long day (especially if you're keen to reach Bodø by nightfall), but one you'll never forget as the road bucks and weaves between the ocean and mountains whose summits remain flecked with snow even into summer.

The pick of the views from the southern end come as the road climbs after the Låvong-Nesna ferry crossing. Further on, as the road nears Mo i Rana, it's a dramatic run in its own right alongside pretty **Ranafjord** to Stokkvågen, soon after which you can roam around the Nazi coastal fort of **Grønsvik**, one of more than 350 defences built along Norway's coastline. Around 1km beyond the fort, a lookout offers more stunning views.

The route crosses the **Arctic Circle** somewhere along the hour-long Kilboghamn–Jektvik ferry crossing. The further north you go, the more spectacular the views, from the snowbound mountains of the Svartisen ice sheet to islands, islets and skerries too numerous to count. Along the way, sea eagles circle above you and spring wildflowers show off their best in the relatively mild climate, warmed by the very last of the Gulf Stream's flow. For long stretches the highway rolls right beside the water.

The best views of Svartisen come after the Ågskardet-Forøy ferry, with dramatic views of the glacier tongues dropping down off the icefields towards the water from the road alongside Holandsfjorden.

To get even closer, a **ferry** (☑47 99 40 30; adult/child return Nkr120/60) makes the 10-minute trip across Holandsfjorden from the small settlement of Holand roughly hourly. You can hire a bike (three/six hours Nkr50/75) to travel the 3km gravel track between the jetty and the tip of the Engebreen glacial tongue.

A 15-minute walk from the ferry landing takes you to the **Svartisen Turistsenter** (☑75 75 10 00; ⊗Jun–mid-Aug) with its cafe, shop and restaurant. It does guided one- to two-hour glacier walks (Nkr500) and longer four- to five-hour treks (Nkr950) from the end of Engabrevatnet lake. Reserve in advance. You can also slog independently up the steep route along the glacier's edge to the Tåkeheimen hut (1171m), near the summit of Helgelandsbukken (1454m). Follow the 'T' markers and allow eight hours out and back. The Turistsenter can also advise on cabin accommodation in the area.

If you've time to spare, consider breaking the journey at **Furøy Camping** (☑75 75 05 25; www.furoycamp.no; Forøy; tent/caravan site Nkr180/200, cabin Nkr500-900). Aside from the magnificent views of the Svartisen glacier across the fjord, this place has a five-star kids' playground (with trampoline and mini-cabins) and a hot tub. It's barely 1km from the Ågskardet-Førøy ferry terminal, but do reserve your cabin in advance; a trail of vehicles heads from the ferry towards reception in summer.

Bodø

POP 49,731

Bodø, the northernmost point of the staggeringly beautiful Kystriksveien Coastal Route and 63km west of Fauske on the Arctic Highway, is the gateway to Norway's true north. It's also the northern terminus of Norway's railway system and a jumping-off point for the Lofoten Islands.

Nordland's largest town, Bodø was founded in 1816 as a trade centre, then turned to fishing in 1860 during an especially lucrative herring boom. The town centre, rebuilt after being almost completely levelled by WWII bombing, is unexciting architecturally and the city's main charm lies in its backdrop of distant rugged peaks and vast skies. Dramatic islands that support the world's densest concentration of white-tailed sea eagles – not for nothing is Bodø known as the Sea Eagle Capital – dot the seas to the north.

◉ Sights

Norwegian Aviation Museum   MUSEUM
(Norsk Luftfartsmuseum; luftfartsmuseum.no; Olav V gate; adult/child/family Nkr110/55/300; ◷10am-4pm Mon-Fri, 11am-5pm Sat & Sun) Norway's aviation museum is huge fun to ramble around if you have even a passing interest in flight and aviation history. Allow at least half a day to roam its 10,000 sq metres. If you're flying into Bodø for real, you'll see that, from above, the striking modern grey and smoked-glass main museum building has the shape of an aeroplane propeller. Exhibits include a complete control tower and hands-on demonstrations.

The affiliated Norwegian Air Force Museum has plenty of examples of historic military and civilian aircraft from the Tiger Moth to the U2 spy plane (the ill-fated US plane that was shot down over the Soviet Union in 1960, creating a major diplomatic incident, was en route from Peshawar in Pakistan to Bodø). Children and kids-at-heart will thrill and shudder at the small simulator, which, for an extra charge, takes you on some pretty harrowing virtual flights, including piloting a fighter jet. Head south along Bankgata, then 750m eastwards along Olav V gate.

Nordlandmuseet   MUSEUM
(www.nordlandsmuseet.no; Prinsens gate 116; adult/child Nkr50/10; ◷11am-6pm Mon-Fri, to 4pm Sat & Sun Jun-Aug, 9am-3pm Mon-Fri rest of year) Recounting the short history of Bodø, this little gem of a museum has a cheerily entertaining and informative 25-minute film with English subtitles on the town's development. Museum highlights include a mock-up of a fisherman's *rorbu*, a section on Sami culture complete with sod hut and ritual drum, regalia relating to the town's fishing heritage, and a small hoard of 9th-century Viking treasure that was discovered nearby in 1919.

Bodøsjøen Friluftsmuseum   MUSEUM
(☑75 50 35 00; nordlandsmuseet.no/en/bodosjoen-friluftsmuseum; ◷24hr) **FREE** This open-air museum is 3km from town, near Bodøsjøen Camping. Here you'll find 4 hectares of historic homes, farm buildings, boat sheds, WWII German bunkers and the square-rigged sloop, the *Anna Karoline*. You can wander the grounds for free but admission to the buildings is by appointment. Here too is the start of a **walking track** up the river Bodøgårdselva, which eventually leads to the wild, scenic Bodømarka woods.

Cathedral   CATHEDRAL
(◷noon-3pm mid-Jun–Aug) This striking, austere structure, completed in 1956, has a soaring, freestanding tower and spire. Shaped like an inverted ship's hull, the walls of its nave are clad with tufty, multicoloured tapestries and there's a fine stained-glass window.

Bodin Kirke   CHURCH
(Gamle riksvei 68; ◷10am-3pm late Jun–mid-Aug) The charming little onion-domed stone church, around 3km from downtown, dates from around 1240. The Lutheran Reformation brought about substantial changes to

the exterior, including the addition of a tower. A host of lively baroque elements – especially the elaborately carved altar – grace the interior.

🏃 Activities

Norlandsbadet & Spektrum Velvære
SWIMMING
(www.bodospektrum.no; Plassmyrveien; adult/child Nkr145/40; ☺3-9pm Mon, Wed & Thu, 6.30am-9pm Tue & Fri, 10am-6pm Sat & Sun) Here's a fine place to relax, tone, and warm up if it's freezing outside. Exhaust yourself in its six swimming pools (you can zoom down an 85m waterslide) then unwind in its six saunas (the one with therapy music and scents, or does eucalyptus vapour tempt?). Soak yourself to the skin in the tropical rainforest shower or shiver in the ice grotto.

✨ Festivals & Events

Nordland Music Festival
MUSIC
(www.musikkfestuka.no) Ten days of classical music, jazz and opera in the first half of August.

Parken Festival
MUSIC
(www.parkenfestivalen.no) An action-packed, twin-staged fiesta of rock, R&B and pop over a weekend in late August.

🛏 Sleeping

Bodøsjøen Camping
CAMPGROUND €
(🗷75 56 36 80; www.bodocamp.no; Kvernhusveien 1; tent/caravan sites Nkr150/200, plus per person Nkr30, cabin Nkr250-840) At this waterside campground, 3km from the centre, cabins are particularly well equipped. There's an attractive grassy area with picnic tables exclusively for tent campers. Buses 12 and 23 stop 250m away.

City Hotell
HOTEL €
(🗷75 52 04 02; www.cityhotellbodo.no; Storgata 39; dm bed Nkr250, s/d Nkr650/750; @🖭) This hotel has 19 smallish but well-priced standard rooms and plenty of flexibility. Three dorms sleeping three to six cater for backpackers. Beneath the eaves are a couple of very large family rooms and two rooms have a kitchenette.

Bodø Vandrerhjem
HOSTEL €
(🗷75 50 80 48; www.hihostels.no/bodo; Sjøgata 57; dm Nkr350, s/d with private bathroom Nkr745/890; @) At last Bodø has a youth hostel to cater for travellers waiting for the next day's ferry to Lofoten or train! Right beside the station, it couldn't be better positioned and facilities are simple but adequate.

⭐Thon Hotel Nordlys
HOTEL €€
(🗷75 53 19 00; www.thonhotels.no; Moloveien 14; s/d from Nkr720/820; 🖭) Bodø's most stylish hotel, with touches of subtle Scandinavian design throughout, overlooks the marina and runs a reasonable restaurant.

⭐Skagen Hotel
HOTEL €€
(🗷75 51 91 00; www.skagen-hotel.no; Nyholmsgata 11; s/d from Nkr850/1050; @🖭) The Skagen occupies two buildings (one originally a butcher's, though you'd never guess it). Facing each other, they're connected by a passage that burrows beneath the street. Rooms are attractively decorated and a continent away from chain-hotel clones. There's a bar and free afternoon waffles and coffee, and excellent breakfasts. Staff can also give advice on a whole raft of vigorous outdoor activities.

Opsahl Gjestegård
B&B €€
(🗷75 52 07 04; www.opsahl-gjestegaard.no; Prinsens gate 131; s/d Nkr850/1100) On a quiet residential street, this guesthouse has 18 comfortable rooms with decor ranging from flowery to the less florid, and a small bar for guests. It's no cheaper than the larger hotels but still remains an attractive alternative to hotel life. There are also four apartments with mini-kitchens.

Clarion Collection Hotel Grand
HOTEL €€
(🗷75 54 61 00; www.nordicchoicehotels.no; Storgata 3; r Nkr890-1400; 🅿@🖭) At the central Grand, all rooms have parquet flooring and a prim but vaguely old-world air. Rates include both breakfast and light-buffet dinner, and there's a sauna with steam bath (free to guests). Reception staff rank among northern Norway's most cheerful.

Radisson Blu Hotel Bodø
HOTEL €€
(🗷75 51 90 00; www.radissonblu.com; Storgata 2; s/d Nkr750/995; 🅿@🖭) This contemporary hotel has bright rooms and a top-floor bar to better view the harbour and mountains. Breakfast is served in the Sjøsiden restaurant with its picture windows.

🍴 Eating

You can buy inexpensive fresh shrimp at the docks. Inside the Glasshuset shopping centre you'll find a supermarket and several quick-service choices.

Bodø

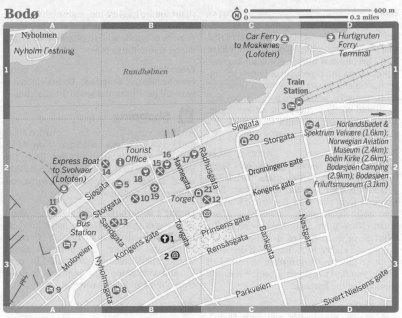

NORDLAND BODØ

Bodø

⊙ Sights

1	Cathedral	B3
2	Nordlandmuseet	B3

🛏 Sleeping

3	Bodø Vandrerhjem	C1
4	City Hotell	D2
5	Clarion Collection Hotel Grand	B2
6	Opsahl Gjestegård	D2
7	Radisson Blu Hotel Bodø	A3
8	Skagen Hotel	B3
9	Thon Hotel Nordlys	A3

🍴 Eating

10	Bjørk	B2
11	Bryggeri Kaia	A2
12	Farmors Stue	C2

13	Kafé Kafka	B3
14	Løvolds	B2
15	Paviljongen	B2

🍷 Drinking & Nightlife

16	G	B2
17	Nissunat	B2
18	Public	B2

🎭 Entertainment

	Fram Kino	(see 10)
19	Nordlænningen	B2

🛍 Shopping

20	Husfliden	C2
21	Ludvig's Bruktbokhandel	B2

Farmors Stue CAFETERIA, NORWEGIAN €
(📞 75 52 78 60; www.farmorsstue.no; Kongens gate 27; mains Nkr60-147; ⊙ 10am-6pm Mon-Fri, 11am-4pm Sat) With all the warmth and charm of an old-fashioned tea room, this lovely little place serves up snacks and light meals, good coffee and a well-priced lunch buffet (Nkr148). Local produce dominates the simple but carefully chosen seasonal menu.

Paviljongen CAFE-RESTAURANT €
(📞 75 52 01 11; Torget; mains around Nkr125; ⊙ 10.30am-midnight Mon-Fri, 10.30am-1am Sat, noon-midnight Sun) This great outdoor spot in the main square is the place to down a coffee or one of its three choices of draught beer; and perhaps nibble on an inexpensive lunch while watching the world pass by.

Løvolds CAFE €€
(www.lovold.no; Tollbugata 9; mains Nkr155-175; ⊙ 9am-6pm Mon-Fri, 9am-3pm Sat) This popular historic quayside cafeteria, Bodø's oldest eating choice, offers sandwiches, grills and hearty Norwegian fare with quality quayside views at no extra charge.

Bjørk
CAFE €€

(www.restaurantbjork.no; Storgata 8, 1st fl, Glasshuset; lunch specials Nkr149-174, pizzas from Nkr157, mains Nkr295-325; ⊙ 10am-10pm Mon-Sat, 3-10pm Sun) This pleasant place has quickly become a popular haunt, especially of Bodø's younger movers and shakers. It serves a variety of creative snacks, wood-fired pizzas, tapas and sushi and partly occupies the sealed bridge above the shopping mall's main alley. It's also a popular spot for an early drink.

Bryggeri Kaia
RESTAURANT-BAR €€

(☑ 75 52 58 08; www.bryggerikaia.no; Sjøgata 1; snacks from Nkr150, mains Nkr195-325; ⊙ 11.30am-3.30am Mon-Sat, noon-3.30am Sun) Bryggeri Kaia is a firm favourite. You can dine well, snack, enjoy its weekday lunch buffet (Nkr175), its Saturday herring buffet (Nkr175) or quaff one of its several beers. Enjoy your choice in its large pub-decor interior, on the street-side terrace or, best of all should you find a seat spare, on the veranda overlooking the harbour.

Kafé Kafka
CAFE €€

(Sandgata 5b; daily specials with coffee Nkr150, sandwiches Nkr125; ⊙ 11am-11pm Mon-Thu, 11am-3.30am Fri & Sat, 3-11pm Sun) You couldn't ask for a wider choice at this stylish contemporary cafe. It brews great coffee 12 different ways (you'll smell the aroma before you enter), offers cafeteria-style snacks and swirls 18 distinct kinds of milkshake. Some weekends, it turns into a club with DJs.

🍷 Drinking & Entertainment

Nissunat
BAR

(Dama Di; Sjøgata 18; ⊙ 10pm-3.30am) With a motto that translates roughly as 'art and chaos bar', Nissunat combines sophistication with an edgy, contemporary feel and eclectic decor.

Public
BAR

(Sjøgata 12; ⊙ 8pm-3.30am) Supersized stills from punk-rock shows line the walls and a life-sized Elvis props up the bar of this minimalist place with its black leather stools.

G
CLUB

(☑ 75 56 17 00; Sjøgata; ⊙ 10pm-3am Fri & Sat) With its cave-like entrance on Sjøgata, below the main square, G is a *discoteka* that packs in the over-25s.

Nordlænningen
LIVE MUSIC

(Torvgata; ⊙ noon-3.30am Mon-Sat, 1pm-3.30am Sun) This low-key basement pub beside the main square has live music six nights a week with karaoke on Sundays – see the signed posters of bands who've played here as you descend into the depths.

Fram Kino
CINEMA

(www.framkino.no; Storgata 8) Bodø's cinema is situated near the entrance to the Glasshuset.

🛍 Shopping

Husfliden
CRAFTS, CLOTHING

(☑ 75 54 43 00; www.norskflid.no; Storgata 23; ⊙ 9.30am-5pm Mon-Fri, 10am-3pm Sat) The Bodø outpost of this national chain has the usual appealing collection of Norwegian knitwear and homewares.

Ludvig's Bruktbokhandel
BOOKS

(Dronningens gate 42) Ludvig has a good selection of used books in English (German, Dutch and Russian, too) and will accept yours in part-exchange. With old LPs, comics and videos too, his shop is a treasure trove for all addicted browsers.

ℹ Information

Tourist office (☑ 75 54 80 00; www.visitbodo.com; Sjøgata 15-17; ⊙ 9am-8pm Mon-Fri, 10am-6pm Sat & Sun mid-Jun–Aug, 9am-3.30pm Mon-Fri rest of year) Publishes the excellent free *Bodø Guide* brochure and has two internet terminals (Nkr60 per hour) as well as free wifi.

ℹ Getting There & Away

AIR

From Bodø's airport, southwest of the city centre, there are at least 10 daily flights to Oslo, Trondheim and Tromsø. Other destinations in northern Norway include Leknes, Narvik, Harstad and Mo i Rana.

BOAT

Bodø is a stop on the Hurtigruten coastal ferry.

Car ferries sail five to six times daily in summer (less frequently during the rest of the year) between Bodø and Moskenes on Lofoten (car including driver/passenger Nkr646/180, three to 3½ hours). If you're taking a car in summer avoid a potential long wait in line by booking in advance (an additional Nkr100; online reservation at www.torghatten-nord.no).

Most days, at least one ferry calls in at the southern Lofoten islands of Røst and Værøy.

There's also an express passenger ferry between Bodø and Svolvær (adult/child Nkr366/183, 3¾ hours) once daily.

BUS

Buses run to/from Narvik (Nkr280, 6½ hours) via Fauske (Nkr90, one hour) twice daily, with extra services to/from Fauske.

TRAIN

Main destinations from Bodø:

Fauske Nkr128, 45 minutes, up to eight daily

Mosjøen Nkr625; 4¼ hours, two to three daily

Mo i Rana Nkr469, three hours, two to four daily

Trondheim Nkr1059, 9¾ hours, two daily

ℹ Getting Around

Local buses cost Nkr40 per ride. The tourist office rents bikes from Nkr100 per day.

Around Bodø

Saltstraumen Maelstrom

You need to plan your day to take in this natural phenomenon, guaranteed to occur four times every 24 hours. At the 3km-long, 150m-wide Saltstraumen Strait, the tides cause one fjord to drain into another, creating the equivalent of a waterfall at sea. The result is a churning, 20-knot watery chaos that shifts over 400 million cubic metres of water one way, then the other, every six hours. It's an ideal environment for plankton, which in turn attract an abundance of fish and therefore anglers. In spring, you can also see the squawking colonies of gulls that nest on the midstream island of Storholmen.

This maelstrom, claimed to be the world's largest, is actually a kinetic series of smaller whirlpools that form, surge, coalesce, then disperse.

At its best – which is most of the time – it's an exhilarating spectacle. Should you be unlucky enough to hit an off day, it may recall little more than the water swirling around your bath plug. The experience is more immediate from the shoreline, but for the best views, stand on the north side of the arching Saltstraumbrua bridge, overlooking the strait at its apex, and watch as the waters swirl like emerald nebulae.

Pick up a tide table in advance from the tourist office in Bodø or your hotel; none are on display at the site itself.

Saltstraumen is 32km south of Bodø by road (and much nearer by boat). There are seven buses daily (two on Saturday and Sunday; one hour) between Bodø and Saltstraumen bridge.

LOFOTEN

You'll never forget your first approach to the Lofoten Islands by ferry. The islands spread their tall, craggy physique against the sky like some spiky sea dragon and you wonder how human beings eke out a living in such seemingly inhospitable surroundings. The beauty of this place is simply staggering.

The main islands, Austvågøy, Vestvågøy, Flakstadøy and Moskenesøy, are separated from the mainland by Vestfjorden, but all are connected by road bridges and tunnels, making getting around easy. On each are sheltered bays, sheep pastures and picturesque villages. The vistas (the whole of the E10 from tip to toe of Lofoten is designated a National Tourist Route, a title bestowed only upon the most scenic roads) and the special quality of the Arctic light have long attracted artists, represented in galleries throughout the islands.

But Lofoten is still very much commercially alive. Each winter the meeting of the Gulf Stream and the icy Arctic Ocean draws spawning Arctic cod from the Barents Sea. For centuries, this in turn drew farmer-fishermen from the mainland's north coast. Although cod stocks have dwindled dramatically in recent years, fishing still vies with tourism as Lofoten's largest industry, as evidenced by the wooden drying racks that lattice nearly every village on the islands.

History

The history of Lofoten is essentially that of its fishing industry. Numerous battles have been fought over these seas, exceptionally rich in spawning cod ever since the glaciers retreated about 10,000 years ago. In 1120 King Øystein set up the first church and built a number of *rorbuer*, basic 4m by 4m wooden cabins for the fisherfolk with a fireplace, earthen floor and small porch area. It wasn't entirely philanthropy: in so doing, he took control of the local economy and ensured rich tax pickings for himself.

In the early 19th century power over the trade fell to local *nessekonger* (merchant squires) who'd bought up property. These new landlords forced the tenants of their *rorbuer* to deliver their entire catch at a price set by the landlords themselves. The Lofoten Act of 1857 greatly diminished the power of the *nessekonger* but not until the Raw Fish Sales Act of 1936 did they lose the power to set prices.

Lofoten

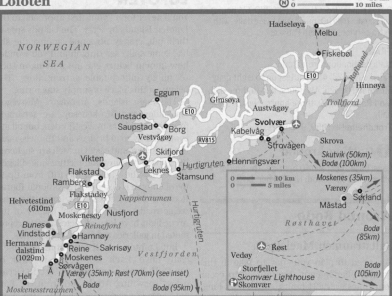

ℹ Information

The official www.lofoten.info website is rich in information about the whole archipelago.

ℹ Getting There & Away

FROM THE SOUTH

Possibilities include:

➜ the car ferry between Svolvær and Skutvik, on the mainland (1¾ hours)

➜ the car ferry between Bodø and Moskenes (three to 3½ hours)

➜ the foot-passenger-only express boat between Bodø and Svolvær (3¾ hours)

FROM THE NORTH

The completion of a couple of tunnels on neighbouring Hinnøya now allows ferry-free access from the mainland. Known as Lofast in Norwegian, this stretch of fast highway has almost halved driving time to Harstad-Narvik Evenes airport and on to Narvik itself and the Arctic Highway.

Otherwise, there's a car ferry between Vesterålen's Hadseløya (Melbu) and Fiskebøl (25 minutes).

ℹ Getting Around

Getting around is easy. The main islands are linked by bridge or tunnel, and buses run the entire E10 from the Fiskebøl–Melbu ferry in the north to Å at road's end in the southwest.

Tourist offices sell an excellent Lofoten cycling guide (Nkr298), full of information for cyclists and including handy pull-out maps.

Austvågøy

POP 9100

Many visitors make their acquaintance with Lofoten on Austvågøy, the northernmost island in the archipelago. It's a pretty enough place with some fascinating attractions, but more appealing as a gateway to the rest of the islands than as a destination in its own right.

Svolvær

POP 4460

The port town of Svolvær is as busy as it gets on Lofoten. The town once sprawled across a series of skerries, but the in-between spaces are being filled in to create a reclaimed peninsula. Although the setting is beautiful with a backdrop of high mountains, the hotch-potch of modern buildings clutter things somewhat.

⊙ Sights

★**Lofoten Krigsminnemuseum** MUSEUM (www.lofotenkrigmus.no; Fiskergata 12; adult/child Nkr80/30; ⊙10am-10pm Mon-Sat, noon-3pm &

KJERRINGØY

It's easy to see why this sleepy peninsula, washed by turquoise seas and with a backdrop of soaring granite peaks, is a regular location for Norwegian film-makers.

Bus 10 connects Bodø and Kjerringøy twice daily. In summer it's possible to squeeze in a return trip on the same day, which allows a good 2½ hours browsing time. Check the current timetable at Bodø's tourist office.

Whether by bus or car, the trip includes the 10-minute ferry crossing between Festvåg and Misten. Along the way, you pass the distinctive profile of **Landegode Island**, the white sandy beaches at **Mjelle** (whose car park is some 20 minutes' walk away) and the dramatic peak **Steigtind**, which rises a few kilometres south of Festvåg.

At the **Kjerringøy Trading Post** (Kjerringøy Handelssted; nordlandsmuseet.no/kjerringoy_handelssted; adult/child Nkr100/50; ⊙11am-5pm late May–late Aug), some 40km north of Bodø, the entrepreneurial Zahl family established an important trading station in the 19th century. The station provided local fishing families with supplies in exchange for their catch. Most of the timber-built structures of this self-contained community have been preserved. The spartan quarters and kitchens of the fishing families contrast with the sumptuous decor of the merchants' housing. There's a 20-minute audiovisual presentation included in the entry price. Admission to the main building is by guided tour.

6-10pm Sun mid-Jun–mid-Aug, shorter hours rest of year) Lofoten War Memorial Museum, privately and passionately run, is a fascinating place. Models in original military uniforms gaze down and there are plenty of artefacts and evocative, largely unpublished WWII-era photos.

★ **Magic Ice**   ICE BAR
(☑76 07 40 11; www.magicice.no; Fiskergata 36; adult/child Nkr130/80; ⊙noon-10.30pm mid-Jun–late-Aug, 6-10pm rest of year) Housed, appropriately, in what was once a fish-freezing plant, this is the ultimate place to chill out, perhaps with something to warm the spirit, served in an ice glass. The 500-sq-metre space is filled with huge ice sculptures, illustrating Lofoten life. If you can't come back to northern Norway in winter, here's a great, if brief, approximation. Admission includes a drink in an ice glass.

Nordnorsk Kunstnersenter   GALLERY
(North Norwegian Artist's Centre; Torget; ⊙10am-6pm mid-Jun–mid-Aug, 10am-4pm Tue-Sun rest of year) **FREE** On the main square and beside the tourist office and Lofoten Kulturhus (lofotenkulturhus.no; a cultural centre housing a cinema and exhibition space), the North Norwegian Artist's Centre hosts changing exhibitions of paintings, sculpture, ceramics and more by artists from northern Norway. Its shop is a good source for a tasteful souvenir of Norway's north.

Lofotenfotografen   GALLERY
(☑95 49 81 50; www.lofotfotografen.no; Vestfjordgata; ⊙10am-4pm & 6.30-8pm Mon-Fri, 10am-3pm & 6.30-8pm Sat mid-Jun–mid-Aug, closed evenings rest of year) **FREE** Stunning photos of the Lofoten Islands in all their brooding glory, most of them for sale, are the work of photographer Anders Finsland. It's worth stopping by even if you don't plan to buy.

Galleri Dagfinn Bakke   GALLERY
(☑76 07 19 98; www.dagfinnbakke.no; Richard Withs gt. 4; ⊙11am-3pm Mon-Wed & Fri, 11am-7pm Thu, 11am-2pm Sat) **FREE** One of Svolvær's more interesting little private galleries, this place showcases works by local artist Dagfinn Bakke, in which the distinctive light and natural formations of Arctic Norway take centre stage, with a range of other painters also on display. As always, many of the pieces are for sale.

Lofoten Temagalleri   MUSEUM, GALLERY
(off Parkgata; ⊙8am-10pm Jun-Aug) **FREE** The Lofoten Theme Gallery is very much the creation of one man, Geir Nøtnes, a keen photographer from a fishing background. The gallery is devoted in the main to cod fishing and whaling, with plenty of photos and equipment. Ask to see the splendid 20-minute DVD about Lofoten through the seasons.

Galleri Stig Tobiassen   GALLERY
(☑47 60 27 22; www.stig-tobiassen.com; Roald Amundsens gate 11; ⊙11am-4pm Mon-Fri, 11am-

Svolvær

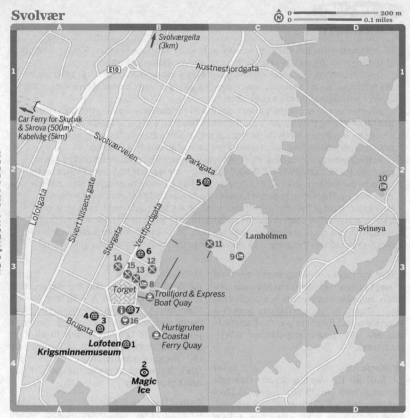

Svolvær

⊙ Top Sights
1 Lofoten Krigsminnemuseum	B4
2 Magic Ice	B4

⊙ Sights
3 Galleri Dagfinn Bakke	A4
4 Galleri Stig Tobiassen	A4
5 Lofoten Temagalleri	B2
6 Lofotenfotografen	B3
7 Nordnorsk Kunstnersenter	B3

🛏 Sleeping
8 Lofoten Suite Hotel	B3
9 Rica Hotel Svolvær	C3
10 Svinøya Rorbuer	D2

Svolvær Sjøhuscamp	(see 5)
Thon Hotel Lofoten	(see 7)

✖ Eating
11 Anker Brygge	C3
12 Bacalao	B3
Børsen	(see 10)
13 Du Verden	B3
14 Hjerterommet Kafe	B3
15 Kringla	B3

◉ Drinking & Nightlife
Bryggabaren	(see 11)
16 Styrhuset	B4

2pm Sat) **FREE** This place is another of Svolvær's fine little galleries that show and sell paintings in which the Lofotens are the focus.

🏃 Activities

★ Svolværgeita
HIKING, CLIMBING

You'll see it on postcards all over Lofoten – some daring soul leaping between two fingers of rock high above Svolvær. To hike up to a point just behind the two pinnacles (355m), walk northeast along the E10 towards Narvik, pass the marina, and then turn left on Nyvcicn, thcn right on Blatind vcg – thc steep climb begins just behind the children's playground.

The climb takes around half an hour, or an hour if you continue up to the summit of Floya. To actually climb Svolværgeita and take the leap, you'll need to go with a climbing guide – ask the tourist office for recommendations or try Northern Alpine Guides (p295).

Trollfjord   CRUISE

(adult/child from Nkr695/300) From the port, several competing companies offer sailings into the constricted confines of nearby Trollfjord, spectacularly steep and narrowing to only 100m. Take the two-hour sea-eagle trip, the three-hour cruise or sign on for a four-hour trip that includes the chance to dangle a line and bring home supper. Buy your ticket at the quayside or at operators such as **Lofoten Explorer** (www.lofoten-explorer.no), **RiB Lofoten** (☑90 41 64 40; www.rib-lofoten. com) or **Trollfjord Cruise** (☑45 15 75 87; www. trollfjordcruise.com).

Kaiser Route   CYCLING

For 83km of breathtaking cycling, head to Holandshamn and make your way back to Svolvær along the Kaiser Route. Lonely shoreline, jagged mountains and abandoned farms will be your constant companions. Unlike the west of Lofoten, this trip takes in parts of the island largely undiscovered by tourists. A long stretch runs parallel to Trollfjord. Ask at the tourist office for information about hiring bikes and getting to Holandshamn.

✦ Festivals & Events

World Cod Fishing Championship CULTURAL (☺Mar) The town's annual World Cod Fishing Championship, a celebration of all things piscatorial, takes place over the last weekend of March and there are hundreds of participants.

🛏 Sleeping

Svolvær Sjøhuscamp SEA HOUSE € (☑76 07 03 36; www.svolver-sjohuscamp.no; Parkgata 12; d/q from Nkr540/880, d with kitchen Nkr590, all without bathroom) This friendly *sjøhus* (sea house) straddling the water is a convivial, excellent-value place to fetch up and meet fellow travellers. There's also a gem of a six-bed apartment with balcony and full facilities (Nkr1900).

★**Svinøya Rorbuer** CABIN €€ (☑76 06 99 30; www.svinoya.no; Gunnar Bergs vei 2; cabins & ste Nkr1150-3200) Across a bridge on the islet of Svinøya, site of Svolvær's first settlement, are several cabins, some historic, most contemporary, and all cosy and comfortable. Reception is a veritable museum, a restored and restocked *krambua* (general store), constructed in 1828, which was Svolvær's first shop. They've properties all over the area and they're some of the best *rorbuer* in Lofoten.

★**Thon Hotel Lofoten** HOTEL €€ (www.thonhotels.no; Torget; r from Nkr973; P🐾) In a pleasing glass edifice overlooking the main square and harbour, Thon's Lofoten outpost has stylish modern rooms, most with fabulous views. Ask for a room on the upper floors (avoid the 2nd and 3rd floors) and facing the town for the best views – the binoculars in

---

LODGING LOFOTEN STYLE

Lofoten's lodging of choice is the *rorbu,* along with its cousin the *sjøhus*. Whereas *rorbu* (plural *rorbuer*) once meant a dingy, tiny red-painted fishing hut, nowadays the name is applied increasingly loosely to just about any wooden ox-blood or ochre-coloured structure, from historic cabins to simple holiday homes to plush, two-storey, multiroom, fully equipped self-catering units.

A *sjøhus* (literally 'sea house') was traditionally a bunkhouse-style building on the docks where fishery workers processed the catch and, for convenience, also ate and slept. While some *sjøhus* retain this style, others have been converted into summer tourist lodges and apartments, usually of the simpler, less-expensive kind.

Lofoten also has a few higher-end hotels and some wonderfully situated campgrounds.

While summer prices tend to be lower in the rest of Norway, the opposite occurs in Lofoten; in hotels you can expect to pay more than Nkr250 per room above the rest-of-the-year prices, although the difference is less pronounced in *rorbuer* and *sjøhus*.

each room are a nice touch. Service is slick and the location couldn't be more central.

Rica Hotel Svolvær
HOTEL €€

(☑76 07 22 22; www.rica.no; Lamholmen; r from Nkr885; P⊜) The Rica here is built on a tiny island, above the water and supported by piles. Room 121 has a hole in the floor so guests can drop a fishing line directly into the water below. Such novelties aside, the rooms are functional rather than memorable – make sure you get one with a balcony.

Lofoten Suite Hotel
BOUTIQUE HOTEL €€€

(☑47 67 01 00; www.lofoten-suitehotel.no; Havnepromenaden; ste from Nkr1500; ⊜) Right on the main harbour in Svolvær, in a lovely wood-and-glass structure, this suites-only hotel has attractive modern rooms with wooden floorboards, most of which have fine harbour views. Most have kitchenettes.

✕ Eating

Hjerterommet Kafe
CAFE €

(Vestfjordgata; snacks from Nkr60; ◎10am-4pm Mon-Fri, 11am-4pm Sat) More a coffee and cake kind of place, this eclectic little cafe is a fine little pitstop. The decor ranges from a bed mattress to cutesy white wood and the whole place is brimful of personality.

Kringla
CAFE €

(☑76 07 03 09; Torget 21; snacks from Nkr80; ◎8am-4pm Mon-Sat) This casual cafe-bakery right on the main square serves up a range of sweet and savoury snacks, from cakes to sandwiches.

Bacalao
BAR, CAFE €€

(☑76 07 94 00; www.bacalaobar.no; Havnepromenaden 2; mains Nkr145-175; ◎10.30am-1am Mon-Thu, 10.30am-2.30am Fri & Sat, noon-1am Sun) With its upbeat interior, Bacalao offers leafy, innovative salads, sandwiches and some equally creative pasta dishes; the *hot reke-pasta* (hot shrimp pasta) will set your taste buds tingling. Bacalao also expresses some of Lofoten's best coffee.

★ Børsen
NORWEGIAN €€€

(☑76 06 99 30; www.svinoya.no; Gunnar Bergs vei 2; mains Nkr289-355; ◎6-10pm) This Arctic Menu–restaurant brims with character. A former fish house, it was called the 'stock exchange' after the harbour-front bench outside, where the older men of the town would ruminate endlessly over the state of the world. In its dining room, with its cracked and bowed flooring, stockfish is the house

speciality – if you try it once, try it here – or the Lofoten lamb.

Du Verden
CAFE, RESTAURANT €€€

(☑76 07 09 75; www.duverden.net; Havnepromenaden; lunch buffet Nkr169, mains Nkr160-325; ◎11am-11pm Sun-Thu, 11am-1am Fri & Sat) With the cafe at street level and more formal dining upstairs, this excellent place is good whatever the occasion. The airy, modern interior and waterfront terrace are the perfect Svolvær setting with everything from sushi and sandwiches to local fish soup on the menu.

Anker Brygge
NORWEGIAN €€€

(Kjøkkenet; ☑76 06 64 80; www.anker-brygge.no; Lamholmen; mains Nkr310-345; ◎4-11pm) Anker Brygge, originally a shack for salting fish and nowadays furnished like an old-time kitchen, is a wonderfully cosy place to dine. The cuisine is just as traditional and the recommended menu choice is of course fish – try the kitchen's signature dish, *boknafisk*, semidried cod with salted fat and vegetables. Or the fried cod tongue...

🍷 Drinking & Nightlife

Styrhuset
PUB

(OJ Kaarsbøs gate 5; ◎7pm-1am Sun-Thu, 6pm-2.30am Fri & Sat) Svolvær's oldest pub is all dark crannies that speak of sailors long gone. There's football on the telly whenever there's a big game.

Bryggabaren
PUB

(Lamholmen) In the same complex as Anker Brygge, this low-beamed, cosy watering hole is bedecked with tools of all kinds. The bar is a lifeboat from a WWII Polish troop ship that washed up in Svolvær in 1946. There's a regular bill of live music from May through to September and sometimes at other times.

ℹ Information

Library (Vestfjordgata; ◎11am-3pm Mon-Sat) Free internet and wi-fi.

Tourist office (☑76 06 98 07; www.lofoten. info; Torget; ◎9am-10pm Mon-Fri, 9am-8pm Sat, 10am-8pm Sun mid-June–mid-Aug, shorter hours rest of year) Provides information on the entire archipelago.

ℹ Getting There & Around

From Svolvær's small airport there are up to six flights daily to Bodø.

Svolvær is a stop on the Hurtigruten coastal ferry. Two other sea routes connect Svolvær to the mainland. For timetables and reservations, visit www.torghatten-nord.no:

To/from Skutvik (car/foot passenger Nkr325/95, 1¾ to 2¼ hours, up to 10 daily) The shortest, most popular crossing (from Skutvik you can connect by bus with Narvik).

To/from Bodø (Nkr366/183, 3½ hours) Daily express passenger boat calling by Skutvik (one hour).

Useful bus routes include the following:

Bus 8 To/from Sortland on Vesterålen (2¼ hours, three to five times daily), via Stokmarknes (1¾ hours).

Bus 9 To/from Leknes (1½ hours, four to six times daily), with connections to Å (3½ hours).

Lofotekspressen To/from Narvik (4¼ hours, twice daily).

Call if you need a **taxi** (☑ 76 07 06 00).

Kabelvåg

Kabelvåg, 5km southwest of Svolvær, is an intimate and cosy place. At its heart is a small square and tiny harbour while its **Storvågen** district, 2km off the E10 to the south, has an enticing trio of museums and galleries.

◎ Sights & Activities

Behind the old prison in Storvågen, a trail climbs to the statue honouring King Øystein. In 1120 he ordered the first *rorbuer* to be built to house fishermen, who previously had been sleeping beneath their overturned rowing boats. His Majesty needed to keep his fisherfolk warm, dry and content since the tax on exported dried fish was the main source of his revenue.

Lofotmuseet   MUSEUM
(www.lofotmuseet.no; adult/child Nkr80/30; ⊙ 10am-6pm Jun-Aug, shorter hours rest of year) The islands' major folk museum is on the site of what could be considered to be the first town in the polar region, where traces of the original *rorbuer* have been excavated. The museum's main gallery was once the merchant's mansion. An easy, undulating, scenic 2km Heritage Path leads from the museum to the centre of Kabelvåg.

Lofoten Aquarium   AQUARIUM
(Lofotakvariet; www.lofotakvariet.no; adult/child Nkr120/60; ⊙ 10am-6pm Jun-Aug, shorter hours rest of year, closed Dec & Jan) Fish and sea animals of the cold Arctic waters inhabit this decent aquarium. Children will particularly enjoy the seal and sea otter feeding frenzies

(noon, 3pm and 6pm) and there's a multimedia show five times daily.

Galleri Espolin   GALLERY
(☑ 76 07 84 05; www.galleri-espolin.no; adult/child Nkr70/30; ⊙ 10am-6pm Jun–mid-Aug, shorter hours rest of year) This gallery features the haunting etchings and lithographs of one of Norway's great artists, Kaare Espolin-Johnson (1907–94). Espolin – his work all the more astounding as he was nearly blind for much of his life – loved Lofoten and often featured its fisherfolk, together with other Arctic themes.

Vågan Kirke   CHURCH
(www.lofotkatedralen.no; Villaveien 9; admission Nkr40; ⊙ 10am-6pm Mon-Sat, noon-6pm Sun late Jun–mid-Aug) Built in 1898 and Norway's second-largest wooden church, Vågan rises above the E10 just north of Kabelvåg. Built to minister to the influx of seasonal fisherfolk, its seating capacity of 1200 far surpasses Kabelvåg's current population.

Northern Alpine Guides   CLIMBING
(☑ 94 24 91 10; alpineguides.no; Havnegata 3) Climbing expeditions in the Lofotens in summer, ski adventures in winter.

🛏 Sleeping

A couple of inlets and 3km west of Kabelvåg, there are a pair of great campgrounds, right beside each other.

Ørsvågvær Camping   CAMPGROUND €
(☑ 76 07 81 80; www.orsvag.no; car/caravan sites Nkr180/220, 4-bed cabins Nkr1000, 7-bed seahouse apt Nkr1400; ⊙ May-Sep) Most *rorbuer* and the sea house are right beside the fjord and offer splendid views. You can rent a motorboat (per hour/day Nkr240/700).

Sandvika Fjord og Sjøhuscamp   CAMPGROUND €
(☑ 76 07 81 45; www.lofotferie.no; car/caravan site Nkr160/200, 4-bed cabins Nkr700-900, sea-house apt Nkr900) This shoreside campground has its own small beach. It rents motorboats (from Nkr220 per hour) and is a base for sea-kayak trips. The camping area is significantly larger than its neighbour's.

Kabelvåg Vandrerhjem & Sommerhotell   HOSTEL €
(☑ 76 06 98 80; www.hihostels.no; Finnesveien 24; dm/s/d with shared bathroom Nkr290/500/710, d with bathroom Nkr995; ⊙ Jun-early Aug; @) Less

than 1km north of the centre, the Lofoten Folkehøgskole school becomes a hostel and hotel outside the teaching year. There's a kitchen for guest use. Hostel rooms have one, two or four beds.

Kabelvåg Hotell HOTEL €€
(☑76 07 88 00; Kong Øysteinsgate 4; summer s/d Nkr850/1250; ☺Jun–mid-Aug & late Feb–Apr) On a small rise close to the centre of Kabelvåg, this imposing seasonal hotel has been tastefully rebuilt in its original art deco style. Rooms overlook either the port or mountains. It also functions as a centre for skiing and a host of other winter activities.

Nyvågar Rorbuhotell CABIN €€€
(☑76 06 97 00; http://www.classicnorway.no/hotell/nyvagar-rorbuhotell; Storvåganveien 22; 4-bed rorbu incl breakfast Nkr2300) At Storvågan, below the museum complex, this snazzy, modern seaside place owes nothing to history, but its strictly contemporary *rorbuer* are attractive and fully equipped. Guests can also rent bikes and motorboats.

Eating & Drinking

Præstengbrygga PUB, CAFE €€
(Torget; mains Nkr130-175) In central Kabelvåg, this friendly pub with its all-wood interior and dockside terracing, front and rear, serves sandwiches, pizzas and tasty mains, including a rich combination platter of marinated salmon, smoked whale, shrimps and salad. There's often live music and, for Nkr35, you can drink coffee all day with free refills.

Lorchstua Restaurant NORWEGIAN €€€
(☑76 06 97 00; mains Nkr195-389, 3-course menus Nkr525; ☺6-10.30pm Jun–mid-Aug) The acclaimed Lorchstua restaurant, run by Nyvågar Rorbuhotell, serves primarily local specialities with a subtle twist, such as baked fillet of halibut in a cod brandade.

Henningsvær

A delightful 8km shore-side drive southwards from the E10 brings you to the still-active fishing village of Henningsvær, perched at the end of a thin promontory. Its nickname, 'the Venice of Lofoten', may be a tad overblown but it's certainly the lightest, brightest and trendiest place in the archipelago.

⊙ Sights & Activities

Ocean Sounds WHALE CENTRE
(☑91 84 20 12; www.ocean-sounds.com; Hjellskjæret; adult/child Nkr200/free; ☺2-6pm Jul–mid-Aug, by request May-Jun & mid-Aug–Oct) Beside the Henningsvær Bryggehotel, this not-for-profit research centre is the initiative of one committed, hugely determined young biologist, Heike Vester. Enjoy a 45-minute multimedia presentation about cod, whales and other Arctic marine mammals, supplemented by an evocative 30-minute slide show featuring whales and other marine animals in the waters around Henningsvær.

Engelskmannsbrygga GALLERY
(www.engelskmannsbrygga.no; Dreyersgate 1; ☺10am-8pm mid-Jun–mid-Aug, noon-4pm Tue-Sun rest of year) FREE Here at 'Englishman's Wharf' is the open studio and gallery of three talented local artists: potter Cecilie Haaland, wildlife photographer and guide John Stenersen and glass-blower Kari Malmberg, with whom you can sometimes try your hand at blowing your own glass.

Lofotens Hus Gallery ART GALLERY
(☑91 59 50 83; www.galleri-lofoten.no; Hjellskjæret; adult/child & concession Nkr85/35; ☺10am-4pm Mar-Apr, 10am-7pm May & 1st half of Sep, 9am-7pm Jun-Aug, by appointment rest of year) In a former fish-processing house, this gallery displays a fine collection from what is known as the golden age of Norwegian painting, between 1870 and 1930, plus canvases by contemporary Norwegian artist Karl Erik Harr. Admission includes an 18-minute slide show of photos by Frank Jenssen, shown on the hour. Revealing the people and landscapes of Lofoten throughout the seasons, it's marred only by the trite, syrupy background music.

North Norwegian Climbing School ROCK CLIMBING
(Nord Norsk Klatreskole; ☑90 57 42 08; www.nordnorskklatreskole.no; Misværveien 10; ☺Mar-Oct) This outfit offers a wide range of technical climbing and skiing courses all around northern Norway. Climbing the peaks with an experienced guide costs around Nkr2200, including equipment, for one to four people.

For a multitude of ideas, check out the thick *Lofoten Rock* by Chris Craggs and Thorbjørn Enevold, the school's director. The last word on climbing in Lofoten, it's on sale at the school's mountaineering shop.

Lofoten Adventure OUTDOORS

(☎90 58 14 75; www.lofoten-opplevelser.no; ☺mid-Jun–mid-Aug) Based in Henningsvær, it offers a cluster of maritime tours and activities between mid-June and mid-August. Advance booking is essential. Tours include sea-eagle safaris (2.30pm, adult/child Nkr550/450, 1½ hours), midnight safaris (10pm, Nkr750, 2½ hours) and snorkelling sorties with equipment provided (11am, Nkr750, two hours).

🛏 Sleeping & Eating

Johs H Giæver
Sjøhus og Rorbuer GUESTHOUSE €

(☎76 07 47 19; www.giaever-rorbuer.no; Hellandsgata 79; rorbuer Nkr650-1200, sea house Nkr500-750) From mid-June to mid-August workers' accommodation in a modern sea house belonging to the local fish plant is hired out to visitors. Spruce rooms (some with space for four) have shared facilities, including a large kitchen and dining area, and are good value. The company also has 10 *rorbuer* with bathrooms in the heart of town.

★Henningsvær Suites APARTMENTS €€

(☎40 17 33 45; www.henningsvarsuites.no; ste Nkr1190-2500; P🛜) These stunning, spacious suites, some of which overlook the water, are a fine option in Henningsvær. With their abundant space and light, and location, it's a great alternative to hotel accommodation.

Henningsvær Bryggehotel HOTEL €€€

(☎76 07 47 19; www.henningsvaer.no; Hjellskjæret; s/d from Nkr1150/1650; 🛜) Overlooking the harbour, this attractive hotel is Henningsvær's finest choice. It's modern, with comfortable rooms furnished in contemporary design, yet constructed in a traditional style that blends harmoniously with its neighbours. Bluefish, its award-winning restaurant, is just as stylish; it serves Arctic Menu dishes and succulent sorbets, using fresh berries in season.

★Fiskekrogen RESTAURANT €€€

(☎76 07 46 52; www.fiskekrogen.no; Dreyersgate 29; mains Nkr195-295, lunch dishes Nkr145-275; ☺1-4pm & 6-11pm Sun, 6-11pm Mon-Sat Jun-Aug, shorter hours rest of year) At the end of a slipway overlooking the harbour, this dockside restaurant, a favourite of the Norwegian royal family, is Henningsvær's other culinary claim to fame. Try, in particular, the outstanding fish soup (Nkr195), but there's

everything else on the menu from fried cod tongues to smoked whale.

ℹ Information

Tourist office (☎91 24 57 02; www.henningsvar.com; ☺10am-6pm Mon-Fri, 11am-4pm Sat & Sun mid-Jun–mid-Nov) Henningsvær's tourist office is beside the main car park.

ℹ Getting There & Away

In summer, bus 510 shuttles between Svolvær (40 minutes), Kabelvåg (35 minutes) and Henningsvær 10 times on weekdays (three services Saturday and Sunday).

Vestvågøy

POP 10,925

The general rule when exploring this central Lofoten island is that the most appealing areas lie away from the main E10. The Viking Museum is an exception. You can cross Vestvågøy in an hour if you drive straight through but you could easily spend the best part of the day exploring.

Stamsund, a Hurtigruten port, is the pick of the traditional fishing villages, while there are fine views if you detour to Eggum and continue on past the town.

👁 Sights & Activities

Lofotr Viking Museum MUSEUM

(www.lofotr.no; adult/child incl guided tour mid-Jun–mid-Aug Nkr160/80, rest of year Nkr120/60; ☺10am-7pm Jun–mid-Aug, shorter hours rest of year) In 1981 at Borg, near the centre of Vestvågøy, a farmer's plough hit the ruins of the 83m-long dwelling of a powerful Viking chieftain, the largest building of its era ever

---

CYCLING IN LOFOTEN

Lofoten is perfect cycling terrain, thanks to its combination of generally flat roads, stunning scenery and enticing detours at frequent intervals.

One of our favourite cycling trails is the Kaiser Route (p293). Another possibility is the 63km from Henningsvær to Stamsund, a lightly trafficked route that takes in some fabulous scenery and quiet beaches en route.

Ask at the tourist office (p294) in Svolvær for further cycling suggestions, and their *Hjulgleder* handbook to cycling in Lofoten.

NORDLAND FLAKSTADØY

> **ⓘ STORVÅGAN COMBINATION TICKET**
>
> A combination ticket (adult/child Nkr180/75) gives entry to Lofoten Museum, Lofoten Aquarium and Galleri Espolin, all in Storvågan. They're an easy walk from each other.

discovered in Scandinavia. The resulting Lofotr Viking Museum, 14km north of Leknes, offers a glimpse of life in Viking times. You can walk 1.5km of trails over open hilltops from the replica of the chieftain's longhouse (the main building, shaped like an upside-down boat) to the Viking-ship replica on the water.

Costumed guides conduct multilingual tours and, inside the chieftain's hall, artisans explain their trades. The Svolvær–Leknes bus passes the museum's entrance.

Galleri 2   GALLERY
(www.galleri2.no; Stamsund; admission Nkr20; ⊙noon-4pm & 7-9.30pm Tue-Sun Jun-Aug, by appointment rest of year) The gallery of Lofoten painter Scott Thoe is barely 175m from the Hurtigruten quay in Stamsund, a short detour from the Rv185. It displays the works of a number of contemporary Norwegian artists, including scale models of his own grand open-air projects.

Lofoten Gårdsysteri   FARM
(☑76 08 96 31; www.lofoten-gardsysteri.no; Unstadveien 235, Bøstad; ⊙11am-5pm Mon-Sat) On the road to Saupstad, this lovely little farm has goats, pigs and chickens that the kids will enjoy. But we like it because it's a working organic farm and cheese factory. They sell their produce, including cheese, handmade sausages and honey – ideal if you're planning a picnic, such as just around the corner, past Eggum.

Unstad to Eggum Hike   HIKING
A popular hike connects these two tiny villages on the island's west coast. A 9km coastal track winds past several headlands, a solitary lighthouse, superb seascapes and the ruins of a fortress by the ocean. Eggum and Unstad are both about 9km from the main road and are served infrequently by buses.

Take care after rain as the trail, particularly around Unstad, can be slick with mud. The tourist office in Svolvær may be able to help with bus timetables, but don't count on it.

🛏 Sleeping & Eating

Justad Rorbuer og Vandrerhjem   HOSTEL €
(☑76 08 93 34; www.hihostels.no/stamsund; dm/s/d with shared bathroom Nkr160/325/460, 4-bed cabins from Nkr600; ⊙Mar–mid-Oct) The island's HI-affiliated youth hostel is a 1.2km walk from the Hurtigruten quay in Stamsund and has its regular clientele who come back year after year – one particularly loyal guest has stayed here over 50 times – so be sure to reserve. It's right beside the water in an old fishing complex.

Roar Justad, the friendly owner, dispenses information about local hiking routes, rents bicycles (from Nkr100 per day) and lends rowing boats and fishing lines for free.

Brustranda Sjøcamping   CAMPGROUND €
(☑76 08 71 44, 916 28 682; www.brustranda.no; Rolvsfjord; car/caravan sites Nkr160/180, 4-bed cabins Nkr500-1400; ⊙mid-May–Aug) This well-tended, beautifully situated seaside campground stretches around a tiny harbour. It's beside the Rv815, 14km northeast of Stamsund.

Skjærbrygga Sjøhus   CAFE, NORWEGIAN €€€
(☑76 05 46 00; dinner mains Nkr215-345; ⊙pub food from 11.30am, dinner 5-10pm) Low-beamed, large yet cosy, this place is right at the water's edge in Stamsund. It has a limited dinner menu (three starters, three fish dishes and two meat mains) that includes all the local favourites such as a starter of smoked whale and tender Lofoten lamb.

ⓘ Information

Tourist office (☑76 08 75 53; Storgata 31; ⊙9am-7pm Mon-Fri, 10am-2pm Sat & Sun mid-Jun–early Aug, 9am-4pm Mon-Fri rest of year) Vestvågøy's tourist office is tucked into the ground floor of Lofotsenteret, a large shopping centre in the lacklustre town of Leknes.

ⓘ Getting There & Away

Up to eight flights daily connect Leknes airport with Bodø. Leknes has bus connections to Å (1¾ hours, four to five daily), Stamsund (25 minutes, three to seven daily) and Svolvær (1½ hours, four to six daily). Stamsund is the island's port for the Hurtigruten coastal ferry.

Flakstadøy

POP 1535

Most of Flakstadøy's residents live along its flat north shore, around the town of Ramberg, but, as with Vestvågøy, it's the craggy south side that has the most dramatic scenery. Many visitors just zip through but it's worth stopping to sun yourself (sandy beaches are the exception in Lofoten) and perhaps to build in a detour to the arty village of Nusfjord.

Nusfjord

A spectacular 6km diversion southwards from the E10 beneath towering bare crags brings you to the cutesy village of Nusfjord (www.nusfjord.no), sprawled around its tiny, tucked-away harbour. Many artists consider it to be the essence of Lofoten but be warned: so do tour operators. As a result, it costs Nkr50 just to walk around plus a further Nkr50 to see *The People & The Fish*, a 12-minute video about Nusfjord, past and present.

In the country store that recently celebrated its centenary, upper shelves are crammed with vintage cans, bottles and boxes while the lower ones are stocked with contemporary fare. There's the old cod-liver oil factory, boat house, sawmill and a cluster of *rorbuer*, most of them modern and many available for rent (from Nkr1260 per night).

To snap the postcard-perfect shot of Nusfjord that you'll see everywhere around the island, you'll need to climb the rocky slope above the closed end of the little harbour. The path can be slippery after rain.

Parking is on a hill at the entrance to the village.

Ramberg & Flakstad

Imagine an arch of tropical white sand fronting a sparkling blue-green bay against a backdrop of snowcapped Arctic peaks. That's pretty much Ramberg and Flakstad **beaches**, on the north coast of Flakstadøy, when the sun shines kindly on them. Should you hit such a day, no one back home will believe that your holiday snaps of this place were taken north of the Arctic Circle, but you'll certainly know it if you stick a toe in the water.

◉ Sights

Flakstad Kirke CHURCH
(guided tours adult/child Nkr40/free; ⊙11am-3pm, late Jun-late Jul) Set back from Flakstad beach and bypassed these days by the E10, the red onion-domed Flakstad Kirke was built in 1780 but has been extensively restored over the years. Most of the original wood was ripped out of the ground by the

Arctic-bound rivers of Siberia and washed up here as driftwood.

Sund Fiskerimuseum MUSEUM
(www.sundfiskerimuseum.no; adult/child Nkr80/10; ⊙10am-4pm or 6pm mid-May–Aug) This fishery museum lies in the village of Sund, 3km off the E10 south of Ramberg. In one dim shack, there's an astounding clutter of boats, ropes and floats while within another is an unlabelled yet fascinating jumble of pots and pans, skis, old valve radios and the like. Tor-Vegard Mørkved, the young resident blacksmith, bashes out cormorants in iron.

Glasshytta GALLERY
(☎76 09 44 42; ⊙10am-7pm May-Aug) A 4km side trip from the E10 at Vareid, north of Flakstad, brings you to Vikten and the gallery of glassblower Åsvar Tangrand. Tangrand is the designer of the Lofoten Rune, the region's seven-pronged logo evoking a longboat, which you'll see all around the islands.

🛏 Sleeping & Eating

Ramberg Gjestegård CAMPGROUND €
(☎76 09 35 00; www.ramberg-gjestegard.no; E10; car/caravan site Nkr170/200, cabin Nkr950-1400) At this welcoming campground, right on the beach, you can rent a bike, kayak, rowing boat or even a motorboat to explore the island. There's a justifiably popular Arctic Menu **restaurant** (mains Nkr220-295) that does mainly fish dishes and its own splendid

---

HORSE RIDING IN LOFOTEN

If the idea of taking in Lofoten's beauty by horseback appeals, there are two operators we recommend.

Hov Hestegård (☎91 76 98 09, 76 07 20 02; www.hovhestegard.no; Gimsøysand; 1hr/2hr/half-day/full-day trail ride per person from Nkr450/850/1250/1950; ⊙May-Nov) Fine trail rides on the small island of Gimsøya, which lies between Vestvågøy and Austvågøy and is accessible off the E10.

Lofothest (☎45 47 33 55, 40 64 00 75; www.lofothest.no; Valbergsveien 966, Rolvsfjord; 3/5hr trips per person from Nkr1250/1950; ⊙May-Nov) From three-hour up to two-day excursions across Vestvågøy, from Rolvsfjord, along the Rv815 north of Stamsund.

WORTH A TRIP

BREAKING FREE FROM THE E10

Instead of continuing to roll along the E10 as it snakes its way through the heart of Vestvågøy island, take the even more attractive, much less travelled and only slightly longer Rv815. It starts just beyond the bridge that links Austvågøy, runs southwestwards for 28km and rejoins the E10 at Leknes. For the most part it hugs the shoreline with sheer mountains rearing to landward.

Flakstad Menu (cod, cured roast lamb and rhubarb compote for dessert). It also offers cheaper lunch specials.

ℹ Information

Tourist office (☑76 09 31 10; henkirk@online.no; ☺9am-7pm mid-May–Aug) Flakstadøy's seasonal tourist office is in Ramberg's Galleri Steinbiten.

Moskenesøy

POP 1225

The 34km-long island of Moskenesøy is the southernmost of the Lofoten Islands. Its spiky, pinnacled igneous ridge, rising directly from the sea and split by deep lakes and fjords, could almost have been conceived by Tolkien. A paradise for mountaineers, some of the tight gullies and fretted peaks of this tortured island – including its highest point, Hermannsdalstind (1029m) – are accessible to ordinary mortals as well.

Activities

The comprehensive *Moskenes Guide* has 14 suggestions for hikes of between one and 10 hours. You'll need to supplement this with Staten Kartverk's *Lofoten* at 1:100,000.

From June to mid-August, you can **deep-sea fish** (from Nkr650) for three to four hours using traditional long lines and hand lines. From the *Hellvåg* in Å and the *Carina* in Reine, both working cod-fishing vessels in winter, you're all but guaranteed a fat catch. Other good spots for fishing around the island include Reinefjord, the waters off Nusfjord, or near the maelstrom off Å.

At sea, there's excellent **birdwatching** and the possibility (albeit dwindling these days as herring stocks fall) of **whale sightings** in season.

ℹ Information

Tourist office (☑76 09 15 99; www.lofoten-info.no; ☺9am-7pm or 10am-5pm) Moskenesøy's tourist office is at Moskenes harbour. It publishes the free, informative *Moskenes Guide*, has an internet terminal and makes reservations for a variety of tours and activities.

ℹ Getting There & Away

Car ferries sail five to six times daily in summer (less frequently during the rest of the year) between Moskenes and Bodø (car including driver/passenger Nkr597/167, 3½ hours). At least one calls in daily at the tiny southern Lofoten islands of Røst and Værøy.

Four to five buses daily connect Leknes and Å (1¾ hours) in summer, stopping in all major villages along the E10.

Å

At the southern tip of Moskenesøy and the Lofoten islands, the bijou village of Å (appropriately, the last letter of the Norwegian alphabet), sometimes referred to as Å i Lofoten, is something of a living museum – a preserved fishing village with a shoreline of red *rorbuer*, cod-drying racks and picture-postcard scenes at almost every turn. It's an almost feudal place, carved up between two families, now living very much from tourism but in its time a significant fishing port (more than 700,000 cod would be hung out to dry here right up to WWII).

Do the village a favour and leave your vehicle at the car park beyond a short tunnel and walk in.

◎ Sights

Norsk Fiskeværsmuseum　　　　　MUSEUM
(Norwegian Fishing Village Museum; adult/child Nkr70/35; ☺10am-6pm mid-Jun–mid-Aug, to 3.30pm Mon-Fri rest of year) This museum takes in 14 of Å's 19th-century boathouses, storehouses, fishing cottages, farmhouses and commercial buildings. Highlights (pick up a pamphlet in English at reception) include Europe's oldest cod-liver oil factory, where you'll be treated to a taste of the wares and can pick up a bottle to stave off those winter sniffles; the smithy, who still makes cod-liver oil lamps; the still-functioning bakery, established in 1844; the old *rorbu* with period furnishings; and a couple of traditional Lofoten fishing boats.

Lofoten Tørrfiskmuseum   MUSEUM
(adult/child Nkr60/40; ⊙11am-4pm or 5pm Jun-Aug) The Lofoten Stockfish Museum is housed in a former fish warehouse. You'll be bowled over by Steinar Larsen, its enthusiastic, polyglot owner, who meets and greets every visitor. This personal collection, a passionate hobby of his, illustrates well Lofoten's traditional mainstay: the catching and drying of cod for export, particularly to Italy. Displays, artefacts and a DVD take you through the process, from hauling the fish out of the sea through drying, grading and sorting to dispatch.

Moskenesstraumen Strait   VIEWPOINT
Beyond the campground at the southern limit of Å, there's an excellent hillside view of Værøy island, across the waters. The mighty **maelstroms** created by tidal flows between the two islands were first described 2000 years ago by Pytheas and later appeared as fearsome adversaries on fanciful early sea charts. They also inspired tales of maritime peril by Jules Verne and Edgar Allan Poe. They're still said to be among the world's most dangerous waters.

🛏 Sleeping & Eating

Moskenesstraumen Camping   CAMPGROUND €
(📝76 09 11 48; camping for 1/2/3 persons Nkr10/160/200, caravans Nkr220, 2-/4-bed cabins from Nkr500/750, with bathroom Nkr750/850; ⊙Jun-Aug) This wonderful cliff-top campground, just south of the village, has flat, grassy pitches between the rocks, just big enough for your bivouac. Cabins too have great views, as far as the mainland on clear days.

Å-Hamna Rorbuer & Vandrerhjem   HOSTEL €
(📝76 09 12 11; www.lofotenferie.com; Å; hostel dm/s/d/tr Nkr250/300/570/750, 4-to 8-bed rorbuer with bathroom Nkr1000-1400) Sleep simple or sleep in more comfort; either way, this is an attractive choice. Newly affiliated to Hostelling International, this place has dorms above the Tørrfiskmuseum and in a quiet villa set in its garden. For more space and privacy, choose one of the restored fishing huts, where prices drop significantly outside high summer.

Å Rorbuer   CABIN €€
(📝76 09 11 21; www.a-rorbuer.com; d Nkr800-1100, apt Nkr1750-2000) *Rorbu* accommodation is dispersed throughout Å's historic buildings, the more expensive ones fully equipped

and furnished with antiques. The newer sea house, above Brygga Restaurant and with trim but plain rooms, has shared bathrooms, despite the hefty price.

Brygga Restaurant   SEAFOOD €€€
(📝76 09 11 21; mains Nkr195-349, lunch specials from Nkr150; ⊙Jun-Sep) Hovering above the water, this is Å's one decent dining choice. The menu, as is right and proper in a village with such a strong fishing tradition, includes mainly things with fins.

Sørvågen

Norsk Telemuseum   MUSEUM
(adult/child Nkr40/20; ⊙11am-5pm mid-Jun–mid-Aug) The Norwegian Telecommunications Museum presents itself as a study in 'cod and communications'. Granted, it's not an immediately winning combination but in fact this small museum commemorates a huge advance in fishing techniques. In 1906, what was Norway's second wireless telephone station was established in this tiny hamlet. From that day on, weather warnings could be speedily passed on and fishing vessels could communicate with each other, pass on news about where the shoals were moving and call up the bait boats.

Maren Anna   SEAFOOD €€€
(📝76 09 20 50; www.marenanna.no; Sørvågen; dinner mains Nkr275-325, lunch mains Nkr125-215) Maren Anna is at once pub, restaurant and cafe. Serving its mainstay of fish, bought daily fresh from the quayside, portions are gen-

---

ARCTIC MENU

To guarantee yourself a good meal in northern Norway, visit a restaurant affiliated to the Arctic Menu scheme. Members, who range from small, family-owned concerns to the restaurants of chain hotels, undertake to use the region's natural ingredients. It may be a sauce simmered with local berries; an Arctic char pulled from the icy waters; reindeer, seal, whale or, of course, cod – every last bit of it from the rich flesh to local delicacies such as the cheek, roe, liver, stomach or tongue.

The scheme's website (www.arktiskmeny.no) has a full list of its (at last count) 35 participants and some tourist offices carry its booklet.

erous. For a table with views over the fishing boats below and what's claimed, tongue in cheek, to be Norway's smallest beach, reserve ahead.

It also has a selection of rooms (singles/doubles Nkr550/850) in a nearby building and a couple of *rorbuer* sleeping five to nine (from Nkr1400).

Moskenes

Moskenes Camping CAMPGROUND €
(☑ 99 48 94 05; www.moskenescamping.no; tent/caravan site Nkr140/220; ☺ May-Aug) In a bleak location yet with great waterside views, Moskenes' only campground is gravel surfaced but has a sheltered grassy area for tent campers. Facilities are continually being upgraded (the owner's a carpenter) and it couldn't be more convenient for an early getaway from the ferry terminal, only 400m away.

Reine & Around

Reine is a characterless place but, gosh, it looks splendid from above beside its placid lagoon and backed by the sheer rock face of Reinebringen. You get a great view from the head of the road that turns to the village from the E10.

In summer, the **M/S Fjordskyss** (www.reinefjorden.no; adult/child return Nkr160/80; every 25min, 3 daily) runs between Reine and Vindstad through scenic Reinefjord.

From Vindstad, it's a one-hour hike across the ridge to the abandoned beachside settlement of **Bunes**, in the shadow of the brooding 610m Helvetestind rock slab.

Aqua Lofoten Coast Adventure AS BOATING
(www.aqualofoten.no; adult/child from Nkr800/500) From June to mid-August, three-hour boat trips are run by Aqua Lofoten to the bird- and fish-rich Moskstraumen maelstrom, as well as other nearby attractions, with snorkelling and fishing also possible.

Eliassen Rorbuer RORBUER €€
(☑ 76 09 23 05; www.rorbuer.no; Hamnøy; rorbuer from Nkr990; ℗ 🛜) This is a terrific collection of 26 *rorbuer* close to Reine, with refurbished interiors; some have great views. Take your time choosing the right one for you – the website is slow but worth persisting with.

Sakrisøy

Museum of Dolls & Toys MUSEUM
(Dagmars Dukke og Leketøy Museum; ☑ 76 09 21 43; www.lofoten.ws; adult/child Nkr60/30; ☺ 10am-6pm May & Sep, 10am-8pm Jun-Aug, by appointment rest of year) In Sakrisøy, Dagmar Gylseth has collected more than 2500 dolls, antique teddy bears and historic toys over 20 years for her Museum of Dolls and Toys. There's also an affiliated antiques shop upstairs.

Sakrisøy Rorbuer CABIN €€
(☑ 76 09 21 43; www.lofoten.ws; cabin Nkr1050-1950) Reserve at the Museum of Dolls & Toys for Sakrisøy Rorbuer, a relatively authentic complex of ochre-coloured cottages hovering above the water. You can also hire motorboats.

Sjømat CAFE €
(☑ 900 61 566; ☺ 10am-4pm mid-Jul–Aug, shorter hours rest of year) For self-catering, the fish shop and cafe Sjømat, across the street from the Doll Museum, is famous for its fish cakes, salmon burgers, smoked salmon, prawns and – go on, be adventurous – seagulls' eggs.

Hamnøy

Hamnøy Mat og Vinbu NORWEGIAN €€€
(☑ 76 09 21 45; Hamnøy; mains Nkr175-295; ☺ late May-early Sep) This welcoming restaurant is run by three generations of the same family. It's well regarded for local specialities, including bacalao and cod tongues. Grandmother takes care of the traditional dishes – just try her fish cakes – while her son is the main chef. Its fish is bought daily from the harbour barely 100m away.

Southern Islands

This remote pair of islands is superb for birdwatching. Værøy, mainly high and rugged, and Røst, flat as a pancake, both offer good walking and relative solitude in well-touristed Lofoten.

Værøy

POP 570

Craggy Værøy, its handful of residents hugely outnumbered by over 100,000 nesting sea birds – fulmars, gannets, Arctic terns, guillemots, gulls, sea eagles, puffins, kittiwakes, cormorants, eiders, petrels and a host of others – is a mere 8km long with white-sand beaches, soaring ridges, tiny, isolated villages, granite-gneiss bird cliffs and sparkling seas.

◉ Sights & Activities

Walking routes approach some of the major **sea-bird rookeries**. The most scenic and popular trail begins at the end of the road around the north of the island, about 6km from **Sørland** and 300m beyond the former airstrip. It heads southward along the west coast, over the Eidet isthmus to the mostly abandoned fishing village of **Måstad**, on the east coast, where meat and eggs from the puffin colonies once supported 150 people.

Fit hikers who relish a challenge may also want to attempt the steep climb from Måstad to the peak of **Måhornet** (431m), which takes about an hour each way. Alternatively, from the quay at Sørland you can follow the road (or perhaps the more interesting ridge scramble) up to the NATO installation at **Håen** (438m).

⌂ Sleeping

Gamle Prestegård GUESTHOUSE €€
(Old Vicarage; ✆ 76 09 54 11; www.varoyrhs.com; s/d with shared bathroom Nkr495/830, with private bathroom Nkr595/930) Værøy's smartest lodging and dining is on the island's north side. It's the large house with a flagpole in the garden beside the church, just where you'd expect the vicar to have lived.

ⓘ Information

Tourist office (✆ 75 42 06 00; ◷ 9am-3pm Mon-Fri mid-Jun–mid-Aug) The tourist office is in the town hall at Sørland, the main village.

ⓘ Getting There & Away

The car ferry runs most days to/from Bodø (passenger/car Nkr167/597), directly or via Moskenes. The ferry also links Værøy with Røst (passenger/car Nkr93/321).

Lufttransport (✆ 75 43 18 00; www.lufttransport.no; one way Nkr845) runs helicopter flights between Bodø and Værøy once or twice daily, February to October.

Røst

POP 625

The 365 islands and skerries of Røst (one for each day of the year) form Lofoten's ragged southern edge. Røst stands in sharp contrast to its rugged neighbours to the north, and were it not for a small pimple in the middle,

the main pond-studded island of Røstlandet would be dead flat. Thanks to its location in the heart of the Gulf Stream, this cluster of islets basks in one of the mildest climates in Norway and attracts 2.5 million nesting sea birds to some serious rookeries on the cliffs of the outer islands.

An unusual view of medieval life on the island is provided in the accounts of a shipwrecked merchant of Venice, one Pietro Querini, who washed up on Sandøy in 1432 and reputedly introduced stockfish to Italy. The tourist office has a sheet outlining the tale.

⌖ Tours

From June to mid-August the M/S *Inger Helen*, belonging to Kårøy Rorbucamping, does five-hour **boat tours** (adult/child Nkr400/200) that cruise past several bird cliffs, including the Vedøy kittiwake colony. Weather permitting, the boat makes a stop for a short walk to the 1887 Skomvær lighthouse or, if you prefer, you can try a little fishing (lines provided).

⌂ Sleeping & Eating

Kårøy Rorbucamping CAMPGROUND €
(✆ 76 09 62 38; www.karoy.no; per person Nkr200; ◷ May–mid-Sep; @) Rooms sleep two, four or six at this authentic *rorbu* on the minuscule island of Kårøy. Bathrooms are communal and there are self-catering facilities. You can borrow a rowing boat for free or rent a motor boat. Phone from the ferry and a boat will be sent to collect you.

Røst Bryggehotel HOTEL €€
(✆ 76 05 08 00; www.rostbryggehotell.no; d Jul–mid-Aug Nkr850, rest of year Nkr1000) This modern development in traditional style is right on the quayside. It has 16 comfortable doubles, and hires out bikes, boats and fishing tackle. It also has a restaurant.

Querini Pub og Restaurant PUB, RESTAURANT €€
(✆ 76 09 64 80; mains from Nkr150; ◷ 6pm-midnight Jun-Aug) Named after the shipwrecked merchant from Venice, this is a reliable choice among Røst's few eating options.

ⓘ Information

Tourist office (✆ 454 92 186; ◷ mid-Jun–mid-Aug) Røst's tourist office is a short walk from the ferry dock.

❶ Getting There & Away

There are flights to/from both Bodø and Le-knes. Røst, like Værøy, is served by the car ferry that runs between Bodø (passenger/car Nkr203/736) and Moskenes (passenger/car Nkr142/507).

VESTERÅLEN

Although the landscapes here aren't as dramatic as those in Lofoten, they tend to be much wilder and the forested mountainous regions of the island of Hinnøya are a unique corner of Norway's largely treeless northern coast.

An Encounter with Vesterålen – Culture, Nature & History (Nkr170), sold at tourist offices, gives a good introduction to the region, its sights and walking routes.

Hadseløya

POP 7950

Vesterålen's link to Lofoten is the southernmost island of Hadseløya, connected by ferry from the port of Melbu to Fiskebøl on Lofoten's Austvågøy. The other main town, Stokmarknes, is best known as the birthplace of the Hurtigruten coastal ferry.

❶ Information

Tourist office (☑76 16 46 60; ◷10am-5pm Mon-Sat, 11am-4pm Sat & Sun mid-Jun–mid-Aug) On the waterfront in Stokmarknes.

❶ Getting There & Around

The Hurtigruten coastal ferry still makes a detour stop in its home port of Stokmarknes.

Buses between Melbu and Stokmarknes run several times daily on weekdays and twice daily at weekends.

Melbu

The main reason to come to Melbu is to catch the ferry from here to Fiskebøl on Lofoten; from Fiskebøl, it's just 32km into Svolvær.

Norwegian Fishing Industry Museum MUSEUM
(Norsk Fiskerindustrimuseum; www.nofi.museum. no; Neptunveien; adult/child Nkr60/free; ◷9am-3pm Mon-Fri) In an abandoned herring-oil factory (romantically named Neptune despite its stark functionality), the Norwegian Fishing Industry Museum traces the life of a fish from the deep sea to the kitchen table. There's also a children's exhibition about the goings-on on the sea floor, and a series of fine photos of sea eagles. Across the harbour from the ferry pier, it's 750m from the E10. In summer there are guided visits, included with the admission fee.

Sommer-Melbu Festival ARTS
(www.sommermelbu.no; ◷Jul) The Sommer-Melbu festival, held each July, is one of northern Norway's liveliest cultural festivals with seminars, lectures, music of all genres, theatre and art exhibitions.

Langøya

POP 14,970

The undoubted highlights of Langøya, Vesterålen's central island, are the historic, little-visited fishing villages at its northern tip. Unappealing Sortland is the island's gateway town.

NORDLAND BOATS

You're bound to come across the uniquely shaped, stubby Nordland boat, which has served local fishing communities from the earliest days of settlement. These informal symbols of the tough, self-sufficient lifestyle of the hardy coastal folk here up north are still in use from Namsos, in Trøndelag, right up to the Kola Peninsula in Arctic Russia, but the greatest concentrations are found in Lofoten.

The smallest versions are known as *færing*, measuring up to 5m, while larger ones are called *hundromsfæring* (6m), *seksring* (7m), *halvfjerderømming* (7.5m), *firroing* (8m), *halvfemterømming* (9m), *åttring* (10m to 11m) and *fembøring* (11m to 13m).

Traditionally, the larger the boat, the greater the status of its *høvedmann* (captain). Whatever the size, Nordland boats are excellent for both rowing and sailing, even in rough northern seas. Until quite recently, sailing competitions, pitting fishing communities against each other, were one of the great social events of the year.

A good place to see museum-quality examples is in the harbour at Å in Lofoten.

Festivals & Events

Arctic Sea Kayak Race SPORTS
(www.askr.no; ☺ Jul) The annual Arctic Sea Kayak Race, held over six days in July, is one of the ultimate challenges in competitive sea-kayaking. Normal beings can opt for less intensive kayak touring or an introductory course in sea-kayaking.

Sortland

POP 9930

Sortland, Vesterålen's commercial centre and transit hub, occupies a nick in the island's east coast. Its mostly chunky, rectangular buildings are painted a soothing sea-blue, perhaps to distract you from the fact that there's very little to detain you as you turn north towards Stø or south towards Lofoten.

✦ Festivals & Events

Sortland Jazz MUSIC
(www.sortlandjazz.no; ☺ Sep) Held in September, Sortland Jazz takes place over a couple of weeks and is a worthy member of Norway's fine jazz festival circuit.

ᗗ Sleeping & Eating

Sortland Camping og Motell CAMPGROUND €
(☑ 76 11 03 00; www.sortland-camping.no; Vestervegen 51; car/caravan site Nkr250/250, cabin Nkr350-2500) Around 1.3km from the centre and signposted off the road to Stokmarknes, this place offers home cooking, strong on northern Norway cuisine. Occupying an extensive, semiwooded area, it produces a useful information sheet about the area.

Sjøhus Senteret GUESTHOUSE, CABIN €€
(☑ 76 12 37 40; www.lofoten-info.no/vesteralen-sjohus; Ånstadsjøen; 5-bed cabins from Nkr1400) Precisely 1.4km north of the bridge that connects Sortland with Hinnøya island, this appealing spot has both comfortable rooms and waterside cabins with views. Its **Sjøstua restaurant** (mains Nkr215-275; ☺ 3-9.30pm Mon-Sat, 1-8.30pm Sun), where owner and chef Marit Asbjørnsen produces a delightful range of à la carte dishes, is worth a visit in its own right.

Intimate and all-wood, it has superb views over the fjord in three directions. Try the cod baked with herbs and garnished with prawns, or the reindeer stew with mushrooms and juniper berries.

ℹ Information

Tourist office (☑ 76 11 14 80; www.visitvesteralen.com; Kjøpmannsgata 2; ☺ 9am-5.30pm Mon-Fri, 10am-3.45pm Sat, noon-3.45pm Sun mid-Jun–mid-Aug, 9am-2.30pm Mon-Fri rest of year) Covers the whole of the Vesterålen region.

ℹ Getting There & Away

Sortland is a stop on the Hurtigruten coastal ferry.

Bus services include:

Andenes Two hours, two to four daily, via Risøyhamn (one hour)

Harstad 2¼ hours, one to three daily

Narvik 3½ hours, three to five daily

Svolvær 2¼ hours, two to four daily

Stø

The small fishing village of Stø clings to Langøya's northernmost tip. It's the sort of place that's so quiet seabirds nest in the low cliffs that abut the main street through town.

People used to come here for two reasons: whale-watching expeditions and the chance to hike one of Vesterålen's prettiest walks. While the latter remains a possibility, the whale safaris have ceased to operate – check with the tourist office in Sortland to see if they've started up again.

Two weekday buses run between Sortland and Stø (1¼ hours).

Queen's Route HIKING
The walk over the headland between Nyksund and Stø, waymarked with red letter Ts, merits a short day of your life. Most hikers prefer to start with the harder part and sweat a little on the outward leg of this five-hour circular trek via the 517m Sørkulen, then breathe easy, returning via the simpler sea-level route. The Sortland tourist office carries a free guide leaflet.

Called the Queen's Route, its name derives from a hike taken by Norway's Queen Sonja in 1994.

Stø Bobilcamp CAMPGROUND €
(☑ 76 13 25 30; www.stobobilcamp.no; campsite Nkr175, cabin Nkr1200; ☺ mid-May–mid-Aug) Small, waterside Stø Bobilcamp is stark indeed and a windy spot to pitch your tent, but it does run an unpretentious little restaurant, serving primarily fish.

① ANDØYA'S ROAD LESS TRAVELLED

Unless you leave Andøya by the seasonal ferry from Andenes to Gryllefjord (in itself a lovely way to go), take the minor, lightly trafficked west coast road from Risøyhamn as you head northwards. Designated a National Tourist Route, it offers magnificent coastal panoramas as it threads along the shoreline. Returning by the Rv82, notice the giant hillocks of peat, extracted, dried and ready to be transported to garden centres around the world.

To experience the route at the pace it deserves, hire a bike from Fargeklatten and ride the coast as far as Sortland, where you can sling your bike on the bus for delivery back to Andenes.

Andøya

POP 5200

Andøya is long, narrow and flat except for the mountains on its western flank, and its main calling card comes, not surprisingly, from the sea. The 1000m-deep, dark, cold waters of its northwestern shore attract abundant stocks of squid, including some very large specimens indeed, and these in turn attract the squid-loving sperm whales. The result is fairly reliable whale-watching from late May to the middle of September, centred on the town of Andenes at the island's northern end.

Andenes is the only place of any size but other nature safaris depart from the tiny ports of Bleik and Stave, about 10km and 25km southwest of the town.

Andenes

The straggling village of Andenes, with its rich fishing history, is northern Norway's main base for whale-watching and there are a host of other nature-based activities possible in the vicinity. The town also has a lonely, end-of-the-road feel – stand on the windswept harbourside quay and stare out into the North Atlantic and you'll see what we mean. That changes somewhat in summer when the seasonal ferry connects Andenes to Senja and the town bustles with uncharacteristic activity.

◉ Sights

★ **Andøya Rocket Range**   MUSEUM
(☑76 14 46 00; www.spaceshipaurora.no; exhibitions adult/child Nkr125/50, virtual missions Nkr350/175; ⊙10am-6pm mid-Jun–mid-Aug, 9am-3pm Mon-Fri rest of year) Located 1km south of the town entrance along the road to Bleik, this innovative space centre has a wide-screen 16-minute movie and other exhibits about the aurora borealis (rockets sent up from here aid in the study of this phenomenon) and Norway's role in space research. To really get into the spirit, you can join a virtual mission (one hour to one hour 45 minutes) aboard the Spaceship Aurora and even send up a virtual rocket. Ring ahead to book.

It's all good, scientific fun and highly recommended.

★ **Hvalsenteret**   MUSEUM
(Havnegate 1; adult/child Nkr70/35; ⊙8.30am-4pm late May–mid-Sep) The Whale Centre provides a perspective for whale-watchers, with displays on whale research, hunting and the life cycle of these gentle giants. Most people visit the centre in conjunction with a whale safari. There's also an onsite restaurant. It sometimes stays open as late as 8pm in July and August.

Hisnakul   MUSEUM
(www.hisnakul.no; Hamnegata 1; ⊙9am-6pm mid-Jun–Aug, 8am-3pm Mon-Fri rest of year) FREE This nature centre shares a restored wooden warehouse with the tourist office. It showcases the natural history of northern Norway, including sea birds, marine mammals, topography, farming, fisheries and local cultures. There's also a 23-minute slide show with spectacular shots of the natural life of northern Norway.

Northern Lights Centre   EXHIBITION
(⊙10am-6pm late Jun-late Aug) FREE Next door to Hisnakul, this impressive high-tech aurora borealis exhibition first featured at the 1994 Winter Olympics in Lillehammer.

Polarmuseet   MUSEUM
(www.museumnord.no; Havnegate; adult/child Nkr50/free; ⊙10am-5pm mid-Jun–mid-Aug) The quaint, Arctic-themed Polar Museum has displays on local hunting and fishing traditions. There's extensive coverage of the 38 winter hunting expeditions in Svalbard undertaken by local explorer Hilmar Nøis, who also collected most of the exhibits.

Andenes Fyr LIGHTHOUSE
(adult/child Nkr50/25; ☉late Jun-Aug) The town's landmark red lighthouse, automated for many years, opened in 1859 and still shines on. To climb up its 40m and 148 steps, ask for the key at the tourist office.

🏃 Activities

In addition to the activities based in Andenes, ask the tourist office about moose safaris in Buksnesfjord and birdwatching possibilities in Bleik. Ask also at the tourist office about sea-kayaking.

★ Whale Safari WILDLIFE-WATCHING
(☎76 11 56 00; www.whalesafari.no; Andenes; adult/child Nkr890/570) Far and away the island's biggest outfit, Whale Safari runs popular whale-watching cruises between late May and mid-September. It also operates the Whale Centre. Tours begin with a guided visit to the centre, followed by a two- to four-hour boat trip. There's a good chance of spotting minke, pilot, humpback and orca (killer whale).

Trips depart at least once daily with more sailings in high summer. Bad weather and/or high seas only rarely prevent a Whale Safari sailing. All the same, try to build in an extra day on the island, just in case you're unlucky. If you fail to spot at least one whale, your money is refunded or you can take another trip for free. Your fee includes a snack, and staff pass around the seasickness pills, just like airline boiled sweets, before takeoff.

Sea Safari Andenes WILDLIFE-WATCHING
(☎91 67 49 60; www.seasafariandenes.no; adult/child Nkr995/800; ☉late-May–mid-Sep) The smaller of Andenes' two whale-watching outfits, this place, with its base on the docks just off the road to the lighthouse, runs 1½-half to three-hour whale-watching trips with up to two daily departures during the season. They also offer shorter seal- and bird-watching trips (adult/child 1½ hours Nkr450/400).

🛌 Sleeping

Hisnakul GUESTHOUSE €
(☎76 14 12 03; www.hisnakul.no; s/d with shared bathroom Nkr350/500) Hisnakul nature centre has well-priced budget rooms above its gallery and there are facilities for self-caterers. It has only 14 beds so phone to reserve.

Andenes Camping CAMPGROUND €
(☎76 11 56 00; www.andenescamping.no; car/caravan sites Nkr125/175; ☉late May-Sep) This basic campground, located 3.5km from town, is on a gorgeous seaside meadow, green and smooth as a golf course. It has a well-equipped kitchen and large common room.

★ Hotell Marena BOUTIQUE HOTEL €€
(☎91 58 35 17; www.hotellmarena.no; Storgata 15; s/d incl breakfast from Nkr800/1000) Hotell Marena is an exciting and particularly tasteful recent addition to Andenes' accommodation choices. Public areas feature nature photographs by local photographer Espen Tollefsen, as do each of the 12 bedrooms, individually designed with colours that match the tones of the blown-up images. There's free coffee around the clock, together with homemade cakes.

STOKMARKNES & THE HURTIGRUTEN

The Hurtigruten coastal ferry was founded in Stokmarknes in 1893 by Richard With. Originally a single ship, the S/S *Vesterålen,* it sailed into nine ports between Trondheim and Hammerfest, carrying post, passengers and vital supplies. Now the line boasts 11 ships, carries half a million passengers annually, serves 35 towns and villages and is a vital link for Norway, providing transport for locals and a scenic cruise experience for tourists.

Hurtigrutemuseet (www.hurtigrutemuseet.no; Markedsgata 1; adult/child Nkr90/35; ☉10am-6pm mid-Jun–mid-Aug, 2-4pm mid-Sep–mid-May) The Hurtigruten Museum portrays the history of the coastal-ferry line in text and image. Hitched to the quayside is the retired ship M/S *Finnmarken,* claimed to be the world's largest museum piece, which plied the coastal route between 1956 and 1993.

Hurtigrutens Hus Turistsenter (☎76 15 29 99; s/d Nkr1175/1475) This friendly extension to the Hurtigruten complex is over the bridge that spans the fjord and has conventional cabins and rooms.

WORTH A TRIP

NYKSUND: A VILLAGE REBORN

The population of the small fishing village of Nyksund was already dwindling when, in the 1960s, the bakery and post office, heart of any community, closed down. Then, after a storm wrought havoc in 1975, nearly everyone else left. Finally, in 1975, the last inhabitant, blacksmith Olav Larsen, packed his bags. The village fell silent. Sheep and vandals moved in.

For many rural communities across Europe, that's where the story ends. But for Nyksund, it was only the beginning of a remarkable story of renewal. Slowly, over the decades, life has been breathed back into this charming, remote settlement that has been reborn as an artists' colony. The crumbling old structures and commercial buildings have been faithfully restored and nowadays modern Nyksund boasts a summer population of around 60 and some half-dozen hardy souls endure throughout the harsh winters.

One of those is Ssemjon Gerlitz, the German owner of **Holmvik Brygge** (☑76 13 47 96; www.nyksund.com; s/d Nkr700/850) ✎, who has lived year-round in Nyksund for a decade and more. Over the years, he and his team of helpers have gleaned, picked and scavenged what could be salvaged from Nyksund's crumbling buildings and incorporated them into the higgledy-piggledy guesthouse, where every room's different, each with its own personality.

Two things in particular keep him here, at road's end. He speaks of the lure of silence, nothing but the rhythm of wind and waves for most of the year and of his sense of communion with long-gone fisherfolk ('Every rusty nail I pull out was hammered in by someone who lived and worked here').

This tiny community manages to support an active summer cultural program and a small **museum** (www.nyksund.as; ☉11am-5pm mid-Jun–mid-Aug).

The route to Nyksund is along a narrow ribbon of road that hugs the shoreline (the last 10km of which is unpaved). Alternatively, walk the Queen's Route (p305), a fine trek over the headland from Nyksund to Stø (three hours return).

Fargeklatten ROOMS, APARTMENTS €€
(☑97 76 00 20; www.fargeklatten.no; Sjøgata 38a; r from Nkr850, 5-bed apt Nkr1600) Rooms in 'Veita', a restored 18th-century home, are attractively furnished in antique style, while apartments are spacious and well equipped at these recently renovated properties at the eastern end of the village.

Hotel Andrikken HOTEL €€
(☑76 14 12 22; www.andrikkenhotell.no; Storgata 53; s/d Nkr900/1200, cabin from Nkr1150; ☎) Although dull and boxy from the outside, Andrikken has comfortable and well-equipped rooms. With far more personality, their Sea Cabins Lankanholmen down by the harbour are excellent value.

✗ Eating

★**Lysthuset** NORWEGIAN €€
(☑76 14 14 99; Storgata 51; mains Nkr165-275) The Lysthuset is the best of Andenes' limited dining options. Ignore the casual cafe at the front – the restaurant proper serves salted local lamb, as well as cod, salmon and whale in various forms. For dessert, indulge in a little 'Sex on the Mountain' – an orgasmic confection of ice cream, cream, blackberries and cloudberries, all doused in eggnog.

Da Vinci ITALIAN €€
(☑76 14 15 00; Sjøgata 19; pizza Nkr110-299, pasta & other mains from Nkr169; ☉11am-11pm Mon-Sat, noon-10pm Sun) The best pizzas on Andøya are found here at this above-average Italian eatery that locals swear by.

Arresten INDIAN €€€
(☑94 98 18 30; Prinsens Gate 6; mains from Nkr209; ☉3-11pm Tue-Thu, 3pm-1am Fri & Sat, 3-9pm Sun) Housed in a delightful 1870s-era Andenes home, this friendly place serves reasonable (if unexciting) Indian cuisine.

❶ Information

Tourist office (☑76 14 12 03; www.andoy-turist.no; Hamnegata 1; ☉10am-6pm mid-Jun–Aug, 10am-4pm 1st half Jun & 1st half Sep, by phone only rest of year) The tourist office covers the whole island and shares premises with the Hisnakul Natural History Centre. It produces a leaflet in English, *Andanes Vær* (Nkr35), which outlines a walking tour of the old quarter. There's internet access (Nkr60 per hour), free wifi and it rents bikes (Nkr150/200 per three hours/day).

❶ Getting There & Around

AIR

The flight between Andenes and Tromsø, via Narvik or Bodø, is a contender for the world's most scenic flight with spectacular aerial views of the landscapes, seas and agricultural patterns.

BICYCLE

Fargeklatten rents bicycles (per hour/day Nkr75/200) as well as cycle trailers and child seats.

BUS

Two to four daily buses run south to Sortland (two hours) via Risøyhamn, where a bus to/from Andenes meets and greets the Hurtigruten.

FERRY

From late May or early June to the end of August, a car ferry (www.senjafergene.no) connects Andenes with the port of Gryllefjord (1¾ hours, two to three daily) on the island of Senja, passing magnificent coastal scenery. It's just a pity it doesn't operate year-round.

Bleik

A long, ash-white beach, one of several claimants to be Norway's longest, extends for almost 3km from the hamlet of Bleik.

Puffin Safari   BIRD-WATCHING, FISHING
(✆ 90 83 85 94; www.puffinsafari.no; puffin safari adult/child Nkr350/200, deep-sea fishing safari Nkr700/200; ☉ Jun–mid-Aug) Puffin Safari, based in Bleik, does warmly recommended, well-presented and informative daily 1½-hour birdwatching boat trips off the island of Bleiksøya, with sightings of puffins and sea eagles guaranteed; more than 150,000 puffins breed around here. You can also bring home dinner from their four-hour deep-sea fishing trips.

Stave

Stave Camping   CAMPGROUND €
(✆ 926 01 257; www.stavecamping.no; camping per person Nkr100, caravans Nkr200, 2-bed cabins with outside bathroom Nkr500, apt Nkr500-1000; ☉ late May-August) Camp at the water's edge overlooking the fjord or take one of the more sheltered set-back sites. The day's exertions over, steep yourself in an ocean hot pool or sweat in the sauna.

Bø

Nordtun Gård   FARM
(✆ 92 64 49 06; www.nordtungard.no; admission Nkr100; ☉ noon-6pm mid-Jun–late Aug) In the hamlet of Bø, on Andøya's west coast, Nordtun Gård is a working farm and dairy where children can play with the animals while adults sample its range of cheeses.

Buksnesfjord

Andøy Friluftssenter   WILDLIFE-WATCHING, HIKING
(✆ 76 14 88 04; andoy-friluftssenter.no; per person Nkr495; ☉ 8.30pm Tue-Fri late Jun–mid-Aug) Andøy Friluftssenter offers summer moose or elk safaris, and is one of few places outside central Norway to do so. The safaris take place from their base at Buksnesfjord, 63km south of Andenes. Bookings can be made at the tourist office in Andenes and they also offer wilderness walks.

Kvalnes

★ **Kvalnesbrygga**   CAMPGROUND €
(✆ 76 14 63 78; www.kvalnesbrygga.no; tent/caravan sites Nkr130/150, d Nkr500; ☉ year-round) This small campground, 22km south of Andenes on the Rv82, is right beside the fjord. The tent area, of soft, springy grass, is tiny. The main building, much modified, was built by the present owner's grandfather over a century ago and has well-equipped guest kitchens for all to use. The six rooms, each named after a local bird, are simply yet tastefully furnished.

Hinnøya

Hinnøya, the largest island off mainland Norway, is the gateway to Vesterålen. Contrasting with the islands to the south, it's mostly forested green upland punctuated by snowcaps and deeply indented by fjords.

Off Hinnøya's west coast, Vesterålen is divided from Lofoten by the narrow Raftsund strait and even narrower, hugely scenic Trollfjorden, whose sheer walls plunge down to the water, dwarfing all below.

Harstad

POP 23,457
On a hillside close to the northern end of Hinnøya, Harstad, the area's largest town, is a small industrial and defence-oriented

DON'T MISS

FARGEKLATTEN

Fargeklatten, meaning 'splash of colour', is a very special place, the creation of Grethe Kvalvik. For years, Grethe was the receptionist at Andrikken Hotell until she lost her sight. After two long years of blindness, partial vision returned and she could again perceive shapes and, above all, colours.

Determined to live a full life anew, she rescued Fargeklatten, at the time earmarked for demolition to make way for a car park. This complex of historical buildings now includes a couple of small **galleries** (www.fargeklatten. no; ☺11am-4pm) displaying the art and crafts of northern Norway and a small **turf museum** (adult/child Nkr50/ free) – plus some attractive accommodation options.

place, full of docks, tanks and warehouses. Contrasting with so many tourism-'n'-fishing towns to the south, it has a certain purposeful bustle.

◉ Sights & Activities

Most sights are on the **Trondenes Peninsula**, some 2.5km north of town.

Trondenes Kirke CHURCH
(☺10am-2pm Mon-Fri Jul–mid-Aug, variable rest of year) FREE Trondenes Church was built by King Øystein around 1150. For a long time it was the northernmost church in Christendom, and still lays claim to being Norway's northernmost medieval *stone* church. Originally of wood, the current stone structure replaced it around 1250 and quickly came to double as a fortification against Russian aggression. Absurdly for one of northern Norway's major cultural sights, it's often locked so do check with the tourist office.

Aside from the robust beauty of the structure itself, the church's jewels are the three finely wrought altars at the east end, all venerating Mary. Most interesting is the central one of the Virgin surrounded by her extended family with infants in arms and children tugging at skirts on all sides. Glance up, too, at the pair of trumpet-wielding cherubs, precariously perched atop the main pillars of the rood screen.

Trondenes Historiske Senter MUSEUM
(☑77 01 83 80; www.stmu.no; Trondenesveien 122; adult/child Nkr85/40; ☺10am-5pm mid-Jun–mid-Aug, 11am-4pm Sun rest of year) Trondenes Historical Centre, just south of the church, has well-mounted and equally well-documented displays and artefacts illustrating the social history of the area from Viking days to the present.

Adolfkanonen HISTORIC SITE
(guided tours adult/child Nkr80/40; ☺9.30am, noon & 4.30pm mid-Jun–mid-Aug) Here's another biggest/furthest claim for Harstad: this formidable WWII weapon is the world's largest land-based big gun, with a calibre of more than 40cm and a recoil force of 635 tonnes. Because it lies in a military area, you're obliged to take a guided tour of the site and to have your own vehicle. Check ahead for times at the tourist office. The bunker also contains a collection of artillery, military equipment and instruments used by Nazi coastal batteries during WWII.

Grottebadet SWIMMING
(☑77 04 17 70; www.grottebadet.no; Håkonsgate 7; adult/child Nkr135/90; ☺4-9pm Mon, Tue & Thu, 4-10pm Wed, 2-8pm Fri, 10am-6pm Sat, 11am-6pm Sun) This heated indoor complex, tunnelled a full 150m into the hillside, has pools, rapids, slides, flume rides, steam rooms and other watery activities. Huge fun for all the family.

★★ Festivals & Events

Festival of North Norway ARTS
(www.festspillnn.no; ☺Jun) Harstad's Festival of North Norway, approaching its 50th incarnation, is a full week of music, theatre and dance in the second half of June.

⨇ Sleeping

Harstad Camping CAMPGROUND €
(☑77 07 36 62; www.harstad-camping.no; Nesseveien 55; car/caravan site Nkr220/280, cabin Nkr450-1200) Follow the Rv83 towards Narvik for 4km, then take a side road to reach this small waterside site, where you can rent rowing boats (per hour/day Nkr95/310) and motorboats (Nkr180/700).

Clarion Collection Hotel Arcticus HOTEL €€
(☑77 04 08 00; www.nordicchoicehotels.no; Havnegata 3; s/d incl breakfast & light evening meal from Nkr800/980; @ ☎) This hotel shares a harmonious modern building with Harstad's cultural centre. A short, pleasant jetty walk

from the centre, it has 75 particularly large rooms. It's extra for a superior standard, waterside room with splendid views over the fjord to the mountains beyond.

Grand Nordic Hotel
HOTEL €€

(☎77 00 30 00; www.rica.no; Strandgata 9; r Nkr845-1395; P @ 🛜) This is the grand dame of Harstad hotels. Request one of the larger, more pleasantly decorated rooms in the newer section.

Thon Hotel Harstad
HOTEL €€

(☎77 00 08 00; www.thonhotels.com/harstad; Sjøgata 11; s/d from Nkr775/975; @🛜) All 141 rooms at this decent chain hotel have attractive parquet flooring and most have views over the port and fjord. Buffet breakfast, taken in the hotel's Egon restaurant, is copious.

🍴 Eating

Take what you can find at the lower end of the budget range, but you're spoilt for choice at the top.

Café & Restaurant De 4 Roser
CAFE, RESTAURANT €€

(☎77 01 27 50; www.de4roser.no; Torvat 7; mains Nkr139-345, 3-/4-course set menu Nkr515/605; ⊙cafe 10am-10pm, restaurant 6-10pm Mon-Sat) On one floor, the Four Roses is a buzzing cafe that offers sandwiches, pasta, burgers and salads and a trio of daily lunch specials. Portions are large. Above the cafe, in more intimate surroundings, the restaurant offers fine gourmet cuisine. The restaurant entrance is also at street level at the other end of the building.

★ Umami
NORWEGIAN €€€

(☎95 09 09 11; www.umamiharstad.no; Havnegata 23a; 3-/5-course set menu Nkr575/695; ⊙6-11pm) A fine recent addition to Harstad's impressive fine-dining scene, Umami is the work of Kim-Havard Larsen and Sigrid Rafaelsem, both of whom have worked in some of Norway's best restaurants. The name 'umami' means 'pleasant and savoury' in Norwegian and the cooking here is creative, assured and changes with the seasons. Their cakes are divine.

★ Hoelstuen
NORWEGIAN €€€

(☎77 06 55 00; www.hoelstuen.com; Rikard Kaarbøs plass 4; mains Nkr315-365, 4-/5-course set menu Nkr645/745; ⊙5-11pm Mon-Sat) This trim place is a candidate for the title of Harstad's best dining experience. Highlights include juniper-perfumed reindeer in a port-wine glaze. It also does a particularly rich and creamy fish soup.

ℹ Information

Tourist office (☎77 01 89 89; www.destinationharstad.no; Sjøgata 1b; ⊙10am-6pm mid-Jun–mid-Aug, 8am-3.30pm Mon-Fri rest of year) The tourist office faces the waterfront, just around the corner from the bus station.

ℹ Getting There & Away

AIR
From the Harstad-Narvik airport at Evenes there are direct flights to Oslo, Bodø, Tromsø and Trondheim.

BOAT
To get to Tromsø, the easiest and most scenic option is by boat. There are two to four express passenger ferries daily between Harstad and Tromsø (three hours), via Finnsnes (1¾ hours).

There's also a seasonal express passenger ferry (www.senjafergene.no) between Stornes, just north of Harstad and Skrolsvik (1¼ hours; two to three daily mid-May to August), at the southern end of Senja island. Here, you'll find bus connections to Finnsnes and then on to Tromsø. Harstad is also a stop on the Hurtigruten coastal ferry.

BUS
Buses to/from Sortland (2½ hours) run one to three times daily. There's one bus to/from Narvik via Harstad-Narvik Evenes airport (2½ hours; daily except Saturday) and a daily service between Harstad and Fauske (5¾ hours).

ℹ Getting Around

Flybussen (Nkr175, 50 minutes) shuttles between the town centre and Harstad-Narvik Evenes airport several times daily.

Buses connect Trondenes with the central bus station approximately hourly, Monday to Saturday.

Call if you need a **taxi** (☎77 04 10 00).

The Far North

Includes ➡

Best Places to Eat

➡ Gammen (p345)

➡ Gapahuken (p341)

➡ Restaurant Haldde (p325)

➡ Emma's Drømekjøkken (p319)

Best Places to Stay

➡ Engholm Husky Design Lodge (p345)

➡ Rica Ishavshotel (p319)

➡ Sollia Gjestegård (p341)

➡ Thon Hotel Kautokeino (p346)

➡ Bungalåven Vertshus (p333)

Why Go?

Norway's northernmost counties of Troms and Finnmark arc across the very top of Europe, where broad horizons share the land with dense forest. Like most of the relatively few visitors who make it this far north, come in summer to enjoy Tromsø, the region's only town of any size. The museums of this sparky, self-confident place will orient you for the Arctic lands beyond. You'll probably respond to the call of Nordkapp (North Cape), the European mainland's self-declared most northerly point. But to really feel the pull of the north, you need to venture further to explore the sparsely populated plateaus of Inner Finnmark and its wild northeastern coast, the Norwegian heartland of the Sami people. For alternative adventure (say, scudding aboard a snowmobile or behind a team of yapping huskies), plan to return in winter, when soft blue light envelops the snowy lands, outsiders are even fewer and the northern lights streak the sky.

When to Go
Tromsø

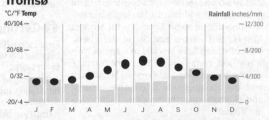

Early Feb Lots of snowy activities and, with luck, the northern lights on tap.

Easter week The Sami party in Kautokeino before dispersing to their summer pastures.

Mid- to late Jun Hotels and sights reopen, and the crowds have yet to come.

TROMS

Troms, where the Gulf Stream peters out, mitigating the harshness of winter, boasts a couple of near-superlative places: Tromsø, the only place large enough to merit the name 'city' in northern Norway; and Senja, Norway's second-largest island, a less trodden rival to the Lofotens for spectacular scenery.

Tromsø

POP 67,300

Simply put, Tromsø parties. By far the largest town in northern Norway and the administrative centre of Troms county, it's lively with cultural bashes, buskers, an animated street scene, a midnight-sun marathon, a respected university, the hallowed Mack Brewery – and more pubs per capita than any other Norwegian town. Its corona of snow-topped peaks provides arresting scenery, excellent hiking in summer and great skiing and dog-sledding in winter.

Although the city lies almost 400km north of the Arctic Circle, its climate is pleasantly moderated by the Gulf Stream. The long winter darkness is offset by round-the-clock activity during the perpetually bright days of summer.

The main part of town stretches along the east shore of the island of Tromsøya, linked to the mainland by a gracefully arched bridge.

◎ Sights

The tourist office's *Summer Activities in Tromsø* and its winter equivalent both provide a comprehensive checklist of tours and activities.

Around town you'll find a number of interesting churches. **Domkirke** (Storgata), the Lutheran Church of Norway's cathedral, is one of Norway's largest wooden churches. Its opening hours are erratic. Up the hill is the town's **Catholic Church** (Storgata 94; ☺9am-7.30pm). Both were built in 1861 and each lays claim to be – here comes yet another superlative – 'the world's northernmost bishopric' of its sect.

★ **Arctic Cathedral**   CHURCH
(Ishavskatedralen; www.ishavskatedralen.no; Hans Nilsensvei 41; adult/child Nkr40/free, organ recitals Nkr70-150; ☺9am-7pm Mon-Fri, 1-7pm Sat & Sun Jun–mid-Aug, 3-6pm Apr, May & mid-Aug–Dec, 2-6pm Feb & Mar) The 11 arching triangles of the Arctic Cathedral (1965), as the Tromsdalen Church is more usually called, suggest glacial crevasses

and auroral curtains. The magnificent glowing stained-glass window that occupies almost the whole of the east end depicts Christ descending to earth. Look back towards the west end and the contemporary organ, a work of steely art in itself, then up high to take in the lamps of Czech crystal, hanging in space like icicles. Take bus 20 or 24.

★ **Fjellheisen**   CABLE CAR
(☎77 63 87 37; www.fjellheisen.no; Sollieveien 12; adult/child Nkr140/60; ☺10am-1am late May–mid-Aug, shorter hours rest of year) For a fine view of the city and midnight sun, take the cable car to the top of Mt Storsteinen (421m). There's a restaurant at the top, from where a network of hiking routes radiates. Take bus 26 and buy a combined bus and cable-car ticket (adult/child Nkr145/65).

★ **Polaria**   MUSEUM, AQUARIUM
(www.polaria.no; Hjalmar Johansens gate 12; adult/child Nkr120/60; ☺10am-7pm mid-May–Aug, to 5pm Sep–mid-May) Daringly designed Polaria is an entertaining multimedia introduction to northern Norway and Svalbard. After an excellent 14-minute film about the latter (screened every 30 minutes), plus another about the northern lights, an Arctic walk leads to displays on shrinking sea ice, a northern lights display, aquariums of cold-water fish and – the big draw – a trio of energetic bearded seals.

M/S Polstjerna   SHIP
(adult/child Nkr25/10; ☺10am-5pm mid-Jun–mid-Aug) Between 1949 and 1981, this historic seal-hunting ship killed (or 'brought home', as the literature euphemistically expresses it) nearly 100,000 seals.

Tromsø University Museum   MUSEUM
(www.uit.no/tmu; Lars Thøringsvei 10; adult/child Nkr50/25; ☺9am-6pm Jun-Aug, 10am-4.30pm Mon-Fri, noon-3pm Sat, 11am-4pm Sun Sep–May) Near the southern end of Tromsøya, this museum has well-presented and documented displays on traditional and modern Sami life, ecclesiastical art and accoutrements, and a small section on the Vikings. Downstairs, learn about rocks of the north and ponder a number of thought-provoking themes (such as the role of fire, the consequences of global warming and loss of wilderness).

There's also a replica 'northern lights machine', or terrella, an early invention that gives you in miniature a sense of the splendour of the aurora borealis.

THE FAR NORTH TROMSØ

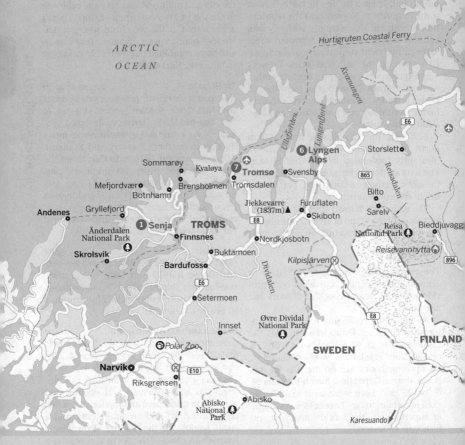

ARCTIC
OCEAN

Hurtigruten Coastal Ferry

Storslett

E6

Kvænangen

Reisadalen

Lyngen
Alps

Svensby

Furuflaten

Bilto

Sarelv

Skibotn

Reisa
National Park

Bieddjuvagg

896

Reisevannhytta

Sommarøy

Kvaløya

Tromsø

Tromsdalen

Jiekkevarre
(1837m)▲

E8

Mefjordvær

Brensholmen

Botnhamn

Andenes

Gryllefjord

Senja

TROMS

Ånderdalen
National Park

Finnsnes

Nordkjosbotn

Skrolsvik

Buktamoen

Bardufoss

Kilpisjärven

E6

Dividalen

Setermoen

Øvre Dividal
National Park

E8

FINLAND

Innset

SWEDEN

Polar Zoo

Narvik

E10

Riksgrensen

Abisko
National
Park

Abisko

Karesuando

Far North Highlights

❶ Cycle or drive the spectacular, lightly trafficked northern coast of the island of **Senja** (p322).

❷ Visit the museums, parliament and knifemakers to learn about the unique culture of the Sami in **Karasjok** (p343).

❸ Explore Alta's **Stone-Age rock carvings** (p323), a Unesco World Heritage Site.

❹ Dog-*mush* through the snow near **Karasjok** (p343), then sleep in a design lodge like no other.

❺ Leave the crowds behind to hike to **Knivskjelodden**

(p332), continental Europe's
northernmost point.

6 Go hiking out into the true
wilderness of the **Lyngen Alps**
(p322).

7 Get a taste for the Arctic in
the museums, take in an organ
recital as the midnight sun
peeks through the windows of
the Arctic Cathedral, then dance
til dawn in **Tromsø** (p313).

8 Be blessed by a walrus
penis at the **Royal & Ancient
Polar Bear Society** (p327) in
Hammerfest.

Other highlights include, in the garden, a *gammen*, or traditional Sami sod house (offers free coffee in summer) and the set of hourglasses, turned to warn the vicar that his sermon time was running out. Take bus 37.

Tromsø Kunstforening GALLERY

(www.tromsokunstforening.no; Muségata 2; ☺noon-5pm Wed-Sun) FREE The Tromsø branch of this national contemporary art foundation makes the most of its late-19th-century premises and promotes rotating exhibitions of contemporary art.

Mack Brewery BREWERY

(Mack Ølbryggeri; ☎77 62 45 80; www.olhallen.no; Storgata 5) This venerable institution merits a pilgrimage. It produces 18 kinds of beer, including the very quaffable Macks Pilsner, Isbjørn, Haakon and several dark beers. At 1pm Monday to Thursday year-round (plus 3pm, June to August) tours (Nkr160, including a beer mug and pint) leave from the brewery's own Ølhallen Pub. Book ahead.

Blåst GLASSWORKS

(☎77 68 34 60; www.blaast.no; Peder Hansens Gate 4; ☺10am-5pm Mon-Fri, to 3pm Sat) Pass by the world's most northerly glass-blowing workshop to see the young team puffing their cheeks and perhaps to pick up an item or two.

Art Museum of Northern Norway GALLERY

(www.nnkm.no; Sjøgata 1; ☺noon-5pm mid-Jun–mid-Aug, 10am-5pm Mon-Fri & noon-5pm Sat & Sun rest of year) FREE The Nordnorsk Kunstmuseum displays mainly 19th-century to present-day sculpture, photography, painting and handicrafts by artists from northern Norway.

> ## ARCHITECTURAL HIGHLIGHTS OF THE FAR NORTH
>
> ➡ Arctic Cathedral (p313), Tromsø
>
> ➡ Northern Lights Cathedral (p324), Alta
>
> ➡ Sámi Parliament (p344), Karasjok
>
> ➡ Hammerfest Kirke (p327), Hammerfest
>
> ➡ Nesseby Church (p335), Nesseby
>
> ➡ Engholm's Husky Design Lodge (p345), Karasjok
>
> ➡ Sorrisniva Igloo Hotel (p326), Around Alta

Bibliotek NOTABLE BUILDING

(Grønnegata 94; ☺10am-4pm Mon-Fri) Tromsø's recently constructed library is a wonderful example of contemporary Norwegian architecture, streaming with light and airiness. There's also free internet access.

Perspektivet HISTORIC BUILDING

(www.perspektivet.no; Storgata 95; ☺11am-5pm Tue-Sun) FREE Dating from 1831, Perspektivet houses a permanent photo exhibition illustrating Tromsø's history and mounts quality temporary displays too. You'll find more early-19th-century timber buildings around the town centre, including a stretch of 1830s shops and merchants' homes along Sjøgata.

★ Polar Museum MUSEUM

(Polarmuseet; www.polarmuseum.no; Søndre Tollbodgata 11; adult/child Nkr50/25; ☺10am-7pm mid-Jun–mid-Aug, 11am-5pm rest of year) The 1st floor of this harbourside museum illustrates early polar research, especially the ventures of Nansen and Amundsen. Downstairs there's a well-mounted exhibition about the hunting and trapping of fuzzy Arctic creatures on Svalbard before coal became king there. Note the exploding harpoons outside; the whale didn't stand much of a chance.

Botanic Gardens GARDENS

(Botanisk Hage; Breivika; ☺24hr) FREE Within the Arctic, Antarctic and alpine areas of Tromsø's carefully maintained and cared-for gardens grows flora from all over the world's colder regions. And yes, it's the world's northernmost. Take bus 20.

Tromsø War Museum MUSEUM

(Tromsø Forsvarsmuseum; ☎77 65 54 40; www.tromsoforsvarsmuseum.no; Solstrandveien; adult/child Nkr50/25; ☺noon-5pm Wed-Sun Jun–mid-Aug, Sun only May & mid-Aug–Sep) The cannons of a Nazi coastal artillery battery and a restored command bunker form the basis of the Tromsø Forsvarsmuseum. It also tells of the giant German battleship *Tirpitz*, sunk nearby in 1944, and the Nazi army's retreat from Leningrad, when many of its 120,000 troops were evacuated by ship from Tromsø. The museum's on the mainland, beside the E6, 4.5km south of Tromsø bridge. Take bus 12 or 28.

🏃 Activities

In and around Tromsø (operators will normally collect you from your hotel), winter activities outnumber those in summer, and include chasing the northern lights, cross-country skiing and snowshoeing, reindeer- and dog-sledding, snowshoe safaris, ice fishing and snowmobiling.

Summer possibilities include hiking, fishing, glacier trekking and sea-kayaking.

Tromsø Villmarkssenter SNOW SPORTS
(🖉77 69 60 02; www.villmarkssenter.no) Tromsø Villmarkssenter offers dog-sled excursions ranging from a one-day spin to a four-day trek with overnight camping. The centre, 24km south of town on Kvaløya island, also offers a range of summer activities such as trekking, glacier hiking and sea-kayaking.

Active Tromsø ADVENTURE SPORTS
(🖉48 13 71 33; activetromso.no) An excellent company offering the full range of summer and winter activities, with dog-sledding expeditions a particular speciality.

Tromsø Friluftsenter ADVENTURE SPORTS
(🖉90 75 15 83; www.tromso-friluftsenter.no) Summer sightseeing, boat trips and a full range of winter activities (including trips to Sami camps). One intriguing possibility is its five-hour humpback-whale safari from mid-November to mid-January.

Arctic Adventure Tours ADVENTURE SPORTS
(🖉45 63 52 88; www.arcticadventuretours.no) A range of activities from dog-sledding and skiing in winter to fishing and hiking expeditions in summer.

Natur i Nord SNOW SPORTS
(🖉97 51 75 83; www.naturinord.no) Natur i Nord runs northern-lights trips in winter, with a midnight sun version in summer.

Tromsø Outdoor OUTDOORS
(🖉97 57 58 75; www.tromsooutdoor.no; Sjøgata 14; ⊙10am-5pm Mon-Fri, to 4pm Sat & Sun Jan, 9am-5pm daily Feb-Apr, to 4pm Mon-Fri & 10am-2pm Sat & Sun May-Aug, shorter hours rest of year) This is for those who prefer a DIY approach to summer or winter activities, with equipment rental for everything from snowshoes and skis to bicycles.

Nordre Hestnes Gård HORSE RIDING
(🖉90 98 26 40; www.nordre-hestnes-gaard.no) Midnight-sun horseback excursions, hikes and other summer (and also winter) activities.

👉 Tours

Ishavstoget RAILWAY
(🖉90 88 16 75; www.ishavstoget.no; adult/child Nkr150/50; ⊙hourly 11am-4pm late May-Aug) Tromsø's version of the toy train trundles around between most of the main sites (although it doesn't cross the bridge to the Arctic Cathedral) with commentary in eight languages. The journey begins and ends at Stortorget square and lasts around 35 minutes.

🎉 Festivals & Events

In summer at the Arctic Cathedral, there are half-hour Midnight Sun Concerts (adult/child Nkr150/50; 11.30pm mid-May to mid-August) and organ recitals (Nkr70; 2pm June and July). The swelling organ and the light of the midnight sun streaming through the huge west window could be one of the great sensory moments of your trip.

The Domkirke holds half-hour organ recitals (Nkr70; 5pm June, 3pm July) of classical music and folk tunes.

Otherwise, Tromsø's two biggest annual bashes take place in deepest winter.

Northern Lights Festival MUSIC
(www.nordlysfestivalen.no; ⊙Jan) Six days of music of all genres. Late January.

Sámi Week CULTURAL
(⊙Feb) Includes the national reindeer sledge championship, where skilled Sami whoop and crack the whip along the main street. Early February.

Midnight Sun Marathon SPORTS
(www.msm.no; ⊙Jun) The world's most northerly marathon. In addition to the full 42km, there's also a half-marathon and a children's race. A Saturday in June.

Insomnia Festival MUSIC
(www.insomniafestival.no; ⊙Oct) A long, loud weekend of electronic music in October.

🛏 Sleeping

Tromsø's peak tourist time is June, when the university's still in full swing, summer tourism has begun and reservations are essential. Check out the home-stay section of the tourist office website (www.visittromso.no) for apartments and rooms in private homes.

Tromsø Camping CAMPGROUND €
(🖉77 63 80 37; www.tromsocamping.no; Tromsdalen; car/caravan sites Nkr240/280, cabins Nkr750-1690; ⊙Oct-Apr; 🅿@) Tent campers enjoy leafy green campsites beside a slow-moving stream. However, bathroom and cooking facilities at this veritable village of cabins are stretched to the limit. Take bus 20 or 24.

Tromsø

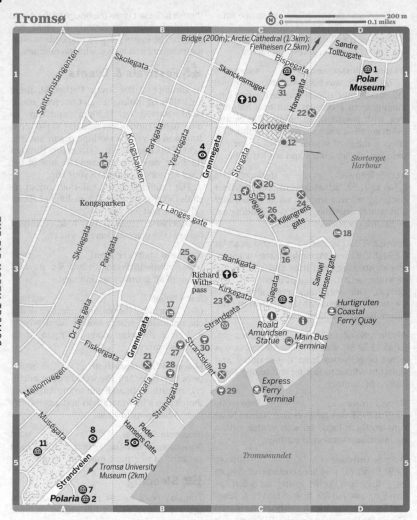

⭐ **Rica Ishavshotel**   HOTEL €€
(📞 77 66 64 00; www.rica.no/ishavshotel; Fredrik Langes gate 2; r Nkr1045-1695; @🅿️) Occupying a prime quayside position, this hotel is immediately recognisable by its mast-like spire. It sometimes swallows as many as five tour groups per day so summer reservations are advisable. Almost half of its attractive rooms, including many singles, have superb views of the sound, and a recent expansion and overhaul of some rooms has added to the appeal.

Both guests and nonguests will enjoy its **Brasseriet** (📞 77 66 64 00; mains Nkr210-375) restaurant and Skibsbroen (p320) bar.

Ami Hotel   HOTEL €€
(📞 77 62 10 00; www.amihotel.no; Skolegata 24; s/d Nkr740/910, with shared bathroom Nkr640/790; 🅿️@🅿️) Located beside a traffic-free road and park, this is a quiet, friendly, family-ly-owned choice. There's a well-equipped kitchen for self-caterers and a couple of communal lounges, each with TV, internet access and free tea and coffee.

Clarion Hotel Aurora   HOTEL €€
(📞 77 78 11 00; www.nordicchoicehotels.no; Sjøgata 19/21; s/d from Nkr900/940; @🅿️) This stylish 121-room waterside hotel, poking towards the sea like the prow of a ship,

Tromsø

THE FAR NORTH TROMSØ

is architecturally stunning with its odd angles, aluminium trim, pictures on bedroom ceilings, sauna – and a top-floor hot tub where you can savour the picturesque harbour and mountain views as you bubble and boil. Its restaurant has great fjord views too.

Radisson Blu Hotel Tromsø   HOTEL €€
(☑77 60 00 00; www.radissonblu.com/hotel-tromso; Sjøgata 7; s/d from Nkr945/1195; P @ 🖙) Bedrooms have recently been comprehensively renovated and an attractive new wing has been grafted onto the solid, rectangular block of the original building. Of its 269 rooms (it's worth the Nkr100 extra for one in the new wing), around half have harbour views. It runs a decent pub, the Rorbua, and a fine Arctic Menu restaurant.

Rica Grand Hotel   HOTEL €€
(☑77 75 37 77; www.rica.no; Storgata 44; r Nkr790-1690; P @ 🖙) The Grand is Tromsø's oldest hotel, but there's little that's antique inside as the place has twice burnt to the ground. Ask for a room on one of the brand-new top two floors. There's a particularly ample breakfast with fresh fruit and hot dishes.

✕ Eating

In Tromsø, the line is blurry between restaurants, cafes and pubs, and many places function in all three modes, simultaneously or at different times of the day.

Driv   CAFE, RESTAURANT €
(www.driv.no; Tollbodgata 3; mains Nkr115-185; ⊙kitchen 11am-6pm, bar 11.30am-1.30am) This student-run converted warehouse serves meaty burgers (try its renowned Driv burger) and great salads. It organises musical and cultural events and has a disco every Saturday. In winter you can steep yourself in good company within its open-air hot tub.

Knoll og Tott   SANDWICHES, €
(Storgata 62; snacks & light meals from Nkr89; ⊙8am-6pm Mon-Fri, 10am-4pm Sat) Run by a cheerful young team, this popular upstairs-downstairs place serving fresh salads, crisp baguettes and house quiches is ideal for a filling midday snack, to eat in or take away.

★**Emma's Under**   NORWEGIAN €€
(☑77 63 77 30; www.emmas.as; Kirkegata; mains Nkr155-295; ⊙11am-10pm Mon-Fri, noon-10pm Sat) Intimate and sophisticated, this is one of Tromsø's most popular lunch spots, where mains include northern Norwegian staples such as reindeer fillet, lamb and stockfish. Upstairs is the more formal **Emma's Drømekjøkken** (☑77 63 77 30; Kirkegata; mains Nkr295-365; ⊙6pm-midnight Mon-Sat), a highly regarded gourmet restaurant where advance booking is essential.

THE FAR NORTH TROMSØ

Aunegården
NORWEGIAN €€

(⌨77 65 12 34; www.aunegarden.no; Sjøgata 29; lunch mains Nkr112-196, dinner mains Nkr246-329; ⊘10.30am-11pm Mon-Sat) You can almost lose yourself in this wonderful cafe-cum-restaurant that's all intimate crannies and cubbyholes. In a 19th-century building that functioned as a butcher's shop until 1996, it's rich in character and serves excellent salads, sandwiches and mains. If you don't fancy a full meal, drop by just to enjoy a coffee and one of its melt-in-the-mouth cakes.

Circa
CAFE €€

(⌨77 68 10 20; www.circa.as; Storgata 36; mains Nkr165-195; ⊘6pm-midnight Mon & Tue, 6pm-1.30am Wed & Thu, 7pm-3am Fri & Sat; 🖥) Circa (Approximately) and its upstairs neighbour Presis (Precisely), under the same ownership, complement each other. Circa is a cavernous bar and light-meal venue. It serves tasty pasta, salads and sandwiches until 5pm. Thereafter, its cool jazz and electronic music attracts a 25- to 35-year-old crowd. There's a great range of quality international beers. Presis (⌨77 68 10 20; www.circa.as; Storgata 36; tapas from Nkr75; ⊘4-11pm Tue-Fri, 6-11pm Sat) is calmer and serves tapas.

Pastafabrikken
ITALIAN €€

(⌨77 67 27 82; Sjøgata 17; pizzas & pasta from Nkr130, mains Nkr135-165; ⊘11am-11pm Mon-Sat, 2-10pm Sun) Drop by for a coffee, a Mack beer or a slice of Italy at this fresh Tromsø choice with its high stools, cosy armchairs and wood everywhere. Pasta (which comes with 17 kinds of sauce) and pizza dough are made on the spot, before your eyes. Everything, from the decor to the food is a significant cut above your average Italian restaurant in Norway.

Fiskekompaniet
SEAFOOD €€€

(⌨77 68 76 00; www.fiskekompani.no; Killengrens gate; mains from Nkr325, 3-course meal Nkr565; ⊘4-11pm) This long-standing Tromsø fish and seafood favourite has a prime portside site. All starters and mains, subtly prepared and enhanced, are from the ocean and the atmosphere is classy and contemporary. Enjoy its delightful range of dinner desserts.

Arctandria
SEAFOOD €€€

(⌨77 60 07 25; www.skarven.no; Strandtorget 1; mains Nkr265-345; ⊘4pm-midnight Mon-Sat) Upstairs and upscale, Arctandria serves filling and supremely fresh ocean catches, including a sample starter of whale steak and

seal. Save a cranny for its crème brûlée with cloudberries dessert.

🍷 Drinking & Nightlife

★Skibsbroen
COCKTAIL BAR

(⊘8pm-2am Mon-Thu, 6pm-3.30am Fri & Sat) For the most exceptional view of the harbour, fjord and mountains beyond, take the lift (elevator) of the Rica Ishavshotel to the 4th floor. Skibsbroen (Ship's Bridge), its intimate crow's-nest bar, has friendly staff, great cocktails – and a superb panoramic view of all below.

Ølhallen Pub
PUB

(⊘9am-6pm Mon-Sat) At Mack Brewery's Ølhallen Pub you can sample its fine ales right where they're brewed. Perhaps the world's only watering hole to be closed in the evening, it carries eight varieties on draught.

Verdensteatret
CAFE

(Storgata 93b; ⊘11am-2am Mon-Thu, 11am-3.30am Fri & Sat, 1pm-2am Sun; 🖥) Norway's oldest film house will satisfy cinephiles and cafe aficionados. The hip bar has free wi-fi and weekend DJs. At other times, the bartender spins from its huge collection of vinyls, so expect anything from classical music to deepest underground. Ask staff to let you peek into the magnificent cinema, its walls painted floor-to-ceiling with early-20th-century murals.

Blå Rock Café
BAR

(Strandgata 14/16; ⊘11.30am-2am) The loudest, most raving place in town has theme evenings, almost 50 brands of beer, occasional live bands and weekend DJs. The music is rock, naturally. Every Monday hour is a happy hour.

Skarven
BAR

(www.skarven.no; Strandtorget 1; ⊘from 11am) Skarven has an extensive waterfront terrace and offers fine bar meals and an agreeable waterside atmosphere.

Tromsø Jernbanestasjon
BAR

(Strandgata 33; ⊘3pm-2am) This engaging railway-themed pub with its ex-train-carriage seating is typical local humour – Tromsø has never, ever had a railway station.

Bastard
BAR, CLUB

(Strandgata 22; ⊘6pm-2am Mon-Sat, 3-11pm Sun) Bastard (with the stress on the second syllable) is a cool basement hang-out with low beams and white, furry walls (no polar bears killed during construction). It engages art-house and underground DJs (Friday and Saturday) and bands (up to three times weekly).

Carrying UK and Norwegian football, it also has a faithful following of fans.

The house sausages, stuffed specially for Bastard, go well with beer or to stave off those wee-hours hunger pangs.

ⓘ Information

Tourist office (☑ 77 61 00 00; www.visittromso.no; Kirkegata 2; ☉ 9am-7pm Mon-Fri, 10am-6pm Sat & Sun mid-May–Aug, shorter hours rest of year) Produces the comprehensive *Tromsø Guide*. Has two free internet points.

ⓘ Getting There & Away

AIR

Destinations with direct Scandinavian Airlines flights to/from **Tromsø Airport** (☑ 77 64 84 00; www.avinor.no), the main airport for the far north, include Oslo, Narvik/Harstad, Bodø, Trondheim, Alta, Hammerfest, Kirkenes and Longyearbyen.

Norwegian (www.norwegian.no) flies to and from London (Gatwick) and Oslo.

BOAT

Express boats connect Tromsø and Harstad (2½ hours), via Finnsnes (1¼ hours), two to four times daily. Tromsø is also a major stop on the Hurtigruten coastal ferry route.

BUS

The main bus terminal (sometimes called Prostneset) is on Kaigata, beside the Hurtigruten quay. There are up to three daily express buses to/from Narvik (Nkr240, 4¼ hours) and one to/from Alta (Nkr560, 6½ hours), where you can pick up a bus for Honningsvåg, and from there, on to Nordkapp.

CAR & MOTORCYCLE

A two- or four-wheeled vehicle is the best way to negotiate Norway's far-northern reaches. All major car-hire companies have offices at the airport. Contrasting with steep rates in summer (when it's essential to reserve in advance), car rental can be very reasonable in winter.

ⓘ Getting Around

TO/FROM THE AIRPORT

Tromsø's airport is about 5km from the town centre, on the western side of Tromsøya island. Flybuss runs between the airport and Rica Ishavshotel (one-way/return Nkr70/100, 15 minutes), connecting with arriving and departing flights and stopping by other major hotels along the way. A privately run minibus service also goes door-to-door to/from many hotels for the same price. Ask at your hotel for details.

> ### HARD DRINKING, TROMSØ-STYLE
>
> It takes stamina to stay the course. With work over, friends will meet for *fredagpils* (Friday drinks to plan the campaign ahead). Then it's time for *vorspiel* (foreplay), a preliminary oiling at a friend's house before setting off around midnight for a club or bar. At the statutory throwing-out time of 3.30am, it's *fyllemat* (fill-up time), when you pick up a burger, kebab or hot dog from one of the street stalls that lurk outside major venues, before heading once more to a friend's pad for a few hours' *nachspiel* (afterplay).
>
> By now it's bed for middle-distance runners while the marathon crowd stamps its feet outside Ølhallen's, waiting for the sliding of bolts that marks its 9am opening. 'If you can stand, we'll serve you', is the bar staff's rule of thumb.

Metered taxis between the airport and centre cost around Nkr200.

CAR & MOTORCYCLE

Tromsø has ample paid parking in the centre. There's also the huge Trygg underground car park tunnelled into the hill; its entrance on Vestregata (closed to trailers and caravans).

Around Tromsø

Sommarøy & Kvaløya

From Tromsø, this half-day trip is more for the drive than the destination. It's an extraordinarily pretty, lightly trafficked run across Kvaløya, much of it down at shore level as far as the small island of Sommarøy.

If you're arriving from Senja by the Botnhamn-Brensholmen ferry (www.senjafergene. no), the vistas as you cross Kvaløya island, heading westwards for Tromsø, are equally stunning.

🛏 Sleeping

Sommarøy Kurs & Feriesenter HOTEL **€€**
(☑ 77 66 40 00; www.sommaroy.no; s/d from Nkr1090/1290, 6- to 8-person cabin Nkr2000-3000; ℗@�(�) Grab a drink or a snack and even overnight at Sommarøy Kurs &

Feriesenter with its restaurant, bar, small children's playground, hot tub and sauna. Rooms are modern and bright without too many frills.

Lyngen Alps

Some of the most rugged alpine heights in all Norway ruck up to form the spine of the heavily glaciated Lyngen Peninsula, east of Tromsø; you get the best views of them from the eastern shore of 150km-long Lyngenfjord. The peaks, the highest of which is Jiekkevarre (1837m), offer plenty of opportunities for climbers but this challenging glacial terrain is strictly for the experienced.

The Lyngsdalen valley, above the industrial village of Furuflaten, is an altogether more accessible and popular hiking area. The usual route begins at the football pitch south of the bridge over the Lyngdalselva and climbs up the valley to the tip of the glacier Sydbreen, 500m above sea level.

The best map for hiking is Statens Kartverk's *Lyngenhalvøya* at 1:50,000.

🏃 Activities

Tour in Lyngen Alps   ADVENTURE SPORTS
(☑91 73 54 97; www.tourinlyngenalps.no) This company offers everything from horse riding (Nkr1645) and mountain hiking (Nkr1095) to sea-kayaking (Nkr1645), fjord fishing (Nkr2095) and glacier hikes (Nkr1195).

Senja

Senja, Norway's second-largest island, rivals Lofoten for natural beauty yet attracts a fraction of its visitors (we meandered the length of its northern coastline and saw only two non-Norwegian vehicles).

A broad agricultural plain laps at Innersida, the island's eastern coast facing the mainland. By contrast, birchwoods, moorland and sweetwater lakes extend beneath the bare craggy uplands of the interior. Along Yttersida, the northwestern coast, knife-ridged peaks rise directly from the Arctic Ocean. Here, the Rv86 and Rv862, declared a National Tourist Route, link isolated, still-active fishing villages such as Hamn and Mefjordvær and traffic is minimal. The now flat, mildly bucking road, almost always within sight of the shore, is a cyclist's dream. On the way, pause at the Tungeneset viewing point and scramble over broad slabs of weathered rock to savour the spiky peaks to the west and, eastwards, more gently sculpted crests.

◎ Sights

Senjatrollet   AMUSEMENT PARK
(www.senjatrollet.no; adult/child Nkr120/80; ⊙9am-9pm Jun-Aug) True, there can't be much competition outside Scandinavia. But the Senja Troll, 18m high and weighing in at 125,000kg, is the world's biggest troll, attested by the *Guinness Book of Records*. There's a tractor and railway carriage for kids to clamber on and a cafe with shelf upon shelf of warty, bucktoothed trolls (and some fine pewterwork on display for mum and dad to look at). You can even enter the bowels of the grinning giant and explore his intestines.

🛏 Sleeping

Hamn i Senja   HOUSE €€
(☑77 85 98 80; www.hamnisenja.no; s/d Nkr915/1130; ℗ 🖥) On the site of a former fishing hamlet, Hamn i Senja is a delightful, self-contained, get-away-from-it-all place that sits in its own little cove. Everything is smart and new, rebuilt after fire ripped through the former premises. Nearby is the small dam that held back the waters for what is claimed to be the world's first hydroelectric plant, established in 1882.

❶ Getting There & Away

➠ Two to three daily buses run from Finnsnes to Tromsø (2¾ hours) and Narvik (three hours) with a connection in Buktamoen.

➠ Express ferries connect Finnsnes with Tromsø (1¼ hours) and Harstad (1¾ hours) two to three times a day.

➠ It's possible to drive the whole of the northwest coast from Gryllefjord (linked by car ferry with Andenes) to Botnhamn, with its car-ferry link to Brensholmen on Kvaløy, then onwards to Tromsø.

➠ Westbound, a summertime car ferry connects Skrolsvik, on Senja's south coast, to Harstad (1½ hours, two to four daily).

➠ Finnsnes is also a stop for the Hurtigruten coastal ferry.

Setermoen & Around

The wooded town of Setermoen is best known to Norwegians as a military training centre and venue for NATO exercises. There's little reason to linger in the town itself.

⊙ Sights

Polar Park ZOO

(www.polarpark.no; adult/child Nkr215/125; ⊘9am-6pm Jun-Aug, 9am-4pm Mon-Fri, noon-4pm Sat & Sun Sep-May) This large open-air zoo is 23km south of Setermoen and 3.3km east of the E6. It features wildlife of the boreal *taiga* (marshy forest) in spacious enclosures that, but for the metal fencing, are scarcely distinguishable from the surrounding birch forests. Here you can watch animals such as brown bears, deer, musk oxen, reindeer, wolves, Eurasian lynx, wolverines, badgers and both red and polar fox.

Follow the keeper around at predator feeding time (normally 1pm; check at reception), with a host of other up-close encounters possible.

Setermoen Church CHURCH

(⊘10am-5pm Mon-Sat late Jun-early Aug) A bell in the porch of this early-19th-century octagonal church dates from 1698. The ingenious heating system, with wood stoves and hot-water pipes beneath the pews, must encourage attendance – or perhaps somnolence – during even the longest sermons.

Forsvarsmuseum MUSEUM

(adult/child Nkr60/free; ⊘10am-3pm Mon-Fri) Those who are aroused by war games will have fun at the Troms Defence Museum with its evocative interior dioramas and over 20 military vehicles to explore outside.

🛏 Sleeping

Bardu Hotell HOTEL €€

(☑77 18 59 40; www.barduhotell.no; Toftakerlia 1; s/d from Nkr1000/1200; 🅿@🛜🏊) The lobby, with pelts splayed across its walls, has a hunting-lodge feel while rooms are decorated in a variety of themes such as the four seasons and Adam and Eve. With plenty of character, it's popular with adventure-tour groups and visiting military, not least for the comfortable bar and its restaurant, Trollstua. There's a sauna, hot tub and year-round heated pool, all free to guests.

WESTERN FINNMARK

Finnmark's wild northern coast is dotted with fishing villages and riven with grand fjords, while the vast interior is dominated by the broad Finnmarksvidda plateau, a stark wilderness.

ⓘ MIND THAT REINDEER

Do keep an eye out for reindeer on the road. They're not dangerous and they're decidedly more charming than annoying. But they might slow your progress and bring you to a very abrupt halt if you hit one at speed. Sometimes wandering alone, now and again in herds, they might not be fazed by your inanimate car. If they refuse to budge, just get out, walk towards them and they'll amble away.

History

Finnmark has been inhabited for around 12,000 years, first by the Komsa hunters of the coastal region and later by Sami fishing cultures and reindeer pastoralists, who settled on the coast and in the vast interior, respectively.

More recently, virtually every Finnmark town was decimated at the end of WWII by retreating Nazi troops, whose scorched-earth policy aimed to delay the advancing Soviets. Towns were soon reconstructed in the most efficient, yet boxy, building style, which is why, in contrast to the spectacular natural surroundings, present-day Finnmark towns are, for the most part, architecturally uninspiring.

Alta

POP 19,822

Although the fishing and slate-quarrying town of Alta lies at latitude N 70°, it enjoys a relatively mild climate. The Alta Museum, with its ancient petroglyphs, is a must-see and the lush green Sautso-Alta canyon, a quick hop away, is simply breathtaking.

Alta, stretching along some 15km of coastline, has a large footprint. Its two main centres are about 2km apart: hilly Bossekop to the west, and Sentrum in – well, just that, with its uninspiring blocks and parking lots and a traffic-free central square.

⊙ Sights

Alta Museum MUSEUM

(www.alta.museum.no; Altaveien 19; adult/child May-Sep Nkr95/25, Oct-Apr Nkr65/15; ⊘8am-5pm May–mid-Jun, to 8pm mid-Jun–Aug, 8am-3pm Mon-Fri, 11am-4pm Sat & Sun Sep-Apr) This superb museum is in Hjemmeluft, at the western end of town. It features exhibits and displays

ØVRE DIVIDAL NATIONAL PARK

Between Setermoen and the Swedish and Finnish borders lies the wild, roadless, lake-studded Øvre Dividal National Park. It's a remote, semiforested, 750-sq-km upland wilderness with plenty of alpine peaks and views. The park is also rich in wildlife, with brown bear, wolf, Arctic fox, Eurasian lynx and one of the densest populations of wolverines anywhere in Europe.

The most popular hike is the eight-day Troms Border Trail, which connects with Abisko National Park, in northern Sweden, where you'll find the start of Sweden's renowned Kungsleden hiking route. The map to use for the Troms Border Trail and the Abisko Link is Statens Kartverk's *Turkart Indre Troms*, at a scale of 1:100,000. In summer the mosquitoes will drive you to distraction; use a head net, smear yourself liberally with repellent and swat every single last buzzing bastard you can, in the interests of those who follow in your footsteps.

Winter visitors can join a dog-sled trip through Arctic Norway led by renowned and resourceful musher **Bjørn Klauer** (huskyfarm.de). In addition to tours through the national park, he runs expeditions deeper into Finnmark. In summer he and his team organise cycle and canoe tours or you can do your own thing and hike the several signed trails that pass nearby. His farm is also a delightful place to stay.

on Sami culture, Finnmark military history, the Alta hydro-electric project and the aurora borealis (northern lights). The cliffs around it, a Unesco World Heritage Site, are incised with around 6000 late–Stone Age carvings, dating from 6000 to 2000 years ago and it's these petroglyphs that will live longest in the memory.

As the sea level decreased after the last ice age, carvings were made at progressively lower heights. Themes include hunting scenes, fertility symbols, bear, moose, reindeer and crowded boats. The works have been highlighted with red-ochre paint (thought to have been the original colour) and are connected by 3km of boardwalks that start at the main building. Although the museum remains open in winter, many of the carvings may be under snow and the entrance fee is reduced as a result.

Northern Lights Cathedral   CHURCH
(Løkkeveien; ◷ 11am-3pm Mon-Fri, 10am-1pm Sat, services 11am Sun) Opened in 2013, the daringly designed Northern Lights Cathedral, next to the Rica Hotel Alta, promises to be one of the architectural icons of the north, with its swirling pyramid structure clad in rippling titanium sheets. The interior is similarly eye-catching, with an utterly modern 4.3m-high bronze *Christ* by Danish artist Peter Brandes – note how the figure gets lighter as your eyes move up the body.

The cathedral is at its best in winter when aglow in floodlights and with the aurora borealis in the sky behind. Stunning.

🎺 Festivals & Events

Borealis Alta   SPRING FESTIVAL
(◷ Mar) Five days of concerts and culture in March, designed to dispel winter's gloom.

Finnmarksløpet 1000km Dog-Sled Endurance Race   SPORTS
(www.finnmarkslopet.no; ◷ Mar) Europe's longest dog-sled race coincides with Borealis Alta.

Alta Blues & Soul Festival   MUSIC
(www.altasoulogblues.no; ◷ Jun) Brings in top Norwegian bands and stars in late May or early June.

🛏 Sleeping

Wisløff Camping   CAMPGROUND €
(☏ 78 43 43 03; www.wisloeff.no; per person/site Nkr30/180, cabins Nkr495-1300) One of three excellent riverside campsites in Ovre Alta, 3.5km south of the E6 along the RV93 to Kautokeino, Wisløff Camping was declared Campground of the Year in 2000, and it still deserves the accolade. Readers too sing its praises.

★ Rica Hotel Alta   HOTEL €€
(☏ 78 48 27 00; www.rica.no; Løkkeveien 61; s/d from Nkr850/1050; ◉ 🖚) Alta's classiest hotel has attractive rooms (some have large photos of the northern lights) and excellent service. Try for one of the west-facing rooms with views over the cathedral. The restaurant is also also excellent and there's a bar (closed Sundays).

Thon Hotel Vica HOTEL €€
(☑78 48 22 22; www.thonhotels.no; Fogdebakken 6; ☺s/d from Nkr820/1120; P@☎) Right from the stuffed brown bear that greets you at the door, the Vica beckons you in. In a timber-built former farmhouse, it was until recently a family-run concern, and still retains a more personal feel than many other hotels in this chain. There's a sauna (Nkr100), steaming outdoor hot tub (wonderful in winter when all around is snow-capped) and a good restaurant.

Bårstua Gjestehus GUESTHOUSE €€
(☑78 43 33 33; www.baarstua.no; Kongleveien 2a; r Nkr770-1000) This friendly B&B is set back from the E6. Its eight rooms, decorated with striking photographs, are spruce and well furnished. Each has self-catering facilities.

✖ Eating & Drinking

Alfa-Omega CAFE €€
(www.alfaomega-alta.no; Markedsgata 14-16; lunch mains from Nkr169, dinner mains Nkr216-329; ☺11am-midnight Mon-Sat) As its name suggests, this place has two parts: Omega, its contemporary cafe, open 11am to midnight, serves salads, sandwiches, pastas and cakes. Sink your teeth into its hugely popular Ole Mattis reindeer steak sandwich. Alfa, a pleasant, casual bar, comes into its own from 8pm. There's also a terrace, ideal for taking a little summer sunshine, overlooking Alta's bleak central square.

Rica Hotel Alta Restaurant NORWEGIAN €€
(☑78 48 27 00; ww.rica.no; Løkkeveien 61; mains Nkr150-312; ☺6-11pm) The Rica's restaurant serves up Arctic specialities such as Arctic char and some creative salmon interpretations.

★Restaurant Haldde NORWEGIAN €€€
(mains Nkr249-349; ☺4-10pm Mon-Thu, 4-11pm Fri & Sat, 1-10pm Sun) ✿ This quality restaurant within Thon Hotel Vica relies almost entirely upon local ingredients in the preparation of choice dishes such as reindeer steak, grilled stockfish and its Flavour of Finnmark dessert of cloudberries and cowberry-blueberry sorbet.

Barila BAR
(Parksentret Bldg, Sentrum; ☺11am-1am Mon-Thu, 11am-3am Fri & Sat, 6pm-1am Sun) This chic, sassy little place serves great coffee, good beer and exotic cocktails.

---

❶ WHICH LOOP?

Alta Museum's short walking loop (1.2km; allow around 45 minutes, including viewing time) is the most visited. A longer one (2.1km, taking around 1¼ hours) begins with a steepish descent, followed by a pleasant seaside walk that takes in more sites.

❶ Information

Tourist office (www.alta-kommune.no; Markedsgata 3; ☺10am-7pm Mon, Tue & Thu, 10am-4pm Wed & Fri, 11am-3pm Sat Jun-Aug, to 3.30pm Mon-Sat rest of year) In the library.

❶ Getting There & Away

Alta's **airport** (☑78 44 95 55; www.avinor.no) is 4km northeast of Sentrum at Elvebakken. SAS has direct flights to/from Oslo, Tromsø, Hammerfest, Lakselv and Vadsø. Norwegian connects Alta with Oslo.

Buses leave from the terminal in Sentrum.
Hammerfest Nkr315, 2¼ hours, two daily
Honningsvåg Nkr475, four hours, one daily
Karasjok Nkr475, 4¾ hours, two daily except Saturday
Kautokeino Nkr280, 2¼ hours, one daily except Saturday
Tromsø Nkr560, 6½ hours, one daily

❶ Getting Around

Fortunately, this sprawling town has a local bus to connect its dispersed ends. On weekdays, buses run more or less hourly between the major districts and to the airport. Services are less frequent on Saturday and don't run at all on Sunday.

Taxis (☑78 43 53 53) cost about Nkr150 from the airport into town.

Around Alta

☉ Sights

Sautso-Alta Canyon CANYON
The Altaelva hydroelectric project has had very little effect on the most scenic stretch of river, which slides through 400m-deep Sautso, northern Europe's grandest canyon.

Kåfjord
At its peak in the 1840s, the tiny settlement of Kåfjord, 18km west of Alta, was a prosperous town of over 1000 inhabitants thanks to the copper works (Kåfjord Kobberverk), which were then Norway's largest.

You can follow an easy 1.3km signed trail around the little that remains (you'll find plenty more information in Alta Museum; p323). Half hidden in the grass opposite the explanatory panel is a plaque in memory of three British midget submarines that entered the fjord and severely damaged the *Tirpitz* in 1943.

To the right of the E6, a 9km cart track begins 250m north of the parish church and leads past copper-mine tailings up to the observatory at the summit of **Mt Hald-de** (904m), a mountain venerated by the Sami.

Tirpitz Museum
MUSEUM

(☎92 09 23 70; www.tirpitz-museum.no; adult/child/concession Nkr70/35/60; ☉10am-5pm Jun-Aug) Kåfjord's Tirpitz Museum, commemorating the *Tirpitz*, once the world's largest battleship, is the achievement of local resident Even Blomkvist, who has single-handedly collected, bought, begged and borrowed the artefacts, uniforms, memorabilia and nearly 3000 evocative photographs relating to the battleship. It hid away deep in Kåfjord from March 1943 to October 1944, then sneaked out and was sunk in waters near Tromsø.

🏃 Activities

Boat Trips

Sorrisniva
BOAT TOURS, ACTIVITIES

(☎78 43 33 78; www.sorrisniva.no) Sorrisniva runs several riverboat rides along the Altaelva river (one/two hours Nkr750/950). Boats set out at noon daily from June to mid-September. To reach Sorrisniva, head 16km south of Alta along the Rv93, then a further 6.5km along a marked road.

Sorrisniva has 80 snowmobiles, the largest such herd in northern Norway. It offers guided outings (one-/two-person snowmobile Nkr1350/1550), and, your exertions over, you can relax in its steaming hot tub.

Gargia Fjellstue also offers a range of summer and winter outdoor activities.

Holmen Husky
DOG-SLEDDING

(☎78 43 66 45; www.holmenhusky.no) Holmen Husky specialises in dog-sledding (dog-carting in summer), with outings ranging from three hours to five days.

Northern Lights Husky
DOG-SLEDDING

(☎45 85 31 44; www.northernlightshusky.com; Gargiaveien 29) Dog-sledding trips from 2½ hours to multiday expeditions.

Alta Adventure
ADVENTURE SPORTS

(☎78 43 40 50; www.alta-adventure.no) Trekking, canoeing, fishing. Also, on request and not something you'll do around home, ptarmigan hunting.

Gløk
ADVENTURE SPORTS

(☎99 79 42 56; www.glod.as) Both a summer and winter player (its name means 'Glow'), Gløk can lay on ice fishing, dog-sledding, snowshoe trekking and other icy fun.

Sarves Alta Alpinsenter
SKIING

(www.altaski.no; ☉Dec-Apr) Alta's ski centre at Rafsbotn, 10km northeast of Alta along the E6, has five downhill runs and plenty of snowboarding possibilities. Equipment rental is easy to arrange at the centre and a semiregular bus connects Rafsbotn to Alta during the season – ask at the tourist office.

Hiking

For experienced hikers, Alta makes a good launching pad for long-distance hiking trails that follow historic routes across the Finnmarksvidda plateau to the south. Alta's tourist office (p325) can advise.

🛏 Sleeping

Sorrisniva Igloo Hotel
HOTEL €€€

(☎78 43 33 78; www.sorrisniva.no; B&B s/d Nkr2550/4500; ☉early Jan–mid-Apr; P) The 30 bedrooms – and beds too – are made entirely of ice, as are the chapel, bridal suite (no complaints of wedding night frigidity so far) and stunning ice bar with its weird-and-wonderful sculptures lit by fibre optics. Then again, you might just want to drop by and visit (adult/child Nkr200/50).

Gargia Fjellstue
LODGE €€

(☎78 43 33 51; www.gargia-fjellstue.no; r from Nkr800) Around 25km south of Alta, direction Kautokeino, this mountain lodge offers a forest getaway, plenty of activities year-round, and the best foot access to the Sautso-Alta canyon.

Hammerfest

POP 10,287

Welcome to Norway's, and perhaps even the world's, northernmost town – other Norwegian communities, while further north, are, Hammerfest vigorously argues, too small to qualify as towns!

If you're arriving on the Hurtigruten coastal ferry, you'll have only 1½ hours to pace around, pick up an Arctic souvenir and scoff some fresh shrimp at the harbour. For most visitors that will be ample. The town's most unusual experience is to be found at the Royal & Ancient Polar Bear Society.

History

Because of its strategic location and excellent harbour, Hammerfest has long been an important way station for shipping, fishing and Arctic hunting. In its heyday, the ladies here wore the finest Paris fashions and in 1890 Europe's first electric street lighting was installed.

Neither man nor nature has been kind to the town: it was set alight by the British in 1809, decimated by a gale in 1856, burned severely in 1890, then torched again by the Nazis in 1944. Its parish church has gone up in flames five times over the centuries. All the same, God may at last be smiling on the town in a way that is having a huge impact.

A 143km-long undersea pipeline starts beneath the Barents Sea, fed from the huge natural gas fields of Snøhvit (Snowhite: one great, friendly, evocative name for such a giant industrial project). It runs to the small island of Melkøya out in the bay, where the gas is liquefied and transported by tanker to Europe and the US. With estimated reserves of 193 billion (yes, billion) cu metres, the pumps, which came on tap in 2007, are expected to pound for at least 25 years.

◉ Sights

★ Royal & Ancient
Polar Bear Society   MUSEUM

(Isbjørklubben; www.isbjornklubben.no; ⊙ 8am-6pm Jun & Jul, 9am-4pm Mon-Fri, 10am-2pm Sat & Sun Aug-May) FREE Dedicated to preserving Hammerfest culture, the Royal & Ancient Polar Bear Society (founded in 1963) features exhibits on Arctic hunting and local history and shares premises with the tourist office. For Nkr180, you can become a life member, and get a certificate, ID card, sticker and pin. At times, the link to polar bears here can feel a little tenuous. But if you think of the place in terms of the Norwegian name (Isbjørklubben, simply Polar Bear Club), you're less likely to be disappointed.

Membership (there are around 250,000 members worldwide) entitles you to attend the annual general meeting of the society in January. And not everyone can join, it seems. In 1973, one Elvis Presley wrote to the society asking to join, but his application was refused – to become a member, one must be physically present in Hammerfest.

If simple membership is not enough, for Nkr220 you also receive a schnapps glass and get dubbed with the large bone from a walrus's penis. Honestly. It's well worth the extra for the conversation this unique honour will generate down the pub, once you're home.

One of the exhibits covers Adolf Henrik Lindstrøm, a Hammerfest-born cook who accompanied Roald Amundsen and Fridtjof Nansen (among others) and ended up travelling on more polar expeditions that any other person on earth, great explorers included. The town has plans to erect a statue of Lindstrøm in time for the 150th anniversary of his birth in 2016.

★ Hammerfest Kirke   CHURCH

(Kirkegata 33; ⊙ 7.15am-3pm Mon-Fri, 11am-3pm Sat, noon-1pm Sun mid-Jun–mid-Aug) The design of Hammerfest's contemporary church, consecrated in 1961, was inspired by the racks used for drying fish in the salty sea air all across northern Norway. Behind the altar, the glorious stained-glass window positively glows in the summer sun, while the wooden frieze along the organ gallery depicts highlights of the town's history. The chapel in the cemetery across the street is the only building in town to have survived WWII.

Gjenreisningsmuseet   MUSEUM

(Reconstruction Museum; www.kystmuseene.no; Kirkegata 21; Feb-Nov adult/child Nkr50/free, Dec & Jan free; ⊙ 10am-4pm early Jun-late Aug, 10am-2pm

---

WHAT'S WITH THE POLAR BEARS?

A wild polar bear hasn't been seen in Hammerfest for thousands of years, and yet polar bears adorn the city's coat of arms, statues of polar bears guard various public buildings and there's even the Royal & Ancient Polar Bear Society. Cashing in without cause? Well, not quite. In the 19th and 20th centuries, Hammerfest was a major base for Arctic hunting expeditions to the Norwegian territory of Svalbard (or Spitsbergen as it was better known). Returning expeditions brought back numerous captive polar bears (particularly cubs) and from Hammerfest they were shipped to zoos around the world.

DON'T MISS

SLEEPING IN A SNOW HOTEL

There really is nothing like sleeping in one of the Far North's two ice or snow hotels, the Sorrisniva Igloo Hotel (p326) near Alta or the Kirkenes Snow Hotel (p341). In both cases, in our view it's the stunning ice carvings and considerable novelty of the whole experience, rather than any thought of a comfortable night's sleep, that make it worthwhile.

Although there are differences between the two, the experience is broadly similar. For a start, the interior of each room, most of which are separated from the corridor by a curtain rather than a solid door, is kept at a really rather chilly -3° to -7°. Some hotels use reindeer skins, others mattresses atop the ice-block beds, but either way you'll be sleeping in an Arctic-strength sleeping bag. That means shedding (as quickly as you can!) most of your clothing before making a dash for the sleeping bag. Needless to say, we recommend going to the toilet just before bedding down for the night, and this is not an experience for those unable to sleep without a stray limb poking out from beneath the covers!

Mon-Fri, 11am-2pm Sat & Sun rest of year) Hammerfest's Reconstruction Museum is a great little museum with particularly thoughtful and sensitive panels and captions (each section has a synopsis in English). It recounts the forced evacuation and decimation of the town during the Nazi retreat in 1944; the hardships that its citizens endured through the following winter; and Hammerfest's postwar reconstruction and regeneration.

Kulturbanken Galleri GALLERY
(☑ 95 19 98 97; www.syvstjerna.no; Sjøgata 15; ⏰ 10am-4pm Mon-Wed & Fri, to 5pm Thu, to 2pm Sat) Local artist Eva Arnesen designed the Nobel Peace Prize diploma that was awarded to Jody Williams and the campaign to ban landmines. Arnesen's paintings evoke the colours of the region from the northern lights to the bright palette of summer and you can see her work in this newly opened gallery in the town centre.

The handsome pair of carved and silvered **polar bears** on Rådhus Plass, and the sealskin chairs in the Royal & Ancient Polar Bear Society museum, were fashioned by her husband, woodcarver Knut Arnesen.

Kulturhuset CULTURAL CENTRE
(Strandgata 30) FREE Hammerfest's recently completed Kulturhuset is worth a brief visit, simply to savour its striking architecture. Within, there's a theatre, a couple of cinemas and a small cafe that does a decent cup of coffee.

St Michaels Catholic Church CHURCH
(cnr Strandgata & Mellomgata) With a strong claim to being the world's most northerly Catholic church, St Michaels, serving a congregation of barely 90 souls, is immediately recognisable by the striking mosaic of the eponymous saint that extends the length of its facade.

Salen Hill VIEWPOINT
For panoramic views over the town, coast and mountains (there's a free pair of binoculars for viewing), climb Salen Hill (86m), topped by the Turistua restaurant (p330), a couple of Sami turf huts and a lookout point. The 15-minute uphill walking trail begins at the small park behind the *rådhus* (town hall).

Meridian Monument HISTORIC SITE
(Meridianstøtta) FREE On the Fuglenes peninsula, just across the harbour, there's the **Meridianstøtta**, a marble column commemorating the first survey (1816–52) by Russian scientist Friedrich Georg Wilhelm Struve to determine the arc of the global meridian and thereby calculate the size and shape of the earth. It forms part of a Unesco World Heritage–listed site known as the Struve Geodetic Arc.

Nearby are the rather thin foundations of the **Skansen Fortress**, which dates from the Napoleonic Wars, when the British briefly held and plundered the town.

☞ Tours

The tourist office (p330) runs one-hour tours of the city at 11am daily for Nkr250 per person. It coincides with the arrival of the Hurtigruten ferry and its exact starting time depends on when the boat docks. Book ahead.

🛏 Sleeping

Camping Storvannet CAMPGROUND €
(☑ 78 41 10 10; storvannet@yahoo.no; Storvannsveien; car/caravan sites Nkr200/210, 2-/4-bed cabins Nkr450/500; ⏰ Jun-Sep) Beside a lake and

Hammerfest

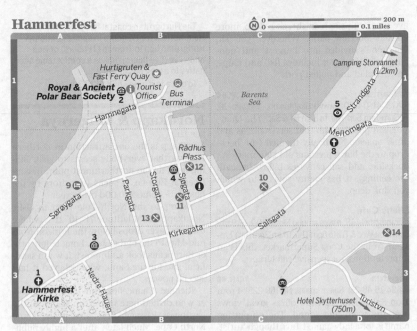

Hammerfest

overlooked by a giant apartment complex, this pleasant site, Hammerfest's only decent camping option, is small so book your cabin in advance.

Rica Hotel Hammerfest HOTEL €€
(🕿 78 42 57 00; www.rica.no; Sørøygata 15; d Nkr890-1605; 🅿@🛜) Constructed in agreeable mellow brick, this hotel has an attractive if somewhat dated bar and lounge and well-furnished rooms – they're worth it if you get a harbour view, but overpriced if not. Its Arctic Menu restaurant, Skansen Mat og Vinstue (p330), serves excellent local fare.

Hotel Skytterhuset HOTEL €€
(🕿 78 42 20 10; http://4service.no/rom-og-restaurant/hammerfest/skytterhuset-hotell; Skytterveien 24; s/d from Nkr595/845; 🅿@🛜) The three

spurs of this secluded hotel overlooking the town look decidedly like barracks from the outside and with good reason; it was originally built as living quarters for summertime fishwives from Finland who worked in the large Findus processing factory. Long ago converted to a friendly, cosy hotel, it's a good option with a solarium and free sauna.

✕ Eating & Drinking

★ Redrum CAFE €
(www.redrum.no; Storgata 23; snacks & mains Nkr69-190; ⏱11am-2pm Mon, to 6pm Tue-Thu, 11am-3am Fri, to 5pm & 9pm-3am Sat) A couple of blocks back from the waterfront, Redrum, with its attractive contemporary decor and flickering candles, saves its energy for weekend wildness, when there's regularly

live music. To the rear, there's a deep, more relaxed wooden patio. Wherever you sit, the menu's divided into 'burgers' and 'non-burgers' – the latter includes fish and chips, Caesar salad and pulled pork.

Kaikanten   PUB €

(🖉78 41 04 70; www.kaikanten.no; Sjøgata 19; ☉3pm-1am Sun-Thu, to 3am Fri & Sat) The Quay-side is a popular pub that serves pizzas and other snacks. Nautically themed (the back-drop to the bar represents old Hammerfest's dockside, and sail canvases billow beneath the ceiling), it has comfy sofas into which you sink deep.

Ellens Café   CAFE €

(Strandgata 14-18; mains around Nkr80-100; ☉9am-5pm Mon-Wed & Fri, to 6pm Thu, 10am-3pm Sat) Up-stairs from the Coop Supermarket, this is an unpretentious, inexpensive cafeteria.

Turistua   CAFE €€

(🖉94 15 46 25; Salen; mains Nkr160-225) From atop Salen Hill, Turistua offers great views over the town and sound. The off-putting name is for a lady named Turi, though 'turist' buses often stop here too.

Qa Spiseri   CAFE €€

(🖉97 07 00 10; Sjøgata 8; mains from Nkr139; ☉10am-midnight Sun-Fri, 11am-1am Sat) Just off Sjøgata and run by a young team, this popu-lar place offers reliable cuisine with a great price-to-quality ratio. There's a choice of Norwegian, Italian and Thai dishes.

Skansen Mat og Vinstue   NORWEGIAN €€€

(🖉78 42 57 00; Sørøygata 15; mains Nkr190-349; ☉6-11pm) A cut above most of the other res-taurants in town, the Rica Hotel's Skansen Mat og Vinstue serves up fine local speciali-ties such as king-crab soup or reindeer stew. Sea views are thrown in for good measure.

❶ Information

Tourist office (www.hammerfest-turist.no; Hamnegata 3; ☉8am-6pm Jun-Jul, 9am-4pm Mon-Fri, 10am-2pm Sat & Sun Aug-May) Has free internet access and rents out electric bikes for Nkr130/325 per hour/day.

❶ Getting There & Around

Buses run to/from Alta (Nkr315, 2¼ hours, two daily), Honningsvåg (Nkr425, 3½ hours, one to two daily) and Karasjok (Nkr410, 4¼ hours, twice daily except Saturday), with one service extend-ing to Kirkenes (Nkr1050, 10¼ hours) via Tana Bru (Nkr740, eight hours) four times weekly.

The Hurtigruten coastal ferry stops in Hammerfest for 1½ hours in each direction. A Hurigruten hop to Tromsø (11 hours) or Hon-ningsvåg (five hours) makes a comfortable alter-native to a long bus journey.

To call a taxi, ring 🖉78 41 12 34.

Nordkapp & Magerøya

POP 3213

Nordkapp is the one attraction in northern Norway that everybody seems to visit. Bill-ing itself as the northernmost point in con-tinental Europe, it sucks in visitors by the busload – some 200,000 every year.

Nearer to the North Pole than to Oslo, Nordkapp sits at latitude 71° 10' 21"N, where the sun never drops below the horizon from mid-May to the end of July. Long before oth-er Europeans took an interest, it was a sacri-ficial site for the Sami, who believed it had special powers.

Richard Chancellor, the English explor-er who drifted here in 1553 in search of the Northeast Passage, first gave it the name North Cape. Much later, after a highly publi-cised visit by King Oscar II in 1873, Nordkapp became a pilgrimage spot for Norwegians. It's also, bizarrely, one for Thais, thanks to a visit by King Chulalongkorn in 1907.

Now here's a secret: Nordkapp isn't con-tinental Europe's northernmost point. That award belongs to Knivskjelodden, an 18km-round-trip hike away, less dramatic, inac-cessible by vehicle – and to be treasured all the more for it. And Nordkapp technically inhabits an island – *mainland* Europe's northernmost point is away to the east, at Kinnarodden on the Nordkyn Peninsula.

❶ Getting There & Away

There are a few options for getting to and from Nordkapp and Magerøya.

The Hurtigruten coastal ferry calls by Hon-ningsvåg. Its 3½-hour northbound stop allows passengers a quick buzz up to Nordkapp.

An express bus connects Honningsvåg with Alta (Nkr475, four hours, one to two daily) and there's also a run to/from Hammerfest (Nkr425, 3½ hours, one to two daily).

The road approach from the E6 is via Old-erfjord, where the E69 branches north.

❶ Getting Around

CAR & MOTORCYCLE

Until the blacktop road to Nordkapp was con-structed in the mid-1950s, all access was by boat. Nowadays, the route winds across a rocky (and often snowbound) plateau past herds of grazing reindeer. Depending upon snow conditions, it's open to private traffic from April to mid-October. In fringe months, ring the tourist office if the weather looks dicey.

In Honningsvåg, **Avis** (☑ 78 47 62 22; Nordkappveien 14B) has a special five-hour deal on car hire for Nkr975, including petrol and insurance.

PUBLIC TRANSPORT
Between mid-May and late August, a local bus (adult/child Nkr490/245, 45 minutes) runs daily at 11am and 9.30pm between Honningsvåg and Nordkapp. It sets off back from the cape at 1.15pm and 12.45am (so that you can take in the midnight sun at precisely midnight). From 1 June to 15 August, there's a supplementary run at 5pm, though this returns at 6.15pm, giving you barely half an hour at Nordkapp unless you want to hang around for the service that returns at 12.45am. Check precise departure times with the tourist office. Ticket prices include the Nkr245 per-passenger Nordkapp entry fee.

If you're on a budget, scan carefully the terms of any all-inclusive tours, which probably charge considerably more for similar services.

A taxi to/from Nordkapp from Honningsvåg costs at least Nkr1400, including an hour of waiting at the cape – plus that Nkr245 admission charge per passenger.

Nordkapp & Around

Yes, it's a rip-off (more on that in a moment), but Nordkapp is a stunning, hauntingly beautiful place. Even after the novelty wears off, it's the view that thrills the most. In reasonable weather – which is a lot of the time – you can gaze down at the wild surf 307m below, watch the mists roll in and simply enjoy the moment.

However, to reach the tip of the continent – by car, by bike, on a bus or walking in – you have to pay a toll (adult/child Nkr245/85). This allows unlimited entry over two days but it's small compensation for the majority who simply roll in, look around, take a snap or two and roll out.

This vast bunker of a place, topped by a giant, intrusive golf ball, provokes a love/hate response. Within are a tediously detailed account of WWII naval actions off the cape, a cafeteria and restaurant, the striking Grotten bar with views of Europe's end through its vast glass wall, a one-room Thai museum, the St Johannes chapel ('the world's northernmost ecumenical chapel'), a post office (for that all-important Nordkapp

postmark) and an appropriately vast souvenir shop. A five-screen, 120-degree theatre runs an enjoyable 17-minute panoramic film.

There is a cheaper fee listed on the ticket office window (adult/child Nkr160/80), which allows you to visit the site without entering the exhibits, but you may have to argue for it – the ticket officer on the day we visited had no idea of this cheaper fee's existence.

🛏 Sleeping

Astoundingly, you can spend the night in your motor home or caravan at Nordkapp itself (fill up on water and electricity though, because you won't find any there for the taking).

Kirkeporten Camping   CAMPGROUND €
(☑ 78 47 52 33; www.kirkeporten.no; Storvannsveien 2, Skarsvåg; per person/site Nkr30/175, cabins Nkr450-825; ☺ May-Oct) Just outside the hamlet of Skarsvåg, this welcoming campsite is a favourite of British adventure tour groups. Its claim to be the 'world's northernmost camping' stands up; there's a rival on Svalbard but it's without cabins. The cosy cafe does reindeer, a fresh-fish daily special, as well as soup and pizzas.

Honningsvåg
POP 2450
Honningsvåg is by far the island's largest settlement and most people visiting Nordkapp either stay or stock up on supplies and souvenirs here.

◎ Sights & Activities

Nordkapp Museum   MUSEUM
(☑ 78 47 72 00; www.nordkappmuseet.no; Fiskeriveien 4; adult/child Nkr50/10; ☺ 10am-7pm Mon-Sat, noon-7pm Sun Jun–mid-Aug, 11am-3pm Mon-Fri mid-Aug–May) Honningsvåg's Nordkapp Museum, upstairs and in the same block as the tourist office, illustrates the impact of early visitors to the cape, the hard days in

WORTH A TRIP

KNIVSKJELODDEN

The continent's real northernmost point, Knivskjelodden, is mercifully inaccessible to vehicles and devoid of tat. Lying about 3km west of Nordkapp, it sticks its finger a full 1457m further northwards. You can hike to the tip of this promontory from a marked car park 6km south of the Nordkapp toll booth – the trails are likely to be snowbound (and hence impassable) deep into May and possibly as early as September.

The 9km track, waymarked with giant cairns, isn't difficult despite some ups and downs, but it's best to wear hiking boots since it can be squelchy. When you get to the tall beehive-shaped obelisk at latitude N 71° 11' 08", down at sea level, sign the guest book. Should you wish, note down your reference number from the book and you can buy – nothing but the hike comes free on this island – a certificate (Nkr50) authenticating your achievement from Nordkapp Camping or the tourist office. Allow five to six hours round trip.

the immediate aftermath of WWII and the daily life of a town that, until the advent of tourism, lived primarily from the sea.

Church
CHURCH

(Kirkegata; ⊘8am-10pm mid-May–mid-Sep) The 19th-century church was the only building in town to survive the Nazis' scorched-earth retreat in 1944. For a time it was a communal dwelling until the first new houses were built.

🛏 Sleeping

Northcape Guesthouse
HOSTEL €

(☑47 25 50 63; www.northcapeguesthouse.com; Elvebakken 5a, Honningsvåg; dm Nkr250, s/d/f with shared bathroom Nkr550/700/1400; ⊘May-Aug; P🛜) A 15- to 20-minute walk from the Hurtigruten quay, this bright, modern hostel is an excellent budget choice. There's a cosy lounge, washing machine, well-equipped kitchen for self-caterers, and great views over the town. It's often full so book well in advance.

Nordkapp Camping
CAMPGROUND €

(☑78 47 33 77; www.nordkappcamping.no; E69, Skipsfjorden; per person/site Nkr50/150, d Nkr650, 2-/4-bed cabins with outdoor bathroom Nkr595/635, cabins with bathroom Nkr120-1540; ⊘May–mid-Sep; 🛜) The well-equipped communal kitchen, friendly service and variety of lodging options more than compensate for the stark location of this campsite, the nearest to Honningsvåg.

Rica Hotel Honningsvåg
HOTEL €€€

(☑78 47 72 20; www.rica.no; Nordkappgata 4; r from Nkr1290; P🛜) The big plus of this hotel, reliable as all others in this Norway-wide chain, is its position, right beside the docks. Grillen, its à la carte restaurant, is well worth a visit, whether you're staying at the hotel or elsewhere.

🍴 Eating & Drinking

Corner
CAFE €€

(☑78 47 63 40; www.corner.no; Fiskerveien 1; mains Nkr195-275; ⊘10am-11pm) Corner serves the usual pizzas and snacks, but also offers great seafood such as crispy cod tongues, whale stew or, more conventionally, fried fillet of cod. It also offers plenty of meaty mains and has a bar with an inviting outdoor terrace overlooking the water.

Artico
ICE BAR

(www.articoicebar.com; Sjøgata 1a; adult/child Nkr139/40; ⊘11am-4pm Apr–mid-May, 10am-7pm late May, 10am-9pm Jun–mid-Aug, 10am-7.30pm late Aug, 11am-3pm Sep) For a shiver in summer and a sense of how Nordkapp must hit the senses in winter, visit this ice bar. Owner, Spaniard José Milares, himself a polar photographer and adventurer, talks with passion of the shapes, bubbles and inadvertent abstract art in the pure ice that he garners freshly each season. The kids can crawl into an igloo that he constructs each year.

Nøden Pub
PUB

(☑78 47 27 11; Larsjorda 1; ⊘8pm-2am Tue-Sun) This local favourite near the Rica Hotel often has live music.

❶ Information

Tourist office (☑78 47 70 30; www.nordkapp. no; Fiskeriveien 4, Honningsvåg; ⊘10am-10pm Mon-Fri, noon-8pm Sat & Sun mid-Jun–mid-Aug, 11am-2pm Mon-Fri rest of year) Right on the waterfront and signposted all over town.

Gjesvær
POP 155

It's a stunning drive to the remote fishing village of Gjesvær, 34km northwest of Honningsvåg and 21km off the Honningsvåg–Nordkapp road, where you'll find two excellent birdwatching outfits. Rolling tundra, punctuated by dark pools and cropped by reindeer, gives way to a stark, rocky landscape, and then a sudden view of low *skerries* (islets) and the Gjesværstappan islands.

🏃 Activities

Bird Safari
BIRDWATCHING

(✆41 61 39 83; www.birdsafari.com; adult/youth/child Nkr550/275/free) Bird Safari sails two to three times daily between June and late August to the bird colony on the Gjesværstappan islands. There are an estimated three *million* nesting birds, including colonies of puffins, skuas, razorbills, kittiwakes, gannets and white-tailed eagles. Bird Safari also has simple seafront accommodation and can arrange fishing.

Stappan Sjøprodukter
BIRDWATCHING, FISHING

(✆95 03 77 22; www.stappan.com; ⊙ Jun-Aug, rest of year by reservation) Fisherman Roald Berg, who built the Stappan Sjøprodukter complex with his own hands, will take you birdwatching (adult/child Nkr600/300) in *Aurora*, his small boat (two departures daily). Or join him for a 2½-hour fishing expedition (Nkr3000, maximum four passengers). He also organises northern lights safaris in winter and king-crab safaris year-round.

He and his photographer partner also run a splendid waterside summer cafe-restaurant offering reindeer stew, king crab, cloudberries and cream, and waffles with homemade blueberry jam. He also has two well-furnished apartments (Nkr1000 for two people, plus Nkr100 per person for bedding and towels).

Lakselv & Around

POP 3125

The plain fishing village of Lakselv, at the head of long, slim Porsangerfjord, has little to detain you. The name means 'salmon stream', which reflects its main appeal for Norwegian holidaymakers. Unless you're here to fish, drive right on by.

🛏 Sleeping

★ Bungalåven Vertshus
CABINS €

(✆92 64 04 23; www.bungalaaven.com; Børselv; 2-bed cabins Nkr550; ⊙ Jun-Sep) Some 40km up the Rv98 northeast of Lakselv, take a signed turning and continue 2km to reach this convivial converted farmhouse. It serves dinner in summer with traditional food for a bargain Nkr250. The lounge is a cosy haven and the owner plays a mean squeezebox so you may find yourself up and dancing. There's also a small camping space too (site Nkr250).

Lakselv Vandrerhjem
HOSTEL €

(✆90 74 53 42; www.hihostels.no/lakselv; dm/s/d Nkr300/400/550, cabins with bathroom & kitchen Nkr700-800; ⊙ mid-Jun–mid-Aug) This HI-affiliated hostel is in a secluded site amid the trees and surrounded by small lakes. It makes a great base for gentle strolls and has self-catering facilities. Follow the E6 southwards from Lakselv for 6km, then take a dirt road to the left for 2km.

Lakselv Hotell
HOTEL €€

(✆78 46 54 00; www.lakselvhotell.no; Karasjokveien; s/d Nkr1050/1365; P@) Just 2km south of town beside the E6, this hotel has cosy rooms, hilltop fjord views, a sauna that's free for guests and a restaurant that does a good summertime dinner buffet (Nkr325). Guests can rent bikes (per day Nkr100).

🍴 Eating

Åstedet Café & Bistro
CAFE €€

(✆78 46 13 77; mains around Nkr150) Don't expect anything fancy to eat in Lakselv itself.

WORTH A TRIP

KAMØYVÆR

A short detour from the E69 between Honningsvåg and Nordkapp brings you to this tiny, sheltered fishing hamlet, its pastel-shaded cottages and cabins encircling the small harbour.

Arran (✆78 47 51 29; www.arran.as; s Nkr750-900, d Nkr1000-1150; ⊙ mid-May–Aug; P🛜) has 44 rooms spread over three quayside buildings. The Sami family who run it bake their own bread and the menu is always the freshest of fish, hauled from the seas off Magerøya. To vary the cuisine, there's also a reindeer special.

If you find it full, several other houses in the village advertise rooms. And should you need a cultural fix, call by the **Gallery East of the Sun** (✆78 47 51 37; www.evart.no; Duksfjordveien 4, Arran; ⊙ noon-9pm mid-May–mid-Aug), featuring the sinuous shapes and bright canvases of artist Eva Schmutterer.

The pick is probably Åstedet, beside Porsanger Versthus Hotel and the Stat Oil petrol station. Both pub and cafe-restaurant, it serves a range of meaty mains plus the usual burgers, pizzas and salads.

ⓘ Getting There & Away

Lakselv's North Cape Airport, an important link for central Finnmark, has up to three daily flights to/from Tromsø.

In summer, a daily bus running between Nordkapp and Rovaniemi via Ivalo (both in Finland) calls by.

Within Finnmark, services running Sunday to Friday include the following:

Alta Nkr365, 3¼ hours, four daily
Honningsvåg Nkr340, three hours, three daily
Karasjok Nkr170, 1¼ hours, three daily

Stabbursnes

At Stabbursnes, 16km north of Lakselv and beside one of the most attractive sectors of Porsangerfjord, there are a couple of important protected areas.

The **Stabbursnes Naturhus og Museum** (☑78 46 47 65; stabburs@online.no; ◷9am-8pm mid-Jun–mid-Aug, 11am-6pm early Jun & late Aug, 9am-3pm Tue & Thu, noon-6pm Wed Sep-May) serves both the nature reserve and national park. It sells field guides, maps and fishing permits and has a well-mounted exhibition about the birds, animals and geology of the interior high plateau, river valleys and coast.

Stabbursnes Nature Reserve

The Stabbursnes Nature Reserve extends over the wetlands and mudflats at the estuary of the River Stabburselva. Birdwatchers come to observe the many species of ducks, geese, divers and sandpipers that rest in the area while migrating between the Arctic and more temperate zones. Among the more exotic species are the bar-tailed godwit, dunlin, knot and the increasingly rare lesser white-fronted goose. Coastal marshes are closed to visitors during the nesting season (May and June) and also from mid-August to mid-September. Ask the nature centre for a full list of birds recorded in the reserve and their seasons.

A signed nature trail (6.4km round trip) leads along the estuary and beside the shore of Porsangerfjord. Ask at the visitors centre for its useful trail description in English.

Stabbursdalen National Park

No roads cross through the 747 sq km of Stabbursdalen National Park, which offers a spectacular glacial canyon and excellent hiking in the world's most northerly pine forest. For hikers, there is one mountain hut, Ivarstua in the park's north; otherwise, you'll need to camp. Two signed trails run across the north – the park's south is rocky, mountainous and hard-going. For longer treks, consult the Stabbursnes visitors centre, which carries the relevant walking maps, Statens Kartverk's *Stabbursdalen* and *Laksdal*, both at 1:50,000. Less arduously, there are three signed trails, the longest requiring around four hours.

The park is a haven for elk (moose), wolverine and the Eurasian lynx, although you'll be lucky to spot the latter two species.

Beside the salmon-rich River Stabburselva and packed with gumbooted fisherfolk in quest of 'The Big One' (the cafe's TV relays live, real-time images from the riverbed), the extensive **Stabbursdalen Feriesenter** (☑78 46 47 60; www.stabbursdalen.no; car/caravan sites Nkr150/200, plus per person Nkr30, 2-bed cabins with outdoor bathroom Nkr500, 2- to 6-bed cabins with bathroom Nkr750-950; ◷mid-May–mid-Sep) campsite enjoys a beautiful position. Facilities, however, are stretched in high season.

EASTERN FINNMARK

Welcome to one of the most remote corners of Europe. For those who make it out here, eastern Finnmark, heartland of the Eastern Sami culture, has some charming coastal villages and a unique frontier history that encompasses Finns, explorers and wartime destruction.

Tana Bru
POP 645

Tiny Tana Bru takes its name from the bridge over the great Tana River, the only one for miles up- and downstream. Here, on one of Europe's best salmon reaches, locals use the technique of constructing barrages to obstruct the upstream progress of the fish; the natural barrage at Storfossen falls, about 30km upstream, is one of the finest fishing spots in all of Norway. Test its waters, though you'll need singular good luck to pull out anything to compare with the record 36kg specimen that was once played ashore.

🛏 Sleeping

Elva Hotel
HOTEL €€€

(☎78 92 82 22; www.elvahotel.no; campsites Nkr180, s/d Nkr1300/1700; ☺mid-Jun–mid-Aug; P🅿🛜) You'll find a campsite, comfortable – though overpriced – rooms, a restaurant and bar at Hotel Tana, a convenient staging post in a classic wooden building at the junction of the Rv98 and E6/E75. Hotel rates include a light evening meal. It also organises salmon-fishing outings.

🛍 Shopping

Tana Gull og Sølvsmie
JEWELLERY

(☎78 92 80 06; www.tanagullogsolv.com; ☺10am-6pm Mon-Sat) Tana Gull og Sølvsmie was established over 30 years ago as eastern Finnmark's first gold- and silversmith. Andreas Lautz creates some very fine gold, silver and bronze jewellery, inspired by traditional Sami designs. The shop also displays quality textiles, ceramics and glassware, as well as traditional Sami knives.

ⓘ Getting There & Away

There are daily buses to/from Kirkenes (2½ hours) and Vadsø (1¼ hours). Westbound, the Kirkenes to Alta bus passes through four times weekly.

Sami Museums

Between Tana Bru and Vadsø are two Sami treasures, each worth a brief visit.

Varanger Sami Museum
MUSEUM

(Várjjat Sámi Musea; varjjat.org; adult/child Nkr50/30; ☺10am-6pm mid-Jun–mid-Aug, to 3pm Mon-Fri rest of year) In Varangerbotn, close to where the E6 meets the E75 17km east of Tana Bru, this is a fun, informative and high-tech display about Sami life and culture, with Sami-related temporary exhibitions and artwork by contemporary Sami artists. Outside is a small, permanent open-air display of Sami turf huts, fishing equipment and domestic life.

Ceavccageadge
HISTORIC SITE

(☺11am-4pm mid-Jun–late Aug) At **Mortens-nes**, on the E75, about 15km east of Verangerbotn, you can stroll towards the shore amid traces of early Sami culture. At the western end, past burial sites, the remains of homesteads and a reconstructed turf hut, is the namesake *ceavccageadge,* a pillar standing near the water, which was smeared with cod-liver oil to ensure luck while fishing. On a hill to the east the Bjørnstein, a rock resembling a bear, was revered by early Sami inhabitants.

Vadsø
POP 6250

The administrative centre of Finnmark, Vadsø has a mixed Norwegian and Finnish heritage thanks to large-scale immigration from Finland in the 19th century. A monument at the north end of Tollbugata commemorates this cultural heritage. Vadsø is also renowned as a site for polar exploration, with several expeditions having started or ended here. Like other Finnmark towns, it was badly mauled in WWII, by both Russian bombers and retreating Nazi troops.

Birders take note: if visiting in early summer, watch for the distinctive Steller's eider, a duck that nests hereabouts.

◉ Sights

Tuomainengården
MUSEUM

(www.varangermuseum.no; Slettengate 21; adult/child Nkr50/free; ☺10am-5pm Mon-Fri, to 4pm Sat & Sun mid-Jun–mid-Aug, to 3pm Mon-Fri rest of year) This historic Finnish farmhouse, built in 1840, had its own bakery, sauna and blacksmith.

Esbensengården
MUSEUM

(www.varangermuseum.no; Hvistendalsgata; adult/child Nkr50/free; ☺10am-5pm Mon-Fri, to 4pm Sat & Sun mid-Jun–mid-Aug, to 3pm Mon-Fri rest

---

DON'T MISS

NESSEBY CHURCH

Along one of the prettiest stretches of the E75 (a nationally designated Tourist Route, see www.turistveg.no), the lovely white church of Nesseby sits far out on the shoreline against the dramatic backdrop of distant mountains. The church itself was built in 1858 and was one of the few in Finnmark to survive the ravages of WWII. The church is signposted off the main road, 0.8km along a quiet road. Alongside the church is a small nature reserve beloved by birders.

NORDKYN PENINSULA

While the hordes rush for Nordkapp, the rarely visited Nordkyn Peninsula makes a strong claim to be Norway's true north and is, in any event, a treasure trove for collectors of 'northernmosts'.

The church-shaped rock formation known as the **Finnkirka** marks the entrance to the village of **Kjøllefjord** and provides a majestic introduction to this remote corner of Finnmark. Across the peninsula, the tiny coastal village of **Gamvik** claims the world's northernmost **museum** (www.kystmuseene.no/gamvik-museum; Strandveien 94; adult/child Nkr50/10; ⏲10am-4pm daily mid-Jun–Aug, to 4pm Mon-Fri rest of year). In a former fish-drying shed, it reveals the fishing cultures of these far-flung environs. Nearby, a birdwatchers' trail runs through the **Slettnes Nature Reserve**, frequented by nesting and migrating ducks and wading birds (accessible only on foot or by private vehicle). **Slettnes Fyr** is the world's northernmost mainland lighthouse.

In the centre are **Kinnarodden**, the northernmost point of mainland Europe (Nordkapp is, technically, on an island) and the town of **Mehamn**, unremarkable except as the site of one of Norway's earliest environmental movements. In 1903 troops were brought in to subdue local fishermen, who protested that whaling was exterminating the whales that had historically made fishing easy by driving cod towards the shore.

Kjøllefjord and Mehamn are both brief stops on the Hurtigruten coastal ferry.

of year) Constructed in the mid-19th century, and just around the corner from Tuomainengården, is this opulent merchant's dwelling, complete with stable and servants' quarters.

Kjeldsen Fish Factory
MUSEUM

(adult/child Nkr50/free; ⏲noon-6pm mid-Jun–mid-Aug) This old fish factory is at Ekkerøy, 15km east of town. The complex retains its old stores and lodgings, a mass of arcane fishing equipment, the former shrimp processing and bottling room, and a vast black vat and boiler for extracting cod-liver oil. Plan to arrive when hunger is beginning to bite and you can enjoy an excellent fish meal in the **Havhesten Restaurant** (☎90 50 60 80; mains Nkr125-225; ⏲2-10pm Tue-Sun), housed in one of the outbuildings.

Its maritime artefacts could be an extension of the museum and, if the wind isn't whipping, you can dine on the jetty with the sea sloshing beneath you.

Luftskipsmasta
HISTORIC SITE

This oil-rig-shaped airship mast on Vadsø island was built in the mid-1920s as an anchor and launch site for airborne expeditions to the polar regions. The expedition of Roald Amundsen, Umberto Nobile and Lincoln Ellsworth, which floated via the North Pole to Alaska in the airship *Norge N-1,* first used it in April 1926.

Two years later it was the launch site for Nobile's airship, *Italia,* which attempted to repeat the journey but crashed on Svalbard.

Amundsen – together with 12 steamships, 13 planes and 1500 men – joined the rescue expedition and disappeared in the attempt, becoming a national martyr as well as a hero. It's well worth the breezy 600m stroll across the grass flats to savour the rich variety of aquatic birds in the small lake just beyond.

Vadsø Church
CHURCH

(Amtmannsgate 1b; ⏲8.30am-3pm Mon-Fri mid-Jun–mid-Aug) As so often is the case in these small Finnmark communities, the church is the most interesting structure architecturally – and all too often the only building to have survived the devastation wreaked by retreating Nazi forces. Vadsø's didn't. Built anew in 1958, it's simple enough yet rich in symbolism. The twin peaks are intended to recall an iceberg, the Orthodox-inspired altarpiece looks metaphorically over the frontier and the rich stained glass depicts the seasons.

🛌 Sleeping

Vestre Jakobselv Camping
CAMPGROUND €

(☎78 95 60 64; www.vj-camping.no; Lilledalsveien; per person/site Nkr10/150, cabins/r from Nkr500/450; ⏲May-Sep) Rooms and cabins are very reasonably priced at Vadsø's nearest campsite, 17km west of town. Only 200m from a fast-flowing salmon river, it's a popular venue for fisherfolk.

Rica Hotel Vadsø
HOTEL €€

(☎78 95 25 50; www.rica.no; Oscarsgate 4; d Nkr945-1355; 🅿@🛜) Plumb in the town centre, the friendly Rica has spruce rooms with parquet flooring. Complete with free sauna and minigym, it represents Vadsø's best choice.

Vadsø Fjordhotell HOTEL €€
(☑ 45 06 03 45; www.vadsoefjordhotell.no; Brugata 2; s/d from Nkr950/1050; P☎) Popular with birdwatchers and close to the trailhead for the Luftskipsmasta, this friendly place has simple but comfy rooms, most of which look out over the water.

✗ Eating

Hildonen CAFE €
(Kirkegata 20; ☺ 9am-4pm Mon-Fri, to 2pm Sat) The aroma of warm bread and sweet cakes draws you into this bakery and cafe, hugely popular with locals and bang opposite the tourist office.

Indigo INDIAN €€
(☑ 78 95 39 99; Tollbugata 12; mains Nkr149-275; ☺ noon-10pm Tue-Sat) It makes no such claim but surely the long-established Indigo must rank as Europe's, if not the world's, northernmost Indian restaurant. Its related takeaway adjunct is something of a culinary UN, dishing up kebabs, burgers, pizzas and Tex-Mex as well as curries.

Oscar Mat og Vinhus NORWEGIAN €€€
(☑ 78 95 25 50; www.rica.no; Oscarsgate 4; mains Nkr190-349; ☺ 6-10.30pm) Oscar Mat og Vinhus, the Rica Hotel's restaurant, is the town's finest, offering a daily fish or meat special to go with its regular cast of reliable Norwegian specialities, including reindeer.

ℹ Information

Vadsø Tourist Office (☑ 78 94 04 44; www.varanger.com; Tollbugata 16; ☺ 10am-6pm Mon-Fri, to 4pm Sat & Sun mid-Jun–mid-Aug) Summer only, and next to the Rica Hotel.

ℹ Getting There & Away

Vadsø is a stop only on the northbound Hurtigruten coastal ferry, which heads for Kirkenes at 8am. There are at least two buses daily to/from Tana Bru (1¼ hours) and Vardø (1½ hours).

Vardø

POP 2274
It's a pancake-flat 75km drive between Vadsø and Vardø, well off the beaten track for all but the most die-hard travellers. But the ribbon of road has a lonely charm as it threads its way between the shoreline, hardy grasses and tough, low shrubs.

Vardø qualifies as Norway's easternmost town. Although this butterfly-shaped island is connected to the mainland by the 2.9km-long Ishavstunnelen (Arctic Ocean tunnel), locals maintain that theirs is the only 'mainland' Norwegian town lying within the Arctic climatic zone (its average temperature is below 10°C). Once a stronghold of trade with the Russian Pomors, it's now a major fishing port and home to many Russian and, strangely, Sri Lankan immigrants.

◉ Sights & Activities

Vardøhus Festning FORT
(Festningsgate 20; admission Nkr40; ☺ 8am-9pm mid-Apr–mid-Sep, 10am-6pm rest of year) The star-shaped Vardøhus Fortress – yes, of course, it's the world's most northerly – was constructed in 1737 by King Christian VI. For a fortress, it's painted in unusually gentle fairy-tale colours. Stroll around the flower-festooned bastions, past turf-roofed buildings and Russian cannons after you've paid the admission fee either at the guard office or by dropping it into the WWII sea mine that guards the entrance.

Pomor Museum MUSEUM
(☑ 40 48 03 32; Kaigata; adult/child Nkr50/25; ☺ 11am-5pm mid-Jun–mid-Aug) This small museum recalls the historic trade between Russia and Norway. Based principally upon the bartering of fish against corn, it lasted until the Bolshevik Revolution in 1917.

Hornøya BIRDWATCHING
(return Nkr200) In summer there are regular **boat trips** from the port to the island of Hornøya with its picturesque lighthouse and teeming bird cliffs. To be all alone after the last shuttle pulls out, reserve one of only three beds at the **lighthouse** (☑ 78 98 72 75; Nkr450).

⌂ Sleeping

Kiberg Bed & Boat GUESTHOUSE €
(☑ 41 32 86 79; Havnegata 37, Kiberg; s/d with shared bathroom Nkr420/575) In Kiberg, 13km south of Vardø, genial owner Ronny Larsen runs these renovated fisherfolk's sleeping quarters, with lounge and well-equipped guest kitchen. Rooms are trim and tidy and there's no better place in all of Norway to suck on the limbs of a giant king crab (around Nkr350). Ronny can organise four-hour fishing trips and birdwatching walks.

WITCHCRAFT IN VARDØ

Between 1621 and 1692, around 90 Vardø women were accused of witchcraft and burned; a sign and flag at Kristian IV gate 24 commemorates the site. On **Domen**, a hill about 2km south of town on the mainland, is the cave where they were supposed to have held their satanic rites and secret rendezvous with the devil.

Reception is open between the hours of 6pm and midnight.

Vardø Hotell HOTEL €€
(☑78 98 77 61; www.vardohotel.no; Kaigata 8; s/d from Nkr900/1000) The staff are willing and cheerful at Vardø's only hotel. However, rooms and corridors are decidedly threadbare and passé. On the plus side, many rooms overlook the harbour and a couple are equipped for travellers with disabilities.

✖ Eating & Drinking

Asia Burger Café CAFE €€
(Kristian IV gate 3; mains from Nkr150; ☺noon-9pm Tue-Sun Feb-Nov) Disregard the off-putting name, shun the burgers and order a dish of tasty, authentic Thai cooking in – you've guessed it – mainland Europe's most northerly Thai restaurant. Accompany this with one of the 36 kinds of bottled beer on offer, including equally authentic Thai Singha beer.

Nordpol Kro PUB
(Kaigata 21; ☺10am-midnight) Dating from 1858 with wooden boards and antique bric-a-brac, Nordpol Kro lays good claim to being northern Norway's oldest eatery. Your friendly landlord, Bjørn Bredesen, has what must be just about anywhere's most comprehensive collection of beer mats. Pick the right night and you can enjoy live music too.

ℹ Information

Vardø Tourist Office (☑78 98 69 07; www.varanger.com; Havnepromenaden; ☺9am-5pm Mon-Fri, 2-5pm Sat & Sun mid-May–Sep) Summer only, and right next to the waterfront.

ℹ Getting There & Away

Vardø is a stop on the Hurtigruten coastal ferry route. Buses follow the scenic seaside route between Vadsø and Vardø (1½ hours) at least twice daily and two services run to Kirkenes (3½ hours) daily except Saturday.

Kirkenes
POP 3680

This is it: you're as far east as Cairo, further east than most of Finland, a mere 15km from the border with Russia – and at the end of the line for the Hurtigruten coastal ferry. It's also road's end for the E6, the highway that runs all the way down to Oslo.

This tiny, nondescript place, anticlimactic for many, has a distinct frontier feel. You'll see street signs in Norwegian and Cyrillic script and hear Russian spoken by trans-border visitors and fishermen, who enjoy better prices for their catch here than in their home ports further to the east.

The town reels with around 100,000 visitors every year, most stepping off the Hurtigruten to spend a couple of hours in the town before travelling onward. But you should linger a while here, not primarily for the town's sake but to take one of the many excursions and activities on offer.

History

The district of Sør-Varanger, with Kirkenes as its main town, was jointly occupied by Norway and Russia until 1926, when the Russian, Finnish and Norwegian borders were set.

In 1906 iron ore was discovered nearby and Kirkenes became a major supplier of raw materials for artillery during WWI. Early in WWII the Nazis coveted its resources and strategic position not far from the Russian port of Murmansk. They occupied the town and posted 100,000 troops there. As a result, tiny Kirkenes was, after Malta, the most bombed place during WWII, with at least 320 devastating Soviet raids. The town was also an internment site for Norwegians from all over the country who did not cooperate with the Nazi occupiers.

The retreating forces burned to the ground the little left of Kirkenes before advancing Soviet troops liberated its ruins in October 1944. Subsequently rebuilt, the mines continued to supply iron ore to much of Europe, but became economically unviable in 1996; they reopened in 2009, this time run by Northern Iron Ltd, an Australian company.

Kirkenes

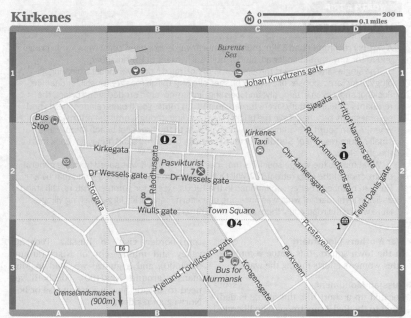

Sights

Grenselandsmuseet   MUSEUM
(Førstevannslia; adult/child Nkr60/free; ⊙10am–6pm Jul–mid-Aug, to 2pm rest of year) This well-presented frontier museum, 1km from Kirkenes centre, illustrates the geography and culture of the border region, with special displays on WWII and mining. Within it, the **Savio collection** displays the distinctive woodblock prints of local Sami artist John A Savio (1902–38), whose works evoke the tension between indigenous life and the forces of nature.

Gabba Reindeer & Husky Park   ANIMAL PARK
(Sandnesdalen 14; adult/child Nkr300/50; ⊙10am–3pm Jun-Sep) This may not be so much of a treat for the children if you've been driving in eastern Finnmark and have stopped to relate to communing roadside reindeer. But it's worth the visit if you've just rolled in on the Hurtigruten; they'll enjoy petting the huskies too.

Andersgrotta   HISTORIC BUILDING
(Tellef Dahls gate; admission Nkr120; ⊙visits 10.30am & 11am) Drop down the steep stairs of Andersgrotta into this cave that once served as an air-raid shelter and bunker as wave upon wave of Russian bombers sought

to knock out the Nazi ore-shipping facility. There's a multilingual presentation, and a nine-minute video also tells the tale. Wrap up warmly as the temperature here is 3°C, even in summer.

Bear Sculptures   SCULPTURE
Outside the Russian consulate, there are two engaging little sculptures of a bear mounting – in every sense of the word, it would appear – a lamp post.

WORTH A TRIP

HAMNINGBERG

A warmly recommended 88km round trip northwards along the coast from Vardø brings you to the tiny, semiabandoned, timber-built settlement of Hamningberg.

The single-lane road runs through some of northern Norway's most fascinating geology: inky tarns; copses of scrubby bushes clinging to the meagre topsoil for dear life; flecks of snow even in late July; and looming, lichen-covered eroded stone pillars, the remnants of sedimentary layers turned on end. En route, you'll pass reindeer herds and several sandy beaches. Save the bucket-and-spading, though, until the return journey when, 7.3km south of Hamningberg, you can walk to the broadest beach through the small nature reserve of **Sandfjordneset**, with its protected sand dunes set back from the shoreline.

What makes the village special is that, being so remote, it was saved from the general destruction of the Nazi retreat in WWII. Only one house was destroyed – and that by a Russian bomber. The rest, abandoned in the 1960s except for summer visitors, still stand as living reminders of what was once one of eastern Finnmark's largest fishing villages. Here where the road ends, there's a small summertime cafe.

War Mothers Monument   STATUE
In the town square, this statue commemorates women's efforts during the war.

Russian Monument   STATUE
Located up a short hill, this statue is dedicated to the Red Army troops who liberated the town in 1944.

 Activities

For such a small place, Kirkenes offers a wealth of tours and activities in and around town. For an overview according to season, pick up one of the comprehensive brochures, *Summer Activities* and *Winter Activities,* from your hotel

There's a summertime reservation point in the lobby of the Rica Hotel, or book directly with tour operators.

Tour agencies can arrange in-town or hotel pick-ups.

Arctic Adventure   ADVENTURE TOURS
(☑78 99 68 74; www.arctic-adventure.no; Jarfjordbotn) Summer and winter activities, eg snowmobiling, dog-sledding and king-crab safaris.

Barents Safari   ADVENTURE TOURS
(☑90 19 05 94; www.barentssafari.no) Barents Safari runs a three-hour boat trip (at least twice daily from June to mid-September) along the Pasvik River to the Russian border at the historic village of Boris Gleb (Borisoglebsk in Russian). It also organises snowmobiling, king-crab safaris and summer quad biking.

Pasvikturist   ADVENTURE TOURS
(www.pasvikturist.no; Dr Wessels gate 9) Offers a wealth of tours including a one-day trans-border visit to Russia's Pechenga valley and mining city of Nikel (around Nkr1500), and a guided weekend in Murmansk (around Nkr2400). For both you need to already have a Russian visa or be a Norwegian resident.

Radius   ADVENTURE TOURS
(www.kirkenessnowhotel; Sandnesdalen 14) A full range of tours and safaris at the home of the Kirkenes Snow Hotel.

Summer Activities
The following activities are popular from late June to mid-August.

➡ King-crab safari (adult/child Nkr1300/600)

➡ Quad-bike safari (single/double Nkr1500/2500)

➡ Half-day tours of the Pasvik Valley (adult/child Nkr900/450)

➡ Visiting the Russian border and iron-ore mines (adult/child Nkr550/275)

➡ Boat trips along the Pasvik river (adult/child Nkr1090/500, including meal)

Winter Activities
Activities to try between December and mid-April:

➡ Snowmobile safaris (s/d Nkr1790/1990)

➡ Ice fishing (from Nkr850)

➡ Snowshoe walks (from Nkr850)

➡ Dog-sledding (from Nkr1990)

➡ King-crab safari (adult/child Nkr1300/600)

🛏 Sleeping

Kirkenes Camping
CAMPGROUND €

(☑78 99 80 28; www.kirkenescamping.no; Maggadalen, Hesseng; tent/caravan sites Nkr150/200, plus per person Nkr50, 4-bed cabins with outside bathroom Nkr450-600, with bathroom Nkr1000-1700; ⊙Jun-Aug) Beside the E6, 8km west of Kirkenes, this is the sole option for campers. Reception opens only between 9am and 7pm (no way to run a campsite in high season) so reserve in advance if you're after a cabin.

★ Sollia Gjestegård
HOTEL €€

(☑78 99 08 20; www.storskog.no; 1-/2-bed apt Nkr1090/1490, 2- to 4-bed cabins Nkr1050-1690, s/d Nkr650/800, breakfast Nkr95) The Sollia, 13km southeast of Kirkenes, was originally constructed as a tuberculosis sanatorium and you can see why. The air could scarcely be more pure or the atmosphere more relaxed at this wonderful getaway haven. The whole family can sweat it out in the sauna and outdoor tub, while children will enjoy communing with the resident huskies. Just below, beside the lake, its Gapahuken restaurant is just as enticing.

Thon Hotel Kirkenes
HOTEL €€

(☑78 97 10 50; www.thonhotels.no/kirkenes; s/d from Nkr595/795; ☎) This newish waterside hotel is Thon-boxy from the exterior. Within, though, it's open, vast and exciting, offering great views of the sound and a cluster of laid-up Russian trawlers. The restaurant is just as architecturally stimulating, and you could easily dangle a line from the open-air terrace.

Rica Arctic Hotel
HOTEL €€

(☑78 99 11 59; www.rica.no/arctic; Kongensgate 1-3; d from Nkr990; 🅿@⚭) The Rica Arctic, a pleasing modern block, boasts Norway's most easterly swimming pool, heated and open year-round. The other special attribute, its Arctic Menu restaurant (summer buffet Nkr350), is the best of the town's hotel dining options.

Kirkenes Snow Hotel
HOTEL €€€

(☑78 97 05 40; www.kirkenessnowhotel.com; s/d half board & sauna incl transfer from Kirkenes Nkr2500/5000; ⊙20 Dec-mid-Apr) Yes, the price is steep but you'll remember the occasion for life. And bear in mind that 25 tonnes of ice and 15,000 cu metres of snow are shifted each winter to build this ephemeral structure. For dinner, guests cook reindeer sausages over an open fire, then enjoy a warming main course of baked salmon.

🍴 Eating

The best in-town meals are in the Rica Arctic Hotel.

Ritz
PIZZA €€

(☑78 99 34 81; www.ritzkirkenes.no; Dr Wessels gate 17; pizzas Nkr193-269; ⊙3-11.30pm) Has an all-you-can-eat dinnertime taco buffet (Nkr128) on Wednesday and pizza buffet (Nkr150) each Friday.

★ Gapahuken
NORWEGIAN €€€

(☑78 99 08 20; mains Nkr220-550, buffet Nkr400; ⊙4-10pm Tue-Sat, 3-7pm Sun mid-Jun–Aug, on demand rest of year) From the broad picture windows of Gapahuken, Sollia Gjestegård hotel's restaurant, there's a grand panorama of the lake at its feet and the Russian frontier post beyond. Discriminating diners drive out from Kirkenes to enjoy gourmet Norwegian cuisine made with fresh local ingredients such as reindeer, king crab, salmon and halibut. Sunday is buffet only.

🍷 Drinking & Nightlife

Galleri Artika
CAFE

(☑95 16 31 48; Wiulls gate 1; ⊙10.30am-3pm Mon-Fri) The motto here is 'art, coffee and chocolate' and this engaging little space is Kirkenes' most agreeable cafe.

Havna
PUB

(Johan Knudtzens gate 1; ⊙6pm-1am Wed-Sun) An earthy sailors' hang-out overlooking the harbour and a rusting Russian hulk. A great place to play pool or darts.

Ritz
PUB

(Dr Wessels gate; ⊙11pm-late Fri & Sat) A disco and pub attracting a mainly younger crowd.

ℹ Information

Kirkenes has no functioning tourist office – their website still works, but it's years out of date. Your best bet for information and brochures are the hotels or tour operators.

Library (Bibliotek; Sjøgata; ⊙10am-4pm Mon-Fri) Has free internet access.

ℹ Getting There & Away

From **Kirkenes airport** (☑67 03 53 00; www.avinor.no), there are direct flights to Oslo (SAS and Norwegian) and Tromsø (Widerøe).

Kirkenes is the terminus of the Hurtigruten coastal ferry, which heads southwards again at 12.45pm daily. A bus (Nkr100) meets the boat and runs into town and on to the airport.

ⓘ A FORBIDDING FRONTIER

Don't even think about stepping across the Russian border for a photo. Nowadays, in addition to vestiges of old Cold War neuroses on both sides, Norway, as a Schengen Agreement country, is vigilant about keeping illegal immigrants from entering. Both Norwegian and Russian sentries are equipped with surveillance equipment and the fine for illegal crossing, even momentarily, starts at a whopping Nkr5000. Using telephoto or zoom lenses or even a tripod all qualify as violations. As the guidance document sternly warns: 'It is prohibited to intentionally make contact with, or act in an insulting manner towards persons on the other side of the border and to throw items across the borderline. Any attempts at violations will be punished as if they had been carried out'. You have been warned!

Buses run four times weekly to Karasjok (five hours), Hammerfest (10¼ hours), Alta (10½ hours) and many points in between.

Independent travellers armed with a Russian visa (which you'll need to get in your home country) can hop aboard one of the two daily buses to Murmansk (one way/return Nkr450/Nkr700, five hours).

ⓘ Getting Around

The airport, 13km southwest of town, is served by the Flybuss (Nkr85, 20 minutes), which connects the bus terminal and Rica Arctic Hotel with all arriving and departing flights.

Kirkenes Taxi (☑ 78 99 13 97) charges Nkr300/350 for a day/evening run between town and the airport.

There are car-rental agencies at the airport or ask at your hotel.

Grense Jakobselv

The first settlement at Grense Jakobselv, 60km northeast of Kirkenes, probably appeared around 8000 years ago, when the sea level was 60m lower than it is today. Only a small stream separates Norway and Russia here, and along the road you can see the **border obelisks** on both sides. The only real attraction – apart from the chance to gaze over the magic line – is the isolated 1869 **stone church**. It was constructed within sight of the sea to cement Norway's territorial claims after local people complained to the authorities that Russian fishing boats were illegally trespassing into Norwegian waters; it was thought that the intruders would respect a church and change their ways. During school holidays, you can make a day trip between Kirkenes and Grense Jakobselv (1½ hours) on Monday, Wednesday and Friday. The bus leaves at 9am and departs Grense Jakobselv at 11.30am, allowing an hour to explore.

Pasvik River Valley

Even when diabolical mosquito swarms make life hell for warm-blooded creatures, the remote lakes, wet tundra bogs and, to their south, Norway's largest stand of virgin *taiga* forest lend appeal to little **Øvre Pasvik National Park**, in the far reaches of the Pasvik River valley.

Some 100km south of Kirkenes and 200 sq km in area, this last corner of Norway seems more like Finland, Siberia or even Alaska. Here, wolves, wolverines and brown bears still roam freely. The park is also home to some of the most northerly elks in Europe, Eurasian lynx and a host of relatively rare birds such as the Siberian jay, pine grosbeak, redpoll and smew.

The Stone Age Komsa hunting culture left its mark here in the form of hunters' pitfall traps around lake Ødevann and elsewhere in the region; some date from as early as 4000 BC. Nearer to our own times in the mid-19th century, farmers from southern Norway established homesteads here with government support, opening up these near-virgin lands and helping to assert this ill-defined frontier territory as Norwegian.

⊙ Sights

Sør-Varanger Museum   MUSEUM
(www.varangermuseum.no/no/sor-varanger; adult/child Nkr50/free; ⊙9.30am-2pm Jul–mid-Aug) It's worth a stop at the Strand branch of the Sør-Varanger Museum, which preserves Norway's oldest public boarding school and illustrates the region's ethnic mix. Visit, too, the timber-built **Svanvik chapel** dating from 1934, and a couple of 19th-century farms, **Bjørklund** and **Nordre Namdalen**.

Høyde 96   VIEWPOINT
The Cold War lookout tower Høyde 96 offers a view eastward to the bleak Russian mining town of Nikel.

⚡ Activities

Numerous Kirkenes operators run boat and snowmobile safaris down the Pasvik Valley.

For hiking, douse yourself liberally in mosquito repellent before heading off into the wilds. The most accessible route is the poor road that turns southwest 1.5km south of Vaggatem and ends 9km later at a car park near the northeastern end of Lake Sortbrysttjørna. There, a marked track leads southwestward for 5km, passing several scenic lakes, marshes and bogs to end at the **Ellenvannskoia hikers' hut**, beside the large lake, Ellenvatn.

Also from the Ødevasskoia car park, it's about an 8km walk due south to **Krokfjell** (145m) and the **Treriksrøysa**, the monument marking the spot where Norway, Finland and Russia meet. Although you can approach it and take photos, you may not walk around the monument, which would amount to an illicit border crossing!

The topographic sheet to use is Statens Kartverk's *Krokfjellet*, which conveniently covers the entire park at 1:25,000.

🛏 Sleeping

Øvre Pasvik Café & Camping CAMPGROUND €
(📞 95 91 13 05; pasvikcamping.no; Vaggetem; tent/ caravan sites from Nkr100/200, cabins Nkr550-650) This place rents out canoes and bicycles, and provides information on local wilderness and attractions.

ℹ Information

Øvre Pasvik National Park Centre (📞 46 41 36 00; ⏰ 8am-8pm mid-Jun–mid-Sep, 9am-3pm Mon-Fri rest of year) The Øvre Pasvik National Park Centre is set in lovely gardens near Svanvik, about 40km south of Kirkenes.

ℹ Getting There & Away

Two weekday buses leave Kirkenes for Skogfoss (1½ hours) via Svanvik and one continues to Vaggatem (2¼ hours).

INNER FINNMARK

Nestled against the Finnish border, Norway's 'big sky country' is a place of lush greenery in summer and deep ice-blues in winter. It's also the epicentre of the Sápmi, the 'land of the Sami'. Kautokeino, a one-street town if ever there was one, is the traditional heart of the region, although Karasjok is altogether livelier and has more Sami institutions.

Karasjok

POP 2875

Kautokeino may have more Sami residents, but Karasjok (Kárášjohka in Sami) is Sami Norway's indisputable capital. It's home to the Sami Parliament and library, NRK Sami Radio, a wonderful Sami museum and an impressive Sami theme park. This is also one of the best places in Norway to go dog-sledding.

It's a lovely forested drive between Karasjok and Kautokeino, following, for the most spectacular stretch, the River Jiešjokka.

⊙ Sights

Sápmi Park AMUSEMENT PARK, MUSEUM
(www.visitsapmi.no; Porsangerveien; adult/child Nkr130/65; ⏰ 9am-7pm mid-Jun–mid-Aug, 9am-4pm late Aug, 9am-4pm Mon-Fri, 11am-3pm Sat Sep–mid-Dec, 10am-2pm Mon-Fri Jan-May) Sami culture is big business here, and this impressive theme park includes a wistful, high-tech multimedia introduction to the Sami in the 'Magic Theatre', plus Sami winter and summer camps and other dwellings to explore in the grounds. There's also, of course, a gift shop and cafe – and **Boble Glasshytte**, Finnmark's only glass-blowing workshop and gallery.

The overall effect is actually very good as it presents the Sami as the normal fellow human beings they are, rather than as exotic anachronisms. If you want more substance, the smaller Sami museums in Karasjok and Kautokeino are less flash and more academic.

Sámi National Museum MUSEUM
(Sámiid Vuorká Dávvirat; 📞 78 46 99 50; www. rdm.no; Museumsgata 17; adult/child Nkr75/free; ⏰ 9am-6pm Jun–mid-Aug, 9am-6pm Mon-Fri, 10am-4pm Sat & Sun late Aug, 9am-3pm Mon-Fri Sep–mid-Jun, 9am-3pm Tue-Fri mid-Aug–May) Exhibits at the Sámi National Museum, also called the Sami Collection, include displays of colourful, traditional Sami clothing, tools and artefacts, and works by contemporary Sami artists. Outdoors, you can roam among a cluster of traditional Sami constructions and follow a short trail, signed in English, that leads past and explains ancient Sami reindeer-trapping pits and hunting techniques. In summer, a guided walk is included in the ticket price.

Sámi Parliament
NOTABLE BUILDING

(Sámediggi; Kautokeinoveien 50; ⊙ hourly tours 8.30am-2.30pm except 11.30am late Jun–mid-Aug, 1pm Mon-Fri rest of year) **FREE** The Sámi Parliament was established in 1989 and meets four times annually. In 2000 it moved into a glorious new building, encased in mellow Siberian wood, with a birch, pine and oak interior. The main assembly hall is shaped like a Sami tent, and the **Sami library**, lit with tiny lights like stars, houses over 35,000 volumes, plus other media. Tours last 30 minutes. There are similar Sami parliaments in Finland and Sweden.

Gamlekirke
CHURCH

Finnmark's oldest timber church, constructed in 1807, was the only building in town to survive WWII destruction.

Activities

Engholm's Husky
DOG-SLEDDING

(www.engholm.no; 1hr dog-sledding Nkr1000, 1-/4-/5-/8-day winter husky safari Nkr1700/7300/9800/16,800) Engholm's Husky, in the lodge bearing the same name, offers winter dog-sled tours. These are sometimes run by Sven Engholm, one of dog-sledding's most celebrated names. Staff can also arrange summer walking tours with a dog to carry at least some of your gear. Consult the website for the full range of activities.

Turgleder
OUTDOORS

(☑ 91 16 73 03; www.turgleder.com) Run out of Engholm Husky Design Lodge by Sven Engholm's daughter Liv, this fine outfit offers a year-round range of activities, from four- to six-hour cross-country skiing excursions (per person Nkr950) to 24-hour 'Scout-for-a-day' experiences (Nkr1900).

Ássebákti Cultural & Nature Trail
WALKING

On the Rv92, 12km south of Karasjok heading for Kautokeino, this 3.5km trail (signed 'Kulturminner' on the highway) is well worth undertaking for a taste of the forest even though, despite its name, it doesn't actually have much that's cultural. This said, around 25 minutes out (allow two hours for the full out-and-back route), there are traces of trappers' pits, store mounds and, across the river, turf huts.

Sleeping

Karasjok Camping
CAMPGROUND €

(☑ 78 46 61 35; www.karacamp.no; Kautokeinoveien; per person/site Nkr20/120, dm Nkr200, cabins Nkr370-1100) Friendly Karasjok Camping occupies a hillside site with river views and a range of cabins. Campers can pitch their tents on its particularly lush, springy grass. Everyone can lie back on reindeer

---

SAMI CULTURE & TRADITIONS

For centuries Sami life was based on hunting and fishing, then sometime during the 16th century reindeer were domesticated and the hunting economy transformed into a nomadic herding economy. While reindeer still figure prominently in Sami life, only about 15% of Sami people are still directly involved in reindeer herding. These days, a mere handful of traditionalists continue to lead a truly nomadic lifestyle. The majority these days fish or are engaged in tourist-related activities.

A major identifying element of Sami culture is the *joik* (or *yoik*), a rhythmic poem composed for a specific person to describe their innate nature and considered to be owned by the person it describes. Other traditional elements include the use of folk medicine, artistic pursuits such as woodcarving and silversmithing, and striving for ecological harmony.

The Sami national dress is the only genuine folk dress that's still in casual use in Norway, and you might see it on the streets of Kautokeino and Karasjok. Each district has its own distinct features, but all include a highly decorated and embroidered combination of red-and-blue felt shirts or frocks, trousers or skirts, and boots and hats. On special occasions, the women's dress is topped off with a crown of pearls and a garland of silk hair ribbons.

To learn more, look out for *The Sami People* published by Davvi Girji (1990) or *The Sami: Indigenous People of the Arctic* by Odd Mathis Hælta, both available in English translations. *The Magic of Sami Yoik* by Dejoda is one of several CDs devoted to this special genre, while the tracks on *Eight Seasons* by Mari Boine, a Karasjok singer, offer a greater variety of Sami music.

skins to the crackle of the nightly birch-wood fire in the cosy *lavvo* (Sami tent).

★**Engholm Husky Design Lodge** CABINS €€
(☑91 58 66 25; www.engholm.no; s/d full board from Nkr1400/2400, s/d hut only from Nkr700/1000; P🐕) *About 6km from Karasjok along the Rv92, Sven Engholm has built this wonderful haven in the forest with his own hands. Each rustic cabin is individually furnished with great flair, with every item (from reindeer-horn toilet brushes to creative lampshades) hand-carved by Sven. All have kitchen facilities and two have bathrooms. You sink into sleep to the odd bark and yelp from the sled dogs.

A plentiful dinner costs Nkr300. Signed trails lead through the forest and barely a five-minute stroll away there's a salmon stream with a fine beach, where you can rent a double canoe (Nkr400 per day). You can also join the team on their daily puppy walk or, for Nkr500, enjoy a boat ride on a nearby lake as the adult huskies run, yap and swim alongside. There's also a sauna and a wood-heated outdoor hot tub.

Rica Hotel Karasjok HOTEL €€
(☑78 46 88 60; www.rica.no; Porsangerveien; d Nkr760-1560; P@🐕) Adjacent to Sápmi Park, this is Karasjok's premier hotel lodging, with handsome rooms and Sami motifs throughout, plus, outside in summertime, Gammen, an impressive Arctic Menu restaurant.

✖ **Eating**

Biepmu Kafeà CAFE €€
(☑78 46 61 51; Finlandsveien; mains Nkr130-225; ☺2-8pm) This simple cafeteria in the centre of town serves up hearty local dishes and snacks, with daily specials (starting at Nkr175) including reindeer on Sunday and a Wednesday fish buffet. There are also other dishes such as shredded reindeer meat. The heavy wooden benches resemble church pews and it's very much locals only in attendance.

★**Gammen** NORWEGIAN €€€
(☑78 46 88 60; mains Nkr225-385; ☺11am-10pm mid-Jun–mid-Aug) It's very much reindeer or reindeer plus a couple of fish options at this summer-only rustic complex of four large interconnected Sami huts run by the Rica Hotel. Although it may be busy with bus-tour groups, it's an atmospheric place to sample traditional Sami dishes from reindeer stew

to fillet of reindeer or simply to drop in for a coffee or beer.

🛍 **Shopping**

Knivsmed Strømeng HANDICRAFTS
(☑78 46 71 05; Badjenjárga; ☺9am-4pm Mon-Fri) This shop calls on five generations of local experience to create original handmade Sami knives for everything from outdoor to kitchen use. They're real works of art, but stay true to the Sami need for durability, made with birch-and-brass handles and varying steel quality. Prices start at Nkr840 for a Sami kid's knife up to Nkr1840 for the real deal.

To get here, turn southwest on Route 92 towards Ivalo at the lower of two main roundabouts along the E6 in the centre of town. It's on your left after crossing the bridge.

ℹ **Information**

Tourist office (☑78 46 88 00; ☺9am-7pm Jun–mid-Aug, closed rest of year) The summer-only tourist office is in Sápmi Park, near the junction of the E6 and the Rv92. It will change money if you're stuck with euros after crossing the border from Finland.

ℹ **Getting There & Away**

Twice-daily buses (except Saturday) connect Karasjok with Alta (Nkr475, 4¾ hours) and Hammerfest (Nkr410, 4¼ hours). There's a service to Kirkenes (Nkr529, five hours) four times weekly.

A daily Finnish Lapin Linjat bus runs to Rovaniemi (Nkr700, eight hours) via Ivalo (Nkr280, 3½ hours), in Finland.

Kautokeino
POP 3050

While Karasjok has made concessions to Norwegian culture, Kautokeino, the traditional winter base of the reindeer Sami (as opposed to their coastal kin), remains more emphatically Sami; some 85% of the townspeople have Sami as their first language and you may see a few non-tourist-industry locals in traditional national dress.

The town is, frankly, dull in summer since so many of its people are up and away with the reindeer in their warm-weather pastures (in winter, by contrast, around 100,000 reindeer live hereabouts). What makes a visit well worthwhile is Juhls' Sølvsmie (Juhls' Silver Gallery), just out of town and a magnificent example of the best of Scandinavian jewellery design.

History

From as early as 1553, during the gradual transition between nomadic and sedentary lifestyles, records reveal evidence of permanent settlement in the Kautokeino area. Christianity took hold early and the first church was built in 1641.

The first road to Kautokeino didn't arrive here until the 1960s.

◉ Sights & Activities

The Thon Hotel Kautokeino organises a number of winter excursions (including snowmobile safaris and trips to local Sami camps) and fishing in summer.

★ **Juhls' Sølvsmie**   GALLERY
(Juhls' Silver Gallery; ☑ 78 48 43 30; www.juhls.no; Galaniitoluodda; ☻ 9am-8pm mid-Jun–mid-Aug, to 6pm rest of year) This wonderful building, all slopes and soft angles, was designed and built by owners Regine and Frank Juhls, who first began working with the Sami over half a century ago. Their acclaimed gallery creates traditional-style and modern silver jewellery and handicrafts. One wing of the gallery has a fine collection of oriental carpets and artefacts, reminders of their work in support of Afghan refugees during that blighted country's Soviet occupation. Staff happily show you around and you're welcome to buy items.

Juhls' Silver Gallery sits on a hill above the southern end of the town and is clearly signposted.

Kautokeino Museum   MUSEUM
(☑ 40 61 14 06; Boaronjárga 23; adult/child Nkr40/ free; ☻ 9am-6pm Mon-Sat, noon-6pm Sun mid-Jun–mid-Aug, 9am-3pm Tue-Fri rest of year) Outside, this little museum has a fully fledged traditional Sami settlement, complete with an early home, temporary dwellings, and outbuildings such as the kitchen, sauna, and huts for storing fish, potatoes and lichen (also called 'reindeer moss' and prime reindeer fodder). Pick up a sheet with a site plan and description on the reverse at reception as nothing's signed. Inside is a fascinating, if cluttered, display of Sami handicrafts, farming and reindeer-herding implements, religious icons and winter transport gear.

Kautokeino Kirke   CHURCH
(Suomalvodda; ☻ 9am-8pm Jun–mid-Aug) The timbered Kautokeino church, which dates from 1958, is one of Norway's most frequented, particularly at Easter. Its cheery interior, alive with bright Sami colours, has some fixtures salvaged from the earlier 1701 church that was torched in WWII. You may find it open outside the summer months, but don't count on it – clearly Sunday morning offers your best chance.

✯ Festivals & Events

Sami Easter   RELIGIOUS, CULTURAL
Easter week is a time for weddings and an excuse for a big gathering to mark the end of the dark season, before folk and flocks disperse to the summer grazing. It's celebrated with panache: the reindeer-racing world championships, the Sami Grand Prix – no, not a souped-up snowmobile race but the premier *joik* and Sami pop contest – and other traditional Sami and religious events.

🛏 Sleeping & Eating

Arctic Motell & Camping   CAMPGROUND €
(☑ 78 48 54 00; www.kauto.no; Suomaluodda 16; car/caravan sites Nkr200/250, cabins Nkr400-1800, motel r from Nkr900; ☻ Jun-Aug) At the southern end of town, this is a hyperfriendly place where campers and cabin dwellers have access to a communal kitchen. Its *lavvo* is a warm and cosy spot to relax by a wood fire and sip steaming coffee, laid on nightly at 8pm. If you ask, the small cafe will also rustle up *bidos,* traditional reindeer-meat stew.

★ **Thon Hotel Kautokeino**   HOTEL €€
(☑ 78 48 70 00; www.thonhotels.no; Biedjovagge-luodda 2; s/d from Nkr1120/1320; 🅿@🛜) This impressive contemporary hotel is a lovely structure with an exterior of mellow wood, built low to blend with its surroundings. Within, rooms are cheerful and cosy. **Duot-tar** (lunch mains Nkr165-175, dinner mains Nkr220-335), its gourmet restaurant, serves fine cuisine. The main item on the menu, as you'd expect in such a town, is reindeer, served in several guises. For dessert, enjoy the delightful fusion of cloudberry *panna cotta* soused in a brandy syrup.

Kautokeino Villmarksenter   CAFE €€
(☑ 78 48 76 02; isakmathis@hotmail.com; Han-noluohkka 2; mains Nkr175-215) Set above the

main road is this functional, cheerless sort of hostel (single/double Nkr800/950, four-bed cabins Nkr600), the main asset of which is its cafe-restaurant, with an attractive open-air deck.

🔒 Shopping

In addition to Juhls' Sølvsmie (p346), there are a number of smaller shops and work-shops where you can pick up local Sami crafts.

Avzi Design   HANDICRAFTS
(☑95 80 88 39; www.avzidesign.com; ⊘10am-5pm Mon-Fri, 10am-3pm Sat) Around 8km east of town in the tiny hamlet of Avzi (ask at the tourist office for directions), this friendly little showroom sells Sami mittens, shawls and other textiles.

Kautokeino Sølvsmie   JEWELLERY
(www.kautokeinosolvsmie.no; Boaronjárga; ⊘9am-4pm Mon-Fri, 10am-2pm Sat) Next to the mu-seum, this place offers finely crafted silver jewellery and other pieces inspired by Sami culture and the local environment.

Samekniv   HANDICRAFTS
(☑97 95 75 17; Boaronjárga; ⊘9am-8pm Jun-Aug, 9am-4pm rest of year) Samekniv, on the road to the museum, is a small workshop with a small range of traditional and modern knives.

ℹ Information

Tourist Office (☑78 48 70 00; ⊘10am-6pm Mon-Fri, 10am-5pm Sun mid-Jun–mid-Aug) The tourist office has occupied five different venues on our last five visits. You might still find it on the ground floor of the Thon hotel.

ℹ Getting There & Away

Public transport to Kautokeino is slim. Buses run between Kautokeino and Alta (Nkr280, 2¼ hours) daily except Saturday. From July to mid-August, the Finnish Lapin Linjat bus connects Kautokeino with Alta (1¾ hours) and Rovaniemi (eight hours), in Finland once daily.

Reisa National Park

Although technically in Troms county, Reisa National Park (803 sq km) is equally acces-sible by road from Kautokeino. Of the park's

BEST FOR SAMI HANDICRAFTS

➡ Juhls' Sølvsmie (p346), Kautokeino

➡ Knivsmed Strømeng (p345), Karasjok

➡ Kautokeino Sølvsmie (p347), Kautokeino

➡ Avzi Design (p347), Kautokeino

wildlife, the most charismatic inhabitants are the wolverine and Eurasian lynx. The Sami name for part of the gorge, Njállaáv-zi, means 'Arctic Fox Gorge', which suggests that Arctic foxes were once present here.

The **national park centre** (☑77 77 05 50; www.reisa-nasjonalpark.no; Storslett; ⊘9am-8pm mid-Jun–mid-Aug, 11am-6pm early Jun and late Aug, 9am-3pm Tue & Thu, noon-6pm Wed Sep-May) is in Storslett.

🏃 Activities

For hikers, the 50km route through this remote Finnmarksvidda country is one of Norway's wildest and most physically de-manding challenges. The northern trailhead at Sarelv is accessible on the Rv865, 47km south of Storslett, and the southern end is reached on the gravel route to Reisevannhy-tta, 4km west of Bieddjuvaggi on the Rv896, heading northwest from Kautokeino.

Most people walk from north to south. From Bilto or Sarelv, you can either walk the track up the western side of the cleft that channels the Reisaelva (Reisa River) or hire a riverboat for the three-hour 27km trip up-stream to Nedrefoss, where there's a DNT hut. En route, notice the 269m Mollesfossen waterfall, east of the track on the tributary stream Molleselva. From Nedrefoss, the walking route continues for 35km south to the Reisevannhytta hut on Lake Reisajávri, near the southern trailhead.

Reisa 20/40 Pound Club   FISHING
(☑45 28 01 00; www.reisa20-40.no; Nyvoll Gard, Storslett; ⊘late Jun-Aug) Salmon fishing in the Reisaelva is a wonderful way to get out and explore the wilderness. Based in Storslett along the E6, this is a well-run place with English-speaking owners.

Svalbard

POP 2642 / HIGHEST ELEV 1713M

Best Places to Eat

➜ Huset (p357)

➜ Kroa (p357)

➜ Mary-Ann's Polarrigg (p357)

➜ Brasseri Nansen (p357)

Best Places to Stay

➜ Basecamp Spitsbergen (p357)

➜ Svalbard Hotell (p356)

➜ Spitsbergen Guesthouse (p356)

➜ Radisson SAS Polar Hotel (p357)

Why Go?

Svalbard is the Arctic North as you always dreamed it existed. This wondrous archipelago is a land of dramatic snow-drowned peaks and glaciers, of vast icefields and forbidding icebergs, an elemental place where the seemingly endless Arctic night and the perpetual sunlight of summer carry a deeper kind of magic. One of Europe's last great wildernesses, this is also the domain of more polar bears than people, a terrain rich in epic legends of polar exploration.

Svalbard's main settlement and entry point, Longyearbyen, is merely a taste of what lies beyond and the possibilities for exploring further are many: boat trips, glacier hikes, and expeditions by snowmobile or led by a team of huskies. Whichever you choose, coming here is like crossing some remote frontier of the mind: Svalbard is as close as most mortals can get to the North Pole and still capture its spirit.

When to Go
Longyearbyen

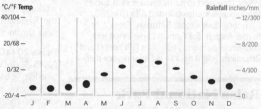

Dec & Jan A jazz festival and deep immersion in the polar night.

Mar & Apr The light returns with week-long festivities.

Jun-Aug Days without end and an array of activities in the summer light.

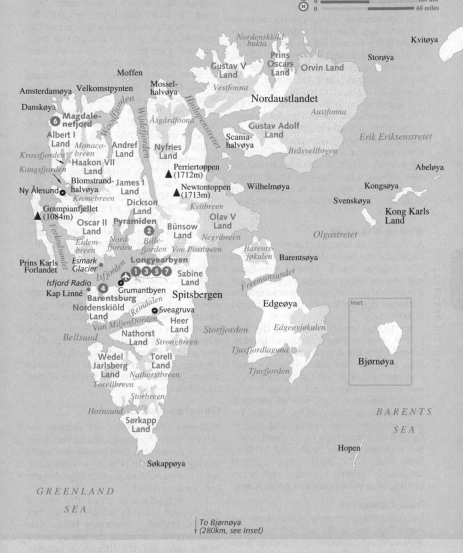

Svalbard Highlights

1 Explore the Arctic wilderness by **hiking** (p354) under the midnight sun.

2 Travel into the fjords of inner Svalbard with a boat trip to **Pyramiden** (p360) and the Nordenskjöldbreen glacier.

3 Experience the polar silence like the explorers of old on a winter **dog-sledding expedition** (p354).

4 Listen to the echo of the Soviet Union on a day trip to the Russian settlement of **Barentsburg** (p359).

5 Feel the exhilaration of racing through the icy wastes on a winter **snowmobiling expedition** (p355).

6 Spend a sunny morning surrounded by the brilliant glaciers and turquoise waters of **Magdalenefjord** (p361).

7 Immerse yourself in the natural and human history of Svalbard at the **Svalbard Museum** (p352) and **Spitsbergen Airship** (p352).

History

The first mention of Svalbard occurs in an Icelandic saga from 1194. Officially, however, the Dutch voyager Willem Barents, while in search of a northeast passage to China, is regarded as the first visitor from the European mainland (1596). He named the islands Spitsbergen, or 'sharp mountains'. The Norwegian name, Svalbard, comes from the Old Norse for 'cold coast'. Today, Spitsbergen is the name of Svalbard's largest island. In 1920 the Svalbard Treaty granted Norway sovereignty over the islands and restricted military activities. Initially signed by nine nations, it now has over 40 adherents, whose citizens enjoy the same rights and obligations on the islands as Norwegians themselves.

Whaling & Hunting

At the time of Barents' discovery, the archipelago was uninhabited. From 1612 to 1720 English, Dutch, French, Norwegian and Danish ships engaged in whaling off the western coast of Spitsbergen island; it's estimated that the Dutch alone slaughtered 60,000 whales.

An English group undertook the first known overwintering at Bellsund in 1630, followed by a Dutch group at Smeerenburg three years later; the following winter, however, scurvy took its toll and the settlement was abandoned for winter, leaving behind a small caretaker team, who all perished. From the early 18th century, Russian Pomor (coast-dwelling) hunters and traders focused their attentions on Svalbard, hunting walruses, moose, seals and belugas. From around 1795 Norwegians exploited the islands' wildlife resources and began hunting both polar bears and Arctic foxes.

Polar Exploration

Longyearbyen is precisely 1338km from the North Pole, and in the late 19th and early 20th centuries a series of explorers used Svalbard to launch attempts on the North Pole using airships and balloons; most met with failure. Roald Amundsen and Umberto Nobile were successful in 1926, but two years later Amundsen and his crew died while on a rescue mission to find Nobile, who had disappeared on a similar expedition and was later rescued.

Coal Mining

Perhaps as early as 1612 whalers had discovered coal at Ny Ålesund, but the first modern mine wasn't opened until 1906, when the Arctic Coal Company (ACC) began extracting coal from a rich seam. The settlement that grew up around this mine was named for the ACC's US owner, John Munroe Longyear. In 1916 ACC sold out to the Store Norske Spitsbergen Kull Compani (SNSK). Over the next few years, two other Norwegian companies set up operations on the archipelago's southernmost island, Bjørnøya, and the Kings Bay Kull Compani opened a mine at Ny Ålesund.

Mining was halted during WWII and on 3 September 1941 the islands were evacuated. Even so, the Nazis bombed Longyearbyen and the settlements of Barentsburg and Sveagruva (Mine No 2, just east of Longyearbyen, was shelled and set alight and continued to burn for 14 years). When the Nazis surrendered in 1945, Norwegian civilians returned, Longyearbyen was rebuilt and the Russians resettled and again mined in Pyramiden and Barentsburg.

Mine No 7 has been in operation for nearly 40 years and nowadays is the only one around Longyearbyen still producing; it yields around 70,000 tonnes per year. The big one these days is the Svea Nord coalfield, 60km southeast of Longyearbyen. It produces around 3 million tonnes annually, extracting more in two days than Mine No 7 does in a year. There are estimated reserves of over 30 million tonnes.

Geography & Climate

Svalbard's vital statistics are suitably impressive: 13% vegetation, 27% barren stone and an astonishing 60% glacier. Svalbard's latitude ranges from 74°N at Bjørnøya in the south to over 80°N on northern Spitsbergen and Nordaustlandet.

The archipelago is about the size of Ireland and consists mainly of glaciated and eroded sedimentary layers that were deposited beneath the sea up to 1.2 billion years ago. It's difficult to imagine but between 300 million and 60 million years ago, Svalbard was lush and tropical. Rich layers of organic matter built up on the surface, then metamorphosed under great heat and pressure into coal. Continental drift shifted it to its present polar location, and most present-day landforms were created during the ice ages of the past two million years. Its highest points are Newtontoppen (1713m) and Perriertoppen (1712m).

Most of Svalbard's glaciers are retreating: Austre Brøggerbreen has lost almost 20m since 1977, while Midre Lovenbreen isn't far behind.

The archipelago enjoys a brisk polar-desert climate, with only 200mm to 300mm of precipitation annually. Although the west coast remains ice-free for most of the summer, pack ice hovers just north of the main island year-round. Snow and frost are possible at any time of year; the mean annual temperature is -4°C, and in July it's only 6°C. On occasion, however, you may experience temperatures of up to 20°C. In January the mean temperature is -16°C, but temperatures of -30°C aren't uncommon.

In Longyearbyen the midnight sun lasts from 19 April to 23 August, while it never even peeks above the horizon between 28 October and 14 February.

Wildlife

In addition to polar bears, Svalbard is home to other emblematic Arctic species. The species you're most likely to see are the Arctic fox (also known as the polar fox) and Svalbard's unusually squat reindeer.

Svalbard's reindeer are genetically akin to their distant Canadian cousins and some have been found bearing Russian tags, proving that they walked in over the ice. Unlike their cousins on the mainland, they don't live in herds but in family groups of two to six animals. As they have no predators other than humans they thrive and the estimated population of around 10,000 is kept constant by an annual cull. Most Svalbard reindeer starve slowly to death when they're about eight years old, their teeth having been ground to stumps by the stones and pebbles they mouth along with sprigs of edible matter.

Despite having been hunted to the brink of extinction in centuries past, whales can still be seen on occasion in Svalbard's waters, while seals are also common. Walruses, too, suffered from relentless hunting, although a population of between 500 and 2000 still inhabits Svalbard.

Dangers & Annoyances

Don't let your desire to see Svalbard's symbol, the polar bear, blind you to the fact that a close encounter with these iconic creatures rarely ends well. As the signs on the outskirts of Longyearbyen attest, polar bears are a real danger almost everywhere in Svalbard. If you're straying beyond Longyearbyen's confines, you're strongly advised to go with an organised tour. Walk leaders carry a gun and know how to use it. Standard equipment too, especially if you're camping, are trip wires with flares and distress flares too – to fire at the ground in front of the bear, not to summon help, which could be hours away. The last bear fatality was in 2011 in the vicinity of the Von Post glacier, 40km from Longyearbyen. The previous fatality, in 1995, happened only 2km from Longyearbyen...

☞ Tours

For reasons of security and sheer logistics, it's difficult to arrange independent trips on Svalbard and we endorse the governor's advice that you should book organised tours through recognised operators. Fortunately, there's a huge range of options.

Longyearbyen

POP 2100

Svalbard's only town of any size, Longyearbyen enjoys a superb backdrop including two glacier tongues, Longyearbreen and Lars Hjertabreen. The town itself is fringed by abandoned mining detritus and the waterfront is anything but beautiful, with shipping containers and industrial buildings. The further you head up the valley towards the glaciers, the more you'll appreciate being here. Even so, Longyearbyen is a place to base yourself for trips out into the wilderness rather than somewhere to linger for its own sake.

History

Although whalers had been present here in previous centuries, the town of Longyearbyen was founded in the early 20th century as a base for Svalbard's coal-mining activities; the town's gritty coal-mining roots still show through, commemorated in the statue of a grizzled miner and his pick near the Lompensenteret. For decades, Store Norsk, owner of the pits, possessed the communal mess, company shop, transport in and out, and almost the miners' souls. Then in 1976 the Norwegian state stepped in to bail the company out from bankruptcy. Today, most of the few people who live here year-round enjoy one-year tax-free contracts. There are at least seven mines dotted around Longyearbyen and the surrounding area, although only one, Mine No 7, 15km east of town, is still operational.

Reflecting the days when miners would remove their coal-dust-encrusted boots at the threshold, local decorum still dictates that people take off their shoes upon entering most buildings in town. Exceptions include the majority of shops and places to eat. Guns must also be left at the door just about everywhere.

◉ Sights

Svalbard Museum   MUSEUM
(☑79 02 64 92; www.svalbardmuseum.no; adult/student/child Nkr75/50/15; ☺10am-5pm Mar-Sep, noon-5pm Oct-Feb) Museum is the wrong word for this impressive exhibition space. Themes include the life on the edge formerly led by whalers, trappers, seal and walrus hunters and, more recently, miners. It's an attractive mix of text, artefacts and birds and mammals, stuffed and staring. There's a cosy book-browsing area, too, where you can lounge on sealskin cushions and rugs.

Spitsbergen Airship Museum   MUSEUM
(North Pole Expedition Museum; ☑91 38 34 67; www.spitsbergenairshipmuseum.com; adult/child Nkr75/40; ☺9am-1pm) This fascinating private museum houses a stunning collection of artefacts, original newspapers and other documents relating to the history of polar exploration. With labels in English and intriguing archive footage, you could easily spend a couple of hours here reliving some of the Arctic's most stirring tales. Opening hours are in a state of flux. It's across the road from the rear of the museum and tourist information office.

Galleri Svalbard   GALLERY
(adult/child/concession Nkr70/20/40; ☺11am-5pm Mar-Sep, 1-5pm Tue-Sat & 11-3pm Sun Oct-Feb) Galleri Svalbard features the Svalbard-themed works of renowned Norwegian artist Kåre Tveter, so pure and cold they make you shiver, as well as works by other artists such as Olav Storø (www.storoe.no). It also has fascinating reproductions of antique maps of Svalbard, historical drawings with a Svalbard focus, temporary ex-

POLAR BEARS UNDER THREAT

Polar bears are one of the most enduring symbols of the Arctic wilderness – loners, immensely strong and survivors in one of the world's most extreme environments. But for all the bears' raw power, some scientists predict that they could be extinct by the end of this century if the world continues to heat up.

Polar bear numbers had been in decline since the late 19th century, when intensive hunting began. But ever since the 1973 treaty for the Conservation of Polar Bears and their Habitat, signed by all the countries whose lands impinge upon the Arctic, polar bear numbers have been gradually increasing again and latest estimates suggest that there are between 20,000 and 25,000 left in the wild; Svalbard has a population of between 3000 and 3500.

But as is the case throughout the Arctic, Svalbard's glaciers are retreating and the ice sheet, their natural habitat and prime hunting ground for seals, the mainstay of their diet (an adult bear needs to eat between 50 and 75 seals every year), is shrinking. Although polar bears are classified as marine mammals and are powerful swimmers, many risk drowning as they attempt to reach fresh ice floes that are ever more separated by open water. Less sea ice also means that some populations will become isolated and inbred, their genetic stock weakened. The birth rate may also fall since females need plenty of deep snow to dig the dens in which they will whelp. And hungry bears, on the prowl and desperate for food, could lead to increasing confrontations with humans.

Your chances of seeing one, unless you're on a cruise and observing from the safety of a ship, are minimal, especially in summer. In any event, contact is actively discouraged, both for your and the bear's sake (if a snowmobiler gives chase, for example, he or she will be in for a stiff fine). Bears under pressure quickly become stressed and overheat under their shaggy coats and may even die of heat exhaustion if pursued.

Should you come within sight of one on land, don't even think of approaching it. An altogether safer way to track polar bears is to log onto www.panda.org/polarbears, managed by the World Wildlife Fund. Here, you can track the movements of bears that scientists have equipped with a collar and satellite transmitter.

SVALBARD GLOBAL SEED VAULT

Deep inside the mountain, down beneath the permafrost, a vast man-made cavern, already dubbed the Doomsday Vault or a vegetarian Noah's Ark, was opened in 2008. It's a repository with a capacity for up to four million different seed types (and up to 2.25 billion seeds in all), representing the botanical diversity of the planet. Samples from seed banks and collections all over the world are kept here at a constant temperature of -18°C so that, should a species become extinct in its native habitat, it can be revived and won't be lost for eternity. The vault is built into the mountain above the airport, 130m above sea level to ensure the vault survives any future rise in sea levels; Svalbard was chosen due to its lack of tectonic activity and the preservative powers of its permafrost. As of mid-2014, the vault was home to over 700,000 different seed varieties, with approximately 250 million individual seeds in all – it already holds the most diverse collection of food crop seeds on earth.

hibitions, and a marvellous 10-minute film, *The Arctic Nature of Svalbard*. The gallery has a small cafe and an excellent shop.

Attached to the gallery is the **Kunstnersenteret** (Artists' Centre; ⊙ 11am-5pm Mar-Sep, 1-5pm Tue-Sat & 11-3pm Sun Oct-Feb) FREE which serves as a workshop for local artists with many of the works on sale.

Historic Sites

The original site for Longyearbyen was on the rise above the west bank of the stream that runs down to the fjord from the two glaciers. Today the rise is dominated by the wooden **Svalbard Kirke**, which was first built in the 1920s but later rebuilt after being destroyed in the German invasion during WWII; it's usually left open.

Some 50m south of the church stand five weathered **wooden steps**, all alone, and a sign, 'Sykhustrappa' (Hospital Stairs). They're all that remain of Longyearbyen's first hospital and they have a special significance for the town's residents. Traditionally, a week of celebrations to dispel the weeks of winter darkness begins once the first of the spring sun's rays touched the forehead of someone standing on the top step.

South of the church and the steps, **wooden pillars** emerging from the permafrost are all that remain of the original settlement; again, the houses that once stood here were burned to the ground during WWII.

Further into the valley to the south lies a haunting little **graveyard** with simple white, wooden crosses with dates. It dates from the early 20th century and includes the bodies of seven young men in Longyearbyen who were struck down by the Spanish flu in October 1918, a virus that killed 40 million people in Europe, Asia and North America.

From here there's a fine view across the valley to the evocative remains of former **Mine No 2**.

🏃 Summer Activities

You'll be disappointed if you restrict yourself to scruffy Longyearbyen; you'll leave with little sense of the sheer majesty of Svalbard's wilderness. Fortunately, there's a dizzying array of short trips and day tours that vary with the season. The tourist office has an extensive weekly activities list. All outings can be booked through individual operators (directly or via their websites; visit www. svalbard.net).

Birdwatching

More than 160 bird species have been reported in Svalbard, with the overwhelming number of these present during the summer months; the only species to overwinter in the archipelago is the Svalbard ptarmigan. If you're in Longyearbyen in summer, among the common species you're likely to see are the barnacle goose, king eider, common eider, Arctic tern, purple sandpiper, glaucous gull and snow bunting; the best chance for sighting these species is in the Adventdalen delta southeast of the centre on the road to Mine No 7. A little further afield, especially on the boat trips to Barentsburg or Pyramiden, the little auk, black guillemot, puffin and fulmar are among the most commonly sighted species. Some tour operators run short boat trips to the 'bird cliffs' close to Longyearbyen, while birders should buy the booklet *Bird Life in Longyearbyen and Surrounding Area* (Nkr50), which is available from the tourist office.

SVALBARD TOUR COMPANIES

The following are the main companies offering tours around Svalbard, starting with day excursions from Longyearbyen to longer boat cruises and multiday expeditions out into the wilderness. All of the following operate in both summer and winter.

Svalbard Wildlife Expeditions offers many of the usual and several unusual trips, while Spitsbergen Travel, one of the giants of the Svalbard travel scene, has a staggering array of options.

Arctic Adventures (☑ 79 02 16 24; www.arctic-adventures.no) Small company offering the full range of activities.

Basecamp Spitsbergen (☑ 79 02 46 00; www.basecampspitsbergen.com) Basecamp Spitsbergen has a large portfolio of adventure trips and mainly offers winter activities, including a stay aboard the *Noorderlicht*, a Dutch sailing vessel that's set into the fjord ice as the long freeze begins each autumn. It also offers winter and summer stays at Isfjord Radio, the ultimate remote getaway on an upgraded, one-time radio station at the western tip of Spitsbergen.

Green Dog Svalbard (☑ 79 02 61 68; www.greendog.no; 4hr trips Nkr1250) A range of dog-sledding adventures.

Poli Arctici (☑ 79 02 17 05; www.poliartici.com) Poli Arctici is the trading name of Stefano Poli, originally from Milan, who has more than 15 years as a Svalbard wilderness guide.

Spitsbergen Outdoor Activities (☑ 91 77 65 95; www.spitsbergenoutdooractivities.com) Specialists in hiking, both on glacier and otherwise.

Spitsbergen Tours (☑ 79 02 10 68; www.terrapolaris.com) The owner of Spitsbergen Tours, Andreas Umbreit, is one of the longest-standing operators on the archipelago.

Svalbard Husky (☑ 98 87 16 21, 98 40 40 89; www.svalbardhusky.no; 4hr trips Nkr1350) Year-round dog-sledding.

Svalbard Villmarkssenter (☑ 79 02 17 00; www.svalbardvillmarkssenter.no; 3hr trips Nkr980; ⊙ 10am & 2pm) Experts in dog mushing, whether by sledge over the snow or on wheels during summer.

Boat Trips

The main boat-trip excursions are to the Russian settlements of Barentsburg and Pyramiden, with shorter trips to nearby bird cliffs and glacier tongues.

Polar Charter BOAT TOURS
(☑ 97 52 32 50; www.polarcharter.no) Polar Charter sends out the *MS Polargirl* to Barentsburg and the Esmark Glacier (Nkr1300, eight to 10 hours) four times a week, and to Pyramiden and Nordenskjöldbreen (Nkr1300, eight to 10 hours); prices include a lunch cooked on board. On Fridays, it also organises five-hour trips to the Borebreen glacier (Nkr900).

Henningsen Transport & Guiding BOAT TOURS
(☑ 91 85 37 56, 79 02 13 11; www.htg.svalbard.no) Henningsen Transport & Guiding runs excellent trips to Barentsburg and Pyramiden (Nkr1550). En route, they tend to sail closer to shore than other companies, rather than sailing down the middle of the fjord. It also runs six-hour Friday-evening trips to Bore glacier for Nkr1190.

Spitsbergen Travel BOAT TOURS
(www.spitsbergentravel.com; 3/6hr Nkr640/990) One of the giants of the Svalbard travel scene, Spitsbergen Travel has a staggering array of tour options. They arrange up to 13 weekly boat cruises around Isfjord, which take in birdwatching, fossil-hunting and glacier views.

Dog-Sledding

The following companies offer half-day excursions with wheeled sleds pulled by pack dogs. There are up to 38 weekly departures in summer.

➡ **Svalbard Villmarkssenter** (p354)

➡ **Green Dog Svalbard** (p354)

➡ **Svalbard Husky** (p354)

Hiking & Fossil-Hunting

Summer hiking possibilities are endless and any Svalbard tour company worth its salt can organise half-, full- and multiday hikes. The easiest options are three-hour fossil-hunting hikes (from Nkr500), some of which take you up onto the moraine at the base of the Longyearbreen glacier.

Popular destinations for other hikes, many of which include glacier hikes, include Platåberget (three hours, Nkr450), up onto the Longyearbreen glacier (five hours, Nkr650), Sarkofagen (525m above sea level; six hours, Nkr620) and Hiorthfjellet (900m above sea level; 10 hours, Nkr1225).

Spitsbergen Outdoor Activities and Poli Arctici are among the better smaller operators.

Horse Riding

Spitsbergen Outdoor Activities organises three-hour, twice-daily horse-riding expeditions in the country beyond Longyearbyen for Nkr750 per person.

Kayaking

Svalbard Wildlife Expeditions　　　　　ADVENTURE TOURS
(☑ 79 02 22 22; www.wildlife.no) Offering many of the usual and several unusual trips, including seven-hour kayaking expeditions to Hiorthamn (Nkr950), with an additional 10-hour hiking and kayaking challenge to Hiortfjellet (Nkr1225). Other options are the various excursions along Adventdalen.

🏃 Winter Activities

Basecamp Spitsbergen (p354) and Spitsbergen Travel (p354) offer some truly epic, multiday cross-country ski expeditions.

Dog-Sledding

The environmentally friendly rival to snowmobiling, dog-sledding is in many ways the iconic Svalbard winter activity – the soundtrack of huskies barking and the scrape of the sled across the ice are a far more agreeable accompaniment in the wilderness than the drone of a snowmobile engine. Expect to pay around Nkr1290 for a four-hour excursion, although longer expeditions are possible.

Dedicated dog-sledding operators include:

➡ **Svalbard Husky** (p354)

➡ **Svalbard Villmarkssenter** (p354)

➡ **Green Dog Svalbard** (p354)

➡ **Basecamp Spitsbergen** (7hr trips adult/child Nkr1990/995)

Snowmobiling

Riding or driving a snowmobile is the main way of getting around Svalbard in winter and it certainly enables you to cover a greater distance and see more than is otherwise possible.

Before setting out, pick up a copy of *Driving a Snowmobile in Svalbard* from the tourist office. To drive a snowmobile scoot, you'll need to flash your home driving licence. Check with the tourist office; many areas are off-limits for snowmobiles. Daily rates range from Nkr1000 to Nkr1250 for the basic model.

Most companies will offer snowmobile safaris. Spitsbergen Travel has a particularly wide range of excursions, while **Svalbard Snøscooterutleie** (☑ 79 02 46 61; www.scooterutleie.svalbard.no) offers snowmobile rental.

Sample expeditions include (prices may vary between companies):

➡ Northern Lights Safari (three hours, Nkr1650)

➡ Coles Bay (four hours, Nkr1750)

➡ Elveneset (four hours, Nkr1750)

MULTIDAY BOAT CRUISES AROUND SVALBARD

To really get a taste for the inner and outer reaches of Svalbard in a short space of time, there's no alternative to a multi-day coastal boat cruise. They don't come cheap, but these are once-in-a-lifetime journeys. Any of the following run such cruises:

➡ **Basecamp Spitsbergen**

➡ **Discover the World** (www.discovertheworld.co.uk)

➡ **GAP Adventures** (www.gapadventures.com)

➡ **Hurtigruten** (www.hurtigruten.com)

➡ **Naturetrek** (www.naturetrek.co.uk)

➡ **Spitsbergen Travel**

➡ East Coast Spitsbergen (10 hours, Nkr2350)

➡ Von Post Glacier (eight hours, Nkr2250)

➡ Pyramiden (11 hours, Nkr2350)

➡ Barentsburg (eight hours, Nkr2250)

👉 Tours

Svalbard Maxi Taxi
BUS TOURS

(✆79 02 13 05; per person Nkr295; ⊘10am & 4pm Jun-Aug) This local taxi company offers two-hour minibus tours that take you further than you might think possible around Long-yearbyen. From a number of the places they take you there are stunning views when the weather's fine, and you can get much further than you would on foot, without needing a gun and guide.

Arctic Tapas
BUS TOURS

(✆46 27 60 00; www.arctictapas.com; tours per adult/child Nkr550/400; ⊘6.30-9pm Tue-Sat) This tour bus with a difference offers a sightseeing tour of Longyearbyen accompanied by an on-board four-course meal with a focus on northern Norwegian produce and specialities.

🎉 Festivals & Events

Polar Jazz
MUSIC

(www.polarjazz.no) A long winter weekend of jazz, held in February.

Sunfest
CULTURAL

(www.solfest.no) Week-long celebrations beginning on 8 March to dispel the polar night.

Blues Festival
MUSIC

(www.svalbardblues.com) Five-day jam session in October to warm you up before the onset of winter.

🛏 Sleeping

To sleep in a hammock strung out above one of the husky kennels (per person Nkr350), contact Svalbard Villmarkssenter (p354).

Basecamp Spitsbergen (p354) has a number of remote lodges – they're mostly available for groups, but check out their website for more details.

Spitsbergen Guesthouse
GUESTHOUSE €

(✆79 02 63 00; www.spitsbergentravel.no; dm Nkr305-375, s Nkr510-900, d Nkr815-1210; ⊘mid-Mar–mid-Sep; 🛜) This guesthouse is a subsidiary of Spitsbergen Travel (p354) and can accommodate up to 136 people. Spread over four buildings, one of which houses a large

breakfast room (once the miners' mess hall), the rooms are simple, come with no frills and are terrific value for money.

Gjestehuset 102
GUESTHOUSE €

(✆79 02 57 16; www.gjestehuset102.no; dm Nkr310-340, s with shared bathroom Nkr400-580, d with shared bathroom Nkr750-920; ⊘Mar-Nov; 🛜) Friendly Guesthouse 102 (which occupies building 7) was once sardonically nicknamed 'Millionaire's Residence'. As the former accommodation for mine workers, the rooms are simplicity itself. They come with washbasins and there's a kitchen for self-caterers.

Longyearbyen Camping
CAMPGROUND €

(✆79 02 10 68; www.longyearbyen-camping.com; campsites per adult/child under 13yr Nkr120/free; ⊘Apr & mid-Jun–mid-Sep) Near the airport on a flat stretch of turf, this particularly friendly campsite overlooks Isfjorden and the glaciers beyond and has a kitchen and showers. It's about an hour's walk from town. You can also hire a tent (per night Nkr150), mattress (Nkr10) and sleeping bag (Nkr50). There are no cabins, but it does issue certificates for those who bathe naked in the fjord...

★ Svalbard Hotell
HOTEL €€

(✆79 02 50 00; svalbardbooking.com/Accommodation/Svalbard-Hotell; s Nkr990-2190, d Nkr1190-2590; 🛜) Svalbard's newest hotel offers stylish rooms with dark Scandinavian wood tones offset by stunning large photos above the beds and splashes of colour in the linens. There are flat-screen TVs, and you couldn't be more central for the main shops and restaurants of Longyearbyen

Spitsbergen Hotel
HOTEL €€

(✆79 02 62 00; www.spitsbergentravel.no; s Nkr835-2580, d Nkr990-2900; ⊘Feb-Oct; 🛜) This comfortable place (sink yourself low into the leather armchairs of its salon), run by the respected Rica Hotel chain, is where the mine bosses once lived. Rooms are comfortable with a vaguely old-world air.

Mary-Ann's Polarrigg
HOTEL, GUESTHOUSE €€

(✆79 02 37 02; www.polarriggen.com; Skjæringa; s Nkr775-995, d Nkr995-2250) Run by the ebullient Mary-Ann and adorned with mining and hunting memorabilia, the Polarrigg brims with character, although most of this is in the public areas; rooms are quite simple. In the main wing, rooms have corridor bathrooms and doubles come with bunk beds. There are two large, comfortably furnished lounges, while in the smart, if somewhat overpriced, annexe, rooms have every comfort.

Haugen Pensjonat
PENSION €€

(✍79 02 17 05; www.haugenpensjonat.no; s with shared bathroom Nkr600-800, d Nkr850-1200; ⊗) Run by the people at Poli Arctici (p354), Haugen Pensjonat, close to the Spitsbergen Hotel, has nine good-sized rooms with double bed and sofa. Shared bathroom facilities work out at roughly one bathroom per two rooms.

Svalbard Lodge
APARTMENTS €€

(✍79 02 50 00; www.scooterutleie.svalbard.no; per person Nkr550-950) From the same stable as Svalbard Hotell and located right in the heart of Longyearbyen, these two- and three-room modern apartments are a good base. There's a two-night, three-person minimum-stay requirement.

★Basecamp Spitsbergen
LODGE €€€

(✍79 02 46 00; www.basecampexplorer.com; s Nkr1100-2500, d Nkr1590-2890; ⊗) Imagine a recreated sealing hut, built in part from recycled driftwood and local slate. Add artefacts and decorations culled from the local refuse dump and mining cast-offs. Graft on 21st-century plumbing and design flair and you've got this fabulous place, also known as Trapper's Lodge. The 16 cabin-like rooms are the definition of cosiness and comfort, and the breakfasts are splendid. It's a special place and easily the most atmospheric choice in Longyearbyen.

Radisson SAS Polar Hotel
HOTEL €€€

(✍79 02 34 50; www.radissonsas.com; s Nkr1370-2890, d Nkr1570-3200; ⊗) This 95-room chain hotel ('the world's northernmost full-service hotel') is the town's premier address, although the rooms are functional and extremely comfortable rather than luxurious. It costs Nkr200 extra for a 'superior room' with partial views of the fjord and Hiorthfjellet mountain beyond, and a coffee machine. The annexe was originally accommodation for the Lillehammer Winter Olympic Games, then transported here.

✗ Eating

Fruene Kaffe og Vinbar
CAFE €

(The Missus; ✍79 02 76 40; Lompensenteret; lunch mains from Nkr79; ⊗10am-6pm Mon-Fri, 10am-5pm Sat, 11am-5pm Sun; ⊗) 'The Missus', run by three sprightly young women, is a welcoming and popular cafe, serving decent coffee, baguettes, pizza and snacks. There's free wi-fi, the walls are hung with stunning photography and the food's good – lunch specials usually include a soup, or a salad. The soups are particularly outstanding.

★Huset
NORWEGIAN €€

(✍79 02 50 02; www.huset.com; cafe mains Nkr138-238, restaurant mains Nkr295-369, 4-/5-/6-course Arctic menus Nkr695/765/895; ⊗cafe 4-10pm Sun-Fri, 2-10pm Sat, restaurant 7-10pm) It's something of a walk up here but it's worth it. Dining in the cafe-bar is casual, with well-priced pasta, pizza and reindeer stew on the menu. Its signature dish is *hamburger med alt* (Nkr105) – a meaty burger with all the trimmings, so juicy, a researcher told us, that lonely scientists in their tents dream of it. The daily specials (Nkr109) are wonderful.

In the same building, the highly regarded restaurant serves up dishes such as terrine of Svalbard reindeer, fillet of reindeer and quail. Its wine cellar has over 20,000 bottles.

Kroa
NORWEGIAN €€

(✍79 02 13 00; www.kroa-svalbard.no; lunch mains Nkr85-138, dinner mains Nkr206-245; ⊗11.30am-2am) This pub-restaurant was reconstructed from the elements of a building brought in from Russian Barentsburg (the giant white bust of Lenin peeking from behind the bar gives a clue), and it feels like a supremely comfortable and spacious trapper's cabin. Service is friendly and mains verge on the gargantuan.

Decent soups, hearty mains (steak and fish) and starters such as smoked minke whale and cured tenderloin of reindeer were on the menu when we passed through. Less formal dishes such as pizza and hamburgers are also possible. In high season, it's worth booking a table if you don't want to wait. The kitchen closes at 11pm.

Mary-Ann's Polarrigg
THAI, NORWEGIAN €€

(✍79 02 37 02; www.polarriggen.com; Skjæringa; mains Nkr145-285; ⊗4-10pm) This excellent restaurant offers up spicy Thai rice dishes in a wonderful glasshouse setting, festooned with living plants that, unlike their nati... Svalbard counterparts, entwine and cli... much more than 2cm high. It also se... some local Norwegian specialities, incl... Svalbard reindeer or seal steak.

Brasseri Nansen
HOTEL REST...

(✍79 02 37 02; www.radissonblu.c... Nkr259-299, 4-course Svalbard set m...

10.30pm) The restaurant at the Radisson SAS Polar Hotel serves up an outstanding Svalbard set menu, with seal, whale, reindeer and other local specialities making a regular appearance on the fine à la carte menu.

🍷 Drinking & Nightlife

Although alcohol is duty-free in Svalbard, it's rationed for locals, and visitors must present a valid onward airline ticket in order to buy beer and spirits (but not wine...). The **Nordpolet** (☎ 79 02 25 33; ⏱ 10am-6pm Mon-Fri, 10am-3pm Sat) booze outlet is at the back of the Coop Supermarket. A surprisingly good buy is 'XO Svalbard Cognac' (avoid the VSOP variety) – it makes an original gift for friends back home.

In addition to the following places, three hotel bars – the Radisson's **Barents Pub & Spiseri** (⏱ 4pm-2am Mon-Thu, 2pm-2am Fri-Sun), the Spitsbergen Hotel's **Funken Bar** (⏱ 11am-2am), and **Peisen Bar** (Mary-Ann's Polarrigg; Mary-Ann's Polarrigg; ⏱ noon-2am) at Mary Ann's Polarrigg – can also get lively in season. Basecamp Spitsbergen (p357) also has a stunning, glass-roofed 'Cognac Loft', which is perfect for watching the Northern Lights in winter – it's for guests only, but they may relax that when things are quiet.

Kroa   BAR
(The Pub; ⏱ 11.30am-2am) Bustling Kroa, with metal bar stools fashioned from old mine stanchions and sealskin rugs, is enduringly popular.

Karls-Berger Pub Café   BAR
(Lompensenteret; ⏱ 5pm-2am Sun-Fri, 3pm-2am Sat) Enter this place, put on your shades and prepare to be dazzled at the sight of over 1000 bottles of whisky, brandy and sundry spirits shimmering behind the bar of this snug pub. They also serve pub meals.

Svalbar   BAR
(⏱ 11am-2am Mon-Fri, 1pm-2am Fri & Sat) A relative newcomer to the Longyearbyen bar scene, Svalbar is your fairly standard Norwegian bar with a dartboard, billiard table and full menu of food until 11pm. It's popular a younger crowd.

     BAR
se; ⏱ bar 4-11pm Mon-Sat, 2-11pm Sun, 10pm-4am Fri & Sat) Huset is your night spot, with a bar and week-

end nightclub (cover charge Nkr100) where live acts take to the stage on weekends.

🔒 Shopping

Skinnboden   HANDICRAFTS, CLOTHING
(☎ 95 97 31 46; www.skinnboden.no; ⏱ 10am-6pm Mon-Fri, 10am-3pm Sat, noon-3pm Sun) The range of 'Arctic Products' at this place is something of a catch-all for all manner of rather unusual products – reindeer-skin boots, seal-skin gloves, hats and vests, and even a range of rugs made from the pelts of musk ox and other Arctic creatures. They also have a small range of jewellery. It won't be everyone's cup of tea, but at least it's different.

ℹ️ Information

Sysselmannen På Svalbard (☎ 79 02 43 00; www.sysselmannen.no; ⏱ 8.30am-3.30pm Mon-Fri) For independent hiking and gun permits.
Tourist Office (☎ 79 02 55 50; www.svalbard.net; ⏱ 10am-5pm May-Sep, noon-5pm Oct-Apr) Produces a helpful weekly activities list and has other information about the archipelago.

ℹ️ Getting There & Away

SAS (www.flysas.com) flies from Longyearbyen to/from Oslo directly in summer (three flights weekly) or via Tromsø (three to five times weekly) year-round.

Norwegian (www.norwegian.com) also flies three times a week between Oslo-Gardermoen and Longyearbyen.

ℹ️ Getting Around

AIRPORT BUS
The SAS Flybussen (Nkr60) connects with flights and runs between the airport and all of the hotels.

BICYCLE
Bicycles can be rented for between Nkr150 and Nkr300 from Poli Arctici (p354) or Basecamp Spitsbergen (p357) and various other, well-signposted outlets around town.

TAXI
Svalbard Maxi Taxi (☎ 79 02 13 05) and **Longyearbyen Taxi** (☎ 79 02 13 75) charge Nkr100 to Nkr150 for the journey between town and airport.

Around Longyearbyen

Although on the cusp of Longyearbyen, even these short hikes carry the risk of a polar bear encounter. For that reason, you'll either need to seek permission (to hike *and* carry a gun) from the governor's office or, more likely, join an organised group with an armed guide.

Platåberget & Bjørndalen

The extensive upland region that overlooks Longyearbyen to the west is known as Platåberget (commonly called the Plateau) and makes for a popular day hike. Either ascend a steep, scree-covered route from near the governor's office or sneak up Blomsterdalen, not far from Mine No 3. You can also get onto Platåberget via Bjørndalen (yes, it means 'bear valley'), south of the airport. Once on the plateau it's possible to continue to the summit of Nordenskiöldsfjellet (1050m), where a Swedish observatory is said to have once operated.

Longyearbreen

The prominent glacier tongues licking at the upper, southwestern outskirts of Longyearbyen have scoured and gouged through many layers of sedimentary material, including fossil layers, created when Svalbard enjoyed a more tropical climate. The terminal moraine churns up plant fossils – leaves and twigs that left their marks 40 to 60 million years ago. Several guided walks build in time for a little foraging.

The trail leads up past the Huset and up the river's true left bank, past the abandoned mine buildings, and onto a rough track. After the remains of a bridge (on your left), you'll approach the terminal moraine and cross a stream that flows down from your left. The track then traverses some steep slopes, crosses the river and continues upstream to its end at the fossil fields. The 5km return hike from Huset takes about 1½ hours, not counting fossicking time.

Adventdalen

Stark, wide-open Adventdalen beckons visitors with wild Arctic landscapes. After leaving town, you'll pass the pungent husky kennels; Isdammen, a freshwater lake that provides drinking water for Longyearbyen and an important habitat for the barnacle goose; then a northern lights station. With a car or bike, you can also cruise out to the defunct **coal mine Nos 5 and 6** and pass **No 7** (the only one that still functions). Above mine No 7 is a satellite station.

Barentsburg
POP 471

Visiting the Russian mining settlement of Barentsburg is like stumbling upon a forgotten outpost of the Soviet Union somewhere close to the end of the earth. Although efforts are being made to spruce it up, the bleakness of its Soviet-era architecture in the icy north still seems like a grim evocation of Arctic Siberia.

The first thing you see upon arrival is its power-station chimney, belching dark black smoke into the blue sky. This isolated village continues to mine coal against all odds and still produces up to 350,000 tonnes per year – the seam is predicted to last at least another decade. With its signing in Cyrillic script, still-standing bust of Lenin, murals of muscly workers in heroic pose and a run-down and dishevelled air, the overwhelming feeling is of a settlement whose time has past.

History

Barentsburg, on Grønfjorden, was first identified as a coal-producing area around 1900, when the Kullkompaniet Isefjord Spitsbergen started operations. Several other companies also sank shafts and in 1920 the town was founded by the Dutch company Nespico. Twelve years later it passed to the Soviet Trust Arktikugol.

Barentsburg, like Longyearbyen, was partially destroyed by the British Royal Navy in 1941 to prevent it falling into Nazi hands (ironically, the German navy itself finished the job later). In 1948 it was rebuilt by Trust Arktikugol and embarked on a period of growth, development and scientific research that lasted until the fall of the Soviet Union.

Barentsburg, like every other pit on Svalbard, has known tragedy. In 1996 many of those who perished in a plane crash during a blizzard near Adventdalen were miners' families from the Ukraine. Then, a year later, 23 miners died in a mine explosion and fire.

◎ Sights

Pomor Museum MUSEUM
(admission Nkr50; ◷ when tour boats are in port)
This simple, appealing little museum ou
lines (in Russian only) the historic Por
trade with mainland Russia, plus Rus
mining and history on Svalbard. Espe
worthwhile are the excellent geologi
hibits and the collection of artefacts
ing Russian activity in Svalbard pri

archipelago's accepted European 'discovery' by Willem Barents.

Chapel
CHAPEL

The small wooden Orthodox chapel above the football pitch commemorates the twin disasters of 1996 and 1997.

🛏 Sleeping & Eating

Barentsburg Hotel
HOTEL €€

(☑ 79 02 10 80, 79 02 18 14; d Nkr800) The Barentsburg Hotel (the settlement's only accommodation for visitors) has reasonable rooms that are, like Barentsburg itself, a fine evocation of former Societ times. That said, the rooms were renovated in 2012 and make for a comfortable and atmospheric stay. Your best bet is to contact one of the boat-tour companies to ask about prices and making a reservation.

The restaurant serves traditional Russian meals, featuring such specialities as boiled pork with potatoes and Arctic sorrel, parsley and sour cream. Bookings in advance for both rooms and meals are essential. In the bar, you can enjoy a deliciously affordable and generous slug of vodka or a Russian beer. It also sells large tins of the Real McCoy caviar at prices you'll never find elsewhere in the West, let alone Norway.

🔒 Shopping

A small souvenir shop you'll be taken to sells babushka dolls, Lenin lapel badges and some Soviet army surplus.

❶ Getting There & Away

Two companies offer summertime nine- to 10-hour boat excursions to Barentsburg from Longyearbyen – Henningsen Transport & Guiding (p354) and Polar Charter (p354). The boats head across the fjord to the vast Esmark glacier on the homeward journey. The price includes 1½ hours in Barentsburg, mostly occupied by a guided tour.

In winter, it's possible to travel between Longyearbyen and Barentsburg as part of a snow-mobile safari. Spitsbergen Travel (p354) is one of many operators offering this excursion.

ʸramiden

⋯rly Russia's second settlement ⋯lbard, Pyramiden, named for the ⋯-shaped mountain that rises nearby, ⋯rding day trip from Longyearbyen.

In the mid-1910s coal was discovered here and operations were set up by the same Swedish concern that exploited Sveagruva. In 1926 it was taken over by a Soviet firm, Russkiy Grumant, which sold out to the Soviet Trust Arktikugol, exploiters of Barentsburg, in 1931. In the 1950s there were as many as 2500 Russian residents, well exceeding the population of Longyearbyen today. During its productive heyday in the early 1990s it had 60km of shafts, 130 homes, agricultural enterprises similar to those in Barentsburg and the world's most northerly hotel and swimming pool. But with the mine no longer yielding enough coal to be profitable and with Russia no longer willing or able to subsidise the mine, Pyramiden was abandoned in 1998. A skeleton staff of (at last count) eight Russians still live at Pyramiden to keep the flag flying, but the sense of abandonment in this remote corner of Svalbard is poignantly evocative.

The former hotel has recently reopened; contact one of the boat-tour companies to ask about prices and making a reservation.

◉ Sights

As with other sights around Svalbard, there are startling juxtapositions between the near-pristine surroundings and the apparent meltdown of industrial infrastructure all across Pyramiden. Focal points for your walk around town are the 1970s-era **Soviet architecture**, a prominent **bust of Lenin** and the **sports hall**. There's a small shop in the **hotel** selling a small selection of Soviet memorabilia and a bar serving up vodka shots.

Across Billefjorden to the east, **Nordenskjöldbreen** is a stunning glacier running as a broad front from the Svalbard interior to the fjord shoreline; most boat excursions from Longyearbyen draw near for photos. The boat journey itself from Longyearbyen is a stunning trip, passing striated cliffs and accompanied by puffins and fulmar.

❶ Getting There & Away

In summer, at least two Longyearbyen-based tour agencies offer 10-hour day cruises to Pyramiden – Henningsen Transport & Guiding (p354) and Polar Charter (p354).

In winter, snowmobile safaris between Longyearbyen and Pyramiden are possible.

Ny Ålesund

POP POP 30–130

Despite its inhospitable latitude (79°N), you'd be hard pressed to find a more awesome backdrop anywhere on earth than the scientific post of Ny Ålesund, 107km northwest of Longyearbyen. Founded in 1916 by the Kings Bay Kull Compani, Ny Ålesund likes to claim that it's the world's northernmost permanently inhabited civilian community (although you could make a case for three other equally minuscule spots in Russia and Canada).

Throughout much of the 20th century Kings Bay mined for coal. As many as 300 people once lived and worked here but, after the last of several lethal explosions resulted in 21 deaths, mining stopped in 1963. Ny Ålesund has since recycled itself as a prominent scientific post, with research stations of several nations, including Japan, France, the British Antarctic Survey and China (bizarrely, in this land of polar bears and Arctic foxes, two marble lions stand watch over the Chinese quarters). There's a hardy year-round population of around 30 scientists, rising to 130 in summer (never more as that's the number of beds available) as researchers from about 15 countries fly in.

◉ Sights

There's a 1.5km trail with multilingual interpretive panels that takes you around the main sites of this tiny settlement.

In the early 20th century several polar explorers set off from Ny Ålesund, including the likes of Roald Amundsen, Lincoln Ellsworth, Admiral Byrd and Umberto Nobile. The anchor pylon was used by Nobile and Amundsen to launch the airship *Norge* on their successful flight over the North Pole to Alaska in 1926; it came in handy again two years later, when Nobile returned to launch the *Italia* on his ill-fated repeat attempt. You'll see memorials to these missions around the settlement.

Perhaps the most unusual sight is the stranded steam locomotive near the dock. In 1917 a narrow-gauge railway was constructed to connect the coalfields with the harbour and it remained in use until 1958. The restored locomotive is, naturally, the world's northernmost railway relic.

The town also supports a neat little Mine Museum (Gruvemuseum; donation suggested; ⊙24hr) in the old Tiedemann's Tabak (tobacco) shop, relating the coal-mining history of this area.

All nonprofessional visitors arrive in Ny Ålesund on tourist cruises and linger for an hour or two.

Around Ny Ålesund

Kongsfjorden

Ny Ålesund's backdrop, Kongsfjorden (the namesake for the Kings Bay Kull Compani) spectacularly contrasts bleak grey-brown shores with expansive white icefields. The distinctive Tre Kroner peaks, Dana (1175m), Svea (1226m) and Nora (1226m) – named in honour of Denmark, Sweden and Norway, respectively – jut from the ice and are among Svalbard's most recognisable landmarks.

Blomstrandhalvøya

Gravelly Blomstrandhalvøya was once a peninsula but, in the early 1990s, it was released from the icy grip on its northern end and it's now an island. In summer the name Blomstrand ('flower beach'), would be appropriate, but it was in fact named for a Norwegian geologist. Ny London, at the southern end of the island, recalls one Ernest Mansfield of the Northern Exploration Company who attempted to quarry marble in 1911 only to discover that the stone had been rendered worthless by aeons of freezing and thawing. A couple of buildings and some forlorn machinery remain.

Magdalenefjord

The lovely blue-green bay of Magdalenefjord in Nordvest Spitsbergen, flanked by towering peaks and intimidating tidewater glaciers, is the most popular anchorage along Spitsbergen's western coast and is one of Svalbard's prettiest corners. In the 17th century, this area saw heavy Dutch whaling; at Graveneset, near the mouth of the fjord, you can still see the remains of two stoves used to boil the blubber. There are numerous protected graves of 17th- and mid-18th-century whalers.

Prins Karls Forlandet

On the west coast of Spitsbergen, the oddly shaped 86km-long island of Prins Karls

Forlandet is a national park set aside to protect breeding walruses, seals and sea lions. The alpine northern reaches, which rise to Grampianfjellet (1084m), are connected to Saltfjellet (430m), at the southern end, by a long flat plain called Forlandsletta.

Krossfjorden

Thanks to Lillehöökbreen (its grand tidewater glacier) and several cultural relics, Krossfjorden attracts quite a few cruise ships. At Ebeltoftbukta, near the mouth of the fjord, you can see several whalers' graves, as well as a heap of leftover junk from a 1912 German telegraph office that was shifted wholesale to Ny Ålesund after only two years of operation. Opposite the entrance rise some crowded bird cliffs overlooking one of Svalbard's most verdant spots, with flowers, moss and even grasses.

Danskøya

One of the most intriguing sites in northwest Spitsbergen is Virgohamna, on the bleak, gravelly island of Danskøya, where the remains of several broken dreams now lie scattered across the lonely beach. Among them are the ruins of three blubber stoves from a 17th-century whaling station, as well as eight stone-covered graves from the same era. You'll also find the remains of a cottage built by English adventurer Arnold Pike, who sailed north in his yacht *Siggen*

and spent a winter subsisting on polar bears and reindeer.

The next adventurer at Virgohamna was Swedish engineer Salomon August Andrée, who set off from Virgohamna in an airship in the summer of 1897, hoping to reach the North Pole. The fate of his expedition was not known until 1930, when sailors from a seal-hunting ship put ashore and stumbled across their last site on Kvitøya.

Then, in 1906, journalist Walter Wellman, who was sponsored by a US newspaper, attempted to reach the North Pole in an airship, but failed. The next year, when he returned to try again, his ship was badly damaged in a storm. On his third attempt, in 1909, he floated to within 60km of the pole, met with technical problems and gave up for good, mainly because he'd heard that Robert Peary had already reached the pole anyway (although that claim is now largely discredited). All of the remaining junk (including dozens of rusted 44-gallon fuel drums) is protected. Erosion damage, caused by the few visitors who manage to get here, has been considerable, so do the right thing and stick strictly to the marked paths.

Moffen Island

Gravelly Moffen Island is known for its walrus population, though the 300m boat-exclusion zone around the island means that any views of these great beasts are distant at best.

Understand
Norway

Norway Today

Few countries can look to the future with quite the same confidence as Norway – economic crises are, after all, something that other countries have. Norway is nonetheless facing some important issues that threaten to cause, if not a crisis, then at the very least widespread ripples of disquiet across Norwegian society. Primary among them are the still-distant (but now imaginable) end of the oil boom and the challenges of building a truly multicultural society.

Best in Print

The Almost Nearly Perfect People (Michael Booth; 2014) Entertaining look at modern Scandinavia with Norway at centre stage.

Island Summers: Memories of a Norwegian Childhood (Tilly Culme-Seymour; 2013) Love letter to the Norwegian coast.

The Ice Museum (Joanna Kavenna; 2006) Vividly captures our fascination with the Arctic North.

Fellowship of Ghosts (Paul Watkins; 2004) Solo foot journeys through Norway's high country.

Rowing to Latitude (Jill Fredston; 2002) A journey by rowboat along Norway's coast.

Best on Film

North of the Sun (2013) Documentary depicting nine months on a remote stretch of Arctic coast.

Max Manus (2009) Rollicking film about the Norwegian Resistance.

Cross My Heart and Hope to Die (1994) Prize-winning evocation of an Oslo childhood.

Wives (1985) Rueful portrayal of three friends reunited at an Oslo school reunion.

Nine Lives (1957) Widely ranked among the best Norwegian films of all time.

A Multicultural Norway?

On 22 July 2011, Norway lost its innocence. That was the day when Anders Behring Breivik detonated a car bomb in Oslo aimed at the nation's political class (eight people were killed), and then, disguised as a policeman, gunned down 69 young political activists on the island of Utøya. When later captured, Breivik claimed that he had acted to save Norway and Europe from being taken over by Muslims. Norway's measured response to the most deadly attack in modern Norwegian history was praised around the world and the country united in condemning the attacks and its motives.

And yet, the massacre left deep scars in a country wholly unaccustomed to political violence, let alone terrorism of any kind on its home soil. More than that, it brought to the forefront a debate that had been simmering for a long time. In 1970, just 1.5% of people living in Norway were immigrants. Now, one out of every eight residents of Norway was either born overseas or was born to two immigrant parents. This radical demographic shift has changed the way that Norwegians think about their country.

On the one hand, mass immigration is a central pillar in Norway's own national story – in the dark days of the 19th century, Norwegians emigrated in their thousands to escape hardship. Later, the fabulous oil wealth of the late 20th century nurtured the deeply held belief that Norway, as one of the richest countries on earth, had to serve as an example of a responsible and tolerant global citizen, and modern Norwegians are rightfully proud of their tolerance and generosity in assisting troubled countries get back on their feet.

At the same time, there is unease in some quarters about what the rise in immigrant numbers means for ethnic Norwegians and their sense of national identity. At parliamentary elections in 2005, 2009 and again in

2013, the Fremskrittspartiet (Progress Party) – which advocates a crackdown on immigration – polled more than 20% of the vote. In the process it has easily become the second-largest party in the country and, since the 2013 elections, the Progress Party has been part of the coalition government. Its leader, Siv Jensen, who has warned of the 'Islamisation of Norway', is currently Norway's Minister of Finance.

Breivik was convicted and is likely to spend the rest of his life in prison. But whether the sense of national unity that followed the massacre can survive remains to be seen.

End of the Boom?

Norway weathered the global financial crisis with aplomb. Yes, growth rates stalled as world oil prices fell, but the economy soon bounced back and its numbers remain the envy of the world – unemployment below 4%, inflation below 2% and a budget seemingly forever in surplus. Norway remains the world's ninth-largest oil exporter and the third-largest exporter of natural gas (providing in the process around one-fifth of the EU's supplies), and the foresight of successive governments has seen the creation of the world's largest pension fund (expected to reach US$1 trillion by 2019). Few countries have prepared better for the day when the oil runs out.

Even so, there are growing concerns that Norway's oil boom could be coming to an end decades earlier than expected. New oil discoveries are increasingly rare, unemployment has been creeping up in recent years and analysts are beginning to warn that Norway's economy is in urgent need of diversification – oil and natural gas accounts for a third of government revenues and more than half of export revenues. If the oil and natural gas were to dry up tomorrow – which is, of course, unlikely – Norway would have a seriously lopsided economy with some of the highest wages and shortest working hours (less than 33 hours a week on average) in the world.

While most countries in the world would give anything to have to confront such problems, and Norway continues to face the future from a position of formidable strength, the fact that Norwegians are having this conversation at all suggests that the country's economic miracle may have finally peaked.

POPULATION: **5.15 MILLION**

GDP: **US$55,400**

UNEMPLOYMENT: **3.6%**

GDP GROWTH: **1.6% (2013)**

LIFE EXPECTANCY: **81.6 YEARS**

AREA: **386,224 SQ KM**

if Norway were 100 people

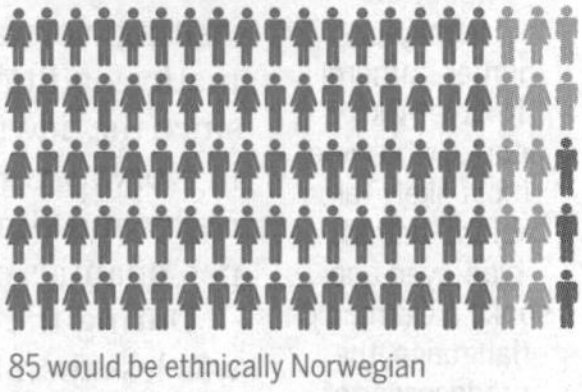

85 would be ethnically Norwegian
12 would be immigrants
3 would be born to 2 immigrant parents

belief systems

(% of population)

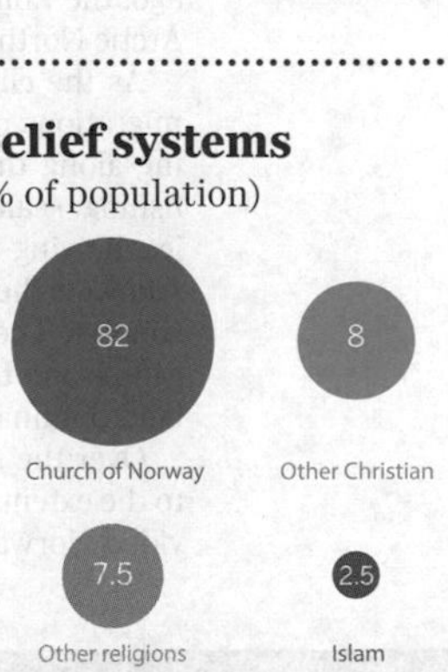

82
Church of Norway
8
Other Christian
7.5
Other religions
2.5
Islam

population per sq km

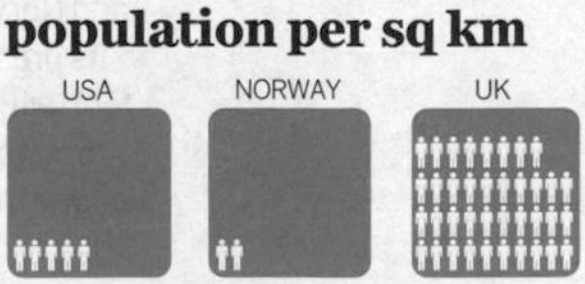

USA
NORWAY
UK
≈ 7 people

History

Norway may have become the epitome of a modern, peaceful country, but its history is soaked in blood. It is a story peopled with picaresque characters and recurring grand themes, from the Vikings to the battle for supremacy in Scandinavia, from the struggles of the Sami to the dark days of World War II, from extreme poverty to previously unimaginable riches. How it all happened is one of world history's great epics.

Darkness & Ice

Little is known about the nomadic, hunter-gatherer Nøstvet-Økser people, who were most likely tall, blond-haired, blue-eyed and spoke a Germanic language, the predecessor of modern Scandinavian languages.

Some of the most lasting impressions travellers carry with them after visiting Norway – a land of snow and ice, a bountiful coast, extreme climatic conditions and a thinly populated land – have been present here since the dawn of Scandinavian civilisation. Indeed, the human presence in Norway was for thousands of years overshadowed by Norway's geography and climate, which have strong claims to being the most enduring personalities of Norwegian history.

During the last ice age, Norway was barely habitable. But if Norway was less than hospitable, it was a paradise compared to northern Russia at the time and, as the ice began to melt, it was from the east that the first major, lasting migration to Norway took place when, around 11,000 years ago, the Komsa, who would later become the Sami, arrived in Norway's Arctic North.

As the climate warmed and Norway became increasingly habitable, migrations of the Nøstvet-Økser people of central Europe began arriving along the southern Norwegian coast, drawn by relatively plentiful fishing, sealing and hunting. Wild reindeer also followed the retreating ice, moving north into the still ice-bound interior, and the hunters that followed them were the first humans to traverse the Norwegian high country. Their presence was, however, restricted to itinerant, seasonal camps and there remained few human footholds in an otherwise empty land dominated by glaciers and frozen wastes.

Over the millennia that followed, settled cultures began to take root, to the extent that during the later years of the Roman Empire, Rome provided Norway with fabric, iron implements and pottery. The iron tools allowed farmland to be cleared of trees, larger boats were built with the aid of iron axes and a cooling climate saw the establishment of more permanent structures built from stone and turf. By the 5th century Norwegians had learned how to smelt their own iron from ore found in the southern Norwegian bogs. Norway's endless struggle to tame its wild landscape had begun.

Here Come the Vikings

Few historical people have captured the imagination quite like the Vikings. Immortalised in modern cartoons (*Asterix* and *Hägar the Horrible*, to name just two) and considered to be the most feared predators of ancient Europe, the Vikings may have disappeared from history, but as a seafaring nation with its face turned towards distant lands, they remain very much the forerunners of modern Norway. But who were these ancient warriors who took to their longboats and dominated Europe for five centuries?

Conquest & Expansion

Under pressure from shrinking agricultural land caused by a growing population, settlers from Norway began arriving along the coast of the British Isles in the 780s. When the boats returned home to Norway with enticing trade goods and tales of poorly defended coastlines, the Vikings began laying plans to conquer the world. The first Viking raid took place on St Cuthbert's monastery on the island of Lindisfarne in 793. Soon the Vikings were spreading across Britain, Ireland and the rest of Europe with war on their minds and returning home with slaves *(thrall)* in their formidable, low Norse longboats.

The Vikings attacked in great fleets, terrorising, murdering, enslaving, assimilating or displacing local populations. Coastal regions of Britain, Ireland, France (Normandy was named for these 'Northmen'), Russia (as far east as the river Volga), Moorish Spain (Seville was raided in 844), and the Middle East (they even reached Baghdad) all came under the Viking sway. Well-defended Constantinople (Istanbul) proved a bridge too far – the Vikings attacked six times but never took the city. Such rare setbacks notwithstanding, the Viking raids transformed Scandinavia from an obscure backwater on Europe's northern fringe to an all-powerful empire.

For all of their destruction elsewhere, Vikings belonged very much to the shores from which they set out or sheltered on their raids. Viking raids increased standards of living at home. Emigration freed up farmland and fostered the emergence of a new merchant class, while captured slaves provided farm labour. Norwegian farmers also crossed

HISTORY HERE COME THE VIKINGS

Archaeological Museums

Bryggens Museum (p154), Bergen

Arkeologisk Museum (p199), Stavanger

Historisk Museum (p51), Oslo

Museum of Natural History & Archaeology (p256), Trondheim

Alta Museum (p323), Alta

The History of Norway – From the Ice Age to Today, by Oivind Stenersen and Ivar Libæk, provides more than enough historical detail for most travellers and is available at larger bookshops in Norway.

2500 BC	AD 787	793	871
The wonderfully named Battle-Axe, Boat-Axe and Funnel-Beaker people, named after the stone tools they used, enter southern Norway from Sweden. They traded amber for metals from mainland Europe.	The earliest account of Norse seafaring appears in the *Anglo Saxon Chronicle* for 787, describing how three ships came to Britain, piloted by sailors who were described as Northmen.	The dawn of the Viking age comes when Vikings plunder St Cuthbert's monastery on the island of Lindisfarne, off the coast of Northumberland in Britain.	Tønsberg in southern Norway is founded around this year, making it the oldest still-inhabited town in Norway. It later served as a royal court and an important trading town.

Viking Sites

Stiklestad

Tønsberg

Kaupang (Larvik; p90)

Eidfjord

Kinsarvik

Haugesund

Karmøy island

Balestrand

Leka

Lindesnes

the Atlantic to settle the Faroes, Iceland and Greenland during the 9th and 10th centuries. The world, it seemed, belonged to the Vikings.

Harald Fair-Hair

Harald Hårfagre (Harald Fair-Hair), son of Hvaldan Svarte (Halvdan the Black), was more than the latest in a long line of great Viking names. While most Viking chieftains made their name in foreign conquest, Harald Fair-Hair was doing something that no other leader had managed before – he united the disparate warring tribes of the Viking nation.

Harald's greatest moment came in 872 at Hafsfjord near Haugesund when he emerged victorious from one of world history's few civil wars to be decided at sea. When the dust settled, Norway had become a single country.

The reign of Harald Hårfagre was such an odd and entertaining time that it was recorded for posterity in the *Heimskringla,* the Norwegian kings' saga, by Icelander Snorre Sturluson. According to Snorre, Harald's unification of Norway was inspired by a woman who taunted the king by refusing to have relations with a man whose kingdom wasn't even as large as tiny Denmark. Through a series of confederations and trade agreements, he extended his rule as far north as what is now Trøndelag. His foreign policies were equally canny, and he even sent one of his sons, Håkon, to be reared in the court of King Athelstan of England. There is no record of whether the woman in question was sufficiently impressed. Harald died of plague at Avaldsnes on Karmøy island around 930.

The king who unified the country could do little about his own family, however. He had 10 wives and fathered a surfeit of heirs, thereby creating serious squabbles over succession. The one who rose above them all was Erik, his last child and only son with Ragnhild the Mighty, daughter of the Danish King Erik of Jutland. The ruthless Erik eliminated all of his legitimate brothers except Håkon (who was safe in England). Erik, whose reign was characterised by considerable ineptitude, then proceeded to squander his father's hard-won Norwegian confederation. When Håkon returned from England to sort out the mess as King Håkon den Gode (Håkon the Good), Erik was forced to flee to Britain where he took over the throne of York as King Erik Blood-Axe.

Christianity & the Viking Decline

The Vikings gave Norwegians their love of the sea and it was during the late Viking period that they bequeathed to them another of their most enduring national traits – strong roots in Christianity. However, this overturning of the Viking pantheon of gods did not come without a struggle.

So ferocious were the Vikings that the word berserk comes from 'bare sark', which means 'bare shirt' and refers to the way that ancient, bare-chested Norsemen used to fight.

872	997	c 1000	1024
Harald Hårfagre (Harald Fair-Hair) fights his fellow Viking chieftains in the Battle of Hafrsfjord and unites Norway for the first time. Some 20,000 people flee to Iceland.	Trondheim is founded at the mouth of the Nid River and is the first major settlement in the country; it becomes the first capital of the fledgling kingdom.	Almost five centuries before Columbus, Leifur Eiríksson, son of Eiríkur Rauðe (Eric the Red), explores the North American coast, which he names Vinland, meaning the 'land of wine'.	Olav II founds the Church of Norway and establishes it as Norway's state religion throughout his realm, a situation that continues to this day.

King Håkon the Good, who had been baptised a Christian during his English upbringing, brought the new faith (as well as missionaries and a bishop) with him upon his return to Norway. Despite some early success, most Vikings remained loyal to Thor, Odin and Freyr. Although the missionaries were eventually able to replace the names of the gods with those of Catholic saints, the pagan practice of blood sacrifice continued unabated. When Håkon the Good was defeated and killed in 960, Norwegian Christianity all but disappeared.

Christianity in Norway was revived during the reign of King Olav Tryggvason (Olav I). Like any good Viking, Olav decided that only force would work to convert his countrymen to the 'truth'. Unfortunately for the king, his intended wife, Queen Sigrid of Sweden, refused to convert.

THE SECRETS OF VIKING DOMINATION

The main god who provided strength to the Viking cause was Odin (Oðinn), the 'All-Father' who was married to Frigg. Together they gave birth to a son, Thor (Þór), the God of Thunder. The Vikings believed that if they died on the battlefield, the all-powerful Odin would take them to a paradise by the name of Valhalla, where Viking men could fight all day and then be served by beautiful women.

Not surprisingly, it was considered far better for a Viking to die on the battlefield than in bed of old age and Vikings brought a reckless abandon to their battles that was extremely difficult for enemies to overcome – to die or to come away with loot, the Vikings seemed to say, was more or less the same. Equally unsurprising was the fact that the essential Viking values that emerged from their unique world view embodied strength, skill in weapons, heroic courage, personal sacrifice and a disregard for death.

But the Vikings were as much the sophisticates of the ancient world as they were its fearless warriors. Viking ships were revolutionary, fast, manoeuvrable vessels capable of withstanding torrid and often long ocean journeys. Longboats were over 30m long, had a solid keel, flexible hull, large, square sails and could travel up to 12 knots (22km) per hour; they enabled the Vikings to launch and maintain a conquest that would go largely unchallenged for 200 years.

Perhaps the most curious aspect of Viking voyages, however, was the navigational tool they employed to travel through uncharted territory. Norse sagas mention a mysterious device known as a *solarsteinn* (sunstone), which allowed navigation even when the sky was overcast or the sun was below the horizon and celestial navigation was impossible.

It is now generally agreed that the *solarsteinn* was a crystal of cordierite, which is found around Scandinavia and has natural polarising qualities. When observed from below and rotated, light passing through the crystal is polarised blue when the long axis is pointed towards the source of the sunlight. Even today, jet planes flying over polar regions, where magnetic compasses are unsuitable, use a sky compass that determines the position of the sun by filtering sunlight through an artificial polarising lens.

1030	1049	1066	1261
After being sent into exile by King Canute (Knut) of Denmark in 1028, King Olav II returns, only to be killed in Trøndelag at the Battle of Stiklestad.	Harald III (Harald Hardråde, or Harald 'Hard-Ruler'), half-brother of St Olav, founds Oslo and uses it as a base to launch far-ranging raids across the Mediterranean.	The Viking age draws to a close after Harald III dies at the hands of King Harold of England at the Battle of Stamford Bridge in England.	Greenland joins the Kingdom of Norway, followed a year later by Iceland, reflecting Norway's growing influence over the affairs of Europe's far north.

The Haugelandet region of western Norway is considered by many to be the cradle of Viking culture and Karmøy island, south of Haugesund, has a Viking Festival in June (www.vikingfestivalen.no). The Viking Kings website (www.vikingkings.com) covers the region's Viking history.

Olav cancelled the marriage contract and Sigrid married the pagan king, Svein Forkbeard of Denmark. Together they orchestrated Olav's death in a great Baltic sea-battle, then took Norway as their own.

Christianity was finally cemented in Norway by King Olav Haraldsson, Olav II, who was also converted in England. Olav II and his Viking hordes allied themselves with King Ethelred and managed to save London from a Danish attack under King Svein Forkbeard by destroying London Bridge (from whence we derive the song 'London Bridge Is Falling Down'). Succeeding where his namesake had failed, Olav II spread Christianity with considerable success. In 1023 Olav built a stone cross in Voss, where it still stands, and in 1024 he founded the Church of Norway. After an invasion by King Canute (Knut) of Denmark in 1028, Olav II died during the Battle of Stiklestad in 1030. For Christians, this amounted to martyrdom and the king was canonised as a saint; the great Nidaros Cathedral (p254) in Trondheim stands as a memorial to St Olav and, until the Protestant Reformation, the cathedral served as a destination for pilgrims from all over Europe. His most lasting legacy, however, was having forged an enduring identity for Norway as an independent kingdom.

Of the kings who followed, none distinguished themselves quite as infamously as Harald III (Harald Hardråde, or Harald 'Hard-Ruler'), half-brother of St Olav. Harald III raided throughout the Mediterranean, but it was a last hurrah for the Vikings. When he was killed during an ill-conceived raid in England in 1066, the Viking air of invincibility was broken.

No Longer Independent

The Vikings may have been fast disappearing into history, but Viking expansionism, along with the coming of Christianity, planted the seeds – of success, of decline – for what was to come. As Norway's sphere of international influence shrank, Norway's neighbours began to close in, leaving this one-time world power having to fight for its own independence.

Trouble Abroad, Trouble at Home

The word 'Viking' derives from vik, an Old Norse word that referred to a bay or cove, a reference to Vikings' anchorages during and after raids.

In 1107 Sigurd I led an expedition of 60 ships to the Holy Land. Three years later, he captured Sidon, in modern-day Lebanon. But by this stage foreign conquest had become a smokescreen for serious internal problems. Sigurd died in 1130 and the rest of the century was fraught with brutal civil wars over succession to the throne. The victorious King Sverre, a churchman-turned-warrior, paved the way for Norway's so-called 'Golden Age', which saw Bergen claim the title of national capital, driven by Norway's perennial ties to foreign lands and, in particular, trade between coastal towns and the German-based Hanseatic League.

1319	1349	1469	1537
Magnus becomes King of Sweden and unites Sweden and Norway. This ends Norwegian independence and the royal line of Harald Fair-Hair, and begins two centuries of decline.	Bubonic plague (the Black Death) arrives in Bergen and quickly spreads throughout the country, forever altering Norway's social fabric.	The Orkney and Shetland islands, along with the Isle of Man, are sold to the Scots, bringing to an end centuries of Norwegian expansion.	The Reformation that sweeps across Europe reaches Norway, after which the incumbent Catholic faith is replaced with Lutheran Protestantism.

Perhaps drawn by Norway's economic boom, Greenland and Iceland voluntarily joined the Kingdom of Norway in 1261 and 1262, respectively.

But Norway's role as a world power was on the wane and Norway was turning inward. Håkon V built brick and stone forts, one at Vardø to protect the north from the Russians, and another at Akershus (p51), in 1308, to defend Oslo harbour. The transfer of the national capital from Bergen to Oslo soon followed. When Håkon V's grandson Magnus united Norway with Sweden in 1319, Norway began a decline that would last for 200 years. Once-great Norway had become just another province of its neighbours.

In August 1349 the Black Death arrived in Norway on board an English ship via Bergen. The bubonic plague would eventually kill one-third of Europe's population. In Norway, land fell out of cultivation, towns were ruined, trading activities faltered and the national coffers decreased by 65%. In Norway, as much as 80% of the nobility perished. Because their peasant workforce had also been decimated, the survivors were forced to return to the land, forever changing the Norwegian power-base and planting the seeds for an egalitarianism that continues to define Norway to this day.

By 1387 Norway had lost control of Icelan. Ten years later, Queen Margaret of Denmark formed the Kalmar Union of Sweden, Denmark and Norway, with Eric of Pomerania as king. Margaret's neglect of Norway continued into the 15th century, when trade links with Iceland were broken and Norway's Greenland colonies mysteriously disappeared without a trace.

In 1469 Orkney and Shetland were pawned – supposedly a temporary measure – to the Scottish Crown by the Danish-Norwegian King Christian I, who had to raise money for his daughter's dowry. Just three years later the Scots annexed both island groups.

Buffeted by these winds of change, Norway had become a shadow of its former self. The only apparent constant was the country's staunch Christian faith. But even in the country's faith there were fundamental changes afoot. In 1537, the Reformation replaced the incumbent Catholic faith with Lutheran Protestantism and the transformation from the Norway of the Vikings was all but complete.

Denmark & Sweden – the Enemies

Talk to many Norwegians and you'll quickly find that there's no love lost between them and their neighbours, Denmark and Sweden. Here's why.

A series of disputes between the Danish Union and the Swedish crown were played out on Norwegian soil. First came the Seven Years War (1563–70), followed by the Kalmar War (1611–14). Trondheim, for

Viking Museums

Vikingskipshuset (p55), Oslo

Lofotr Viking Museum (p297), Vestvågøy, Lofoten

Nordvegen Historiesenter (p196), Karmøy island

HISTORY NO LONGER INDEPENDENT

The mystery behind the disappearance of the Greenland colonies is examined in Jared Diamond's *Collapse: How Societies Choose to Fail or Survive.*

1596	**1612**	**1720**	**1814**
Willem Barents, a Dutch explorer searching for a northeast sea passage to Asia, becomes the first European to set foot on Svalbard. He names the archipelago Spitsbergen ('sharp mountains').	Commercial whaling begins on Svalbard, with English, Dutch, Norwegian, French and Danish fleets driving many whale and other marine species to the brink of extinction in the centuries that follow.	After 150 years of conflict on Norwegian soil (the Seven Years War, the Kalmar War and the Great Nordic War), Sweden is finally defeated, although Danish and Swedish influence remains strong.	Norway is presented to Sweden in the so-called 'Union of the Crowns'. Disgruntled Norwegians draft their first constitution, an event still celebrated as Norway's first act of independence.

example, was repeatedly captured and recaptured by both sides and during the Kalmar War an invasion of Norway was mounted from Scotland.

In two further wars during the mid-17th century Norway lost a good portion of its territory to Sweden. The Great Nordic War with the expanding Swedish Empire was fought in the early 18th century and in 1716 the Swedes occupied Christiania (Oslo). The Swedes were finally defeated in 1720, ending over 150 years of warfare.

Despite attempts to re-establish trade with Greenland through the formation of Norwegian trading companies in Bergen in 1720, Danish trade restrictions scuppered the nascent economic independence. As a consequence, Norway was ill-equipped to weather the so-called 'Little Ice Age', from 1738 to 1742. The failure of crops ensured a period of famine and the death of one-third of Norwegian cattle, not to mention thousands of people.

During the Napoleonic Wars, Britain blockaded Norway, causing the Danes to surrender on 14 January 1814. The subsequent Treaty of Kiel presented Norway to Sweden in a 'Union of the Crowns'. Tired of having their territory divided up by foreign kings, a contingent of farmers, businesspeople and politicians gathered at Eidsvoll Verk in April 1814 to draft a new constitution and elect a new Norwegian king. Sweden wasn't at all happy at this show of independence and forced the new king, Christian Frederik, to yield and accept the Swedish choice of monarch, Karl Johan. War was averted by a compromise that provided for devolved Swedish power. Norway's constitution hadn't lasted long, but it did suggest that Norwegians had had enough.

Independent Norway

Norway may have spent much of the previous centuries as the subservient vassal of foreign occupiers and its days as a world power had long ago ended, but not all was doom and gloom. It took almost a century after their first constitution, not to mention nine centuries after Harald Fair-Hair first unified the country, but Norwegians were determined to once and for all become masters of their own destiny.

A Confident Start

During the 19th century, perhaps buoyed by the spirit of the 1814 constitution, Norwegians began to rediscover a sense of their own, independent cultural identity. This nascent cultural revival was most evident in a flowering of musical and artistic expression led by poet and playwright Henrik Ibsen, composer Edvard Grieg and artist Edvard Munch.

Language also began to play its part with the development of a standardised written form of Norwegian known as *landsmål* (or *Nynorsk*). Norway's first railway, from Oslo to Eidsvoll, was completed in 1854 and

According to some linguists, Viking gods gave their names to the days of the week in English – Tuesday (Tyr's Day), Wednesday (Odin's Day), Thursday (Thor's Day) and Friday (Freyr's Day).

Books about Vikings

A History of the Vikings, Gwyn Jones

The Vikings, Magnus Magnusson

The Oxford Illustrated History of the Vikings, Peter Sawyer (Ed)

The Vikings, Else Roesdahl

1861	1870s	1895	1905
Fridtjof Nansen, an explorer, scientist, diplomat and winner of the Nobel Peace Prize, is born near Oslo (then called Christiania). He would become a symbol for Norway's growing international influence.	Emissaries from London gentlemen's clubs journey to Norway's western fjords to find blue ice for the clubs' drinks. Soon after, Thomas Cook begins the first tourist cruises into the fjords.	Alfred Nobel's will decrees that the interest on his vast fortune be awarded each year 'to those who, during the preceding year, shall have conferred the greatest benefit on mankind'.	Norwegians vote overwhelmingly for independence and against union with Sweden. Norway becomes independent, with its own constitutional monarchy.

Norway began looking at increased international trade, particularly tied to its burgeoning fishing and whaling industries in the Arctic North.

Norway was still extremely poor – between 1825 and 1925, over 750,000 Norwegians resettled in the USA and Canada – but the surge of national pride and identity would not be stopped.

In 1905 a constitutional referendum was held. As expected, almost 80% of voters favoured independence from Sweden. The Swedish king, Oskar II, was forced to recognise Norwegian sovereignty, abdicate and reinstate a Norwegian constitutional monarchy, with Haakon VII on the throne. His descendants rule Norway to this day, with decisions on succession remaining under the authority of the *storting* (parliament). Oslo was declared the national capital of the Kingdom of Norway.

Newly independent Norway quickly set about showing the world that it was a worthy international citizen. In 1911 the Norwegian explorer Roald Amundsen reached the South Pole. Two years later Norwegian women became among the first in Europe to be given the vote. Hydroelectric projects sprang up all around the country and prosperous new industries emerged to drive the increasingly growing export economy.

Having emerged from WWI largely unscathed – Norway was neutral, although some Norwegian merchant vessels were sunk by the Germans – Norway grew in confidence. In 1920 the *storting* voted to join the newly formed League of Nations, a move that was opposed only by the Communist-inspired Labour Party that dominated the *storting* by 1927. The 1920s also brought new innovations, including the development of factory ships, which enabled processing of whales at sea and caused an increase in whaling activities, especially around Svalbard and in the Antarctic.

Trouble, however, lay just around the corner. The Great Depression of the late 1920s and beyond almost brought Norway to its knees. By December 1932 there was 42% unemployment and farmers were hit especially hard by the economic downturn.

Norway at War

Norway chose a bad time to begin asserting its independence. The clouds of war were gathering in Europe and by the early 1930s fascism had begun to spread throughout the continent. Unlike during WWI, Norway found itself caught up in the violent convulsions sweeping across Europe and in 1933 the former Norwegian defence minister Vidkun Quisling formed a Norwegian fascist party, the *Nasjonal Samling*. The Germans invaded Norway on 9 April 1940, prompting King Haakon and the royal family to flee into exile, while British, French, Polish and Norwegian forces fought a desperate rearguard action.

Sweden and Visions of Norway: Politics and Culture 1814–1905, by H Arnold Barton, offers a detailed analysis of the enmity and uneasy neighbourliness between Norway and Sweden in the pivotal 19th century.

1911	1913	1914	1940
Norwegian explorer Roald Amundsen becomes the first person to reach the South Pole, highlighting a period of famous Norwegian explorers going to the ends of the earth.	Norway introduces universal suffrage for women, 15 years after men but long before many other European countries and begins a tradition of gender equality that has become a hallmark of modern Norway.	Norway, Sweden and Denmark announce that they will remain neutral during WWI, thereby sparing Scandinavia the devastation that the war visited upon much of the rest of Europe.	On 9 April Nazi Germany invades Norway. King Haakon and the royal family flee into exile, first to the UK and then to Washington, DC, where they remain throughout the war.

Six southern towns were burnt out and despite some Allied gains the British, who were out on a limb, abandoned Arctic Norway to its fate. In Oslo, the Germans established a puppet government under Vidkun Quisling, whose name thereafter entered the lexicon as a byword for those collaborators who betray their country.

Having spent centuries fighting for a country to call their own, the Norwegians didn't take lightly to German occupation. In particular, the Norwegian Resistance network distinguished itself in sabotaging German designs, often through the assistance of daring Shetland fishermen who smuggled arms across the sea to western Norway. Among the most memorable acts of defiance was the famous commando assault of Febru-

ROALD AMUNDSEN

The Norwegian explorer Roald Amundsen played a pivotal role in forging a proud sense of Norwegian identity in the early 20th century.

Born into a family of shipowners and captains in 1872 at Borge, near Sarpsborg in southern Norway, Amundsen sailed in 1897 to the Antarctic as first mate on the Belgian Belgica expedition. Their ship froze fast in the ice and became – unintentionally – the first expedition to overwinter in the Antarctic.

Amundsen then set his sights on the Northwest Passage and the study of the Magnetic North Pole. The expedition, which set out from Oslo in June 1903, overwintered in a natural harbour on King William Island, which they named Gjøahavn. By August 1905 they emerged into waters that had been charted from the west, becoming the first vessel to navigate the Northwest Passage.

Amundsen dreamed of becoming the first man to reach the North Pole, but in April 1909 Robert Peary took that honour. In 1910 Amundsen headed instead for the South Pole. In January 1911, Amundsen's ship dropped anchor at Roosevelt Island, 60km closer to the South Pole than the base of Robert Falcon Scott's Terra Nova expedition. With four companions and four 13-dog sleds, Amundsen reached the South Pole on 14 December 1911, beating Scott by a month and three days.

In 1925 Amundsen launched a failed attempt to fly over the North Pole. He tried again the following year aboard the airship Norge, this time with Lincoln Ellsworth, Hjalmar Riiser-Larsen and Italian explorer Umberto Nobile. They left Spitsbergen on 11 May 1926 and, 16 hours later, dropped the Norwegian, US and Italian flags on the North Pole. On 14 May they landed triumphantly at Teller, Alaska, having flown 5456km in 72 hours – the first ever flight between Europe and North America.

In May 1928 Nobile attempted another expedition in the airship Italia and, when it crashed in the Arctic, Amundsen joined the rescue. Although Nobile and his crew were subsequently rescued, Amundsen's last signals were received just three hours after take-off from somewhere over the Barents Sea. His body has never been found.

1945	1945	1949	1950s
On 7 May the last foreign troops on Norwegian soil, the Russians, withdraw from Arctic Norway, following the devastation wrought across the country by the retreating German army.	Norway becomes a founding member of the UN. This membership would later provide a platform for Norwegian foreign policy, with Norway an important mediator in numerous international conflicts.	Norway joins NATO and aligns itself with the USA despite fears in the West that left-leaning Norway would turn towards the Soviet Union.	A Norwegian government commission declares that 'the chances of finding oil on the continental shelf off the Norwegian coast can be discounted'. How wrong they were.

HEADING INTO EXILE

When German forces invaded Norway in April 1940, King Haakon and the Norwegian government fled northwards from Oslo. They halted in Elverum and on 9 April the parliament met at the folk high school and issued the Elverum Mandate, giving the exiled government the authority to protect Norway's interests until the parliament could reconvene. When a German messenger arrived to impose the Nazis' version of 'protection' in the form of a new puppet government in Oslo, the king rejected the 'offer' before heading into exile. Two days later, Elverum became the first Norwegian town to suffer massive bombing by the Nazis and most of the town's old wooden buildings were levelled. By then the king had fled to Nybergsund (close to Trysil), which was also bombed, but he escaped into exile.

ary 1943 on the heavy water plant at Vemork, which was involved in the German development of an atomic bomb.

The Germans exacted bitter revenge on the local populace and among the civilian casualties were 630 Norwegian Jews who were sent to central European concentration camps. Serbian and Russian prisoners of war were coerced into slave labour on construction projects in Norway, and many perished from the cold and an inadequate diet. The high number of worker fatalities during the construction of the Arctic Highway through the Saltfjellet inspired its nickname, the *blodveien* (blood road).

Finnmark suffered particularly heavy destruction and casualties during the war. In Altafjorden and elsewhere, the Germans constructed submarine bases, which were used to attack convoys headed for Murmansk and Arkhangelsk in Russia, so as to disrupt the supply of armaments to the Russians.

In early 1945, with the Germans facing an escalating two-front war and seeking to delay the Russian advance into Finnmark, the German forces adopted a scorched-earth policy that devastated northern Norway, burning fields, forests, towns and villages. Shortly after the German surrender of Norway, Quisling was executed by firing squad and other collaborators were sent off to prison.

The Oil Years

Although there were initial fears in the postwar years that Norway would join the Eastern Bloc of Communist countries under the Soviet orbit – the Communist party made strong gains in postwar elections and even took part in coalition governments – the Iron Curtain remained firmly in place at the Russian border. More than that, Norway made a clear statement of intent in 1945 when it became a founding member of the UN. Ever conscious of its proximity to Russia, the country also abandoned its

The first Allied victory of WWII occurred in late May 1940 in Norway, when a British naval force retook Narvik and won control over this strategic iron ore port. It fell again to the Germans on 9 June.

Late 1960s	1993	1994	2001
Oil is discovered, transforming Norway into one of the richest countries in the world. Oil revenues have provided the basis for an all-encompassing system of social welfare and generous foreign aid.	In defiance of international opinion and contrary to a 1986 moratorium, Norway resumes commercial whaling operations, thereby complicating its claims to be a model environmental citizen.	Norwegians vote against joining the EU. The 'no' vote (52%) draws on the concerns of family farms, fishing interests and the perceived loss of national sovereignty that membership would supposedly bring.	A rare victory for a conservative-liberal coalition after the Labour-led government suffers a massive fall in its vote in national elections; no single party wins enough votes to form government.

neutrality by joining NATO in 1949. Letting bygones be bygones, Norway joined with other Scandinavian countries to form the Nordic Council in 1952.

There was just one problem: Norway was broke and in desperate need of money for reconstruction, particularly in the Arctic North. At first, it appeared that the increasingly prosperous merchant navy and whaling fleet would provide a partial solution, but in truth Norway struggled through (postwar rationing continued until 1952) as best it could.

That would soon change in the most dramatic way possible. It was the discovery of the Ekofisk oilfield on Norway's Continental shelf, in the North Sea southwest of Stavanger in 1969, that turned Norway into a major oil-producing nation (the world's 14th-largest in 2013, with 2.79% of world reserves). The economy boomed, transforming Norway from one of Europe's poorest countries to one of its richest.

Modern Norway

Since the transformation, the Norwegian economy following the discovery of oil, successive socialist governments (and short-lived conservative ones) have used the windfalls (alongside high income taxes and service fees) to foster one of the most extensive social welfare systems in history, with free medical care and higher education, as well as generous pension and unemployment benefits. And there looks to be no end in sight for the era of government largesse – its rapidly rising oil fund for future generations has soared to around US$700 billion. It all adds up to what the government claims is the 'most egalitarian social democracy in Western Europe'.

Thanks in part to its oil wealth, Norway wields a level of influence on the international stage far out of proportion to its relatively small population. Its energetic participation in a range of international institutions, its pivotal involvement in peace processes from the Middle East to Sri Lanka, and its role as a leading player in assisting refugees around the world, in particular, have won international plaudits.

At the same time, Norway remains, by choice, on the fringes of the continent that it inhabits and has yet to join the European Union. Casting an eye over Norwegian history, it's not difficult to understand why Norwegians remain wary of forming unions of any kind with other countries. Having narrowly voted against EU membership in 1972 and again in 1994 despite Norwegian governments pressing for a 'yes' vote, Norway remains on the outside looking in.

2005	2009	22 July 2011	2013
A 'red-green' coalition wins parliamentary elections, overturning a conservative-led coalition government that had won power in 2001.	A centre-left coalition led by Jens Stoltenberg, who had led Labour to its 2001 election defeat, wins closely contested parliamentary elections.	Right-wing extremist Anders Breivik kills 77 people in Oslo and on the nearby island of Utøya in protest of Norway's multicultural policies. He is later sentenced to the maximum 21 years in prison.	A four-party, centre-right coalition unseats the red-green coalition of Prime Minister Jens Stoltenberg, winning 96 out of 169 parliamentary seats. Erna Solberg becomes prime minister.

Landscapes & National Parks

Norway's geographical facts tell quite a story. The Norwegian mainland stretches 2518km from Lindesnes in the south to Nordkapp in the Arctic North with a narrowest point of 6.3km wide. Norway also has the highest mountains in northern Europe and the fourth largest landmass in Western Europe (behind France, Spain and Sweden). But these are merely the statistical signposts to the staggering diversity of Norwegian landforms, from glacier-strewn high country and plunging fjords to the tundralike plains of the Arctic North.

The Coast

Seeming to wrap itself around Scandinavia like a protective shield from the freezing Arctic, Norway's coastline appears to have shattered under the strain, riven as it is with islands and fjords cutting deep fissures inland. Geologists believe that the islands along Norway's far northern coast were once attached to the North American crustal plate – such is their resemblance to the landforms of eastern Greenland. Further north, Svalbard is geologically independent of the rest of Europe and sits on the Barents continental plate deep in the polar region.

In the North Sea lie two rift valleys that contain upper Jurassic shale bearing the extravagantly rich deposits of oil and gas.

Geological history can seem to move at a speed indiscernible to the human eye, but Norway's coastline remains in a state of flux. In the early 1990s, Blomstrandhalvøya in northwestern Svalbard ceased to be a peninsula and became an island.

Fjords

Norway's signature landscape, the fjords rank among the most astonishing natural landforms anywhere in the world. The Norwegian coast is cut deeply with these inlets distinguished by plunging cliffs, isolated farms high on forested ledges and an abundance of ice-blue water extending deep into the Norwegian interior.

Norway's fjords are a relatively recent phenomenon in geological terms. Although Norwegian geological history stretches back 1.8 billion years, the fjords were not carved out until much later. During the glacial periods over this time, the elevated highland plateaus that ranged across central Norway subsided at least 700m due to an ice sheet up to 2km thick. The movement of this ice, driven by gravity down former river courses, gouged out the fjords and valleys and created the surrounding mountains by sharpening peaks and exposing high cliffs of bare rock. The fjords took on their present form when sea levels rose as the climate warmed following the last Ice Age (which ended around 10,000 years ago), flooding into the new valleys left behind by melting and retreating glaciers. Sea levels are thought to have risen by as much as 100m, creating fjords whose waters can seem impossibly deep.

In 2005, Unesco inscribed Geirangerfjord and Nærøyfjord on their World Heritage List because they 'are classic, superbly developed fjords', which are 'among the most scenically outstanding fjord areas on the planet'.

Glacier Museums

Norwegian Glacier Museum (p221), Fjærland

Breheimsenteret Visitors Centre (p223), Nigardsbreen

BIGGEST & HIGHEST

Jostedalsbreen is continental Europe's largest icecap.

Sognefjorden, Norway's longest fjord at 203km (second only in the world to Greenland's Scoresby Sund) is 1308m deep, making it the world's second-deepest fjord (after Skelton Inlet in Antarctica). Hardangerfjord, at 179km, is the third-longest fjord network in the world.

Galdhøpiggen (2469m) is the highest mountain in northern Europe.

Hardangervidda, at 900m above sea level, is Europe's largest and highest plateau.

Utigårdsfossen, a glacial stream that flows into Nesdalen and Lovatnet from Jostedalsbreen (not readily accessible to tourists), is placed by some authorities as the third-highest waterfall in the world at 800m, including a single vertical drop of 600m. Other Norwegian waterfalls among the 10 highest in the world are Espelandsfossen (703m; Hardangerfjord); Mardalsfossen (655m; Eikesdal); and Tyssestrengene (646m in multiple cascades), near Odda.

Glacier Hikes

Jotunheimen National Park

Hardangerjøkulen glacier, Hardangervidda

Folgefonna National Park

Nigardsbreen

Briksdalsbreen

Bødalsbreen

Saltfjellet-Svartisen National Park

Svalbard

Glaciers

Ranking high among the stand-out natural highlights of the country, Norway's glaciers cover some 26,092 sq km (0.7% of mainland Norwegian territory and 60% of the Svalbard archipelago) – at last count there were 2534 glaciers. But this is a far cry from the last Ice Age, when Norway was one vast icefield; the bulk of the ice melted around 8800 years ago.

Not only are glaciers a stunning tourist attraction, they also serve an important purpose in Norway's economy: 15% of Norway's electricity derives from river basins below glaciers.

Concerns about shrinking glaciers and ice sheets in the Arctic have taken on added urgency in recent years as the impact of global warming takes hold. Some of Norway's glaciers retreated by up to 2.5km in the 20th century, while glacial ice is also thinning at an alarming rate. In 2013, for example, northern Norway experienced its hottest summer on record, following on from above-average temperatures during much of the preceding decade, thereby accelerating the melting of Norway's glaciers. Inland glaciers are considered to be at far greater risk than Norway's coastal glaciers. A few Norwegian glaciers have grown in recent decades – the thickness of the ice on the Nigardsbreen glacier grew by 13.8m from 1977 to 2007, although it later retreated by 136m in the years to 2011.

Jostedalsbreen is mainland Europe's largest icecap and it feeds some of Norway's largest glaciers, among them Nigardsbreen, Briksdalsbreen and Bødalsbreen. Another spectacular example is Folgefonn, while central Norway's Jotunheimen National Park is home to 60 glaciers.

Arctic North

If the fjords have drama, Norway's Arctic North has an irrevocable sense of mystery. From Svalbard to the Arctic Highway that carries you north into Arctic Norway, Norway's far north is rich in phenomena that seem to spring from a child's imagination.

The first thing you'll likely notice is the endless horizon that never quite seems to frame a landscape of austere, cinematic beauty. Or perhaps what you'll remember most is the astonishing night sky in winter when the weird and wonderful aurora borealis, also called the northern lights, can seem like an evocation of a colourful ghost story writ large.

The midnight sun and seemingly endless polar night can be similarly disorienting, adding a strange magic to your Norwegian sojourn.

Also part of Norway's Arctic mix is the lichen-strewn tundra landscape of Svalbard.

The Aurora Borealis

There are few sights as mesmerising as an undulating aurora. Although these appear in many forms – pillars, streaks, wisps and haloes of vibrating light – they're most memorable when taking the form of pale curtains wafting on a gentle breeze. Most often, the Arctic aurora appears as a faint green or light rose but, in periods of extreme activity, can change to yellow or crimson.

The visible aurora borealis, or northern lights, are caused by streams of charged particles from the sun, called the solar wind, which are directed by the earth's magnetic field towards the polar regions. Because the field curves downward in a halo surrounding the magnetic poles, the charged particles are drawn earthward. Their interaction with electrons in nitrogen and oxygen atoms in the upper atmosphere releases the energy creating the visible aurora. During periods of high activity, a single auroral storm can produce a trillion watts of electricity with a current of 1 million amps.

The Inuit (Eskimos) call the lights *arsarnerit* ('to play with a ball'), as they were thought to be ancestors playing ball with a walrus skull. The Inuit also attach spiritual significance to the lights, and some believe that they represent the capering of unborn children; some consider them gifts from the dead to light the long polar nights and others see them as a storehouse of events, past and future.

The Arctic – The Complete Story, by Richard Sale, is arguably the best of recent books about the Arctic, with world-class photography and informative text.

LANDSCAPES & NATIONAL PARKS ARCTIC NORTH

MIDNIGHT SUN & POLAR NIGHT

Because the Earth is tilted on its axis, polar regions are constantly facing the sun at their respective summer solstices and are tilted away from it in the winter. The Arctic and Antarctic Circles, at 66° 33' north and south latitude respectively, are the northern and southern limits of constant daylight on their longest day of the year.

The northern half of mainland Norway, as well as Svalbard and Jan Mayen Island, lie north of the Arctic Circle, but during summer, between late May and mid-August, nowhere in the country experiences true darkness. In Trondheim, for example, the first stars aren't visible until mid-August.

Conversely, winters here are dark, dreary and long, with only a few hours of twilight to break the long polar nights. In Svalbard, not even a twilight glow can be seen for over a month. During this period of darkness, many people suffer from SAD syndrome, or 'seasonal affective disorder'. Its effects may be minimised by using special solar-spectrum light bulbs for up to 45 minutes after waking up. Not surprisingly, most northern communities make a ritual of welcoming the sun the first time it peeks above the southern horizon.

TOWN/AREA	LATITUDE	MIDNIGHT SUN	POLAR NIGHT
Bodø	67° 18'	4 Jun–8 Jul	15 Dec–28 Dec
Svolvær	68° 15'	28 May–14 Jul	5 Dec–7 Jan
Narvik	68° 26'	27 May–15 Jul	4 Dec–8 Jan
Tromsø	69° 42'	20 May–22 Jul	25 Nov–17 Jan
Alta	70° 00'	16 May–26 Jul	24 Nov–18 Jan
Hammerfest	70° 40'	16 May–27 Jul	21 Nov–21 Jan
Nordkapp	71° 11'	13 May–29 Jul	18 Nov–24 Jan
Longyearbyen	78° 12'	20 Apr–21 Aug	26 Oct–16 Feb

National Parks

⊕ N

━━━ 0 200 km
━━━ 0 100 miles

↑ Svalbard (840km)
(See Inset)

NORWEGIAN SEA

RUSSIA

FINLAND

SWEDEN

Gulf of Bothnia

Varangerhalvøya

Øvre Pasvik

Seiland

Lakselv

Stabbursdalen

Øvre Anarjåkka

Reisa

Tromsø

Øvre Dividal

Andørdalen

Møysalen

Rago

Junkerdal

Sjunkhatten

Bodø

Saltfjellet-Svartisen

Mosjøen

Lomsdal-Visten

Børgefjell

ØVRE PASVIK NATIONAL PARK

Norway's last refuge for the brown bear in an otherworldly tongue of Norwegian territory within sight of Russia. (p342)

REISA NATIONAL PARK

Remote park in Norway's High Arctic with multi-day hiking routes, a soul-stirring river valley and unusual wildlife you may not see elsewhere. (p347)

SALTFJELLET-SVARTISEN NATIONAL PARK

Sits astride the Arctic Circle with fabulous glaciers, but also upland moors, Sami archaeological sites and glorious scenery. (p276)

Arctic Circle

Svalbard

Nordvest Spitsbergen

Indre Wijdefjorden

Sassen-Bünsow Land

Forlandet

Nordre Isfjorden

Nordenskiold Land

Sør Spitsbergen

━━━ 0 300 km
━━━ 0 150 miles

JOSTEDALSBREEN NATIONAL PARK

Europe's largest icecap tumbles down into the fjords in a series of glaciers that are among Norway's most accessible. (p222)

JOTUNHEIMEN NATIONAL PARK

The roof of Norway with more than 275 peaks over 2000m, year-round skiing and arguably Norway's best hiking. (p148)

FOLGEFONNA NATIONAL PARK

A year-round taste of winter, with an icecap as ideal for skiing as it is for glacier hiking. (p192)

DOVREFJELL-SUNNDALSFJELLA NATIONAL PARK

Stark upland plateau that's home to wild reindeer, primeval musk ox and eerily beautiful scenery. (p138)

FEMUNDSMARKA NATIONAL PARK

Wild land of lakes, marshes and mountains close to the Swedish border. The hiking is superb, and there's reindeer and musk ox in residence. (p134)

RONDANE NATIONAL PARK

Home to some of Norway's shapeliest peaks and an excellent park for wildlife-watching and hiking, with some intriguing archaeological sites. (p139)

HARDANGERVIDDA NATIONAL PARK

Vast, pre-Arctic scenery with tundra-like landscape perfectly suited to wildlife (including Norway's largest population of wild reindeer), hiking, mountain-biking and skiing. (p184)

FINLAND

HELSINKI

TALLINN

ESTONIA

LITHUANIA

Baltic Sea

STOCKHOLM

SWEDEN

Gulf of Bothnia

Grong ○ Lierne
Blåfjella-
Skjækerfjella
Skäckerfjällen
Skarvan og
Trondheim ○ Roltdalen
Forollhogna
Røros ○
Femundsmarka
Dovrefjell-
Sunndalsfjella ○ Dovre ○ Koppang
Rondane
Ormtjernkampen
Lillehammer ○

ATLANTIC OCEAN

Ålesund
Reinheimen
Jostedalsbreen
Breheimen ○ Lom
Jotunheimen
Hallingskarvet ○ Geilo
Hardangervidda
Bergen ○ Folgefonna

OSLO

Ytre Hvaler
Larvik ○

Stavanger ○

DENMARK

MAJOR NATIONAL PARKS

NATIONAL PARK	FEATURES	SIZE (SQ KM)	ACTIVITIES	BEST TIME
Børgefjell	alpine vegetation, Arctic fox	1447	birdwatching	Jun-Aug
Breheimen	high country	1691	hiking	Jun-Aug
Dovre	every Norwegian flora type present within its borders; highest elevation 1700m	289	hiking	Jun-Aug
Dovrefjell-Sunndalsfjella	musk ox, reindeer, Snøhetta (2286m) highlands, Fokstumyra marshes	1693	hiking, climbing, birdwatching, wildlife safaris	May-Sep
Femundsmarka	glaciers, highlands, musk ox, reindeer	573	hiking, boat trips	mid-Jun–Aug
Folgefonna	glaciers, Folgefonna icecap	545	glacier-hiking, summer skiing	May-Sep
Forlandet	waterbird, seal & walrus breeding grounds on Prins Karls Forlandet in Svalbard	4647	birdwatching	Jul & Aug
Hallingskarvet	wild reindeer	450	hiking	Jul & Aug
Hardangervidda	vast upland plateau, largest wild reindeer herd in Europe	3422	Nordic skiing, hiking	Jun-Aug
Jostedalsbreen	Jostedalsbreen icecap (487 sq km), glaciers	1310	hiking, ice-climbing, kiting, boat trips	Jun-Aug
Jotunheimen	Norway's highest mountains, glaciers	1151	hiking	Jul & Aug
Nordvest Spitsbergen	Kongsbreen icefield, Magdalenefjord, archaeological sights, caribou & marine-mammal breeding grounds	9914	hiking, kayaking	Jul & Aug
Øvre Pasvik	Norway's largest stand of virgin taiga forest, last Norwegian habitat of brown bear	119	hiking	year-round
Rago	high peaks, plunging valleys & waterfalls	171	hiking	Jul & Aug
Reinheimen	wild reindeer	1969	hiking	Jun-Aug
Reisa	Reisa Gorge, waterfalls, wildlife	803	hiking	Jun-Aug
Rondane	reindeer, Rondane massif, archaeological sites	963	hiking, wildlife safaris	Jun-Aug
Saltfjellet-Svartisen	straddles Arctic Circle, upland moors, icecaps, Sami archaeological sites	2102	hiking	Jul & Aug
Sør Spitsbergen	Norway's largest park, 65% ice coverage, sea-bird breeding grounds	13,282	wildlife	Jul & Aug
Stabbursdalen	world's northernmost pine forest, lynx, wolverine	747	hiking	Jul & Aug

The best time of year to catch the northern lights in Norway is from October to March, although you may also see them as early as August.

Fata Morgana

If the aurora inspires wonder, the Fata Morgana may prompt a visit to a psychiatrist. The clear and pure Arctic air ensures that distant features do not appear out of focus. As a result, depth perception becomes impossible and the world takes on a strangely two-dimensional aspect where distances are indeterminable. Early explorers meticulously charted islands, headlands and mountain ranges that were never seen again. An amusing example of distance distortion described in *Arctic Dreams,* by Barry Lopez, involves a Swedish explorer who was completing a description in his notebook of a craggy headland with two unusual symmetrical valley glaciers, when he discovered that he was actually looking at a walrus.

Fata Morganas are apparently caused by reflections off water, ice and snow, and when combined with temperature inversions, create the illusion of solid, well-defined features where there are none. On clear days off the outermost coasts of Lofoten, Vesterålen, northern Finnmark and Svalbard, you may well observe inverted mountains or nonexistent archipelagos of craggy islands resting on the horizon. It's difficult indeed to convince yourself, even with an accurate map, that they're not really there! Normal visibility at sea is less than 18km, but in the Arctic, sightings of islands and features hundreds of kilometres in the distance are frequently reported.

High Country

If you think Norway is spectacular now, imagine what it was like 450 million years ago when the Caledonian Mountain Range, which ran along the length of Norway, was as high as the present-day Himalayas. With time, ice and water eroded them down to their current form of mountains and high plateaux (some capped with Europe's largest glaciers and icefields) that together cover more than half the Norwegian land mass.

Norway's highest mountains are in the Jotunheimen National Park, where Galdhøpiggen soars to 2469m. Nearby Glittertind (2465m, and shrinking) was for a long time the king of the Norwegian mountains, but its melting glacier sees its summit retreat a little further every year.

National Parks

At last count, Norway had 44 national parks (including seven in Svalbard where approximately 65% of the land falls within park boundaries). Thirteen new national parks have been created since 2003, with further parks as well as extensions to existing park boundaries planned. Around 15% of the country lies within protected areas.

The focus of Norway's national parks is the preservation of remaining wilderness areas from development, rather than the managed interaction between humans and their environment, although a few interpretation centres do exist.

Further national park information is available at local tourist offices and from the Norwegian Environment Agency (www.miljodirektoratet.no/nasjonalparker) in Trondheim.

Northern Lights: The Science, Myth, and Wonder of Aurora Borealis by Calvin Hall et al combines hard science with historical legend and stunning photography to help unlock one of Norway's great mysteries.

Written in 1986, *Arctic Dreams,* by Barry Lopez, is the enduring classic of Arctic landscapes, wildlife and peculiarly northern phenomena. It covers the entire Arctic, rather than simply Norway's Arctic territories, but there is no finer exploration of the Arctic.

Wildlife

Norway is home to some of Europe's most charismatic fauna and tracking them down can be a highlight of your trip. While Norway's unique settlement pattern spreads the human population thinly and limits wildlife habitat, Norway more than compensates with its variety of iconic northern European species – from polar bears, walrus and Arctic fox in Svalbard to musk ox, reindeer and elk on the mainland. And offshore, whales have survived the best efforts of hunters to drive them to extinction.

Arctic Fox: Life at the Top of the World, by Garry Hamilton, combines fascinating detail with fine photos.

Land Mammals

Arctic Fox

Once prolific throughout Arctic regions, the Arctic fox may be Norway's most endangered land mammal. Numbers of Arctic fox have scarcely risen in the decades since it was officially protected in 1930; the species' greatest threat now comes from the encroachment of the much larger and more abundant red fox. Børgefjell National Park, north of Rørvik and just south of the Arctic Circle, is home to one of mainland Norway's few viable populations, although the species survives in more substantial numbers in Svalbard – sightings are possible even in Longyearbyen. A small population is believed to survive in the Dovrefjell-Sunndalsfjella National Park in central Norway and a tiny number have recently been reintroduced onto the Hardangervidda Plateau: Europe's southernmost Arctic fox population.

The Arctic fox is superbly adapted to harsh winter climates and is believed capable of surviving temperatures as low as minus 70°C thanks to its thick insulating layer of underfur. Almost perfectly white in winter, the Arctic fox can in summer have greyish-brown or smoky-grey fur. In Arctic regions it inhabits the sea ice, often cleaning up the scraps left by polar-bear kills.

Musk Oxen & Elk

Elk Safaris

Oppdal

Dombås

Rjukan

Evje

Andøya, Vesterålen

After being hunted to extinction in Norway almost two millennia ago, the downright prehistoric *moskus-okse* (musk oxen) were reintroduced into Dovrefjell-Sunndalsfjella National Park from Greenland in the 1940s and have since extended their range to the Femundsmarka National Park near Røros. Fewer than 100 are believed to survive in the two Norwegian herds, although their numbers remain more prolific in Greenland, Canada and Alaska; in North America, the Inuit word for the musk ox is *oomingmaq*, which means 'the animal with skin like a beard'. Wherever it is found, the musk ox is one of the most soulful of all Arctic and sub-Arctic species.

From the forests of the far south to southern Finnmark, *elg* (elk; moose in the USA), Europe's largest deer species, are fairly common, although given the Norwegian fondness for elk meat, they wisely tend to stay clear of people and roads.

Reindeer

Wild *reinsdyr* (reindeer) exist in large herds across central Norway, usually above the treeline and sometimes as high up as 2000m. The prime viewing areas are on the Hardangervidda Plateau, where you'll find Europe's largest herd (around 7000). Sightings are also possible in most national parks of central Norway, as well as the inland areas of Trøndelag. For a fine interpretation centre, visit the Norwegian Wild Reindeer Centre (p138) in Dovrefjell-Sunndalsfjella National Park.

The reindeer of Finnmark in Norway's far north are domestic and owned by the Sami, who drive them to the coast at the start of summer, then back to the interior in winter. The smaller *svalbardrein* (Svalbard caribou or reindeer) is native only to Svalbard.

Polar Bears

Isbjørn (polar bears), the world's largest land carnivore, are found in Norway only in Svalbard, spending much of their time on pack or drift ice. Since the ban on hunting came into force in 1973, their numbers have increased to between 3000 and 3500, although they remain extremely difficult to see unless you're on a cruise around Svalbard. Despite weighing up to 720kg and measuring up to 2.5m long, polar bears are swift and manoeuvrable, thanks to the hair on the soles of their feet, which facilitates movement over ice and snow and provides additional insulation.

A polar bear's diet consists mostly of seals, beached whales, fish and birds, and only rarely do they eat reindeer or other land mammals (including humans). Polar-bear milk contains 30% fat (the richest of any carnivorous land mammal), which allows newborn cubs to grow quickly and survive extremely cold temperatures.

Other Land Mammals

Like many of Norway's larger mammal species, *bjørn* (brown bears) have been persecuted for centuries, and Norway's only permanent population is in Øvre Pasvik National Park in eastern Finnmark, although sightings do happen from time to time in Reisa and Stabbursdalen National Parks in Finnmark.

A forest-dweller, the solitary and secretive Eurasian lynx is northern Europe's only large cat. It is found throughout the country but rarely seen.

Lemen (lemmings) occupy mountain areas through 30% of the country and stay mainly around 800m altitude in the south and lower in the north. They measure up to 10cm and have soft orange-brown and black fur, beady eyes, a short tail and prominent upper incisors. If you encounter a lemming in the mountains, it may become enraged, hiss, squeak and attempt to attack!

Other smaller mammal species that are more difficult to see include *hare* (Arctic hares), *pinnsvin* (hedgehogs; mainly in southern Trøndelag), *bever* (beavers; southern Norway), *grevling* (badgers), *oter* (otters), *jerv* (wolverines), *skogmår* (pine martens), *vesel* (weasels) and *røyskatt* (stoats).

Marine Mammals

Whales

The seas around Norway are rich fishing grounds, due to the ideal summer conditions for the growth of plankton. This wealth of nutrients also attracts fish and baleen whales, which feed on the plankton, as well as other marine creatures that feed on the fish. Sadly, centuries of whaling in the North Atlantic and Arctic Oceans have reduced several whale species to perilously small populations. Apart from the minke whale, there's

---

The excellent *Ice Bear: A Natural and Unnatural History of the Polar Bear*, by Kieran Mulvaney, is packed with information and polar bear anecdotes.

Polar Bears International (www.polarbears-international.org) is dedicated to the polar bear, with educational information, details on threats and campaigns to save it.

Although polar bear numbers have remained stable since 2001, US government scientists estimate that two-thirds of the world's polar bears (now numbering between 20,000 and 25,000) will disappear by 2050 due to diminishing summer sea ice, and that the remainder could die out by the end of the 21st century.

WILDLIFE MARINE MAMMALS

Marine Mammals of the North Atlantic by Carl Christian Kinze is an excellent field guide to 51 marine mammals, almost all of which are present in Norway.

no sign that the numbers will ever recover in this area. Given this history, the variety of whale species in Norway's waters is astonishing.

Minkehval (minke whales), one of the few whale species that is not endangered, measure around 7m to 10m long and weigh between 5 and 10 tonnes. They're baleen whales, which means that they have plates of whalebone baleen rather than teeth, and migrate between the Azores area and Svalbard.

Between Ålesund and Varangerhalvøya, it's possible to see *knolhval* (humpback whales), baleen whales that measure up to 15m and weigh up to 30 tonnes. These are among the most acrobatic and vocal of whales, producing deep songs that can be heard and recorded hundreds of kilometres away.

Spekkhogger (killer whales), or orcas, are the top sea predators and measure up to 7m and weigh around 5 tonnes. There are around 1500 off the coast of Norway, swimming in pods of two or three. They eat fish, seals, dolphins, porpoises and other whales (such as minke), which may be larger than themselves.

The long-finned *grindhval* (pilot whales), about 6m long, may swim in pods of up to several hundred and range as far north as Nordkapp. *Hvithval* (belugas), which are up to 4m long, are found mainly in the Arctic Ocean.

The grey and white *narhval* (narwhal), which grow up to 3.5m long, are best recognised by the peculiar 2.7m spiral ivory tusk that projects from the upper lip of the males. This tusk is in fact one of the whale's two teeth and was prized in medieval times. Narwhal live mainly in the Arctic Ocean and occasionally head upstream into freshwater.

The endangered *seihval* (sei whales), a baleen whale, swim off the coast of Finnmark and are named because their arrival corresponds with that of the *sei* (pollacks), which come to feast on the seasonal plankton. They can measure 18m and weigh up to 30 tonnes (calves measure 5m at birth). The annual migration takes the *sei* from the seas off northwest Africa and Portugal (winter) up to the Norwegian Sea and southern Barents Sea in summer.

Finhval (fin whales) measure 24m and can weigh 80 tonnes. These whales were a prime target after the Norwegian Svend Føyn developed the exploding harpoon in 1864 and unregulated whaling left only a few thousand in the North Atlantic. Fin whales are also migratory, wintering between Spain and southern Norway and spending summer in northern Norway.

Spermsetthval (sperm whales), which can measure 19m and weigh up to 50 tonnes, are characterised by their odd squarish profile. They subsist mainly on fish and squid and usually live in pods of 15 to 20. Their numbers were depleted by whalers seeking whale oil and the valuable spermaceti wax from their heads. The fish-rich shoals off Vesterålen attract quite a few sperm whales and they're often observed on boat tours.

The largest animal on earth, *blåhval* (blue whales), measure around 28m and weigh in at a staggering 110 tonnes. Although they can live to 80 years of age, 50 is more common. Heavily hunted for its oil, the species finally received protection, far too late, from the International Whaling Commission in 1967. Prior to 1864, there were between 6000 and 9000, but only a few hundred remain in the world's oceans (although some Norwegian estimates put the number at around 11,000). Recent evidence suggests that a few hardy blue whales are making a comeback in the northeast Atlantic.

Grønlandshval (bowhead whales), or Greenland right whales, were virtually annihilated by the end of the 19th century for their baleen, which was used in corsets, fans and whips, and because they are slow

Possibly the largest animal to ever inhabit the earth, the longest blue whale ever caught measured 33.58m; 50 people could fit on its tongue alone.

swimmers and float when dead. In 1679 Svalbard had around 25,000 bowheads, but only a handful remains and worldwide numbers are critically low.

Other Marine Mammals

Norway's waters shelter reasonable populations of bottlenose, white-beaked, Atlantic white-sided and common dolphins.

Seals are also commonly seen near the seashore throughout Norway and some inland fjords. The main species include *steinkobbe* (harbour seals), *havert* (grey seals), *ringsel* (ringed seals), *grønlandssel* (harp seals), *klappmyss* (hooded seals) and *blåsel* (bearded seals).

The much larger *hvalross* (walruses), which in Norway live only in Svalbard, measure up to nearly 4m and weigh up to 1450kg; their elongated canine teeth can measure up to 1m long in males. Although once heavily hunted for their ivory and blubber, the Svalbard population has increased to around 1000 since they became a protected species in 1952.

Birds

Norway is an excellent destination for ornithologists. The greatest bird populations are found along the coastline, where millions of sea birds nest in cliff faces and feed on fish and other sea life. The most prolific species include terns, *havsule* (gannets), *alke* (razorbills), *lundefugl* (puffins), *lomvi* and *teist* (guillemots), *havhest* (fulmars), *krykkje* (kittiwakes), *tjuvjo* and *fjelljo* (skuas) and *alkekonge* (little auks).

The standout species among Norway's host of wading and water birds include the *storlom* (black-throated wading birds), *smålom* (red-throated divers; called 'loons' in North America), *horndykker* (horned grebes), *åkerrikse* (corncrakes) and Norway's national bird, the *fossekall* (dippers), which make their living by diving into mountain streams.

Norway is also home to at least four species of owls: *jordugle* (short-eared owls), *spurveugle* (pygmy owls), *snøugle* (snowy owls), and *hubro* (eagle owls).

The most dramatic of Norway's raptors is the lovely *havørn* (white-tailed eagle), the largest northern European raptor, with a wingspan of up to 2.5m; there are now at least 500 nesting pairs along the Nordland coast, Troms and Finnmark. Around the same number of *kongeørn* (golden eagles) inhabit higher mountain areas. The rare *fiskeørn* (ospreys) have a maximum population of 30 pairs and are seen only in heavily forested areas around Stabbursdalen and Øvre Pasvik National Parks, both in the far north.

Birdwatching Sites

Femundsmarka National Park

Fokstumyra marshes, Dovrefjell-Sundalsfjella National Park

Gjesvær (Nordkapp)

Øvre Pasvik National Park

Runde Island

Stabbursnes

Lovund Island

Værøy

Svalbard

WILDLIFE BIRDS

Environmental Issues

Norway and the environment are like everyone's model couple – from the outside, they seem like a perfect match even if you suspect that they conceal the occasional dark secret. Indeed, the story of how Norway has been acclaimed for promoting environmental sustainability while being one of the world's largest producers of fossil fuels (oil is the elephant in the room) is a fascinating tale. In short, it's a complicated picture.

Climate Change

The Arctic: An Anthology, edited by Elizabeth Kolbert, brings together some of the most inspiring historical writings about the Arctic, with an emphasis on the exploration of Norwegian and other wilderness areas.

Global warming is by no means a solely Norwegian problem, but few countries have committed to doing as much about it as Norway. In 2007 the Norwegian government promised to 'be at the forefront of the international climate effort' and announced plans to become 'carbon neutral' and cut net greenhouse gas emissions to zero by 2050. This will mostly involve offsetting its annual carbon dioxide emissions by purchasing carbon credits on international markets. The government also agreed to cut actual emissions by 30% by 2030.

Around 98% of Norway's electricity supplies come from renewable (primarily hydro power) sources, with fossil fuels accounting for just 2%. Norway also has targeted tax regimes on carbon dioxide emissions, and allocates billions of kroner to carbon dioxide capture and storage schemes and climate-related initiatives, both within Norway and abroad.

For all such good news, it is worth remembering that Norway's greenhouse gas emissions increased by around 5% between 1990 and 2013 and the average Norwegian emits 11.7 metric tonnes of greenhouse gases, twice the world average, although in line with most other developed countries.

Climate change in Norway is most evident in the worrying signs that its glaciers may be under threat. As ever, Norway's principled position on Arctic pollution is undermined by its production of fossil fuels – the government's strict provisions protecting the environment in Svalbard have won praise, even as it continues to make exemptions for coal production on the archipelago. At the same time, the Svalbard Global Seed Vault is also seen as an important resource in protecting biodiversity in the event of a large rise in global temperatures.

A DANGEROUS ENVIRONMENTAL HAZARD – MOOSE FARTS

According to a report in London's *Times* newspaper in August 2007, by doing nothing more than farting and belching every year, a single adult moose releases the methane equivalent of 2100kg of carbon dioxide emissions, equal to about 13,000km of travel in a car. With an estimated 120,000 wild moose roaming the Norwegian wilds – the Norwegian authorities authorise an annual nationwide hunting quota of around 37,000 – that adds up to a disturbingly high output of methane, not to mention a heightened state of nervousness among otherwise innocent moose.

Commercial Fishing

Fishing and aquaculture (fish farming) remain the foundation of Norway's coastal economy, providing work for an estimated 30,000 people in the fishing fleet, and a host of secondary industries. With an annual catch of around 2.5 to 3 million tonnes, Norway is the 10th-largest fishing nation in the world and one of the world's largest exporters of seafood.

And yet centuries of fishing have severely depleted fish stocks among species that were once the mainstays of the Norwegian economy. By the late 1970s, for example, herring stocks were nearly wiped out. In addition, overfishing depleted stocks of cod all across the North Atlantic. Three decades of conservation measures later, including strict quotas, the herring-fishery industry is recovering. Cod-fishing regulations are now in place, although it will be many years before the numbers return.

It's fair to say that Norwegians usually view the critical depletion of fish stocks in Norwegian waters as much through the prism of economic self-interest as they do a strictly environmental concern. Still Norway's second-largest export earner, it was one of the country's few commercial resources in the days before oil – an essential context to understanding many of Norway's environmental policies as they relate to fishing.

Fish Farming

The aquaculture industry, which has thrived for at least two decades and was born out of the depletion of wild-fish stocks, concentrates mainly on Atlantic salmon and trout, but there have also been experiments with Arctic char, halibut, catfish and scallops. Currently, fish farming amounts to around 500,000 tonnes of fish per annum, but the export of pen-raised salmon and trout constitutes 55% of the value of Norway's fish exports.

This ready-made alternative to ocean fishing does carry attendant and potentially serious consequences. The main drawback is that diseases in captive stock spread to wild populations whenever fish escape from the pens, thereby threatening wild populations. Tightened government regulations have reduced escapes in recent years, but it remains an issue of major concern.

Sealing

In Norway seal hunting is restricted to the harp seal. The government's support for seal hunting – it provides funding for sealing vessels and sets an annual quota of between 30,000 and 50,000 seals – is mainly driven by the needs of the fishing community, which wishes to restrict the competition between fishing boats and marine mammals that depend on fish and eat up to 2.5kg per day. Seal meat is also considered a delicacy in many regions of coastal Norway. Even so, the Norwegian sealing industry is in serious decline, with actual culls amounting to barely 10% of the allocated quota.

To mitigate protests, regulations limit seal hunters to only two tools: a rifle and a *hakapik,* or gaff; the former is for adult seals and the latter for pups (which may not be hunted while suckling). Hunters are also required to take courses and shooting tests before each sealing season. Such regulations notwithstanding, media reports suggest that the injuring of young seals abandoned during the hunt was widespread.

Whaling
The International Context

In 1986, as a result of worldwide campaigns expressing critical concern over the state of world whale populations, the International Whaling Commission (IWC) imposed a moratorium on whale hunting. Although

The Future History of the Arctic by Charles Emmerson is an engaging exploration of the politics of the Arctic with a particular focus on the big issues of energy security, environmental protection and the exploitation of the region's natural resources.

State of the Environment Norway (www.environment.no) is a comprehensive site covering everything from biodiversity and international agreements to statistics and Svalbard.

In the respected Environmental Performance Index for 2010, operated by the Yale Center for Environmental Law and Policy (epi.yale.edu), Norway ranked 10th out of 178 countries (down from second in 2008).

SUSTAINABLE NORWAY 2015

In 2007, Norway's government announced its flagship manifesto on sustainable tourism. Entitled 'Sustainable Norway 2015', it aims to increase awareness of sustainable tourism (both within the industry and wider community), as well as place sustainability at the heart of all new and existing tourism developments. Run through the quasi-government Innovation Norway (www.innovasjonnorge.no/no/english), the program is both a marketing tool and a code of practice for the tourism industry, although its impact upon (and visibility for) your average tourist remains minimal. The four destinations chosen for the pilot phase of the project are two Unesco World Heritage–listed sites, Vega and Røros, as well as fjordside Lærdal (scene of a spectacular fire in 2014) and the ski resort of Trysil.

Harpoon – Into the Heart of Whaling by Andrew Darby is an erudite (and unashamedly anti-whaling) account of whaling in all its manifestations, from the history of uncontrolled slaughter to the more complicated political debates of the present.

it has largely held, two key elements in recent years have placed the moratorium under threat.

The first has been the decision by the three major whaling nations – Norway, Japan and Iceland – to resume commercial whaling or, in the case of Japan and Iceland, to threaten to withdraw from the IWC unless the moratorium is replaced by a management plan that allows some whaling.

The second development threatening world whale stocks is a concerted campaign that has seen nations with no history of whaling – including Mauritania, Ivory Coast, Grenada, Tuvalu and even landlocked Mongolia, San Marino and Mali – joining the commission. The result has seen a change from nine pro-whaling votes out of 55 in 2000 to an almost 50% split among its 88 members currently (a 75% majority is required to change IWC policy). Allegations that pro-whaling votes have been rewarded with development aid have not been denied by the Japanese.

Norway, for its part, sees the moratorium as unnecessary and outdated. It argues that, unlike in the past when whalers drove many whale species to the verge of extinction (in the 17th century alone, Dutch whalers killed an estimated 60,000 whales in the waters off Svalbard), modern whalers have a better and more informed perspective, that they adhere to a sensible quota system and now adopt more humane methods of killing. The Norwegians claim that they support only traditional, family-owned operations and have no intention of returning to industrial whaling.

For a Norwegian perspective on whaling, stop by the Whaling Museum (p90) in Sandefjord, along Norway's southern coast.

Norway's Recent Practice

Follow the whaling debate at Greenpeace UK (www.greenpeace.org.uk), the Whale and Dolphin Conservation Society (www.wdcs.org) and the Norwegian Ministry of Fisheries (fisheries.no).

Norway resumed commercial whaling of minke whales in 1993 in defiance of an international whaling ban but under its registered objection to the 1986 moratorium. While Norway supports the protection of threatened species, the government contends that minke whales, with a northeast Atlantic population of an allegedly estimated 100,000, can sustain a limited harvest. Despite condemnation by international environmental groups such as Greenpeace and the Whale and Dolphin Conservation Society, the Norwegian government maintains an annual minke-whale quota of 1286, although in recent years whalers have killed less than half their allocated quota.

Japan and Norway resumed trading in whale meat in 2004 and it tends to be the export market that drives the industry rather than domestic consumption, although whale meat is openly sold in fish markets (especially Bergen) – a good moment to decide where you stand on the issue.

Forestry

Forests cover an estimated 38% of mainland Norway, but forests set aside for cultivation account for around 25% of Norwegian territory. Government-protected wilderness areas account for less than 1% of Norway's forests, well below the international standard of 5%. More than 1000 forest-dwelling species are considered to be endangered and areas of old-growth forest are extremely rare.

One remaining stand of old-growth Norwegian forest that has caught the attention of environmentalists is Trillemarka-Rollagsfjell, about 100km west of Oslo and covering 205 sq km. Declared a nature reserve in 2002, it shelters the endangered species such as the lesser spotted woodpecker, tree-toed woodpecker, Siberian jay and golden eagle, as well as threatened plant life.

Although no forestry operation can be entirely environmentally sound, Norway currently has one of the world's most sustainable forestry industries and much of the visible damage to the forests is due to agricultural clearing and timber overexploitation between the 17th and 20th centuries.

Wilderness Areas

Norway may have one of the lowest population densities in Europe, but due to its settlement pattern – which is unique in Europe, and favours scattered farms over villages – even the most remote areas are inhabited and a large proportion of the population is rural-based.

As a result, the natural world has been greatly altered by human activities and the landscape is criss-crossed by roads that connect remote homes, farmsteads and logging areas to more populated areas. All but a couple of the country's major rivers have been dammed for hydroelectric power and even the wild-looking expanses of Finnmarksvidda and the huge peninsulas that jut into the Arctic Ocean serve as vast reindeer pastures. As a result, apart from the upland icefields and Norway's impressive network of national parks, real wilderness is limited to a few forested mountain areas along the Swedish border, scattered parts of Hardangervidda and most of Svalbard.

Recycling

Norwegians strongly support the sorting of household waste for collection and recycling, and travellers are encouraged to do likewise. A mandatory deposit scheme for glass bottles and cans has been a success and about 96% of beer and soft-drink bottles are now returned. Supermarkets give money back for returned aluminium cans and plastic bottles (usually Nkr1 to Nkr1.50).

Since the early 1970s, however, the average annual level of household waste generated per person has nearly doubled to around 375kg, a rise that coincides with the golden years of Norway's oil-fuelled prosperity boom. Although it took a while to catch on, around 50% of household waste and two-thirds of industrial waste is now recycled, while Norway is a world leader when it comes to recycling electrical and electronics products. Methane from waste nonetheless still accounts for 7% of Norway's greenhouse gas emissions and Norwegians consume more than 130,000 tonnes of plastic packaging every year.

Norway's Sami

The formerly nomadic, indigenous Sami people are Norway's largest ethnic minority and can reasonably claim to be Norway's longest-standing residents – they have inhabited northern Scandinavia and northwestern Russia for millennia. Of the approximately 60,000 Sami, around 40,000 reside in Norway, primarily inhabiting the far northern region of Finnmark (scattered groups live in Nordland, Trøndelag and other regions of central Norway). The Sami, who refer to their traditional lands as Sápmi or Samiland, are also present in Sweden, Finland and Russia. They were formerly known as Lapps, although that term now carries negative connotations.

Sami History

The Sámi People: Traditions in Transition by Veli-Pekka Lehtola takes you on a journey through Sami history and is a study of how Sami culture has adapted to the needs of the modern world.

Although it's believed that the Sami migrated to Norway from Siberia as early as 11,000 years ago, the oldest written reference to the Sami was penned by the Roman historian Tacitus in AD 98. In AD 555 the Greek Procopius referred to Scandinavia as Thule (the 'furthest north'), and its peoples as *skridfinns,* who hunted, herded reindeer and travelled about on skis. The medieval Icelandic sagas confirm trading between Nordic peoples and the Sami; the trader Ottar, who 'lived further north than any other Norseman', served in the court of English king Alfred the Great and wrote extensively about his native country and its indigenous peoples.

During medieval times, the Sami people lived by hunting and trapping in small communities known as *siida*. While the 17th- and 18th-century colonisation of the north by Nordic farmers presented conflicts with this

NILS MIKKEL SOMBY: SAMI REINDEER HERDER

Nils Mikkel Somby has spent his life in the rolling hill country above the Iešjokha River west of Karasjok. He continues to herd his family's 3000 reindeer and migrates with them to Nordkapp every April, returning around October.

It must be a tough life being a Sami. My mother was out herding reindeer on her own in winter when she was 10 and my father, who is 74, is still out herding every day.

There must have been many changes in the Sami way of life. In the old times, life for the Sami was very difficult. We had to do everything on skis or on foot and we had to be camped out in the mountains during the winter. Now we have cabins with heating. But if one thing has made Sami life easier, it is the snowmobile – we can use it to check on the reindeer, to bring supplies, and then return to our huts. So in that way, life is much better for us. But now there are too many rules, how many reindeer we can have and so on.

The winters must be very long. Life in winter is hard because of the cold and because it's always dark and you can only track the reindeer by looking for their footprints in the snow. But this is also my favourite time of the year. Can you see how beautiful it is here, with sun shining and no other people in sight?

And the next generation? The modern world needs so much, things like roads and resources from remote places. And with so many distractions for young Sami, it's difficult to keep our culture alive. Fifty years from now, I hope that there will still be Sami up here. I am not so sure.

Sami Cultural Area & Dialects

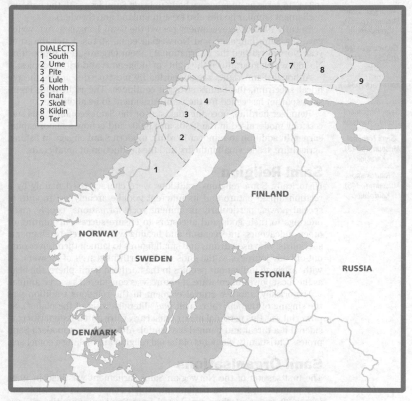

DIALECTS
1 South
2 Ume
3 Pite
4 Lule
5 North
6 Inari
7 Skolt
8 Kildin
9 Ter

FINLAND

NORWAY

SWEDEN

ESTONIA

RUSSIA

DENMARK

system, many newcomers found that the Sami way of life was better suited to the local conditions and adopted their dress, diet and customs.

Around 1850, with Sami traditions coming under increasing threat from missionary activity, reforms were introduced, restricting the use of the Sami language in schools. From 1902 it became illegal to sell land to any person who couldn't speak Norwegian; this policy was enforced zealously and Sami culture seemed to be on the brink of extinction.

After WWII, however, official Norwegian government policy changed direction and began to promote internal multiculturalism. By the 1960s the Sami people's right to preserve and develop their own cultural values and language was enshrined across all government spectra. Increasingly, official policy viewed the Sami as Norwegian subjects but also an ethnic minority and separate people. Their legal status improved considerably and the government formed two committees: the Samekulturutvalget to deal with Sami cultural issues; and the Samerettsutvalget to determine the legal aspects of Sami status and resource ownership.

From 1979 to 1981, an increasingly bitter Sami protest in Oslo against a proposed dam on Sami traditional lands drew attention to the struggle for Sami rights. In 1988 the Norwegian government passed an enlightened constitutional amendment stating: 'It is the responsibility of the authorities of the State to create conditions enabling the Sami people to preserve and develop its language, culture and way of life.' It

According to Norway's national statistics bureau, just under 10% (or around 3000) of Norway's Sami are involved in reindeer herding, primarily in the Finnmark region of Norway's far north, including roughly equal numbers of men and women.

also provided for the creation of an elected 39-member Sami Parliament (p344) to serve as an advisory body to bring Sami issues to the national parliament (similar bodies also exist in Finland and Sweden).

In early 1990 the government passed the Sami Language Act, which gave the Sami language and Norwegian equal status. Later the same year, Norway ratified the International Labour Organisation proposition No 169, which guaranteed the rights of indigenous and tribal peoples.

Although Sami rights are supported by most parties across the political spectrum, the Sami's struggle continues. The right-wing Fremskrittspartiet has called for the Sami Parliament to be abolished.

Reindeer herding, once the mainstay of the Sami economy, was successfully modernised in the 1980s and 1990s and is now a major capital earner. In addition to reindeer herding, modern Sami engage in fishing, agriculture, trade, small industry and the production of handicrafts.

Sami Religion

Historically, Sami religious traditions were characterised mainly by a relationship to nature and its inherent godlike archetypes. In sites of special power, particularly prominent rock formations, people made offerings to their gods and ancestors to ensure success in hunting or other endeavours. Intervention and healing were affected by shamanic specialists, who used drums and small figures to launch themselves onto out-of-body journeys to the ends of the earth in search of answers. As with nearly all indigenous peoples in the northern hemisphere, the bear, as the most powerful creature in nature, was considered a sacred animal.

Historically, another crucial element in the religious tradition was the singing of the *joik* (also spelt *yoik*; literally 'song of the plains'). So powerful was this personal mantra that early Christian missionaries considered it a threat and banned it as sinful. Although most modern Sami profess Christianity, elements of the old religion are making a comeback.

Sami Organisations

The first session of the Norwegian Sami Parliament was held in 1989. The primary task of the parliament, which convenes in Karasjok and whose 39 representatives are elected from Sami communities all over Norway every four years, is to protect the Sami language and culture.

The Norwegian Sami also belong to the **Saami Council** (www.saami-council.net), which was founded in 1956 to foster cooperation between political organisations in Norway, Sweden, Finland and Russia. In Tromsø in 1980, the Saami Council's political program adopted the following principles:

> We, the Sami, are one people, whose fellowship must not be divided by national boundaries. We have our own history, tradition, culture and language. We have inherited from our forebears a right to territories, water and our own economic activities. We have an inalienable right to preserve and develop our own economic activities and our communities, in accordance with our own circumstances and we will together safeguard our territories, natural resources and national heritage for future generations.

The Sami participate in the Arctic Council and the World Council of Indigenous Peoples, which encourages solidarity and promotes information exchange between indigenous peoples.

The **Sami University College** (www.samiskhs.no) at Kautokeino was established as the Nordic Sami Institute in 1974 and promotes Sami language, culture and education, as well as research, economic activities and environmental protection.

To be officially considered Sami and (if 18 or over) be able to vote in elections for the Sami Parliament, a person must regard themselves as Sami, speak Sami as their first language or at least one of their parents, grandparents or great-grandparents must have spoken Sami as their first language.

Arts & Architecture

Norway is one of Europe's cultural giants, producing world-class writers, composers and painters in numbers far out of proportion to its size. Norwegian artists and performers, too, excel in the realms of popular culture, from dark and compelling crime fiction to musical strands as diverse as jazz, electronica and heavy metal. And when it comes to architecture, Norway is as known for its stave churches as it is for the zany contemporary creations that are also something of a national speciality.

Arts

Literature

The Golden Age

The late 19th and early 20th centuries were the golden age of Norwegian literature. Although most of the attention centres on Henrik Ibsen, it was Bjørnstjerne Bjørnson (1832–1910) who in 1903 became the first Norwegian writer to win the Nobel Prize for Literature. Bjørnson's work included vignettes of rural life (for which he was accused of romanticising the lot of rural Norwegians). His home at **Aulestad** (☑61 22 41 10; www.aulestad.no; Follebu; adult/child Nkr110/55; ☺10am-4pm late-May-Aug, weekends only Sep) is open to visitors.

Knut Hamsun (1859–1952) won the Nobel Prize for Literature in 1920. Hamsun's elitism, his appreciation of Germanic values and his idealisation of rural life led him to side with the Nazis in WWII. Only now is his reputation being rehabilitated and he is widely recognised as belonging to the tradition of Dostoevsky and Joyce. To find out more, visit the Hamsunsenteret (p279), the museum in Hamarøy dedicated to his life.

Henrik Ibsen Sites

Ibsen Museum (p51), Oslo

Ibsenhuset Museum (p96), Grimstad

Henrik Ibsenmuseet (p111), Skien

National Theatre (p75), Oslo

CULTURAL ICON: HENRIK IBSEN

Born in Skien in southern Norway, Henrik Johan Ibsen (1828–1906) became known internationally as 'the father of modern drama', but to Norwegians he was the conscience of a nation. Norwegians are extremely proud of Ibsen, but from 1864 until 1891 he lived in disenchanted exile, decrying the small-mindedness of Norwegian society of the day. The enormously popular *Peer Gynt* (1867) was Ibsen's international breakthrough. In this enduring epic, an ageing hero returns to his Norwegian roots after wandering the world and is forced to face his own soul.

His best-known plays include *The Doll's House* (1879), the highly provocative *Ghosts* (1881), *An Enemy of the People* (1882), *Hedda Gabler* (1890) and, his last drama, the semi-autobiographical *When We Dead Awaken* (1899).

Throughout his life, Ibsen was always more than a chronicler of Norwegian society and saw himself as the very reflection of 19th-century Norwegians: 'He who wishes to understand me must know Norway. The magnificent but severe natural environment surrounding people up there in the north forces them to keep to their own. That is why they become introspective and serious, they brood and doubt – and they often lose faith. There, the long, dark winters come with their thick fogs enveloping the houses – oh, how they long for the sun!'

Sigrid Undset (1882–1949) became the third of Norway's Nobel Literature laureates in 1928 and is regarded as the most significant female writer in Norwegian literature. Undset began by writing about the plight of poor and middle-class women. **Bjerkebæk** (Map p124; ☎61 28 89 00; www.maihaugen.no/bjerkebek; Sigrid Undsetsveg 1; adult/child/family Nkr110/55/275; ⊘10am-4pm mid-May–Aug, 10am-3pm Sat & Sun Sep), her former home in Lillehammer, is open to the public.

Fiddling for Norway: Revival and Identity, by Chris Goertzen, looks at the revival of folk-fiddling in Norway, the history of Norwegian folk music and its influence on the world folk-music scene.

Contemporary Literature

One of the best-known modern Norwegian writers is Jan Kjærstad (b 1953), whose *The Seducer* (2003) combines the necessary recipe for a best seller – a thriller with a love affair and a whiff of celebrity – with seriously good writing. It won the 1999 Nordic Prize for Literature among other international prizes. Other Norwegian winners of the prestigious Nordic Prize include Per Petterson (b 1952) and Lars Saabye Christensen (b 1953). Another world-renowned author is Jostein Gaarder (b 1952), whose first best-selling novel, *Sophie's World* (1991), sold over 15 million copies worldwide. Dag Solstad (b 1941) is the only Norwegian author to win the Norwegian Literary Critics' Award three times.

In the crime-fiction genre, Gunnar Staalesen and Karin Fossum have devoted international followings. But it's Jo Nesbø (jonesbo.com/en) who is considered the king of Norwegian crime fiction. His stories are darker than many in the genre and are almost all set in Norway from World War II to the present.

Music

Classical Music

The 19th century was an extraordinarily rich time for Norwegian music. It was at this time that Edvard Grieg, who is regarded as one of history's greatest composers, emerged. Of arguably equal importance was the virtuoso violinist Ole Bull, known throughout Europe as the 'Nordic Paganini'. Bull is credited with critically encouraging the careers of Edvard Grieg and Henrik Ibsen, bringing the Hardanger folk fiddlers to Bergen concert halls and reviving Europe-wide interest in Norwegian folk music.

There are fine philharmonic orchestras in Oslo, Bergen (dating from 1765), Trondheim and Stavanger; the Norwegian Opera Company (established in 1958) is based in Oslo.

Folk Music

Folk music is a central pillar of Norwegian music, and the Hardanger fiddle – which derives its distinctive sound from four or five sympathetic strings stretched out beneath the usual four strings – is one of Europe's best-loved folk instruments.

Edvard Grieg Experiences

Edvard Grieg Museum (p158), Bergen

Open-air concerts, Bergen

Grieghallen (p170), Bergen

Some of the hottest folk acts include Tore Bruvoll and Jon Anders Halvorsen, who perform traditional Telemark songs *(Nattsang);* the live Norwegian performances of Bukkene Bruse (heavy on the Hardanger fiddle; *Spel);* Rusk's impressively wide repertoire of music from southeastern Norway *(Rusk);* Sigrid Moldestad and Liv Merete Kroken, who bring classical training to bear on the traditional fiddle *(Spindel);* and Sinikka Langeland, whose *Runoja* draws on ancient runic music. In 2009, Alexander Rybak, a Norwegian composer, fiddler and pianist of Belorussian descent won the Eurovision Song Contest.

Sami Music

The haunting music of the Sami people of northern Norway is enjoying a revival. Recent Sami artists such as Aulu Gaup, Sofis Jannock, Mari

Boine Persen and Nils Aslak Valkeapää have performed, recorded and popularised traditional and modern versions of the traditional *joik* (personal songs). Boine in particular has enjoyed international air-time and her distinctive sound blends folk-rock with *joik* roots.

Contemporary Music

Jazz

Norway has a thriving jazz scene, with world-class festivals held throughout the year all over the country.

Jazz saxophonist Jan Garbarek is one of the most enduring Norwegian jazz personalities and is one of the biggest names on the international stage, quite apart from his fame within Norway. His work draws on classical, folk and world-music influences and he has recorded 30 albums, some including collaborations with renowned artists across a range of genres. His daughter, Anja Garbarek, is seen as one of the most exciting and innovative performers on the Norwegian jazz scene, bringing pop and electronica into the mix.

Other well-known performers include pianists Bugge Wesseltoft and Ketil Bjørnstad, saxophonist Trygve Seim, guitarist Terje Rypdal and female jazz singers Solveig Slettahjell, Sidsel Endresen and Karin Krog. Supersilent, the Christian Wallumrod Ensemble and the cutting-edge Jaga Jazzist rank among Norway's best-loved jazz groups.

Jazzbasen (www.jazzbasen.no/index_eng.html) is the internet's true home of Norwegian jazz.

Electronica

Norway is at once one of Europe's most prolific producers, and most devoted fans, of electronica. Although much of the energy surrounding Norwegian electronica has shifted to Oslo in recent years, the so-called Bergen Wave was largely responsible for putting Norway on the world electronica circuit in the first years of the 21st century. Röyksopp (royksopp.com) in particular took the international electronica scene by storm with its debut album *Melody A.M.* in 2001 and the group has never really left the dance-floor charts since. The Bergen Wave was not just about electronica; it also produced internationally acclaimed bands Kings of Convenience (www.kingsofconvenience.com) and Ephemera (www.ephemera.no).

In recent years Oslo has taken up the electronica mantle with *Sunkissed*, spun by G-Ha and Olanskii. It remains the hottest thing to hit Norwegian dance music since Röyksopp.

Metal

Metal is a genre that Norway has taken to heart and Bergen tends to be the home city for much of the action. Two venues famous throughout Europe are Hulen (p170), an almost mythical venue among European heavy and indie rock fans; and Garage (p168), another iconic rock-heavy venue.

Norway is particularly known for its black-metal scene which, for a time in the early 1990s, became famous for its anti-Christian, Satanist philosophy. A handful of members of black-metal bands were involved in the burning down of churches such as the Fantoft Stave Church near Bergen. Among the better-known (or more notorious) Norwegian black-metal bands are Darkthrone, Mayhem, Enslaved, Gorgoroth, Satyricon and Arcturus.

Painting & Sculpture

Nineteenth-century Norway gave birth to two extraordinary talents: painter Edvard Munch and sculptor Gustav Vigeland, whose work adorns Oslo's public spaces.

ARTS & ARCHITECTURE ARTS

For a wonderful overview of traditional Norwegian folk music, the 2007 CD *Norway: Traditional Music* excavates long-lost music from the vaults of Norwegian Public Radio.

Jazz Festivals

Polar Jazz (p356), Longyearbyen

Vossajazz (p181), Voss

May Jazz (p199), Stavanger

Night Jazz (Nattjazz; p160), Bergen

Kongsberg Jazz (p108), Kongsberg

Moldejazz (p247), Molde

Canal Street Jazz & Blues (p95), Arendal

International Jazz (p67), Oslo

Silda Jazz (p195), Haugesund

Lillehammer Jazz (p123), Lillehammer

Of the crop of contemporary Norwegian artists, Olav Jensen, Anne Dolven, Ørnulf Opdahl, Bjørn Tufta, Håvard Vikhagen, Odd Nerdrum and Anders Kjær have all created a minor stir with their return to abstract and expressionist forms. Their works often feature harsh depictions of the Norwegian landscape. Norwegian sculptors who've distinguished themselves include Bård Breivik, Per Inge Bjørlo and Per Barclay.

Cinema

Norway has a small, but internationally respected, film industry. Pioneering the industry's claims to international recognition were the Oscar-nominated Nils Gaup and Arne Skouen. Other directors to catch the international eye include Marius Holst, Berit Nesheim, Anja Breien and Jens Lien.

The only Norwegian feature film to win an Academy Award was Thor Heyerdahl's *Kon-Tiki* for Best Documentary Feature in 1951. In 2006 *The Danish Poet*, which was directed by Norway's Torill Kove and narrated by Liv Ullmann, won the Oscar for Best Animated Short Film, and became the second Norwegian production to receive an Academy Award.

Architecture
Traditional Architecture

Timber and stone are the mainstays of traditional Norwegian architecture; nowhere is this more evident than in the former mining village of Røros, where many of the colourful timber houses date back to the 17th and 18th centuries. For an overview of Norwegian architectural styles down through the centuries, it's worth making a detour to Lillehammer to visit Maihaugen, or any of the excellent folk museums dotted around the country.

Sami Architecture

In the far north, where both wood and stone were in short supply, the early nomadic Sami ingeniously built their homes out of turf, which provided excellent insulation against the cold. The temporary shelter that the Sami used on their travels is popularly known as the *lavvo* (although it has different names in various Sami dialects). Less vertical (and hence more stable in the winds of the high Arctic) than the North American teepee, the *lavvo* was held aloft by a tripod of three notched poles with a cover of reindeer skins (and later canvas).

CULTURAL ICON: EDVARD MUNCH

Edvard Munch (1863–1944), Norway's most-renowned painter, was a tortured soul: his mother and elder sister died of tuberculosis and his younger sister suffered from mental illness from an early age. Munch's first great work, *The Sick Child,* was a portrait of his sister Sophie shortly before her death. In 1890 he produced the haunting *Night,* depicting a lonely figure in a dark window. The following year he finished *Melancholy* and began sketches of what would become his best-known work, *The Scream,* which graphically represents Munch's own inner torment.

In 1892 Munch buried himself in a cycle of angst-ridden, atmospheric themes collectively entitled *Frieze of Life – A Poem about Life, Love and Death.* Beyond the canvas, his obsession with darkness and doom cast a long shadow over his life. Alcoholism, chronic emotional instability and a tragic love affair culminated in the 1907 work *Death of Marat,* and, a year later, he checked into a Copenhagen mental-health clinic for eight months.

After leaving the clinic, Munch settled on the coast at Kragerø. It became clear that Munch's post-clinic work was to be altogether different, dominated by a sunnier, more hopeful disposition dedicated to humans in harmony with their landscape.

The *lavvo* formed at once a centrepiece of Sami life and a refuge from the elements. The *lavvo* also holds considerable modern symbolism for the Sami: in the early 1980s, the Oslo police bulldozed a Sami *lavvo* that had been set up outside Norway's parliament building to protest against a proposed dam that would have inundated Sami herding lands. These events provided a catalyst for a reassessment of Sami rights and which led indirectly to the foundation of the Sami parliament. The stunning modern Sami Parliament (p344) building in Karasjok was inspired by the traditional *lavvo* form.

Stave Churches

Seemingly conceived by a whimsical child-like imagination, the stave church is an ingenious adaptation to Norway's unique local conditions. Originally dating from the late Viking era, these ornately worked houses of worship are among the oldest surviving wooden buildings on earth, albeit heavily restored. Named for their vertical supporting posts, these churches are also distinguished by detailed carved designs and dragon-headed gables resembling the prows of classic Viking ships. Of the 500 to 600 that were originally built, only about 20 of the 28 that remain retain many of their original components.

Contemporary Architecture

Due to the need to rebuild quickly after WWII, Norway's architecture was primarily governed by functionalist necessity (the style is often called *funkis* in the local vernacular) rather than any coherent sense of style. Nowhere is this exemplified more than in the 1950, red-brick Oslo Rådhus (p51). As the style evolved, functionality was wedded to other concerns, such as recognising the importance of aesthetics in urban renewal (for example in Oslo's Grünerløkka district), and ensured that architecture once again sat in harmony with the country's environment and history.

Tromsø's Ishavskatedralen (Arctic Cathedral; p313), designed by Jan Inge Hovig in 1964, mimics Norway's glacial crevasses and auroral curtains. Another beautiful example is the Sami Parliament in Karasjok, where Arctic building materials (birch, pine and oak) lend the place a sturdy authenticity, while the use of lights to replicate the Arctic night sky and the structure's resemblance to a Sami *lavvo* are extraordinary. The creative interpretation of historical Norwegian shapes also finds expression at the Viking Ship Sports Arena (p126) in Hamar, while Oslo's landmark new opera house (p47) powerfully evokes a fjord-side glacier.

ARTS & ARCHITECTURE ARCHITECTURE

Norwegian Cuisine

Norwegian food can be excellent. Abundant seafood, local specialities such as reindeer, and a growing trend in cutting-edge cooking are undoubtedly the highlights. The only problem (and it's a significant one) is that prices are prohibitive, meaning that a full meal in a restaurant may become something of a luxury item for all but those on expense accounts. As a result, you may end up leaving Norway pretty uninspired by its food, which is such a shame considering what's on offer.

Roots web (www.rootsweb.com/~wgnorway/recipe.html) has easy-to-follow recipes of traditional Norwegian foods passed down through generations of people of Norwegian descent.

Food

Meat

Norway is that rare place where signature wildlife species also provide some of the country's most memorable meals. Norwegians love their meat. Roast reindeer *(reinsdyrstek)* is something every nonvegetarian visitor to Norway should try; despite its cost (starting from around Nkr275 and often much higher), you'll likely order it again as it's one of the tastier red meats, and that's how it should be ordered – nice and red. In the far north, or if you're fortunate enough to be invited to a Sami wedding, you'll also come across traditional reindeer stew *(bidos)*. Another popular local meat is elk *(elg)*, which comes in a variety of forms, including as a steak or burger.

Other meat-based dishes include *bankebiff* (slices/chunks of beef simmered in gravy), *dyrestek* (roast venison) and *lammebog* (shoulder of lamb). Meats are often cured, one variety of which is *spekemat* (cured lamb, beef, pork or reindeer, often served with scrambled eggs). Other dishes include *kjøttpålegg* (cold meat cuts), *fårikål* (lamb in cabbage stew), *syltelabb* (boiled, salt-cured pig's trotter), *lapskaus* (a thick stew of diced meat and vegetables) and *pytt i panne* (eggs with diced potato and meat).

Surprisingly few Norwegian restaurants offer the kind of meals that Norwegians eat at home, or at least used to when their mothers and grandmothers cooked for them. One such dish is traditional Norwegian meatballs served with mushy peas, mashed potatoes and wild-berry jam.

Seafood

One Norwegian contribution to international cuisine that you shouldn't miss is salmon (grilled, *laks;* or smoked, *røykelaks*). Whereas other Norwegian foods may quickly empty your wallet, salmon remains blissfully cheap, although this applies only to farmed salmon; wild salmon is considerably more expensive. The quality is consistently top-notch. An excellent salmon dish, *gravat laks* is made by marinating salmon in sugar, salt, brandy and dill, and serving it in a creamy sauce.

Other Norwegian freshwater seafood specialities include brown trout, perch, Arctic char, Arctic grayling, bream and eel.

The most common ocean fish and seafood that you're likely to eat are cod *(torsk* or *bacalao;* often dried) and boiled or fresh shrimp. Herring (once the fish of the poor masses and now served pickled in onions, mustard or tomato sauce) is still served in some places, but it's becoming rarer. Also popular is *fiskesuppe,* a thin, creamy, fish-flavoured soup.

Fish Markets

Bergen

Stavanger

Kristiansand

Trondheim

Narvik

IF YOU DARE...

Norway has its share of strong-tasting culinary oddities that the brave among you may wish to try:

➡ Whale steak *(hvalbiff)* – a reasonably common sight on restaurant menus and in harbourside markets (eg in Bergen), although it may grate against your environmental sensibilities.

➡ Brown cheese *(Gudbrandsdalsost)* – made from the whey of goat's and/or cow's milk and has a slightly sweet flavour despite its off-putting caramel-coloured appearance.

➡ Reconstituted cod, mackerel or saithe balls *(lutefisk)* – more common in homes than restaurants and something of a staple for older folk.

➡ Cod tongues *(torsketunger)* – these are hugely popular in Lofoten and, strangely enough, nowhere else.

➡ Fermented trout *(rakfisk)* – some Norwegians swear by it, but some Lonely Planet authors are happy to leave them to it.

Other Specialities

Potatoes feature prominently in nearly every Norwegian meal and most restaurants serve them boiled, roasted or fried with just about every dish.

The country's main fruit-growing region is around Hardangerfjord, where strawberries, plums, cherries, apples and other orchard fruits proliferate. The most popular edible wild berries include strawberries, blackcurrants, red currants and raspberries; blueberries (huckleberries), which grow on open uplands; blue, swamp-loving bilberries; red high-bush and low-bush cranberries; and muskeg crowberries. The lovely amber-coloured *moltebær* (cloudberries) are highly prized and considered a delicacy. They grow one per stalk on open swampy ground and in Norway some cloudberry patches are zealously guarded. Warm cloudberry jam with ice cream is simply fantastic!

Norwegian cheeses have come to international attention as a result of the mild but tasty Jarlsberg, a white cheese first produced in 1860 on the Jarlsberg estate in Tønsberg.

One scheme worth watching out for in northern Norway is the Arctic Menu, an attempt by an association of restaurants to revive interest in local ingredients and recipes.

Vegetarian & Vegan Food

Norwegians are not the most vegetarian of people. That said, most restaurants offer some vegetarian options, sometimes just a cheese-and-onion omelette or a pasta with cream sauce, but increasingly you'll find creative salads (although vegans won't appreciate the widespread use of cheese) and a range of crepes or pancakes to add some variety to your diet. The predominance of potatoes on most Norwegian restaurant menus almost always provides a fall-back option.

In general, the rule is that the larger the town, the wider your choices of vegetarian fare. Tapas restaurants are a recurring theme in larger towns and most have vegetable-only options. Pizza restaurants also always have at least one vegetarian dish.

Drinks

Hot Drinks

If Norway has a national drink, it's coffee: it is drunk in such staggering quantities that one can only wonder how people can remain so calm under the influence of so much caffeine. Most Norwegians drink it black

Norwegian National Recipes: An Inspiring Journey in the Culinary History of Norway by Arne Brimi can be hard to track down, but there's no finer study of Norwegian food covering all regions, and it's written by one of Norway's premier chefs.

Every Thursday from September to May, many Bergen restaurants serve *raspeballer,* a powerful traditional meal with salted meat, potatoes and mashed turnip – an acquired taste perhaps, but hearty winter food.

and strong, but foreigners requiring milk and/or sugar are normally indulged. Teas and infusions are also available all over the country.

Alcoholic Drinks

Beer & Wine

Beer is commonly sold in bars in 400mL or 500mL glasses (about 30% and 15% less than a British pint, respectively). The standard Norwegian beer is pils lager, with an alcohol content of around 4%, and it's still brewed in accordance with the 16th-century German purity law. The most popular brands are the lagers Ringsnes in the south and Mackin in the north, while micro-breweries are a growing trend. Munkholm is a fairly pleasant alcohol-free beer. Note that when friends go out drinking, people generally buy their own drinks rather than rounds.

Norwegians increasingly drink wine with meals. According to one study, wine makes up one-third of Norway's alcohol intake, compared to just 12% in 1974. Quality restaurants increasingly offer extensive wine lists with wines from across Europe and sometimes further afield. In some cities, wine bars are all the rage.

Aquavit

The national spirit, aquavit (or *akevitt*) is a potent dose of Norwegian culture made from potatoes and caraway liquor. The name is derived from the Latin *aqua vitae,* the 'living waters'. Although caraway is an essential ingredient, modern distilleries augment the spicy flavour with any combination of orange, coriander (cilantro), anise, fennel, sugar and salt. The confection is aged for three to five years in 500L oak barrels.

Perhaps the most esteemed version of this libation is *linje aquavit,* or 'line aquavit', which first referred to stores that had crossed the equator. In the early days, ships carried oak barrels of aquavit abroad to trade, but the unsold barrels were returned to Norway and offered for sale. When it was discovered that the product had improved with age and travel, these leftovers became highly prized commodities. Today, bottles of *linje aquavit* bear the name of the ship involved, its route and the amount of time the barrels have aged at sea.

Authentic Norwegian Cooking by Astrid Karlsen Scott emphasises the practical and has been endorsed by none other than Ingrid Espelid, the Betty Crocker or Delia Smith of Norway. *The Norwegian Kitchen* by K Innli (ed) brings together more than 350 favourite recipes of members of the Association of Norwegian Chefs.

THE TROUBLE WITH ALCOHOL

Norway must be one of few countries in the world where the population actually voted *for* prohibition (in a 1919 referendum)! The ban on alcohol remained in force until 1927, by which time half the Norwegian population was involved either in smuggling or illegally distilling home brew, including, no doubt, many who had voted in favour of the ban. Under the state monopoly system, state alcohol outlets called Vinmonopolet (or just 'pole' to its friends) remain the only place, outside of bars and restaurants, where wine and spirits may be purchased.

And the old prohibitionist streak still runs deep in some corners of the country. Alcohol sales are strictly controlled and a few towns have even implemented virtual prohibition. In some places, drinking beer in public incurs a hefty fine and/or prison time, although we're yet to hear of any tourist doing time for enjoying a quiet pint.

Norway's official attitude towards alcohol borders on paranoia, especially as alcohol consumption by Norwegians is among the lowest in Europe, although whether this is because of the strict laws or in spite of them it's difficult to tell. Yes, Norwegian alcohol consumption has increased from 3.4L per person per week in 1960 to 6.2L in recent years, but these figures are still barely more than half the consumption levels in Germany or the UK.

Eating in Norway

Habits & Customs

The Norwegian day starts with coffee (always!), a boiled egg and some sort of bread or dry crispbread (normally Ryvita) topped with cheese, cucumber, tomato and a type of pickled herring.

For lunch, most people opt for an open sandwich, a slice of bread topped with sardines, shrimp, ham, olives, cucumber or egg. In the midafternoon Norwegians often break for coffee and one of the highlights of the day, waffles with cream and jam. Unlike Belgian waffles, Norwegian waffles are flower-shaped, soft and often strongly flavoured with cardamom.

The main meal is eaten between 4pm and 6pm, considerably later in summer. Usually the only hot meal of the day, it normally includes a meat, seafood or pasta dish, with boiled potatoes, a scoop of vegetables and perhaps even a small salad or green garnish.

Where to Eat & Drink

Hotel breakfasts in Norway often consist of a gargantuan buffet that is dominated by continental-style choices, with a few hot dishes (usually bacon, eggs and/or sausages) and some Scandinavian options (such as pickled herrings) thrown in. If you're staying somewhere where breakfast is not included, your best bet is a bakery where bread, pastries, sandwiches and bagels are well priced.

If you love fresh fish, any of Norway's fish markets are fabulous places to eat; buy what you want as a takeaway and find a quiet vantage point alongside the water.

Norwegians love to eat out and just about every town in Norway has at least one sit-down restaurant. Although it's more usual to eat a light lunch and save the main meal for dinner, many Norwegian restaurants, especially in larger towns, serve cheaper lunch specials (often around Nkr79). These are often filling and well sized for those wanting more than a sandwich. Sometimes these are signed as a *dagens rett* (daily special).

Food & Drink Glossary

bacalao	cod (see also *torsk*)
bankebiff	slices/chunks of beef simmered in gravy
bidos	traditional reindeer stew (Sami)
brisling	sardine
brus	soft drink
dagens rett	daily special
dyrestek	roast venison
elg	elk or moose
fårikål	lamb in cabbage stew
fiskebolle	fish balls
fiskegrateng	fish casserole
fiskesuppe	thin, creamy, fish-flavoured soup
frokost	breakfast
frukt	fruit
gaffelbitar	salt- and sugar-cured sprat/herring fillets
gatekjøkken	food wagons or kiosks
gravat laks	salmon marinated in sugar, salt, brandy and dill and served in a creamy sauce
grønnsak	vegetable
Gudbrandsdalsost	brown cheese made from the whey of goat's and/or cow's milk

hvalbiff	whale steak
hvitvin	white wine
jordbær	strawberry
kaffe	coffee
kjøtt	meat
kjøttpålegg	cold meat cuts
klippfisk	salted and dried cod
kylling	chicken
laks	salmon, usually grilled
lammebog	shoulder of lamb
lapskaus	thick stew of diced meat, potatoes, onions and other vegetables
lunsj	lunch
lutefisk	reconstituted cod, mackerel or saithe ball
melk	milk
meny	menu
mineralvann	mineral water
moltebær	cloudberries
nøtter	nuts
øl	beer
oksekjøtt	beef
ost	cheese
pinneribbe	mutton ribs steamed over birch or juniper branches at Christmas
pølse	sausage, hot dog
potet	potato
pytt i panne	eggs with diced potato and meat
rakfisk	fermented trout
reinsdyrstek	roast reindeer
reker	shrimp
rødvin	red wine
rømmegrøt	sour-cream variant on porridge, served at Christmas
røykelaks	smoked salmon
rupa	ptarmigan or grouse
salat	salad
sauekjøtt	lamb
sild	herring
sildesalat	salad with slices of herring, cucumber, onions etc
skinke	ham
sopp	mushroom
spekemat	cured lamb, beef, pork or reindeer, often served with scrambled eggs
spekeslid	salted herring, often served with pickled beetroot, potatoes and cabbage
svinekjøtt	pork
syltelabb	boiled, salt-cured pig's trotter
torsk	cod (see also *bacalao*)
torsketunger	cod tongues
tunfisk	tuna

Survival Guide

Directory A–Z

Accommodation

Norway offers a wide range of accommodation, from camping, hostels and pensions to international-standard hotels. You'll pay a lot more for what you get compared with other countries, but standards are high. Most hotels have wi-fi access.

Reservations

Although it's rare that you'll arrive in a town to find that all of the accommodation is full – festival times are an exception – it's always advisable to book in advance to ensure that you get the accommodation of your choice.

Most places in Norway accept phone or email reservations (you'll often have to leave a credit-card number for the latter). Many hostels are happy to book beds at your next destination for a small fee (around Nkr20).

Many tourist offices can help you find accommodation, usually for a fee of around Nkr50; apart from in some larger tourist offices, this service usually operates only if you're physically present in the tourist office and not for advance bookings.

Seasons

The main tourist season runs from around the middle of June to the middle of August. Unusually, this is when accommodation prices are at their lowest and many hotels offer their best deals. In some areas, the season begins in mid-May and/or hangs on until mid-September.

Winter, particularly in northern Norway where travellers come for activities such as snowmobiling and dog-sledding, is also a popular time to visit although, unlike in summer, prices rarely drop as a consequence. Some hotels and the overwhelming majority of campsites close during the winter months, while that rare breed, ice hotels – there are examples in Kirkenes and Alta – only open in winter.

Prices

Prices vary widely throughout the year. Discounted high-season prices apply in July only. The sometime exception to high-season lower prices is the southern Norwegian coast, where beach resorts raise their prices to cash in on the school-holiday influx.

During the rest of the year, the assumption seems to be that the only people travelling are those doing so for business and on expense accounts, and prices can soar accordingly (by as much as 40%). The exception is weekends (usually Friday and Saturday nights, but sometimes also Sunday) when, year-round, prices can drop to their much more reasonable summer rates. If you're travelling outside the summer months, ask your hotel about special offers to see if discounts are available.

Prices for single rooms are generally not much less than the rates for double rooms. Remember that if you're making enquiries in advance about prices, they're often quoted *per person* for double rooms, so always check.

Staying within a tight budget is difficult in Norway, and you'll either need to stay at campsites (in a tent or a simple cabin), hostels or guesthouses; within the budget category, it's rare that you'll have your own private bathroom. Midrange and top-end rooms are usually very comfortable and almost always have a private bathroom.

BOOK YOUR STAY ONLINE

For more accommodation reviews by Lonely Planet authors, check out http://lonelyplanet.com/hotels/. You'll find independent reviews, as well as recommendations on the best places to stay. Best of all, you can book online.

Bed & Breakfasts

Some places operate as B&Bs, where prices (usually with shared bathrooms) start from Nkr450/600 per single/double and can go up to Nkr650/900.

Bed & Breakfast Norway (www.bbnorway.com) Has extensive online listings for B&Bs throughout Norway; it also sells *The Norway Bed & Breakfast Book*, with listings throughout the country.

Camping

Norway has more than 1000 campsites. Tent space costs from Nkr100 at basic campsites up to Nkr225 for those with better facilities or in more popular areas, such as Oslo and Bergen. Quoted prices usually include your car, motorcycle or caravan. A per-person charge is also added in some places, electricity often costs a few kroner extra and almost all places charge Nkr10 for showers.

Most campsites also rent simple cabins with cooking facilities, starting at around Nkr400 for a very basic two- or four-bed bunkhouse. Bring a sleeping bag, as linen and blankets are only provided at an extra charge (anywhere from Nkr50 to Nkr100).

Unless you opt for a more expensive deluxe cabin with shower and toilet facilities (Nkr750 to Nkr1300), you'll also have to pay for showers and washing water (there are a few exceptions). Normally, cabin occupants must clean their cabin before leaving or pay an additional cleaning charge (around Nkr150).

Note that although a few complexes remain open year-round, tent and caravan sites are closed in the off-season (normally early September to mid-May).

For a comprehensive list of Norwegian campsites, pick up a copy of the free *Camping* (available at some tourist offices, campsites and from Norsk Camping); it has hundreds of listings, but most entries are in Norwegian.

NAF Camp (www.nafcamp. no) An excellent online resource listing more than 250 campsites around Norway.

Norsk Camping (www. camping.no) A useful resource for general camping info, as well as the comprehensive *Camping* guide, available in book (they charge Nkr90 to send it out to you) or PDF format (free).

DNT & Other Mountain Huts

Den Norske Turistforening (DNT, Norwegian Mountain Touring Club; Map p56; www. turistforeningen.no; Storget 3; ⏱10am-5pm Mon-Wed & Fri, to 6pm Thu, to 3pm Sat) maintains a network of 460 mountain huts or cabins located a day's hike apart along the country's 20,000km of well-marked and maintained wilderness hiking routes. Of these, over 400 have beds for sleeping, with the remainder reserved for eating, rest stops or emergency shelter.

DNT huts range from unstaffed huts with two beds to large staffed lodges with more than 100 beds and renowned standards of service. At both types of huts, DNT members receive significant discounts.

Most DNT huts are open from 16 February to 14 October. Staffed DNT lodges also open from the Saturday before Palm Sunday until Easter Monday, but staffed huts along the Oslo–Bergen railway and a few others open for the cross-country ski season as early as late February. DNT can provide lists of opening dates for each hut.

Members/nonmembers who prefer to camp outside the huts and use the facilities will pay Nkr50/60.

There are also numerous private hikers' huts and lodges peppered around most mountain areas, but not all are open to the public. Some offer DNT members a discount.

SLEEPING PRICE RANGES

The following price ranges relate to a double room with private bathroom in high season and, unless stated otherwise, include breakfast:

€ less than Nkr750

€€ Nkr750-1400

€€€ more than Nkr1400

UNSTAFFED DNT HUTS

All unstaffed huts offer cooking facilities, but in most places you must have your own sleeping bag or hostel-style sleeping sheet.

For unstaffed huts, you must pick up keys (Nkr150 to Nkr200 deposit) in advance from a DNT office or a staffed hut. To pay, fill out a Once-Only Authorisation slip and leave either cash or a valid credit-card number in the box provided. There are two classes of unstaffed huts. Self-service chalets are stocked with blankets and pillows and have wood stoves, firewood, gas cookers and a wide range of tinned or freeze-dried food supplies for sale (on the honour system). At other unstaffed huts, users must carry in their own food. In unstaffed huts, DNT members/nonmembers pay Nkr220/325 for a bed.

STAFFED DNT HUTS

At staffed huts, which are concentrated in the south, you can simply turn up and pay your fees. In compliance with international mountain hospitality, no one is turned away, even if there's only floor space left; DNT members over 50 years of age are guaranteed a bed, even if it means displacing a younger hiker! Huts tend to be packed at Easter and are consistently busy throughout summer.

PRACTICALITIES

⇒ **Currency** Norwegian kroner (Nkr)

⇒ **Weights & Measures** Metric. Watch out for the use of *mil* (mile), which is a Norwegian mile (10km).

⇒ **Newspapers & Magazines** The most respected Norwegian-language daily is **Aftenposten** (www.aftenposten.no), while **VG** (www.vg.no) and **Dagbladet** (www.dagbladet. no) are other national mass-circulation dailies. **Morgenbladet** (www.morgenbladet. no) is a Norwegian-language weekly, while **The Norway Post** (www.norwaypost.no) is a good source of news in English, although the print version is not widely available. Major international newspapers and magazines are available a day after publication in cities.

⇒ **Smoking** Forbidden in enclosed public spaces, including hotels, restaurants and bars.

⇒ **TV & Radio** Government-run NRK (one TV and four radio channels) competes with TV2 and TV Norge networks and satellite broadcasts of TV3. Foreign-language programs are subtitled. Hotels often have cable TV.

⇒ **DVD** Norway uses the PAL (Region 2) DVD system.

Staffed lodges don't normally have cooking facilities for guests, but a self-service section with cooking facilities is available at some lodges when they are unstaffed. Sleeping sheets are often sold or included in the price at staffed huts.

For the full range of options and prices at staffed huts, see the DNT website.

Guesthouses & Pensions

Many towns have *pensjonat* (pensions) and *gjestehus* (guesthouses) and some, especially the latter, are family-run and offer a far more intimate option than the hostel or hotel experience. Prices for a single/double with shared bathroom usually start at Nkr500/750 but can cost significantly more; linen and/or breakfast will only be included in the higher-priced places.

Hostels

In Norway, reasonably priced hostels (*vandrerhjem*) offer a dorm bed for the night, plus use of communal facilities that usually include a self-catering kitchen (you're advised to take your own cooking and eating utensils), internet access and bathrooms. Some also have single or double rooms with either shared or private bathroom facilities, but these often represent poor value.

While some hostels have quite comfortable lodge-style facilities and are open year-round, a few are used for school accommodation and others are the cheaper wing of a hotel; occasionally prices work out to be more expensive than a cabin or budget hotel. In most hostels, guests must still bring their own sleeping sheet and pillowcase, although most hire sleeping sheets for a one-off fee (starting from Nkr50) regardless of the number of nights.

Most hostels have two- to six-bed rooms, and beds cost from Nkr200 to Nkr400. The higher-priced hostels usually include a buffet breakfast, while other places may charge from Nkr50 to Nkr125 for breakfast. Some also provide a good-value evening meal for around Nkr125.

A welcome recent addition to the budget end of the market are chains such as Citybox, Smarthotels and Basic Hotels. These hostel-hotel hybrids are slick and excellent value, but you'll only find them in larger cities.

Several hostel guides are available, including HI's annually updated Europe guide.

Hostelling International (HI; www.hihostels.com) Although not all Norwegian hostels belong to the Hostelling International network, many do. HI members pay 15% less than nonmembers. Check the HI website to find its office in your home country so that you can join and qualify for members' prices in Norway.

Norske Vandrerhjem (☎23 12 45 10; www.hihostels. no) The Norwegian hostelling association, Norske Vandrerhjem is HI-affiliated and publishes the free *Hostels in Norway*, which contains a full listing of hostels and updated prices for the 77 hostels on its books; it's available from hostels and some tourist offices.

Hotels

Norway's hotels are generally modern and excellent, although those with any character are pretty thin on the ground. Comfortable nationwide chain hotels are the norm and the rooms can all start to look the same after a while, whether you're sleeping in Oslo or Kirkenes. The advantage of these chains or hotel networks, however, is that some offer hotel passes, which can entitle you to a free night if you use the chain enough times; some passes only operate in summer.

Best Western (www.best-western.no) The Best Western Rewards system operates at all Best Western hotels in Norway and beyond, in addition to occasional summer deals.

Nordic Choice Hotels (www.nordicchoicehotels.no) Covering Clarion, Quality and Comfort Hotels, with the Nordic Choice Club you can earn free nights if you stay in enough member hotels. In some Comfort Hotels, you get a light evening buffet included in the price. Watch out for their new upmarket, boutique brand, the Clarion Collection.

De Historiske (☑55 31 67 60; www.dehistoriske.no) Although it's less a chain than a collection of historic hotels and there are no membership options, it's always worth checking out the worthwhile De Historiske network, which links Norway's most historic old hotels and restaurants. The quality on offer is consistently high, every hotel is architecturally distinguished and many are family-run. Admittedly, they can be expensive, but they are almost always worth it.

Fjord Pass (www.fjordpass. no; 2 adults & unlimited children under 15yr Nkr150) The Fjord Pass enables discounts at 120 hotels, guesthouses, cabins and apartments year-round; no free nights, but the discounts on nightly rates are considerable. Works best if you book in advance through its website, rather than simply turning up and hoping for a discount.

Scandic Hotels (Rica Hotels; www.scandichotels.no) Scandic recently bought the Rica brand. The process of rebranding will take some time, but expect the Rica name to disappear. The shape of the new rewards program is still being considered.

Thon Hotels (www.thonhotels.com) This program has free membership that qualifies you for discounts or free nights.

Private Homes

Tourist offices in some towns have lists of private rooms, which are among the cheapest places to stay. In some cases, they allow you to stay with a Norwegian family. Prices vary, but you'll rarely have to pay more than Nkr400/500 for a single/double; breakfast isn't normally included. Showers sometimes cost Nkr10 to Nkr20 extra.

Along highways, you'll occasionally see *rom* signs, indicating informal accommodation typically costing from Nkr250 to Nkr450 per room (without breakfast); those who bring their own sheets or sleeping bags may get a discount.

Summer Homes & Cabins

Most tourist offices in popular holiday areas keep lists of private huts, cabins and summer homes that are rented out to holidaymakers when the owners aren't using them; these arrangements sometimes also apply in the ski season. The price for a week's rental starts from around Nkr1500 for a simple place in the off-season to around Nkr15,000 for the most elaborate chalet in midsummer. Most cabins sleep at least four people, and some accommodate as many as 12; if you have a group, it can be an economical option. Advance booking is normally required, and you'll probably have to pay a deposit of around Nkr750 or 20% of the total fee, whichever is less.

Dansommer (☑in Denmark 39 14 33 00; www.dansommer.com) Privately run Danish agency that act as a clearing house for hundreds of self-catering cabins and chalets in Norway and elsewhere in Scandinavia.

Customs Regulations

Alcohol and tobacco are extremely expensive in Norway. To at least get you started, it's worth importing your duty-free allotment: 1L of spirits and 1L of wine (or 2L of wine), plus 2L of beer per person. Note that drinks with an alcohol content of over 60% may be treated as narcotics! You're also allowed to import 200 cigarettes duty-free. Importation of fresh food and controlled drugs is prohibited.

Svalbard is a duty-free zone and many items are considerably cheaper there than in mainland Norway as they're subject to neither VAT nor customs duties.

Discount Cards

A Hostelling International membership card will get you a 15% discount at youth hostels.

Senior Cards

Honnør (senior) discounts are available to those aged 67 years or over for admission to museums, public pools, transport etc. The discounted price usually amounts to 75% of the full price. You don't require a special card, but those who look particularly youthful may, apart from enjoying the compliment, need proof of their age to qualify.

Student Cards

Discounts (usually 75% of the normal fee) are often available for students. You will need some kind of identification (eg an International Student Identity Card; www.isic.org) to prove student status. Some travellers have reported being refused access with their normal university cards (unless it's from a Norwegian university), so the ISIC card is a good investment. It can provide discounts on many forms of transport (including airlines, international ferries and local public transport) and in some internet cafes, reduced or free admission to museums and sights, and cheap meals in some student restaurants.

Electricity

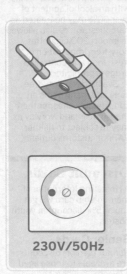

230V/50Hz

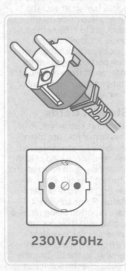

230V/50Hz

Embassies & Consulates

Australian Embassy The nearest Australian embassy is in Copenhagen; contact the UK embassy in an emergency.

Canadian Embassy (☑22 99 53 00; norway.gc.ca; 4th fl, Wergelandsveien 7, Oslo)

Danish Embassy (☑22 54 08 00; www.amboslo.um.dk; Olav Kyrres gate 7, Oslo)

Finnish Embassy (☑22 12 49 00; www.finland.no; Thomas Heftyes gate 1, Oslo)

French Embassy (☑22 28 46 00; www.ambafrance-no. org; Drammensveien 69, Oslo)

German Embassy (☑22 27 54 00; www.oslo.diplo.de; Oscars gate 45, Oslo)

Irish Embassy (☑22 01 72 00; www.embassyofireland.no; Haakon VII's gate 1, Oslo)

Japanese Embassy (☑22 01 29 00; www.no.emb-japan. go.jp; Haakon VII's gate 9, Oslo)

Netherlands Embassy (☑23 33 36 00; www.netherlands-embassy.no; Oscars gate 29, Oslo)

New Zealand Embassy The UK embassy handles consular affairs; the nearest New Zealand embassy is in The Hague.

Russian Embassy (☑22 55 32 78; www.norway.mid.ru; Drammensveien 74, Oslo)

Swedish Embassy (☑24 11 42 00; www.sverigesambassad. no; Nobelsgata 16, Oslo)

UK Embassy (☑23 13 27 00; www.gov.uk/government/ world/norway; Thomas Heftyes gate 8, Oslo)

US Embassy (☑22 44 85 40; www.usa.no; Henrik Ibsens gate 48, Oslo) A new embassy is being built in the Oslo district of Huseby. Check the website for updates.

Food

Although lunch is usually served from noon to 3pm and dinner from 6pm to 11pm, many restaurants (and their kitchens) remain open from noon to 11pm.

This book classifies eating venues into the following budget ranges. Prices refer to a standard main course.

€ less than Nkr125
€€ Nkr125-200
€€€ >more than Nkr200
For information on Norway's cuisine, see p400.

Gay & Lesbian Travellers

Norwegians are generally tolerant of alternative lifestyles. Homosexuality has been legal in Norway since 1973 and on 1 January 2009 Norway became the sixth country in the world to legalise same-sex marriage when its parliament passed a gender-neutral marriage law. The new law granted full rights to church weddings, adoption and artificial insemination to married couples regardless of their sexual orientation.

All of that said, public displays of affection are not common practice, except perhaps in some areas of Oslo. Oslo is generally the easiest place to be gay in Norway, although even here there have been occasional recent attacks on gay couples holding hands, especially in the central-eastern areas of the capital. You're most likely to encounter difficulties wherever conservative religious views predominate, whether among newly arrived Muslim immigrant communities or devoutly Lutheran communities in rural areas.

Oslo has the liveliest gay scene, and it's worth stopping by **Use-It** (Map p56; ☑24 14 98 20; www.use-it.no; Møllergata 3, Oslo; ◔10am-6pm Mon-Fri, noon-5pm Sat Jul-early Aug, 11am-5pm Mon-Fri, noon-5pm Sat rest of year), where you can pick up its excellent annual *Streetwise* booklet, which has a 'Gay Guide' section.

Organisations & Websites

Global Gayz (www. globalgayz.com) The Norway page has some interesting background information and practical information.

Landsforeningen for Lesbisk og Homofil Frigjøring (LLH; ☑23 10 39 39; www.llh. no; Valkyriegaten 15, Oslo) The Norwegian National Association of Lesbian and Gay Liberation; website only in Norwegian.

Night Tours (www.nighttours. com/oslo) A gay guide to the Oslo night.

Visit Oslo (www.visitoslo. com) Click on 'Gay Olso' for some useful links.

Health

Norway is, in general, a very healthy place and no special precautions are necessary when visiting. The biggest risks are likely to be viral infections in winter, sunburn and insect bites in summer, and foot blisters from too much hiking.

Availability & Cost of Health Care

If you do fall ill while in Norway, you will be very well looked after as health care is excellent.

Most medications are available, but they may go by a different name than at home, so be sure to have the generic name, as well as the brand name. If carrying syringes or needles, be sure to have a physician's letter documenting their medical necessity. For minor illnesses, pharmacists can dispense valuable advice and over-the-counter medication.

Like almost everything else, medical care can be prohibitively expensive in Norway and insurance is a must.

Water

Tap water is always safe to drink in Norway, but it's wise to beware of drinking from streams, as even the clearest and most inviting water may harbour giardia and other parasites. For extended hikes where you must rely on natural water sources, the sim-

plest way of purifying water is to boil it thoroughly; at high altitude water boils at a lower temperature, so germs are less likely to be killed. Boil it for longer in these environments (up to 10 minutes).

If you cannot boil water, it should be treated chemically. Chlorine tablets (Puritabs, Steritabs or other brands) will kill many pathogens, but not giardia and amoebic cysts. Iodine is more effective in purifying water and is available in tablet form (such as Potable Aqua). Too much iodine can be harmful.

Insurance

A travel-insurance policy to cover theft, loss, medical problems and cancellation or delays to your travel arrangements (due to illness, ticket loss, industrial action etc) is a good idea. Paying for your ticket with a credit card can often provide limited travel-accident insurance and you may be able to reclaim the payment if the operator doesn't deliver.

Note that some policies specifically exclude 'dangerous activities' such as motorcycling, skiing, mountaineering, snowmobiling or even hiking. Make sure the policy covers ambulances and an emergency flight home. A policy that pays doctors or hospitals directly may be preferable to one where you pay on the spot and claim later. If you have to claim later, make sure you keep all documentation.

In Norway, EU citizens may be required to pay a service fee for emergency medical treatment, but presentation of an E111 form will certainly expedite matters and minimise the amount of paperwork involved. Inquire about these at your national health service or travel agent well in advance.

Worldwide travel insurance is available at lonelyplanet.com/bookings. You can buy, extend and claim

online anytime – even if you're on the road.

Internet Access

Internet Cafes

With wi-fi widely available, good cybercafes that last the distance are increasingly hard to find; ask at the local tourist office. Prices per hour range from Nkr25 to Nkr75; students sometimes receive a discount.

Public Libraries & Tourist Offices

The scarcity of internet cafes is compensated for by having free internet access available in most municipal libraries (biblioteket). As it's a popular service, you may have to reserve a time slot earlier in the day; in busier places, you may be restricted to a half-hour slot. Internet access is also available at some tourist offices around the country; it's sometimes free but there's usually a small fee.

Wi-Fi

Wi-fi is widely available at most hotels, cafes and tourist offices, as well as some restaurants; it's generally (but not always) free and you may need to ask for a password. Connection speed often varies from room to room in hotels, so always ask when you check in. Airports have wi-fi but generally charge around Nkr60 for the first hour. In our reviews, hotels offering wi-fi are indicated with the 🛜 icon. Hotels offering public-access computer terminals are indicated with the @ icon.

Language Courses

Berlitz Language Services (☑23 00 33 60; www.berlitz. no; 7th fl, Akersgata 16, Oslo) Convenient location in the heart of town.

Folkeuniversitetet Oslo (☑22 47 60 00; www.fuoslo.no;

5th fl, Torggata 7, Oslo) Centrally located language school.

International Summer School, University of Oslo (✆22 85 63 85; www.uio.no/english/studies/summerschool; 6th fl, Gaustadalléen 25, Oslo) Northwest of the centre at the university.

Oslo Adult Education (Oslo Voksenopplæring;✆23 47 00 00; www.english.oslovo.no; Karoline Kristiansens vei 8, Oslo) Language school east of the city centre.

Maps

Most local tourist offices distribute user-friendly and free town maps.

Country Maps

Bilkart over Norge (1:1,000,000) by Nortrabooks is one of the best maps of Norway for general travellers. It includes useful topographic shading and depicts the entire country on one sheet. *Michelin Norway – 752* (1:1,250,000) is also good, although the last update was in January 2007 and the font size can be a problem.

Hiking Maps

Den Norske Turistforening (DNT, Norwegian Mountain Touring Club; Map p56; www.turistforeningen.no; Storget 3; ⊙10am-5pm Mon-Wed & Fri, to 6pm Thu, to 3pm Sat) is the best source of hiking maps. Hikers can pick up topographic sheets at any DNT office, although the offices in larger cities have a wider selection beyond the local area. National-park centres and nearby tourist offices are good sources for the excellent Turkart or Statens Kartverk (www.statkart.no) hiking maps. Statens Kartverk, Norway's official mapping authority, covers the country in 21 sheets at a scale of 1:250,000.

Road Maps

The best road maps are the Cappelens series, which are sold in Norwegian bookshops. There are three maps at 1:335,000 scale: *No 1 Sør-Norge Sør, No 2 Sør-Norge Nord* and *No 3 Møre og Trøndelag*. Northern Norway is covered in two sheets at 1:400,000 scale: *No 4 Nordland og Sør-Troms* and *No 5 Troms og Finnmark*. The *Veiatlas Norge* (*Norwegian Road Atlas*), published by Statens Kartverk, is revised every two years.

Money

The most convenient way to bring your money is in the form of a debit or credit card, with some extra cash for use in case of an emergency.

ATMs

'Mini-Banks' (the Norwegian name for ATMs) are widespread and most accept major credit cards as well as Cirrus, Visa Electron and/or Plus bank cards, although check with your bank before leaving about which banks charge the lowest withdrawal fees.

Changing Money

Don't assume that all banks will change money and in some places you may need to shop around to find one that does. Rates at post offices and tourist offices are generally poorer than at banks, but can be convenient for small amounts outside banking hours.

Credit & Debit Cards

Visa, Eurocard, MasterCard, Diners Club and American Express cards are widely accepted throughout Norway. If your card is lost or stolen in Norway, report it immediately.

American Express (✆22 96 08 00)

Diners Club (✆21 01 53 00)

MasterCard (✆21 01 52 22, 80 01 26 97)

Visa (✆80 01 20 52)

Currency

The Norwegian krone is most often represented either as Nkr (preceding the number), NOK (preceding the number) or simply kr (following the amount). One Norwegian krone (Nkr1) equals 100 øre.

Taxes & Refunds

For goods that cost more than Nkr315 (Nkr290 for food items) at shops displaying the 'Tax Free' logo, you're entitled to a 'Refund Cheque' for the 25% MVA (the equivalent of value-added or sales tax) or 15% for food items. At the point of sale, you fill out the cheque with your name, address and passport number, and then, at your departure point from the country, you present your sealed goods, passport and Refund Cheque to collect the refund; ferry passengers normally collect their refund from the purser during limited hours once the boat has sailed.

For more information, pick up the *How to Shop Tax Free* brochure from most tourist offices and some tourist shops, which explains the procedure and lists border crossings at which refunds can be collected, or visit www.globalblue.com/destinations/norway.

Tipping

Service charges and tips are included in restaurant bills and taxi fares; tipping on a North American scale is not expected. It is, however, customary to round up the bill. If the service has been particularly helpful, feel free to leave more.

Travellers Cheques

Post offices, some tourist offices and banks accept all brands of travellers cheques, which command a better exchange rate than cash by about 2% (but this is often cancelled out by commission fees).

Opening Hours

These standard opening hours are for high season (mid-June to mid-September) and tend to decrease outside that time. Many businesses close completely over Christmas and Easter; this is particularly the case outside larger cities.

Banks 8.15am to 3pm Monday to Wednesday and Friday, 8.15am to 5pm Thursday

Central Post Offices 8am to 8pm Monday to Friday, 9am to 6pm Saturday; otherwise 9am to 5pm Monday to Friday, 10am to 2pm Saturday

Restaurants noon to 3pm and 6pm to 11pm

Shops 10am to 5pm Monday to Wednesday and Friday, 10am to 7pm Thursday, 10am to 2pm Saturday

Supermarkets 9am to 9pm Monday to Friday, 9am to 6pm Saturday

Photography

Although few Norwegians are camera-shy, you should always ask permission before taking a photo in Sami areas, where you may encounter some camera sensitivity, as well as in villages where whaling is a mainstay (people may be concerned that the photos will be used against them in the media).

For comprehensive advice on taking terrific photos, check out Lonely Planet's Guide to Travel Photography by Richard I'Anson.

Public Holidays

New Year's Day (Nyttårsdag) 1 January

Maundy Thursday (Skjærtorsdag) March/April

Good Friday (Langfredag) March/April

Easter Monday (Annen Påskedag) March/April

Labour Day (Første Mai, Arbeidetsdag) 1 May

Constitution Day (Nasjonaldag) 17 May

Ascension Day (Kristi Himmelfartsdag) May/June, 40th day after Easter

Whit Monday (Annen Pinsedag) May/June, 8th Monday after Easter

Christmas Day (Første Juledag) 25 December

Boxing Day (Annen Juledag) 26 December

Safe Travel

Your personal belongings are safer in Norway than in most people's home countries, and the cities – even east Oslo, which has a relatively poor reputation – are reasonably safe at all hours of the night. However, don't become blasé about security: be careful near the nightclubs in the Rosenkrantz gate area of Oslo and beware of pickpockets around the Torget area of Bergen. Normally, the greatest nuisance value will come from drug addicts, drunks and/or beggars (mainly in Oslo) who can spot a naive tourist a block away. Although dope may be readily available in places, it isn't legal.

If you're planning on hiking out into the Norwegian wilds, remember that Norway's weather can, even in summer, change rapidly.

Telephone

Mobile Phones

There aren't too many places where you can't get GSM mobile (cell) access; there's coverage in close to 90% of the country. This doesn't, of course, apply to wilderness areas and the hiking trails of most national parks.

If you want to use your home-country mobile in Norway, always check with your carrier about the cost of roaming charges to avoid a nasty surprise when your next bill arrives; in theory, if you're using a phone from an EU country, there should be no roaming charges, but check first.

If you wish to use your mobile, but with a Norwegian SIM card, check with your network before leaving home that this is possible, as some phones sold by some networks are blocked from using other carriers. If your phone will accept a foreign SIM card, these can be purchased from any 7-Eleven store and some Narvesen kiosks. However, as the connection instructions are entirely in Norwegian, you're better off purchasing the card from any Telehuset outlet, where they'll help you connect on the spot. SIM cards start from Nkr200, which includes Nkr100 worth of calls.

There are three main service providers.

NetCom (www.netcom. no) Norway's second-largest operator.

Mobile Norway (www. mobilenorway.no) Also known as Network Norway.

Telenor Mobil (www.telenor. com) The largest mobile-service provider.

Phone Codes

All Norwegian phone numbers have eight digits. Numbers starting with ☎800 usually indicate a toll-free number, while those beginning with ☎9 are mobile (cell) phone numbers. There are no local area codes (these are incorporated into listed numbers).

Directory assistance (☎180; calls cost Nkr9 per minute

International access code (☎00

Norway country code (☎47

Phonecards

International calls can be prohibitively expensive. Although there are Telekort (Telenor phonecards), they're increasingly hard to find (ask for the cards at post offices and Narvesen kiosks), as are card and coin phones. Your best bet is to go for one of the phonecards issued by private companies. Usually costing Nkr100, they allow you to make over six hours' worth of calls using a scratch PIN number on the back and a local access number. The only drawback is that they, too, can be difficult to find – some kiosks sell them, but the easiest place to look is an 'ethnic' grocery store.

For international calls, internet-connected calls (eg www.skype.com) are the way to go; unfortunately few internet cafes are Skype-enabled. You cannot make phone calls from municipal library computers.

Time

Note that when telling the time, Norwegians use 'half' as signifying *half before* rather than half past. Always double-check unless you want to be an hour late! Although the 24-hour clock is used in some official situations, you'll find people generally use the 12-hour clock in everyday conversation.

Norway shares the same time zone as most of Western Europe (GMT/UTC plus one hour during winter, and GMT/UTC plus two hours during the daylight-saving period). Daylight saving starts on the last Sunday in March and finishes on the last Sunday in October.

Note the following time differences:

Australia During the Australian winter (Norwegian summer), subtract eight hours from Australian Eastern Standard Time to get Norwegian time; during the Australian summer, subtract 10 hours.

Finland One hour ahead of Norway.

Russia One hour ahead of Norway.

Sweden & Denmark Same time as Norway.

UK & Ireland One hour behind Norway.

USA Norwegian time is USA Eastern Time plus six hours and USA Pacific Time plus nine hours.

Toilets

Most towns (and many roadside stops) have public facilities. However, at some shopping malls, train stations, bus terminals and even some (but not many) restaurants, you may have to pay up to Nkr10.

Tourist Information

It's impossible to speak highly enough of tourist offices in Norway. Most serve as one-stop clearing houses for general information and bookings for accommodation and activities. Nearly every city and town has its own tourist office, and most tourist offices in reasonably sized towns or major tourist areas publish comprehensive booklets giving the complete, up-to-date low-down on their town.

Offices in smaller towns may be open only during peak summer months, while in cities they're open year-round, but with shorter hours in the off-season.

Tourist offices operate under a variety of names – *turistkontor* and *reiseliv* are among the most common – but all have the information symbol prominently displayed outside and are easy to identify and find.

Norwegian Tourist Board (Norges Turistråd; ☎22 00 25 00; www.visitnorway.com; PO Box 448, Sentrum, N-0158 Oslo) For general info on travelling in Norway.

Travellers with Disabilities

Norway is generally well set up for travellers with disabilities and all newly constructed public buildings are required by law to have wheelchair access. That said, like in most countries, the situation remains a work-in-progress. As a result, anyone with special needs should plan ahead.

Most Norwegian tourist offices carry lists of wheelchair-accessible hotels and hostels, but your best bet is to contact the Norwegian Association for the Disabled. Nearly all street crossings are equipped with either a ramp or a very low kerb (curb), and crossing signals produce an audible signal – longer beeps when it's safe to cross and shorter beeps when the signal is about to change.

Most (but not all) trains have carriages with space for wheelchair users and many public buildings have wheelchair-accessible toilets.

Organisations & Tours

Access-able Travel Source (www.access-able. com) US information portal with 25 listings for Norway.

Accessible Travel & Leisure (☑01452-729739; www. accessibletravel.co.uk; Avionics House, Newhaven Rd, Quedgeley, Gloucester GL2 2SN, UK) Claims to be the biggest UK travel agent dealing with travel for those with disabilities; encourages independent travel.

Norwegian Association for the Disabled (Norges Handikapforbund; Map p56; ☑24 10 24 00; www.nhf.no; Schweigaards gate 12, Grønland, Oslo) For information on disabled travel and sites of special interest to disabled travellers in Norway.

Society for Accessible Travel & Hospitality (☑212-447 7284; www.sath. org; 347 Fifth Ave, Ste 605, New York, NY 10016, USA) Provides advice on how to travel with a wheelchair, kidney disease, sight impairment or deafness.

Visas

Norway is one of 26 member countries of the Schengen Convention, under which 22 EU countries (all but Bulgaria, Cyprus, Ireland, Romania and the UK) plus Iceland, Norway, Liechtenstein and Switzerland have abolished checks at common borders. The process towards integrating Bulgaria, Cyprus and Romania has slowed but they may join sometime in the not-too-distant future.

The visa situation for entering Norway is as follows:

Citizens of Denmark, Finland, Iceland and Sweden No visa or passport required.

Citizens or residents of other EU & Schengen countries No visa required.

Citizens or residents of Australia, Canada, Israel, Japan, New Zealand and the USA No visa required for tourist visits of up to 90 days.

Other countries Check with a Norwegian embassy or consulate.

To work or study in Norway A special visa may be required – contact a Norwegian embassy or consulate before travel.

Women Travellers

Women travellers will have few worries in Norway, and sober Norwegian men are normally the very picture of decorum. While alcohol-impaired men may become tiresome or obnoxious, they're probably no different from the same breed you'll encounter in your home country. Some of the oil towns (such as Stavanger, Haugesund and Kristiansund) can be male-dominated and may feel slightly intimidating for first-time female travellers in some areas, particularly late at night.

Journeywoman (www. journeywoman.com) Of the general websites dedicated to women travellers, Journeywoman is outstanding.

Krisesenter (☑90 57 91 18, 23 01 03 00; www.krisesenter. com) Women who have been attacked or abused can contact the Krisesenter in Oslo or dial ☑112 nationwide.

Work

In order to work in Norway, knowledge of basic Norwegian is required at the very least. As a member of the European Economic Area (EEA), Norway grants citizens of other EEA countries the right to look for work for a three-month period without obtaining a permit; those who find work have the right to remain in Norway for the duration of their employment. For other foreigners, it's very difficult and an application for a work permit must be made through the Norwegian embassy or consulate in your home country before entering Norway.

In Oslo, **Use-It** (Map p56; ☑24 14 98 20; www.use-it.no; Møllergata 3, Oslo; ◷10am-6pm Mon-Fri, noon-5pm Sat Jul-early Aug, 11am-5pm Mon-Fri, noon-5pm Sat rest of year) is a useful resource.

Norwegian Labour & Welfare Organisation (☑55 55 33 33, 80 03 31 66; www. nav.no) For help with looking for work, the best places to start are the Norwegian Labour & Welfare Organisation, which produces extensive online information for free.

Transport

GETTING THERE & AWAY

Norway is well linked to other European countries by air. There are also regular bus and rail services to Norway from neighbouring Sweden and Finland (from where there are connections further afield to Europe), with less regular (and more complicated) services to/from Russia. Regular car and passenger ferries also connect southern Norwegian ports with Denmark, Sweden and Germany.

Flights, cars and tours can be booked online at www.lonelyplanet.com/bookings.

Entering Norway

Crossing most borders into Norway is usually hassle-free. That's particularly the case if you're arriving by road where, in some cases, you may not even realise that you've crossed the border.

If you're arriving in Norway from a non-Schengen or non-EU country, expect your papers to be checked carefully. If you're from a non-Western country, expect that you and your baggage will come under greater scrutiny than other travellers at airports and some of the staffed border crossings; this also applies for all travellers crossing by land into Norway from Russia.

Passport

All travellers – other than citizens of Denmark, Iceland, Sweden and Finland – require a valid passport to enter Norway.

Air

Airports & Airlines

For a full list of Norwegian airports, visit www.avinor.no; the page for each airport has comprehensive information.

The main international Norwegian airports are Gardermoen (Oslo), Flesland (Bergen), Sola (Stavanger), Tromsø, Værnes (Trondheim), Vigra (Ålesund), Karmøy (Haugesund), Kjevik (Kristiansand) and Torp (Sandefjord).

Dozens of international airlines fly to/from Norwegian airports. There are direct flights to Norway from East Coast USA and the UK. If coming from Australia or New Zealand, you'll need to connect via an airport in Asia, the Middle East or Europe.

Norwegian (www.norwegian. com) Low-cost airline with an extensive and growing domestic and international network.

SAS (www.sas.no) The largest international network of Norway's carriers.

Land

Norway shares land borders with Sweden, Finland and Russia.

Train travel is possible between Oslo and Stockholm, Gothenburg, Malmö and

---

CLIMATE CHANGE & TRAVEL

Every form of transport that relies on carbon-based fuel generates CO_2, the main cause of human-induced climate change. Modern travel is dependent on aeroplanes, which might use less fuel per kilometre per person than most cars but travel much greater distances. The altitude at which aircraft emit gases (including CO_2) and particles also contributes to their climate change impact. Many websites offer 'carbon calculators' that allow people to estimate the carbon emissions generated by their journey and, for those who wish to do so, to offset the impact of the greenhouse gases emitted with contributions to portfolios of climate-friendly initiatives throughout the world. Lonely Planet offsets the carbon footprint of all staff and author travel.

Hamburg, with less frequent services to northern and central Swedish cities from Narvik and Trondheim.

Eurolines (www.eurolines.com) The main operator for many international bus services to/from Norway is Eurolines, which acts as a feeder for national companies.

Nor-Way Bussekspress (www.nor-way.com) Nor-Way Bussekspress has a reasonable range of international routes.

Finland
BUS
Eskelisen Lapin Linjat (☑in Finland 016-342 2160; www.eskelisen-lapinlinjat.com) Most cross-border services between northern Norway and northern Finland are operated by the Finnish company Eskelisen Lapin Linjat.

CAR & MOTORCYCLE
The E8 highway extends from Tornio, in Finland, to Tromsø; secondary highways connect Finland with the northern Sami towns of Karasjok and Kautokeino. Regular buses serve all three routes.

Russia
Russia has a short border with Norway and buses run twice daily between Kirkenes in Norway and Murmansk in Russia (one way/return Nkr400/Nkr675, five hours). Once in Murmansk, trains connect to St Petersburg and the rest of the Russian rail network.

To cross the border, you'll need a Russian visa, which must usually be applied for and issued in your country of residence.

Sweden
BUS
Swebus Express (☑in Sweden 0771-21 82 18; www.swebus.se) has the largest (and cheapest) buses between Oslo and Swedish cities.

Among the numerous cross-border services along the long land frontier between Sweden and Norway, there are twice-daily services between Narvik and Riksgränsen (one hour), on the border, and Kiruna (three hours).

There are also less frequent services between Bodø and Skellefteå, and along the Blå Vägen (Blue Highway), between Mo i Rana and Umeå.

TRAIN
Rail services between Sweden and Norway are operated by **Norges Statsbaner** (Norwegian State Railways; NSB; ☑81 50 08 88; www.nsb.no) or **Swedish Railways** (SJ; ☑in Sweden 0771-75 75 99; www.sj.se).

It's worth noting that some of the Stockholm–Oslo services require a change of train in the Swedish city of Karlstad.

It's also possible to travel from Trondheim to Sweden via Storlien and Östersund, although you'll need to change trains at the border.

Sea
Ferry connections are possible between Norway and Denmark, Germany, Iceland, the Faroe Islands and Sweden; sadly the ferry services between the UK and Norwegian ports have been discontinued. Most ferry operators offer package deals that include taking a car and passengers, and most lines offer substantial discounts for seniors, students and children. Taking a bicycle incurs a small extra fee.

If you're travelling by international ferry and plan on drinking at all while in Norway, consider picking up your maximum duty-free alcohol allowance on the boat.

FINLAND & SWEDEN TO NORWAY BUSES
Options for bus travel between Finland and Norway include the following (some in summer only).

FROM	TO	FARE (€)	DURATION (HR)
Rovaniemi	Alta	82	10
Rovaniemi	Karasjok	66	7
Rovaniemi	Tromsø (Jun-Sep only)	93	8-10
Rovaniemi	Nordkapp	123	12
Saariselkä	Kirkenes	42	3

Buses operate from the following Swedish destinations to Oslo.

FROM	FARE (SKR)	DURATION (HR)	FREQUENCY (PER DAY)
Gothenburg (Göteborg)	from 189	3¾	5-10
Malmö	from 339	8	4-7
Stockholm	from 329	8-13	5

Denmark

The following companies operate ferries between Norway and Denmark.

Color Line (www.colorline. com) Sails from Hirtshals to Kristiansand (once or twice daily; 3¼ hours) and Larvik (once or twice daily; 3¾ hours).

DFDS Seaways (www. dfdsseaways.com) Copenhagen to Oslo (once daily; 17 hours).

Fjord Line (✆in Denmark 97 96 30 00, in Norway 51 46 40 99; www.fjordline.com) Hirtshals to Kristiansand, Bergen, Stavanger and Langesund (Oslo).

Stena Line (✆in Norway 02010; www.stenaline.no) Fredrikshavn to/from Oslo.

Germany & Sweden

Color Line (✆in Germany 0431-7300 300, in Norway 81 00 08 11, in Sweden 0526-62000; www.colorline.com) connects Norway with Germany and Sweden. Check the website for different fare and accommodation types. From Oslo to Kiel, Germany, there are seven weekly departures (from €279, 20 hours), while ferries from Sandefjord to Strömstad in Sweden depart up to 20 times weekly (from €4, 2½ hours).

Tours

Given the expenses involved in Norwegian travel, it may be worth looking into an organised tour.

Some of the more reputable international operators include the following:

Bentours International (www.bentours.com.au) One of the few Australian travel agencies specialising in Scandinavia, with organised tours and options for independent travellers.

Brekke Tours (www.brekketours.com) US company with excellent escorted and independent tours.

SWEDEN–NORWAY TRAINS

Train services between Sweden and Norway include the following. Most require a change en route.

FROM	TO	FARE	DURATION (HR)	FREQUENCY (PER DAY)	OPERATOR
Gothenburg (Göteborg)	Oslo	from Nkr204/ SEK221	4-6	2-4	Norwegian Railways & Swedish Railways
Malmö	Oslo	from Skr530	7½-9	3-6	Swedish Railways
Stockholm	Oslo	from Skr341	6-7½	4	Swedish Railways
Stockholm	Narvik	from Skr916	20-22	0-3	Swedish Railways

DENMARK–NORWAY FERRIES

Ferry services between Denmark and Norway include the following. Fares and weekly departures are for high season (mid-June to mid-August); at other times, fares can be half the high-season price but departures are much less frequent. Depending on the route, there are a range of prices and accommodation types and, in most cases, you can transport your car.

FROM	TO	FARE PER PERSON (€)	DURATION (HR)	WEEKLY DEPARTURES	FERRY OPERATOR
Copenhagen	Oslo	from 99	16½	7	DFDS Seaways
Fredrikshavn	Oslo	from 31	12	7	Stena Line
Hirtshals	Bergen	from 26	19½	3	Fjord Line
Hirtshals	Kristiansand	from 18	2¼-3¼	up to 14	Color Line & Fjord Line
Hirtshals	Larvik	from 20	3¾	up to 14	Color Line
Hirtshals	Stavanger	from 20	12	4	Fjord Line

Norway Transport

Discover the World (www.discover-the-world.co.uk) UK operator formerly known as Arctic Experience, with a handful of winter and summer trips.

Grand Nord Grand Large (www.gngl.com) French company with cruises and hiking in Svalbard and Lofoten, among other destinations.

Nordic Experience (www.nordicexperience.co.uk) UK-based company with a wide range of well-run, year-round tours.

Scanam World Tours (www.scandinaviantravel.com) US operator with cruises and shorter upmarket tours.

Scantours (www.scantours.com) US company with an extensive range of short tours in Norway.

Taber Holidays (www.taber-hols.co.uk) Year-round tours from the UK.

GETTING AROUND

Norway has an extremely efficient public-transport system and its trains, buses and ferries are often timed to link with each other. The handy *NSB Togruter*, available free at most train stations, details rail timetables and includes information on connecting buses. Boat and bus departures vary with the season and the day (services on Saturday are particularly sparse, although less so in the summer high season), so pick up the latest *ruteplan* (timetable) from regional tourist offices.

Rail lines reach as far north as Bodø (you can also reach Narvik by rail from Sweden); further north you're limited to buses and ferries. A fine alternative to land travel is the Hurtigruten coastal ferry, which calls in at every sizeable port between Bergen and Kirkenes.

Air

Due to the time and distances involved in overland travel, even budget travellers may want to consider a segment or two by air. The major Norwegian domestic routes are quite competitive, meaning that it is possible (if you're flexible about departure dates and book early) to travel for little more than the equivalent train fare.

Keep an eye out for *minipris* return tickets, which can cost just 10% more than full-fare one-way tickets. In addition, spouses (including gay partners), children aged two to 15, travellers aged under 26, students and senior citizens over 67 years of age may be eligible for significant discounts on some routes – always ask.

Airlines in Norway

Three airlines fly domestic routes.

Norwegian (www.norwegian.com) Low-cost airline with an extensive and growing domestic network that now includes Longyearbyen (Svalbard).

SAS (www.sas.no) Large domestic network on mainland Norway, plus flights to Longyearbyen (Svalbard).

Widerøe (www.wideroe.no) A subsidiary of SAS with smaller planes and a handful of flights to smaller regional airports.

Bicycle

Given Norway's great distances, hilly terrain and narrow roads, only serious cyclists engage in extensive cycle touring, but those who do rave about the experience.

Assuming that you've steeled yourself for the challenge of ascending mountain after mountain, the long-distance cyclist's biggest headache will be tunnels, and there are thousands of them. Most of these, especially in the western fjords, are closed to nonmotorised traffic; in many (although not all) cases there are outdoor bike paths running parallel to the tunnels. If no such path exists, alternative routes may involve a few days' pedalling around a long fjord or over a high mountain pass.

Rural buses, express ferries and nonexpress trains carry bikes for various additional fees (around Nkr150), but express trains don't allow them at all and international trains treat them as excess baggage (Nkr300). Nor-Way Bussekspress charges a child's fare to transport a bicycle!

The Norwegian government takes cycling seriously enough to have developed an official **Cycling Strategy** (www.sykkelby.no), one of the primary goals of which is to increase cycling in larger Norwegian cities.

Hire

Some tourist offices, hostels and campsites rent out bicycles to guests, while bicycle shops *(sykkelbutikken)* are another good place to ask. Rental usually starts at around Nkr60 for an hour and is rarely more than Nkr350 per day, although the per-day price drops if you rent for a few days.

Boat

Norway's excellent system of ferries connects otherwise inaccessible, isolated communities with an extensive network of car ferries criss-crossing the fjords; express boats link the country's offshore islands to the mainland. Most ferries accommodate motor vehicles, but some express coastal services normally take only foot passengers and cyclists, as do the lake steamers.

Long queues and delays are possible at popular crossings in summer. They do, however, run deep into the night, especially in summer, and some run around the clock, although departures in the middle of the night are less frequent. Details on schedules and prices for vehicle ferries and lake steamers are provided in the timetables published by the Norwegian Tourist Board, or *Rutebok for Norge*. Tourist offices can also provide timetables for local ferries.

Canal Trips

Southern Norway's Telemark region has an extensive network of canals, rivers and lakes. There are regular ferry services or you can travel using your own boat.

Hurtigruten Coastal Ferry

For more than a century, Norway's legendary **Hurtigruten Coastal Ferry** (☑81 00 30 30; www.hurtigruten.com) has served as a lifeline linking coastal towns and villages and it's now one of the most pop-

---

THE HURTIGRUTEN – SLOW TRAVEL?

Although the Hurtigruten route is a marvellous journey, it's worth remembering that the ferry usually only stops in ports for 15 to 60 minutes and these times can be cut shorter if the ferry is behind schedule. As one traveller noted: 'There was only one stop which gave any opportunity to visit a town, Trondheim, but that was at 6am till 9.30am... The attitude of the ship was geared to meeting the route times.' It is important to keep in mind that even though the majority of passengers are tourists, the Hurtigruten is a regular ferry service not a tour.

ular ways to explore Norway. Year in, year out, one of 11 Hurtigruten ferries heads north from Bergen every night of the year, pulling into 35 ports on the way to Kirkenes, where it then turns around and heads back south.

The northward journey takes six days, the return journey takes 11 days and covers a distance of 5200km. In agreeable weather (which is by no means guaranteed) the fjord and mountain scenery along the way is nothing short of spectacular. Most of the ships are modern, others are showing their age; the oldest ship dates from 1956, but all were substantially remodelled in the 1990s.

Onboard, meals are served in the dining room and you can buy snacks and light meals in the cafeteria.

FARES

Long-haul Hurtigruten trips can be booked online, while all tickets can be purchased from most Norwegian travel agencies. The Hurtigruten website carries a full list of international sales agents. You can also purchase tickets through **Fjord Tours** (✆81 56 82 22; www.fjordtours.no).

Summer fares, which run from mid-April to mid-September, are considerably more expensive than winter prices. Prices depend on the type of cabin, which range from those without a view to supremely comfortable suites. Sample fares (per person in a twin-bedded cabin):

Bergen–Kirkenes–Bergen From €1652 (November to February) up to €4411 (June and July).

Bergen–Kirkenes €847 to €2528.

Kirkenes–Bergen €778 to €2483.

It is also possible, of course, to book shorter legs, although you'll probably need to do this once you're in Norway; the Hurtigruten website makes shorter-haul bookings near-on impossible. Cars can also be carried for an extra fee. Children aged four to 16, students, and seniors over the age of 67 all receive a 50% discount,

as do accompanying spouses and people aged 16 to 25. Ask also about cheaper, 21-day coastal passes if you're aged between 16 and 26 years.

EXCURSIONS

It's possible to break up the trip with shore excursions, especially if you're travelling the entire route. Each of the excursions, which are organised by the shipping company, may only be available on either northbound or southbound routes: there are 24 northbound and 15 southbound excursions, although many are seasonal. Options range from city tours, cruises deep into the interior fjord network, a bus up to Nordkapp, or a trip to the Russian border from Kirkenes, to activities such as dog-sledding and snowmobiling. The Hurtigruten website has a full list, with prices.

These excursions offer fairly good value but, in a few cases, you'll miss segments of the coastal scenery.

Bus

Buses on Norway's extensive long-distance bus network are comfortable and make a habit of running on time.

In addition to the larger networks, there are a number of independent long-distance companies that provide similar prices and levels of service. In northern Norway there are several Togbuss (train–bus) routes, while elsewhere there's a host of local buses, most of which are confined to a single *fylke* (county). Most local and some long-distance bus schedules are drastically reduced everywhere in Norway on Saturday, Sunday and in the low season (usually mid-August to mid-June).

To get a complete listing of bus timetables (and some prices) throughout the country, pick up a copy of the free *Rutehefte* from any reasonably sized bus station and some tourist offices. All bus stations and tourist offices have smaller timetables for the relevant routes passing through town.

Nor-Way Bussekspress

(www.nor-way.no) Nor-Way Bussekspress operates the largest network of express buses in Norway, with routes connecting most towns and cities.

Lavprisekspressen (www. lavprisekspressen.no) The cheapest buses are operated by Lavprisekspressen, which sells tickets over the internet. Its buses run along the coast between Oslo and Stavanger (via Kristiansand and most towns in between) and along two north–south corridors linking Oslo with Trondheim.

If you're online at the right moment, fares between Oslo and Trondheim can cost as little as Nkr99, and even its more expensive tickets are often significantly cheaper than those of its competitors.

Nettbuss (www.nettbuss. no) Nettbuss has a big network which includes the subsidiaries TIMEkspressen, Nettbuss Express and Bus4You (Bergen to Stavanger).

Costs & Reservations

Advance reservations are rarely required in Norway. That said, you're more likely to find cheaper fares the earlier you book. Buying tickets over the internet is usually the best way to get the cheapest fare (special *minipris* tickets are frequently offered in summer), and online bookings are often the only option for Lavprisekspressen buses. Tickets are also sold on most buses or in advance at the bus station, and fares are based on the distance travelled. Some bus companies quote bus fares excluding any ferry costs, so always check.

Many bus companies offer student, child, senior and family discounts of 25% to 50%, so it pays to ask when purchasing. Groups (including two people travelling together) may also be eligible for discounts.

In northern Norway, holders of InterRail and Eurail passes are also often eligible for discounts on some routes.

Car & Motorcycle

There are no special requirements for bringing your car to Norway. Main highways, such as the E16 from Oslo to Bergen and the entire E6 from Oslo to Kirkenes, are open year-round; the same cannot be said for smaller, often more scenic mountain roads that generally only open from June to September, snow conditions permitting.

Vegmeldingssentralen (📞175; www.vegvesen.no) Vegmeldingssentralen, Statens Vegvesen's 24-hour Road User Information Centre, provides up-to-date advice on road closures and conditions throughout the country.

Automobile Associations

Norges Automobil-Forbund (NAF;📞92 60 85 05; www.naf.no) By reciprocal agreement, members affiliated with Alliance Internationale de Tourisme (AIT) national automobile associations are eligible for 24-hour breakdown recovery assistance from the NAF. NAF patrols ply the main roads from mid-June to mid-August. Emergency phones can be found along motorways, in tunnels and at certain mountain passes. Ask your automobile association for a *lettre de recommendation* (letter of introduction), which entitles you to services offered by affiliated organisations in Norway, usually free of charge. These services may include touring maps and information, help with breakdowns, technical and legal advice etc.

Driving Licence

Short-term visitors may hire a car with only their home country's driving licence.

Fuel

Leaded and unleaded petrol and diesel are available at most petrol stations. Although prices fluctuate in keeping with international oil prices, prevailing prices at the time of research ranged from around Nkr13 per litre up to Nkr16. Diesel usually costs around Nkr1 per litre less. You can pay with major credit cards at most service stations.

In towns, petrol stations may be open until 10pm or midnight, but there are some 24-hour services. In rural areas, many stations close in the early evening and don't open at all on weekends. Some have unstaffed 24-hour automatic pumps operated with credit cards.

A word of warning for those driving a diesel vehicle: don't fill up at the pump labelled '*au-giftsfri diesel*', which is strictly for boats, tractors etc.

Hire

Norwegian car hire is costly and geared mainly to the business traveller. Walk-in rates for a compact car (with 200km per day included) typically approach Nkr1200 per day (including VAT, but insurance starts at Nkr75 per day extra), although per-day rates drop the longer you rent.

In summer always ask about special offers, as you may be able to get the smallest car (eg VW Polo) for a three- to five-day period for Nkr500 per day with 50km free, or Nkr600 per day with 200km free; each extra kilometre costs Nkr2.50, which quickly adds up. Some major rental agencies also offer weekend rates, which allow

---

NATIONAL TOURIST ROUTES

The Norwegian Public Roads Administration has 18 specially designated roads (covering 1850km) known as **National Tourist Routes** (www.nasjonaleturistveger.no/en), each one passing through signature Norwegian landscapes. Many already have regular lookouts and information points along these pre-existing routes, with more such facilities planned. Of most interest to visitors is the easy identification of some of Norway's most scenic routes, and help in planning and making the most of your trip along Norway's most picturesque drives.

Of the 18 roads, following are some of our favourites:

➡ Sognefjellet Rd (Rv55; p219)

➡ Rv86 and Rv862 on the island of Senja (p322)

➡ Kystriksveien Coastal Route between Stokkvågen, west of Mo i Rana, and Storvik, south of Bodø (p281)

➡ E10 through Lofoten (p289)

➡ West coast road through Vesterålen from Risøyhamn to Andenes (p306)

➡ Gamle Strynefjellsvegen between Grotli in Oppland and Videseter in Sogn og Fjordane (Rv258; p229)Trollstigen, south of Åndalsnes

➡ Two routes through Hardanger from Halne in the east to Steinsdalfossen (Rv7) and Jondal (Rv550) in the west (p183)

ROAD DISTANCES (KM)

	Ålesund	Alta	Bergen	Bodø	Florø	Hammerfest	Harstad	Kautokeino	Kirkenes	Kristiansand	Kristiansund	Lillehammer	Narvik	Odda	Oslo	Røros	Stavanger	Tromsø
Alta	1701																	
Bergen	384	2071																
Bodø	1008	814	1378															
Florø	201	1970	248	1277														
Hammerfest	1845	144	2215	959	2114													
Harstad	1186	557	1556	300	1455	701												
Kautokeino	1827	131	2197	941	2096	276	684											
Kirkenes	2215	519	2585	1329	2484	498	1072	451										
Kristiansand	811	2226	492	1533	652	2370	1711	2352	2740									
Kristiansund	142	1609	517	916	329	1753	1094	1735	2123	867								
Lillehammer	382	1756	439	1063	466	1900	1241	1882	2270	473	396							
Narvik	1190	511	1560	304	1459	655	119	637	1025	1715	1098	1245						
Odda	416	2064	159	1371	320	2208	1549	2190	2578	333	549	362	1553					
Oslo	533	1909	478	1216	512	2053	1394	2035	2423	322	562	168	1398	357				
Røros	401	1569	635	876	535	1713	1054	1695	2083	704	327	263	1058	624	382			
Stavanger	603	2251	179	1558	426	2395	1736	2377	2765	245	736	587	1740	187	453	836		
Tromsø	1440	290	1810	554	1709	435	296	417	805	1965	1348	1495	250	1803	1648	1308	1990	
Trondheim	287	1414	657	721	556	1558	899	1540	1928	812	195	342	903	650	495	155	837	1153

you to pick up a car after noon on Friday and keep it until 10am on Monday for around Nkr1200 – be sure it includes unlimited kilometres.

Auto Europe (www.auto-europe.com) Online rental agency which acts as a clearing house for cheap rates from major companies.

Autos Abroad (www.autos-abroad.com) UK-based clearing house for major companies.

Avis (☏81 56 30 44; www.avis.no)

Bislet Bilutleie (☏22 60 00 00; www.bislet.no)

Budget (☏81 56 06 00; www.budget.no)

Europcar (☏67 16 58 20; www.europcar.no)

Hertz (☏67 16 80 00; www.hertz.no)

Ideamerge (www.ideamerge.com) Information on the Renault company's car-leasing plan, motor-home rental and more.

Rent-a-Wreck (☏81 52 20 50; www.rent-a-wreck.no)

Sixt (☏81 52 24 66; www.sixt.no)

Insurance

Third-party car insurance (unlimited cover for personal injury and Nkr1,000,000 for property damage) is compulsory and, if you're bringing a vehicle from abroad, you'll have fewer headaches with an insurance company Green Card. Ensure that your vehicle is insured for ferry crossings.

If you're renting, it's worth paying extra for comprehensive insurance – in the case of even a small accident, the difference between having to pay Nkr1000 and Nkr10,000 is considerable.

Road Conditions

If Norway were Nepal they'd have built a road to the top of (or underneath) Mt Everest. There are roads that can

inspire nothing but profound admiration for the engineering expertise involved. The longest tunnels link adjacent valleys, while shorter tunnels drill through rocky impediments to straighten routes.

Although the roads are generally excellent, plan on taking longer than you expect to get where you're going, especially in summer high season. Speed limits rarely reach, let alone exceed, 80km/h, and you'll share most roads with trucks, campervans and buses with very few overtaking lanes in sight.

Road Hazards

Older roads and mountain routes are likely to be narrow, with multiple hairpin bends and very steep gradients. Although most areas are accessible by car (and very often tour bus), some of the less-used routes have poor or untarred surfaces only suitable for 4WD vehicles, and some seemingly normal roads can narrow sharply with very little warning. On some mountain roads, caravans and campervans are forbidden or advisable only for experienced drivers, as it may be necessary to reverse in order to allow approaching traffic to pass.

If you're expecting snowy or icy conditions, use studded tyres or carry snow chains.

Vegdirektoratet (☑02030; www.vegvesen.no) outlines on a map the restricted roads for caravans; its website also has a handy route planner.

Road Rules

For more detail than you probably need, there's a downloadable PDF of Norway's road rules on the website for **Vegdirektoratet** (☑02030; www. vegvesen.no); follow the links to 'Traffic', then 'Traffic Rules'.

Blood-alcohol limit The limit is 0.02%. Mobile breath-testing stations are reasonably common, and violators are subject to severe fines and/or imprisonment. Because establishments serving alcohol may legally share liability in the case of an accident, you may not be served even a small glass of beer if the server or bartender knows you're driving.

Foreign vehicles Should bear an oval-shaped nationality sticker on the back. UK-registered vehicles must carry a vehicle registration document (Form V5), or a Certificate of Registration (Form V379, available from the DVLA in the UK). For vehicles not registered in the driver's name, you'll require written permission from the registered owner.

Headlights The use of dipped headlights (including on motorcycles) is required at all times and right-hand-drive vehicles must (in theory) have beam deflectors affixed to their headlight in order to avoid blinding oncoming traffic.

Legal driving age for cars 18 years.

Legal driving age for motorcycles & scooters Ranges from 16 to 21 (depending on the motorcycle's power). A licence is required.

Motorcycle parking Motorcycles may not park on the pavement (sidewalk) and are subject to the same parking regulations as cars.

Red warning triangles Compulsory in all vehicles for use in the event of a breakdown.

Roundabouts (traffic circles) Give way to cars coming from the right, which are liable to shoot across your bows 'like a troll from a box', as one Norwegian told us.

Side of the road Drive on the right side.

Speed limits The national speed limit is 80km/h on the open road, but pass a house or place of business and the limit drops to 70km/h or even 60km/h. Through villages limits range from 50km/h to 60km/h and, in residential areas, the limit is 30km/h. A few roads have segments allowing 90km/h, and you can drive at 100km/h on a small part of the E6 – bliss! The speed limit for caravans (and cars pulling trailers) is usually 10km/h less than for cars.

Road Signs

Most road signs are international, but a white M on a blue background indicates a passing place on a single-track road (the 'm' stands for *møteplass*). Others worth watching out for:

➡ *All Stans Forbudt* (No Stopping)

➡ *Enveiskjøring* (One Way)

➡ *Kjøring Forbudt* (Driving Prohibited or Do Not Enter)

➡ *Parkering Forbudt* (No Parking)

➡ *Rekverk Mangler* (Guardrail Missing)

Road Tolls & Speed Cameras

ROAD TOLLS

Around one-quarter of Norway's road-construction budget comes from road tolls – you'll soon become accustomed to the ominous 'Bomstasjon – Toll Plaza' signs.

TUNNELS IN NORWAY

In November 2000 the world's longest road tunnel, from Lærdal to Aurland (24.51km long, 7.59km longer than the St Gotthard tunnel in Switzerland), was completed at a total cost of Nkr1082 million. There are no tolls to use the tunnel as it was paid for entirely by the national government. The two-lane tunnel, part of the vital E16 road connecting Oslo and Bergen, reduces the difficulties of winter driving and replaces the lengthy Gudvangen–Lærdal ferry route. It was drilled through very hard pre-Cambrian gneiss, with over 1400m of overhead rock at one point. Motorists should tune into NRK radio when driving through the tunnel (yes, there are transmitters inside!) in case of emergency.

In addition to Lærdal, there's also the Gudvangentunnelen in Sogn og Fjordane (11.43km, also on the E16), Folgefonntunnelen in Hardanger (11.15km, on Rv551 passing beneath the Folgefonn icecap) and the new Jondalstunnelen (10.4km), which helps connect Odda with Jondal, also in Hardangerfjord.

Norway also has a number of undersea tunnels, which typically bore over 200m below the seabed; Eiksund-tunnelen (7.76km long, connecting Eika island to the mainland in Møre og Romsdal) is the world's deepest undersea road tunnel at 287m below sea level.

Apart from some smaller country roads, most of Norway's toll stations are automated. If you're driving a Norwegian rental car, it'll be fitted with an automatic sensor – after you return your car, the hire company adds up the accumulated tolls and then charges it to your credit card.

If, however, you're driving a foreign-registered car (including some rental cars from other countries), you're expected to either register your credit card in advance online at www.autopass.no (whereupon you pay a Nkr200 deposit) and the tolls are later deducted. The alternative is to stop at one of the pay stations (sometimes the first petrol station after the toll station) to pay the fee there. If you don't pay, the authorities will, in theory, attempt to track you down once you return to your home country (often as much as six months later) and you'll be expected to pay both the toll and a penalty fee of Nkr300.

SPEED CAMERAS

The lethargy-inspiring national speed limits may seem laborious by your home standards, but avoid the temptation to drive faster as they're taken very seriously. Mobile police units lurk at the side of the roads. Watch for signs designating *Automatisk Trafikkontrol*, which means that there's a speed camera ahead; these big and ugly grey boxes have no mercy at all – you'll be nabbed for even 5km/h over the limit. Fines range from Nkr1000 to well over Nkr10,000.

If you're in a rental car, the fine will be deducted from your credit card. If you're in a foreign-registered vehicle, you may be tracked back to your home country.

Vehicle Ferries

While travelling along the scenic but mountainous, fjord-studded west coast may be spectacular, it also requires numerous ferry crossings that can prove time-consuming and costly. For a complete list of ferry schedules and fares, get hold of the *Rutebok for*

Norge, a phone-book-sized transport guide sold in bookshops and larger Narvesen kiosks.

Hitching

Hitching isn't entirely safe and we don't recommend it. Travellers who decide to hitch should understand they're taking a potentially serious risk. People who choose to hitch will be safer if they travel in pairs and let someone know where they're planning to go.

If you're determined to hitch, you'll find Norwegians generally friendly, and they understand that not all foreigners enjoy an expense-account budget or earn Norwegian salaries. Your chances of success are better on main highways, but you still may wait for hours in bad weather. One approach is to ask for rides from truck drivers at ferry terminals and petrol stations; that way, you'll normally have a place to keep warm and dry while you wait.

Local Transport

Bus

Nearly every town in Norway supports a network of local buses, which circulate around the town centre and also connect it with outlying areas. In many smaller towns, the local bus terminal is adjacent to the train station, ferry quay and/or long-distance bus terminal. Fares range from Nkr20 to Nkr35 per ride. Day- or multitrip tickets are usually available.

Taxi

Taxis are best hailed around taxi ranks, but you can also reserve one by phone; hotels and tourist offices always have the numbers for local companies. If you're phoning for a taxi immediately, remember that charges begin at the moment the call is taken. Daytime fares, which apply from 6am to 7pm on weekdays and from 6am to 3pm on Saturday, cost from around Nkr45 at flagfall (more in larger cities), plus Nkr18 to Nkr28 per kilometre.

Weekday evening fares are 22% higher, and in the early morning, on Saturday afternoon and evening, and on Sunday, they're 30% higher. On holidays, you'll pay 45% more. In some places, you may find 'maxi-taxis', which can carry up to eight passengers for about the same price.

Train

Norges Statsbaner (Norwegian State Railways, NSB; 📞press 9 for English 81 50 08 88; www.nsb.no) operates an excellent, though limited, system of lines connecting Oslo with Stavanger, Bergen, Åndalsnes, Trondheim, Fauske and Bodø; lines also connect Sweden with Oslo, Trondheim and Narvik. Most train stations offer luggage lockers and many also have baggage storage rooms.

Most long-distance day trains have 1st- and 2nd-class seats and a buffet car or refreshment trolley service. Public phones can be found in all express trains and most intercity trains. Doors are wide and there's space for bulky luggage, such as backpacks or skis.

Reservations sometimes cost an additional Nkr50 and are mandatory on some long-distance routes.

Classes & Costs

On long-distance trains, 2nd-class carriages provide comfortable reclining seats with footrests. First-class carriages, which cost 50% more, offer marginally more space and often a food trolley, but they're generally not worth the extra expense.

Travelling by train in Norway is (like everything else) expensive. Indeed, the fact that it often costs less to fly than it does to catch a train puts a dint in Norway's impressive environmental credentials. However, if you learn how to work the *minipris* system, or the train passes, train travel suddenly becomes affordable. And think of the scenery...

There's a 50% discount on rail travel for people aged 67

MINIPRIS – A TRAVELLER'S BEST FRIEND

If you plan to travel on longer routes by train through Norway and you know your itinerary in advance, the following information will save you hundreds of kroner. On every route, for every departure, Norges Statsbaner (Norwegian State Railways) sets aside a limited number of tickets known as *minipris*. Those who book the earliest can get just about any route for just Nkr249. Once those are exhausted, the next batch of *minipris* tickets goes for Nkr349 and so on. These tickets cannot be purchased at ticket counters and must instead be bought over the internet (www.nsb.no) or in ticket-vending machines at train stations. Remember that *minipris* tickets may only be purchased in advance (minimum one day), reservations are non-refundable and cannot be changed once purchased. In peak seasons (especially from mid-June to mid-August) on popular routes, you may need to book up to three weeks in advance to get the cheapest fares. That said, the savings are considerable, often as much as 75% off the full fare.

and older, for travellers with disabilities, and for children aged between four and 15; children under four travel free. Students get discounts of between 25% and 40%.

On long-distance overnight routes, sleeper compartments (you pay for the whole two-bed compartment) are additional to the standard fares.

Train Passes

Rail passes are available for Norway (but should be bought before you arrive in the country). Eurail has a pass that includes only Norway.

Details about rail passes can also be found at www.railpass.com or www.raildude.com.

INTERRAIL PASSES

InterRail passes are available to people who have lived in Europe for six months or more. They can be bought at most major stations and student travel outlets, as well as online.

InterRail has a Global Pass encompassing 30 countries that comes in four versions, ranging from five days of travel that must be taken within 10 days to a full month's travel. These, in turn, come in three prices: adult 1st class, adult 2nd class and youth 2nd class. The one-month pass costs, respectively, €1050/668/442; children (aged four to 11 years) travel for half the cost of the adult fare. Youth passes are for people aged 12 to 25. Children aged three and under travel for free.

The InterRail one-country pass for Norway can be used for three, four, six or eight days in one month. For the 2nd-class, eight-day pass you pay €326/163/216 per adult/child/youth.

EURAIL PASSES

Eurail (www.eurail.com) passes are for those who've been in Europe for less than six months and are supposed to be bought outside Europe. They're available from leading travel agencies and online.

Eurail Global Passes are good for travel in 21 European countries (not including the UK); forget it if you intend to travel mainly in Norway. Passes are valid for 10 or 15 days within a two-month period, 15 or 21 consecutive days, or for one, two or three months.

The Eurail Select Pass provides between five and 15 days of unlimited travel within a two-month period in three to five bordering countries (from a total of 19 possible countries). As with Global Passes, those aged 26 and over pay for a 1st-class pass, while those aged under 26 can get a cheaper 2nd-class pass.

Eurail also offers a Norway national pass, a two-country regional pass (Norway and Sweden) and a Scandinavia Rail Pass (valid for travel in Norway, Sweden, Finland and Denmark). For these passes, you choose from between three and 10 days' train travel in a one- or two-month period. The adult eight-day national pass (valid for one month) costs €259/304 in 2nd/1st class. Regional passes come in three versions: 1st-class adult, 2nd-class adult saver (for two or more adults travelling together), and 2nd-class youth.

Language

The official language of Norway is Norwegian, which belongs to the North Germanic (or Scandinavian) group of languages.

There are two official written forms of Norwegian, known as *Bokmål* (literally 'book language') and *Nynorsk* (or 'new Norwegian'). They are actually quite similar and understood by all speakers. Both varieties are written standards, and are used in written communication (in schools, administration and the media), whereas the spoken language has numerous local dialects. *Bokmål* is predominant in the cities, while *Nynorsk* is more common in the western fjords and the central mountains. It's estimated that out of the five million speakers of Norwegian around 85% use *Bokmål* and about 15% use *Nynorsk*. In this chapter we've used *Bokmål* only.

In northern Norway, around 20,000 people speak Sami, a language of the Finno-Ugric group. It's related to Finnish, Estonian and Hungarian. There are three distinct Sami dialects in Norway – Fell Sami (also called Eastern or Northern Sami), Central Sami and South Sami. Fell Sami is considered the standard Sami language. Most Sami speakers can also communicate in Norwegian.

Pronunciation

Most Norwegian sounds have equivalents in English, and if you read our coloured pronunciation guides as if they were English, you'll be understood. Length is a distinctive feature of Norwegian vowels, as each vowel can be either long or short. Generally, they're long when followed by one consonant and short when followed by two or more consonants. Note that the eu in the pronunciation guides is like the 'ur' in 'nurse', and that ew is pronounced like the 'ee' in 'see' but with pursed lips.

Most Norwegian words have stress on the first syllable, and sometimes there's more than one stressed syllable in a word. In our pronunciation guides the stressed syllables are indicated with italics.

BASICS

Hello.	God dag.	go·*daag*
Goodbye.	Ha det.	*haa*·de
Yes.	Ja.	yaa
No.	Nei.	ney
Thank you.	Takk.	tak
Please.	Vær så snill.	veyr saw snil
You're welcome.	Ingen årsak.	*ing*·en *awr*·saak
Excuse me.	Unnskyld.	ewn·shewl
Sorry.	Beklager.	bey·*klaa*·geyr

How are you?
Hvordan har du det?   vor·dan haar doo de

Fine, thanks. And you?
Bra, takk. Og du?   braa tak aw doo

What's your name?
Hva heter du?   vaa *hey*·ter doo

My name is ...
Jeg heter ...   yai *hay*·ter ...

Do you speak English?
Snakker du engelsk?   sna·ker doo eyng·elsk

I don't understand.
Jeg forstår ikke.   yai fawr·*stawr* i·key

ACCOMMODATION

Do you have a ... room?	Finnes det et ...?	*fi*·nes de et ...
single	enkeltrom	eyn·kelt·rom
double	dobbeltrom	daw·belt·rom

How much is it per night/person?
Hvor mye koster det pr dag/person?   vor *mew*·e *kaws*·ter de peyr daag/peyr·son

campsite	campingplass	keym·ping·plas
guesthouse	gjestgiveri	yest·gi·ve·ree
hotel	hotell	hoo·*tel*

youth hostel	ungdoms-herberge	ong·dawms·heyr·beyrg
air-con	luftkjøling	luft·sheu·ling
bathroom	bad	baad
window	vindu	vin·du

DIRECTIONS

Where is ...?
Hvor er ...?   vor ayr ...

What is the address?
Hva er adressen?   va ayr aa·dre·seyn

Could you write it down, please?
Kan du skrive det?   kan doo skree·ve de

Can you show me (on the map)?
Kan du vise meg (på kartet)?   kan du vee·se ma (paw kar·te)

at the corner	på hjørne	paw yeur·ney
at the traffic lights	i lyskrysset	ee lews·krew·sey
behind	bak	baak
far	langt	laangt
in front of	foran	faw·ran
left	venstre	vens·trey
near (to)	nær	neyr
next to	ved siden av	vey see·den aav
opposite	ovenfor	aw·ven·fawr
right	høyre	hoy·rey
straight ahead	rett fram	ret fram

EATING & DRINKING

A table for (four), please.
Et bord til (fire), takk.   et bawr til (fee·re) tak

What would you recommend?
Hva vil du anbefale?   va vil doo an·be·fa·le

What does it include?
Hva inkluderer det?   va in·kloo·dey·re de

I don't eat (meat).
Jeg spise ikke (kjøtt).   yai (spi·se) i·key (sheut)

Cheers!
Skål!   skawl

I'd like the bill, please.
Kan jeg få regningen, takk.   kan yai faw rai·ning·en tak

Key Words

bar	bar	bar
bottle	flaske	flas·ke
breakfast	frokost	fro·kost

Hello.	Buorre beaivi.
Hello.	Ipmel atti. (reply)
Goodbye.	Mana dearvan. (to person leaving)
Goodbye.	Báze dearvan. (to person staying)
Thank you.	Giitu.
You're welcome.	Leage buorre.
Yes.	De lea.
No.	Li.
How are you?	Mot manna?
I'm fine.	Buorre dat manna.

1	okta
2	guokte
3	golbma
4	njeallje
5	vihta
6	guhta
7	cieza
8	gávcci
9	ovcci
10	logi

cold	kald	kal
cup	kopp	kawp
dinner	middag	mi·da
food	mat	maat
fork	gaffel	ga·fel
glass	glass	glas
grocery store	matbutikk	maat·boo·tik
hot (warm)	het	heyt
knife	kniv	kniv
lunch	lunsj	loonsh
market	marked	mar·ked
menu	meny	me·new
restaurant	restaurant	res·tu·rang
spoon	skje	shai
vegetarian	vegetariansk	ve·ge·ta·ree·ansk
with/without	med/uten	mey/u·ten

Signs

Åpen	Open
Damer	Women
Forbudt	Prohibited
Herrer	Men
Informasjon	Information
Inngang	Entrance
Stengt	Closed
Toaletter	Toilets
Utgang	Exit

Meat & Fish

beef	oksekjøtt	ook·se·sheut
chicken	kylling	chew·ling
cod	torsk	tawshk
fish	fisk	fisk
hake	lysing	lew·sing
halibut	hellefisk	he·le·fisk
ham	skinke	shin·ke
herring	sild	seel
lamb	sauekjøtt	sow·e·sheut
mackerel	makrell	ma·krel
meat	kjøtt	sheut
pork	svinekjøtt	svee·ne·sheut
sardine	brisling	brees·ling
sausage	pølse	peul·se
shrimp	reker	rey·ker
tuna	tunfisk	tun·fisk

Fruit & Vegetables

apple	eple	ep·le
banana	banan	baa·naan
fruit	frukt	frookt
grapes	druer	droo·er
mushroom	sopp	sop
onion	løk	leuk
orange	appelsin	aa·pel·sin
pineapple	ananas	aa·naa·nas
potato	potet	po·tet
strawberries	jordbær	yor·bar
tomato	tomat	too·maat
vegetable	grønnsak	greun·sak

Other

butter	smør	smour
cake	kake	ka·ke
casserole	gryterett	grew·te·ret
cheese	ost	ost
chocolate	sjokolade	sho·kaa·laa·de
cold buffet	koldtbord	kolt·bawr
cream	fløte	fleu·te
eggs	egg	eg
ice cream	is	ees
jam	syltetøy	sewl·te·toy
nuts	nøtter	neu·ter
pancake	pannekake	pa·ne·kaa·ke
pâté	postei	po·stai
salad	salat	sa·lat
sugar	sukker	soo·ker
sweetbread	brissel	bri·sel

Drinks

beer	øl	eul
coffee	kaffe	kaa·fe
(orange) juice	(appelsin)jus	(a·pel·seen·)joos
milk	melk	melk
red wine	rødvin	reu·veen
soft drink	brus	broos
tea	te	te
(mineral) water	(mineral)vann	(mi·ne·ral·)van
white wine	hvitvin	veet·veen

EMERGENCIES

Help!
Hjelp! — yelp

Go away!
Forsvinn! — fawr·svin

I'm lost.
Jeg har gått meg vill. — yai har gawt mai vil

There's been an accident.
Det har skjedd en ulykke. — de har shed en oo·lew·ke

Call ...! — Ring ...! — ring ...
  a doctor — en lege — en le·ge
  the police — politiet — po·lee·tee·ay

I'm ill.
Jeg er syk. — yai er sewk

It hurts here.
Det gjør vondt her. — de yeur·vont heyr

I'm allergic to (antibiotics).
Jeg er allergisk mot   yai eyr a·ler·gisk mot
(antibiotika).   (an·ti·bi·o·ti·ka)

SHOPPING & SERVICES

I'm looking for ...
Jeg leter etter ...   yai ley·ter e·ter ...

May I look at it?
Kan jeg få se på det?   kan yai faw se paw de

I don't like it.
Det liker jeg ikke.   de lee·ker yai i·key

How much is it?
Hvor mye koster det?   vor mew·e kaws·ter de

That's too expensive.
Det er for dyrt.   de eyr fawr dewrt

What's your lowest price?
Hva er din absolutt   va eyr deen ab·saw·lut
laveste pris?   la·ves·te prees

There's a mistake in the bill.
Det er en feil på   de eyr en fail paw
regningen.   rai·ning·en

ATM	minibank	mee·ni·bank
credit card	kredittkort	kre·dit·kawrt
internet cafe	Internettkafé	in·ter·net·ka·fe
post office	postkontor	pawst·kawn·tawr
mobile phone	mobiltelefon	mo·beel·te·le·fon
tourist office	turist-informasjon	tu·reest·in·fawr·ma·shawn

TIME & DATES

What time is it?
Hva er klokka?   vaa eyr klaw·ka

It's (two) o'clock.
Klokka er (to).   klaw·ka eyr (taw)

Half past (one).
Halv (to).   haal (taw)
(lit: half (two))

in the morning
om formiddagen   awm fawr·mi·dan

in the afternoon
om ettermiddagen   awm e·ter·mi·dan

in the evening
om kvelden   awm kve·len

yesterday	i går	ee gawr
today	i dag	ee daag
tomorrow	i morgen	ee maw·ren
Monday	mandag	maan·daa
Tuesday	tirsdag	teers·daa
Wednesday	onsdag	awns·daa
Thursday	torsdag	tawrs·daa
Friday	fredag	frey·daa
Saturday	lørdag	leu·daa
Sunday	søndag	seun·daa
January	januar	yaa·nu·aar
February	februar	fe·broo·aar
March	mars	maars
April	april	aa·preel
May	mai	mai
June	juni	yoo·nee
July	juli	yoo·lee
August	august	ow·goost
September	september	sep·tem·ber
October	oktober	awk·taw·ber
November	november	naw·veym·ber
December	desember	de·seym·ber

TRANSPORT

Public Transport

boat	båt	bawt
bus	buss	bus
plane	fly	flew
taxi	drosje	draw·shey
train	tåg	tawg
1st class	førsteklasse	feur·ste·kla·se
economy class	økonomi-klasse	eu·ko·no·mi·kla·se
one-way ticket	enveisbillett	en·veys·bee·let
return ticket	returbillett	re·toor·bee·let

I want to go to ...
Jeg skal til ...   yai skaal til ...

At what time does it arrive/leave?
Når ankommer/   nawr an·kaw·mer/
går den?   gawr den

How?	Hvordan?	vor·dan
What?	Hva?	vaa
When?	Når?	nawr
Where?	Hvor?	vor
Which?	Hvilken?	veel·keyn
Who?	Hvem?	vem
Why?	Hvorfor?	vor·fawr

Numbers		
1	*en*	en
2	*to*	taw
3	*tre*	trey
4	*fire*	fee·re
5	*fem*	fem
6	*seks*	seks
7	*sju*	shoo
8	*åtte*	aw·te
9	*ni*	nee
10	*ti*	tee
20	*tjue*	shoo·e
30	*tretti*	trey·tee
40	*førti*	feur·tee
50	*femti*	fem·tee
60	*seksti*	seks·tee
70	*sytti*	sew·tee
80	*åtti*	aw·tee
90	*nitti*	nee·tee
100	*hundre*	hun·dre
1000	*tusen*	tu·sen

Does it stop at (Majorstua)?
Stopper denne på (Majorstua)? — staw·per dey·ne paw (maa·yoor·stu·a)

Please tell me when we get to (Oslo).
Kan du si fra når vi kommer til (Oslo)? — kan doo see fraa nawr vee kaw·mer til (os·law)

Please stop here.
Vær så snill å stoppe her. — veyr saw snil aw sto·pe heyr

first	*første*	feur·ste
last	*siste*	si·ste
next	*neste*	ne·ste

| **baggage claim** | *bagasjeskranke* | ba·gaa·shes·kran·ke |

bus stop	*busstopp*	bus·stawp
cancelled	*avbestillt*	av·be·stilt
delayed	*forsinket*	fawr·sin·ket
left-luggage office	*gjenglemt bagasjes kranke*	yen·glemt ba·gaa·shes· kran·ke
reservation	*reservasjon*	re·ser·va·shawn
train station	*stasjon*	staa·shawn

Driving & Cycling

I'd like to hire a ...	*Jeg vil gjerne leie en ...*	yai vil yer·ne lai·e·en ...
4WD	*fire-hjulstrekk*	fee·re·hyools·trek
bicycle	*sykkel*	sew·kel
car	*bil*	beel
motorcycle	*motor-sykkel*	maw·tor·sew·kel
child seat	*barnesete*	bar·na·se·te
diesel	*diesel*	dee·sel
mechanic	*verksted*	verk·stey
petrol/gas	*bensin*	ben·seen
service station	*bensin-stasjon*	ben·seen·staa·shawn

Is this the road to (Gol)?
Er dette veien til (Gol)? — eyr de·tey vai·en til (gol)

(How long) Can I park here?
(Hvor lenge) Kan bilen min stå her? — (vor leng·e) kan bee·len min staw her

I have a flat tyre.
Jeg har punktert. — yai haar poonk·tert

I've run out of petrol.
Jeg har gått tom for bensin. — yai haar gawt tawm fawr ben·seen

I've had an accident.
Jeg har vært i en ulykke. — yai haar veyrt ee en oo·lew·ke

GLOSSARY

You may encounter some of the following terms and abbreviations during your travels in Norway. Note that although the letters ø and å fall at the end of the Norwegian alphabet, we have included them under 'o' and 'a' respectively to make things easier for non-Norwegian-speaking readers.

allemannsretten – 'every man's right'; a tradition/law allowing universal access to private property (with some restrictions), public lands and wilderness areas

apótek – pharmacy

Arctic Menu – scheme to encourage the use of the region's natural ingredients in food served by restaurants

arête – a sharp ridge between two valley glaciers

arsarnerit – name given by Inuit (Eskimos) to aurora borealis

aurora borealis – northern lights

automatisk trafikkontrol – speed camera

bakke – hill

berg – mountain

bibliotek – library

billett – ticket

bilutleie – car-hire company

blodveien – literally 'blood road'; nickname given to the Arctic Highway during construction due to the high number of worker fatalities

bokhandel – bookshop

bro, bru – bridge

brygge – quay, wharf

bryggeri – brewery

bukt, bukta – bay

bunad – the Norwegian national costume; each region has its own version

by – town

calving – the breaking off of icebergs from tidewater glaciers

cirque – an amphitheatre scoured out by a glacier

crevasse – a fissure in moving ice, which may be hidden under snow

dal – valley

DNT – Den Norske Turistforening (Norwegian Mountain Touring Club)

domkirke – cathedral

dressin – rail bikes or bicycles on bogies

elg – elk (moose)

elv, elva – river

Fata Morgana – Arctic phenomenon whereby distant features do not appear out of focus

fell, fjall, fjell – mountain

festning – fort, fortress

fiskeskrue – fish press

fjord – drowned glacial valley

fonn – glacial icefield

forening – club, association

foss – waterfall

friluft – outdoor, open-air

Fv – Fylkesvei; county road

fylke – county

fyr – lighthouse

galleriet – gallery, shopping arcade

gamla, gamle, gammel – old

gamlebyen – the 'old town'

gamma, gammen – Sami tent or turf hut, sometimes partially underground

gård, gard – farm, courtyard

gata, gate – street (often abbreviated to g or gt)

gatekjøkken – literally 'street kitchen'; street kiosk/stall/grill

gjestehavn – 'guest harbour'; the area of a port town where visiting boats and yachts moor

gjestehus – guesthouse

gravlund – cemetery

grønlandssel – harp seal

gruva, gruve – mine

hage – garden

halvøya – peninsula

Hanseatic League – association of German traders that dominated trade in Bergen from the 12th to 16th centuries

hav – ocean

havn – harbour

honnør – senior citizen

Hurtigruten – literally 'the Express Route'; a system of coastal steamers plying the route between Bergen and Kirkenes

hus – house

hval – whale

hvalross – walrus

hytte – cabin, hut or chalet

hytteutleie – hut-hire company

ice floe – a flat chunk of floating sea ice or small iceberg

icecap, icefield – a stable zone of accumulated and compressed snow and ice, and a source of valley glaciers; an icecap generally covers a larger area than an icefield

isbjørn – polar bear

jernbanestasjon – train station

jerv – wolverine

joik – 'song of the plains'; religious Sami tradition

jul – Christmas

kai, kaia – quay

kart – map

kerk, kirke, kirkja, kirkje – church

kort – card

krambua – general store

krone – Norwegian currency unit

kulturhus – a large complex containing cinemas, public library, museums etc

kvadraturen – the square grid pattern of streets measuring six long blocks by nine shorter blocks

kyst – coast

landsmål – Norwegian dialect

lavvo, lavvu – tepee; Sami tent dwelling

legevakten – clinic

lemen – lemming

libris – books; indicates a bookshop

lundefugl – puffin

magasin – department store

marka – the forested hills around Oslo

mil – Norwegian mile measuring 10km

minipris – cheaper fares, usually for transport

MOMS – Value Added Tax/ sales tax

moskus-okse – musk oxen

M/S – motorskip or motor ship; designates ship names

museet – museum

MVA – see *MOMS*

nasjonalpark – national park

navvy – railway worker

nord – north

nordlys – northern lights (aurora borealis)

Norge – Norway

Norges Turistråd – Norwegian Tourist Board, formerly NORTRA

Norsk – Norwegian

Norway in a Nutshell – a range of tours that give high-speed travellers a glimpse of the best of Norway in one or two days

NSB – Norges Statsbaner (Norwegian State Railways)

ny – new

Nynorsk – see *landsmål*

og – and

øst – east

oter – otter

øvre – upper

øy – island

pack ice – floating ice formed by frozen seawater, often creating an impenetrable barrier to navigation

pensjonat – pension, guesthouse

plass – plaza, square

polarsirkelen – Arctic Circle; latitude 66°33′N

Pomor – Russian trading and fishing community from the White Sea, which prospered in northern Norway in the 17th century

rådhus – town hall

reinsdyr – reindeer

reiseliv – local tourist office

riksdaler – old Norwegian currency

rom – signs on roads indicating private rooms/cabins for rent

rorbu – cabin/fishing hut

rutebilstasjon – bus terminal

ruteplan – transport timetable

Rv – Riksvei; national highway

schøtstue – large assembly room where employees of the Hanseatic League met and ate

sentrum – town centre

siida – small Sami communities or bands that hunted and trapped together

sild – herring

sjø – sea

sjøhus – fishing bunkhouse on the docks; many are now available for tourist accommodation

skalds – metaphoric and alliterative works of Norwegian court poets in the 9th and 10th centuries

skerries – offshore archipelago of small rocky islets

skog – forest

sla låm – slope track

slott – castle, palace

snø – snow

solarsteinn –Viking navigational tool used when the sky was overcast or the sun below the horizon

sør – south

spekkhogger – killer whale (orca)

stabbur – raised storehouse

stasjon – station

Statens Kartverk – State Mapping Agency

stavkirke – stave church

steinkobbe – harbour seal

storting – parliament

strand – beach

stuer – trading firm

sund – sound, strait

Sverige – Sweden

sykkel – bicycle

sykkelutleie – bicycle-hire company

taiga – marshy forest

tårn – tower

teater – theatre

telekort – Telenor phone cards

tog – train

togbuss – bus services in Romsdalen and Nordland run by NSB to connect railheads with other popular destinations

torget, torvet – town square

turistkontor – tourist office

ulv – wolf

utleie – hire company

vandrerhjem – youth hostel

vann, vannet, vatn, vatnet – lake

veg, vei – road (often abbreviated to v or vn)

vest – west

vetter – mythical Norwegian guardian spirits of the wildest coastline

vidda, vidde – plateau

Vinmonopolet – government-run shop selling wine and liquor

yoik – see *joik*

Behind the Scenes

SEND US YOUR FEEDBACK

We love to hear from travellers – your comments keep us on our toes and help make our books better. Our well-travelled team reads every word on what you loved or loathed about this book. Although we cannot reply individually to your submissions, we always guarantee that your feedback goes straight to the appropriate authors, in time for the next edition. Each person who sends us information is thanked in the next edition – the most useful submissions are rewarded with a selection of digital PDF chapters.

Visit **lonelyplanet.com/contact** to submit your updates and suggestions or to ask for help. Our award-winning website also features inspirational travel stories, news and discussions.

Note: We may edit, reproduce and incorporate your comments in Lonely Planet products such as guidebooks, websites and digital products, so let us know if you don't want your comments reproduced or your name acknowledged. For a copy of our privacy policy visit lonelyplanet.com/privacy.

OUR READERS

Many thanks to the travellers who used the last edition and wrote to us with helpful hints, useful advice and interesting anecdotes:

Alan Quinn, Ankur Agarwal, Anthony Smith, Axel Nelms, Bart de Boer, Bitte Giæver, Catherine Ward, Chai Sia, Christian Stranger-Johannessen, Christopher Eva, Cornelia Pabijan, Dave Whitfield, David Souyris, Egil Hogrenning, Ellen IJspeert, Esteban Ara, Gidon Morein, Gloria Thompson, Idun Urdal, Isaiah Bier, Jennifer Marsh, Jennita Dankelman, Jeremy Fischer, Jim Hill, Jonathan Baines, Jørgen Berentsen-Deem, Judith Harper, Kate Martin, Kathleen Hanley, Kenneth Lew, Lars Wara, Lies Offeciers, Linn Dahle, Magnus Nørsett, Maja Branovacki, Martin Williams, Marvin Finnley, Matthias Schroeter, Matthijs van Vulpen, Melissa Reading, Niklas Aas Skovdahl, Niklas Barre, Peter Andrews, Rachel Lim, Ragnar Augestad, Sain Alizada, Sally Amis, Sam Joffe, Stephanie Johnston, Terje Løkke, Tom Day, Tony Geerts, Vidar Hovlid, Zaf Kowolski.

AUTHOR THANKS
Anthony Ham

Special thanks to Gemma Graham; to my fine co-authors Stuart and Donna; to Miles Roddis; to Ron and Elaine for first igniting my love of Norway. As always, so many Norwegians I met were unfailingly helpful ambassadors for their country – I am deeply grateful to all of them.

And it gets harder with each journey to be away from my family – to Marina, Carlota and Valentina, heartfelt thanks for enduring my absences. Os quiero.

Stuart Butler

Once again I'd like to thank my wife, Heather, and children Jake and Grace for their patience with this project. I'd also like to thank everyone in Norway who, knowingly or unknowingly, helped with my research, as well as my co-authors Anthony and Donna and, back at Lonely Planet HQ, Gemma.

Donna Wheeler

Norway as a whole deserves thanks for being such a wonderfully decent, civil, and, yes, warm place. A big takk to the Bergenvegger: the incredibly generous, welcoming Eirik Glambek Bøe, along with Live Ø Danielsen, Jo, Martin and Yorick, for all your suggestions and company. That extends to the Rønning family in Åndalsnes, Sissel Thompson, Anne-Marie and Marte in Stavanger and Carlos Inglesias and Johan Jr in Haugesund. And, finally, thanks to mio bell' uomo, Joe Guario, for doing it again.

ACKNOWLEDGMENTS

Climate map data adapted from Peel MC, Finlayson BL & McMahon TA (2007) 'Updated World Map of the Köppen-Geiger Climate Classification', Hydrology and Earth System Sciences, 11, 1633–44.

Cover photograph: Winter cabin, Oppland. Vegard Røine Stenerud, Getty Images.

BEHIND THE SCENES

THIS BOOK

This 6th edition of Lonely Planet's *Norway* guidebook was researched and written by Anthony Ham, Stuart Butler and Donna Wheeler. The 5th edition was written by Anthony Ham, Stuart Butler and Miles Roddis, and the 4th edition by Anthony Ham, Miles Roddis and Kari Lundgren. This guidebook was produced by the following:

Destination Editor Gemma Graham

Product Editor Bruce Evans

Coordinating Editor Lauren O'Connell

Senior Cartographer Valentina Kremenchutskaya

Book Designer Clara Monitto

Assisting Editors Judith Bamber, Melanie Dankel, Victoria Harrison, Charlotte Orr, Sally Schafer

Cartographer James Leversha

Cover Researcher Naomi Parker

Thanks to Ryan Evans, Larissa Frost, Jouve India, Elizabeth Jones, Benjamin Little, Claire Naylor, Karyn Noble, Martine Power, Dianne Schallmeiner, Samantha Tyson

Index

Map Legend

Sights

- Beach
- Bird Sanctuary
- Buddhist
- Castle/Palace
- Christian
- Confucian
- Hindu
- Islamic
- Jain
- Jewish
- Monument
- Museum/Gallery/Historic Building
- Ruin
- Shinto
- Sikh
- Taoist
- Winery/Vineyard
- Zoo/Wildlife Sanctuary
- Other Sight

Activities, Courses & Tours

- Bodysurfing
- Diving
- Canoeing/Kayaking
- Course/Tour
- Sento Hot Baths/Onsen
- Skiing
- Snorkelling
- Surfing
- Swimming/Pool
- Walking
- Windsurfing
- Other Activity

Sleeping

- Sleeping
- Camping

Eating

- Eating

Drinking & Nightlife

- Drinking & Nightlife
- Cafe

Entertainment

- Entertainment

Shopping

- Shopping

Information

- Bank
- Embassy/Consulate
- Hospital/Medical
- Internet
- Police
- Post Office
- Telephone
- Toilet
- Tourist Information
- Other Information

Geographic

- Beach
- Hut/Shelter
- Lighthouse
- Lookout
- Mountain/Volcano
- Oasis
- Park
- Pass
- Picnic Area
- Waterfall

Population

- Capital (National)
- Capital (State/Province)
- City/Large Town
- Town/Village

Transport

- Airport
- Border crossing
- Bus
- Cable car/Funicular
- Cycling
- Ferry
- Metro station
- Monorail
- Parking
- Petrol station
- S-Bahn/S-train/Subway station
- Taxi
- T-bane/Tunnelbana station
- Train station/Railway
- Tram
- Tube station
- U-Bahn/Underground station
- Other Transport

Note: Not all symbols displayed above appear on the maps in this book

Routes

- Tollway
- Freeway
- Primary
- Secondary
- Tertiary
- Lane
- Unsealed road
- Road under construction
- Plaza/Mall
- Steps
- Tunnel
- Pedestrian overpass
- Walking Tour
- Walking Tour detour
- Path/Walking Trail

Boundaries

- International
- State/Province
- Disputed
- Regional/Suburb
- Marine Park
- Cliff
- Wall

Hydrography

- River, Creek
- Intermittent River
- Canal
- Water
- Dry/Salt/Intermittent Lake
- Reef

Areas

- Airport/Runway
- Beach/Desert
- Cemetery (Christian)
- Cemetery (Other)
- Glacier
- Mudflat
- Park/Forest
- Sight (Building)
- Sportsground
- Swamp/Mangrove

OUR STORY

A beat-up old car, a few dollars in the pocket and a sense of adventure. In 1972 that's all Tony and Maureen Wheeler needed for the trip of a lifetime – across Europe and Asia overland to Australia. It took several months, and at the end – broke but inspired – they sat at their kitchen table writing and stapling together their first travel guide, *Across Asia on the Cheap*. Within a week they'd sold 1500 copies. Lonely Planet was born.

Today, Lonely Planet has offices in Franklin, London, Melbourne, Oakland, Beijing and Delhi, with more than 600 staff and writers. We share Tony's belief that 'a great guidebook should do three things: inform, educate and amuse'.

OUR WRITERS

Anthony Ham
Coordinating Author, Spectacular Norway, Trøndelag, Nordland, The Far North, Svalbard

Anthony fell in love with Norway the first time he laid eyes on it, and there aren't many places in Norway he hasn't been, from Lindesnes in the south to the remote fjords of Svalbard in the far north. His true passion is the Arctic north, whether dog-sledding and spending time with the Sami around Karasjok or drawing near to glaciers and scouring the horizon for polar bears in the glorious wilderness of Svalbard. When he's not travelling for Lonely Planet to the Arctic (or, his other great love, Africa), he lives in Melbourne and Madrid and writes and photographs for magazines and newspapers around the world. Anthony's website is www.anthonyham.com.

Read more about Anthony at:
lonelyplanet.com/members/anthony_ham

Stuart Butler
Oslo, Central Norway, Travel with Children

Stuart's first contacts with Norway were very cold ones – a surf trip in the shadow of Nordkapp one frozen November where he rode waves under the glow of the Northern Lights. Fortunately, the short days meant he didn't have to spend long in the water! Once he had thawed out, his interest in Norway was piqued and he has since returned numerous times to hike the central mountains, travel the fjords, hang out in Oslo and, deciding that Nordkapp wasn't quite cold enough, go on a surf trip to Svalbard... Today he lives with his wife and two young children on the much warmer beaches of southwest France. Stuart's website is www.stuartbutlerjournalist.com.

Read more about Stuart at:
lonelyplanet.com/members/stuartbutler

Donna Wheeler
Southern Norway, Bergen & the Southwestern Fjords, The Western Fjords

Donna Wheeler first came to Norway in search of the northern lights, insanely ambitious architecture and Arctic silence. She was happy to return and again immerse herself in the Norwegian sublime, easily found deep in the fjords, up mountain passes, in summer's first strawberries and on a Bergen dancefloor. Donna is based in Melbourne, where she also writes for My Art Guides, *National Geographic Traveler* and other publications. Her features, photographs and experiential travel projects can be found at donnawheeler.com.

Published by Lonely Planet Publications Pty Ltd
ABN 36 005 607 983
6th edition – May 2015
ISBN 978 1 74220 207 5
© Lonely Planet 2015   Photographs © as indicated 2015
10 9 8 7 6 5 4 3 2 1
Printed in China